D0224668

MCSA Guide to
Installation, Storage, and Compute with Windows Server® 2016

MCSE/MCSA

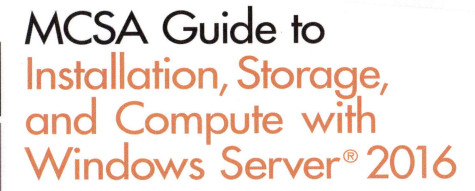

Exam #70-740

MCSA Guide to
Installation, Storage, and Compute with Windows Server® 2016

MCSE/MCSA

Exam #70-740

CENGAGE

Australia • Brazil • Mexico • Singapore • United Kingdom • United States

Greg Tomsho

MCSA Guide to Installation, Storage, and Compute with Windows Server 2016, Exam 70-740
Greg Tomsho

SVP, GM Science, Technology & Math:
  Balraj S. Kalsi

Senior Product Director: Kathleen McMahon

Product Team Manager: Kristin McNary

Associate Product Manager: Amy Savino

Senior Director, Development: Julia Caballero

Senior Product Development Manager:
  Leigh Hefferon

Senior Content Developer:
  Michelle Ruelos Cannistraci

Product Assistant: Jake Toth

Marketing Director: Michelle McTighe

Production Director: Patty Stephan

Senior Content Project Manager:
  Brooke Greenhouse

Art Director: Diana Graham

Cover image: iStockPhoto.com/Stavklem

Production Service/Composition: SPi Global

For product information and technology assistance, contact us at
Cengage Customer & Sales Support, 1-800-354-9706

For permission to use material from this text or product, submit all requests online at **www.cengage.com/permissions**.
Further permissions questions can be e-mailed to
permissionrequest@cengage.com

Library of Congress Control Number: 2017945198

Student Edition ISBN: 978-1-337-40066-4
Loose-leaf Edition ISBN: 978-1-337-68595-5

Cengage
20 Channel Center Street
Boston, MA 02210
USA

Cengage is a leading provider of customized learning solutions with employees residing in nearly 40 different countries and sales in more than 125 countries around the world. Find your local representative at **www.cengage.com**.

Cengage products are represented in Canada by Nelson Education, Ltd.

To learn more about Cengage platforms and services, register or access your online learning solution, or purchase materials for your course, visit **www.cengage.com**.

Notice to the Reader
Publisher does not warrant or guarantee any of the products described herein or perform any independent analysis in connection with any of the product information contained herein. Publisher does not assume, and expressly disclaims, any obligation to obtain and include information other than that provided to it by the manufacturer. The reader is expressly warned to consider and adopt all safety precautions that might be indicated by the activities described herein and to avoid all potential hazards. By following the instructions contained herein, the reader willingly assumes all risks in connection with such instructions. The publisher makes no representations or warranties of any kind, including but not limited to, the warranties of fitness for particular purpose or merchantability, nor are any such representations implied with respect to the material set forth herein, and the publisher takes no responsibility with respect to such material. The publisher shall not be liable for any special, consequential, or exemplary damages resulting, in whole or part, from the readers' use of, or reliance upon, this material.

Printed at CLDPC, USA, 01-20

Brief Contents

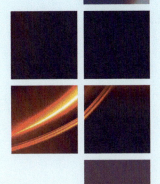

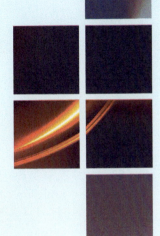

Table of Contents

CHAPTER 12

Nano Server and Windows Containers 473

Introduction

MCSA Guide to Installation, Storage, and Compute with Windows Server® 2016, Exam 70-740, gives you an in-depth coverage of the 70-740 certification exam objectives and focuses on the skills you need to install and configure Windows Server 2016. With more than 80 hands-on activities and dozens of skill-reinforcing case projects, you'll be well prepared for the certification exam and learn valuable skills to perform on the job.

After you finish this book, you'll have an in-depth knowledge of Windows Server 2016, including installation, local and remote management, file and storage services, Hyper-V virtualization, and high availability. You'll also get hands-on experience working with Microsoft's newest server features including Storage Spaces Direct, PowerShell Direct, Nano Server, and Windows containers. This book is written from a teaching and learning point of view, not simply as an exam study guide. The chapters guide readers through the technologies they need to master to perform on the job, not just to pass an exam.

Intended Audience

MCSA Guide to Installation, Storage, and Compute with Windows Server® 2016, Exam 70-740 is intended for people who want to learn how to configure and manage a Windows Server 2016 computing environment and earn the Microsoft Certified Solutions Associate (MCSA) certification. This book covers in full the objectives of exam 70-740, one of three required for the MCSA: Windows Server 2016 certification. Exam 70-740 is also one of the four exams needed for the MCSE: Cloud Platform and Infrastructure certification. This book serves as an excellent tool for classroom teaching, but self-paced learners will also find that the clear explanations, challenging activities, and case projects serve them equally well. Although this book doesn't assume previous experience with Windows servers, it does assume a familiarity with current Windows operating systems, such as Windows 10. Networking knowledge equivalent to an introductory networking course or Network+ is highly recommended.

What This Book Includes

- A lab setup guide is included in the "Before You Begin" section of this introduction to help you configure a physical or virtual (recommended) lab environment for doing the hands-on activities.
- Step-by-step hands-on activities walk you through tasks ranging from a basic Windows Server 2016 installation to complex multi-server cluster configurations. All activities have been tested by a technical editor.
- Extensive review and end-of-chapter materials reinforce your learning.
- Critical thinking case projects require you to apply the concepts and technologies learned throughout the book.

- Abundant screen captures and diagrams visually reinforce the text and hands-on activities.
- A list of 70-740 exam objectives is cross-referenced with chapters and sections that cover each objective (inside cover and Appendix A).

Note 📎

This text does not include Windows Server 2016 software. However, 180-day evaluation versions of Windows Server 2016 are available at no cost from *https://www.microsoft.com/en-us/evalcenter/evaluate-windows-server-2016*. More specific instruction can be found in "Using an Evaluation Version of Windows Server 2016" in the Before You Begin section of this Introduction.

About Microsoft Certification: MCSA

This book prepares you to take one of the three exams in the Microsoft Certified Solutions Associate (MCSA) Windows Server 2016 certification. The MCSA Windows Server 2016 certification is made up of three exams, which can be taken in any order:

- Exam 70-740: Installation, Storage and Compute with Windows Server 2016
- Exam 70-741: Networking with Windows Server 2016
- Exam 70-742: Identity with Windows Server 2016

Note 📎

This text focuses on Exam 70-740. Companion texts focus on Exam 741 and Exam 742, respectively: *MCSA Guide to Networking with Windows Server 2016* (Cengage, 2018) and *MCSA Guide to Identity with Windows Server 2016* (Cengage, 2018).

Microsoft Certified Solutions Expert (MCSE): The Next Step

After achieving the MCSA Windows Server 2016 certification, you can move on to the MCSE certification. For the MCSE: Cloud Platform and Infrastructure certification, the MCSA Windows Server 2016 certification is a prerequisite. You then have the option of taking one of the ten exams to complete the MCSE. To see the list of exams you can take to complete the MCSE, see *https://www.microsoft.com/en-us/learning/mcse-cloud-platform-infrastructure.aspx*.

Chapter Descriptions

This book is organized to familiarize you with Windows Server 2016 features and technologies and then provide an in-depth coverage of Windows Server 2016 installation, management, storage, and virtualization. It wraps up by discussing Nano Server and Windows containers, two new features included in Windows Server 2016. The 70-740 exam objectives are covered throughout the book, and you can find a mapping of objectives and the chapters in which they're covered on the inside front cover, with a more detailed mapping in Appendix A. The following list describes this book's chapters:

- **Chapter 1**, "Introducing Windows Server 2016," describes the role of a server operating system and provides an overview of Windows Server 2016 core technologies, such as the NTFS file system, Active Directory, disk management, Hyper-V, and PowerShell. You'll also be introduced to server roles and new features in Windows Server 2016.

> **Note**
>
> Chapter 1 of this book is available as a PDF for free download by students and instructors from the Cengage website. If you are starting with one of the other Windows Server 2016 MCSA books (70-741 or 70-742), you can use Chapter 1 of this book as an introductory chapter to Windows Server 2016 before beginning those books.

- **Chapter 2**, "Installing Windows Server 2016," discusses the details of planning a Windows Server 2016 installation, including installing the first server on a new network, expanding an existing network, and upgrading to Windows Server 2016, including server role migration. The Server Core installation option is discussed next, followed by optimizing an installation by using Features on Demand.
- **Chapter 3**, "Configuring and Managing Windows Server 2016," explains how to work with server roles and features and how to manage servers remotely. You'll also learn how to work with Windows install images and configure Windows services.
- **Chapter 4**, "Configuring Storage and File Systems," describes the methods available for storage provisioning, including working with local and virtual disks and using disk partition and format options. You learn about the types of volumes you can create on a Windows server and how to work with virtual disks. This chapter also discusses how Windows implements file sharing. This chapter also explains default and administrative shares and how to manage shared folders. Finally, you learn how to secure access to files by using permissions and see how permission inheritance works.
- **Chapter 5**, "Configuring Advanced Storage Solutions," discusses how to implement Storage Spaces, a method for providing flexible and fault-tolerant storage without using expensive RAID controllers. Next, you learn to configure an iSCSI Storage Area Network (SAN) with Windows as the iSCSI client and iSCSI server. You'll also explore data deduplication and Storage Replica. Data deduplication helps reduce storage requirements by eliminating duplicated data, while Storage Replica provides server-to-server and cluster-to-cluster volume replication for high-availability applications.
- **Chapter 6**, "Implementing Virtualization with Hyper-V: Part 1," focuses on how to use the Hyper-V server role for a virtualization platform. You learn the requirements for installing Hyper-V and how to install and configure the Hyper-V role. You'll learn how to manage Hyper-V both locally and remotely, create virtual machines, and manage and optimize virtual machines. In the next chapter, you'll learn how to work with Hyper-V virtual disks and Hyper-V virtual networks.
- **Chapter 7**, "Implementing Virtualization with Hyper-V: Part 2," covers virtual hard disks including dynamically expanding, fixed, differencing, and pass-through disks. You also look at shared VHDX files. Next, you examine the three types of virtual switch and deployment scenarios for each. Along with configuring virtual switches, you'll learn about configuring virtual network adapters including hardware acceleration and advanced features such as MAC address spoofing, protected network, and port mirroring. You'll also learn how to create and configure NIC teaming both on the host server and in a virtual machine. In addition, you'll learn how to properly configure your Hyper-V host to enable nested virtualization, and finally, you'll briefly look at deploying Linux and FreeBSD VMs in Hyper-V.
- **Chapter 8**, "Implementing High Availability: Server Clusters," discusses two high-availability options in Windows Server 2016: network load balancing and failover clustering. You'll learn about the requirements for implementing a NLB cluster and install the Network Load Balancing feature. Next, you'll examine the requirements for network and storage to implement workgroup, single domain, and multi-domain clusters.

- **Chapter 9**, "Implementing High Availability: Advanced Failover and Virtual Machines," covers advanced failover cluster configurations including quorum settings, adding and removing cluster nodes, moving core cluster resources, and configuring Active Directory-detached clusters. Next, you'll learn to configure highly available virtual machines and implement several virtual machine movement technologies.
- **Chapter 10**, "Maintaining Server Installations," discusses the Windows Update program for downloading and installing available updates with Windows Server Update Services (WSUS). This chapter discusses how to install the WSUS role and then configure the role and the client computers using WSUS. Microsoft's solution to malware is Windows Defender. This chapter discusses how to configure Windows Defender using Group Policy and PowerShell and how to integrate WSUS with Windows Defender to ensure your antimalware software and definitions are up to date on all computers throughout the enterprise.
- **Chapter 11**, "Server Monitoring and Backup," covers backup and restore features in Windows Server 2016 that can help IT administrators sleep better knowing they can recover a system from failure or data loss. You learn about Windows Server Backup, and strategies for backing up server roles, including file servers, domain controllers, virtualization servers, and web servers.
- **Chapter 12**, "Nano Server and Windows Containers," discusses Nano Server, a new headless deployment option for Windows Server 2016 that has a very small footprint, consumes few resources, and starts very quickly. It has limited usage scenarios because it supports only a few server roles and features, but it's likely to find a niche in virtual and cloud applications. Next, you'll learn about containers, and the open source container management environment called Docker. Like Nano Server, containers are likely to be deployed in highly virtualized and cloud computing environments, but they may might also find a spot in a moderately sized datacenter.
- **Appendix A**, "MCSA 70-740 Exam Objectives," maps each 70-740 exam objective to the chapter and section where you can find information on that objective.

Features

This book includes the following learning features to help you master the topics in this book and the 70-740 exam objectives:

- *Chapter objectives*—Each chapter begins with a detailed list of the concepts to be mastered. This list is a quick reference to the chapter's contents and a useful study aid.
- *Hands-on activities*—More than 80 hands-on activities are incorporated into this book, giving you practice in setting up, configuring, and managing a Windows Server 2016 server. The activities give you a strong foundation for carrying out server installation and configuration tasks in production environments. Much of the learning about Windows Server 2016 comes from doing the hands-on activities, and a lot of effort has been devoted to making the activities relevant and challenging.
- *Requirements for hands-on activities*—A table at the beginning of each chapter lists the hands-on activities and what you need for each activity.
- *Screen captures, illustrations, and tables*—Numerous screen captures and illustrations of concepts help you visualize theories and concepts and see how to use tools and desktop features. In addition, tables are used often to give you details and comparisons of practical and theoretical information and can be used for a quick review.
- *Chapter summary*—Each chapter ends with a summary of the concepts introduced in the chapter. These summaries are a helpful way to recap and revisit the material covered in the chapter.
- *Key terms*—All terms in the chapter introduced with bold text are gathered together in the Key Terms list at the end of the chapter. This list gives you a way to check your understanding of all important terms. All key term definitions are listed in the Glossary at the end of the book.
- *Review questions*—The end-of-chapter assessment begins with review questions that reinforce the concepts and techniques covered in each chapter. Answering these questions helps ensure that you have mastered important topics.

- *Critical Thinking*—Each chapter closes with one or more case projects to provide critical thinking exercises. Many of the case projects build on one another, as you take a small startup company to a flourishing enterprise.
- *Exam objectives*—Major sections in each chapter show the exam objective or objectives covered in that section, making it easier to find the material you need when studying for the MCSA exam.

Text and Graphics Conventions

Additional information and exercises have been added to this book to help you better understand what's being discussed in the chapter. Icons throughout the book alert you to these additional materials:

Tip

Tips offer extra information on resources, how to solve problems, and time-saving shortcuts.

Note

Notes present additional helpful material related to the subject being discussed.

Caution ⚠

The Caution icon identifies important information about potential mistakes or hazards.

Activity

Each hands-on activity in this book is preceded by the Activity icon.

Critical Thinking

The end-of-chapter case projects are scenario-based assignments that ask you to apply critical thinking skills to what you have learned in the chapter.

Certification

- Certification icons under chapter headings list exam objectives covered in that section.

Instructor Companion Site

Everything you need for your course in one place! This collection of book-specific lecture and class tools is available online via *www.cengage.com/login*. Access and download PowerPoint presentations, images, the Instructor's Manual, and more.

- *Electronic Instructor's Manual*—The Instructor's Manual that accompanies this book includes additional instructional material to assist in class preparation, including suggestions for classroom activities, discussion topics, and additional quiz questions.
- *Solutions Manual*—The instructor's resources include solutions to all end-of-chapter material, including review questions and case projects.
- *Cengage Testing Powered by Cognero*—This flexible, online system allows you to do the following:
  - Author, edit, and manage test bank content from multiple Cengage solutions.
  - Create multiple test versions in an instant.
  - Deliver tests from your LMS, your classroom, or wherever you want.
- *PowerPoint presentations*—This book comes with Microsoft PowerPoint slides for each chapter. They're included as a teaching aid for classroom presentation, to make available to students on the network for chapter review, or to be printed for classroom distribution. Instructors, please feel free to add your own slides for additional topics you introduce to the class.
- *Figure files*—All the figures and tables in the book are reproduced in bitmap format. Similar to the PowerPoint presentations, they're included as a teaching aid for classroom presentation, to make available to students for review, or to be printed for classroom distribution.

MindTap

MindTap for Tomsho/*MCSA Guide to Installation, Storage, and Compute with Windows Server 2016, Exam 70-740* is a personalized, fully online digital learning platform of content, assignments, and services that engages students and encourages them to think critically, while allowing instructors to easily set the course through simple customization options.

MindTap is designed to help students master the skills they need in today's workforce. Research shows employers need critical thinkers, troubleshooters, and creative problem solvers to stay relevant in our fast-paced, technology-driven world. MindTap helps you achieve this with assignments and activities that provide hands-on practice, real-life relevance, and certification test prep. Students are guided through assignments that help them master basic knowledge and understanding before moving on to more challenging problems.

The live virtual machine labs provide real-life application and practice. Based on the textbook's Hands-On Projects, the live virtual machine labs provide more advanced learning. Students work in a live environment via the Cloud with real servers and networks that they can explore. The IQ certification test prep engine allows students to quiz themselves on specific exam domains, and the pre- and post-course assessments are mock exams that measure exactly how much they have learned. Readings and labs support the lecture, while "In the News" assignments encourage students to stay current.

Instant Access Code: (ISBN: 9781337400688)
Printed Access Code: (ISBN: 9781337400695)

Acknowledgments

I would like to thank Cengage Product Team Manager Kristin McNary and Associate Product Manager Amy Savino for their confidence in asking me to undertake this challenging project. In addition, thanks go out to Michelle Ruelos Cannistraci, the Senior Content Developer, who assembled an outstanding team to support this project. A special word of gratitude goes to Deb Kaufmann, the Development Editor, who took an unrefined product and turned it into a polished manuscript. Danielle Shaw, the Technical Editor tested chapter activities diligently to ensure that labs work as they were intended, and for that, I am grateful. I also want to include a shout-out to a former student of mine, Shaun Stallard, who was instrumental in the creation of the end of chapter material including Chapter Summary, Key Terms, and Review Questions.

Finally, my family: my beautiful wife, Julie, lovely daughters Camille and Sophia, and son, Michael, deserve special thanks and praise for going husbandless and fatherless 7 days a week, 14 hours a day, for the better part of a year. Without their patience and understanding and happy greetings when I did make an appearance, I could not have accomplished this.

About the Author

Greg Tomsho has more than 30 years of computer and networking experience and has earned the CCNA, MCTS, MCSA, Network+, A+, Security+, and Linux+ certifications. Greg is the director of the Computer Networking Technology Department and Cisco Academy at Yavapai College in Prescott, AZ. His other books include *MCSA Guide to Networking with Windows Server 2016, Exam 70-741; MCSA Guide to Identity with Windows Server 2016, Exam 70-742; Guide to Operating Systems; MCSA Guide to Installing and Configuring Windows Server 2012/R2, Exam 70-410; MCSA Guide to Administering Windows Server 2012/R2, Exam 70-411; MCSA Guide to Configuring Advanced Windows Server 2012/R2 Services, Exam 70-412; MCTS Guide to Microsoft Windows Server 2008 Active Directory Configuration; MCTS Guide to Microsoft Windows Server 2008 Applications Infrastructure Configuration; Guide to Networking Essentials; Guide to Network Support and Troubleshooting; and A+ CoursePrep ExamGuide.*

Contact the Author

I would like to hear from you. Please email me at w2k16@tomsho.com with any problems, questions, suggestions, or corrections. I even accept compliments! Your comments and suggestions are invaluable for shaping the content of future books. You can also submit errata, lab suggestions, and comments via email. I have set up a website to support my books at http://books.tomsho.com, where you'll find lab notes, errata, web links, and helpful hints for using my books. If you're an instructor, you can register on the site to contribute articles and comment on articles.

Before You Begin

Windows Server has become more complex as Microsoft strives to satisfy the needs of enterprise networks. In years past, you could learn what you needed to manage a Windows Server-based network and pass the Microsoft certification exams with a single server, some good lab instructions, and a network connection. Today, as you work with advanced technologies—such as Hyper-V, Storage Spaces, and failover clusters, just to name a few—your lab environment must be more complex, requiring several servers. Setting up this lab environment can be challenging, and this section was written to help you meet this challenge. Using virtual machines in Hyper-V on Windows 10 or Windows Server 2016 is highly recommended; other virtual environments work, too, but you'll want to choose one that allows nested virtualization, which means running a virtual machine within a virtual machine so you can do some of the Hyper-V activities that require it. Using virtual machines is also highly recommended because it allows you to easily change the storage and network configuration of your servers and allows you to revert your lab to its original state for each chapter.

> **Note**
>
> The MindTap digital online learning platform for this text includes access to live virtual machine labs based on the textbook's Hands-On Projects, without the need to set up your own lab environment.

Lab Setup Guide

Because of the flexibility and availability of using a virtual environment, the lab setup guide is designed with the assumption that virtualization is used, whether Hyper-V, VMware, VirtualBox, or some other product. The lab environment is designed so that the initial configuration of the virtual machines will take you through any chapter except for Chapter 9, which requires the successful completion of Chapter 8 activities. Each chapter (except for Chapter 9) starts with an activity that instructs the reader to revert the virtual machines used in the chapter to the initial configuration using a saved snapshot/checkpoint.

A total of five virtual machines (VMs) with Windows Server 2016 installed are used throughout the book. However, they are not all used at the same time; some activities use as many as four VMs while some require only one or two. No client OS is used. This decision was made primarily on the basis that many readers will be using evaluation versions of Windows on their VMs and the evaluation period for Windows client OSs such as Windows 10 is very short compared to Windows Server 2016's evaluation period. In addition, Windows 10 is continually being upgraded and the upgrades may affect the outcome of some of the activities. Therefore, any activities that require a client will use a VM that has Windows Server 2016 installed. Readers should see little to no difference between using Windows Server 2016 as a client OS and using Windows 10.

There are two configurations for the lab activities. Configuration 1 uses four VMs running Windows Server 2016 in which one server is a domain controller (DC) and two servers are domain members. The fourth server is configured as a stand-alone server that is operating in workgroup mode. Configuration 1 will be used in the activities in most of the chapters. Some activities require your VMs to access the Internet. An easy way to accommodate this is to install the Remote Access role on your Hyper-V host (if you're using Hyper-V and Windows Server 2016 for your host computer) and configure NAT so your Hyper-V host can route packets to the physical network and the Internet. After installing the Remote Access role with the Routing role service, configure NAT and select the interface connected to the physical network as the public interface and the interface connected to the Hyper-V internal switch as the private interface. The interface connected to the Hyper-V internal switch should be configured with address 192.168.0.250/24. Figure 1 shows a diagram of this network.

Configuration 2 uses one VM running Windows Server 2016 with the Hyper-V role installed and some VMs pre-installed (see Figure 2). Configuration 2 is used in the Hyper-V chapters (Chapters 6 and 7) and for activities in which the reader installs Windows Server 2016.

A few words about this diagram:

- The router address is an example; you can use a different address. You can do most activities without a router to the Internet, except those requiring Internet access.
- ServerDC1 is a domain controller for domain MCSA2016.local and has both the Active Directory Domain Services (AD DS) and DNS server roles installed.
- The host Hyper-V server is the only physical server, and it is running routing and remote access with routing and NAT to allow the VMs access to the physical network and the Internet.
- Specific installation requirements for each server are explained in the following sections.

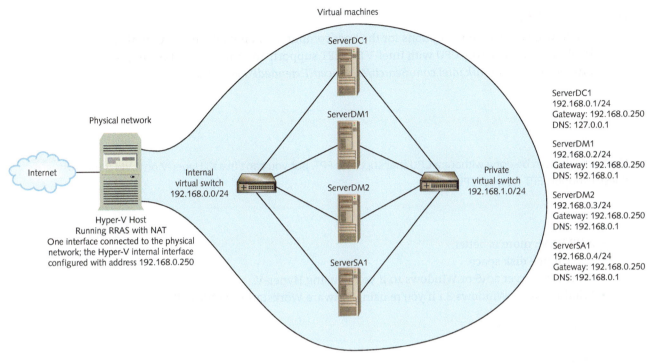

Figure 1 A diagram of lab Configuration 1

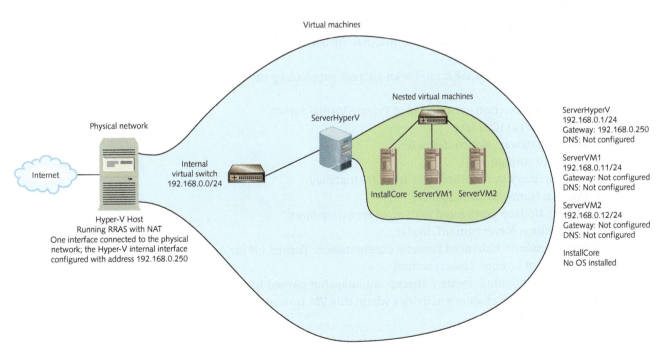

Figure 2 A diagram of lab Configuration 2

Host Computer Configuration

The following are recommendations for the host computer when you're using virtualization:

- Dual-core or quad-core CPU with Intel-VT-x/EPT support. You can see a list of supported Intel processors at *http://ark.intel.com/Search/Advanced?ExtendedPageTables=True*.

Note:

Most activities can be done without a CPU that supports EPT, but you can't install Hyper-V on a VM if the host doesn't support EPT for Intel CPUs.

- 8 GB RAM; more is better.
- 200 GB free disk space.
- Windows Server 2016 or Windows 10 if you're using Hyper-V.
- Windows 10 or Windows 8.1 if you're using VMware Workstation or VirtualBox.

Configuration 1

ServerDC1

This virtual machine should be configured as follows:

- Windows Server 2016 Datacenter—Desktop Experience
- Server name: ServerDC1
- Administrator password: Password01
- Memory: 2 GB or more
- Hard disk 1: 60 GB or more
- Ethernet connection—connected to Internal Virtual Switch
  - IP address: 192.168.0.1/24
  - Default gateway: 192.168.0.250 (or an address supplied by the instructor)
  - DNS: 127.0.0.1
- Ethernet 2 connection—connected to Private Virtual Switch
  - IP address: 192.168.1.1/24
  - Default gateway: Not configured
  - DNS: Not configured
- Active Directory Domain Services and DNS installed:
  - Domain Name: MCSA2016.local
- Windows Update: Configured with most recent updates
- Power Setting: Never turn off display
- Internet Explorer Enhanced Security Configuration: Turned off for Administrator
- User Account Control: Lowest setting
- After fully configured, create a checkpoint/snapshot named InitialConfig that will be applied at the beginning of each chapter's activities where this VM is used. Turn off the VM before you create a checkpoint/snapshot.

ServerDM1

This virtual machine should be configured as follows:

- Windows Server 2016 Datacenter—Desktop Experience
- Server name: ServerDM1
- Administrator password: Password01
- Memory: 2 GB or more

- Hard disk 1: 60 GB or more
- Hard disk 2: 20 GB
- Hard disk 3: 15 GB
- Hard disk 4: 10 GB
- Ethernet connection—connected to Internal Virtual Switch
  - IP address: 192.168.0.2/24
  - Default gateway: 192.168.0.250 (or an address supplied by the instructor)
  - DNS: 192.168.0.1 (the address of ServerDC1)
- Ethernet 2 connection—connected to Private Virtual Switch
  - IP address: 192.168.1.2/24
  - Default gateway: Not configured
  - DNS: Not configured
- Member of domain: MCSA2016.local
- Windows Update: Configured with most recent updates
- Power Setting: Never turn off display
- Internet Explorer Enhanced Security Configuration: Turned off for Administrator
- User Account Control: Lowest setting
- After fully configured, create a Checkpoint/Snapshot named InitialConfig that will be applied at the beginning of each chapter's activities where this VM is used.

ServerDM2

This virtual machine should be configured as follows:

- Windows Server 2016 Datacenter—Server Core
- Server name: ServerDM2
- Administrator password: Password01
- Memory: 2 GB or more
- Hard disk 1: 60 GB or more
- Hard disk 2: 20 GB
- Hard disk 3: 15 GB
- Hard disk 4: 10 GB
- Ethernet connection—connected to Internal Virtual Switch
  - IP address: 192.168.0.3/24
  - Default gateway: 192.168.0.250 (or an address supplied by the instructor)
  - DNS: 192.168.0.1 (the address of ServerDC1)
- Ethernet 2 connection—connected to Private Virtual Switch
  - IP address: 192.168.1.3/24
  - Default gateway: Not configured
  - DNS: Not configured
- Member of domain: MCSA2016.local
- Windows Update: Configured with most recent updates
- Power Setting: Never turn off display
- Internet Explorer Enhanced Security Configuration: Turned off for Administrator
- User Account Control: Lowest setting
- After fully configured, create a Checkpoint/Snapshot named InitialConfig that will be applied at the beginning of each chapter's activities where this VM is used.

ServerSA1

This virtual machine should be configured as follows:

- Windows Server 2016 Datacenter—Desktop Experience
- Server name: ServerSA1
- Administrator password: Password01

- Memory: 2 GB or more
- Hard disk 1: 60 GB or more
- Hard disk 2: 20 GB
- Hard disk 3: 15 GB
- Hard disk 4: 10 GB
- Ethernet connection—connected to Internal Virtual Switch
  - IP address: 192.168.0.4/24
  - Default gateway: 192.168.0.250 (or an address supplied by the instructor)
  - DNS: 192.168.0.1 (the address of ServerDC1)
- Ethernet 2 connection—connected to Private Virtual Switch
  - IP address: 192.168.1.4/24
  - Default gateway: Not configured
  - DNS: Not configured
- Workgroup: MCSA2016 (The workgroup name doesn't matter)
- Windows Update: Configured with most recent updates
- Power Setting: Never turn off display
- Internet Explorer Enhanced Security Configuration: Turned off for Administrator
- User Account Control: Lowest setting
- After fully configured, create a Checkpoint/Snapshot named InitialConfig that will be applied at the beginning of each chapter's activities where this VM is used.

Configuration 2

ServerHyperV

This virtual machine should be configured as follows:

- Windows Server 2016 Datacenter—Desktop Experience
- Server name: ServerHyperV
- Administrator password: Password01
- Memory: 4 GB or more (Dynamic memory disabled)
- Hard disk 1: 100 GB or more
- DVD: Assigned to D: drive and mapped to the Windows Server 2016 installation media ISO file
- Nested virtualization must be configured before installing Hyper-V. If you are using Hyper-V on the host server, use the following steps:

From a PowerShell window:

```
Set-VMProcessor -VMName ServerHyperV -ExposeVirtualizationExtensions
  $true
Get-VMNetworkAdapter -VMName ServerHyperV | Set-VMNetworkAdapter
  -MacAddressSpoofing On
```

- Configure the firewall to allow ping messages:

```
Set-NetFirewallRule FPS-ICMP4-ERQ-In -Enabled True
```

- Ethernet connection—connected to Internal Virtual Switch
  - IP address: 192.168.0.1/24 (You can also use 192.168.0.5 if you might have ServerDC1 running at the same time)
  - Default gateway: 192.168.0.250 (or an address supplied by the instructor)
  - DNS: Not configured
- Hyper-V role installed
- Workgroup: MCSA2016 (The workgroup name doesn't matter)
- Windows Update: Configured with most recent updates
- Power Setting: Never turn off display
- Internet Explorer Enhanced Security Configuration: Turned off for Administrator
- User Account Control: Lowest setting

Hyper-V should be configured as follows:

1. Create a private virtual switch named PrivateNet
2. Create a virtual machine named InstallCore with a 40 GB HDD and 1 GB RAM; the VM should be located in a folder named C:\VMs. This VM will be used to install Windows Server Core in Chapter 2.
3. Create two Generation 2 VMs named ServerVM1 and ServerVM2 for use in Chapters 6 and 7 activities:

ServerVM1:

- Windows Server 2016 Datacenter—Desktop Experience
- Server name: ServerVM1
- Memory: 1 GB
- Hard disk: 40 GB
- Ethernet connection—connected to PrivateNet
  - IP address: 192.168.0.11/24
  - Default gateway: Not configured
  - DNS: Not configured
- Configure the firewall to allow ping messages:

```
Set-NetFirewallRule FPS-ICMP4-ERQ-In -Enabled True
```

ServerVM2:

- Windows Server 2016 Datacenter—Desktop Experience
- Server name: ServerVM2
- Memory: 1 GB
- Hard disk: 40 GB
- Ethernet connection—connected to PrivateNet
  - IP address: 192.168.0.11/24
  - Default gateway: Not configured
  - DNS: Not configured
- Configure the firewall to allow ping messages:

```
Set-NetFirewallRule FPS-ICMP4-ERQ-In -Enabled True
```

4. After fully configured, create a Checkpoint/Snapshot named InitialConfig that will be applied at the beginning of each chapter's activities where these VMs are used.

Using an Evaluation Version of Windows Server 2016

You can get a 180-day evaluation copy of Windows Server 2016 from the Microsoft Evaluation Center at *https://www.microsoft.com/en-us/evalcenter/evaluate-windows-server-2016/*. You will need to sign in with your Microsoft account or create a new account. You can download an ISO file that can then be attached to your virtual machine's DVD drive to install Windows Server 2016.

If your evaluation version of Windows Server 2016 gets close to expiring, you can extend the evaluation period (180 days) up to five times. To do so, follow these steps:

1. Open a command prompt window as Administrator.
2. Type **slmgr -xpr** and press **Enter** to see the current status of your license. It shows how many days are left in the evaluation. If it says you're in notification mode, you need to rearm the evaluation immediately.
3. To extend the evaluation for another 180 days, type **slmgr -rearm** and press **Enter**. You see a message telling you to restart the system for the changes to take effect. Click **OK** and restart the system.
4. After you have extended the evaluation period, you should take a new checkpoint/snapshot and replace the InitialConfig checkpoint/snapshot.

Where to Go for Help

Configuring a lab and keeping everything running correctly can be challenging. Even small configuration changes can prevent activities from running correctly. The author maintains a website that includes lab notes, suggestions, errata, and help articles that might be useful if you're having trouble, and you can contact the author at these addresses:

- Website: *http://books.tomsho.com*
- Email: *w2k16@tomsho.com*

CHAPTER 1

INTRODUCING WINDOWS SERVER 2016

After reading this chapter and completing the exercises, you will be able to:

Explain the role a server operating system has in a network

Describe Windows Server 2016 roles and features

Explain the core technologies of Windows Server 2016

Summarize the new features of Windows Server 2016

Windows Server 2016 builds upon previous Windows Server versions, particularly in the areas of virtualization, workload management, and cloud computing. This new version is chockfull of new tools and features designed to help server administrators increase the availability of network services and limit security risks. Windows Server 2012 was all about the "private cloud" with a heavy emphasis on virtualization and virtual storage and using software to help you get more out of the hardware. Windows Server 2016 continues that trend and can be summed up as being all about the software-defined datacenter with new features such as Nano Server, containers, and Storage Spaces Direct.

Most networks are set up so that the people using computers on them can communicate with one another easily. One of a server's functions is to facilitate communication between computers and, therefore, between people. The administrator of a computer network has the job of configuring servers and computers on the network to provide services that facilitate this communication. These services include, but aren't limited to, file sharing, device sharing (such as printers and storage), security, messaging, remote access, web services, and many other services that work in the background to ensure a user-friendly and secure experience.

This chapter discusses the roles a server operating system plays in a computer network and the many features in Windows Server 2016 designed to perform these roles. As the Windows Server operating system (OS) becomes more complex with more features to facilitate the software-defined datacenter, there is less emphasis on the core technologies upon which Windows Server is built. This chapter introduces you to those core features such as NTFS, Active Directory, and Hyper-V while other chapters or other books in the MCSA series will cover them in more detail. Finally, we take a brief look at the new features in Windows Server 2016, most of which are front and center in the Microsoft MCSA certification exams. All of these new features will be covered in detail in other chapters.

About the Hands-On Activities 📎

Be sure to read and complete the activities in the "Before You Begin" section in the Introduction to this book. The hands-on activities in this chapter and all that follow require setting up your lab environment so that it's ready to go. The hands-on activities in this chapter use a Windows Server 2016 Standard or Datacenter Edition computer that's already installed and initially configured. The "Before You Begin" section gives you step-by-step instructions on setting up your lab for use with all activities in this book.

Completing the hands-on activities in this book is important because they contain information about how Windows Server 2016 works and the tools to manage it that are best understood by hands-on experience. If for some reason you can't do some of the activities, you should at least read through each one to make sure you don't miss important information. Table 1-1 summarizes the requirements of the hands-on activities in this chapter.

Table 1-1   Activity requirements

Activity	Requirements	Notes
Activity 1-1: Resetting Your Virtual Environment	ServerSA1	You need to perform this activity only if you are using virtual machines with snapshots and you are performing the activities in this chapter an additional time.
Activity 1-2: Reviewing System Properties and Exploring Server Manager	ServerSA1	Windows Server 2016 Datacenter Edition is installed according to instructions in "Before You Begin" section of this book's Introduction.
Activity 1-3: Examining NTFS Permissions and Attributes	ServerSA1	
Activity 1-4: Working with MMCs	ServerSA1	
Activity 1-5: Creating a Volume and Sharing a Folder	ServerSA1	
Activity 1-6: Exploring Windows Networking Components	ServerSA1	
Activity 1-7: Working with PowerShell	ServerSA1	

The Role of a Server Operating System

A server or collection of servers is usually at the center of most business networks. The functions a server performs depend on several factors, including the type of business using the server, size of the business, and extent to which the business has committed to using technology to aid operations. The latter factor is the crux of the matter. Technology is designed to help a person or an organization do things more efficiently or more effectively, and a server is used to provide services a business has deemed can help its operations. Before you explore these services in more detail, a few definitions are in order.

Server: Hardware or Software?

When most people hear the word *server*, they conjure up visions of a large tower computer with lots of hard drives and memory. This image is merely a computer hardware configuration that may or may not be used as a server, however. In short, a computer becomes a server when software is installed on it that provides a network service to client computers. In other words, you could install certain software on an inexpensive laptop computer and make it act as a server. By the same token, a huge tower computer with six hard drives and 128 gigabytes (GB) of random access memory (RAM) could be used as a workstation for a single user. So although some computer hardware configurations are packaged to function as a server and others are packaged as desktop computers, what makes a computer a server or desktop computer is the software installed on it.

Of course, with modern operating systems (OSs), the lines between desktop and server computers are blurred. OSs such as Windows 10 and its predecessors are designed to be installed on desktop computers or workstations (and in the case of Windows 10, tablet computers and phones); to run web browser, word processing, spreadsheet, and similar programs; and generally to act as a personal computer. However, these OSs can perform server functions, such as file and printer sharing, and even act as a web server. Although Windows Server 2016 and its predecessors are designed as **server operating systems**, there's nothing to stop you from installing a word processor or web browser and using Windows Server 2016 on your desktop computer. So what are the differences between a desktop OS, such as Windows 10, and a server OS, such as Windows Server 2016? The following section explains.

Server Operating Systems Versus Desktop Operating Systems

Both Windows Server 2016 and Windows 10 can perform some server functions and some desktop functions, but important differences distinguish them. Windows 10 is configured to emphasize the user interface and is performance-tuned to run desktop applications. Windows Server 2016, on the other hand, deemphasizes many of Windows 10's user interface bells and whistles in favor of a less flashy and less resource-intensive user interface. In fact, Microsoft makes the Server Core version with no graphical user interface the default Windows Server 2016 installation option. And, as you will see, a new Windows Server 2016 installation option, known as "Nano Server," nearly strips away the user interface altogether. In addition, Windows Server 2016 is performance-tuned to run background processes so that client computers can access network services faster. Speaking of network services, most Windows Server 2016 editions can run the following network services, among others:

- File and Printer Sharing
- Web Server
- Routing and Remote Access Services (RRAS)
- Domain Name System (DNS)
- Dynamic Host Configuration Protocol (DHCP)
- File Transfer Protocol (FTP) Server
- Active Directory
- Distributed File System (DFS)
- Hyper-V
- Fax Server

Of these services, Windows 10 supports only Hyper-V, File and Printer Sharing, Web Server, and FTP Server and in a limited capacity. In addition, Windows 10 is restricted to 20 signed-in network users, whereas on a Windows Server 2016 computer running Standard or Datacenter Edition, signed-in users are limited only by the number of purchased licenses and available resources. In addition, because a server is such a critical device in a network, Windows Server 2016 includes fault-tolerance features, such as a redundant array of independent disks (RAID) 5 volumes, load balancing, and clustering, which aren't standard features in Windows 10 or other Windows desktop OSs. Windows Server 2016 is also capable of supporting up to 64 processors; Windows 10 supports a maximum of 2.

Windows Server 2016 Roles and Features

In Windows, a **server role** is a major function or service that a server performs. Probably the best known and most common server role is a file server (the File Server role in Windows Server 2016), which allows the server to share files on a network. **Role services** add functions to the main role. For example, with the File and Storage Services role, you can install role services such as Distributed File System, Server for NFS, and File Server Resource Manager. Windows server roles and role services are installed in Server Manager by clicking Manage and clicking Add Roles and Features (see Figure 1-1).

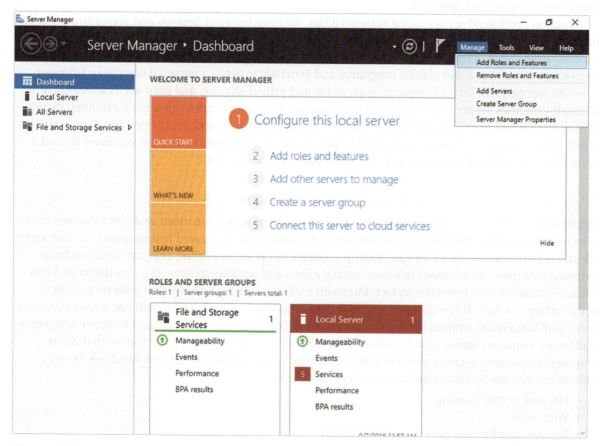

Figure 1-1   Adding roles and features with Server Manager

You can also add **server features**, which provide functions that enhance or support an installed role or add a standalone function. For example, you can add the Failover Clustering feature to provide fault tolerance for a file server or database server. An example of a standalone feature is Internet Printing Client, which enables clients to use Internet Printing Protocol to connect to printers on the Internet. A server can be configured with a single role or several roles, depending on the organization's needs and the load a role puts on the server hardware. Figure 1-2 shows the list of available server roles in Windows Server 2016. Several of these roles, particularly those covered in Exam 70-740, are explained in detail in later chapters.

Windows Server 2016 Core Technologies

Many of the topics of this book require that you understand the core technologies in Windows Server 2016. Some of these core technologies are discussed in more detail in this book or in one of the other MCSA titles (*MCSA Guide to Networking with Windows Server 2016, Exam 70-741* and *MCSA*

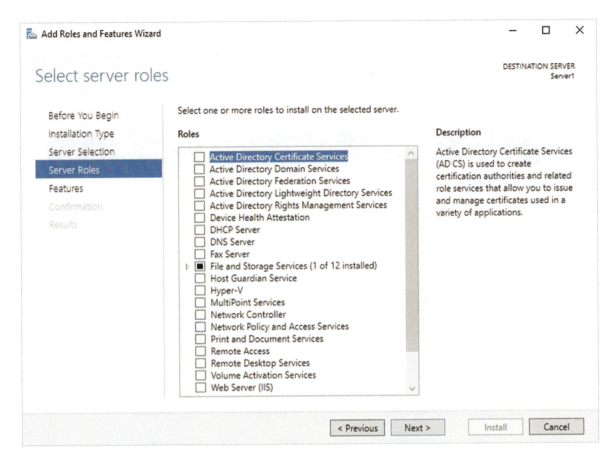

Figure 1-2 Available server roles in Windows Server 2016

Guide to Identity with Windows Server 2016, Exam 70-742 [Cengage, 2018]). However, this section gives you a brief overview of these technologies so you will be familiar with them when you need to use them later on. The following is a list of some of the technologies on which Windows Server 2016 is built:

- Server Manager
- NT File System (NTFS)
- Active Directory
- Microsoft Management Console (MMC)
- Disk Management
- File and Printer Sharing
- Windows networking
- PowerShell
- Hyper-V and cloud computing
- Storage Spaces

The following sections describe these technologies briefly; some are covered in detail in later chapters.

Server Manager

Server Manager provides a single interface for installing, configuring, and removing a variety of server roles and features on your Windows server. It also summarizes your server's status and configuration and includes tools to diagnose problems, manage storage, and perform general configuration tasks. Server Manager can be used to manage all servers in your network and access all the server administration tools from a single console.

When you start Server Manager, you see the Dashboard view, shown in Figure 1-3. The Dashboard shows a list of tasks you can perform, summarizes the installed roles, and shows the servers that are available to manage. The Welcome section can be hidden after you're familiar with Server Manager. This tool is used to access most of the configuration and monitoring tools for administering Windows servers, and you learn more about it throughout this book.

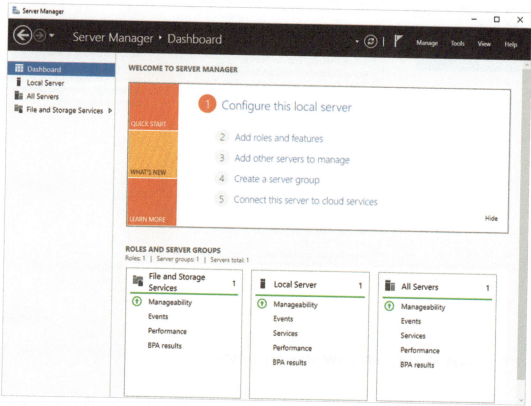

Figure 1-3   Server Manager Dashboard view

The forward and backward arrows at the upper left are used to navigate through recently opened windows. Moving to the right, your current location is displayed, followed by the refresh button and the notifications icon (shaped like a flag) that you click to view recent messages from Server Manager. Next is the Manage menu, used to perform major tasks, such as adding and removing roles and features and creating server groups. The Tools menu gives you quick access to administrative tools, such as Computer Management, Event Viewer, and Task Scheduler. Management consoles for server roles or features that you install are added to this menu. You can use the View menu to choose a magnification option for fonts in Server Manager, and the Help menu is self-explanatory.

The left pane of Server Manager displays the major views: Dashboard (described previously), Local Server, and All Servers. You use the Local Server view to manage just the server where you're running Server Manager and the All Servers view to manage aspects of all servers. To add servers you want to manage, right-click All Servers and click Add Servers or use the Manage menu. Under the All Servers item in the left pane is a node for each installed server role. In Figure 1-3, you see File and Storage Services, which is a preinstalled role. Clicking a server role puts Server Manager into role management mode so that you can manage each role in the Server Manager interface. When you're managing a role, the options for the role are displayed.

NT File System (NTFS)

One of a server's main jobs is to store a variety of file types and make them available to network users. To do this effectively, a server OS needs a robust and efficient file system. **NT File System (NTFS)** was introduced in Windows NT in the early 1990s. Although it has been updated throughout the years, NTFS has remained a reliable, flexible, and scalable file system. Its predecessor was File Allocation Table (FAT)/FAT32, which had severe limitations for a server OS. It lacked features such as native support for long file names, file and folder permissions, support for large files and volumes, reliability, compression, and encryption. NTFS supports all these features and more.

Perhaps the most important feature of NTFS is the capability to set user and group permissions on both folders and files. With this feature, administrators can specify which users can access a file and what users can do with a file if they're granted access, which increase a server environment's security. FAT/FAT32 has no user access controls.

> **Note** 📎
>
> The exFAT file system is similar to FAT/FAT32 except that you can create volumes larger than 32 GB; with FAT32, you are limited to a maximum volume size of 32 GB.

An NTFS volume has a number of advantages over a FAT/FAT32 volume. So what good is a FAT or FAT32 volume? One reason to use FAT or FAT32 on a Windows computer now is having a volume that will be used by another OS that might not support NTFS. In addition, removable drives, USB flash drives, and flash memory cards are often formatted with FAT32 or, for larger removable drives, exFAT. NTFS and other supported file systems are covered in detail in Chapter 4.

> **Tip** ⓘ
>
> A FAT/FAT32-formatted disk can be converted to NTFS without losing existing data by using the `convert` command-line utility.

Microsoft Management Console

A server OS requires a multitude of tools that administrators must use to manage, support, and troubleshoot a server system. One challenge of having so many tools is the numerous user interfaces an administrator has to learn. Microsoft has lessened this challenge by including the Microsoft Management Console (MMC), a common framework for running most administrative tools The MMC alone isn't very useful; it's just a user interface shell, as you can see in Figure 1-4. What makes it useful is the bevy of snap-ins you can install. Each snap-in is designed to perform a specific administrative task, such as the Disk Management snap-in shown in Figure 1-5.

Figure 1-4   The Microsoft Management Console

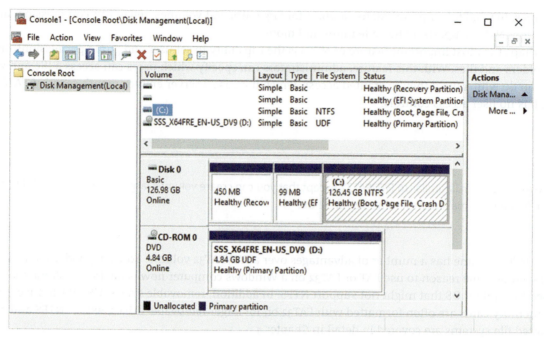

Figure 1-5   An MMC with the Disk Management snap-in

A number of MMCs are available in Server Manager's Tools menu, depending on the roles and features installed on the server. For example, after you install Active Directory, several new MMCs for managing it are created and added to the Tools menu. Not all administrative functions can be accessed from these prebuilt MMCs, however; you might have to create a customized MMC to access some functions or keep an MMC handy on your desktop with the administrative snap-ins you use most often. An important feature of an MMC is the capability to connect to servers remotely. Using this feature, you can install management tools on a Windows 10 workstation, for example, and manage a Windows Server 2016 computer without having to sign in at the server console.

Disk Management

To manage the disks and volumes on a Windows Server 2016 computer, you might use the Disk Management snap-in or the File and Storage Services role, which is integrated into Server Manager. With these tools, you can monitor the status of disks and volumes, initialize new disks, create and format new volumes, and troubleshoot disk problems. Both tools enable you to configure redundant disk configurations, such as RAID 1 and RAID 5 volumes. File and Storage Services also lets you create storage pools for Storage Spaces, discussed later in the "Storage Spaces" section of this chapter. These tools are also covered in more detail in Chapter 4, and Activity 1-5 walks you through using Disk Management.

File and Printer Sharing

Probably the most common reason for building a network and installing a server is to enable users to share files, printers, and other resources. Windows Server 2016 has a full-featured system for file and printer sharing, offering advanced features such as shadow copies, disk quotas, and the Distributed File System (DFS). At its simplest, sharing files or a printer is just a few clicks away. More complex configurations that offer redundancy, version control, and user storage restrictions are also readily available. Windows Server 2016 offers myriad tools and options for configuring file sharing; most are discussed in more detail in Chapter 4.

Windows Networking Concepts

Administering a Windows server requires extensive knowledge of networking components and protocols as well as a solid understanding of the network security models used in Windows. In a Windows network environment, computers can be configured to participate in one of two network security models: workgroup or domain.

The Workgroup Model

A **Windows workgroup** is a small collection of computers with users who typically have something in common, such as the need to share files or printers with each other. A workgroup is also called a *peer-to-peer network* sometimes because all participants are represented equally on the network with no single computer having authority or control over another. Furthermore, logons, security, and resource sharing are decentralized, so each user has control over his or her computer's resources. This model is easy to configure, requires little expertise to manage, and works well for small groups of users who need to share files, printers, an Internet connection, or other resources. A Windows Server 2016 server that participates in a workgroup is referred to as a **standalone server**.

The Domain Model

A **Windows domain** is a group of computers that share common management and are subject to rules and policies defined by an administrator. The domain model is preferred for a computer network that has several computers and/or requires centralized security and resource management. Unlike the workgroup model, a domain requires at least one computer configured as a domain controller running a Windows Server OS. In the domain model, a computer running a Windows Server OS can perform one of two primary roles: a domain controller or a member server.

A **domain controller** is a Windows server that has Active Directory installed and is responsible for allowing client computers access to domain resources. The core component of a Windows domain is Active Directory. A **member server** is a Windows server that's in the management scope of a Windows domain but doesn't have Active Directory installed.

Windows Networking Components

Every OS requires these hardware and software components to participate on a network: a network interface, a network protocol, and network client or network server software. Current OSs usually have both client and server software installed. In Windows, this collection of networking components working together is a **network connection**.

Network Interface

A **network interface** is composed of two parts: the network interface card (NIC) hardware and the device driver software containing specifics of how to communicate with the NIC. In Windows Server 2016, you configure the network interface in the Network Connections window (see Figure 1-6). To open it from Server Manager, click Local Server, and then click the address next to the Ethernet label. Alternatively, right-click Start and click Network Connections.

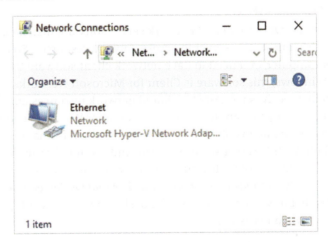

Figure 1-6   The Network Connections window

If you right-click a network connection and click Properties, a Properties dialog box similar to Figure 1-7 opens. The network interface used in this connection is specified in the Connect using text box. You can view details about the interface, including the device driver and configurable settings, by clicking the Configure button.

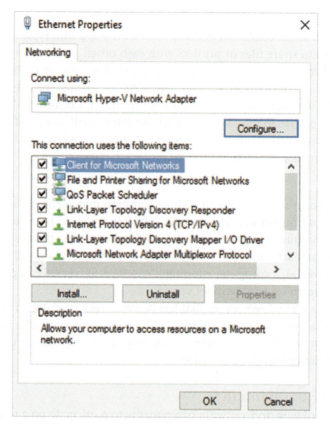

Figure 1-7   Properties of a network connection

Network Protocol

A **network protocol** specifies the rules and format of communication between network devices. Several years ago, network administrators may have had to understand and support two, three, or more protocols on their networks. Today, most administrators need to work with only TCP/IPv4 and more recently, TCP/IPv6. Both versions of TCP/IP are installed by default on Windows computers. To configure a network protocol, select it and click the Properties button.

Network Client and Server Software

Windows systems have both network client and network server software installed. A **network client** is the part of the OS that sends requests to a server to access network resources. So if you want to access a file shared on a Windows computer, you need to have network client software that can make a request for a Windows file share. In Windows, this software is Client for Microsoft Networks. **Network server software** is the part of the OS that receives requests for shared network resources and makes these resources available to a network client. So if you want to share files that other Windows computers can access, you need to have network server software installed that can share files in a format that Client for Microsoft Networks can read. In Windows, this server software is File and Printer Sharing for Microsoft Networks.

Windows networking is quite robust with a number of client and server components and a variety of configuration options. The *MCSA Guide to Networking with Windows Server 2016, Exam 70-741* covers TCP/IP configuration in depth, but you need to know the basics so you can configure and troubleshoot a server's network connection when necessary.

Active Directory Domain Services

Active Directory is the foundation of a Windows network environment. With Active Directory, you transform a limited, nonscalable workgroup network into a Windows domain with nearly unlimited scalability. The Active Directory Domain Services (AD DS) role installs Active Directory and turns a Windows Server 2016 computer into a domain controller. The main purpose of AD DS is to handle authentication and authorization for users and computers in a Windows domain environment. Active Directory stores information in a centralized database, giving administrators a tool for deploying user and computer policies, installing software, and applying patches and updates to client computers in the domain. Some server roles and functions require Active Directory to operate, such as certain types of failover clusters and Windows Server Update Services, so you need to learn the basics of Active Directory so you can install it and perform basic configuration tasks when you need to. However, you will learn about Active Directory in detail in the *MCSA Guide to Identity with Windows Server 2016, Exam 70-742* book. To summarize, the following are Active Directory's main purposes and features:

- To provide a single point of administration of network resources, such as users, groups, shared printers, shared files, servers, and workstations
- To provide centralized authentication and authorization of users to network resources
- Along with DNS, to provide domain naming services and management for a Windows domain
- To enable administrators to assign system policies, deploy software to client computers, and assign permissions and rights to users of network resources

PowerShell

PowerShell is a command-line interactive scripting environment that provides the commands for almost any management task in a Windows Server 2016 environment. It can be used much like a command prompt, where you enter one command at a time and view the results, or as a powerful scripting engine that enables you to create and save a series of commands for performing complex tasks. To say that PowerShell scripts are like a command-prompt batch file is like saying a two-seat propeller plane is similar to an F-35 fighter jet. Yes, they both fly, but the F-35 is much more powerful.

In a command-prompt environment, commands you type are called simply *commands*; PowerShell uses the term *cmdlets* (pronounced "command-lets"). Hundreds of cmdlets are available in PowerShell, ranging from performing simple tasks, such as displaying the date and time, to managing aspects of Active Directory and almost every other server role. In addition, new cmdlets can be created and imported as modules for extending the capabilities of PowerShell. PowerShell cmdlets aren't limited to managing the local computer; you can use PowerShell to remotely manage Windows servers and desktops. Remote management using PowerShell is particularly useful when you are managing Server Core or Nano Server computers that have limited to no user interface.

Getting the most out of PowerShell requires some effort because the number of available cmdlets is staggering. Learning to use this powerful tool is no longer just an option, however; it's a requirement for enterprise server administrators. PowerShell 1.0 was introduced as a downloadable product in late 2006, and version 2.0 became an important part of Windows 7 and Windows Server 2008 R2. PowerShell 3.0 is an integrated component of Windows Server 2012 and Windows 8, and Windows Server 2012 R2 and Windows 8.1 are equipped with PowerShell 4.0. Microsoft has continued updating PowerShell in Windows Server 2016, which sports PowerShell 5.0 and a new feature, called PowerShell Direct, for managing virtual machines with PowerShell directly from the host computer.

Using PowerShell

The names of PowerShell cmdlets are structured as *verb–noun* pairs with most cmdlets having one or more parameters that are specified after the cmdlet name. For example, the following cmdlet lists the available disks on the computer with the output shown in Figure 1-8:

```
Get-Disk
```

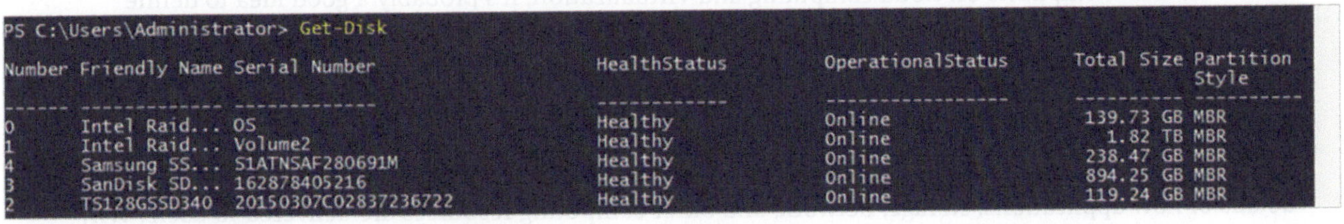

Figure 1-8   Output of the Get-Disk cmdlet

Note that capitalization doesn't matter when you type a cmdlet, but as a convention, the cmdlets are written using capital letters at the beginning of recognizable terms in the cmdlet name. If you want to see information about just a particular disk, you could use the following cmdlet:

```
Get-Disk -Number 1
```

In the preceding cmdlet, `-Number` is called a *parameter*. A **parameter** is an input to a cmdlet; in this case, the input is the disk number. The `1` that follows `-Number` is a value for the `-Number` parameter. Not all parameters require values, but many of them do. In some cases, the value for a parameter can be stored in a variable. A **variable** is a temporary storage location that holds values, whether numeric, strings, or objects. In PowerShell, variables are names that start with a dollar sign ($). For example, the previous cmdlet could be executed using the following PowerShell commands:

```
$DiskNum = 1
Get-Disk -Number $DiskNum
```

This is not a very useful example of using a variable, but you will see later that variables can make using PowerShell easier and more powerful.

Some of the cmdlets and parameters have quite long names. To reduce the amount of typing required, PowerShell has some shortcuts. You can begin typing a cmdlet or parameter and press the Tab key, and PowerShell will complete the name of the cmdlet or parameter. However, you must type enough of the cmdlet for PowerShell to understand what you mean; otherwise, it will complete the name with the first one in alphabetical order that it finds. For example, if you type `Get` and press Tab, PowerShell will finish the cmdlet with the first cmdlet that starts with `Get`, which in this case is `Get-Acl`. If you type `Get-Di` and press Tab, the cmdlet will be completed with `Get-Disk`. That example doesn't save much typing, but if you type `Get-NetI` and press Tab, the cmdlet will be completed with `Get-NetIPAddress`, which saves some typing. As in the command prompt, if you press the Up Arrow in PowerShell, the last command you typed is repeated and you can edit the command if necessary. This feature comes in really handy when you have typed a long cmdlet with several parameters and PowerShell returns an error indicating a typo.

Here are a few more useful tips for using PowerShell:

- To list all the cmdlets that start with `Get`, type `Get-Command Get-*`.
- To list all the cmdlets that have the word *disk* in them, type `Get-Command *disk*`.
- To get help on a cmdlet, type `Get-Help cmdlet` where `cmdlet` is the name of the cmdlet. Power-Shell may display limited help information at first. To update the help files, type `Update-Help`.
- PowerShell can take the output of one cmdlet and pipe it to another cmdlet. To do this, you use the pipe character (|). For example, if you want to stop all instances of Internet Explorer, type `Get-Process iexplore | Stop-Process`. You can also use the pipe character to filter the results from a cmdlet. For example, if you want to list all disks that are offline, type `Get-Disk | Where-Object IsOffline -eq $True`.

This book doesn't aim to make you a PowerShell guru, but with the new emphasis on remote administration of servers, many of the tasks you learn to do in the graphical user interface (GUI) are also shown as PowerShell cmdlets and scripts, and some tasks are performed only in PowerShell. You'll learn more PowerShell techniques as you work through the book.

Hyper-V and Cloud Computing

With Microsoft's emphasis on cloud computing and virtualization, it's probably a good idea to define some terms used when talking about these topics. Many of these terms and concepts are expanded on later as you learn about the technologies behind them, but this section should give you a running start.

So what exactly is cloud computing? This question isn't as easy to answer as it might seem, and you're likely to get different answers from different people. However, most networking professionals are likely to agree with this definition: **Cloud computing** is a collection of technologies for abstracting the details of how applications, storage, network, and other computing resources are delivered to users. Why the term *cloud*? It comes from network diagrams that included the Internet (see Figure 1-9), and because the Internet is a vast collection of different technologies, no single networking symbol could be used to represent it. So a cloud symbol conveys that a lot of complex network services are involved, but the details are unimportant at this time. One goal of cloud computing is to abstract the details of how things get done so that people can get on with their work. For example, do users really care that the X drive is mapped to ServerA by using the SMB protocol over TCP/IP? No, they want to store their files in a place they know is reliable and secure and do not need to know the details of how this task is done.

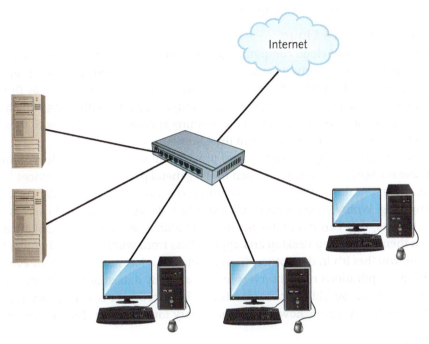

Figure 1-9   Network diagram with a cloud symbolizing the Internet

However, as an IT professional, you do need to know some details because setting up this technology is your job. A core technology of cloud computing is **virtualization**, which uses software (usually aided by specialized hardware) to emulate multiple hardware environments so that multiple operating systems can run on the same physical server simultaneously. Virtualization has its own terms for its operation and components. Some are defined in the following list:

- A **virtual machine (VM)** is the virtual environment that emulates a physical computer's hardware and BIOS. A **guest OS** is the operating system running in a VM.
- A **host computer** is the physical computer on which VM software is installed and VMs run.
- **Virtualization software** is the software for creating and managing VMs and creating the virtual environment in which a guest OS is installed. Microsoft Hyper-V Manager or VMware Workstation are examples of virtualization software.
- The **hypervisor** is the virtualization software component that creates and monitors the virtual hardware environment, which allows multiple VMs to share physical hardware resources. (In some software, this component is the Virtual Machine Monitor [VMM].) The hypervisor on a host computer acts in some ways like an OS kernel, but instead of scheduling processes for access to the central processing unit (CPU) and other devices, it schedules VMs to have that access.

The preceding list covers the basic terms you'll need to know when discussing virtualization, and when you learn more about Hyper-V in Chapters 6 and 7, you'll run across more terms that are particular to Hyper-V.

Hyper-V is virtualization software that can be installed as a server role in Windows Server 2016. It provides services for creating and managing virtual machines running on a Windows Server 2016 computer. As mentioned, a virtual machine is a software environment that simulates the computer hardware that an OS requires for installation. In essence, a virtual machine creates in software all the hardware you find on a computer, including BIOS, disk controllers, hard drives, DVD drives, serial ports, USB ports, RAM, network interfaces, video cards, and even processors. An OS can be installed on a virtual machine by using the same methods for installing an OS on a physical machine. Once installed, you can run the OS in the virtual machine and perform all the same tasks as with the OS running on a physical server. It's important to note that you can run as many virtual machines (VMs) in Hyper-V as there are resources available on the host computer. For example, you can set up a virtual environment that includes two Windows Server 2016 VMs, two Windows Server 2012 VMs, and a Windows 10 VM, all running on a Windows Server 2016 host computer.

Public Cloud Versus Private Cloud

There are two broad categories of cloud computing: public and private. The **public cloud** is a cloud computing service provided by a third party, whereas a **private cloud** is a cloud computing service provided by an internal IT department. Examples of public cloud computing are services such as DropBox and OneDrive, which provide storage as a cloud service, and Google Apps and Office 365, which offer office applications as a cloud service. You don't have to do anything special to have access to these services (some of which are free) other than have access to the Internet.

With a private cloud, a company's IT department provides all services for employees and perhaps customers, but these services aren't generally open to the general public. Typical services include virtual desktops, storage, and applications. **Virtual desktop infrastructure (VDI)** is a rapidly growing sector of private cloud computing. With VDI, users don't run a standard desktop computer to access their data and applications. Instead, they connect to the private cloud with a web browser or downloaded client software. They can then access their desktop and applications from wherever they happen to have an Internet connection, whether it's in their office, from a laptop in a local coffee shop, or even from a tablet computer. The OS and applications run on servers in the company datacenter rather than on the local computer. The key feature for building private clouds in Windows Server 2016 is Hyper-V. All the core technologies in Windows Server 2016, however, are necessary for running a cloud infrastructure.

Storage Spaces

Software-defined storage (SDS) is one component of the software-defined datacenter (SDDC) paradigm, along with software-defined networking (SDN) and, now, software-defined everything (SDE). SDS simply decouples the physical storage hardware from the storage requirements of the applications that use it, providing a flexible software-defined storage solution with advanced features such as deduplication (the ability to store duplicate, or repeating, data only once), thin provisioning, and replication. In a nutshell, that is what Storage Spaces does.

Storage Spaces is a tool first introduced in Windows Server 2012 that is designed to make the most of local storage on servers. It uses the power of virtual disks to give you a platform for creating volumes from storage pools that can be dynamically expanded and fault tolerant without the usual physical disk restrictions placed on volume creation. Volumes can be created from multiple drive types, including USB, SATA, and SAS. Drives can be internal or external, and RAID volumes need not be created from same-sized disks. By using virtual disks, Storage Spaces permits **thin provisioning**, which means the physical disk space isn't allocated for a volume until it's actually needed. Storage Spaces is covered in detail in Chapter 4.

Activity 1-1: Resetting Your Virtual Environment

Note 📎

> The activities in this book are based on the use of virtual machines in a Windows Server 2016 Hyper-V environment. Other virtualization platforms such as VMware and VirtualBox should work for most activities. See the "Before You Begin" section of this book's Introduction for more information about using virtualization.

Note

You need to perform this activity only if you are using virtual machines with snapshots and you are per-forming the activities in this chapter an additional time. If you are using your virtual machines for the first time, they will already be in the initial configuration state.

Time Required: 5 minutes
Objective: Reset your virtual environment by applying the InitialConfig checkpoint or snapshot.
Required Tools and Equipment: ServerSA1
Description: Apply the InitialConfig checkpoint or snapshot to ServerSA1.

1. Be sure ServerSA1 is shut down. In your virtualization program, apply the InitialConfig checkpoint or snapshot to ServerSA1.
2. When the snapshot or checkpoint has finished being applied, continue to the next activity.

Activity 1-2: Reviewing System Properties and Exploring Server Manager

Time Required: 10 minutes
Objective: View system properties in Windows Server 2016.
Required Computers: ServerSA1 with Windows Server 2016 Datacenter Edition installed according to instructions in "Before You Begin" section of this book's Introduction
Description: You learn to find basic information about a Windows Server 2016 installation, such as the server edition, network adapter settings, processors, installed RAM, and disk drives.

1. Start ServerSA1, and sign in as **Administrator** with the password **Password01**. Server Manager starts automatically.
2. In the left pane of Server Manager, click **Local Server**. You see the Properties window for ServerSA1 shown in Figure 1-10.

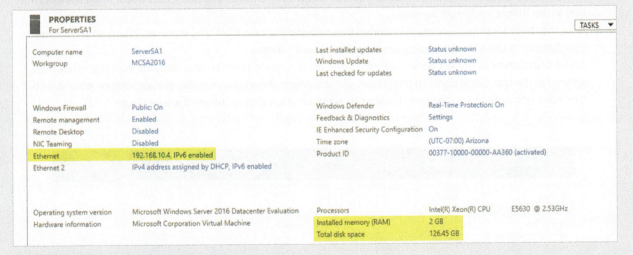

Figure 1-10   The Local Server Properties window

3. Review the fields highlighted in Figure 1-10 : Ethernet, Installed memory (RAM), and Total disk space. Your settings may differ depending on your environment.
4. Scroll down to explore other information available in Server Manager, such as a list of recent events, a summary of services, and a list of installed roles and features at the bottom.
5. Click **Dashboard** in the left pane. (Notice the icon next to Dashboard; you'll need it to navigate back to this view later.) The Dashboard is divided into two sections: Welcome and Roles and Server Groups. The Welcome

section lists common tasks you can access easily, including adding roles and features, adding other servers to manage, and creating server groups. This section can be hidden if desired.

6. Scroll down, if necessary, to see the Roles and Server Groups section. This section contains a box for each installed role, a box for the local server, and a box for each server group (see Figure 1-11). Each box contains information about manageability, which tells you whether Server Manager can contact the role or server to perform management tasks. You can double-click other items in these boxes to get details about events, services, performance, and Best Practices Analyzer (BPA) results. In the File and Storage Services box, click **Events**. Any events related to this role are then displayed in the resulting dialog box. Click **Cancel** to close the Events Detail View box for File and Storage Services.

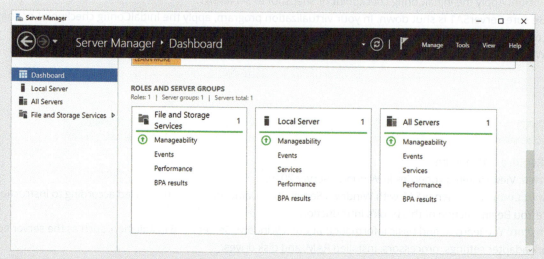

Figure 1-11   The Roles and Server Groups section

7. Scroll up to see the Welcome section, if necessary. In the Welcome section, click **Add roles and features** to start the Add Roles and Features Wizard; you use this wizard often in this book's activities. Read the information in the Before you begin window.

8. Note the three tasks that are recommended before installing new roles and features. When you're finished, click **Cancel** to close the Add Roles and Features Wizard window.

9. Click **Local Server** in the left pane. The right pane is then divided into several sections with the Properties section at the top. Scroll down to the Events section, which shows the most recent warning or error events that have occurred in your system. Clicking an event displays a description of it (see Figure 1-12).

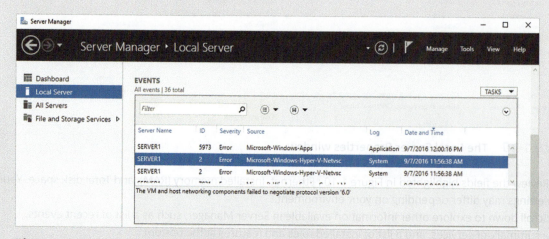

Figure 1-12   The Events section

10. Scroll down to the Services section, which displays a list of services installed on the server along with their status. You can start and stop services by right-clicking them and then selecting an action in the menu.

11. Scroll down to the Best Practices Analyzer section. The Best Practices Analyzer (BPA) is used to make sure a server role is installed in compliance with best practices to ensure effectiveness, trustworthiness, and reliability. Run a BPA scan by clicking the **TASKS** drop-down arrow, and then clicking **Start BPA Scan**. After a while, you see the results and any best practices suggestions will be displayed. There may not be any warning or errors, which means the server is completely in compliance!

12. Scroll down to the Performance section. You can view and configure performance alerts for CPU and memory use. Performance monitoring is covered in more detail in Chapter 11.

13. Scroll down to the Roles and Features section to see a list of roles and features installed on the local server. They're listed in the approximate order in which they were installed. You will see a list of roles and features that are installed by default on Windows Server 2016 since you haven't installed any yet.

14. In the left pane, click **All Servers**. The right pane has the same sections as Local Server except the top section, which is Servers instead of Properties. In the Servers section, you can select one or more servers and see information about them in the other sections of this window. As of now, you have only one server that can be managed with Server Manager.

15. In the left pane, click **File and Storage Services**. This server role is installed by default. The window changes to show you specific tools for working with this role. Click **Volumes** to see a summary of the server's volumes (see Figure 1-13). Click **Disks** to see information about the physical disks installed. Click **Storage Pools**. This feature in Windows Server 2016 is explained later in this chapter in the "Storage Spaces" section of this chapter and in more detail in Chapter 4.

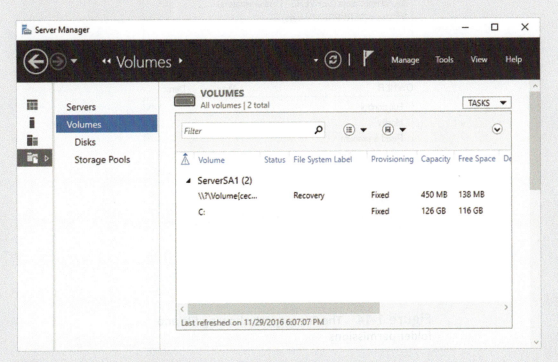

Figure 1-13   The Volumes window in Server Manager

16. Click the **Dashboard** icon in Server Manager to return to the Dashboard view.

17. Let's add a shortcut to Server Manager on the taskbar. Close Server Manager. Open Server Manager again by clicking the **Search Windows** icon next to Start (it looks like a magnifying glass) and typing **server** and then clicking **Server Manager** in the results window. To add the shortcut to the taskbar, right-click the **Server Manager** icon on the taskbar and click **Pin to taskbar**.

18. Continue to the next activity.

Activity 1-3: Examining NTFS Permissions and Attributes

Time Required: 10 minutes

Objective: View NTFS file permissions and attributes.

Required Tools and Equipment: ServerSA1

Description: In this activity, you familiarize yourself with the features of NTFS.

1. Sign in to ServerSA1 as **Administrator** if necessary.
2. Click the **File Explorer** icon on the taskbar, and then click **This PC** in the left pane.
3. Right-click the **(C:)** drive in the right pane and click **Properties**.
4. Click the **General** tab, if necessary. You see that the file system is NTFS, which is the only option for the drive where Windows is installed. FAT/FAT32 lacks the security and features required by Windows.
5. Click the **Security** tab (see Figure 1-14).

Figure 1-14   The Security tab showing file and folder permissions

6. Click each item in the Group or user names section, and view the permission settings for each in the bottom pane.
7. Next, click the **Quota** tab. The quotas feature allows you to set the maximum space a user's files can occupy on a volume. You see that disk quotas are disabled, the default configuration.
8. Now click the **Previous Versions** tab. This feature enables you to restore previous versions of a file and must be enabled on each volume on which you want to use the feature.
9. Last, click the **General** tab again. Note the two check boxes at the bottom for enabling file indexing and compression, which are features of NTFS.
10. Click **Cancel** to close the Properties dialog box.

11. In the left pane, click the **Documents** folder. Right-click in the right pane, point to **New**, and click **Text Document**.
12. Right-click **New Text Document** and click **Properties**. Notice the two check boxes at the bottom labeled Read-only and Hidden. They are common file attributes in both the FAT/FAT32 and NTFS/ReFS file systems. Click **Advanced**.
13. In the Advanced Attributes dialog box, notice four more check boxes for attributes. Only the archiving attribute is available with FAT/FAT32 volumes. The other three, for file indexing, file compression, and encryption, are available only with NTFS volumes.
14. Close all open windows and continue to the next activity.

Activity 1-4: Working with MMCs

Time Required: 15 minutes
Objective: Explore the Tools menu in Server Manager and work with MMCs.
Required Tools and Equipment: ServerSA1
Description: Familiarize yourself with the management tools on your server work with prebuilt MMCs, and create a custom MMC.

1. Sign in to ServerSA1 as **Administrator** and start Server Manager, if necessary.
2. In Server Manager, click **Tools**, **Computer Management** from the menu (you can also access Computer Management by right-clicking **Start**). You might notice that some tools in the Computer Management MMC, such as Task Scheduler and Event Viewer, are also available as separate MMCs in the Tools menu.
3. To explore a tool in Computer Management, click the tool name in the left pane. Some tools have an arrow next to them to indicate additional components. Each tool is called a "snap-in."
4. Click the arrow next to **Services and Applications** to expand it, and then click the **Services** snap-in. This snap-in is also available as a standalone tool in the Tools menu.
5. In Services, find and double-click **Windows Firewall**. Review the properties for this service, which are typical for most services. Click **Cancel** to close the Windows Firewall Properties window.
6. Explore several snap-ins in the left pane of Computer Management such as Performance and Disk Management so you are familiar with the server. Close Computer Management.
7. Now, you'll create a custom MMC. Right-click **Start** and click **Run**. Type **mmc** in the Open text box, and then click **OK**.
8. Click **File**, **Add/Remove Snap-in** from the MMC menu.
9. In the Available snap-ins list box, click **Device Manager**, and then click **Add**.
10. Note your choices in the next dialog box. You can decide whether to use the selected snap-in on the local computer or another computer. If you select the *Another computer* option, you can manage this computer remotely with your MMC. Leave the **Local computer** option selected, and then click **Finish**.
11. Repeat Steps 9 and 10, but this time add the **Disk Management** and **Task Scheduler** snap-ins instead of Device Manager. Click **Finish** after adding Disk Management and then **OK** after adding Task Scheduler. Then click **OK** to close the Add or Remove Snap-ins dialog box.
12. To name your MMC, click **File**, **Save As** from the menu.
13. In the Save As dialog box, click the **Desktop** icon, type **DevDiskTask** for the file name, and then click **Save**. You now have a customized MMC on your desktop. Close the **DevDiskTask MMC**. When prompted to save the console settings, click **No**.
14. Continue to the next activity.

Note 📎

If you are using virtual machines with snapshots, you will be restoring the configuration of all the servers at the beginning of each chapter, so changes you make such as adding the custom MMC to the desktop will be erased when you restore the snapshot for the ServerSA1 server.

Activity 1-5: Creating a Volume and Sharing a Folder

Time Required: 15 minutes
Objective: Create a volume using the Disk Management snap-in; then create and share a folder.
Required Tools and Equipment: ServerSA1
Description: Use the Disk Management snap-in to create a volume. Then create a folder on the new volume and share it.

> **Note** 📎
>
> If your server is configured according to instructions in the "Before You Begin" section of the Introduction, you should have four physical disks. Disk 0 has the Windows OS installed, and the others are empty and offline.

1. Sign in to ServerSA1 as **Administrator** if necessary.
2. From the desktop, open the MMC you created in Activity 1-4. (You can also access Disk Management by right-clicking **Start** and clicking **Disk Management**).
3. Click the **Disk Management** snap-in in the left pane. There are two panes in Disk Management: The upper pane shows a summary of configured volumes and basic information about each volume. The lower pane shows installed disks and how each disk is being used.
4. Right-click the **(C:)** volume in the upper pane and note some of the options you have.
5. In the lower pane, find Disk 1. If its status is online and initialized, skip to the next step; otherwise, right-click **Disk 1** and click **Online**. Right-click it again and click **Initialize Disk** to open the dialog box shown in Figure 1-15. Leave the default option **GPT (GUID Partition Table)** selected, and click **OK**.

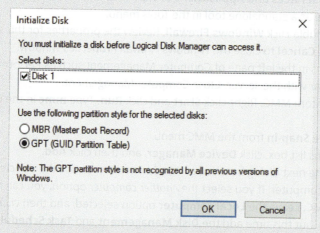

Figure 1-15 Initializing a disk in Disk Management

6. Right-click the unallocated space of **Disk 1**, and notice the options for making the unallocated space into a new volume.
7. Click **New Simple Volume** to start the New Simple Volume Wizard. In the welcome window, click **Next**.
8. In the Specify Volume Size window, type **500** to make a 500 MB volume, and then click **Next**.
9. In the Assign Drive Letter or Path window, you have the option to assign a drive letter or mount the new volume into a folder on another volume. Click the drive letter to open the selection box, click drive letter **S**, and then click **Next**.
10. In the Format Partition window, click the **File system** list arrow, and note the available options. Click **NTFS** to select it as the file system. In the Volume label text box, type **DataVol1**, and then click **Next**.

11. Review the settings summary, and then click **Finish**. Watch the space where the new volume has been created. After a short pause, the volume should begin to format. When formatting is finished, the volume status should be Healthy (Primary Partition).

12. Close the management console; click **No** when prompted to save the settings.

13. Open **File Explorer** and click **This PC** in the left pane to view the available drives.

14. Double-click the **S:** drive. Click the folder icon at the upper left to create a new folder. Type **DocShare** for the folder name and press **Enter**.

15. Double-click the **DocShare** folder to open it. Create a text file in the folder by right-clicking empty space in File Explorer, pointing to **New**, and clicking **Text Document**. Type **file1** for the file name and press **Enter**.

16. In the left pane, click the **S:** drive so you see DocShare in the right pane again. Right-click the **DocShare** folder, point to **Share with**, and click **Specific people**.

17. Click the selection arrow, click **Everyone**, and click **Add**. Notice that the default permission level is set to Read (see Figure 1-16), which allows all users with an account on the network to open or copy files in the DocShare folder, but not to change them.

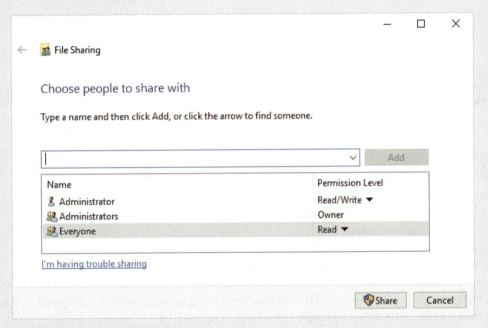

Figure 1-16   **Sharing a folder**

18. Click **Share**. (If you see a Network discovery and file sharing message, click **No, make the network I am connected to a private network**.) You see a message confirming that the folder is shared and the path to your new share is \\ServerSA1\DocShare. This is called the Universal Naming Convention (UNC) path. Click **Done**.

19. To verify that you can access the share using the UNC path, right-click **Start**, click **Run**, type **\\ServerSA1\ DocShare** (note that capitalization is not important), and click **OK** or press **Enter**. A File Explorer window opens and you see the file you created earlier. The UNC path is how someone on another computer would access the shared folder.

20. Close both **File Explorer** windows and open **Server Manager** if necessary. Click **File and Storage Services** in the left pane.

21. You should see that new tools have been added to the left pane: Shares, iSCSI, and Work Folders. (If you don't see these new tools, press **F5**, or click the **Refresh** button at the top of Server Manager, or close and restart Server Manager.) When you created a share, the File Server role service was installed automatically along with additional tools.

22. Click **Shares** to see a list of shares on your server (see Figure 1-17).

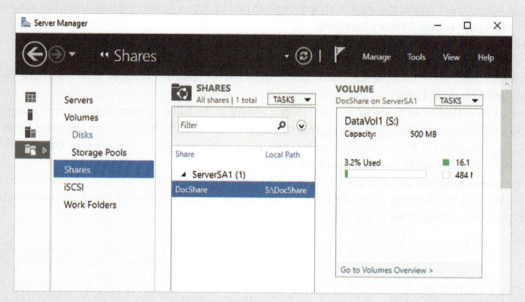

Figure 1-17 Viewing shares in Server Manager

23. Continue to the next activity.

Activity 1-6: Exploring Windows Networking Components

Time Required: 15 minutes

Objective: Explore features of Windows networking components.

Required Tools and Equipment: ServerSA1

Description: Manage various aspects of a network connection on your server.

1. Sign in to ServerSA1 as **Administrator** if necessary.
2. Right-click the **network connection** icon in the notification area and click **Open Network and Sharing Center**.
3. Active networks are listed at the top of the window. Depending on your network configuration, your network might have a name or be shown as simply Network as in Figure 1-18.

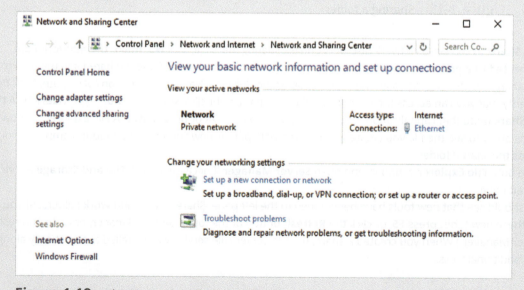

Figure 1-18 The Network and Sharing Center

4. Click the **Ethernet** link on the right to display information about your network connection and the number of bytes being sent and received (see Figure 1-19).

Figure 1-19   Viewing the status of a network connection

5. Click the **Details** button to view address information about TCP/IP and physical address information about your NIC, and then click **Close**.
6. Click the **Properties** button to see details on installed protocols, clients, and services. Each protocol and service has a check box for enabling or disabling it on the connection.
7. Click **Internet Protocol Version 4 (TCP/IPv4)**. (Don't clear the check box, or you'll disable the protocol.) Then click **Properties** to open a dialog box where you can change your server's IP address settings. For now, leave the settings as they are. Click **Cancel**, and then click **Cancel** again. Click **Close**.
8. Close all open windows and continue to the next activity.

Activity 1-7: Working with PowerShell

Time Required: 15 minutes
Objective: Work with Windows PowerShell cmdlets and features.
Required Tools and Equipment: ServerSA1
Description: Open a PowerShell prompt and work with some cmdlets and features of PowerShell.

1. Sign in to ServerSA1 as **Administrator**, if necessary.
2. Click the **Search Windows** icon and type **power** and click **Windows PowerShell** in the search results. A PowerShell window opens.
3. Type **Get-Verb** and press **Enter**. You see a list of verbs that can begin PowerShell cmdlet names.
4. Type **Get-Command** and press **Enter**. You see a list of all PowerShell cmdlets.

5. Press the **Up Arrow** and Get-Command is repeated. Press the **Backspace** key until you see only **Get-Com** and then type **p** and press **Tab**. Get-ComputerInfo is displayed. Press **Enter** to see information about the computer. Scroll through the information as there is quite a lot of detailed information about your computer shown.

6. Type **Get-Command *info*** and press **Enter** to see all cmdlets and command prompt commands that have the string "info" as part of their name.

7. Type **Get-Disk** and press **Enter**. You see a list of all disks on the computer. Type **Get-Disk | Where-Object IsOffline –eq $False** and press **Enter** to see a list of disks that are online.

8. Type **Get-Disk | Where-Object IsSystem –eq $True | fl** and press **Enter**. You see information about the system disk. The | fl part of the command means Format-List and provides more details about an object.

9. Type **Get-NetI | Where Int –eq Ethernet** and press **Enter**. Be sure to press the **Tab** key where it says and don't type a space before the Tab key.

10. Use a variable to store a value. Type **$interface = "Ethernet"** and press **Enter**.

11. Press the **Up Arrow** twice so that the command from Step 9 is shown. Press **Backspace** until the word Ethernet is erased and type **$interface** and press **Enter**.

12. Use a variable to store an object. Type **$interfaces = Get-NetIPAddress** and press **Enter**.

13. Type **$interfaces.IPAddress** and press **Enter** to see a list of addresses for all interfaces.

14. You have an introduction to PowerShell. Close the PowerShell window and shut down the server.

New Features in Windows Server 2016

Microsoft has added several new features and improved a host of existing features to make Windows Server 2016 a secure, highly available, enterprise-class server OS. Microsoft's emphasis on virtualization and the cloud is clear with several features focused on this burgeoning sector of IT. Some of the new features, discussed briefly in the following sections, are covered in more detail in later chapters; others are covered in *MCSA Guide to Networking with Windows Server 2016, Exam 70-741*, and *MCSA Guide to Identity with Windows Server 2016, Exam 70-742*.

- Nano Server
- Windows containers
- Storage Spaces Direct
- Storage Replica
- PowerShell Direct
- Nested Virtualization

Nano Server

Continuing on the theme of "less is more" that Microsoft started with the introduction of the GUI-less version of Windows called Server Core, the company has introduced an even lighter-weight server, Nano Server. While Server Core is designed to be installed on physical hardware or in a virtual machine, Nano Server is geared toward virtual machines, although installing it on a physical computer is an option. Nano Server is not intended to be a full-fledged server but is targeted at specific uses, such as the following:

- A server that provides processing, storage, networking, and memory resources needed to run an application, usually as a virtual machine and often as a cluster member, referred to by Microsoft as a **compute host**
- A cloud-based application server
- A file server as part of a cluster (a scale-out file server) or standalone
- A web server
- A DNS server

Nano Server is not a general-purpose Windows server that can be used to deploy any one of dozens of server roles and features. Instead, it is intended to be used as a tool to deploy (usually) a single well-defined service. Note that the uses listed here are likely to be a part of almost any network, large or small. Nano Server is not installed in the traditional method by booting to an installation DVD or DVD image; rather, you create a virtual disk from files included on your Windows Server 2016 installation media using PowerShell and using that virtual disk as the basis for a new virtual machine you create in Hyper-V. As mentioned, it is possible to deploy Nano Server on a physical computer as well.

Nano Server has no real user interface other than the Nano Server Recovery Console (see Figure 1-20), which you use to configure a network interface so you can manage the server remotely. Nano Server is a big step in the new paradigm of Microsoft's idea that network servers are to be considered commodity items that can be deployed and removed quickly and easily depending on the current computing needs of the organization or of a particular application. The details of installing and working with Nano Server are discussed in Chapter 12.

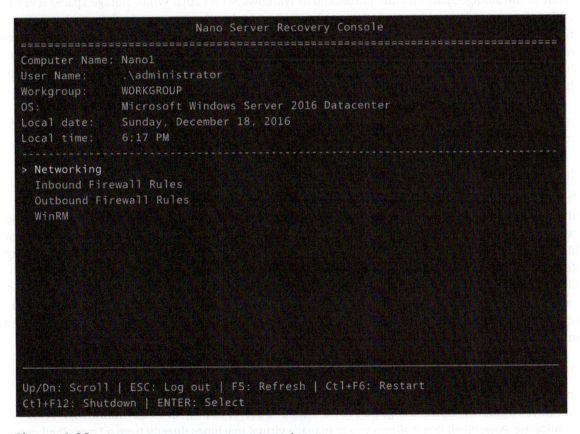

Figure 1-20   The Nano Server Recovery Console

Windows Containers

In computer and operating system terms, a container is a software environment in which an application can run but is isolated from much of the rest of the operating system and other applications. So, if operating system components that the application depends on are somehow corrupted or otherwise compromised, only the application in the container is affected. Take, for example, the registry, the integrity of which both applications and the OS rely on. If a regular application corrupts the registry, all running applications and services are likely affected. But an application running in a container has its own private copy of the registry. Any changes to it affect only that application, not other parts of the system. The same protection mechanism applies to other components used by applications such as dynamic link libraries (DLLs) and the file system. In other words, almost everything an application needs to run is "contained" in the container, so any changes made to those components affect only that application.

Aside from isolating applications, containers make applications completely portable between Windows systems. In other words, once an application is installed in a container, that application, container and all, can be moved to another Windows server (that supports containers, of course) without the usual installation process that can so often be fraught with problems.

A container sounds a little like a virtual machine, and there are similarities but also important differences. One or more containers deployed on Windows Server 2016 still share a single Windows Server 2016 kernel between the host OS and all other containers. So, for example, you can't deploy a container created for Windows Server 2016 on a different operating system such as Linux. There is much to be said about containers, and Chapter 12 is dedicated to this important new feature.

Storage Spaces Direct

Although Storage Spaces isn't new, Storage Spaces Direct expands upon the software-defined storage nature of the Storage Spaces feature introduced in Windows Server 2012. While Storage Spaces leverages local storage on an individual server, Storage Spaces Direct takes that one step further and leverages the storage contained on a network of servers. So, if you have three servers, each with three hard disks available for storage (not already allocated by existing volumes), Storage Spaces Direct can use all nine of those disks in its storage pool to create any number of different volume types (e.g., mirrored and striped) that are available to all servers on the network.

This feature adds a new level of fault tolerance to server storage because fault tolerant volumes can now be spread among multiple servers, not just multiple disk drives. Storage Spaces Direct is targeted primarily at highly available applications and is discussed in detail in Chapter 9.

Storage Replica

Continuing the storage theme, Storage Replica is a new feature that provides the storage manager with peace of mind in the event of a disaster. Storage Replica enables block-level data replication to occur automatically between datacenters located across the hall or across the ocean. While many replication strategies rely on file-based replication, where changes to files are replicated to other servers hosting the same files, Storage Replica uses block-level replication, which is much more efficient and less susceptible to data loss due to files being locked while in use. With block-level replication, only the data blocks that have changed need be replicated rather than entire files. Storage Replica utilizes synchronous replication techniques so data is replicated as soon as it changes with no delays inherent in file-level replication. Storage Replica can be used in failover cluster scenarios and with standalone servers. This new feature is covered in Chapter 5.

PowerShell Direct

PowerShell Direct is more a new method of utilizing an existing feature than an actual new feature. But, since PowerShell is such a large part of the Windows Server management environment, it bears mentioning. PowerShell Direct allows you to manage virtual machines directly from a PowerShell prompt running on the Hyper-V host. With PowerShell Direct, you can run PowerShell commands directly on a virtual machine from the host server without having to configure the firewall, security policies, or even a network interface on the virtual machine. Valid credentials for the virtual machine must still be provided, but other than that, it's like you are running a PowerShell session directly on the virtual machine console. PowerShell Direct is used to manage virtual machines, not other physical computers, and it is discussed in Chapter 6.

Nested Virtualization

Nested virtualization is exactly what it sounds like: the ability to run a virtual machine on a virtual machine. While this capability has been available with other virtualization platforms for some time,

Hyper-V started supporting it only with Hyper-V running on Windows 10. Although it is not intended for production applications, nested virtualization is important for training and test environments. In the past, if you wanted to experiment with Hyper-V, you had to install Windows Server 2008 or 2012 on a physical computer (or a different virtualization platform such as VMware). Now, since Hyper-V supports nested virtualization, you can install Windows Server 2016 in a virtual machine on a Windows Server 2016 computer running Hyper-V and install Hyper-V on the virtual machine. This functionality allows you to, for example, test virtual machine movement scenarios such as live migration and Hyper-V clusters without having to actually set up multiple physical servers.

This preceding list of new features is by no means exhaustive; there are many improvements and much added functionality to existing features in Windows Server 2016, but this chapter covered the major enhancements to the latest version of Windows Server, in particular those that you will need to know when taking the Windows Server 2016 MCSA/MCSE exams. As you can tell from the focus on virtualization and software-defined storage, Microsoft aims to make Windows Server 2016 the foundation of your software-defined datacenter.

Chapter Summary

- A server is largely defined by the software running on the computer hardware rather than the computer hardware on which the software is running. Although most client OSs now provide some server services, such as file and printer sharing, a true server OS is usually defined as providing these important network services: directory services, DNS, remote access, DHCP, and robust network application services. In addition, current server OSs include hardware support for multiple processors, disk fault tolerance, and clustering.

- Windows Server 2016 includes more than a dozen primary server roles and many supporting role services and features. Administrators can configure a server as a narrowly focused device, providing just one or two specific services, or as a general, do-it-all system that's the center of a Windows network.

- The technologies that make up the core functions of Windows Server 2016 include Server Manager, NTFS, the Microsoft Management Console, disk management, file and printer sharing, Windows networking, Active Directory, PowerShell, Hyper-V, and Storage Spaces.

- Microsoft has added several new features and improved a host of existing features to make Windows Server 2016 a secure, highly available, enterprise-class server OS. New features include Nano Server, Windows containers, Storage Spaces Direct, Storage Replica, PowerShell Direct, and nested virtualization.

Key Terms

Active Directory
cloud computing
compute host
domain controller
guest OS
host computer
hypervisor
member server
nested virtualization
network client
network connection

network interface
network protocol
network server software
NT File System (NTFS)
parameter
PowerShell
private cloud
public cloud
role services
server features
server operating system

server role
standalone server
thin provisioning
variable
virtual desktop infrastructure (VDI)
virtual machine (VM)
virtualization
virtualization software
Windows domain
Windows workgroup

Review Questions

1. Which of the following best defines a computer used as a server?
   a. Computer hardware that includes fast disk drives and a lot of memory
   b. A computer with OS software that has a web browser and Client for Microsoft Networks
   c. A computer with OS software that includes directory services and domain name services
   d. A computer with Linux installed

2. Which of the following best describes a Windows client OS?
   a. Supports up to 64 processors
   b. Includes fault-tolerance features, such as RAID-5 and clustering
   c. Supports network connections based on the number of purchased licenses
   d. Supports a limited number of signed-in network users

3. Which of the following is a service supported by Windows 10? (Choose all that apply.)
   a. File and Printer Sharing
   b. Active Directory
   c. Hyper-V
   d. Distributed File System

4. Which server feature provides fault tolerance?
   a. FTP
   b. Failover clustering
   c. DNS
   d. Internet Printing Protocol

5. Which Windows Server core technology can you use to install, configure, and remove server roles and features?
   a. AD DS
   b. NTFS
   c. Microsoft Management Console
   d. Server Manager

6. With which Windows Server core technology do you use snap-ins?
   a. AD DS
   b. NTFS
   c. Microsoft Management Console
   d. Server Manager

7. You are signed in to a server named Mktg-Srv1 that is a part of the Marketing workgroup. What kind of server are you signed in to?
   a. Domain controller
   b. Member server
   c. Standalone server
   d. Cluster server

8. The IT department sent out a memo stating that it will start delivering desktop computer interfaces through the IT datacenter via a web browser interface. What technology is the IT department using?
   a. Public cloud computing
   b. Server clustering
   c. Directory server
   d. Virtual desktop infrastructure

9. Which component of a network connection specifies the rules and format of communication between network devices?
   a. Network protocol
   b. Network interface card
   c. Network client
   d. Device driver

10. Which type of networking component is File and Printer Sharing for Microsoft Networks?
    a. Network protocol
    b. Server software
    c. Client software
    d. Device driver

11. What feature of Windows Server 2016 allows you to run command on a virtual machine directly from the host server?
    a. PowerShell Direct
    b. Windows containers
    c. Nano Server
    d. Nested virtualization

12. You're a consultant for a small business with four computer users. The company's main reason for networking is to share the Internet connection, two printers, and several documents. Keeping costs down is a major consideration, and users should be able to manage their own shared resources. Which networking model best meets the needs of this business?
    a. Domain
    b. Workgroup
    c. Management
    d. Client/Server

13. Which networking component includes a device driver?
    a. Network server software
    b. Network client software
    c. Network protocol
    d. Network interface

14. If you want to share files on your computer with other Windows computers, what should you have installed and enabled on your computer?
    a. Client for Microsoft Networks
    b. File and Printer Sharing for Microsoft Networks
    c. Active Directory
    d. Domain Name System

15. If you want to make a computer a domain controller, which of the following should you install?
    a. Client for Microsoft Networks
    b. File and Printer Sharing for Microsoft Networks
    c. Active Directory
    d. Domain Name System

16. Which new feature in Windows Server 2016 is not a full-fledged server but is targeted at specific use cases such as a DNS server or web server?
    a. PowerShell Direct
    b. Windows containers
    c. Nano Server
    d. Nested virtualization

17. Which of the following is the common framework in which most Windows Server 2016 administrative tools run?
    a. Windows Management Center
    b. Microsoft Management Console
    c. Server Configuration Manager
    d. Windows Configuration Manager

18. You have been asked to advise a business on how best to set up its Windows network. Eight workstations are running Windows 10. The business recently acquired a new contract that requires running a network application on a server. A secure and reliable environment is critical to run this application, and security management should be centralized. There are enough funds in the budget for new hardware and software if necessary. Which Windows networking model should you advise this business to use?
    a. A Windows domain using Active Directory
    b. A Windows workgroup using Active Directory
    c. A peer-to-peer network using File and Printer Sharing
    d. A peer-to-peer network using Active Directory

19. Which new feature in Windows Server 2016 isolates applications and shares the host OS kernel?
    a. PowerShell Direct
    b. Windows containers
    c. Nano Server
    d. Nested virtualization

20. Which of the following roles should you install if you want to create and manage virtual machines?
    a. Network Policy and Access Services
    b. Server Manager
    c. Hyper-V
    d. DHCP Server

Critical Thinking

The following activities give you critical thinking challenges. Case Projects offer a scenario with a problem to solve for which you supply a written solution.

Case Project 1-1: Recommending a Network Model

You're installing a new network for CSM Tech Publishing, a new publisher of technical books and training materials. There will be 10 client computers running Windows 10, and CSM Tech Publishing plans to run a web-based order processing/inventory program that for now is used only by in-house employees while they're on site. CSM Tech Publishing wants to be able to manage client computer and user policies and allow employees to share documents. Sign in and security should be centrally managed. What network model, workgroup, or domain, should be used? Explain your answer, including any server roles you may need to install.

Case Project 1-2: Preserving Disk Space

CSM Tech Publishing has been operating for six months, and business is good. You do a spot check on server resources and find that RAM use is at 50%, which is fine, but the data volume on the server used by employees to store and share documents is approaching 90% full. There are two volumes on this server: one for OS and program files and one for data storage. You inspect the data volume and find that some users are storing large amounts of data on the server. You check with the owner and determine that each user should require only about 4 GB of storage on the server for necessary documents. Because some users are clearly exceeding this limit, you're asked to come up with a solution. What file system option can you use, and which file system format must be used with this option?

Case Project 1-3: Explaining Cloud Computing

The owner of CSM Tech Publishing is always thinking about how he can use technology to improve the operation of his business. He read an article about cloud computing and has asked you to explain what cloud computing is and whether he needs it now or in the future for more efficient operations. Write a memo explaining what cloud computing is and whether you recommend using any form of it now or in the future.

CHAPTER 2

INSTALLING WINDOWS SERVER 2016

After reading this chapter and completing the exercises, you will be able to:

Determine appropriate Windows Server 2016 installation requirements and editions

Plan a Windows Server 2016 installation

Install and configure Windows Server Core

Install and remove features using Features on Demand

Once an arduous and sometimes intimidating task, installing a Windows server has become an easy, straightforward process. The installation process in Windows Server 2016 is similar to the Windows 10 process and requires little user interaction from start to finish.

The real work of a Windows Server 2016 installation takes place before you actually begin—in the planning phase. This chapter covers the actual installation process, but more important, it describes the planning that should go into installing a server in a production environment. Answers to questions about which edition of Windows Server 2016 you should use, how the server will be used, whether the installation is an upgrade or a new installation, and what roles the server will play in the network factor into how you decide to install the operating system. After installing the server, you need to undertake a number of postinstallation tasks right away, many of which depend on decisions you made in the planning phase. This book doesn't cover in detail the tools for deploying Windows Server 2016 in large numbers; instead, it focuses on the planning process for both small and large installations and the postinstallation tasks.

Other installation options in Windows Server 2016 also affect installation-planning decisions, depending on whether you want a server with a full graphical user interface (GUI) or the Server Core option. This chapter explores these options plus server upgrades, Features on Demand, and server role migration so that you can make wise choices when you deploy Windows Server 2016 on your network.

Windows Server 2016 Editions and Requirements

- 70-740 – Install Windows Servers in host and compute environments:
  Install, upgrade, and migrate servers and workloads

Table 2-1 summarizes what you need for the hands-on activities in this chapter.

Table 2-1   Activity requirements

Activity	Requirements	Notes
Activity 2-1: Resetting Your Virtual Environment	ServerHyperV	
Activity 2-2: Creating a New Virtual Machine for Server Installation	ServerHyperV	
Activity 2-3: Installing Windows Server 2016 Desktop Experience	ServerHyperV, InstallDE	InstallDE is a virtual machine you create in Activity 2-1
Activity 2-4: Performing Postinstallation Tasks	ServerHyperV, InstallDE	
Activity 2-5: Installing Server Core	ServerHyperV, InstallCore	
Activity 2-6: Performing Postinstallation Tasks in Server Core	ServerHyperV, InstallCore	

In the realm of server operating systems (OSs), Microsoft has an edition for all types of businesses, large and small. Businesses can choose the best solution for their size and the services they require. From a simple file-sharing server to a massive virtualization server, Windows Server 2016 has it covered. The editions are listed here:

- Datacenter
- Standard
- Essentials
- MultiPoint Premium Server
- Storage Server
- Hyper-V Server

Why the need for several editions? One size doesn't fit all is the short answer. For example, a small organization with a dozen users who mainly need a centralized network sign-in along with file and printer sharing can probably use Essentials Edition. A medium to large company or one that needs a robust application server might opt for Standard Edition. A company with hundreds or thousands of users that's implementing a private cloud solution will likely opt for Datacenter Edition. MultiPoint Premium Server is intended for volume licensing customers in academic institutions while Storage Server and Hyper-V Server are special-use editions. The following sections review the features and requirements of these six Windows Server 2016 editions.

Datacenter Edition

For organizations using virtualization on a large scale, **Datacenter Edition** is clearly the best fit. A Datacenter Edition license allows you to install an unlimited number of virtual instances of the OS, meaning you can install Datacenter Edition with Hyper-V on a physical server and then install as many instances of Windows Server 2016 Datacenter Edition in virtual machines as you need. A properly licensed Datacenter Edition also gives you the right to install an unlimited number of Windows Server or Hyper-V containers.

Features found in Datacenter that are not found in Standard Edition include Storage Spaces Direct, Storage Replica, Shielded Virtual Machines, and aspects of the networking stack that are based on the Microsoft Azure cloud computing system.

Standard Edition

Standard Edition has most of the features of Datacenter Edition except Storage Spaces Direct, Storage Replica, Shielded Virtual Machines, and the new networking stack based on Azure. The other distinction is that a Standard Edition license permits only two virtual instances or Hyper-V containers, so when you purchase Standard Edition, you can install it on a server, install the Hyper-V role, and then install Standard Edition on up to two virtual machines or create two Hyper-V containers. Except as noted, all Windows Server 2016 server roles and features are supported in both editions, and either edition can be configured as a domain controller, member server, or standalone server.

Essentials Edition

The **Essentials Edition** is aimed at small businesses with 25 or fewer users. It supports most of the roles and features in Standard and Datacenter editions, but some roles have restrictions or limited functions. For the price of the license, you can install Essentials Edition one time on a physical server or a virtual machine, but not both. Essentials Edition is automatically configured as a **root domain controller**, which is the first domain controller installed in an Active Directory forest. However, you are limited to 50 devices that can be managed by Active Directory. During installation of Essentials Edition, you're asked for the domain name, and Active Directory is installed automatically. Several other services are configured automatically in this edition: Active Directory Certificate Services, Domain Name System (DNS), File Services, Web Server (IIS), Network Policy Server, and Remote Desktop Services. In addition, Essentials Edition comes with a front-end management interface called Dashboard that serves as a simplified server manager. Other features particular to this edition include client backups and Remote Web Access. This edition supports up to two physical processors and 64 GB random access memory (RAM) and can't be installed in Server Core mode. No client access licenses (CALs) are required.

> **Note**
>
> You can install the Windows Server Essentials Experience server role in Standard and Datacenter editions. It includes the features and functions of Windows Server 2016 Essentials (such as automatic Active Directory configuration, the Dashboard view of Server Manager, client backup, and Remote Web Access), along with other preconfigured roles and features, and doesn't have the user and hardware limitations of Essentials Edition.

MultiPoint Premium Server

MultiPoint Premium Server Edition is for volume licensing customers in academic markets only. MultiPoint Premium Server allows multiple users to share one Windows computer, each with its own Windows environment settings. Each user station can connect to the server directly using video cables, USB, or a local area network (LAN) connection. Because this version is uniquely tailored to academic applications, it is not discussed in detail here. You can achieve the functionality of MultiPoint Premium Server with Windows Server 2016 Standard Edition and Datacenter Edition by installing the MultiPoint Services role.

Storage Server

Windows Storage Server is singularly focused on making a computer a storage appliance. Storage Server can be configured as a network-attached storage device for file-sharing applications or as a block-level Internet Small Computer System Interface (iSCSI) storage device for shared storage applications such as storage area networks (SANs) and server clusters. Many of the server roles you can install on Windows Server 2016 Standard or Datacenter editions are not available on Storage Server. For example, you can't install Active Directory or configure Storage Server as an application server, but you can install roles such as Dynamic Host Configuration Protocol (DHCP) and DNS.

Hyper-V Server

Microsoft Hyper-V Server 2016 is a free download with no licensing costs that allows you to make a server a Hyper-V virtualization server. Once installed, you can perform basic administrative tasks on the Hyper-V console so you can connect to and manage Hyper-V servers remotely using PowerShell or the Hyper-V Manager console. Hyper-V Server has all the features of the Hyper-V server role that you can install on Standard or Datacenter editions. Although there are no licensing costs for Hyper-V Server itself, you must license any guest operating systems you install in virtual machines.

General Licensing Considerations

Windows Server 2016 Standard and Datacenter editions use a core-based licensing model instead of the processor-based model used with previous releases of Windows Server. What this means is that each processor core must be licensed regardless of the number of physical processors. Each physical server requires a minimum of 16 core licenses for up to two physical processors with up to 8 cores each. So, even if your server has one physical processor with 2 cores, you must purchase licenses for 16 cores. Additional cores must also be licensed and are sold in packs of two. To get an idea of how it works, look at these examples:

> **Note** 🔗
>
> The terms *central processing unit (CPU)* and *processor* are often used interchangeably. A physical processor is a chip that installs in a socket on a motherboard. However, today's physical processors might have multiple processor cores, and each core can perform nearly the same work as a single-core physical processor.

- A physical server has one processor with 2 cores. You must purchase eight 2-core licenses for a total of 16 core licenses.
- A physical server has two processors, each with 4 cores for a total of 8 cores. You must purchase eight 2-core license packs for a total of 16 core licenses.
- A physical server has two processors, each with 8 cores for a total of 16 cores. You must purchase eight 2-core license packs for a total of 16 core licenses.
- A physical server has four processors, each with 4 cores for a total of 16 cores. You must purchase sixteen 2-core licenses for a total of 32 cores because each processor requires a minimum of eight core licenses.
- A physical server has two processors, each with 10 cores for a total of 20 cores. You must purchase ten 2-core license packs for a total of 20 core licenses.

> **Note** 🔗
>
> As of this writing, the retail price for eight 2-core packs for Standard Edition is about $880 and for Datacenter Edition about $6,100.

Standard Edition allows two **operating system environments (OSEs)** or two Hyper-V containers for each fully licensed server. An OSE is all or part of an operating system instance or all or part of a virtual operating system instance, which includes Windows Server 2016 installed as a virtual machine or a Hyper-V container. For each two additional OSEs or Hyper-V containers, all cores must be licensed again. Datacenter Edition allows an unlimited number of OSEs and Hyper-V containers.

> **Note**
>
> You can look at an OSE as simply a virtual machine with Windows Standard or Datacenter installed as the guest OS.

Additionally, both Standard and Datacenter editions require CALs for each client device or user that will be accessing the server. You can purchase per-user CALs or per-device CALs. Per-user CALs make the most sense if you have individual users who might access the server from multiple devices. Per-device CALs make the most sense if you have multiple users that share a device (such as shift workers or students in an academic environment). A CAL licenses a user or device to access any Windows Server running any edition no matter how many servers they might be accessing. So, for example, if you have already purchased per-device CALs for Windows 10 computers to access Windows Server 2012 servers, you do not need to purchase new CALs for those same Windows 10 computers to access Windows Server 2016 unless you install additional Windows client computers.

> **Note**
>
> Windows Server 2016 Essentials, MultiPoint Premium Server, and Storage Server are licensed using a processor-based system with a license required for each two physical processors regardless of the number of cores on each processor.

Windows Server 2016 Standard and Datacenter Edition Requirements

Table 2-2 summarizes the system requirements for the Standard and Datacenter Editions of Windows Server 2016.

Table 2-2   Windows Server 2016 minimum system requirements for Standard and Datacenter Editions

Component	Requirement
Processor	Minimum: 1.4 GHz 64-bit CPU Recommended: 3.1 GHz or faster 64-bit multicore
Memory	Minimum: 512 MB RAM Recommended: 2 GB RAM or more
Available disk space	Minimum: 32 GB Recommended: 60 GB or more for the system partition PCI Express SATA, SAS, or SCSI disk controller (PATA/IDE not supported)
Additional drives	DVD drive (required only if installing from DVD media)
Network interface card	PCI Express Gigabit (10/100/1000 BaseT) Ethernet Adapter supporting PXE boot
Display and peripherals	Super VGA or higher Keyboard and mouse Internet access

> **Note**
>
> To install Windows Server 2016 in a virtual machine (VM), the VM must have at least 800 MB RAM. After installation, you can change the RAM to 512 MB if desired.

Planning a Windows Server 2016 Installation

 **Certification**

- **70-740 – Install Windows Servers in host and compute environments:**
  Install, upgrade, and migrate servers and workloads

The actual process of installing Windows Server 2016 is simple enough that you might be inclined to get out the DVD and forge ahead without much forethought. However, this temptation could be a time-consuming and costly mistake if you don't have a well-thought-out plan for using the technologies in Windows Server 2016. Aside from selecting an edition, choosing an upgrade or a new install, and deciding whether to use a domain controller, among other decisions, you must also consider your installation options such as whether to do a Server Core installation, a GUI installation, or a Nano Server installation. In addition, you can install your server on physical hardware or as a virtual machine.

Admittedly, a single server installation for a small business with 25 users doesn't pose a major challenge requiring weeks of careful consideration and planning. You can make a few decisions and get on with it. However, situations such as installing 400 servers or bringing a branch office online, which requires integrating its server with the existing network, involve more planning. This section doesn't attempt to cover every possible server installation you might encounter. Instead, it gives you the knowledge you need to understand some potential issues and arms you with questions you need to answer before proceeding.

The network environment in which you're deploying a server and the roles a server will play on the network are the key considerations in planning Windows Server 2016 installations. In the following sections, you examine these common installation situations and learn some of the issues and options involved in:

- Installing the first server in a new Windows network
- Expanding a network by adding a second server or installing a server in a branch office
- Upgrading from earlier Windows versions

Installing the First Server in a New Network

Installing Windows Server 2016 in a new network that doesn't already have Windows servers operating is usually the most straightforward installation situation. The following descriptions assume you're installing the first server in a small network with fewer than 100 users.

One issue to consider for any server installation is hardware features. The following list describes a few of these features:

- *CPU architecture*—The major CPU manufacturers typically have a workstation line and a server line of processors. The server line includes Intel Xeon and AMD Opteron. Depending on the expected server workload, you must also consider how many physical processors and how many cores each processor should have. As noted, the number of cores plays into the cost of licensing your server. Server virtualization, which has special CPU requirements, is also a factor. To sum up, here are some of the CPU architecture options:
  - Workstation or server line of processors: Typically, the workstation line supports only 1 or at most 2 physical CPUs; the server line supports 64 or more.
  - Total number of physical processors: You can buy a system with one processor now and add more later if the system supports multiple physical processors. Be aware, however, that you must use identical processors in multiprocessor systems, and finding an identical match 3 or 4 years later can be difficult. Also, keep in mind the Windows Server 2016 edition you plan to install because the maximum number of processors supported varies. Again, licensing costs also play a factor.
  - Number of cores in each processor: Server CPUs are multicore processors with typically between 4 and 24 cores as of this writing, and the core count keeps increasing.

- Option of 32-bit versus 64-bit processors: This is no longer an issue for Windows Server products starting with Windows Server 2008 R2 because Microsoft no longer makes a 32-bit version of its server OS. In addition, unless you're using a very old processor, it's a moot point because any server or workstation processor manufactured after 2004 supports 64-bit processing.
- Virtualization extensions: With a 64-bit processor, chances are good that it supports virtualization extensions, but you need to be certain if you want to run Hyper-V. On Intel processors, look for the Intel Virtualization Technology (Intel-VT) label, and on AMD processors, look for AMD-V. These extensions are prerequisites to installing the Hyper-V role. The processor must also support second-level address translation (SLAT), a feature referred to as Extended Page Table (EPT) by Intel and Nested Page Table (NPT) by AMD.

> **Tip** ⓘ
>
> You can run `systeminfo` from a command prompt, and it reports on your computer's ability to run Hyper-V. You can also download and run a small program, Coreinfo, which displays many of the features and capabilities of your processor and processor cores. You can find this program at *https://technet.microsoft.com/en-us/sysinternals/cc835722.aspx*.

- *Disk subsystem*—Before the arrival of SATA drives, the only real choice of hard drives for servers was SCSI. Between these two standards is SAS. Current knowledge indicates that for entry-level or departmental servers, SATA is a good choice because it's inexpensive and offers excellent performance. For enterprise servers or servers accessed 24/7, SAS drives have a performance and reliability advantage. SAS disks are generally designed for continuous use; SATA drives tend to be designed more for consumer use than around-the-clock use. Doing research on current technology and your network's needs before deciding is best.
- *Hot-add/hot-replace features*—Say you've noticed that memory use has increased to dangerously high levels after installing a new database application on your server. You need to add memory to the server before it crashes; in the past, this process meant shutting down the server first. Not so with Windows Server 2016 Standard and Datacenter editions because both support **hot-add** memory, meaning the server doesn't have to shut down for this procedure. Unfortunately, the server hardware must also support this feature, and you find it only in high-end, enterprise-class servers. Some servers even support adding or replacing a processor without a system shutdown. The capability to hot-add disk drives is more common and can be found in almost all server classes. If you need more disk space or need to replace a failed disk in a redundant array of independent disks (RAID) configuration, you can simply install the new drive without shutting down the server. All editions support disk **hot-replace** or hot-add if the hardware supports it.

This list covers just a few of the server hardware features you should consider before installing a new server. The best advice is to forge a good relationship with a knowledgeable vendor you can consult when you need to make a purchase. This way, you can focus on managing your server, and your vendor can focus on keeping up with the latest hardware options.

> **Tip** ⓘ
>
> To make sure your hardware selections are compatible with Windows Server 2016, check the Windows Server Catalog at *www.windowsservercatalog.com*. Microsoft tests and certifies a number of preconfigured servers for use with Windows Server 2016. You can also check the compatibility of individual components.

When installing the first server in a new network, you must make some decisions shortly after finishing the installation. Some are fairly straightforward, but others take some thought and consultation. Here's a list of some decisions you need to make:

- *What should you name the server?* This decision is more important than it sounds. Every computer needs a name so that it can be identified on the network. A server name must be unique on the network and should include some description, such as its location or primary function. Server names should also be simple and easy to remember because users often access servers by name.

Tip ⓘ

Even if you expect the server to be the only server on the network, you shouldn't use just "Server" as the name. Situations often change and require adding a server, so at least give it a number, such as Server1. Subsequent server names can be a bit more descriptive, such as Mail1, Accounting1, or Building19DC.

- *Which network protocols and addresses should you use?* By default, Windows installs both TCP/IPv4 and TCP/IPv6 in Windows Server 2016. You can't uninstall them, but you can disable them in a network connection's Properties dialog box. TCP/IPv4 is still the predominant LAN protocol, but it won't be long before IPv6 takes hold in networks.

Caution ⚠

Although you might be tempted to disable IPv6 on your network connections if you're not using it, don't do it in Windows Server 2016. Some features, such as DirectAccess, depend on IPv6.

- *How should I assign an IP address to the server?* By default, Windows Server 2016 uses automatic IP addressing, but a server should have a static IP address. Some server roles (such as DHCP) actually require assigning a static address. If you haven't devised your addressing scheme, now is the time to do that. Generally, server administrators assign one of the first or last addresses in an address range, such as 192.168.1.1 or 192.168.1.254. Whatever you decide, be consistent so that when more servers are added, you can assign IP addresses easily. After configuring networking on a server, most people test the configuration by using Ping, a network testing and troubleshooting tool that sends a series of Echo Request packets to a destination IP address to see whether there's a reply. If the Echo Request reaches the destination computer, an Echo Reply packet is sent back to the sender.
- *Should I use the workgroup or domain model?* As discussed in Chapter 1, the Windows domain model has a number of advantages in usability, manageability, and security. If you've invested in a Windows Server OS, it makes sense to get the most out of it by using the domain model and installing Active Directory. With a small network of only a few users, however, the workgroup model is a viable option, particularly if the main administrator isn't familiar with Active Directory. With either model, you need a workgroup or domain name unless you're using the workgroup model and keep the default name Workgroup. If you're using the domain model, the domain name you use should be registered with the Internet Corporation for Assigned Names and Numbers (ICANN; *www.icann.org*). If the Internet name isn't already registered, make sure the name you have in mind is still available.

> **Note** 📎
>
> For testing purposes and for domains that don't need a public Internet presence, you can use top-level names, such as .local, .example, and .test (mycompany.local, mycompany.example, or mycompany.test). For a production network that requires an Internet presence, however, you should use only valid top-level domain names and registered second-level domain names.

- *What server roles should you install?* This decision is one of the most important because it determines how the server will be used and what network services will be available to users. Chapter 1 discussed some of the available roles and features you can install. For a first-server installation, however, there are some clear choices. With the domain model, you must install the Active Directory Domain Services (AD DS) role. AD DS requires DNS, so the DNS Server role is installed automatically. Other basic roles to consider on a first server include DHCP (for IP address configuration) and File and Storage Services, which includes tools for sharing and managing file storage. Many other roles and features can be installed to meet your network and business needs; several are discussed in later chapters.

Now that you have a plan, it's time to move on to the actual installation of Windows Server 2016.

Performing a Clean Installation

A **clean installation** is one in which the OS is installed on a new disk partition and isn't an upgrade from any previous version of Windows. For the first server installation on a new network, you usually use a DVD, or you can perform a network-based installation. If you are installing from DVD, make sure the BIOS is set to boot from the CD/DVD drive first if you have an OS already installed. After installation begins, a message is displayed to let you know that Windows is loading files. Next, you see the window shown in Figure 2-1, where you choose the language, time, and keyboard configuration.

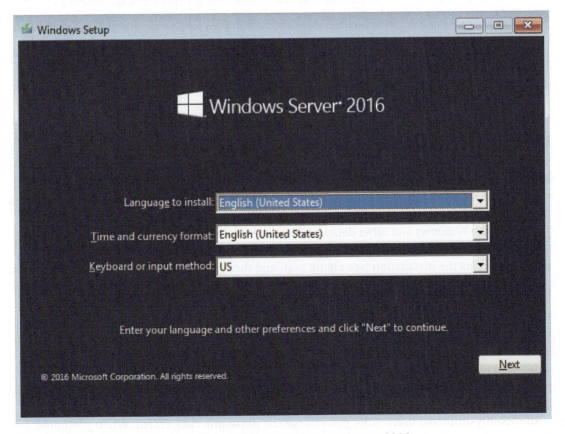

Figure 2-1   The initial installation window for Windows Server 2016

After clicking Next, a window is displayed with the options Install now or Repair your computer.

After you click Install now, you're prompted to enter the product code (unless you're using an evaluation edition). The next window asks which edition you want to install and whether you want to install the Desktop Experience (see Figure 2-2). The default installation option is the Server Core install that does not include a GUI. The Desktop Experience includes the standard Windows graphical user interface you find on Windows 10. This section covers a Desktop Experience installation, and you perform a Server Core installation later in Activity 2-5. In subsequent windows, you accept the license terms and select an upgrade or a custom installation. The upgrade option is available only if a supported version of Windows is already installed. A custom installation, described in this section, performs a clean install of Windows.

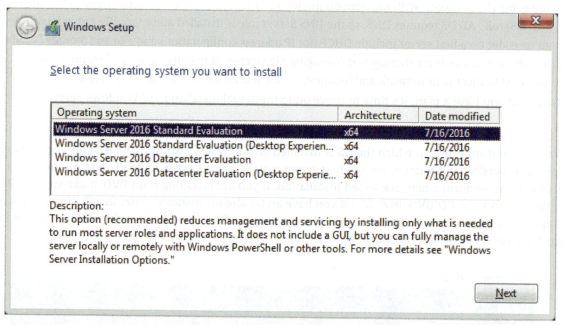

Figure 2-2   Choosing the edition and installation type

After selecting the custom option, choose from a list of disks and partitions to specify where you want to install Windows (see Figure 2-3). You can use the Load driver link to install a driver for a disk controller if your disk isn't shown. If you click the New link, you're prompted to create a new volume from the selected disk. If you select just a disk and click Next, Windows creates two volumes: one of about 350 MB for system boot files (which isn't assigned a drive letter) and the other for the C: drive, where the Windows and other default folders are located. The entire disk is used and is formatted with NTFS.

Windows begins the installation (see Figure 2-4), and then your computer typically restarts at least once. After the installation is finished, you're prompted to set the password for the built-in administrator account (see Figure 2-5). The password you choose must include three of the following types: uppercase letters, lowercase letters, numerals, and special symbols, such as @, /, and #. When you first assign the password for the Administrator account, you can use as few as three characters as long as they are of the different types just mentioned. However, you should always use a longer and more complex password than just three characters for a production server. After the initial password assignment, future password changes require that you use the minimum number of characters defined in the password policy. You can use the icon at the lower-left corner to select ease of access options for hearing-, sight-, or mobility-impaired users. After you change the password, click Finish. When prompted, press Ctrl+Alt+Delete to sign in. Server Manager starts automatically.

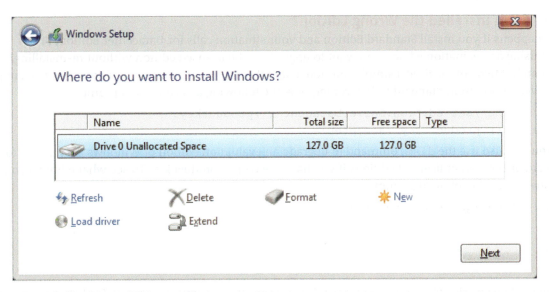

Figure 2-3   Specifying where to install Windows

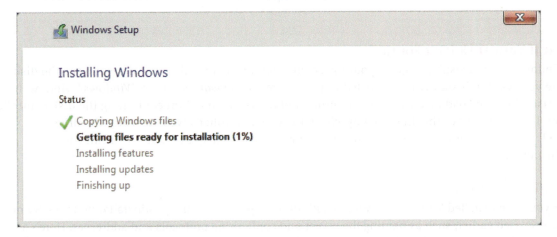

Figure 2-4   Installation begins

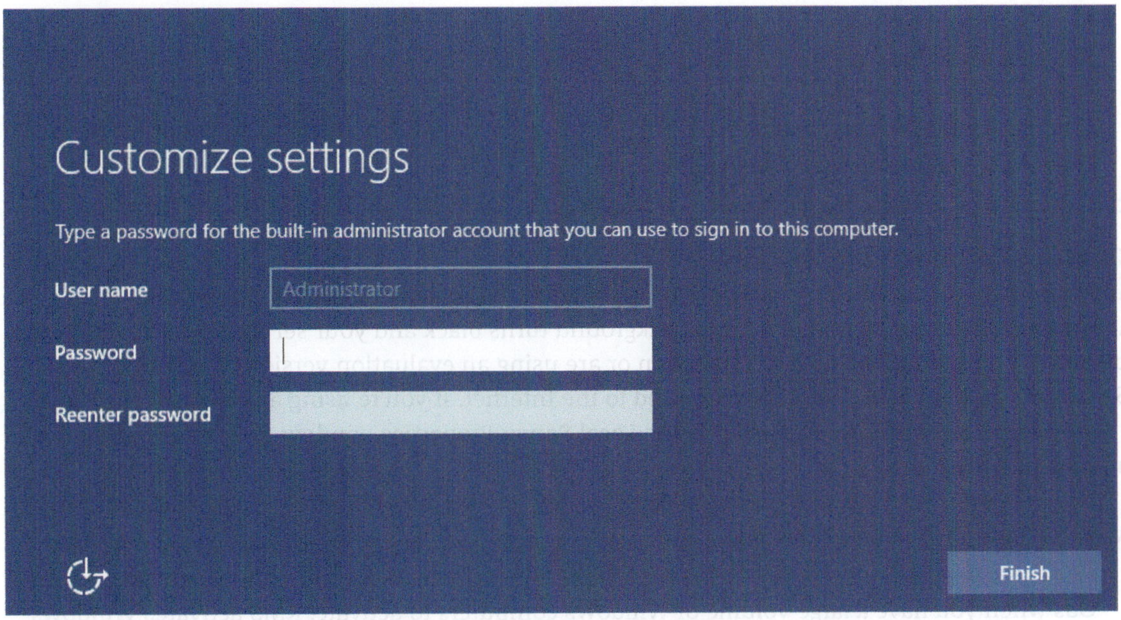

Customize settings

Type a password for the built-in administrator account that you can use to sign in to this computer.

User name	Administrator
Password	
Reenter password	

Finish

Figure 2-5   Setting the administrator password

What If You Installed the Wrong Edition?

What happens if you install Standard Edition and your situation calls for Datacenter Edition, or you're using an evaluation edition and want to upgrade to the licensed edition without re-installing? Fortunately, Microsoft devised a simple solution: using the `dism.exe` command. If you need to change the server edition from Standard to Datacenter, type the following at a command prompt:

```
dism /online /set-edition:ServerDatacenter /productkey:
  datacenter product key /accepteula
```

You can also use the `dism` command to upgrade an evaluation edition of Windows Server 2016 to Standard or Datacenter licensed editions if you have the correct product key. To see what editions you can upgrade to, use the following command:

```
dism /online /get-targeteditions
```

> **Tip** ⓘ
>
> For information on using the `dism.exe` command, type `dism /?` at a command prompt. For help on a specific `dism` option, type `dism /option /?`. For example, for help on the `/online` option, type `dism /online /?`.

What If Your Disk Isn't Found?

If Windows setup doesn't recognize your disk controller during installation, you won't see the disk where you want to install Windows listed in the *Where do you want to install Windows?* window. In this case, click the Load driver link. You're prompted to insert a medium containing the disk controller driver. If you don't have the driver handy, check the disk controller's website. After the driver is loaded, the disk or disks connected to the controller should be displayed, and you can continue the installation.

Postinstallation Tasks

After you have installed Windows Server 2016, it's time to attend to some postinstallation tasks. Some were discussed earlier, such as naming the server and configuring protocols and addresses. Here's a summary of the tasks you should perform immediately on the first server in a network:

- Activate Windows Server 2016.
- Set the correct date, time, and time zone.
- Assign a static IP address.
- Assign a computer name.
- Configure automatic updates.
- Download and install available updates.

All these tasks can be accessed from Server Manager when you click Local Server in the left pane.

Activating Windows Server 2016

Windows Server 2016 requires **activation** within 10 days after installation. If you haven't activated Windows Server after 10 days, the desktop background turns black and your server restarts every hour. If you entered a product key during installation or are using an evaluation version, Windows Server 2016 activates automatically if you're connected to the Internet. If you're using a volume license copy, you need to activate Windows manually in the Local Server Properties window or use the `slmgr.vbs` command-line program.

There are several activation models for Windows Server 2016 in addition to automatic and manual activation. These include the following:

- *Key Management Service (KMS)*—You can use KMS to activate many Windows client and server OSs when you have a large volume of Windows computers to activate. KMS activates Windows using a computer configured as a KMS host instead of having to connect with Microsoft servers via the Internet. You must have several computers to activate to use KMS; the minimum number of server OSs is 5 and the minimum number of client OSs is 25. KMS is used in situations when your organization has purchased a volume license agreement with Microsoft. You can configure a Windows Server 2016 computer as a KMS host by installing the Volume Activation Services server role.

- *Active Directory-Based Activation (ADBA)*—ADBA allows Windows computers that have a volume license key installed to activate when the computer joins the domain. ADBA has benefits over KMS in that there is no minimum number of server or client OSs that must be activated at one time. Since activation information is stored in Active Directory, you have automatic fault tolerance as long as you have one domain controller. ADBA can be configured to work across multiple domains. You can configure ADBA by installing the Volume Activation Services server role.

- *Automatic Virtual Machine Activation (AVMA)*—AVMA lets you install Windows Server 2016 in Hyper-V virtual machines without having to manage the product key for each virtual machine. You can activate VMs running Datacenter, Standard, or Essentials editions of Windows Server 2016 or Windows Server 2012 R2. The server running Hyper-V must be already be activated and must be running Windows Server 2012 R2 Datacenter or Windows Server 2016 Datacenter. After the guest OS is installed, activate the VM by running the command: `slmgr /ipk AVMA_key` where *AVMA_key* is a key you can get from the Microsoft Technet website for the specific version and edition of Windows Server you are installing. Virtual machines can be activated with or without an Internet connection.

Setting the Time Zone and Date

Setting the correct time zone isn't really a decision but a task you must complete because having the wrong time zone can cause all manner of problems, particularly in a domain environment. Certain functions in a domain network, such as user authentication, depend on client and server computers having their clocks well synchronized.

Assigning an IP Address

As discussed, you should already have in mind your IP addressing scheme and the address you will assign to your server. Remember that Windows Server 2016 configures the network interface to use DHCP by default, so your server may already have an IP address assigned via DHCP. However, servers should have a static IP address since they are frequently accessed. You can use the GUI, the `netsh` command prompt command, or the `New-NetIPaddress` PowerShell cmdlet to set your IP address. You'll need the address of your default gateway and DNS servers as well. If this server will be a DNS server, you can set the DNS server address to 127.0.0.1, and the server will use its own DNS service once installed. If this computer will be a domain member, the DNS server address is usually the address of one of the domain controllers.

Assigning a Computer Name

The name of the computer, as mentioned, holds some importance since administrators, and sometimes users, will access shared resources using the computer name. You should devise a naming scheme for your servers so when you install a second, third, and beyond server, you already have a good idea how to name it. Even if your organization has only a single location, you might want to include something about the location of the server in its name in the event your organization expands. Valid Windows computer names can be from 1 to 15 characters in length and must follow the rules of DNS host names. They cannot contain the following characters: ` ~ ! @ # $ % ^ & ( ) = + _ [ ] { } ; . ' , \ / : * ? " < > |.

Configuring and Installing Updates

One of the most important administrative tasks is installing updates. Almost immediately after an OS is released, bugs and security vulnerabilities are found and fixed. These fixes, normally released as **patches**, can be installed through Windows Update. Windows Update also downloads and installs new drivers and service packs. A **service pack** is generally a collection of all bug fixes and security updates made since the OS release. Service packs can also add features and performance enhancements or change the functioning of existing features, so you must understand the effects of a service pack on your server before installing it. Testing a service pack extensively on a test server is highly recommended before deploying it on production machines.

By default, Windows Update is set to download updates only. On a desktop computer, the default setting is to download and install updates, which is usually what you want. Since updates may require a restart, you want to be able to control when updates are installed on a server so the restart doesn't disrupt network services.

To configure Windows Update and view installed updates, click the link in the Local Server Properties window next to Windows Update to open the Update status window (see Figure 2-6).

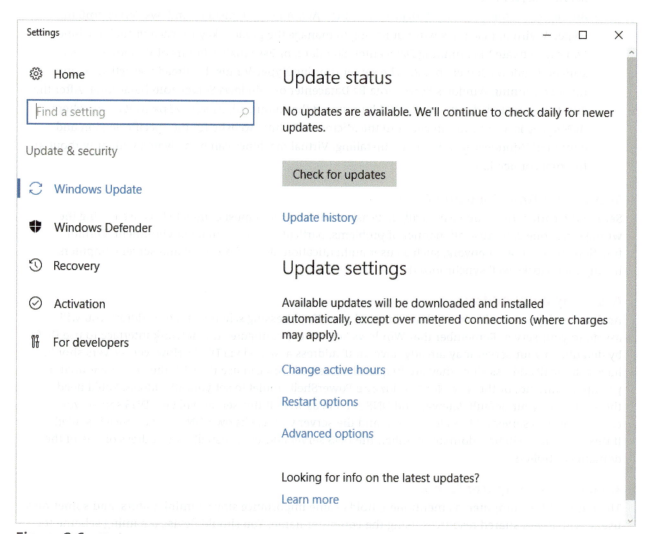

Figure 2-6   Update status

From the Update status window, you have the following options:

- *Check for updates*—Windows immediately checks to see if updates are available. A connection to the Internet or a Windows server running the Windows Server Update Services role must be available.
- *Update history*—This shows a list of updates installed or that have been downloaded and are ready to install. From the Update history screen, you can also uninstall updates, which is useful if an update causes a known problem.

- *Change active hours*—On the Active hours screen, you can specify the start and end times when the computer is usually active. Windows won't restart the computer due to an update during those hours. On a server, the active hours might be 24 hours a day, but you can set the active hours for up to only 12 hours per day.
- *Restart options*—If you turn this option on, you can specify a custom time and day to restart the server if an update requires a restart. Note that the restart options apply only to a pending restart, not to future updates that require a restart.
- *Advanced options*—From the Advanced options window (see Figure 2-7), you have the following options:
    - Give me updates for other Microsoft products when I update Windows: This option will update other installed Microsoft products such as Microsoft Office, SQL Server, System Center, and so forth.
    - Defer feature updates: This option allows you to defer upgrades that change, add, or remove features from Windows Server 2016. You can defer this type of upgrade, referred to as *feature updates*, for several months, but security updates will still be installed on a regular basis.

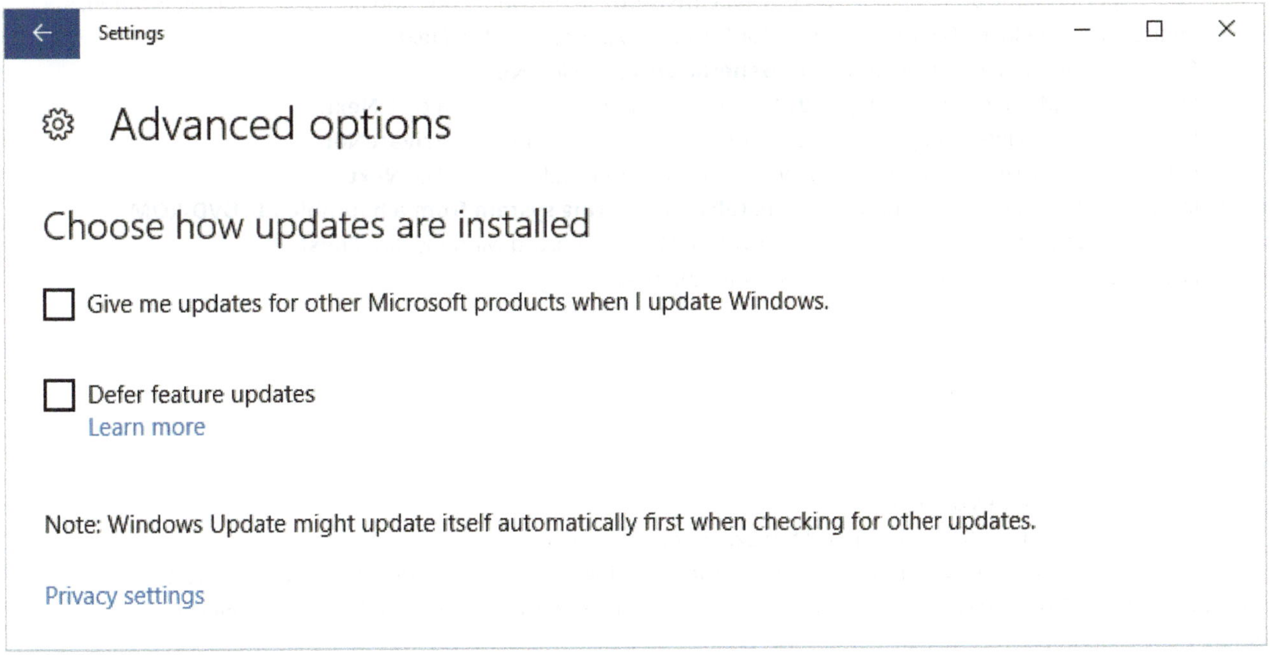

Figure 2-7   Windows Update Advanced options window

Activity 2-1: Resetting Your Virtual Environment

Time Required: 5 minutes
Objective: Reset your virtual environment by applying the InitialConfig checkpoint or snapshot.
Required Tools and Equipment: ServerHyperV
Description: Apply the InitialConfig checkpoint or snapshot to ServerHyperV.

1. Be sure ServerHyperV is shut down. In your virtualization program, apply the InitialConfig checkpoint or snapshot to ServerHyperV.
2. When the snapshot or checkpoint has finished being applied, continue to the next activity.

Activity 2-2: Creating a New Virtual Machine for Server Installation

Time Required: 10 minutes

Objective: Create a virtual machine for Windows installation.

Requirements: ServerHyperV virtual machine configured according to the instructions in the "Before You Begin" section of the Introduction to this book. This configuration assumes that your virtualization environment supports Hyper-V nested virtualization (running a Hyper-V virtual machine in a virtual machine).

Description: Create a virtual machine for Windows Server 2016 installation. You will install the Desktop Experience installation. You will create a virtual machine with the following specifications:

- Virtual machine name: InstallDE
- Memory 1024 MB
- Private network
- Minimum 40 GB HD

1. Start the virtualization server and sign in with an administrator account. From Server Manager, click **Tools**, **Hyper-V Manager**.
2. Hyper-V Manager starts. In the Actions pane, click **New**, **Virtual Machine**.
3. In the Before You Begin window, click **Next**.
4. In the Specify Name and Location window, type **InstallDE** in the Name box and accept the default location. (In the VM name InstallDE, the DE stands for Desktop Experience.) Click **Next**.
5. On the Specify Generation window, click **Generation 1** and click **Next**.
6. In the Assign Memory window, type **1024** in the Startup memory box and click **Next**.
7. In the Configure Networking window, click the selection arrow, and click **PrivateNet**.
8. In the Connect Virtual Hard Disk window, accept the default values and click **Next**.
9. In the Installation Options window, click **Install an operating system from a bootable CD/DVD-ROM**, and click **Next**. In the Completing the New Virtual Machine Wizard window, click **Finish**.
10. Leave ServerHyperV running and continue with the next activity.

Activity 2-3: Installing Windows Server 2016 Desktop Experience

Time Required: 30 minutes or more

Objective: Install Windows Server 2016 Desktop Experience version.

Requirements: ServerHyperV with the InstallDE virtual machine prepared according to Activity 2-2. The Windows Server 2016 Installation media should be attached to ServerHyperV's DVD drive, or the ISO file should be mounted.

Description: You're ready to install Windows Server 2016 on your network. You have verified the hardware configuration and have the installation media. There is no existing OS on the hard drive so the computer should attempt to boot from the DVD without changing the BIOS boot order.

1. Power on InstallDE. On many computers and virtual machines, you will be prompted to press a key to boot from DVD; if so, do that now.
2. You see a progress bar as files are loaded from the DVD. In the first installation window (shown previously in Figure 2-1), verify the language, time, and keyboard choices for your environment. Make changes if necessary, and click **Next**.
3. In the next window, click **Install now**.
4. If you are using an evaluation version of Windows Server 2016, you will not be prompted for a product key, so skip to Step 5. If you are prompted for your product key, enter it, and then click **Next**.
5. The next window might differ slightly from Figure 2-2, but you should click **Windows Server 2016 Standard (Desktop Experience)**, and then click **Next**. (If you are using the evaluation version, the version will be Windows Server 2016 Standard Evaluation [Desktop Experience].)

6. Click the option to accept the license agreement, and then click **Next**. In the next window, click **Custom: Install Windows only (advanced)**.

7. In the Where do you want to install Windows? window, you can manipulate drive partitions and load drivers for a disk controller, if needed. If you simply click Next with an unallocated disk selected, Windows uses the entire disk and formats it as NTFS. Click to select **Drive 0 Unallocated Space**, and then click **Next**. Now you can just sit back and let Windows do the rest. Your computer restarts at least once.

> **Tip** ⓘ
>
> In the Where do you want to install Windows? window, you can press Shift+F10 to open a command prompt window in the MINWINPC environment. From this command prompt, you can use a host of utilities, including `diskpart` for performing advanced disk configuration tasks.

8. In the Customize settings window, set the Administrator password by typing **Password01** twice, and then clicking **Finish**. You see a message that Windows is finalizing your settings.

9. When prompted, press **Ctrl+Alt+Delete** to sign in. Type **Password01**, and press **Enter**. After a short time, you see the desktop, Server Manager opens, and you're ready to go.

10. Continue to the next activity.

Activity 2-4: Performing Postinstallation Tasks

Time Required: 30 minutes
Objective: Perform typical postinstallation tasks.
Requirements: ServerHyperV with the InstallDE virtual machine with Windows Server 2016 installed
Description: You have finished the Windows installation and now it's time for the typical postinstallation tasks. These include setting the time, date, and time zone, assigning a static IP address, assigning a computer name, and configuring automatic updates.

1. Sign in to InstallDE as **Administrator**, if necessary. When Server Manager starts, click **Local Server** in the left pane to open the Properties window.

2. Click the **Time zone** link to open the Date and Time dialog box.

3. Click **Change date and time** and make changes, if necessary. Click **OK**.

4. Click **Change time zone**, and select your time zone in the drop-down list, if necessary. If your region observes daylight saving time, make sure the **Automatically adjust clock for Daylight Saving Time** check box is selected, and then click **OK**.

5. Click the **Additional Clocks** tab where you can tell Windows to display the time in other time zones when you hover the mouse pointer over the taskbar clock.

6. Click the **Internet Time** tab where you can select the option to synchronize with a time server on the Internet. By default, Windows Server 2016 is set to synchronize with *time.windows.com*, and synchronization occurs weekly. Click **Change settings** to use a different time server or disable Internet time synchronization. You can choose from a list of time servers or enter the name of another server. You can also tell Windows to synchronize now by clicking **Update now**. If time synchronization isn't working, your company firewall might be blocking it.

7. Click **OK** twice to close the Date and Time dialog box.

8. Now you will set the IPv4 address. Find Ethernet in the Local Server Properties dialog box and click **IPv4 address assigned by DHCP, IPv6 enabled**. The Network Connections window opens.

9. Right-click **Ethernet**, and click **Properties** to open the Ethernet Properties dialog box (see Figure 2-8).

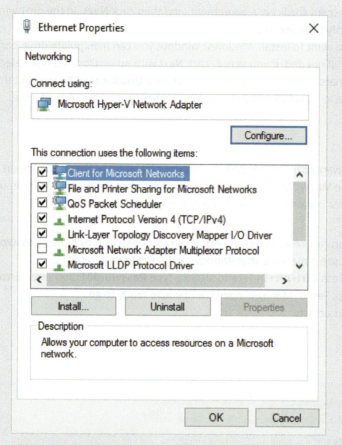

Figure 2-8 The Ethernet Properties dialog box

10. Notice that both TCP/IPv4 and TCP/IPv6 are installed and enabled (scroll down to see TCP/IPv6 if necessary), but you're going to configure only TCP/IPv4. Click **Internet Protocol Version 4 (TCP/IPv4)**, being careful not to clear the check box next to it. Click the **Properties** button.

11. In the Internet Protocol Version 4 (TCP/IPv4) Properties dialog box, click the **Use the following IP address** option button shown in Figure 2-9.

12. Fill in the following information (see Figure 2-9):
    IP address: 192.168.0.10
    Subnet mask: 255.255.255.0
    Default gateway: 192.168.0.250 (or an address supplied by your instructor)

Note

If you're using a different IP addressing scheme, see your instructor for these values.

13. Click **OK**, and then **OK** again. If you see the Networks box asking if you want to allow your PC to be discoverable, click **No**.

14. To verify your settings, right-click **Ethernet** and click **Status**. Then click the **Details** button to open the Network Connection Details dialog box.

15. Verify all the information, and then click **Close** twice. Close the Network Connections window.

16. Now, you will set the computer name. Find Computer name in the Local Server Properties box and click the name of the computer to open the System Properties dialog box.

17. Click the **Computer Name** tab, if necessary, and then click the **Change** button. In the Computer name text box, type **InstallDE**. Click **OK**.

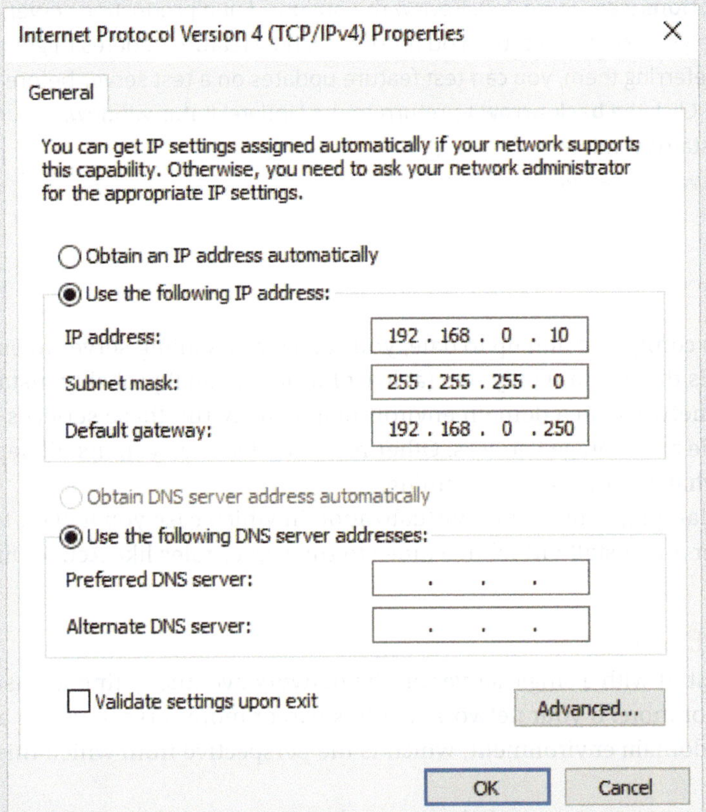

Figure 2-9   Configuring IP address settings

18. When prompted to restart your computer, click **OK**. Click **Close**, and then click **Restart Now**.
19. When Windows restarts, sign in as **Administrator**.
20. After Server Manager starts, verify your changes in the Local Server Properties window. You can also right-click **Start** and click **System** to open the System dialog box, which displays the computer name, workgroup or domain, and other system information.
21. It's time to check for updates and configure Windows Update as necessary. From the Local Server Properties window, find Windows Update. Notice the current configuration is Download updates only, using Windows Update. Click that link to open the Update status window.

> **Note** 📎
>
> You don't install updates in this activity because of the amount of time installation takes and because you might install an update that unexpectedly changes how Windows Server 2016 works. In a production environment, however, you should install updates on a new server.

22. If you were connected to the Internet, Windows will have already checked for updates and may be downloading them already. In this activity, you aren't connected to the Internet. Under Update settings, click **Change active hours** where you can change the hours during which the device is expected to be active. Windows won't restart after installing an update during these hours. Click **Cancel**.
23. Click **Restart options**. Here, you can configure a time when Windows restarts if an update requires it. Since there are no updates, the options are grayed out. Click the **back arrow** to return to the Update status window.

24. Click **Advanced options** (see Figure 2-7). Review the options. For a production server, the Defer feature updates option is a good choice because you don't know how feature updates might affect the operation of the server. By deferring them, you can test feature updates on a test server before deploying them to a production server. Click the **back arrow** to return to the Update status window.
25. Close the Update status window.
26. Sign out or shut down the server.

What's Next?

After your computer is configured and up to date, you can start installing server roles and additional features. If this server is the first and only one (at least for now), you'll probably install several roles on it. As discussed, most networks in a domain environment usually run these services at a minimum: AD DS, DNS, DHCP, and File and Storage Services. Other roles and features you install depend on how the network is used and what applications are running.

You may also be planning to use server virtualization in which case you'll want to install the Hyper-V role on your first server and install virtual machines to run server roles like Active Directory and DHCP.

Expanding Your Network

Many businesses that start with a single server on the network eventually find a reason to install a second or third server or more. If your network requires two or more servers, you're almost certainly running in a domain environment, which is the perspective from which this topic is discussed.

When you're adding a server to an existing network, you must answer many of the same planning questions that you did for the first server. You need to decide on an IP address, a server name, and what roles the new server will play on the network. However, you probably don't need to choose a domain name because this new server will likely be part of the existing domain or a standalone server. What you must decide is whether the new server will be one of the following:

- A domain controller (DC) in the existing domain
- A member server in the existing domain
- A standalone server

If you're installing the second server in the network, there are some good arguments for making it a domain controller. The second server can share the load of managing directory services and handling user sign-ins and provide fault tolerance for Active Directory should the first domain controller go offline.

A member server belongs to the domain and falls under domain management but doesn't run Active Directory or participate in managing directory services. Making a server a member server rather than a DC is best when you already have at least two DCs at a location or when you plan to run resource-intense applications on it that shouldn't share server resources with other services.

A standalone server, as the name implies, doesn't fall under the domain's management umbrella; instead, it's configured as part of a workgroup. Configuring a standalone server makes sense when, for example, the server will be acting as a public Web server, providing services (such as DNS or DHCP) for a group of non-Windows clients or serving as a departmental server when you want local management.

Some reasons you need to add servers to a network include the following:

- Company growth
- Excessive load on existing servers
- Need to isolate an application
- Need for fault tolerance
- Addition of branch offices

A company that's growing, particularly in the number of users, should plan ahead for the inevitable network slowdowns caused by increased activity. A server that has been humming along smoothly with 25 users might not perform as well when this number doubles. Ideally, if growth is foreseen, new resources are put in place before the server becomes taxed. Even without additional users on a network, existing users' use tends to increase over time as they and administrators find more functions for the server to handle. This gradual increase in network and server use can sneak up on you. A server that was running fine 6 months ago can gradually bog down, sapping user productivity as it takes longer to sign in to the network or access shared files. Monitoring a server's performance regularly before this problem becomes a crisis is a good idea.

Sometimes a network application works best when no other major services are competing for a server's CPU and memory resources. Even if your existing server isn't overused, introducing such an application into your network might prompt you to install it on its own server. Isolating applications in this way has the added benefit of not disturbing other network services when you perform maintenance on the server. The converse is also true: When you perform maintenance on other servers, you don't disturb the isolated application.

Access to network resources is so critical in business environments that loss of access to a server's functions can reduce productivity and increase costs. Even in a smoothly running network where no server has an excessive load, adding a server for fault tolerance might still be wise. Load balancing or fault tolerance are built into several Windows server roles, such as AD DS, DNS, and file sharing with DFS. If you need a complete hot replacement for an existing server, you can use failover clustering in which a group of servers is connected by both cabling and software, so if one server fails, another takes over to provide those services.

When a business opens a branch office connected to the main office through a wide area network (WAN), installing a server at the branch office might be prudent. This setup can reduce WAN traffic created by authentication and authorization on a domain controller, DNS lookups, DHCP address assignment, access to shared files, and more. IT administrators are often concerned about security when installing a branch office server because a separate secure room to house the server might not be available. The server might be placed in somebody's office or a common area, which leaves it vulnerable to theft or even attacks by employees. Having physical access to a server makes compromising the server's security much easier. To address this problem, administrators can use Read Only Domain Controllers (RODCs). RODCs have many of the benefits of a standard DC, but administrators can filter what information is replicated to the RODC, including passwords. Therefore, an administrator can configure the RODC to keep only local users' passwords, which limits what damage could be done if someone were able to compromise the server. In addition, you can create a local administrator for an RODC so that maintenance activities can be carried out without giving the local administrator domainwide administrative capabilities. Another option for a branch office server is using the Server Core installation mode to diminish the overall security risk.

Upgrading to Windows Server 2016

When you upgrade to Windows Server 2016, you can use two main methods: an in-place upgrade and server role migration. With an **in-place upgrade**, you boot to the existing OS and run `setup.exe` from the Windows Server 2016 installation medium. With **server role migration**, you perform a clean install of Windows Server 2016 and migrate the server roles that the old OS version performed. Here's an overview of in-place upgrade considerations, followed by available upgrade paths in Table 2-3:

- The only previous Windows versions supported for upgrade are Windows Server 2012 and Windows Server 2012 R2.
- If you're running Server Core, you can upgrade only to Windows Server 2016 Server Core installation. In Windows Server 2012, you had the option to install the GUI after Server Core was installed, but that option is no longer available. If you are running a Windows Server 2016 Server Core installation, you must do a clean install if you want the GUI instead.
- You can't upgrade to a different language.

Table 2-3	Windows Server 2016 upgrade paths
Current edition	**Server 2016 upgrade path**
Windows Server 2012 Datacenter	Windows Server 2016 Datacenter
Windows Server 2012 Standard	Windows Server 2016 Standard or Datacenter
Windows Server 2012 R2 Standard	Windows Server 2016 Standard or Datacenter
Windows Server 2012 R2 Datacenter	Windows Server 2016 Datacenter
Windows Server 2012 R2 Essentials	Windows Server 2016 Essentials

If you're considering an in-place upgrade, Microsoft recommends removing any third-party software the manufacturer doesn't specifically support for an upgrade before performing the upgrade. In addition, make sure your system meets the minimum CPU, RAM, and disk requirements for Windows Server 2016.

An upgrade is similar to a clean installation with a few exceptions. First, you must boot the existing OS and sign in. Then you can start the `setup.exe` program from the installation medium. Next, you're asked whether Windows should go online to get the latest updates for installation. This option is recommended. You aren't prompted for the language, time, currency format, or keyboard layout; they must match the settings for the Windows Server 2016 edition being installed. In addition, in an upgrade, you aren't prompted for the location to install Windows. It's installed on the same disk partition as the OS you booted to.

Before an upgrade begins, Windows runs a compatibility check and produces a compatibility report. Any application, hardware, or driver issues discovered during the check are noted, and you can't continue the installation until you address issues known to prevent a successful upgrade.

Migrating from an Earlier Version

As you can see, in-place upgrades are somewhat limiting, and you could run into software incompatibility problems. In addition, upgrading isn't always possible if the specified upgrade path isn't available. For these reasons, Microsoft recommends a clean installation followed by server role migration when possible. Windows Server 2016 has a number of tools to help with this process, which avoids most of the upgrade path restrictions. For example, migration allows you to do the following:

- Migrate from Windows Server 2008 R2 and later.
- Migrate from a Windows Server 2008 R2 Server Core installation to a GUI installation and vice versa.
- Upgrade the server with no downtime, depending on the roles involved.

Note 🔗

To see which server roles support migration with no downtime, see *https://technet.microsoft.com/en-us/windows-server-docs/get-started/server-role-upgradeability-table*.

Migrating Windows server roles and features isn't an all-or-nothing proposition. You can migrate roles and features from a server running an earlier version to a Windows Server 2016 server, move a role or feature from one Windows Server 2016 server to another, or move a role or feature from a virtual machine to a physical machine or vice versa. However, language migration isn't supported; both server versions must be running the same language package. Before you begin, you should verify that the OSs running on both the source and destination computers have the most current service packs.

A migration is a multistep process. In the following steps, the *destination* computer is the new Windows Server 2016 server you're migrating to, and the *source* computer is the computer you're migrating from:

1. To install the Windows Migration Tools feature on the destination Windows Server 2016 server, use the Add Roles and Features Wizard in Server Manager or the PowerShell command `Install-WindowsFeature Migration`.

2. To create a distribution folder containing the tools the source server needs, use the `smigdeploy.exe` command. The specifics of using this command vary depending on the OS version and the processor architecture running on the source computer. For example, if the source computer is running Windows Server 2008 R2 on an AMD processor, you use the following command to create a distribution folder in the `C:\distr` folder:

   `smigdeploy.exe /package /architecture /amd64 /os WS08R2 /path C:\distr`

   You could also specify a network share in place of `C:\distr`.

3. Use any copying tool to copy the distribution folder created in Step 2 to the source computer.

4. To register Windows Server Migration Tools on the source computer, at an elevated command prompt, change the directory to the distribution folder you copied in Step 3 and enter the `smigdeploy.exe` command.

Note

An elevated command prompt is a command prompt run in Administrator mode. You can access one by right-clicking Start and clicking Command Prompt (Admin).

5. After the command finishes running, a PowerShell window opens, and you can begin using Windows Server Migration Tools cmdlets to migrate roles and features.

Note

The details of migrating individual roles and features are beyond the scope of this book because each role and feature has different procedures to follow. For more information on using Windows Server Migration Tools, refer to *https://technet.microsoft.com/en-us/windowsserver/jj554790.aspx*.

Server Core: Windows That Doesn't Do Windows

Certification

- **70-740 – Install Windows Servers in host and compute environments:**
  Install, upgrade, and migrate servers and workloads

As you learned in Chapter 1, the Server Core installation option provides an environment for running Windows Server without the overhead of a GUI. Server Core's reduced codebase minimizes OS vulnerabilities and lessens maintenance and management tasks. In addition, the overall disk and memory footprint is smaller, thereby requiring fewer hardware resources than a full installation. In addition, the server will require fewer updates since updates related to the graphical desktop won't be needed. The price you pay for these reductions and simplifications is a less user-friendly management interface.

Server Core is the default and preferred operating mode for Windows Server 2016. GUI management is intended to be performed from another Windows Server 2016 server with a GUI or, preferably, from a Windows client OS computer using remote server administration tools (RSAT) and PowerShell. As you will see in Chapter 3, Microsoft has improved and unified its remote administration tools with the goal that you rarely, if ever, need to visit a server's console to manage it. Be aware that while earlier versions of Windows Server allowed you to install and uninstall the GUI according to your preference, you no longer have that option with Windows Server 2016.

Even if you prefer a server with the full GUI in most circumstances, Server Core is a good candidate for deployment in the following situations:

- As a secondary DC to provide redundancy for Active Directory running on a full installation
- As a branch office server when remote administration is likely and the reduced attack surface and maintenance are substantial benefits
- As an RODC for a department or branch office providing many of a standard DC's benefits but with reduced security risks
- As a virtual machine when reduced resource requirements are an important benefit
- As a specialized single-role server providing services such as DNS, DHCP, Web Services, or File and Storage Services
- As a departmental server for many of the same reasons as a branch office server

Although Server Core supports most Windows server roles and features, there are a few it doesn't support. If you need to run any of these server roles or features, you must install the GUI version:

- MultiPoint Services
- Distributed Scan Server
- Internet Printing
- Remote Desktop Services: Gateway, Session Host, and Web Access
- IIS Management Console (however, IIS 6 Management tools are available)
- Direct Play
- Internet Printing client
- LPR Port Monitor
- RAS Connection Manager Administration Kit
- Remote Assistance
- A number of Remote Server administration tools
- Windows Biometric Framework
- Windows Search service
- Simple TCP/IP services
- Windows Deployment services
- Wireless LAN service

Of course, Server Core does not support any features that require a GUI. Server Core's benefits are well and good, but you might be wondering how you carry out server management tasks without a desktop or Server Manager. That brings you to the next topic: performing initial configuration tasks on Server Core.

Server Core Installation

A Server Core installation is nearly identical to a full installation, so there's no need to explain all the steps again. The only real difference is that you choose the Windows Server 2016 option instead of the Windows Server 2016 (Desktop Experience) option (refer to Figure 2-2) when prompted to select the OS you want to install. From there, the process is the same, including changing the administrator password and signing in the first time (although you enter the administrator password in a command prompt instead of a GUI screen). The first major difference you'll probably notice occurs after you sign in when you see no desktop or Server Manager interface, just a command prompt.

Server Core Postinstallation Tasks

The immediate postinstallation tasks for Server Core are the same as in a Desktop Experience installation. The big difference is how you perform these tasks because you can use only command prompt and PowerShell commands. This chapter covers some initial configuration tasks you can perform using a variety of command-line programs and PowerShell. The focus from Microsoft is to use PowerShell for as many tasks as possible, so we'll use PowerShell whenever possible in activities that involve Server Core and even for many activities on servers that have Desktop Experience installed.

> **Note** 📎
>
> In previous versions of Server Core, a command-line menu-driven program, `sconfig`, was available to perform many initial configuration tasks. The program still exists, but according to the Microsoft website, it has been deprecated and may not be available in future updates.

Configuring the Time

As discussed, it's important to be sure that servers have the correct time, date, and time zone settings. From the command prompt, you use the `time` and `date` commands to set the time and date and the `tzutil` command to set the time zone. You can also use PowerShell to set the date and time using the `Set-Date` cmdlet. For example, to set the date and time to October 1, 2017, at 7:00 pm, at a PowerShell prompt, type `Set-Date "10/01/2017 7:00pm"`. You can also just type `Set-Date` and press `Enter`, and you will be prompted to enter the date and time parameters. Remember that if you need help with the command, type `Get-Help Set-Date`. To set the time zone with PowerShell, use the `Set-TimeZone` cmdlet as in `Set-TimeZone "US Mountain Standard Time"`. To see a list of possible time zones, type `Get-TimeZone -ListAvailable`.

Configuring the IP Address

To configure IP address settings, you can use the `netsh` command prompt command or PowerShell. The PowerShell cmdlet to configure the IP address is `New-NetIPAddress` followed by the various parameters for the address, subnet mask (or network prefix), default gateway, and interface name, as you'll see in the next activity. To set the DNS server addresses, use the `Set-DnsClientServerAddress` cmdlet. Remember that for help on how to use any PowerShell cmdlet, type `Get-Help cmdletname` at a PowerShell prompt.

Configuring the Firewall

If you try to ping a computer running a fresh installation of Windows Server, you might not get a reply. However, if you ping from a Windows Server 2016 computer to the default gateway or another computer on the network, you will probably get a response because the Windows Server 2016 firewall blocks incoming ping (Echo Request) packets but allows ping reply (Echo Reply) packets. Though it's not always necessary to allow incoming ping packets, you may want to be able to verify that a server is running and responding on the network using ping. To do so, you need to configure the firewall using the PowerShell cmdlet `Set-NetFirewallRule` or the `netsh` command prompt command. As part of the next activity, you configure the firewall using PowerShell to allow Echo Request packets so that your server can respond to ping packets. To configure the firewall using `netsh`, use the command `netsh firewall set icmpsetting 8`. To block incoming Echo Request packets, use the command `netsh firewall set icmpsetting 8 disable`. The `netsh` firewall command is deprecated but still available; however, it may not be available in future updates. The `netsh advfirewall` command replaces it.

Setting the Computer Name and Workgroup/Domain Membership

The next postinstallation steps for configuring Server Core are setting the computer name and workgroup or domain name. The `sconfig` command can handle these tasks, as can `netdom.exe` and PowerShell commands. `Netdom.exe` is a useful command for working with computer names. You can rename a computer, set the primary DNS suffix, or join a domain by using `netdom.exe` at an elevated command prompt. You can find the current name of the server by typing `hostname` at a command prompt or `$env:computername` in PowerShell. The following command renames a computer. `Currentname` is the current name of the server, and `newname` is the name you want to change it to.

```
netdom renamecomputer currentname /newname:newname
```

The following command sets the primary DNS suffix. `currentname.domainname` is the fully qualified domain name, and `domainname` is the primary DNS suffix:

```
netdom computername currentname /makeprimary:currentname.domainname
```

The following command joins a computer (specified by `computername`) to a domain (specified by `domainname`):

```
netdom join computername /domain:domainname
```

> **Tip** ⓘ
>
> You can get more information about these commands by typing `netdom help`.

To use PowerShell to add a computer to a workgroup or domain, use these commands:

```
Add-Computer -WorkGroupName WorkGroup -Restart
Add-Computer -DomainName Domain -Restart
```

Activating Server Core

You may need to activate your copy of Windows Server 2016 if it didn't activate automatically. Use the `slmgr` command to activate the server. If you entered a product key during installation or you have an evaluation copy, Windows Server should have activated automatically if it has a connection to the Internet. To check on the activation status of a Server Core installation, type `slmgr -dlv` to see a window similar to Figure 2-10. Look for the line near the bottom that starts with "License Status:"; in Figure 2-10, it says "Initial grace period," and the next line gives the time remaining before activation is required. If the time expires, Windows will restart every hour. If Windows is activated, the License Status will be Licensed.

To activate Windows, type `slmgr /ato`; if this is successful, you will see a small dialog box stating that the product was activated successfully. If you did not enter the product key during installation, you can do so using the command `slmgr -ipk` followed by the product key.

> **Note** 📎
>
> The Windows Server 2016 evaluation version is licensed for 180 days and that time period can be renewed up to six times using the `slmgr -rearm` command.

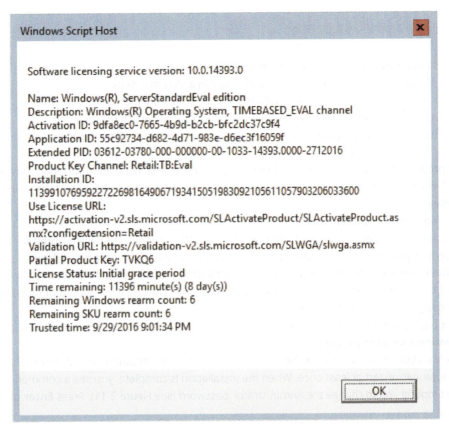

Figure 2-10   Using `slmgr` to view Windows activation status

Configuring Windows Update

Another postinstallation task is configuring Windows Update. By default, Server Core is set to download updates but not install them. The `sconfig` command is an easy way to configure basic settings for Windows Update on a Server Core computer. If you want to configure updates beyond using the default settings, you can edit the Registry. The Registry Editor is one of the few graphical utilities available in Server Core. For details on editing the Registry for Windows Update, consulting a good book on the subject is best. The best method for configuring updates in Server Core and all computers in a Windows domain is to use Group Policy.

When Not to Use Server Core

As you might have noticed, a Server Core installation does have its drawbacks. You need to learn quite a few commands or keep them in a handy reference file. Server Core definitely has its place, especially after you master using remote administration tools, but it's not for all people or all situations. You might not want to use Server Core in situations such as the following:

- When it's the first server in a network
- When you need to install server roles and features that Server Core doesn't support
- When the server administrator isn't well versed in using command-line programs or remote administration tools
- When you absolutely, positively can't live without the Windows GUI running on your server

Because of Server Core's lower resource demands and smaller attack surface, however, it's likely to be a staple in many Windows networks, particularly large networks that use virtualization or have branch offices—that is, after administrators get used to not having a GUI.

Time Required: 30 minutes or longer, depending on the server's speed

Objective: Install Windows Server 2016 using the Server Core installation option.

Required Tools and Equipment: ServerHyperV with the InstallCore virtual machine

Description: Install Windows Server 2016 Server Core on the InstallCore virtual machine.

1. Power on InstallCore. On many computers and virtual machines, you will be prompted to press a key to boot from DVD; if so, do that now.

2. You see a progress bar as files are loaded from the DVD. In the first installation window (shown previously in Figure 2-1), verify the language, time, and keyboard choices for your environment. Make changes if necessary and click **Next**.

3. In the next window, click **Install now**.

4. If you are using an evaluation version of Windows Server 2016, you will not be prompted for a product key, so skip to Step 5. If you are prompted for your product key, enter it now, and then click **Next**.

5. Click **Windows Server 2016 Standard** and then click **Next** (if you are using the evaluation version, the version will be Windows Server 2016 Standard Evaluation). By selecting the option that doesn't include the Desktop Experience, you are installing Server Core.

6. Click the option to accept the license agreement, and then click **Next**. In the next window, click **Custom: Install Windows only (advanced)**.

7. In the *Where do you want to install Windows* screen, accept the default option and click **Next**.

8. Your computer will restart at least once. When the installation is complete, you see a command prompt window prompting you to change the Administrator password (see Figure 2-11). Press **Enter** on the Ok prompt.

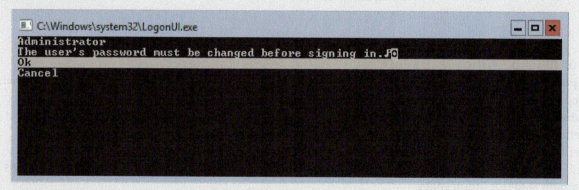

Figure 2-11 Server Core—Changing the Administrator password

9. Type **Password01** at the New password and Confirm password prompts, using the **<Tab>** key to move between them and pressing **Enter** when finished. Press **Enter** on the Ok prompt.

10. You are now signed in. As discussed, Server Core does not have a GUI, so all you see is the command prompt. What happens if you close the command prompt? There is no Start button or other obvious method to restore the prompt. Go ahead and close the command prompt by typing **exit** and pressing **Enter**.

11. To restore the command prompt, press **Ctrl+Alt+Delete**. A command prompt opens, giving you several choices. Press the **Down Arrow** until **Task Manager** is highlighted (see Figure 2-12), and then press **Enter**. In Task Manager, click **More details**. Click **File**, and then click **Run new task**. Type **cmd** in the Create new task dialog box, and then click **OK**. A new command prompt opens. Task Manager is one of the few GUI tools available in Server Core.

Tip ⓘ

If you ever close the command prompt window in a Server Core installation, simply follow the preceding step to restore it. You can also sign out of the server after pressing Ctrl+Alt+Delete, choosing the option to Sign out, and then signing back in.

Figure 2-12   Restoring a command prompt

12. In the next activity, you will configure various aspects of Server Core such as the computer name, IP address, and so forth, so stay signed in.

Activity 2-6: Performing Postinstallation Tasks in Server Core

Time Required: 25 minutes
Objective: Perform a number of postinstallation tasks in Server Core.
Required Tools and Equipment: ServerHyperV with the InstallCore virtual machine
Description: You have finished the Server Core installation, but now you must perform a number of postinstallation tasks. In this activity, you set the time, date, time zone, IP address, and server name.

1. Start InstallCore and sign in as **Administrator**, if necessary. A command prompt window opens.
2. In the command prompt, type **date** and press **Enter**. Type a new date if necessary; otherwise, just press **Enter**.
3. Type **time** and press **Enter**. Type a new time if necessary; otherwise, just press **Enter**.
4. To set the time zone, you first need to see a list of time zones you can use. Type **tzutil /l** and press **Enter**. You will need to use your mouse to scroll up and down in command prompt to see all the time zones. Find your time zone and then type **tzutil /s "US Mountain Standard Time"** and press **Enter**, being sure to replace the time zone string with your time zone. To display the current time zone, type **tzutil /g** and press **Enter**.

Note 📎

Any computer that becomes a member of a domain synchronizes its clock to a domain controller, so setting the time and date is unnecessary in these circumstances. You must still set the correct time zone, however.

5. Next, you set the IP address. At the command prompt, type **ipconfig /all** and press **Enter**. You'll see that the IP address is set via DHCP (or if you don't have a DHCP server on the network, you see an APIPA address in the range 169.254.X.X). If necessary, scroll down in the command prompt to see the rest of the output from the ipconfig command.

6. To work with network settings using PowerShell, start a PowerShell prompt by typing **powershell** and pressing **Enter**. You see the letters PS added to the beginning of the prompt, indicating you are in PowerShell.

7. To see a list of interfaces you can configure with PowerShell, type **Get-NetIPInterface** and press **Enter**. You see a list of interfaces as in Figure 2-13. (Remember that PowerShell commands are not case sensitive, so you can type the command using all lowercase or all uppercase or a combination of both. The commands are written in Microsoft documentation and will be written in this book using a combination of uppercase and lowercase for readability).

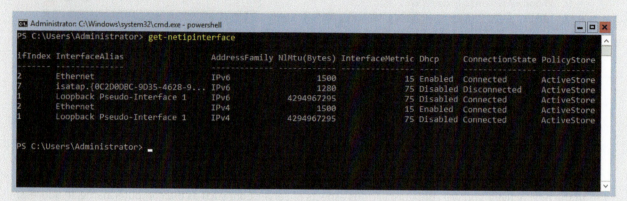

Figure 2-13 The Get-NetIpInterface cmdlet

8. You will see several interfaces listed, but the one you are interested is probably named Ethernet in the Interface Alias column of the output. If the interface is named something else, use that name in place of Ethernet in the following command. To set the IP address to 192.168.0.11 with subnet mask 255.255.255.0, type **New-NetIPAddress 192.168.0.11 -PrefixLength 24 -DefaultGateway 192.168.0.250 -InterfaceAlias Ethernet** and press **Enter**. The command will output the current IP configuration for the Ethernet interface.

9. To configure the DNS server address, type **Set-DNSClientServerAddress -InterfaceAlias Ethernet -ServerAddresses 192.168.0.250** and press **Enter**.

10. You may want to set the firewall on a Server Core computer to allow ICMP echo request (Ping) packets and for remote management purposes. To configure the firewall to allow ICMP echo request packets, type **Set-NetFirewallRule FPS-ICMP4-ERQ-In -enabled True** and press **Enter**.

11. Now, change your computer name. To see your current computer name, type **$env:ComputerName**, and press **Enter** to display the environment variable containing the computer name. You can also type the command `hostname` at a command prompt or PowerShell prompt. To set the computer name, type **Rename-Computer "ServerCore"** and press **Enter**. You see a message that you must restart the computer for the change to take effect.

12. To restart the computer, type **Restart-Computer** and press **Enter**. Your computer shuts down and restarts immediately. Alternatively, if you know you want to restart immediately after you enter the `Add-Computer` cmdlet, you can add the `-Restart` parameter to the `Add-Computer` cmdlet.

13. After the server reboots, sign in and verify your changes using the **ipconfig /all** command. Shut down the server by typing **shutdown /s /t 0** and pressing **Enter**.

> **Note** 📎
>
> In the `shutdown` command used in Step 13, the `/s` parameter specifies shutting down the server. You can use `/r` instead to specify a server restart. The `/t` parameter specifies the time to wait in seconds before the server should shut down. A `0` for the time period means to shut down immediately. From PowerShell, you can shut down the server using the `stop-computer` cmdlet.

Using Features on Demand

 **Certification**

- **70-740 – Install Windows Servers in host and compute environments:**
  Install, upgrade, and migrate servers and workloads

When you install Windows Server 2016, all the files you need to install server roles and features are copied to the C:\Windows\WinSxS folder, so you don't need any installation medium to install new roles and features. However, these files use a lot of disk space. Although disk space is fairly cheap and abundant, it's neither free nor infinite. Besides, one reason for using Server Core is that it has a small footprint. When you're talking about a server hosting several virtual machines, the disk space used for server roles and features can have an impact, and it can be used for better purposes.

To address this problem, Windows Server 2016 has **Features on Demand**, which enables you to remove these files and free up the disk space they normally consume. If the files are needed later, such as for adding a server role, Windows can be directed to a network share, installation medium, or Windows Update to get them. Another advantage of removing features you don't need is that Windows Update runs faster because it doesn't have to update files that have been removed.

Keep in mind that you can't remove these files from a feature that you want to remain installed; Features on Demand is used only to remove features you aren't currently using. For example, say that you have Windows Server 2016 installed with the Active Directory Domain Services and DHCP server roles. You want to remove the files for all other server roles. To remove a role or feature, use the PowerShell cmdlet `Uninstall-Windows-Feature` with the `-Remove` option. For example, to remove the DNS Server role, use the following cmdlet:

```
Uninstall-WindowsFeature DNS -Remove
```

The preceding cmdlet will uninstall a role or feature and then remove the installation files from disk. If the role is not installed, it just removes the installation files. You can use this command on any role, role service, or feature you want. To see a list of available roles and features, use the following command, which yields the output shown in Figure 2-14:

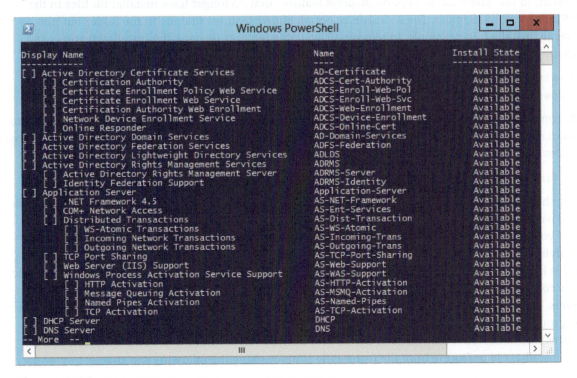

Figure 2-14   List of Windows features and their status

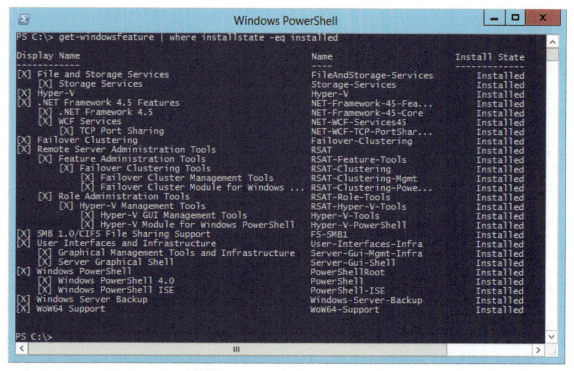

Figure 2-15 Listing only installed features

```
Get-WindowsFeature | more
```

If you want to narrow the display down to only those features that are installed, use the following command to yield the output in Figure 2-15:

```
Get-WindowsFeature | where InstallState -eq Installed
```

You can replace the string `Installed` with `Removed or Available`, depending on the list you want to see. The `Removed` option displays features that no longer have installation files in the C:\Windows\WinSxS folder. The `Available` option shows features that are in the folder but not currently installed. For example, to remove all available features (leaving the installed features as they are) and restart the server, use the following command:

```
Get-WindowsFeature | where InstallState -eq Available|Uninstall-
WindowsFeature -Remove
```

This command creates a list of all features that have an install state of `Available` and pipes this list to the `Uninstall-WindowsFeature` cmdlet, which uninstalls the features (if necessary) and then removes the files from the C:\Windows\WinSxS folder. You can verify the results by using this command:

```
Get-WindowsFeature | where InstallState -eq Removed
```

Using this command also reduces the C:\Windows\WinSxS folder by about 2 GB, which, of course, is the objective.

If you have removed installation files and need to install a role or feature later, you can do so by specifying another location where Windows can find the installation files. The most common way to do this is to create a feature file store (also called a *side-by-side store*). A **feature file store** is a network share containing the files required to install roles, role services, and features on Windows Server 2016 servers. To create a feature file store, create a network share and assign Read permissions for the Everyone group (or a group containing the computer accounts that will access the store). Then copy the Sources\SxS folder from the Windows Server 2016 installation medium to the shared folder. You can then install a role or feature from the feature file store by using the following command:

```
Install-WindowsFeature FeatureName -Source \\Server\Share
```

In this command, you replace *FeatureName* with the name of the role or feature you want to install and *Server**Share* with the UNC path of the share you created for the feature file store.

Now that you're familiar with planning a Windows Server 2016 installation, performing initial configuration tasks, and considering upgrade factors, it's time to get deeper into Windows Server 2016 configuration. Chapter 3 covers many of the more detailed Windows Server 2016 configuration tasks along with options for managing servers remotely.

Chapter Summary

- Microsoft has an edition for all types of business, large and small. Businesses can choose the best solution for their size and the services they require. Editions include Datacenter, Standard, Essentials, MultiPoint Premium Server, Storage Server, and Hyper-V Server.

- Windows Server 2016 Standard and Datacenter editions use a core-based licensing model instead of the processor-based model used with previous releases of Windows Server.

- The process of installing Windows Server 2016 is fairly straightforward. Most of the work takes place in the planning phase. Some issues to consider include the server's CPU architecture, the total number of processors or cores the server requires, the number and types of disks, and advanced hardware features.

- Installing from a DVD is common for a single-server installation. Only a few choices must be made, such as whether to do a full GUI or Server Core installation and deciding which disk or disk partition should be used for installing Windows Server 2016.

- Postinstallation configuration tasks include giving the server a name, configuring network protocols, setting time zone information, selecting a network model (workgroup or domain), and installing and

configuring Windows Updates. After completing these tasks, you can install server roles.

- When adding new servers to an existing network, you must decide whether the new server will be a new domain controller in the existing domain, a member server, or a standalone server. Reasons for adding new servers include company growth, excessive server load, application isolation, fault tolerance, and adding a branch office server.

- You can do an in-place upgrade to Windows Server 2016 only if the existing OS is Windows Server 2012 or Windows Server 2012 R2. A clean install followed by server role migration is recommended.

- Windows Server Core is the default and recommended installation option. The traditional Windows GUI isn't available in Server Core. Initial configuration tasks, such as changing the server name and setting IP address information, must be done from the command prompt, PowerShell, or through remote administration tools. You cannot convert from a Server Core installation to a GUI installation or vice versa.

- Features on Demand enables you to remove Windows feature installation files from the local disk. Removing these unused files makes it possible to save disk space and allows Windows Update to run faster.

Key Terms

activation

Active Directory-Based
    Activation (ADBA)

Automatic Virtual Machine
    Activation (AVMA)

clean installation

Datacenter Edition

Essentials Edition

feature file store

Features on Demand

hot-add

hot-replace

in-place upgrade

Key Management Service (KMS)

Microsoft Hyper-V Server 2016

MultiPoint Premium Server

operating system
    environment (OSE)

patches

root domain controller

server role migration

service pack

Standard Edition

Windows Storage Server

Review Questions

1. Which of the following is *not* a valid Windows Server 2016 installation option?
   a. A clean installation of Windows Server 2016 Datacenter
   b. An upgrade from Windows Server 2012 R2 Server Core to Windows Server 2016 Desktop Experience
   c. An upgrade from Windows Server 2012 Standard to Windows Server 2016 Datacenter
   d. A clean installation of Windows Server 2016 Server Core

2. What is required to install the Hyper-V server role? (Choose all that apply.)
   a. A 64-bit processor
   b. A 32-bit version of Windows Server 2016
   c. AMD-V or Intel-VT extensions
   d. At least 384 MB RAM

3. Which of the following is true when purchasing a motherboard with multiple CPU sockets?
   a. Windows Server 2016 doesn't support multiple CPU sockets.
   b. You must run a 32-bit version of Windows Server 2016.
   c. All installed CPUs must be identical.
   d. Virtualization is not supported on multiple CPUs.

4. You're trying to decide which disk technology to use on your new Windows Server 2016 install. The server will be in heavy use around the clock every day, so high performance is a necessity. Which technology is the best choice?
   a. IDE
   b. ATA-166
   c. SATA
   d. SAS

5. Your company's new physical server has two processors, each with four cores for a total of eight cores. How many Windows Server 2016 licenses need to be purchased for your eight-core server?
   a. Two 2-core license packs for a total of 4 cores
   b. Eight 2-core license packs for a total of 16 core licenses
   c. Four 2-core license packs for a total of 8 core licenses
   d. Sixteen 2-core license packs for a total of 32 cores

6. Which networking protocol is installed by default in Windows Server 2016? (Choose all that apply.)
   a. TCP/IPv4
   b. IPX/SPX
   c. NetBEUI
   d. TCP/IPv6

7. Which of the following is *not* a typical Windows Server 2016 postinstallation task?
   a. Installing the Server Core role
   b. Setting the correct time zone
   c. Setting IP configuration parameters
   d. Changing the server name

8. Which of the following is a task you must do *during* Windows Server 2016 installation?
   a. Name the server.
   b. Choose the disk where it will be installed.
   c. Set the Administrator password.
   d. Set the workgroup or domain.

9. What command allows Echo Request packets through the firewall?
   a. `icmp set icmp-echo enabled`
   b. `Set-NetFirewallRule "Echo Request" -Enabled True`
   c. `netsh firewall set icmpsetting 8`
   d. `ipconfig -allow "ping requests"`

10. Which PowerShell cmdlet allows you to set the date and time for your Server Core installation?
    a. `Set-Time`
    b. `Set-Date`
    c. `Set-Date-Time`
    d. `Set-TimeZone`

11. If the product key was entered during a Server Core installation, which command allows you to activate your copy of Windows Server 2016 Server Core?
    a. `slmgr /ato`
    b. `Add-Computer`
    c. `slmgr -ipk`
    d. `sconfig`

12. Which of the following is a reason for installing a new server? (Choose all that apply.)
    a. Excessive load on existing servers
    b. Fault tolerance
    c. Addition of a new network protocol
    d. Isolation of a new application

13. You approach one of your servers running Server Core and see a completely blank desktop except for the mouse pointer. You need to do some management tasks on the server. What should you do?
    a. Right-click the mouse and click Open a command prompt.
    b. Press Start+X and click Run.
    c. Press Ctrl+Alt+Delete and select Task Manager.
    d. Right-click the desktop, point to New, and click Task.

14. You have just finished installing Windows Server 2016. You have assigned the server a name and finished configuring IP addresses. You have tested your configuration by using `ping` to verify network connectivity with your default gateway and another server on the network, and everything worked fine. However, the next day, a colleague tells you that when she tried to ping the server, her request timed out. You try to ping her computer and receive a reply that it's just fine. Why can't your colleague ping your server successfully?
    a. Your server's default gateway is incorrect.
    b. Windows Firewall is blocking the packets.
    c. Your colleague's IP address configuration is incorrect.
    d. You don't have DNS installed.

15. Which command can you use to restart Windows Server immediately?
    a. `shutdown /r /t 0`
    b. `restart /t 0`
    c. `net stop /r /t 0`
    d. `net computer /reset /t 0`

16. Which of the following is the default setting for Windows Update after you first turn on automatic updates?
    a. Download updates only.
    b. Download and install updates automatically.
    c. Inform when updates are available but do not download updates.
    d. Never check for updates.

17. Which of the following is true about upgrading to Windows Server 2016?
    a. An upgrade from Windows Server 2008 edition requires a clean install.
    b. You can upgrade from a Chinese version to an English version.
    c. A Server Core install always requires a clean installation.
    d. You can upgrade from Windows Server 2008 R2.

18. In which of the following circumstances is server migration required when you want to upgrade to Windows Server 2016 Datacenter? (Choose all that apply.)
    a. When you're running Windows Server 2008 R2
    b. When you're running Windows Server 2012 R2 Standard
    c. When you're running a GUI installation of Windows Server 2008
    d. When you're running Windows Server 2012 Datacenter

19. Which command can you use in Windows Server 2016 Server Core to configure basic settings for Windows Update?
    a. `netsh.exe`
    b. `smigdeploy.exe`
    c. `sconfig`
    d. `command.com`

20. Why would you use Features on Demand?
    a. To free up system RAM
    b. To reduce disk space use
    c. To use the GUI interface
    d. To uninstall Server Core

21. If you want to see a list of available roles and features, which command should you use?
    a. `sconfig`
    b. `Show-WindowsRoles`
    c. `dism.exe`
    d. `Get-WindowsFeature`

Critical Thinking

The following activities give you critical thinking challenges. Case Projects offer a scenario with a problem to solve for which you supply a written solution.

Case Project 2-1: Adding a Server to Your Network

Your client, CSM Tech Publishing, has been running Windows Server 2016 Essentials Edition, which you installed about a year ago, and is using the Active Directory Domain Services, DNS, IIS, and File Services roles. The number of computer clients has grown from 25 to 40 in the past 6 months, and additional growth is expected. CSM Tech just purchased an expensive project management system to help manage project scheduling. This application has hefty memory (8 GB or more) and CPU requirements (recommended 3.0 GHz quad-core processor). All desktop computers will have the project management client application installed. The owner doesn't want to install the client application on mobile users' laptops, so a remote solution is needed for these laptops. The owner also mentions that he's familiar with this application and will need to sign in to the server periodically to do maintenance and monitoring.

The owner tells you that in the future, CSM Tech Publishing might need system fault tolerance to ensure that there's little or no downtime because this critical application will eventually be accessed at all times of the day and night. For now, he's just concerned about getting the system up and running. You check the existing server's capacity and determine that the new application's memory and disk requirements will likely exceed the existing server's 4 GB capabilities. The owner explains that there's enough budget for a new server, so you should plan for growth. As an aside, he mentions that because all his employees sign in at about the same time, the time it takes to sign in has been increasing. You need to come up with specifications for a new server. Describe some hardware features you plan to recommend for this new server, in particular the CPU architecture, number of CPUs, amount of RAM, and disk system. Explain your answers.

Case Project 2-2: Choosing the Right Edition

You have your new server for the CSM Tech Publishing upgrade project and are ready to install Windows Server 2016. Case Project 2-1 describes the current environment and requirements of CSM Tech. Which edition of Windows Server 2016 will you install? Include information on whether it should be a full GUI or Server Core installation. Explain your answer.

Case Project 2-3: Performing Server Postinstallation Tasks

You have finished installing Windows Server 2016 on the new server for CSM Tech. Next, you need to decide what to name the server and how it will participate in the existing domain: as a domain controller, a member server, or a standalone server. The existing server is named CSM-Server1-DC, and the new server will be located near the existing server in the equipment closet. List the postinstallation tasks you must perform on this server, including details on the server name and its role in the domain (if any). Don't include installing specific server roles just yet.

Case Project 2-4: Choosing Server Roles on the Second Server

You have finished postinstallation tasks for the new server, and now you need to decide which server roles to install on it. Reread Case Project 2-1 carefully because it contains most of the information you need to make an informed decision. List which server roles you plan to install and explain why.

CHAPTER 3

CONFIGURING AND MANAGING WINDOWS SERVER 2016

After reading this chapter and completing the exercises, you will be able to:

Work with server roles and features

Manage servers remotely

Work with Windows install images

Configure services

After you have installed a server and performed initial configuration tasks, next comes the task of configuring the server. This chapter covers how to add and remove server roles and features on both local and remote servers. You also learn how to add servers to Server Manager and configure firewall rules to allow remote management.

Some configuration tasks can be done before you actually install Windows if you use Windows Deployment Services. You can create custom install images with the roles and services already installed as well as update existing images, including virtual disk images that will be used with virtual machines. You'll also learn about a powerful feature, Desired State Configuration, in which servers can be configured and maintained using special PowerShell scripts.

You might need to start or stop a Windows service or install and configure a new service; you learn how to perform these tasks using both the GUI and the command line.

Working with Server Roles and Features

Certification

- **70-740 – Install Windows Servers in host and compute environments:**
  Install, upgrade, and migrate servers and workloads

Table 3-1 describes what you need to do the hands-on activities in this chapter.

Table 3-1 Activity requirements

Activity	Requirements	Notes
Activity 3-1 Resetting Your Virtual Environment	ServerDC1, ServerDM1, ServerDM2, ServerSA1	
Activity 3-2: Installing and Removing Server Roles with Server Manager	ServerDC1, ServerDM1	
Activity 3-3: Installing and Uninstalling a Server Role with PowerShell in Server Core	ServerDC1, ServerDM2	
Activity 3-4: Adding Servers to Server Manager and Creating Server Groups	ServerDC1, ServerDM1, ServerDM2	
Activity 3-5: Working with Windows Services	ServerSA1	

Windows Server without roles and features installed is like an iPhone without apps installed. The basic installation does have some limited functions, such as basic file and printer sharing, but not much beyond that. You need to add server roles and features to take advantage of the power Windows Server 2016 offers. This section covers how you work with server roles and features in both a graphical user interface (GUI) installation and a Server Core installation and how to update roles and features installed in offline images.

In Chapter 1, you learned the difference between server roles and features and explored the Add Roles and Features Wizard in Server Manager. In this chapter, you look more closely at the process of adding and removing roles and features.

Managing Server Roles in the GUI

In Server Manager, you can start the Add Roles and Features Wizard in the Welcome window or by clicking Manage, Add Roles and Features from the menu (see Figure 3-1).

In either case, the Add Roles and Features Wizard opens to the Before You Begin window as shown in Figure 3-2. You can bypass this window in the future by selecting the option to skip it. If you're new to Windows Server, however, reading the information in this window is a good idea so that you can make sure you have performed these crucial tasks before installing server roles and features:

- The administrator has a strong password.
- Static IP addresses have been configured. Some server roles, such as Dynamic Host Configuration Protocol (DHCP) and Active Directory, don't work correctly with dynamically assigned addresses. Although not all roles require static IP addresses, using them on servers is a recommended practice.
- Security updates are current.

The next window, Installation Type (see Figure 3-3) has two options:

- *Role-based or feature-based installation*—Use this default option to install a role or feature on a single server or an offline virtual hard disk. In most cases, you choose this option.
- *Remote Desktop Services installation*—Use this option to distribute components of the Remote Desktop Services role across different servers for use in a virtual desktop infrastructure.

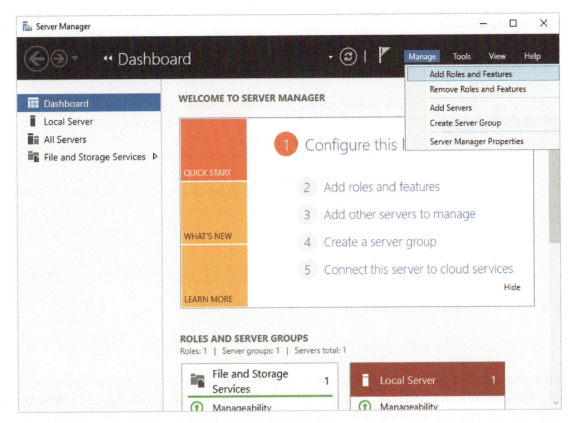

Figure 3-1   Starting the Add Roles and Features Wizard

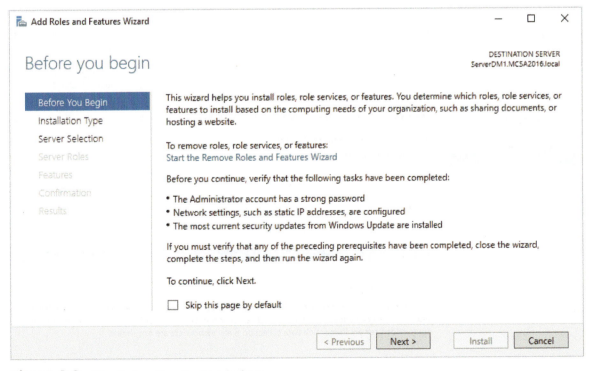

Figure 3-2   The Before You Begin window

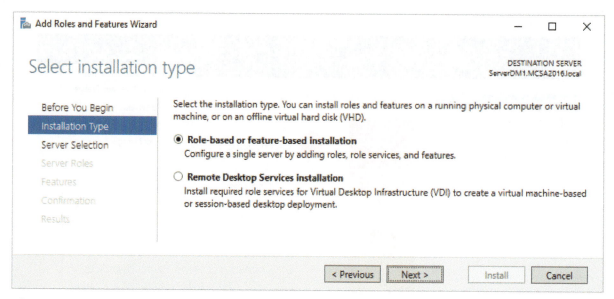

Figure 3-3 Selecting an installation type

In the next window, Server Selection (see Figure 3-4), you choose a server from the server pool for installing roles and features. You learn how to add servers to this list later in the chapter in "Managing Servers Remotely." You can also install roles and features on a virtual hard disk (VHD). If you choose this option, you're prompted to choose a server on which to mount the VHD and specify the path to the VHD file.

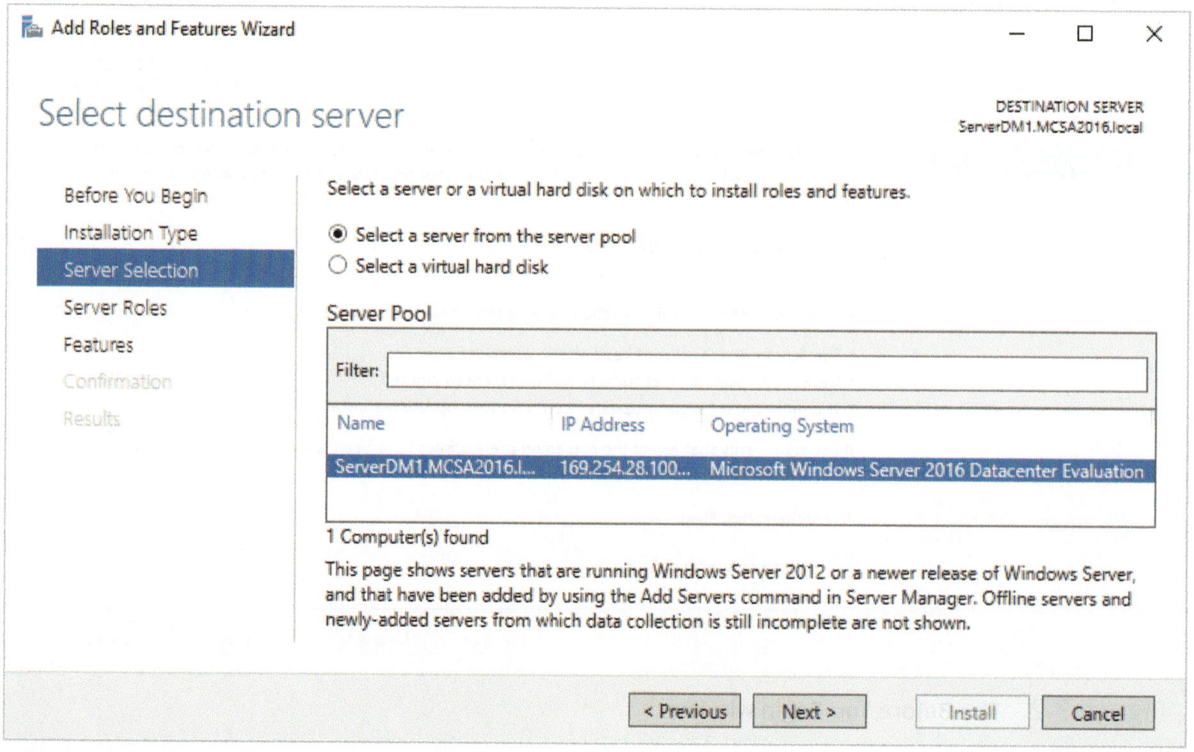

Figure 3-4 Selecting a destination server

The next window, Server Roles, lists all the server roles you can install (see Figure 3-5). Underneath each server role, there may be one or more role service. Next to each role or role service is a box. If it's selected, that role or role service along with any subordinate role services are installed. If the box is shaded, one or more role services or subordinate role services are installed. Figure 3-5 shows File and Storage Services (1 of 12 installed), which means 1 of the 12 role services (and subordinate role services) under File and Storage Services is installed. When you click the box next to a server role, Windows prompts you to include additional features and management tools, if necessary.

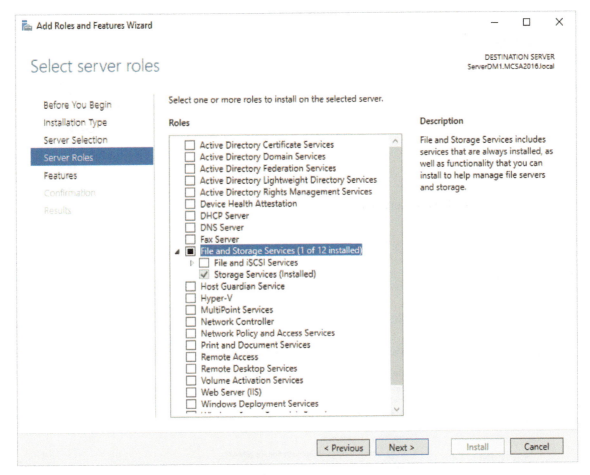

Figure 3-5   Selecting roles to install on a server

The next window, Features, lists the available features and works like the Server Roles window. If you selected a server role with multiple associated role services, the next step is to select which role services you want. For example, the Remote Access server role has three role services associated with it (see Figure 3-6). If a role service requires installing other roles and role services, you're prompted to confirm their installation, too.

In the Confirmation window, shown in Figure 3-7, you can review your selections. Selecting the check box at the top ensures that the server restarts automatically, if needed, during installation. At the bottom of this window are links to two options:

- *Export configuration settings*—Select this option if you want to generate an XML script for installing the selected roles and features on another server with the PowerShell command `Install-WindowsFeature -ConfigurationFilePath` *XMLscript.xml*.
- *Specify an alternate source path*—Select this option to specify a path to an image file containing the installation files for roles and features if the files aren't available locally.

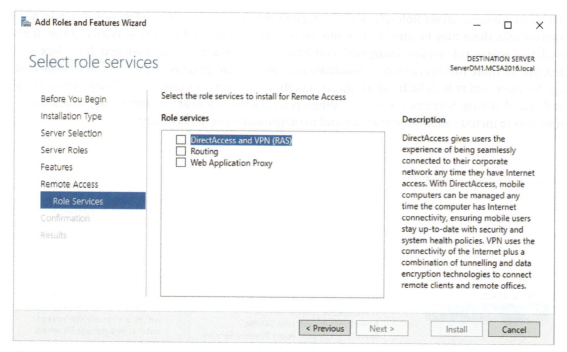

Figure 3-6   Selecting role services

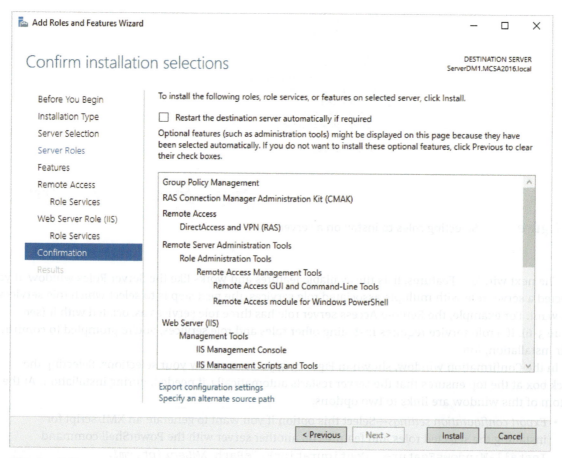

Figure 3-7   Confirming your selections

Clicking the Install button starts installing the server roles or features you've selected, and the Results window shows the progress of the installation.

The procedure for removing roles and features is similar. In Server Manager, click Manage, Remove Roles and Features from the menu to start the Remove Roles and Features Wizard. The main difference from the installation wizard is that you clear the box for the role or feature you want to remove. Roles and features that aren't installed are grayed out and can't be selected.

Managing Server Roles with PowerShell

You can use PowerShell to add and remove server roles from a Server Core or Desktop Experience server if you don't want to use Server Manager. To start PowerShell, type `powershell` at an elevated command prompt or right-click the PowerShell icon and click Run as Administrator. The following PowerShell commands are used to work with server roles and features:

- `Get-WindowsFeature`—Displays a list of available roles and features. You can also use `Get-WindowsFeature | where Installed` to display a list of installed roles and features or `Get-WindowsFeature | where InstallState -eq Available` to display roles and features that are available to be installed.

- `Install-WindowsFeature RoleOrFeatureName`—Installs the server role or feature specified by `RoleOrFeatureName`. To specify multiple roles and features, separate the names with a space. Variations on this command include `Install-WindowsFeature RoleOrFeatureName -IncludeAllSubFeature -IncludeManagementTools`, which installs the specified role or feature and includes necessary subfeatures and management tools, and `Uninstall-WindowsFeature RoleOrFeatureName -IncludeManagementTools`, which uninstalls the specified role or feature along with management tools. Separate the names of multiple roles and features with a space.

> **Tip** ⓘ
>
> Remember that PowerShell commands aren't case sensitive. They're shown with selective capitalization to make them more readable, but you can use all lowercase (or uppercase) letters when typing commands at a PowerShell prompt.

You can also install and uninstall roles and features to and from an offline VHD file by including the option `-VHD pathname` (replacing `pathname` with the path to the VHD file).

Using PowerShell on Remote Servers

All the PowerShell commands discussed in the previous section can be used to install or remove server roles and features on remote servers. You can perform the same commands on remote servers by including the parameter `-ComputerName string`, which specifies the name or IP address of the computer:

```
-ComputerName string
```

For example, if you're on Server1 and want to install the Windows Server Backup feature on a server named Server2, use this command:

```
Install-WindowsFeature Windows-Server-Backup -ComputerName Server2
 -IncludeAllSubFeature -IncludeManagementTools
```

For this command to work, Server2 must be in the same domain as the server where you entered the command. If the remote server isn't in the same domain, it must be added to the TrustedHosts setting, which is explained later in "Managing Servers Remotely."

Working with Offline Images

You can install and uninstall features to and from an offline VHD file by using Server Manager or PowerShell cmdlets, as you have seen. Being able to work with VHD files offline can come in handy when you're maintaining a Hyper-V virtualization host. You might keep a virtual machine (VM) in an offline state until you're ready to deploy it. If you need to add or remove roles and features from a VM, you can do so without having to start it. The ability to deploy roles and features on VHD files without having to start the virtual machine that the VHD is associated with can save time and resources. The procedure for adding roles and features to an offline VHD file with PowerShell is identical to that for a live system (described previously), but you include the `-VHD` option in the command.

You might also need to manage features on an installation image that you deploy with Windows Deployment Server (WDS). For working with install images (`.wim` files), you use the Deployment Image Servicing and Management (`dism.exe`) command. Here's the general procedure for deploying a feature on an offline image (`.wim`) file:

1. Mount the image by entering this command:

```
dism /mount-wim /wimfile:pathtowimfile /index:1 /mountdir:pathtomountedimage
```

2. Install the feature by entering this command:

```
dism /image:pathtomountedimage /enable-feature /featurename:roleorfeaturename
```

3. To commit the changes and dismount the image, enter this command:

```
dism /unmount-wim /mountdir:pathtomountedimage /commit
```

In Step 2, you can replace `/enable-feature` with `/disable-feature` to uninstall a role or feature or `/get-features` to list currently installed roles and features.

Activity 3-1: Resetting Your Virtual Environment

Time Required: 5 minutes

Objective: Reset your virtual environment by applying the InitialConfig checkpoint or snapshot.

Required Tools and Equipment: ServerDC1, ServerDM1, ServerDM2, ServerSA1

Description: Apply the InitialConfig checkpoint or snapshot to ServerDC1, ServerDM1, ServerDM2, and ServerSA1.

1. Be sure the servers are shut down. In your virtualization program, apply the InitialConfig checkpoint or snapshot to ServerDC1, ServerDM1, ServerDM2, and ServerSA1.
2. When the snapshot or checkpoint has finished being applied, continue to the next activity.

Activity 3-2: Installing and Removing Server Roles with Server Manager

Time Required: 15 minutes

Objective: Install a server role with Server Manager.

Requirements: ServerDC1, ServerDM1

Description: You've done the initial configuration on your server, so now it's time to install some roles and features. In this activity, you will install the Print and Document Services role using Server Manager.

1. Start ServerDC1. Start ServerDM1 and sign in as the domain **Administrator** by clicking **Other user** from the sign-in screen, typing **mcsa2016\administrator** in the User name box, and then entering the password in the Password box.
2. On ServerDM1, in Server Manager, click **Manage, Add Roles and Features** from the menu to start the Add Roles and Features Wizard.

3. In the Before You Begin window, read the information to make sure you have the prerequisite tasks completed, and then click **Next**.

4. In the Installation Type window, accept the default option **Role-based or feature-based installation**, and then click **Next**.

5. In the Server Selection window, the only option is ServerDM1 because you haven't added any other servers to be managed from this server. If you were installing the feature on an offline VHD file, you would click the Select a virtual hard disk option button. Accept the default setting **Select a server from the server pool**, and then click **Next**.

6. In the Server Roles window, click the box next to **Print and Document Services**. In the Add Roles and Features Wizard dialog box asking you to confirm the additional features needed for this role (see Figure 3-8), click the **Add Features** button.

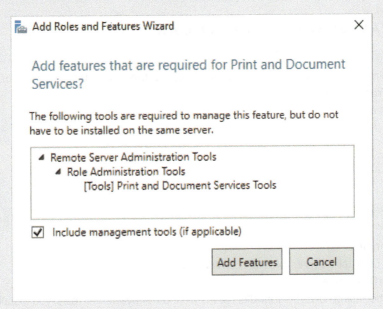

Figure 3-8   Adding features for a role service

7. Click **Next**. In the Features window, scroll through the list of features to review what's available, and then click **Next**.

8. Read the description of the Print and Document Services role in the next window, and then click **Next**.

9. In the Role Services window, you can choose other role services that work with this role, such as Internet Printing. Accept the default option **Print Server** and click **Next**.

10. In the Confirmation window, click **Install**. The Results window shows the progress of the installation. You can close this window without interrupting the installation; if you do, you can restore it to view your progress by clicking Notifications. Wait until the installation is finished, and then click **Close**.

11. A new icon named Print Services is added to Server Manager in the left pane. As shown in Figure 3-9, Print Services is also added in the Roles and Server Groups section.

12. Now, you will remove the role. On ServerDM1, in Server Manager, click **Manage, Remove Roles and Features** from the menu.

13. In the Before You Begin window, click **Next**. In the Server Selection window, click **Next**.

14. In the Server Roles window, click the box next to **Print and Document Services**.

15. In the Remove Roles and Features Wizard dialog box, click **Remove Features**, and then click **Next**. In the Features window, click **Next**.

16. In the Confirmation window, click **Remove**.

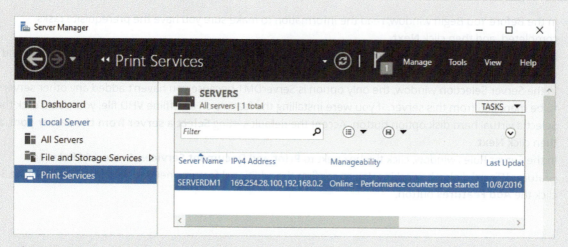

Figure 3-9 Adding Print Services to Server Manager

17. In the Results window, wait until the process is finished, and then click **Close**. Notice that Print Services has been removed from Server Manager.
18. Shut down ServerDM1 but keep ServerDC1 running.

Activity 3-3: Installing and Uninstalling a Server Role with PowerShell in Server Core

Time Required: 10 minutes
Objective: Install and uninstall a server role with PowerShell.
Requirements: ServerDC1, ServerDM2
Description: For practice using PowerShell cmdlets to install and remove server roles, you install Print and Document Services with PowerShell and then uninstall it.

1. Start ServerDM2 and sign in as **Administrator**.
2. At the command prompt, type **powershell** and press **Enter** to start PowerShell. The command prompt changes to PS C:\Users\Administrator>.
3. To see what roles and features are available to install, type **Get-WindowsFeature** and press **Enter**. You see a list of server roles, role services, and features (see Figure 3-10). Installed roles, role services, and features are preceded with an X. The left column shows the display name of the server role, role service, or feature, and the right column is the name you use in PowerShell commands.
4. Scroll up to Print and Document Services. Notice that the name in the right column is Print-Services.
5. Type **Install-WindowsFeature Print-Services -IncludeManagementTools** and press **Enter**.
6. Your progress is shown at the top of the PowerShell window. When the installation is finished, type **Get-WindowsFeature | where Installed** and press **Enter** to see a list of installed roles and features.
7. To uninstall Print and Document Services, type **Uninstall-WindowsFeature Print-Services -IncludeManagementTools** and press **Enter**.
8. When the role has been removed, you see a status message indicating success. Type **Get-WindowsFeature | where Installed** and press **Enter**. You no longer see Print and Document Services in the list of installed features.
9. Continue to the next activity.

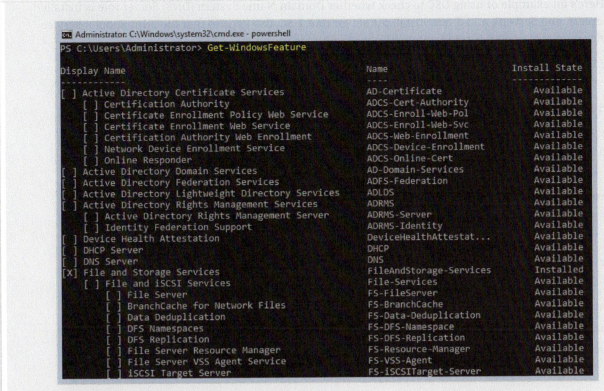

Figure 3-10   Output of `Get-WindowsFeature`

Implementing Desired State Configuration

Starting with PowerShell 4.0 (first appearing in Windows Server 2012 R2), the feature **Desired State Configuration (DSC)** gives you a way to manage and maintain servers with simple declarative statements. DSC's declarative syntax makes it possible for you to just tell the server how it should be configured without using the actual commands for performing configuration steps. DSC can operate in one of two modes:

- *Push mode*—In this mode, a server configuration is manually sent to one or more target servers by an administrator. This mode is best used to test your DSC configuration without having to configure a pull server.
- *Pull mode*—In this mode, instead of DSC configurations having to be sent to remote servers, servers can pull their configurations from a central server by using standard web protocols. This technology eliminates the need to open additional firewall ports.

As mentioned, push mode is a good way to test your DSC configuration without having to set up a DSC pull server. In push mode, you set up the configurations on a desktop computer and manually begin the DSC process by sending configurations to target machines. However, to realize the power of DSC, you set up a pull server and the target computers check with the server every 15 minutes to see if a configuration is available.

You create a DSC script in PowerShell's **Integrated Scripting Environment (ISE)**, a PowerShell development environment that you can open from the Tools menu in Server Manager. The basic steps for using DSC are as follows:

1. Create the script in the PowerShell ISE.
2. Run the script to create configuration files called *management object files (MOF) files*.
3. Enter the `Start-DscConfiguration` cmdlet at a PowerShell prompt.

Here's an example of using DSC to check whether Domain Name System (DNS) Server role is installed on ServerA and ServerB, and if not, install the server role. DSC also verifies that the Print Spooler service (service name is Spooler) is set to automatically start and is running.

```
Configuration DNSSpool
{
Node ServerA, ServerB
{
WindowsFeature DNSserver
{
Name = "DNS"
Ensure = "Present"
}
Service PrintSpooler
{
Name = "Spooler"
StartupType = "Automatic"
State = "Running"


}
}
}
```

Windows Server 2016 comes with DSC version 2 and lets you automate a variety of configuration tasks on a set of computers using scripts like the previous example. Some of the automated tasks include:

- Enabling or disabling server roles and features
- Managing services (e.g., starting and stopping)
- Retrieving the configuration of a server
- Deploying software
- Managing registry settings
- Managing files and folders
- Managing accounts
- Running PowerShell scripts

The configuration tasks you can perform with DSC are based on DSC resources. To see a list of DSC resources, use the Get-DscResources PowerShell cmdlet. A number of DSC resources are built in to DSC, but you can add more resources, and therefore more configuration tasks, by downloading the DSC Resource Kit, available on Microsoft TechNet. In addition to automating server configuration tasks, DSC can also determine whether a server still has the desired configuration and if not, restore it to the desired state. For example, if someone changes the configuration of a server, DSC can determine that it has been changed and then change it back.

At the heart of DSC is the **local configuration manager (LCM)**, which is responsible for sending (pushing) and receiving (pulling) configurations, applying configurations, monitoring, and reporting discrepancies between the desired state and the current state of a server. When a discrepancy exists (a term referred to as *configuration drift* or simply *drift*), DSC is responsible for reapplying the desired state configuration to resolve the drift. One major enhancement in DSC v2 is the ability to split a configuration into multiple configuration files. In this way, multiple people can create different configurations according to their expertise. Each partial configuration can be used independently or combined with any other partial configuration to configure a server. For example, in DSC v1, if you needed to configure a server as a DHCP, DNS, and file and print server, you would create a single DSC script that would be used by each server that required the configuration. If you needed a server with just DHCP and DNS, a different script would be required that excluded the file and print components. With DSC v2, you can create a script for each role and deploy each script independently according to how it is needed. For example, you can deploy the DNS, DHCP, and file and print scripts to all servers that need all three components but only the DNS and DHCP scripts to those servers that don't require file and print components.

> **Tip** (i)
>
> The details of using DSC are beyond the scope of this book, but for a quick primer and examples, take a look at *https://msdn.microsoft.com/en-us/powershell/dsc/overview*.

Managing Servers Remotely

 **Certification**

- **70-740 – Install Windows Servers in host and compute environments:**
  Install, upgrade, and migrate servers and workloads

The server management and configuration tools you have used so far perform tasks on the local server. Most networks have more than one server, and although you can perform a task by signing in to the console at each server or using Remote Desktop, there are more convenient ways to manage a multiserver environment remotely as covered in the following sections. By managing servers remotely, you can take advantage of the benefits of Server Core yet still be able to use a GUI on a remote machine. In addition, remote management reduces the need for a physical keyboard and monitor for each server. Most remote management tasks are handled by using Server Manager, a Microsoft Management Console (MMC), or the PowerShell command line.

Adding Servers to Server Manager

In Windows Server 2016, you can manage all your servers from a single Server Manager interface. In Server Manager, you can manage all roles and features installed on any server and view the status of all servers, including events and performance data. To do this, you must add servers to Server Manager. To start the process, click Manage, Add Servers from the Server Manager menu. If the server where you're running Server Manager is a member of a domain and the server you want to add is also a domain member, you can add it by using any of these methods:

- *Searching Active Directory*—This method is probably the easiest. You can type the first few characters of the server name in the Name text box (see Figure 3-11) and click Find Now, or just click Find Now to see all computers in the domain. Then select one or more servers to manage. (Note that you can't manage computers running a client operating system [OS].)
- *Searching DNS*—Type the server name or IP address in the Search text box on the DNS tab, and select the servers you want to add.
- *Importing a text file*—Browse for and select a text file containing a list of server names or IP addresses on the Import tab, one per line, and all the servers listed in the file are added.

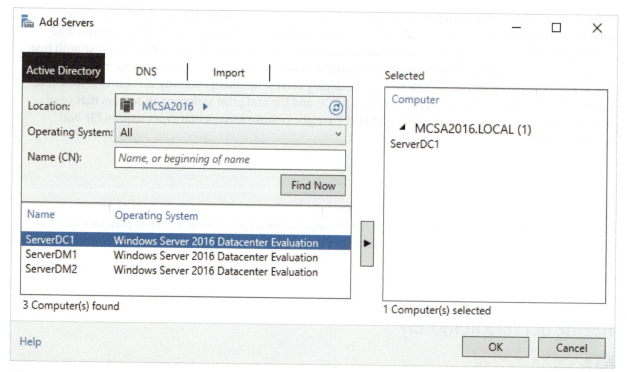

Figure 3-11 Adding a server to Server Manager

In Windows Server 2016, you can manage servers running Windows Server 2003 and later. However, you can't manage a more recent version of Windows Server than the version on which Server Manager is running. For example, you can't manage a Windows Server 2016 server from a Windows Server 2012 server, but you can manage a Windows Server 2012 server from a Windows Server 2016 server.

If the server where you're running Server Manager is a member of a workgroup rather than a domain, or the server you want to manage is a workgroup member, first you need to add the remote server to the TrustedHosts list on the computer running Server Manager. To do this, use the following PowerShell cmdlet while signed in as Administrator:

```
Set-Item wsman:\localhost\Client\TrustedHosts RemoteServerName
 -Concatenate -Force
```

RemoteServerName is the name or IP address of the remote server you want to manage. The -Concatenate option adds the entry to the list instead of overwriting the existing list. After adding the remote server to the TrustedHosts list, you can add the server to Server Manager by using the previously described methods of searching DNS or importing a text file.

Note

If you try to add a standalone server that's not in the TrustedHosts list to Server Manager, Server Manager reports this error: "WinRM Negotiate authentication error."

Using Server Manager Groups

If you have only a few servers to manage, you can add them as described previously and access them by clicking All Servers in Server Manager. If you have dozens or even hundreds of servers to manage, however, you might want to organize them in groups, such as by department, location, or function. For example, you can group all servers related to the Operations Department, all servers in the Phoenix office, or all DNS servers. By organizing servers in this manner, you can see a group's status at a glance. Servers can be a member of more than one group, so you can place a domain controller in the Phoenix office in both the Domain Controllers group and the Phoenix group, for example.

To create a server group in Server Manager, click Manage, Create Server Group from the menu. Give the group a name, and then add servers to the group (see Figure 3-12). You can add servers from the existing list of servers managed by Server Manager, or you can add other servers to manage by using the methods described earlier. After you create a server group, the group name is added to the left pane of Server Manager and can be used just like the All Servers node.

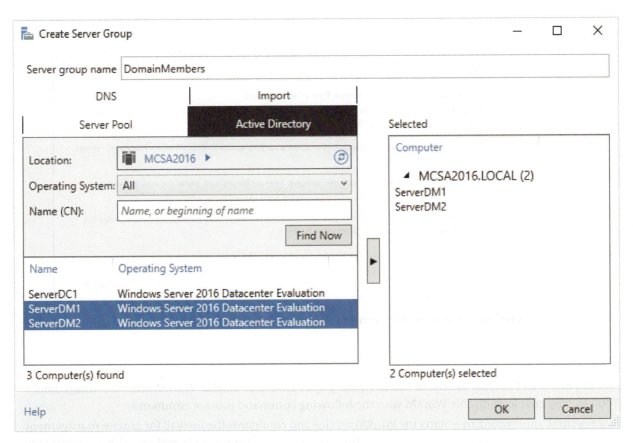

Figure 3-12   Creating a server group

Enabling and Disabling Remote Management

By default, Windows Server 2016 remote management is enabled via **Windows Remote Management (WinRM)**. WinRM provides a command-line interface for performing a variety of management tasks. Running in the background, it allows commands or applications that require Windows Management

Instrumentation (WMI) or PowerShell to access the server remotely. To change the remote management setting, click the setting next to the label Enable remote management in the Local Server Properties window (see Figure 3-13).

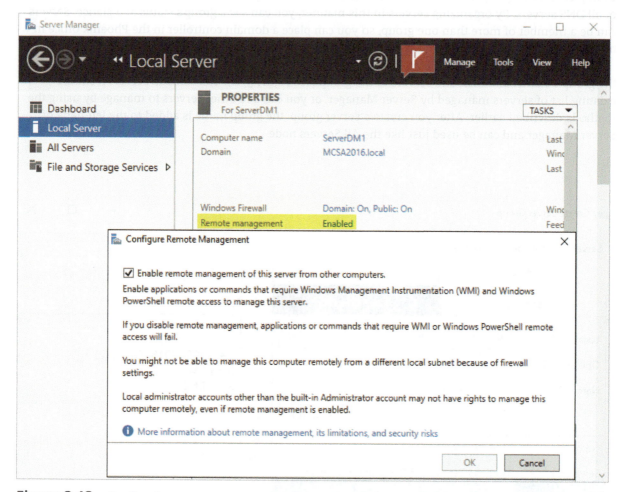

Figure 3-13   Configuring remote management

You can select or clear the check box in Figure 3-13 to enable or disable WinRM remote management. You can also enable or disable WinRM with the following command prompt commands:

- `winrm quickconfig`—Starts the WinRM service and configures the firewall for remote management.
- `Configure-SMRemoting.exe -Get`—Displays the current status of WinRM (enabled or disabled)
- `Configure-SMRemoting.exe -Enable`—Enables WinRM
- `Configure-SMRemoting.exe -Disable`—Disables WinRM. To configure remote management using PowerShell, use the following cmdlets from a PowerShell prompt using the Run as Administrator option:
  - `Enable-PSRemoting`: Enables WinRM
  - `Disable-PSRemoting`: Disables WinRM
  - `Test-WSMan -ComputerName computer`: Tests whether the WinRM service is running on *computer*.

Configure Windows Firewall for Remote Management

Adding a server to Server Manager and enabling WinRM gives you only a few remote management capabilities. You can view the status of a remote server, run PowerShell, add and remove server roles, restart a server, and perform some additional tasks. However, to use an MMC to manage a remote server, you need to make some firewall rule changes on the remote server. To further complicate matters, different MMCs require different firewall rule changes. If you right-click a remote server in Server Manager and click Computer Management, for example, you get an error message that states that you must enable some firewall rules on the remote server (see Figure 3-14).

Figure 3-14   An error when trying to manage a server remotely

Configuring Firewall Rules with Desktop Experience

If the remote server you want to manage is running the Desktop Experience, you can use the Windows Firewall with Advanced Security MMC to configure firewall rules. You need to sign in to the remote server and open the Windows Firewall with Advanced Security console. In the Inbound Rules section, enable the following rules (see Figure 3-15):

- COM+ Network Access (DCOM-IN)
- Remote Event Log Management (NP-In)
- Remote Event Log Management (RPC)
- Remote Event Log Management (RPC-EPMAP)

Enabling the preceding rules makes it possible to run most MMCs and snap-ins for managing a remote server.

Configuring Firewall Rules with the Command Line

You can configure the firewall with the `netsh` command or the `Set-NetwFirewallRule` cmdlet in PowerShell. To enable the four rules highlighted in Figure 3-15 with `netsh`, use the following commands:

```
netsh advfirewall firewall set rule group = "COM+ Network Access"
  new enable=yes
netsh advfirewall firewall set rule group = "Remote Event Log Management"
  new enable=yes
```

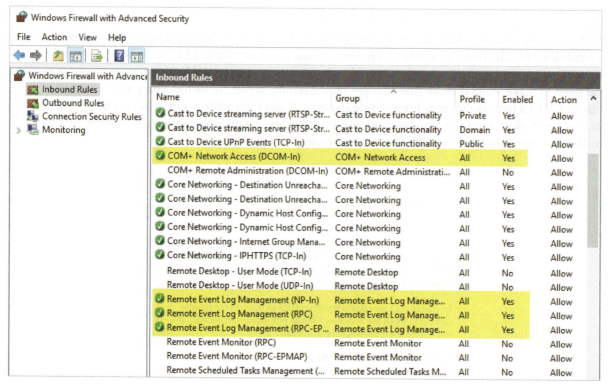

Figure 3-15   Windows Firewall rules for remote management

 Tip ⓘ

Using the `group` keyword in these commands sets all three Remote Event Log Management rules at the same time.

The `netsh` command can be used to configure the firewall remotely, but *first* the Windows Firewall Remote Management group rules must be enabled on the remote computer, and they're disabled by default. To specify a remote computer in the `netsh` command, use the `-r RemoteComputer` parameter (replacing `RemoteComputer` with the name or IP address of the computer you're configuring).

To use PowerShell to configure the firewall, open a PowerShell command prompt window and enter the following commands:

```
Set-NetFirewallRule -DisplayGroup "COM+ Network Access" -enabled True
Set-NetFirewallRule -DisplayGroup "Remote Event Log Management" -enabled True
```

You can issue these commands while signed in to the remote computer or by opening a PowerShell command prompt remotely, as shown in Activity 3-3.

Special Considerations for Server Core

Server Core doesn't have the COM+ Network Access firewall group, and firewall rules for several MMC snap-ins might need to be enabled separately. You might want to enable the necessary firewall rules on the Server Core computer first so that you can manage the firewall remotely with the Windows Firewall with Advanced Security snap-in. To do so, open a PowerShell command prompt window on the Server Core computer and enter the following command:

```
Set-NetFirewallRule -DisplayGroup "Windows Firewall Remote Management" -enabled True
```

After you have enabled the firewall rule, you can create a Windows Firewall with Advanced Security MMC snap-in on a client computer or another server to manage the Server Core computer's firewall. Here are some other firewall rule groups you might want to enable on the Server Core computer for remote management with MMCs:

- *File and Printer Sharing*—Enables use of the Shared Folders snap-in and most of the other snap-ins in Computer Management with the exception of Event Viewer and Device Manager.
- *Remote Event Log Management*—Allows using the Event Viewer snap-in.
- *Remote Volume Management*—Enables you to use the Disk Management snap-in to manage disks remotely. This firewall rule group must be enabled on both the Server Core computer and the computer where you're running Disk Management.
- *Remote Service Management*—Allows using the Services snap-in.
- *Performance Logs and Alerts*—Enables use of the Performance Monitor snap-in.
- *Remote Scheduled Tasks Management*—Allows using the Task Scheduler snap-in.

Note

You can't access Device Manager remotely on Windows Server 2016 systems.

Activity 3-4: Adding Servers to Server Manager and Creating Server Groups

Time Required: 15 minutes
Objective: Add a server to Server Manager and create a server group.
Required Tools and Equipment: ServerDC1, ServerDM1, ServerDM2
Description: You have one server running the Desktop Experience and one running Server Core. You want to manage the server running Server Core with Server Manager, so you add the Server Core server to Server Manager on the server running the Desktop Experience. Next, you create a server group and place both servers into the group.

1. Start all three servers, if necessary: ServerDC1, ServerDM1, and ServerDM2.
2. Sign in to ServerDM1 as the **domain Administrator** (mcsa2016\administrator).
3. In Server Manager, click **Manage**, **Add Servers** from the menu to open the Add Servers window (see Figure 3-16).

Note

If the servers you plan to manage aren't domain members, you must add them to the TrustedHosts list. In PowerShell, type `Set-Item wsman:\localhost\Client\TrustedHosts ServerName —Concatenate -Force`. (The `ServerName` must be the fully qualified domain name or the IP address of the server.)

---

4. Be sure the Active Directory tab is selected and click the **Find Now** button. Click **ServerDM2** and click the arrow to move ServerDM2 to the Selected box (see Figure 3-17). Click **OK**.
5. In Server Manager, click **Dashboard** in the left pane, if necessary. Scroll down to the Roles and Server Groups section. Notice that the File and Storage Services box displays the number 2, indicating that two servers are running the File and Storage Services role. The All Servers box also displays a 2.
6. In the left pane of Server Manager, click **All Servers**. You should see both ServerDM1 and ServerDM2 in the list of servers (see Figure 3-18).
7. Click **ServerDM2**. You see the Events box change to show recent events generated on the ServerDM2 server. Scroll down to view the Services box, which shows the status of services running on ServerDM2.

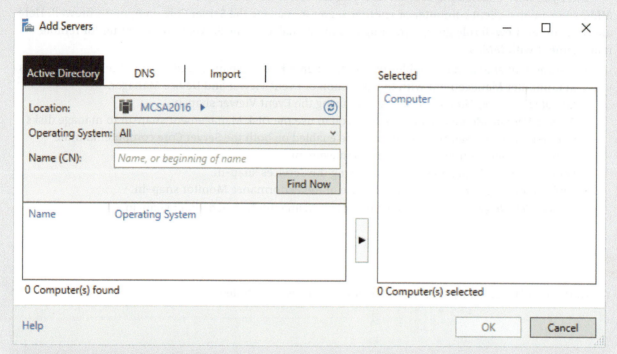

Figure 3-16   The Add Servers window

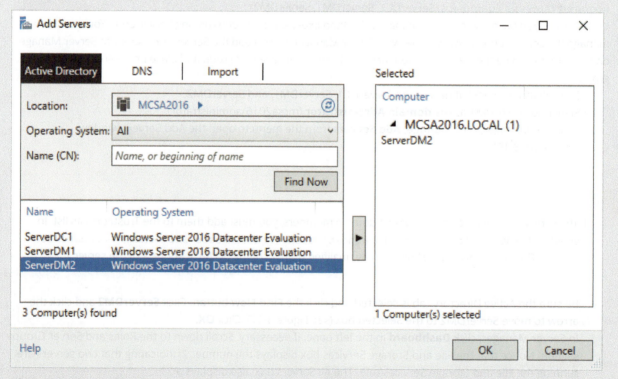

Figure 3-17   Adding a server

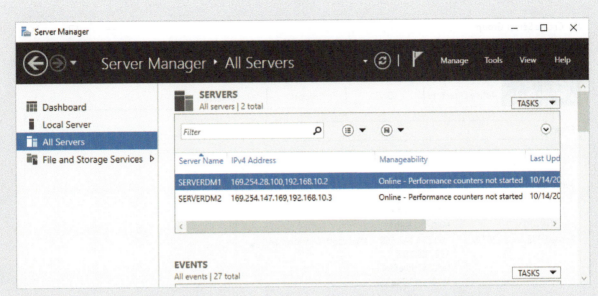

Figure 3-18   The All Servers window

8. Scroll back up to the list of servers and right-click **ServerDM2**. You see a number of management options you can perform on the server, including Add Roles and Features, Restart Server, Computer Management, and so forth. Click **Computer Management**. Before you can use MMCs to manage a remote server, you need to configure Windows Firewall on the remote server, but if the virtual machines were preconfigured with the correct firewall settings, Computer Management will open without error. In either case, in the following steps, you will configure the firewall for remote management. Close the Computer Management window.

9. Right-click **ServerDM2** and click **Windows PowerShell**. Notice that the prompt is prefaced with [ServerDM2. MCSA2016.local], indicating you are connected to ServerDM2. To set the firewall for remote management with the Computer Management MMC, type **Set-NetFirewallRule DisplayGroup "Remote Event Log Management" -enabled True** and press **Enter**. Close the PowerShell window.

10. In Server Manager, right-click **ServerDM2** and click **Computer Management**. The Computer Management MMC opens successfully. Click each snap-in to see which you can use (it may take a while to open each snap-in after you click it). You should be able to use all snap-ins except Device Manager, which can't be remotely managed, and Disk Management, which requires additional firewall configuration. Close Computer Management.

11. In Server Manager, click **Manage**, **Create Server Group** from the menu to open the dialog box in Figure 3-19.

12. In the Server group name text box, type **Domain Members**.

13. In the list of servers, click **ServerDM1**, and then click the right-pointing arrow to move the server over to the Selected list box. Next, add **ServerDM2** to the Selected box. Click **OK**.

14. In Server Manager, click **Domain Members** in the left pane. You see the two servers ServerDM1 and ServerDM2 listed.

15. Next, you'll delete the server group. In the left pane of Server Manager, right-click **Domain Members** and click **Delete Server Group**. When prompted to confirm the deletion, click **OK**.

16. In the left pane of Server Manager, click **All Servers**. Right-click **ServerDM2** and click **Remove Server**. When prompted to confirm the deletion, click **OK**.

17. Shut down all three servers before continuing to Activity 3-5.

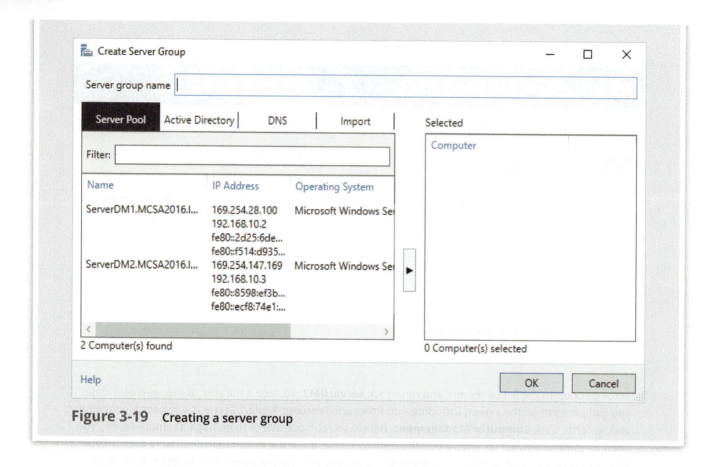

Figure 3-19   Creating a server group

Working with Windows Install Images for Deployment

 **Certification**

- **70-740 – Install Windows Servers in host and compute environments:**
  Create, manage, and maintain images for deployment

Whether you are deploying Windows Server 2016 to physical computers or deploying to virtual machines on a Hyper-V host, Windows has a number of tools to help you configure, update, manage, and deploy installation images. As you have seen, deploying a few servers is a straightforward process, but if you have dozens or hundreds of servers to deploy and maintain, you'll want some tools to help automate and manage the process. This section covers the following topics for Windows image deployment:

- Windows Deployment Services (WDS)
- Working with WDS images
- Updating images
- Managing Images with PowerShell

Windows Deployment Services

Windows Deployment Services (WDS) is a server role that facilitates installing Windows OSs across a network. With WDS, you don't need to have installation media ready and sit at the server console as Windows performs the usually uneventful task of OS installation. In addition, you can configure many OS properties (such as computer name and IP address) before deployment instead of having to perform these tasks at the server console after installation. WDS in Windows Server 2016 can deploy the following OSs: Windows XP, Windows Server 2003, Windows Vista SP1, Windows Server 2008/R2, Windows 7, Windows Server 2012/R2, Windows 8/8.1, Windows 10, and Windows Server 2016.

Before you get into the details of installing and configuring WDS, review the following terms used with this server role:

- *Preboot eXecution Environment*—**Preboot eXecution Environment (PXE)**, pronounced "pixie," is a network environment built into many NICs that allows a computer to boot from an image stored on a network server (referred to as a *network boot*) rather than from local storage. During a network boot, PXE sends packets to the network looking for a WDS server to send it an installation image. PXE uses Dynamic Host Configuration Protocol (DHCP) to acquire an IP address and Trivial File Transfer Protocol (TFTP) to transfer data.
- *Image file*—An **image file** contains other files, much like a zip file contains multiple files. In WDS, an image file is a boot image or an install image. A **boot image** contains the Windows PE (defined in the next bulleted item) that allows a client computer to access a WDS server so that it can access an install image. An **install image** contains the actual OS being deployed to the client computer. A **discover image** can be used to boot a client computer that can't use PXE, usually from a CD/DVD or flash device. A **capture image** is a special boot image that creates an install image from a reference computer (described later in "Working with Boot Images"). WDS supports three image file formats: .wim, .vhd, and .vhdx. Files with the .wim extension are **Windows Imaging Format (WIM)** files, the most common image file type used by WDS and the method for storing installation files on a Windows installation DVD. VHD and VHDX files are virtual disk formats also supported by WDS, but their use in WDS is not covered in this book.
- *Windows Preinstallation Environment*—**Windows Preinstallation Environment (PE)** is a minimal OS that has only the services needed to access the network, work with files, copy disk images, and jump-start a Windows installation. Windows PE also has a command-line interface that can be used for troubleshooting startup problems or recovering from a damaged OS installation. When you boot Windows Server 2016 or Windows 10 into Recovery Mode, you're booting into Windows PE. Windows PE is used in the boot image for remote installation with WDS.
- *Multicasting*—**Multicasting** is a network communication method for delivering data to multiple computers on a network simultaneously. It's used in WDS when the same installation image should be sent to multiple computers on the network at the same time. Multicasting reduces bandwidth use more than unicasting does because with unicasting, you have to send data across the network separately for each computer that should receive it. With multicasting, data is sent once and received by all computers configured to receive it.
- *Network boot*—As discussed, a computer with a PXE-compatible NIC has the capability to boot from the network rather than local storage, called a **network boot**. A computer with a PXE-compatible NIC performs a network boot in the following situations:
  - The computer does not have an OS installed on the local hard drive and there is no bootable media inserted into any of the removable drives.
  - The BIOS/UEFI is configured to attempt a network boot before attempting to boot from local media.
  - The F12 key is pressed during computer startup (but before a locally installed OS boots), which initiates a network boot.
- wdsnbp.com—The bootstrap program **wdsnbp.com** is a WDS component that a WDS client downloads when performing a network boot. It contains basic instructions on how to perform a network boot operation, such as whether F12 must be pressed to continue the network boot and which file to request from the WDS server.

WDS Requirements

The WDS server role doesn't stand on its own; it requires several support technologies on the network:

- *Windows Server 2016*—WDS is also available in Windows Server 2008 and Windows Server 2012, but these requirements apply to installing the role on a Windows Server 2016 server.

- *Active Directory*—Microsoft introduced a standalone option for WDS that doesn't require Active Directory, but installing it on a domain controller or member server is recommended and provides the most features.
- *DHCP Server*—A DHCP server must be available, ideally on a Windows server. Having WDS and DHCP on the same server requires fewer configuration steps because some required DHCP options are configured automatically when WDS is installed.
- *DNS Server*—Part of the WDS process in an Active Directory environment requires user authentication from the client computer; a DNS server is needed for the client to locate a domain controller. Even in a standalone WDS implementation, DNS is required for name resolution.
- *PXE-compatible NICs*—A PXE-compatible NIC on WDS client computers isn't a strict requirement because client computers can be booted to a discover image, but using PXE is preferable. If you are deploying Windows to a Hyper-V virtual machine, you must use a legacy network adapter for generation 1 virtual machines; however, you can use a standard (synthetic) network adapter on generation 2 virtual machines since they support PXE boot starting with Hyper-V running on Windows Server 2012.
- *Suitable storage*—An NTFS volume with enough free space for storing the boot and installation images is required.

Installing and Configuring the WDS Role

You can install WDS, like most Windows server roles, by using Server Manager or PowerShell. The real work begins after the role is installed. WDS is a complex server role and has numerous configuration options and associated tasks. This section covers some of the most common configurations you'll encounter.

In Server Manager, you install the WDS role as you do any other role. In the Role Services window, you're prompted to install the Windows Deployment Services tools, and you have the option to install two role services, both selected by default:

- *Deployment Server*—This role service provides full WDS features and depends on the Transport Server role service to function. In most cases, you install this role service.
- *Transport Server*—This role service provides necessary services for Deployment Server, but it can be used without Deployment Server in advanced deployment environments, such as those without Active Directory and DHCP. In addition, Transport Server supports image multicasting, that is, deploying install images to multiple computers on the network.

You can also install the WDS role with PowerShell. To do so, open a PowerShell command prompt, and enter the following command:

```
Install-WindowsFeature WDS
```

By default, this command installs the necessary features and both role services.

WDS Initial Configuration

After WDS is installed, the management console is added to the Tools menu in Server Manager. Before you can use WDS, you must perform initial configuration. When you first open the Windows Deployment Services MMC, you see a message informing you that WDS isn't configured. To configure WDS, right-click the server name in the left pane and click Configure Server to start the WDS Configuration Wizard. The Before You Begin window explains the requirements for configuring WDS (see Figure 3-20).

The next window gives you the choice of installing WDS integrated with Active Directory or as a Standalone server (see Figure 3-21). The default option, an Active Directory–integrated installation, is recommended if your network includes Active Directory. With this option, you can prestage client computers by creating computer accounts for them in Active Directory. **Prestaging** enables you to do a basic unattended installation by specifying the computer name, selecting the boot and install images

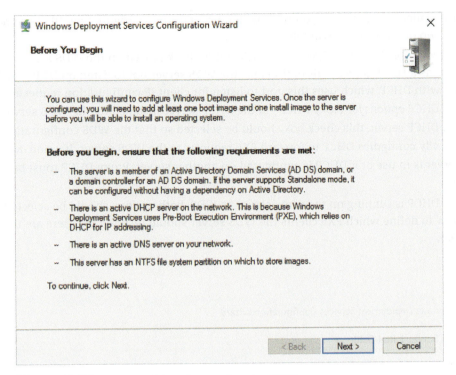

Figure 3-20   Prerequisites for configuring WDS

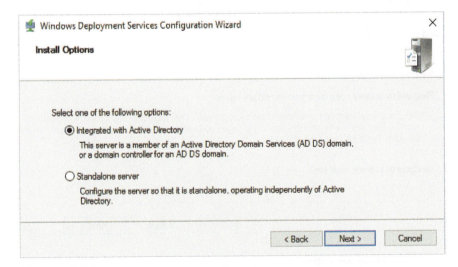

Figure 3-21   Selecting WDS install options

a client should receive, and joining the client to the domain. You can also specify which WDS server a client should use when more than one server is on the network. In addition, you can specify that only prestaged clients can access the WDS server, thereby enhancing security.

In the next window, you decide where to store boot and install images, PXE boot files, and WDS management tools. Install images can be quite large, so you need to choose a folder on an NTFS-formatted volume with plenty of free disk space. By default, this folder is C:\RemoteInstall. For the best performance, you shouldn't choose the System volume (where the \Windows folder is located). If you do, a warning message is displayed, recommending that you choose a folder on a different volume.

If DHCP is installed on the server, you see a window where you configure how DHCP works with WDS. There are two options in this window:

- *Do not listen on DHCP and DHCPv6 ports*—Select this check box when the WDS server is also configured as a DHCP server. This option tells the WDS server not to listen on UDP port 67 to avoid a conflict with DHCP, which uses this port to listen for client IP configuration requests.
- *Configure DHCP options for Proxy DHCP*—If the DHCP server installed on the WDS server is the Microsoft DHCP server, this check box should be selected so that the WDS configuration wizard automatically configures DHCP to forward PXE requests to the WDS server. If a non-Microsoft DHCP server is in use or if DHCP is configured on another server, Proxy DHCP must be configured manually.

If Microsoft DHCP is running on the same server as WDS, both options should be selected. You use the next window to define which PXE clients the WDS server should respond to. There are three options (see Figure 3-22):

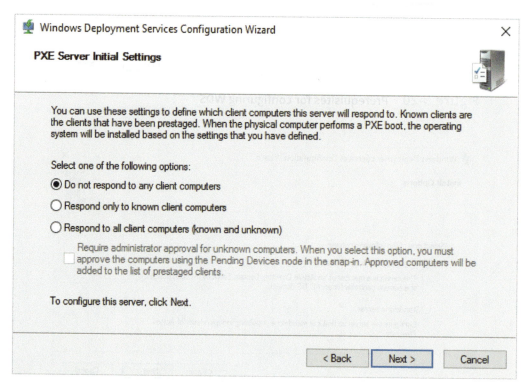

Figure 3-22   PXE server settings

- *Do not respond to any client computers*—This option essentially disables WDS, an option you might want to choose until you have finalized WDS configuration.
- *Respond only to known client computers*—With this option set, WDS responds only to prestaged clients. This option is more secure because it prevents a rogue computer from attempting to acquire an install image, but it requires more up-front configuration.
- *Respond to all client computers (known and unknown)*—WDS responds to all clients that attempt a PXE boot, whether they're prestaged or not. If this option is set, you can choose whether administrator approval is required before WDS responds to unknown computers. Unknown clients requiring administrator approval are placed in the Pending Devices node in the WDS management console.

> **Note** 📎
>
> All the options configured with the WDS configuration wizard can be changed later in the Properties window of the WDS server.

The WDS service attempts to start after the last window of the WDS configuration wizard. If the WDS server is also a DHCP server, a DHCP scope must be configured so that WDS can configure proxy DHCP; otherwise, WDS won't start.

> **Tip** ⓘ
>
> If the WDS service doesn't start after finishing the wizard, right-click the server in the WDS console, point to All Tasks, and click Start.

Working with WDS Images

Now that you're familiar with the WDS server role, it's time to turn your attention to working with WDS images so that you can begin performing remote installations. Images are the heart of the WDS server role. Boot and install images, along with a client that has a PXE-compatible NIC, allow an administrator to install an OS remotely on a computer that has neither an OS installed on its hard disk nor locally bootable media. You can use WDS images customized for your environment, the stock OS installation, or a combination of both, depending on the needs of those using the target client computer. The following sections go into more detail on boot and install images and explain discover images and how to update an existing image.

Working with Boot Images

As discussed, a boot image contains Windows PE and Windows Setup, which a client computer uses to select and download an installation image and begin the OS installation. The boot image used in WDS contains the same code on a Windows installation DVD that a client computer boots from when performing a local installation. The main difference is that with WDS, the installation image is loaded across the network, allowing many installations to occur at the same time without requiring multiple copies of the installation medium.

Adding a boot image is really the first step in working with images because without one, you can't boot clients from the network. After a boot image is configured, you can do testing of your WDS setup. In most cases, you should use the `boot.wim` file on the Windows Server 2016 (or other support Windows version) installation DVD.

Creating and Using a Capture Image

A capture image is a specialized boot image used to capture the state of an OS already installed and configured on a reference computer. A **reference computer** is like a prototype where you have installed an OS, made configuration changes, and installed some applications. It serves as the model for other computers. You then boot the reference computer to the capture image and capture the OS and applications to an install image that's applied to other computers. You create a capture image in the WDS management console, using an existing boot image as a template.

Before you boot the reference computer with the capture image, it must be prepared with `sysprep`, which resets system identifiers and other information unique to the computer (such as computer name). In most cases, when you run `sysprep` (in the \Windows\system32\sysprep folder), you should choose the following options (see Figure 3-23):

- Enter System Out-of-Box Experience (OOBE)
- Generalize
- Shutdown

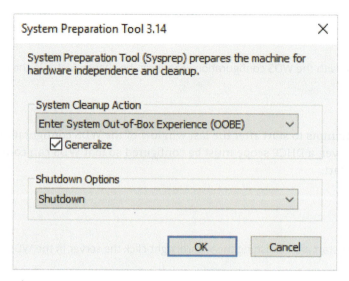

Figure 3-23 Selecting `sysprep` options

You can also run `sysprep` from the command line:

```
C:\windows\system32\sysprep\sysprep /oobe /generalize /shutdown
```

The `/oobe` option causes the computer to start in the usual startup mode, allowing users to perform initial configuration tasks. The `/generalize` option removes the unique identifiers on the system; they're created the next time the system boots. This option also clears system restore points and deletes event logs. The `/shutdown` option causes the target computer to shut down after `sysprep` is finished running. You can also choose `/reboot`, but the `/shutdown` option makes sure your WDS server is ready, and you can be prepared to press F12 to do a network boot. If you miss the network boot, your target system boots into Windows and you need to run `sysprep` again.

One caution when using a capture image on the target computer: There must be enough space on the target to store the resulting install image. A network drive can be used, but it isn't recommended because a failed network link can cause image corruption.

Working with Install Images

Install images, unsurprisingly, contain the data and instructions for installing an OS. You can use the stock install image (`\sources\install.wim`) on the Windows installation DVD, or you can create an install image with a reference computer and a capture image. The `install.wim` file on a Windows installation DVD might contain multiple installation images. For example, a Windows Server `install.wim` file might contain four images: Standard and Datacenter editions in both the Server Core and Desktop Experience versions. While adding the image to WDS, you can select which edition and version you want to include.

Using a Stock Windows Install Image

This section describes adding an install image from a Windows installation DVD. When you use the standard `install.wim` image on the installation DVD, the installation experience is the same as though you booted the client to the installation DVD. The only difference might be the choices of which OS to install. When you boot to the installation DVD, you see all the installation choices on the DVD. However, when you configure the install image with WDS, you can limit which choices the person attending the installation sees.

When you configure an install image in WDS, the image must be added to an image group. An **image group** is just a container where you can organize images with common properties. For example, you can create an image group for Windows Server 2016 install images and one for Windows 10 install images. You can also group images according to which users should have access to them. You can create an image group before adding an install image or by using the Add Image Wizard.

Updating Images

You can make changes to images after they're created. For example, you've created an install image with several customizations and installed applications, and you don't want to go through the same process each time a patch or service pack is released. With the **Deployment Image Servicing and Management (dism.exe)** command-line tool, you can update an image with patches, drivers, hotfixes, and service packs without having to re-create the entire image. The dism.exe command can be used on an offline image that you've mounted by using dism /mount-wim or on an online image if you include the /online switch. It can also be used to display information about an image.

As a typical example of using dism.exe on an existing image, say you've created a Windows Server 2016 custom install image from a reference computer. After creating the image, you learn that Microsoft has published a hotfix containing a security patch for the DNS Server role service. You plan to deploy DNS on several servers that will use the install image, so including the hotfix in the install image is critical. The following steps describe the procedure; each step can take a lot of time because of the size of image files:

1. First, take the image offline by right-clicking it in WDS and clicking Disable. Then right-click the image again and click Export Image. Note where you placed the exported image and the name you gave it. (*Note*: If the image was never added to WDS, you don't need to perform this step.)

2. Create a folder where you'll mount the image. Mounting an image is like mounting a drive, making its contents available as though they were just files and folders on a disk. This example uses C:\mount as the location. Use the following command to mount the install.wim image in the C:\RemoteInstall\Export folder. The /index parameter specifies which installation image to use if the .wim file contains more than one.

```
dism /mount-wim /wimfile:c:\remoteinstall\export\install.wim
 /index:1 /mountdir:c:\mount
```

3. Use the following command to apply the hotfix named DNSfix.cab. After the /image parameter, you specify the folder where you mounted the image but not the image's file name.

```
dism /image:c:\mount /add-package /packagepath:c:\hotfixes\dnsfix.cab
```

4. Use the following command to commit the changes to the .wim file and dismount the image. The /commit option writes the changes to the image file you exported in Step 1. You can use /discard instead of /commit if you don't want to keep the changes you made.

```
dism /unmount-wim /mountdir:c:\mount /commit
```

5. The last step is replacing the image in WDS with the new image and enabling it. Right-click the original image in WDS and click Replace Image. Browse to and select the image you exported in Step 2. Finally, enable the image so that clients can access it.

When you update an image, the updates can be applied to computers that already have installed an OS with WDS. Some updates require a system restart after being applied, but you might not want this action, especially for servers. There are two dism options for dealing with automatic restarts:

- /preventpending—Prevents updates that require a restart from being installed on the target computer.
- /norestart—Allows installing updates that require a restart but prevents an automatic restart; the computer must be restarted manually before the update takes effect.

As mentioned, an image file can contain multiple install images. To see a list of images available in a .wim file, for example, use the /Get-ImageInfo option. To see a list of images in the install.wim file on the Windows Server 2016 installation medium in drive D:, use the following command:

```
dism /get-imageinfo /imagefile:d:\sources\install.wim
```

> **Tip**
>
> Any errors that occur while running `dism.exe` are reported in the Windows log at C:\Windows\Logs\DISM.

Enabling and Disabling Features in Images

As with applying hotfixes and patches, you can enable and disable features in an existing image by using the `dism.exe` command. To enable a feature in an image, it must be taken offline and mounted first. In the following examples, the DHCPServer feature is enabled in the first command and disabled in the second command. The third command displays a list of available features (and indicates whether they're enabled or disabled in the mounted image) and can be used to get the names of features you want to enable or disable.

```
dism /image:c:\mount /enable-feature /featurename:dhcpserver
dism /image:c:\mount /disable-feature /featurename:dhcpserver
dism /image:c:\mount /get-features
```

After you enable or disable features, be sure to commit the changes and dismount the image, and then replace the image in WDS, if necessary.

> **Tip** ⓘ
>
> For more information on `dism.exe`, including its options and parameters, see *http://technet.microsoft.com/en-us/library/dd744382(v=ws.10).aspx*.

Managing Images with PowerShell

There are a number of PowerShell cmdlets available to manage WDS and WDS images. The following is a list of some of the PowerShell cmdlets for working with WDS images:

> `Add-WdsDriverPackage`—Adds a driver package to a driver group or into a boot image.
>
> **Example:** `Add-WdsDriverPackage -Architecture x64 -ImageName "Standard Setup Boot" -Name "Raid Driver"`

The preceding cmdlet adds a driver package named *Raid Driver* to a WDS boot image named *Standard Setup Boot* that uses the Intel x64 architecture. The `-architecture` parameter is required.

> `Disable-WdsBootImage`—Disables a boot image so it will not be available to WDS clients.
>
> **Example:** `Disable-WdsBootImage -Architecture x64 -ImageName "Standard Setup Boot"`

This cmdlet disables a WDS boot image named *Standard Setup Boot* that uses the Intel x64 architecture.

> `Disable-WdsInstallImage`—Disables an install image so it will not be available to WDS clients.
>
> **Example:** `Disable-WdsInstallImage -InstallImageName "Windows Server 2016 Standard Core"`

The preceding cmdlet disables a WDS install image named *Windows Server 2016 Standard Core*.

> `Enable-WdsBootImage`—Enables a boot image so it will be available to WDS clients.
>
> **Example:** `Enable-WdsBootImage -Architecture x64 -ImageName "Standard Setup Boot"`

The preceding cmdlet enables a WDS boot image named *Standard Setup Boot*.

> `Enable-WdsInstallImage`—Enables an install image so it will be available to WDS clients.

> **Example:** `Enable-WdsInstallImage -InstallImageName "Windows Server 2016 Standard Core"`

The preceding cmdlet enables a WDS install image named *Windows Server 2016 Standard Core*.

> `Export-WdsBootImage`—Exports a boot image from WDS to a Windows image file (`.wim`).

> **Example:** `Export-WdsBootImage -Architecture x64 -Destination W:\images\ StandSetup.wim -ImageName "Standard Setup Boot"`

The preceding cmdlet exports a WDS boot image named *Standard Setup Boot* to a file named `StandSetup.wim`.

> `Export-WdsInstallImage`—Exports an install image from WDS to a Windows image file (`.wim`).

> **Example:** `Export-WdsBootImage -Destination W:\images\W2K16StCore.wim ImageName "Windows Server 2016 Standard Core"`

The preceding cmdlet exports a WDS install image named *Windows Server 2016 Standard Core* to a file named `W2K16StCore.wim`.

> `Get-WdsBootImage`—Gets and lists the properties of a boot image.

> **Example:** `Get-WdsBootImage -Architecture x64 -ImageName "Standard Setup Boot"`

The preceding cmdlet gets and lists the properties for a WDS boot image named *Standard Setup Boot*.

> `Get-WdsInstallImage`—Gets and lists the properties of an install image.

> **Example:** `Get-WdsInstallImage -InstallImageName "Windows Server 2016 Standard Core"`

The preceding cmdlet gets and lists the properties for a WDS install image named *Windows Server 2016 Standard Core*.

> `Import-WdsBootImage`—Imports a boot image from a `.wim` file into the WDS image store so it is ready to be used by WDS clients.

> **Example:** `Import-WdsBootImage -Path W:\images\StandSetup.wim -ImageName "Standard Setup Boot"`

The preceding cmdlet imports a WDS boot image named *Standard Setup Boot* into the WDS image store and makes it available for WDS clients.

> `Import-WdsInstallImage`—Imports an install image from a `.wim` file into the WDS image store so it is ready to be used by WDS clients.

> **Example:** `Import-WdsInstallImage -Path W:\images\W2K16StCore.wim -ImageName "Windows Server 2016 Standard Core"`

The preceding cmdlet imports a WDS install image named *Windows Server 2016 Standard Core* into the WDS image store and makes it available for WDS clients.

> `Remove-WdsBootImage`—Removes a boot image from the WDS image store. The image will not be available to WDS clients. After removal, to use the image for WDS clients, it must be imported.

> **Example:** `Remove-WdsBootImage -Architecture x64 -ImageName "Standard Setup Boot"`

The preceding cmdlet removes a WDS boot image named *Standard Setup Boot* from the WDS image store.

> `Remove-WdsInstallImage`—Removes an install image from the WDS image store. The image will not be available to WDS clients. After removal, to use the image for WDS clients, it must be imported.

Example: `Remove-WdsInstallImage -ImageName "Windows Server 2016 Standard Core"`

The preceding cmdlet removes a WDS install image named *Windows Server 2016 Standard Core* from the WDS image store.

    `Set-WdsBootImage`—Sets properties of a boot image in the WDS image store. The image name and description can be changed, the display order can be set, and the image can be enabled for multicast.

Example: `Set-WdsBootImage -Architecture x64 -ImageName "Standard Setup Boot" -Multicast`

The preceding cmdlet configures a WDS boot image named *Standard Setup Boot* for multicast transmission.

    `Set-WdsInstallImage`—Sets properties of an install image in the WDS image store. The image name and description can be changed, the display order can be set, an answer file can be specified, access permissions can be set, and multicast properties can be configured.

Example: `Set-WdsInstallImage -ImageName "Windows Server 2016 Standard Core" -Multicast`

The preceding cmdlet configures a WDS install image named *Windows Server 2016 Standard Core* for multicast transmission.

Note

For a full list of WDS cmdlets, type `Get-Command -Module Wds` at a PowerShell prompt.

Configuring Services

- **70-740 – Install Windows Servers in host and compute environments:**
  Install, upgrade, and migrate servers and workloads

A **service** is a task or process that runs in the background, behind the scenes. Just because you don't see a user interface for a service doesn't mean it doesn't need to be configured, however. Configuring services isn't a task you need to do often, but should the need come up, you must know how it's done. In Server Manager, you can access services via the Local Server node. After clicking Local Server, scroll down until you see the Services window shown in Figure 3-24. If you have added servers to Server Manager, you can click a server and see the Services window for that particular server.

You can use this window to view the status of a service. You can also right-click a service and perform the following actions:

- Start services
- Stop services
- Restart services
- Pause services
- Resume services
- Copy (used to copy text so that you can paste information about a service into a text file)

A Services MMC is also available from the Tools menu in Server Manager, and the Services snap-in is a standard part of the Computer Management MMC. If you need to perform configuration tasks beyond

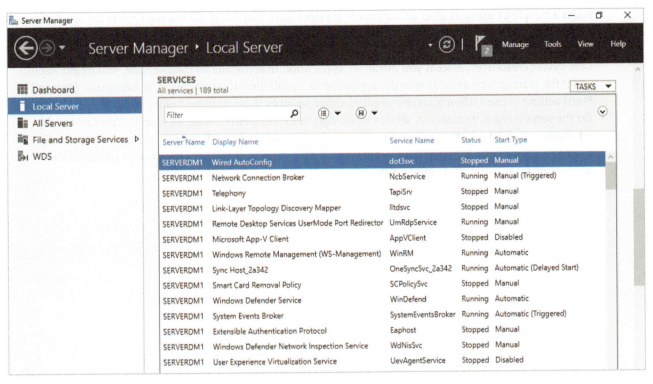

Figure 3-24   The Services window in Server Manager

what's available in the Services window, you must use the Services snap-in. In addition to the actions listed previously, you can use the Services snap-in to perform the following operations:

- *Set the service startup type*—The settings are Automatic, Automatic (Delayed Start), Manual, and Disabled (see Figure 3-25). Manual requires an administrator to start the service. With the Automatic setting, the service starts at system boot. With the Automatic (Delayed Start) setting, the service

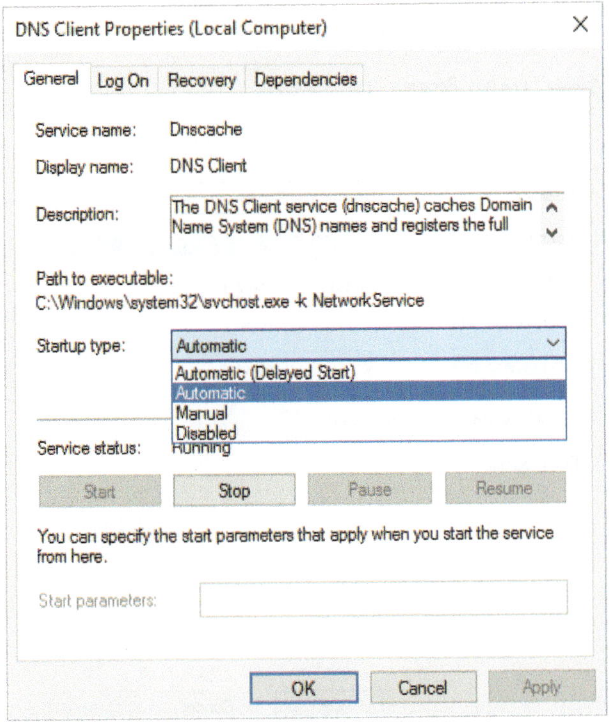

Figure 3-25   Setting the service startup type

starts a couple of minutes after all automatic services have started. If the startup type is Disabled, the service doesn't start. Services that are already installed in Windows usually don't require a change to the startup type; however, on occasion, you might want to disable a service you know isn't used to save system resources. Also, if you install an application that installs its own service, you might need to set the startup type according to the application's installation instructions. The Automatic (Delayed Start) setting is used when a service requires other services to be running before it starts.

- *Set the service logon account*—A service must sign in to a system to interact with it. You can specify an account (see Figure 3-26) or use the Local System account. As with the startup type, you usually need to configure the logon account only when installing a new service. The service installation instructions usually include guidelines.

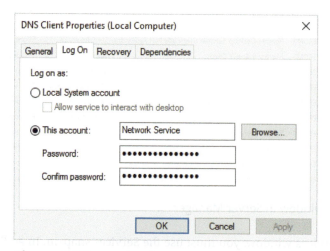

Figure 3-26 Setting the service logon account

- *Set service recovery options*—You can specify how a service should respond if it fails or is unable to start (see Figure 3-27). You can set the following options for the first, second, and subsequent failures: Restart the Service, Take No Action, Run a Program, and Restart the Computer.

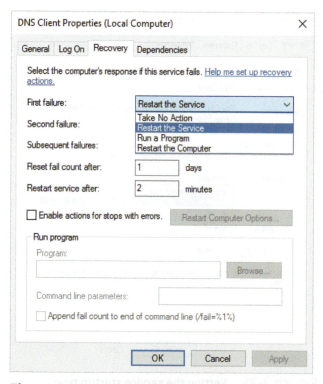

Figure 3-27 Setting service recovery options

- *View service dependencies*—Some services depend on other services to run, which is called **service dependencies**. The Dependencies tab shows other services that the current service depends on, if any, and what system components depend on the current service (see Figure 3-28).

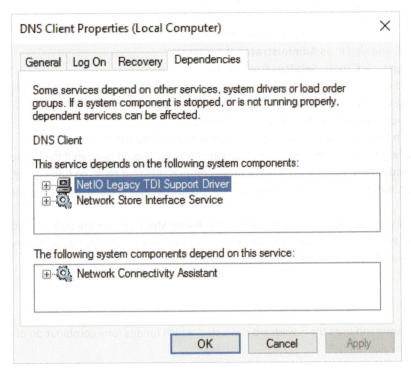

Figure 3-28   Viewing service dependencies

Configuring Services with PowerShell

As with most server functions, there are PowerShell cmdlets for configuring Windows services:

- `Get-Service`—Displays a list of services. To narrow the list, add the `-DisplayName` argument. For example, if you want to see a list of all services related to Hyper-V, use `Get-Service -DisplayName Hy*`.
- `Start-Service`—Starts a specified service. For multiple services, separate the names with a comma.
- `Stop-Service`—Stops a specified service. Separate multiple service names with a comma.
- `Restart-Service`—Stops and then starts a specified service. For multiple services, separate the names with a comma.
- `Suspend-Service`—Pauses a specified running service. For multiple services, separate the names with a comma.
- `Resume-Service`—Resumes a suspended service. For multiple services, separate the names with a comma.
- `Set-Service`—Allows you to change the properties of a service, including its status, description, start mode, and display name. You can also start, stop, and suspend services.
- `New-Service`—Creates a new service.

Tip ⓘ

You can get detailed help on each command by typing `get-help cmdname -detailed` at a PowerShell command prompt (replacing `cmdname` with one of the service commands in the preceding list).

Activity 3-5: Working with Windows Services

Time Required: 10 minutes

Objective: Check the status of services and configure services.

Required Tools and Equipment: ServerSA1

Description: Use the Services MMC and PowerShell to view and modify services.

1. Start ServerSA1, and sign in as **Administrator**, if necessary.
2. In Server Manager, click **Tools**, **Services** from the menu.
3. Scroll down and double-click **Print Spooler**. In the Print Spooler Properties dialog box, click the **Startup type** list arrow to see the available options. Make sure **Automatic** is selected.
4. Click the **Stop** button to stop the Print Spooler service.
5. Click the **Log On** tab where you configure how a service signs into the system.
6. Click the **Recovery** tab. Explore the available options for what should happen if the service fails.
7. Click the **Dependencies** tab. You see a list of other components that must be functioning for Print Spooler to run. Click **OK**. Notice that in the Service MMC, the Status column is blank, indicating that the service isn't running.
8. Open a PowerShell command prompt by clicking the **PowerShell** icon on the taskbar. Type **Get-Service -DisplayName Pr*** and press **Enter**. You see a list of services with a display name beginning with Pr, including the Print Spooler service. Its name is simply Spooler.

> **Note** 🔗
>
> The `Pr*` in the command uses the `*` wildcard character, which means "any combination of characters can follow Pr in the service name."

9. Type **Start-Service Spooler** and press **Enter**. Type **Get-Service Spooler** and press **Enter**. The Print Spooler service is running again. Close PowerShell. Click the **Refresh** icon in the Services MMC to see that Print Spooler's status is Running.
10. Close the Services MMC and shut down ServerSA1.

Chapter Summary

- You need to add roles and features to take advantage of Windows Server 2016's power. You can add and remove roles and features with Server Manager or PowerShell. You can also use PowerShell to query whether a role or feature is installed or available to be installed. You can use PowerShell to act on remote servers by using the `-ComputerName` argument.

- You can add and remove features to and from offline VHD and `.wim` file images with the `dism` command.

- You can add servers to Server Manager and perform most management tasks on remote servers. You can add servers by using Active Directory, DNS, and an import file. Remote computers that aren't domain members must be added to the TrustedHosts file on the managing computer.

- To organize the servers you're managing, create groups in Server Manager. Servers can belong to more than one group.

- WinRM has a command-line interface for performing a variety of tasks. This feature must be enabled to use PowerShell cmdlets remotely. The `Configure-SMRemoting` command enables and disables WinRM.

- You need to configure firewall rules to allow remote management with an MMC. You can use the

Windows Firewall with Advanced Security MMC, the `netsh` command, or PowerShell cmdlets to set firewall rules.

- The WDS server role facilitates installing Windows OSs across a network. In Windows Server 2016, WDS can deploy these OSs: Windows XP, Windows Server 2003, Windows Vista SP1, Windows Server 2008/R2, Windows 7, Windows Server 2012/R2, Windows Server 2016, and Windows 8.

- The WDS process starts with a client computer that has a PXE-compatible NIC. An IP address is assigned to the client via DHCP. A bootstrap file is transferred to the client, which uses it to boot and request a boot image file. Windows Setup is started, and an install image is sent to the client. The client runs the install image, and the OS is installed.

- The WDS server role has two role services: Deployment Server and Transport Server. In most cases, both role services are installed. WDS must be configured before the server can be used. A configuration wizard walks you through basic settings, and then you can make changes in the WDS server's Properties window.

- To use WDS, you need both boot and install images. A boot image contains Windows PE and Windows Setup, which are used to access and run install images. A capture image is a specialized boot image used to create a custom install image from a reference computer. Install images contain the OS deployed to the client computer. The Windows installation DVD contains a standard install image that can be used if no OS customizations are needed. When you add an install image, you must place it in a WDS image group used to organize images and set permissions.

- If you have clients that can't PXE-boot, you can create a discover image, which allows a client to boot from a CD/DVD and access a WDS server for the install image. Discover images are specialized boot images that need to be converted to an ISO file before burning to bootable media.

- Install images can be updated with patches, hotfixes, and service packs by using the `dism.exe` command. Images are generally taken offline, updated with the necessary packages, and then added back to WDS. Using `dism.exe`, you can also enable and disable Windows features.

- You configure services with the Services MMC or PowerShell. In the Services MMC, you can start, stop, and disable services. You can also configure the startup type, service logon account, recovery options, and service dependencies.

Key Terms

boot image
capture image
Deployment Image Servicing and Management (dism.exe)
Desired State Configuration (DSC)
discover image
image file
image group
install image
Integrated Scripting Environment (ISE)

local configuration manager (LCM)
multicasting
network boot
Preboot eXecution Environment (PXE)
prestaging
reference computer
service
service dependencies
wdsnbp.com

Windows Deployment Services (WDS)
Windows Imaging Format (WIM)
Windows Preinstallation Environment (PE)
Windows Remote Management (WinRM)

Review Questions

1. Which of the following is a task you should perform before installing server roles and features? (Choose all that apply.)
   a. Set a strong Administrator password.
   b. Read the Windows Server 2016 user manual.
   c. Configure static IP addresses.
   d. Make sure security updates are current.

2. Which of the following is true about installing roles and features in Windows Server 2016?
   a. You can't install a server role by using the command line.
   b. All server role installations require a server restart.
   c. You can install more than one role at a time.
   d. Server roles can be installed only on online drives.

3. Which PowerShell command shows a list of installed roles and features?
   a. `Installed-WindowsFeature -Show`
   b. `Get-WindowsFeature | where Installed`
   c. `List-InstalledFeature`
   d. `Show-Features .if. Installed`

4. You want to install a feature to an offline image (.wim) file. What do you do first?
   a. Commit the changes.
   b. Install the feature by using `dism`.
   c. Mount the image.
   d. Import the .wim file.

5. You can install and uninstall features to and from an offline VHD file only by using PowerShell cmdlets. True or False?

6. Which of the following commands should be used when working with an install image (.wim file) that will be deployed with Windows Deployment Server (WDS)?
   a. `netsh`
   b. `wimfile`
   c. `Install-WindowsFeature`
   d. `dism`

7. Which of the following modes does Desired State Configuration operate in? (Choose all that apply.)
   a. Push mode
   b. Config mode
   c. State mode
   d. Pull mode

8. Which of the following configuration tasks can be automated when using DSC version 2 in Windows Server 2016? (Choose all that apply.)
   a. Deploying software
   b. Managing Disk Images
   c. Managing registry settings
   d. Running PowerShell scripts

9. Which of the following is a method for adding a server to Server Manager? (Choose all that apply.)
   a. Query NetBIOS.
   b. Search Active Directory.
   c. Import a file.
   d. Search DNS.

10. You add a server to Server Manager but see the error message "WinRM Negotiation authentication error." What should you do?
    a. Add the server with different credentials.
    b. Add the server to the TrustedHosts list.
    c. Install .NET Framework 4.5.
    d. Enter the Configure-SMRemoting command.

11. You're managing 75 servers from a single Server Manager console and find you're wasting a lot of time scrolling through the list of servers to

find the one you want to manage. You have five locations with about 15 servers in each location. What can you do to make managing these servers in Server Manager easier?
    a. Create a group in Active Directory.
    b. Use WinRM.
    c. Enable PowerShell remoting.
    d. Create server groups.

12. In Windows Server 2016, what must be running to allow you to manage a server remotely with PowerShell?
    a. Windows Firewall
    b. LBFO
    c. Telnet
    d. WinRM

13. You right-click a Server Core server in Server Manager and click Computer Management. You see an error indicating that the server can't be managed. What should you do to solve the problem?
    a. Run `configure-SMRemoting.exe -Enable` on the local computer.
    b. Configure Windows Firewall on the remote computer.
    c. Install the GUI Interface on the remote computer.
    d. Disable WinRM on the local computer.

14. You want to be able to manage a Server Core computer's firewall by using the Windows Firewall with Advanced Security snap-in. What should you do?
    a. On the local computer, disable the Windows Firewall Remote Management rule group.
    b. On the remote computer, enter the command `Configure-SMRemoting -ConfigureFirewallRules`.
    c. On the remote computer, use the PowerShell command `Set-NetFirewallRule -DisplayGroup "Windows Firewall Remote Management" -enabled True`.
    d. On the local computer, enable the COM+ Network Access firewall rule.

15. You need to stop a service so that you can do some troubleshooting. Before you stop it, you need to see whether any other services will be affected by this action. What should you do?
    a. Look at the Dependencies tab.
    b. View the service startup type.
    c. Right-click the service and click Show Requirements.
    d. Set the service recovery options.

16. Which cmdlet shows a list of services related to Hyper-V?
    a. `List-Services Hyper-V -all`
    b. `Show-Service -ServiceType Hyper*`
    c. `Get-Help Service Hyper-V`
    d. `Get-Service -DisplayName Hy*`

17. Which operating system can be deployed with WDS in Windows Server 2016? (Choose all that apply.)
    a. Windows 2000
    b. Windows Server 2003
    c. Windows 7
    d. Windows Server 2008/R2

18. Which of the following is a special boot image that creates an install image from a reference computer?
    a. Discover image   c. Install image
    b. Capture image   d. Update Image

19. If you want to deploy an image to multiple client computers at the same time but send data packets only once, what WDS feature should you use?
    a. Boot   c. Advanced
    b. Multicast   d. Client

20. When a client performs a PXE boot, which of the following does it download from the WDS server first?
    a. boot.wim   c. install.wim
    b. PXE-boot.com   d. wdsnbp.com

21. You're creating a reference computer for the purpose of creating a custom install image. You have installed the OS, made your configuration changes, and installed the applications you want. What should you do next?
    a. Boot the reference computer by using boot.wim.
    b. Prestage the reference computer.
    c. Run sysprep on the reference computer.
    d. Use the dism.exe command on the reference computer.

22. Which of the following is true about the Windows Server 2016 install.wim file? (Choose all that apply.)
    a. It's in the C:\Windows directory.
    b. It can contain multiple installation images.
    c. It's on the DVD in the \sources folder.
    d. It always contains a single OS installation.

23. Last week, you created a custom install image from a reference computer with plans to deploy the image tomorrow. The reference computer has already been put into service for other purposes. Today, you discover that a critical security patch for IIS has been released. IIS is a necessary part of your install image. What's the most efficient solution for ensuring that your computers will have this security patch?
    a. Disable IIS in the image, deploy the image, and then install the patch.
    b. Create a new reference computer that includes the patch.
    c. Deploy the image and then run Windows update on all your computers.
    d. Use dism.exe to modify the image before deploying it.

24. Which of the following dism options prevents updates that require a restart from being installed on the target computer?
    a. `/norestart`
    b. `/restartpending`
    c. `/preventpending`
    d. `/preventrestart`

25. Which of the following PowerShell cmdlets sets properties of a boot image in the WDS image store?
    a. `Set-WdsInstallImage`
    b. `Import-WdsBootImage`
    c. `Set-WdsBootImage`
    d. `Import-WdsInstallImage`

Critical Thinking

The following activities give you critical thinking challenges. Case Projects offer a scenario with a problem to solve for which you supply a written solution.

Case Project 3-1: Outfitting a Branch Office with Server Core

You have been supporting CSM Tech Publishing's Windows Server 2016 server network for over a year. The office has two Windows Server 2016 servers running Active Directory and a number of other roles. Management has informed you that a small sales office is opening in the same building three floors up. The sales manager wants to install a sales application on a server located in the sales office. This server will have limited physical security because there's no special room dedicated for it, which means it will be accessible to non-IT personnel and visitors. You're considering installing Windows Server 2016 Server Core on the new server because accessing its console regularly probably won't be necessary, and this server will be managed from one of the other CSM Tech Publishing servers. What are the benefits and drawbacks of using Server Core for this branch office? What are some things you should do to set up this server management environment?

Case Project 3-2: Dealing with Server Core Angst

The owner of CSM Tech Publishing was at the sales office last week and out of curiosity wanted to sign in to the server there. The owner is somewhat tech savvy and has even worked a little with Active Directory in Windows Server 2012. He was shocked when he signed in and didn't see a familiar user interface—only a command prompt. He asked you about this and accepted your explanation of Server Core and why you chose this installation option. However, he was wondering what would happen if you stopped providing support or were unavailable for an extended period, and your replacement wasn't familiar with Server Core. Write a memo explaining how this situation could be handled easily.

Case Project 3-3: Ensuring Proper Server Configuration

You are called to consult with an organization that has well over 100 servers including virtual servers. The manager you spoke with told you that the organization is having problems keeping the servers properly configured. Different administrators make changes to the configuration or add and remove services to keep up with user demand. However, the manager finds that changes are not well documented and often cause problems. The manager would like to know if there is a way to automate control of changes to server roles, features, services, and so forth. What Windows Server 2016 feature can you suggest and why?

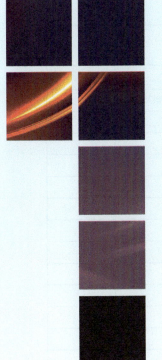

CHAPTER 4

CONFIGURING STORAGE AND FILE SYSTEMS

After reading this chapter and completing the exercises, you will be able to:

Describe server storage

Configure local disks

Work with virtual disks

Describe file sharing

Configure Windows file sharing

Secure access to files with permissions

Configuring a server's storage is usually one of the first tasks you need to perform on a new server after finishing its initial configuration. In the past, server storage was simply a disk controller and one or two hard drives. Now advanced storage solutions are available to provide fault tolerance and high performance. This chapter covers the basics of server storage and then explains configuring local disks. With virtualization becoming such an important part of network environments, it's no surprise that Windows Server 2016 supports creating and mounting virtual disks. This chapter describes the basic steps to work with virtual disks.

Once storage is configured, you'll need to configure the storage for use, which often means sharing it with network users and setting permissions. This chapter discusses a variety of methods for creating and configuring Windows shares and shows you how to properly set permissions to allow users the proper access. Because many networks include Linux/UNIX computers, you'll also learn how to configure Network File System (NFS) shares, the native file-sharing protocol for Linux/UNIX operating systems.

An Overview of Server Storage

Q Certification

- 70-740 – Implement storage solutions:
  Configure disks and volumes

Table 4-1 describes what you need to do the hands-on activities in this chapter.

Table 4-1   Activity requirements

Activity	Requirements	Notes
Activity 4-1: Resetting Your Virtual Environment	ServerSA1, ServerHyperV	
Activity 4-2: Configuring a New Disk	ServerSA1	
Activity 4-3: Working with Volumes in Disk Management	ServerSA1	
Activity 4-4: Working with Virtual Disks in Disk Management	ServerSA1	
Activity 4-5: Working with Virtual Disks in PowerShell	ServerHyperV	
Activity 4-6: Sharing a Folder with Simple File Sharing	ServerSA1	
Activity 4-7: Sharing a Folder with Advanced Sharing	ServerSA1	
Activity 4-8: Creating a Share with File and Storage Services	ServerSA1	
Activity 4-9: Creating a Hidden Share and Monitoring Share Access	ServerSA1	
Activity 4-10: Mapping a Drive	ServerSA1	
Activity 4-11: Examining Default Settings for Volume Permissions	ServerSA1	
Activity 4-12: Experimenting with File and Folder Permissions	ServerSA1	
Activity 4-13: Restricting Access to Subfolders of Shares	ServerSA1	

One of the main reasons that networks and servers were invented was to have a centralized repository for shared files. The need for faster, bigger, and more reliable storage is growing as fast as the technology can keep up. Everything is stored on digital media now—documents, emails, music, photographs, and videos—and this trend is continuing. In addition, people want instant anywhere access to whatever it is they're storing. Just about every large Internet company—from Dropbox to iCloud to OneDrive, and many more—has its own version of cloud storage. Dozens of cloud storage services are competing to store your files, and although these services are convenient and seemingly work by magic, they all start with a server and some disk drives. The following sections cover some basics of server storage: what it is, why you need it, and the common methods for accessing storage.

What Is Storage?

Generally speaking, storage is any digital media data can be written to and retrieved from. Technically, this definition includes random access memory (RAM), but the term *server storage* generally means long-term storage, maintaining data without a power source. Long-term storage includes the following types of media:

- USB memory sticks (flash drives)
- Secure Digital (SD) cards and Compact Flash (CF) cards
- CDs and DVDs
- Magnetic tape
- Solid state drives
- Hard disk drives

This discussion centers on server storage, which is based on hard disk drives (HDDs), although solid state drives (SSDs) are catching up in popularity with HDDs, especially for applications requiring higher speed, smaller size, and lower power requirements. A **solid state drive (SSD)** uses flash memory and the same type of high-speed interfaces (SATA, SAS) as traditional hard disks. An SSD has no moving parts, requires less power, and is faster and more resistant to shock than an HDD, but the cost is still higher per gigabyte than that for an HDD. However, because of the speed advantages of SSDs, you'll often find them alongside HDDs in server systems. Most of the discussion of HDD storage applies to SSDs, too, and as technology progresses and prices drop, you'll see SSDs eventually replace HDDs except in the most storage-centric applications.

> **Note** 📎
>
> Some SSD drives now come with a PCI Express interface that plugs directly into a PCI Express slot. There are other variations of SSDs such as SATA Express, mSATA, and M.2.

Reasons for Storage

Every computer needs some amount of storage, but servers generally require more than client computers because one of the server's main purposes is to store and serve files. The following list isn't exhaustive, but it covers most uses:

- *Operating system files*—The operating system (OS) itself requires a good bit of storage. The files that make up the OS include boot files, the kernel, device drivers, user interface files, and all the files for roles and features you can install. Together, they add up to around 9 GB on a server with the GUI installed and about 5 GB in Server Core.
- *Page file*—A **page file** is used as virtual memory and to store dump data after a system crash. Its size varies depending on how much RAM is installed, memory use patterns, and other factors. In the past, the page file was set to 1.5 times the amount of installed memory, but this formula is no longer valid. By default, the system manages the page file, which can change size depending on needs but is typically close to the amount of installed RAM, up to 4 GB.
- *Log files*—The log files you see in Event Viewer and other log files change size dynamically depending on how the system is used. You can use Event Viewer to configure the maximum size of many log files. Be aware that even if you aren't adding any files to the disk where Windows is installed, log files can slowly eat up disk space unless you keep an eye on them.
- *Virtual machines*—If the server is a virtualization server running Hyper-V, you need plenty of space to store files for virtual hard disks. Virtualization is one of the largest uses of disk space in servers now.
- *Database storage*—If a server is running one or more databases, disk storage requirements vary depending on the size of databases. Because databases can grow dynamically, it's a good idea to store them on a drive separate from the Windows drive, preferably on a volume that can have its capacity expanded if needed.
- *User documents*—If a server is being used to store user files or user profiles, this purpose might be the largest use of disk space. Using disk quotas on servers that store user files is a good idea so that a single user can't monopolize disk space by storing his or her entire collection of movies, for example, on a network server.

When deciding how much disk space you need for a server, you should take all the preceding uses into account. Remember that certain storage benefits from being on separate disks from the disk where Windows is stored. This advice is particularly true of the page file and virtual machines, but ideally, the Windows directory should be on a separate drive from most other storage uses.

Storage Access Methods

The discussion on storage access methods revolves around where storage is located in relation to the server. There are three broad categories of storage access methods:

- Local storage and direct-attached storage (DAS)
- Network-attached storage (NAS)
- Storage area network (SAN)

Local Storage and Direct-Attached Storage

Local storage has been around as long as computers have, but the interfaces to storage media have improved as speed and capacity requirements have grown. Local storage is the focus of this chapter, and disk interface technologies are discussed later in "Configuring Local Disks."

Local storage can be defined as storage media with a direct, exclusive connection to the computer's system board through a disk controller. Local storage is almost always inside the computer's case, attached to a disk controller via internal cables and powered by the computer's internal power supply. The term *local storage* usually refers to HDDs or SSDs instead of CD/DVDs or other types of media. Local storage provides rapid and exclusive access to storage media through ever-faster bus technologies. The downside of local storage is that only the system where it's installed has direct access to the storage medium. Data on disks can be shared through network file sharing, but the system with the installed storage must fulfill requests for shared data.

Direct-attached storage (DAS) is a type of local storage in that it's connected directly to the server using it. In fact, DAS includes hard drives mounted inside the server case. However, DAS can also refer to one or more HDDs in an enclosure with its own power supply. In this case, the DAS device is connected to a server through an external bus interface, such as eSATA, small computer system interface (SCSI), USB, FireWire, or Fibre Channel.

A DAS device with its own enclosure and power supply can usually be configured as a disk array, such as a RAID configuration (discussed later in "Configuring Local Disks"). Although most DAS devices provide exclusive use to a single computer, some have multiple interfaces so that more than one computer can access the storage medium simultaneously. Most of the later discussion in "Configuring Local Disks" also applies to DAS devices because the computer usually sees an externally attached DAS device as local storage.

Note

The term *DAS* was created to distinguish it from storage connected to a network, such as NAS and SAN.

Network-Attached Storage

Network-attached storage (NAS), sometimes referred to as a **storage appliance**, has an enclosure, a power supply, slots for multiple HDDs, a network interface, and a built-in OS tailored for managing shared storage. NAS is designed to make access to shared files easy to set up and easy for users to access. Because NAS is typically dedicated to file sharing, it can be faster than a traditional server in performing this task because a server is often sharing its computing and networking resources among several duties. NAS shares files through standard network protocols, such as Server Message Block (SMB), Network File System (NFS), and File Transfer Protocol (FTP). Some NAS devices can also be used as DAS devices because they often have USB, eSATA, or other interfaces that can be attached directly to a computer.

Storage Area Network

The most complex type of storage is a **storage area network (SAN)**, which uses high-speed networking technologies to give servers fast access to large amounts of shared disk storage. The storage that a SAN manages appears to the server OS as though it's physically attached to the server. However, it's connected to a high-speed network technology and can be shared by multiple servers. The most common network technologies used in SANs are Fibre Channel and iSCSI. These technologies are designed to connect large arrays of hard drive storage that servers can access and share. Client computers access shared data by contacting servers via the usual method, and the servers retrieve the requested data from the SAN devices and pass it along to the client computer. Figure 4-1 shows a SAN using Fibre Channel in which disk arrays are connected to a Fibre Channel switch, and servers are connected to the Fibre Channel network as well as a traditional network. In this arrangement, all servers have access to the storage medium, which can be shared and allocated as needed.

SANs use the concept of **logical unit number (LUN)** to identify a unit of storage. A LUN is a logical reference point to a unit of storage that could refer to an entire array of disks, a single disk, or just part of a disk. To the server using the SAN, the LUN is easier to work with because the server doesn't have to know how the storage is provided; it needs to know only how much it has available. SANs are often used by server clusters so that all cluster members have access to shared storage for the purposes of load balancing and fault tolerance.

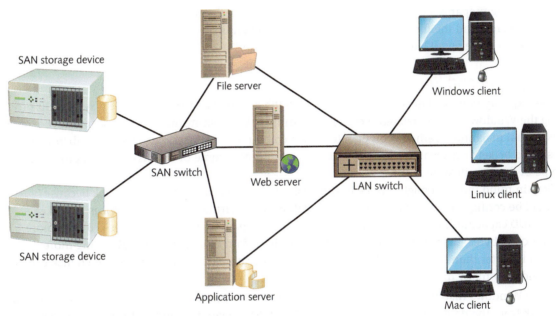

Figure 4-1   A storage area network

Configuring Local Disks

 **Certification**

- **70-740 – Implement storage solutions:**
  Configure disks and volumes

Configuration of local disks can be divided into two broad categories: physical disk properties and logical disk properties. Physical disk properties, which must be considered first before purchasing disk drives for a server, involve disk capacity, physical speed, and the interface for attaching a disk to the system. Logical disk properties include its format and the partitions or volumes created on it. Before you get too far into these properties, however, make sure you're clear on disk storage terminology:

- *Disk drive*—A **disk drive** is a physical component with a disk interface connector (such as SATA or SAS) and a power connector. A mechanical disk drive (usually called an HDD) has one or more circular magnetic platters storing the data's actual bits and one or more read/write heads—one for each side of the magnetic platters. The platters spin at high speed, and the read/write heads move from the inside of the platter to the outside to read data on the disk. An SSD has a disk interface and power connector but has flash memory chips instead of magnetic platters, and there are no read/write heads or other moving parts. Data on SSDs is accessed in a similar fashion as RAM.

- *Volume*—Before an OS can use a disk drive, a volume must be created on the drive. A **volume** is a logical unit of storage that can be formatted with a file system. A disk drive can contain one or more volumes of different sizes. Disk drive space that hasn't been assigned to a volume is said to be unallocated. Volumes can also span two or more disks in an arrangement called *RAID*. Volumes, including RAID volumes, are discussed in more detail later in the section "Volumes and Disk Types."
- *Partition*—This older term means the same thing as *volume* but is used with basic disks. The term **partition** is still used at times, but in Windows, it has largely been replaced by *volume*.
- *Formatting*—Before an OS can use a volume, the volume must be formatted.

Formatting prepares a disk with a file system used to organize and store files. There are different format standards, and the format you choose for a disk depends on how the disk will be used. This topic is discussed in more detail later in the section "Disk Formats."

Disk Capacity and Speed

The disk capacity you need depends entirely on how the disk will be used. Will it be a system disk for storing the Windows OS and related files, a file-sharing disk, a disk storing a database, or maybe one that stores virtual machines? Perhaps you plan to have a combination of uses, but in general, distinct types of data should be kept on separate disks so that you can optimize some of the disk's logical properties for the type of data it will store.

Keep in mind that you might not be basing disk capacity decisions on a single disk because you could be configuring an array of disks in a RAID or using virtual disks with services like Storage Spaces. HDD capacities are now measured in hundreds of gigabytes with 4 terabytes (TB) and more (1 TB = 1000 gigabytes) disks being common. Disk capacity is fairly inexpensive, and having more than you need is better than having less. Here are some considerations for deciding how much disk capacity to buy and how many disks to use in a server:

- The Windows installation (the volume that stores the \Windows folder) should be on a separate disk from the data to be stored on the server. An SSD is a good candidate for the Windows installation.
- The page file should be on its own disk, if possible. An SSD is also a good candidate for the page file. If a separate disk is impractical, at least try to put the page file on its own volume.
- Take fault tolerance into account by using a RAID, which combines multiple disks to make a single volume so that data stored on the volume is maintained even if an individual disk fails. However, overall storage capacity is diminished.

The speed of HDDs is affected by a number of factors. The disk interface technology is an important performance factor that's discussed next. Other factors include rotation speed and the amount of cache memory installed. The rotation speed of disk platters in HDDs ranges from a low of about 4200 revolutions per minute (rpm) to 15,000 rpm with speeds of 7200 and 10,000 rpm in between. A server should be outfitted with an HDD that rotates at a minimum of 7200 rpm, but for high-performance applications, look for 10,000 or 15,000 rpm drives.

The amount of cache in an HDD allows the drive to buffer read and write data locally, which speeds overall disk access. Cache sizes of 32 and 64 MB are common for server-class drives, but some very fast drives might have as little as 16 MB. What you're most interested in for disk performance is how fast data can be read from and written to the disk—the data rate. When researching disks for performance factors, look for the sustained data rate the manufacturer claims, which tells you how fast the drive can transfer data for an extended period.

Disk Interface Technologies

The disk interface connects a disk to a computer system, usually with some type of cable. The cable acts as a bus that carries data and commands between the disk and the computer. The faster the bus, the faster the system can read from and write to the disk. The most common types of disk interfaces for locally attached disks are SATA, SAS, and SCSI. Each technology has advantages and disadvantages, discussed in the following sections.

> **Note** 📎
>
> You might also find a few parallel ATA (PATA) or Integrated Drive Electronics (IDE) drives on older computers and Fibre Channel drives on high-end systems, but for locally attached drives for servers, the most common by far are SATA, SAS, and SCSI. IDE drives are nearly obsolete, and Fibre Channel drives are most likely to be used in SANs.

Serial ATA Drives

Serial ATA (SATA) drives have replaced PATA drives and have several advantages over this older technology, including faster transfer times and smaller cable size. Whereas the PATA interface is limited to about 167 megabytes per second (MB/s), SATA drives boast transfer times up to 6 gigabits per second (Gb/s; 600 MB/s). SATA drives are inexpensive, fast, and fairly reliable. They're a good fit for both client computers and low-end servers. The SATA standard has evolved from SATA 1.0, supporting transfer speeds of 1.5 Gb/s (150 MB/s) to the current SATA 3.2, supporting speeds up to 16 Gb/s (or 1.6 GB/s). However, most readily available devices support SATA 2.0 (3 Gb/s) or SATA 3.0 (6 Gb/s). Even with their high transfer rates, however, SATA drives take a back seat to SAS drives in the enterprise server realm.

SAS and SCSI Drives

Small computer system interface (SCSI) drives were a mainstay in enterprise-class servers for decades, and this drive technology has endured through more than half a dozen upgrades. The most recent SCSI variation, developed in 2003, is Ultra-640 with up to 640 MB/s transfer rates. SCSI is a parallel technology, like PATA, and has probably reached its performance limits. SCSI, however, has always provided high reliability and enterprise-level command features, such as error recovery and reporting. Its successor is **serial attached SCSI (SAS)**, which maintains the high reliability and advanced commands of SCSI and improves performance with transfer rates up to 6 Gb/s and higher speeds underway. SAS has the benefit of having bus compatibility with SATA, so SATA drives can be connected to SAS backplanes. A **backplane** is a connection system that uses a printed circuit board instead of traditional cables to carry signals.

The SAS standard offers higher-end features than SATA drives do. SAS drives usually have higher rotation speeds and use higher signaling voltages, which allow their use in server backplanes. Overall, SAS is considered the more enterprise-ready disk interface technology, but enterprise features come with a price—SAS drives are also more expensive than SATA drives. As with many other things, server disk technologies have a trade-off between performance and reliability versus price.

Volumes and Disk Types

Before data can be stored on a disk drive, space on the drive must be allocated to a volume. On a Windows system, each volume is typically assigned a drive letter, such as C or D. A volume can use some or all of the space on an HDD, or a single volume can span multiple drives. Before you go further, there are two Microsoft-specific volume definitions you need to know:

- *Boot volume*—The **boot volume** is the volume where the \Windows folder is located. It's usually the C drive but doesn't have to be. The boot volume is also called the *boot partition*.

- *System volume*—The **system volume** contains files the computer needs to find and load the Windows OS. In Windows 2008 and later, it's created automatically during installation if you're installing an OS for the first time on the system, and it's not assigned a drive letter, so you can't see it in File Explorer. You can, however, see it in Disk Management (see Figure 4-2). In earlier Windows versions, the system volume was usually the C drive. The system volume is also called the *system partition*.

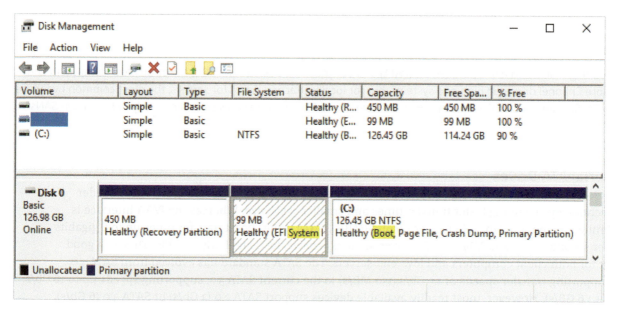

Figure 4-2   Boot and system volumes in Disk Management

In Windows, the types of volumes you can create on a disk depend on how the disk is categorized. Windows defines two disk categories, discussed next: basic and dynamic.

> **Note**
>
> The Windows boot and system volumes can be created only on basic disks.

Basic Disks

As the name implies, a **basic disk** can accommodate only basic volumes, called *simple volumes*. A simple volume is a disk partition residing on only one disk; it can't span multiple disks or be used to create a RAID volume. The volumes on a basic disk are also called *partitions*. The Disk Management snap-in uses both terms in its interface, but the term *partition* is more accurate and distinguishes it from a volume created on a dynamic disk. When Windows detects a new disk drive, it's initialized as a basic disk by default.

You can create a maximum of four partitions on a basic disk. The first three you create with Disk Management are primary partitions. A **primary partition** can be an active partition and can be the Windows system volume. Primary partitions are usually assigned a drive letter but don't have to be as does the Windows system volume. If you create a fourth partition, it's called an **extended partition**, which can be divided into one or more logical drives, each assigned a drive letter. A logical drive on an extended partition can hold the boot volume, but it can't hold the system volume because it can't be marked as active.

Dynamic Disks

If you need more than a simple volume, you must convert a basic disk to a **dynamic disk**. Volumes created on dynamic disks can span multiple disks and be configured for fault tolerance by using RAID. A dynamic disk can hold the Windows boot or system partition but only if you convert the disk to dynamic after Windows is already installed on the volume. You can create up to 128 volumes on a dynamic disk.

To convert a basic disk to dynamic in Disk Management, simply right-click the disk and click Convert to Dynamic Disk. Existing volumes on the basic disk are converted to simple volumes on the dynamic disk, and all data on the disk is maintained. You can convert a dynamic disk to basic in the same manner, but you must first delete existing volumes on the dynamic disk, and existing data will be lost.

> **Note** 📎
>
> If you attempt to create a volume on a basic disk that isn't supported, Windows prompts you to convert it to dynamic before you can proceed.

Partitioning Methods

Windows offers two methods for partitioning disks. The most common method, **Master Boot Record (MBR)**, has been around since DOS. MBR partitions support volume sizes up to 2 TB. MBR-based disks are compatible with all Windows versions as well as most other OSs. When a disk is initialized in Disk Management, it's initialized as an MBR disk by default.

The second and newer method is **GUID Partitioning Table (GPT)**. GPT disks became an option starting with Windows Server 2008 and Vista. They support volume sizes up to 18 exabytes (EB), a million terabytes; however, Windows file systems currently support volume sizes up to only 256 TB. Starting with Windows Server 2016, new disks are initialized using GPT, but you can select MBR if desired. In Disk Management, you can convert an MBR disk to GPT and vice versa, but you must delete existing partitions first, which erases all data. In addition to larger volume sizes, GPT partitions offer improved reliability in the form of partition table replication (a backup copy of the partition table) and Cyclic Redundancy Check (CRC) protection of the partition table.

> **Tip** ⓘ
>
> Systems with an EFI BIOS (virtual machines created in Hyper-V, for example) can boot only to GPT partitions.

> **Note** 📎
>
> GPT partitions contain an area on the disk called the *protective MBR*, which is maintained for backward compatibility with disk utilities that work only with MBR disks.

Disk Sector Sizes

The storage space on disk drives is divided into sectors, and sectors are combined by the file system into clusters when the disk is formatted. Sector sizes have traditionally been 512 bytes in length, and the sectors are combined into cluster sizes in kilobytes (K) of 4K, 8K, 16K, 32K, or 64K. Windows Server 2016 supports disks with 512 byte sectors, referred to as a *Standard Format disk*, but Windows Server 2016 also supports Advanced Format disks that use 4096 byte sectors. The larger sector size allows Windows to support much larger volume sizes than previously possible using 512 byte sectors. Windows Server 2016 also supports a hybrid version of Advanced Format disks called *512e drives* in which the disk is configured with 4096 byte physical sectors but emulates 512 byte sectors to support systems that can't use 4096 byte sectors. You can view the sector size in use on a drive by typing `fsutil fsinfo sectorinfo DriveLetter:` at a command prompt. For example, Figure 4-3 shows the logical sector size as 512 bytes and the physical sector size as 4096 bytes. The command was run on a Hyper-V virtual machine, indicating that Windows formats virtual disks using the larger size sectors but with 512 byte emulation. In general, if your server application requires very large volumes containing large files, the Advanced Format disk is more efficient, but not all OSs support this type of disk.

```
C:\Windows\system32>fsutil fsinfo sectorinfo h:
LogicalBytesPerSector :                                  512
PhysicalBytesPerSectorForAtomicity :                     4096
PhysicalBytesPerSectorForPerformance :                   4096
FileSystemEffectivePhysicalBytesPerSectorForAtomicity :  4096
Device Alignment :                                       Aligned (0x000)
Partition alignment on device :                          Aligned (0x000)
Performs Normal Seeks
Trim Supported
Not DAX capable
```

Figure 4-3   Checking the sector size

Types of Volumes

A basic disk supports only simple volumes, but you can create several volume types on a dynamic disk, including RAID volumes. **Redundant array of independent disks (RAID)** is a disk configuration that uses space on multiple disks to form a single logical volume. Most RAID configurations offer fault tolerance, and some enhance performance. The following are the types of volumes you can create on a Windows Server 2016 system:

- *Simple volume*—A **simple volume**, as mentioned, resides on a single disk, basic or dynamic. On a basic disk, a simple volume can be extended (made larger) if unallocated space is available on the disk. A simple volume can also be shrunk on basic or dynamic disks. A simple volume on a dynamic disk can be extended on the same disk or to multiple disks as long as they have unallocated space. A simple volume can also be made into a mirrored volume by using two dynamic disks.
- *Spanned volume*—A **spanned volume** extends across two or more physical disks, for example, a simple volume that has been extended to a second disk is a spanned volume. When the first disk has filled up, subsequent disks are used to store data. Spanned volumes don't offer fault tolerance; if any disk fails, data on all disks is lost. There's also no performance advantage in using a spanned volume.
- *Striped volume*—A **striped volume** extends across two or more dynamic disks, but data is written to all disks in the volume equally. For example, if a 10 MB file is written to a striped volume with two disks, 5 MB is written to each disk. A striped volume can use from 2 to 32 disks. Striped volumes don't offer fault tolerance, but they do have a read and write performance advantage over spanned and simple volumes because multiple disks can be accessed simultaneously to read and write files. A striped volume is also referred to as a RAID-0 volume. The Windows system and boot volumes can't be on a striped volume.
- *Mirrored volume*—A **mirrored volume** (or RAID-1 volume) uses space from two dynamic disks and provides fault tolerance. Data written to one disk is duplicated, or mirrored, to the second disk. If one disk fails, the other disk has a good copy of the data, and the system can continue to operate until the failed disk is replaced. The space used on both disks in a mirrored volume is the same. Mirrored volumes might have a disk read performance advantage, but they don't have a disk write performance advantage.
- *RAID-5 volume*—A **RAID-5 volume** uses space from three or more dynamic disks and uses disk striping with parity to provide fault tolerance. When data is written, it's striped across all but one of the disks in the volume. Parity information derived from the data is written to the remaining disk.

The system alternates the disk that is used for parity information, so each disk has both data and parity information. Parity information is used to re-create lost data after a disk failure. A RAID-5 volume provides increased read performance, but write performance is decreased because of having to calculate and write parity information. The Windows system and boot volumes can't be on a RAID-5 volume.

> **Note** 📎
>
> Striped, mirrored, and RAID-5 volumes configured in Windows are referred to as *software RAID*. You can also purchase a RAID disk controller that can create RAID disks by using the controller's firmware—called *hardware RAID*. Hardware RAID is done at the disk level, whereas software RAID in Windows is done at the volume level. Hardware RAID typically results in better performance than software RAID. In addition, the restrictions on placing Windows system and boot volumes on RAID volumes apply to software RAID since the OS must be up and running before the RAID is recognized. Hardware RAID configurations don't have these restrictions in most cases. As you'll see in Chapter 5, you can also use Storage Spaces to create fault-tolerant virtual disk configurations.

Disk Formats

Before you can store data on a volume, it must be formatted with a file system. Formatting creates the directory structure needed to organize files and store information about each file. The information stored about each file depends on the file system used.

A **file system** defines the method and format an OS uses to store, locate, and retrieve files from electronic storage media. Windows supports three file systems for storing files on hard disks: File Allocation Table (FAT), NTFS, and Resilient File System (ReFS). NTFS is by far the most important and is dominant on Windows servers. However, FAT is still found occasionally on workstations and servers, and there are valid reasons to use this file system in certain circumstances. ReFS, the comparatively new kid in town, has limited features compared with NTFS.

Before going into detail on these disk formats, reviewing the components of a file system is helpful. Modern file systems have some or all of the following components:

- *File naming convention*—All files stored on a disk are identified by name, and the file system defines rules for how to name a file. These rules include length, special characters that can be used (such as $, #, %, &, and !), and case sensitivity (differentiating uppercase and lowercase letters).
- *Hierarchical organization*—Most file systems are organized as an inverted tree structure with the root of the tree at the top and folders or directories underneath acting as branches. A folder can be empty or contain a list of files and additional folders. In most file systems, folders or directories don't contain the data that makes up the actual file; they contain information about the file along with a pointer to the file's location on the disk. Information for each file is usually called a *directory entry*.
- *Data storage method*—Space on hard disks is divided into one or more partitions with each partition containing its own file system. A partition is typically divided into 512 byte sectors. The file system groups one or more sectors into blocks or clusters, which are used as the basic unit of storage for file data. These blocks are indexed so that the file data they contain can be retrieved easily. A single file can occupy from one to many thousands of blocks. File systems vary in the methods used for indexing and managing these blocks, which affect the efficiency and reliability of data storage and retrieval.
- *Metadata*—Metadata is information about a file beyond its name and the data it contains. This information is generally stored by the directory or folder with the file's name or in a data structure the directory entry points to. Metadata can include time stamps indicating when a file was created, last changed, and last accessed; descriptive information about the file that can be used in searches; file attributes; and access control lists.

- *Attributes*—Attributes are usually on/off settings, such as Read Only, Hidden, Compressed, and so forth. File systems differ in the attributes that can be applied to files and folders.
- *Access control lists (ACLs)*—ACLs determine who can access a file or folder and what can be done with the file (read, write, delete, and so on).

File systems vary in whether and how each component is used. Generally, more advanced file systems have flexible file naming rules, an efficient method of managing data storage, a considerable amount of metadata, advanced attributes, and ACLs. Next, you examine these file systems more closely.

> ### Note
>
> For more information on other file systems and a comparison of features, see *http://en.wikipedia.org/wiki/Comparison_of_file_systems*.

The FAT File System

The FAT file system consists of two variations: FAT16 and FAT32. FAT vaguely describes the structure used to manage data storage. FAT16, usually referred to simply as *FAT*, has been around since the mid-1980s, which is one of its biggest strengths—it's well known and well supported by most OSs. FAT32 arrived on the scene with the release of Windows 95 OSR2 in 1996.

> ### Note
>
> A third variation, FAT12, is the original version of FAT developed in the late 1970s. It was limited to use on floppy disks.

The main difference between FAT16 and FAT32 is the size of the disk partition that can be formatted. FAT16 is limited to 2 GB partitions in most implementations (although Windows NT permits partitions up to 4 GB). FAT32 allows partitions up to 2 TB; however, in Windows 2000 and later, Microsoft limits them to 32 GB because the file system becomes noticeably slower and inefficient with larger partition sizes. This 32 GB limitation applies only to creating partitions. Windows can read FAT32 partitions of any size. FAT16 supports a maximum file size of 2 GB, and FAT32 supports files up to 4 GB.

> ### Note
>
> The number in FAT versions refers to the number of bits available to address disk clusters. Fat16 can address up to 2^{16} disk clusters, and FAT32 can address up to 2^{32} disk clusters. The number of disk clusters a file system can address is directly proportional to the largest size partition it supports.

Already, you can see that FAT has severe limitations in current computing environments. The file size limitation alone prevents storing a standard DVD image file on a FAT file system. The limitations are even more apparent when you consider reliability and security requirements of current OSs. FAT doesn't support file and folder permissions for users and groups, so any user logging on to a computer with a FAT disk has full control over every file on that disk. In addition, FAT lacks support for encryption, file compression, disk quotas, and reliability features, such as transaction recovery and journaling, all of which NTFS supports.

You might think FAT isn't good for much, especially compared with the more robust NTFS, but FAT/FAT32 still has its place. It's the only file system option when using older Windows OSs, such as Windows 9x. In addition, FAT is simple and has little overhead, so it's still the file system of choice on removable media, such as flash drives. For hard drives, however, particularly on Windows servers, NTFS is usually the way to go, although some applications benefit from ReFS.

> **Note** 📎
>
> Chapter 1 mentioned another variation of FAT, exFAT, which has the same features as FAT32 but can be used to format volumes larger than 32 GB, up to a theoretical 64 zettabytes (ZB, a billion terabytes) and file sizes up to 16 EB. When you format a volume larger than 32 GB in Disk Management, exFAT is offered as a format option.

The NTFS and ReFS File Systems

NTFS is a full-featured file system that Microsoft introduced with Windows NT in 1993. Since that time, its features have been expanded to help administrators gain control of ever-expanding storage requirements. NTFS has supported file and folder permissions almost since its inception, which was a considerable advantage over FAT. Many compelling features have been added, particularly starting with Windows 2000:

- *Disk quotas*—Enable administrators to limit the amount of disk space that users' files can occupy on a disk volume. Starting with Windows Server 2008, quotas can also be specified for folders.
- *Volume mount points*—Make it possible to associate the root of a disk volume with a folder on an NTFS volume, thereby forgoing the need for a drive letter to access the volume.
- *Shadow copies*—Enable users to keep historical versions of files so that they can revert a file to an older version or restore an accidentally deleted file.
- *File compression*—Allows users to store documents in a compressed format without needing to run a compression/decompression program to store and retrieve the documents.
- *Encrypting File System (EFS)*—Makes encrypted files inaccessible to everyone except the user who encrypted the file, including users who have been granted permission to the file. EFS protects files even if the disk is removed from the system.

The Resilient File System (ReFS)

The main uses of ReFS is in large file-sharing applications where volumes are managed by Storage Spaces and for storage of virtual disks. Although ReFS is mostly backward compatible with NTFS, it doesn't support file compression, disk quotas, and EFS. Also, Windows can't be booted from an ReFS volume, and the boot volume (the volume that contains the \Windows folder) cannot be ReFS formatted. ReFS can repair minor problems with the file system automatically and supports volume sizes up to 1 yottabyte (YB), a trillion terabytes.

ReFS works with Storage Spaces (discussed in Chapter 5) to automatically repair disk failure caused by corruption whether from software or hardware problems. Unlike other fault-tolerant disk options, such as RAID-1 and RAID-5, that can only recover from failures, ReFS can also correct some types of data corruption automatically. This capability, when used with Storage Spaces, allows building highly reliable and scalable disk systems without using RAID disk controllers and the sometimes wasteful disk allocation schemes that RAID configurations require.

ReFS has been enhanced in Windows Server 2016 and is now the disk format of choice for storing virtual hard disks for use in Storage Spaces and on Hyper-V servers. ReFS is optimized for creating virtual disk files and moving blocks of data between files. For example, a fixed-size virtual disk of 100 GB can be created on an ReFS volume in a little more than 1 second. The same operation on an NTFS volume can take several minutes. In addition, operations such as checkpoint merging and other Hyper-V specific storage operations perform much faster on ReFS.

Because of the features ReFS doesn't support, this file system isn't intended as a replacement for NTFS. ReFS is best for supporting applications that require virtual disks such as Storage Spaces and Hyper-V and on volumes for high-availability applications that use very large files but don't require user-specific features, such as disk quotas and EFS.

Note

A very minor limitation with ReFS volumes: the minimum volume size supported is 640 MB.

Preparing a New Disk for Use

Now that you know most of the options for local disk storage in Windows Server 2016, you can work through adding a disk to a working system. Depending on the system, you might be able to add a new HDD to a server while it's powered on, a process called *hot-add* or *hot-swap*. Windows Server supports hot-adding a hard disk as long as the server hardware supports it. Don't attempt to add a disk to a running server unless you know that the hardware supports it.

After the HDD has been physically attached to the server and the server is running, you need to use the Disk Management snap-in or File and Storage Services to make the disk accessible. By default, new disks must be initialized and brought online from their initial offline state, as explained in Activity 4-1. After the disk is online and initialized, you can create a volume and format it. In Disk Management, you can convert the disk to dynamic or between MBR and GPT partitioning schemes.

Activity 4-1: Resetting Your Virtual Environment

Time Required: 5 minutes
Objective: Reset your virtual environment by applying the InitialConfig checkpoint or snapshot.
Required Tools and Equipment: ServerSA1, ServerHyperV
Description: Apply the InitialConfig checkpoint or snapshot to ServerSA1 and ServerHyperV.

1. Be sure that the servers are shut down. In your virtualization program, apply the InitialConfig checkpoint or snapshot to ServerSA1 and ServerHyperV.
2. When the snapshot or checkpoint has finished being applied, continue to the next activity.

Activity 4-2: Configuring a New Disk

Time Required: 10 minutes
Objective: Configure a new disk for use in a server.
Required Tools and Equipment: ServerSA1
Description: You have just installed a new disk in your server, and you need to prepare it for use. First you bring the disk online and initialize it, and then you create a simple volume and format it. You should already have a disk installed in ServerSA1 for use in this activity.

Note

The size of your disks may not match the size of the disks in the screenshots in this activity.

1. Start ServerSA1, and sign in as **Administrator**.
2. In Server Manager, click **File and Storage Services**, and then click **Disks** to open the Disks window as shown in Figure 4-4.

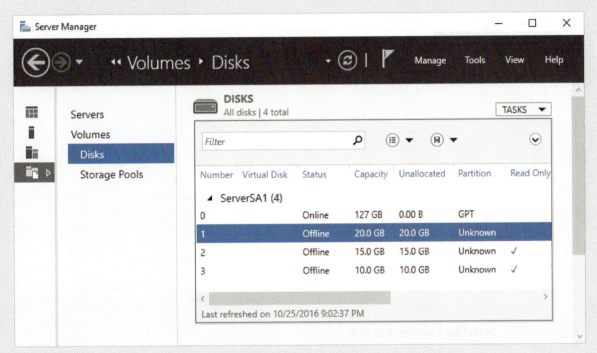

Figure 4-4   The Disks window in File and Storage Services

3. Find the 20.0 GB disk; its status will be Offline. Right-click the disk and click **Bring Online**. In the Bring Disk Online message box, click **Yes**. Repeat this step for the 15.0 GB and 10.00 GB disks.
4. Right-click the 20.0 GB disk again and click **Initialize**. In the Initialize Disk box, leave all three disks checked. Notice that the Initialize Disk message indicates that the disks will be configured as GPT disks. Click **OK** in the Initialize Disk message box.
5. To create a new volume, right-click the **20.0 GB DISK**, and click **New Volume** to start the New Volume Wizard. Read the information in the Before You Begin window, and then click **Next**. (*Note*: File and Storage Services initializes a disk only as a basic disk. If you want a dynamic disk, use Disk Management.)
6. In the Server and Disk window, make sure ServerSA1 and the 20.0 GB disk are selected (see Figure 4-5), and then click **Next**.
7. In the Size window, type **10** in the Volume size text box, and then click **Next**.
8. In the Drive Letter or Folder window, click **H** in the Drive letter list box. Notice that you can also mount the volume in an empty folder or not assign a drive letter or folder at all. Click **Next**.
9. In the File System Settings window, click the **File system** list arrow to see the options for formatting the volume. File and Storage Services lists only NTFS and ReFS as options. In Disk Management, you also have FAT32 as an option (or exFAT for volumes larger than 32 GB).
10. Type **NTFSvol** in the Volume label text box, and then click **Next**.
11. In the Confirmation window, verify your choices, and then click **Create**. The Results window shows you the progress. Click **Close** when the process is finished.
12. In Server Manager, click **Volumes** in the left pane to see the new volume.
13. Stay signed in and continue to the next activity.

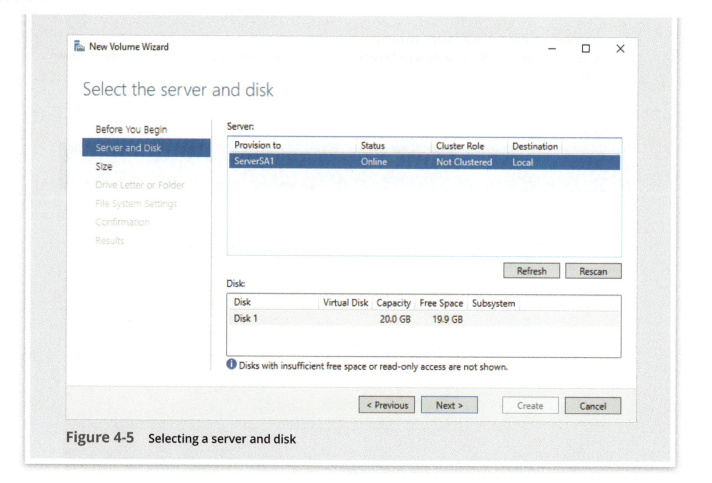

Figure 4-5 Selecting a server and disk

Activity 4-3: Working with Volumes in Disk Management

Time Required: 10 minutes
Objective: Work with basic and dynamic volumes.
Required Tools and Equipment: ServerSA1
Description: In this activity, you examine the options for working with basic and dynamic disks and ReFS and NTFS volumes.

 Note

The size of your disks may not match the size of the disks in the screenshots in this activity.

1. Start ServerSA1, and sign in as **Administrator**, if necessary.
2. Right-click **Start** and click **Disk Management**. Notice that Disk 0 has three volumes: the Recovery Partition, the System partition, and the Boot partition (C:). These volumes contain the Windows OS, so make sure you don't make any changes to Disk 0.
3. Right-click **NTFSvol** and notice the options for working with this volume. Click **Extend Volume**. In the Extend Volume Wizard welcome window, click **Next**.
4. In the Select Disks window, you can add disks to extend to if any are available. If you do so, you're prompted to convert the disk to dynamic because basic disks don't support extending to other disks (disk spanning). In the *Select the amount of space in MB* text box, type **5000**, which makes the volume about 15 GB total. Click **Next**.

5. In the Completing the Extend Volume Wizard window, click **Finish**. The disk is extended to about 15 GB.

6. In Disk Management, right-click **NTFSvol**, and click **Shrink Volume** to open the Shrink H: dialog box. In the *Enter the amount of space to shrink in MB* text box, type **5000** and click **Shrink**. The volume is back to 10 GB.

7. Next, you create an ReFS-formatted volume. Right-click the unallocated space next to NTFSvol, and click **New Simple Volume** to start the New Simple Volume Wizard. Click **Next**.

8. In the Specify Volume Size window, click **Next** to accept the default size, which is the remaining space on the disk. In the Assign Drive Letter or Path window, click the selection arrow next to Assign the following drive letter and click **I**. Click **Next**.

9. In the Format Partition window, click the selection arrow next to File system and click **ReFS**. In the Volume label box, type **ReFSvol**. Click **Next**, and then click **Finish**.

10. Right-click **NTFSvol** and click **Properties**. Review the tabs available to configure the volume. In particular, notice on the General tab the option to compress the drive to save disk space. Also notice the Quota tab where you can set file quotas to restrict the amount of space a user's file can occupy on the volume. Click **Cancel** when you have finished exploring the properties of NTFSvol.

11. Right-click ReFSvol and click **Properties**. Notice that there is no option to compress the drive on the General tab and there are no quota tab and no Shadow Copies tab because ReFS doesn't support these features. Click **Cancel**.

12. Now, you will create a mirror volume. Right-click **NTFSvol** and click **Add Mirror**. There is only one option for creating the mirror because the 10.0 GB disk is a little too small. In the Add Mirror window (see Figure 4-6), click **Disk 2** and click **Add Mirror**.

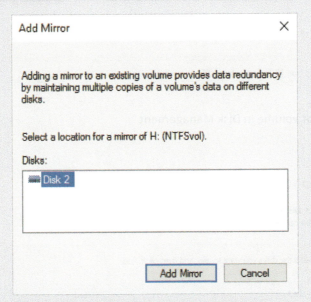

Figure 4-6   Creating a mirror volume

13. You see a Disk Management message explaining that the basic disks will be converted to dynamic disks since dynamic disks are required to support a mirror. Click **Yes**. After a short while, you see the mirror in which the volume is now shown on Disk 1 and Disk 2, and the mirror is colored red to indicate it is a mirror (see Figure 4-7). You see that in the top pane of Disk Management, the Layout column changes to Mirror.

14. Next, you'll create a RAID-5 volume, but you need three disks for a RAID-5 volume, so first you delete the volumes you just created. Right-click **NTFSvol**, click **Delete Volume**, and click **Yes** to confirm. Next, right-click **ReFSvol**, click **Delete Volume**, and click **Yes** to confirm.

15. Right-click **Disk 1** (this should be the 20.0 GB disk, but it may show just under 20.0 GB), click **New RAID-5 Volume**, and click **Next**.

16. In the Select Disks window, click **Disk 2**, click **Add**, click **Disk 3**, and then click **Add** (see Figure 4-8). Notice that the total size of the RAID-5 will be about 20 GB even though you are using 10 GB of space from each disk. This is because a RAID-5 uses the equivalent of the space from one disk for the parity information needed to recreate missing data if a disk fails. Click **Next**.

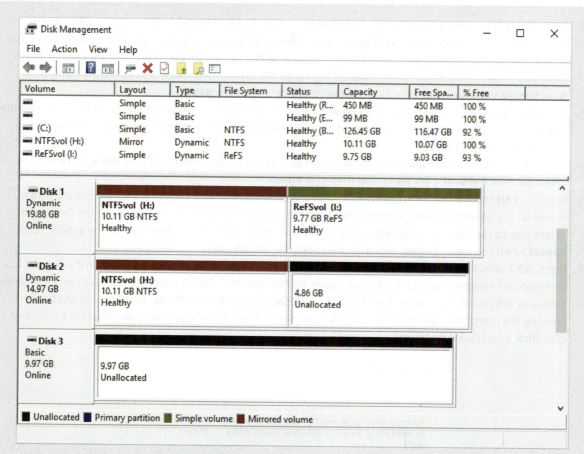

Figure 4-7   A mirror volume in Disk Management

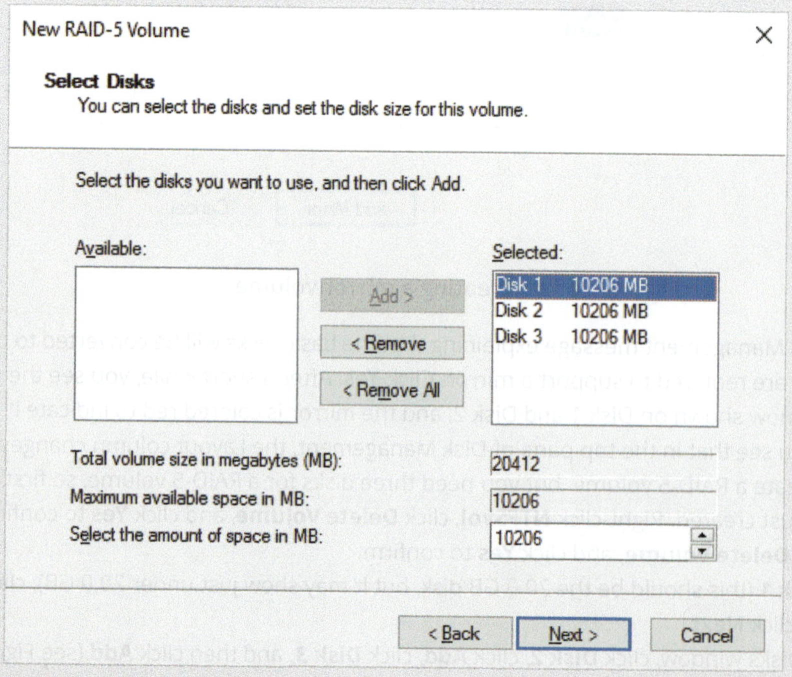

Figure 4-8   Select disks for the RAID-5 volume

17. In the Assign Drive Letter or Path window, click the drive letter selection box, and click **H**. Click **Next**.
18. In the Format Volume window, type **RAID5vol** in the Volume label box and click **Next**. Click **Finish**, and then click **Yes** when prompted to convert basic disks to dynamic (when you deleted the volumes, the disks were converted back to basic disks).
19. After a short while, you see the new RAID-5 volume as in Figure 4-9. It will take a while for the volume to synch between the three disks and format.

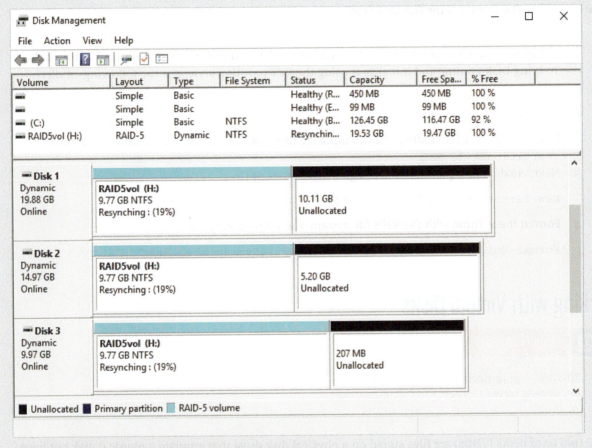

Figure 4-9   A RAID-5 volume in Disk Management

20. You'll be using these disks for other activities, so delete the RAID-5 volume as you did the other volumes. Close Disk Management.

Managing Disks with PowerShell

You may need to manage disks using PowerShell, for example, on a Server Core installation of Windows Server 2016. You can perform all the same tasks on disks using PowerShell as you can using the Disk Management or File and Storage Services GUI tools. To bring a volume online, initialize it, and create a new simple volume formatted as ReFS, and follow these steps using PowerShell cmdlets after opening a PowerShell prompt:

1. Get a list of disks. Type the following into PowerShell with no arguments:

```
Get-Disk
```

You'll see a list similar to Figure 4-10.

```
PS C:\Users\Administrator> get-disk

Number  Friendly Name       Serial Number           HealthStatus      OperationalStatus      Total Size Partition
                                                                                                        Style
------  -------------       -------------           ------------      -----------------      ---------- ---------
0       Msft Virtual Disk                           Healthy           Online                     127 GB GPT
1       Msft Virtual Disk                           Healthy           Offline                     20 GB RAW
2       Msft Virtual Disk                           Healthy           Offline                     15 GB RAW
3       Msft Virtual Disk                           Healthy           Offline                     10 GB RAW

PS C:\Users\Administrator>
```

Figure 4-10   The results of the Get-Disk cmdlet

2. In Figure 4-10, notice the Disk Number column, which you will use for subsequent commands. To bring Disk 1 online and initialize it using the GPT partition style, use the following cmdlets:

    ```
    Set-Disk -Number 1 -IsOffline $false
    Initialize-Disk -Number 1
    ```

    In the Initialize-Disk cmdlet, you can initialize the disk using MBR by including the argument `-PartitionStyle MBR`.

3. Next, create a new partition and assign a drive letter of H:

    ```
    New-Partition -DiskNumber 1 -Size 10GB -DriveLetter H
    ```

4. Format the volume with the ReFS file system and name it ReFSvol:

    ```
    Format-Volume H -FileSystem ReFS -NewFileSystemLabel ReFSVol
    ```

Working with Virtual Disks

 **Certification**

- **70-740 – Implement storage solutions:**
  Implement server storage

Virtual hard disks (VHDs) are files stored on a physical disk drive that emulate a physical disk but have additional capabilities for virtual machines and general Windows storage applications. VHDs are used by virtual machines running in Hyper-V as the primary storage for the OS and data. On a physical computer, Windows can mount VHD files and use them as though they were physical disk volumes. VHDs are also used in Storage Spaces applications to create flexible storage solutions.

You might want to use virtual disks instead of physical volumes to store data. Virtual disks have the advantage of being very portable. Because a virtual disk is just a file on an existing physical volume, you can copy it to any location quickly and easily for the purposes of backing up data on the virtual disk or allowing it to be used by another computer. The Disk Management snap-in has options to create and mount virtual disks, and there are a number of PowerShell cmdlets for working with VHDs.

Note 📎

Virtual disks can have a `.vhd` or `.vhdx` extension. Windows Server 2012/R2 can mount either file type. The VHDX format, introduced in Windows Server 2012 Hyper-V, has more capacity (up to 64 TB), protection from corruption, and performance improvements over the original VHD format.

VHD versus VHDX Format

When you create a virtual disk, you have the option to use the VHD for the VHDX format. The VHD format is the original format used by Hyper-V VMs. You may want to choose this format for backward compatibility with Windows Server 2008. However, for the most features, you should choose the VHDX format. Following is a list of differences between VHD and VHDX:

- VHD supports virtual disks up to 2 TB whereas VHDX supports up to 64 TB virtual disks.
- VHDX uses a 4096 byte logical sector size compared to 512 byte sectors used in VHD. As mentioned, a larger sector size improves performance and increases the maximum disk and volume size.
- With VHDX disks, you can store custom metadata about the disk indicating information such as the OS version or the build number.
- VHDX is resilient to power failures because it tracks updates in the metadata, allowing incomplete writes to be backed out to avoid corruption.

You can convert a VHD disk to VHDX using Hyper-V Manager or PowerShell. Using Hyper-V Manager, click Edit Disk in the Action pane (see Figure 4-11) to start the Edit Virtual Hard Disk Wizard, and then select the disk you wish to edit. You have the option to compact, convert, or expand the disk (see Figure 4-12). Choose Convert and select the VHDX format (you can also choose VHD if you want to convert a VHDX disk to a VHD disk). The conversion process actually copies the original disk to a new file and adjusts the format during the copy process.

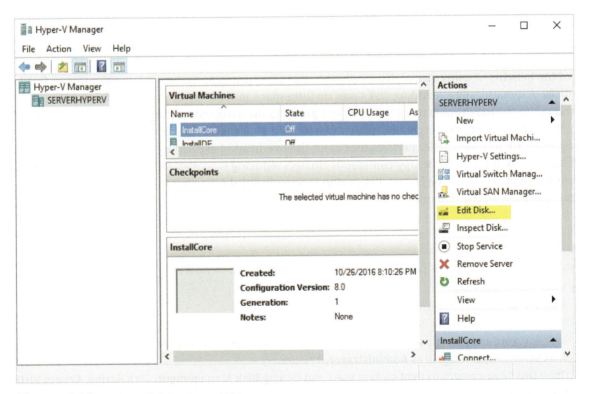

Figure 4-11   Edit a disk in Hyper-V Manager

To convert a disk using PowerShell, use the Convert-VHD cmdlet; for example, to convert a VHD file named Win2K16Boot.vhd to VHDX format, use the following cmdlet from a PowerShell prompt:

```
Convert-VHD -Path D:\Vdisks\Win2k16Boot.vhd -DestinationPath
D:\Vdisks\Win2k16Boot.vhdx
```

The PowerShell cmdlet determines the format you wish to convert to and from by the file name extension (.vhd or .vhdx).

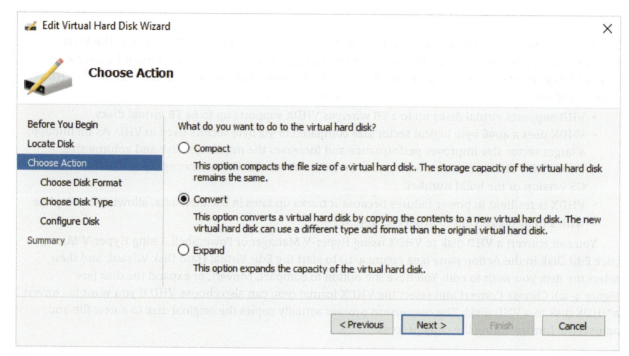

Figure 4-12   Convert a virtual hard disk

Dynamically Expanding and Fixed Size Disks

One of the benefits of using virtual disks is that they can be created as dynamically expanding or fixed size disks. A dynamically expanding disk takes up little space initially (typically less than 100 MB, depending on the maximum size of the disk) and grows to the assigned maximum size as data is stored on it. When a fixed size disk is created, the entire size of the disk is allocated on the host volume. A fixed size disk provides better performance since the overhead of expanding the disk is removed and a fixed size disk will generally occupy contiguous clusters reducing host disk fragmentation. For production environments that require the fastest disk performance, use fixed disks, but for testing and nonspeed critical applications, use dynamic disks.

Activity 4-4: Working with Virtual Disks in Disk Management

Time Required: 10 minutes

Objective: Create and mount a virtual disk.

Required Tools and Equipment: ServerSA1

Description: Create and mount a virtual disk and view it in Disk Management and File Explorer.

1. Start ServerSA1, and sign in as **Administrator**, if necessary.
2. Open Disk Management by right-clicking **Start** and clicking **Disk Management**. Click **Action**, **Create VHD** from the menu.
3. In the Create and Attach Virtual Hard Disk dialog box (see Figure 4-13), you can select the virtual hard disk format and whether the disk is a fixed size or dynamically expanding. Click **Browse**.
4. In the left pane, click **This PC** and then double-click **Local Disk (C:)** in the right pane. Type **Virtual1** in the File name text box. In the Save as type selection box, you can choose the format (.vhd or .vhdx). Accept the default and click **Save**.
5. In the Virtual hard disk size text box, type **5000** to create a 5 GB virtual disk.
6. The virtual hard disk format is VHD by default. Because you're creating a small volume, you can accept this default setting. Click the **Dynamically expanding** option button so that the disk's file size is very small at first and then expands up to the 5 GB you specified as you add data to it. Click **OK**.

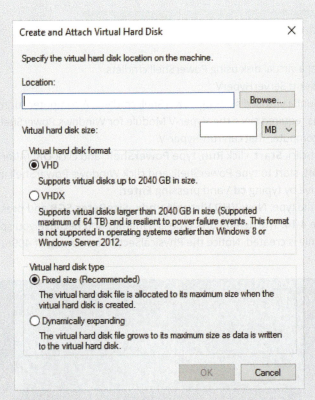

Figure 4-13   Creating a virtual hard disk

7. When you create a VHD file in Disk Management, it's mounted automatically. The disk should be listed as Disk 4, and its status is Not Initialized. Right-click **Disk 4**, and notice the Detach VHD option in the menu. Detaching the disk is the same as unmounting it. Click **Initialize Disk**.

8. In the Initialize Disk dialog box, click **OK**. Your new virtual disk is initialized and ready to have a volume created on it. Notice that the disk icon turns green, indicating it is a virtual disk.

9. Right-click the unallocated space of Disk 4, and click **New Simple Volume**. Follow the New Simple Volume Wizard, using the following settings:

   Volume size: Use the default size.
   Drive letter: Assign drive letter **V:**.
   Format: Use the defaults, but make the volume label **VirtualVol**.

10. When the volume has finished formatting, you can access it. Right-click the volume and click **Explore**.

11. File Explorer treats the virtual disk and volumes in it like any other disk and volume. In File Explorer, click **Local Disk (C:)**. You should see a file named `Virtual1` with a disk icon next to it indicating a virtual disk. Notice the size of the virtual disk file; it is probably around 60 MB. The size of the file will expand up to the maximum of 5 GB as you add data to it.

12. Now, you will copy a file to V:. Right-click **Start** and click **Command Prompt**, type **V:** and press **Enter**. You are now on the V: volume. Type **copy c:\windows\explorer.exe** and press **Enter**. Close the command prompt.

13. In File Explorer, click **Local Disk (C:)**. Notice that the size of file Virtual1 has increased because you have added data to it.

14. Right-click **Virtual1 (V:)** in the left pane of File Explorer and click **Eject**; this action unmounts the disk. The disk is no longer shown in File Explorer or Disk Management.

15. Open File Explorer again and click **Local Disk (C:)**. Right-click **Virtual1** and click **Mount**, or just double-click the file. The volume is mounted again. Dismount the virtual disk again. In File Explorer, delete the Virtual1 file.

16. Close all open windows and shut down ServerSA1.

Activity 4-5: Working with Virtual Disks in PowerShell

Time Required: 10 minutes

Objective: Create and mount a virtual disk using PowerShell cmdlets.

Required Tools and Equipment: ServerHyperV

Description: Create and mount a virtual disk using PowerShell cmdlets. A computer running Hyper-V or at least one capable of running Hyper-V is required since the Hyper-V Module for Windows PowerShell must be installed and the cmdlets will work only on a computer that can run Hyper-V.

1. On ServerHyperV, right-click **Start**, click **Run**, type **PowerShell**, and click **OK**. (Alternatively, you can click the search icon next to Start, start to type PowerShell, and click Windows PowerShell in the search results.) Move to the root of the C: drive by typing **cd ** and pressing **Enter**.

2. To create a new VHDX file type, **New-VHD Virtual1.vhdx -SizeBytes 5GB** and press **Enter**. You will see output similar to that in Figure 4-14. The default disk type is dynamic, and because you specify the .vhdx extension in the file name, a VHDX file is created. Notice the PhysicalSectorSize setting of 4096.

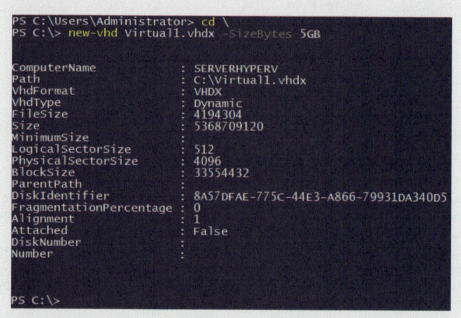

Figure 4-14 Creating a new VHD with PowerShell

3. To create a new VHD file, type **New-VHD Virtual2.vhd -SizeBytes 5GB** and press **Enter**. A VHD format virtual disk is created with PhysicalSectorSize of 512. Recall that VHD files do not support the more efficient 4096 byte sectors.

4. To mount the virtual disk, type **Mount-VHD Virtual1.vhdx**. If there were volumes already created, drive letters would be automatically assigned unless you include the -NoDriveLetter option. At this point, working with the virtual disk is the same as working with a physical disk.

5. In order to work with the disk, you need the disk number assigned to it. Type **Get-Disk** and press **Enter**. Look for the 5 GB disk; it should be assigned number 1.

6. Bring the disk online and initialize it. Type **Set-Disk -Number 1 -IsOffline $false** and press **Enter**. Type **Initialize-Disk -Number 1** and press **Enter**. Type **Get-Disk** and press **Enter** to see the results. Notice that the disk had a Partition Style of Raw before it was initialized and now has a Partition Style of GPT.

7. To create a new volume, type **New-Partition -DiskNumber 1 -Size 4.9GB -DriveLetter V** and press **Enter**. Because the physical disk is only 5 GB, the largest partition you can create is just a little smaller because the disk needs room for holding disk structures like the partition table and sector information.

8. Format the volume. Type **Format-Volume V -FileSystem NTFS -NewFileSystemLabel VirtualVol** and press **Enter**.

9. To see the disk in Disk Management, right-click **Start** and click **Disk Management**. You should see that Disk 1 is the virtual disk you just created and formatted. Close Disk Management.

10. In PowerShell, dismount the disk by typing **Dismount-VHD Virtual1.vhdx** and pressing **Enter**.

11. Delete both virtual disks by typing **del virtual*** and pressing **Enter**.

12. Close all open windows and shut down ServerHyperV.

Although you may find a number of uses for virtual disks in Windows, the most common use of virtual disks is with Storage Spaces and with virtual machines running in Hyper-V, topics discussed in Chapters 5 and 6, respectively. Now, we turn our attention to other storage topics including file sharing and securing access to files with permissions.

An Overview of File Sharing

- **70-740 – Implement storage solutions:**
  Configure disks and volumes

File and print sharing functions in Windows Server 2016 are in the File and Storage Services role and its many role services and related features. As you've seen, the File and Storage Services role is installed in Windows Server 2016 by default, but the only role service installed is Storage Services, which can't be removed. If you create a shared folder on your computer, the File Server role service (under File and Storage Services) is installed automatically.

Windows clients access shared files and printers on a Windows server by using **Server Message Block (SMB)**, a client/server Application-layer protocol that provides network file sharing, network printing, and authentication. A common variation of SMB is Common Internet File System (CIFS), which is called a *dialect* of SMB.

Although SMB is the native file-sharing protocol for Windows clients and servers, Windows Server 2016 also supports **Network File System (NFS)**, the native file-sharing protocol in UNIX and Linux OSs. Server for NFS is a role service found under File and Storage Services that you can install if you need to support clients using the NFS protocol.

> **Note** 📎
>
> Linux supports SMB in a variation of the protocol that Linux calls *Samba*.

Creating Windows File Shares

 **Certification**

- **70-740 – Implement storage solutions:**
  Configure disks and volumes

The File Server role service is required to share folders. You can install this role service via Server Manager, or you can simply share a folder to have the role service installed automatically. Folders in Windows Server 2016 can be shared only by members of the Administrators or Server Operators groups.

Sharing files on the network, as you saw in Chapter 1, isn't difficult in a Windows environment. Nonetheless, you should be familiar with some techniques and options before forging ahead with setting up a file-sharing server. You can use the following methods to configure folder sharing in Windows Server 2012/R2:

- *Simple file sharing*—To use simple file sharing, right-click a folder in File Explorer and click Share with or click Share in the Sharing tab of a folder's Properties dialog box. The File Sharing dialog box (see Figure 4-15) simplifies sharing for novices by using easy-to-understand terms for permissions and by setting file and folder permissions to accommodate the selected share permissions. If you share a file by using this method, the share permissions are always set to Full Control for the Administrators group and Everyone. If you choose the Read permission for a specific user, the file and folder permissions are set to Read & Execute, List Folder Contents, and Read for the specified user or group. If you choose Read/Write, the file and folder permissions are set to Full control for the specified user.

> **Note** 📎
>
> As you'll see later in the chapter, there are two types of permissions: share permissions are assigned to a shared folder through the Sharing tab of the folder's properties, and file and folder permissions are assigned through the Security tab of a file or folder's properties. File and folder permissions are available only on NTFS and ReFS formatted volumes.

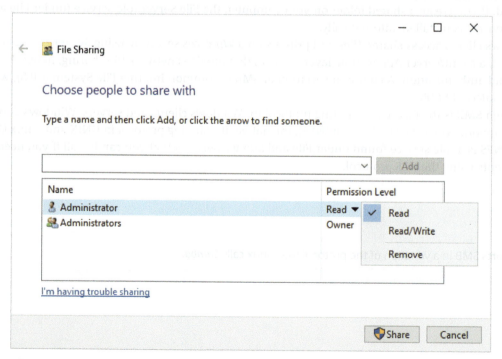

Figure 4-15   Simple file sharing

- *Advanced Sharing dialog box*—To open this dialog box, click Advanced Sharing in the Sharing tab of a folder's Properties dialog box. There are several options in this dialog box (see Figure 4-16):
  - Share this folder: Sharing can be enabled or disabled for the folder by clicking this check box.
  - Share name: The share name is the name users see in the Network folder of File Explorer when browsing the server. To put it another way, the share name is the name you use to access the folder with the UNC path (`\\server\share name`). You can add or remove share names. A single folder can have multiple share names, each with different permissions, a different number of simultaneous users, and different caching settings.
  - Limit the number of simultaneous users: In Windows Server 2016, the default limit is 16,777,216, which is, practically speaking, unlimited. In Windows 10, the maximum number of users who can access a share is 15.
  - Comments: You can enter a description of the share's contents and settings in this text box.
  - Permissions: Click this button to open the Permissions dialog box discussed later in this chapter. In Windows Server 2016, folders shared with advanced sharing are configured with the Everyone special identity, which has Read permission by default.
  - Caching: This option controls how offline files are configured. Offline files enable users to disconnect from the network and still have the shared files they were working with available on their computers. When a user reconnects to the network, the offline and network copies of the file are synchronized.

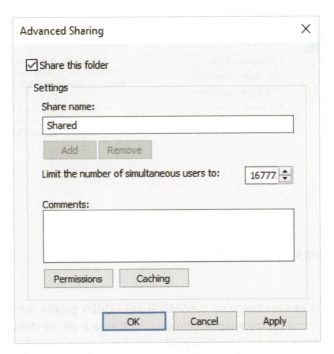

Figure 4-16   The Advanced Sharing dialog box

- *Shared Folders snap-in*—You use this component of the Computer Management MMC to monitor, change, and create shares on the local computer or a remote computer. To create a new share, right-click the Shares node under the Shared Folders snap-in and click New Share. The Create A Shared Folder Wizard walks you through selecting the folder to share or creating a new folder to share, naming the share, configuring offline files, and setting permissions.
- *File and Storage Services*—In Server Manager, click File and Storage Services, and then click Shares (the File Server role must be installed to see the Shares option in File and Storage Services). Click Tasks and then New Share to start the New Share Wizard. This method is the preferred method for creating and managing shares. Creating shares with File and Storage Services is discussed in more detail in the next section.

Creating Shares with File and Storage Services

You can create shares and set a number of sharing options with the New Share Wizard in the File and Storage Services role. To start the wizard, click File and Storage Services in the left pane of Server Manager, and then click Shares. In the Tasks list box, click New Share. The first window in the File Share Wizard is for setting the share profile (see Figure 4-17), which has five options:

- *SMB Share - Quick*—Creates a standard Windows share with default settings and permissions that you can customize by using the wizard or later in the shared folder's properties.
- *SMB Share - Advanced*—Allows you to create a Windows share with advanced options for setting the folder owner, the ability to classify data, and quotas. This option requires the File Server Resource Manager role service.
- *SMB Share - Applications*—Creates a Windows share that's suitable for Hyper-V, databases, and other applications.
- *NFS Share - Quick*—Creates an NFS share for Linux/UNIX clients with standard options.
- *NFS Share - Advanced*—Offers advanced options for creating a Linux/UNIX-style share.

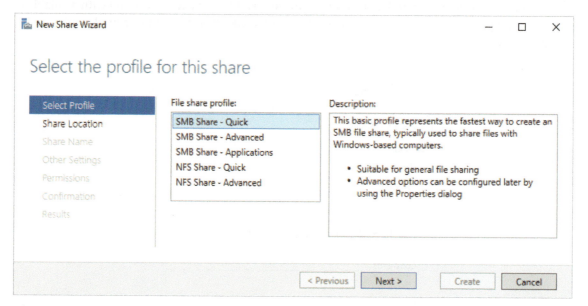

Figure 4-17 Selecting a profile for a share

The next windows described are based on the SMB Share - Quick profile. After selecting the profile, you choose a server and volume for the share's location (see Figure 4-18). By default, the share is created in the \Shares directory, but you can set a custom path.

Next, you specify a share name and, if you like, add a description. The local and remote paths are displayed, as shown in Figure 4-19.

In the next window, you can set the following additional options for an SMB share (see Figure 4-20):

- *Enable access-based enumeration*—If enabled, **access-based enumeration (ABE)** shows only the files and folders to which a user has at least Read permission. If the user doesn't have at least Read permission, the files and folders in the share are hidden from the user. If ABE isn't enabled, users can still see files and folders they don't have access to but can't open them. ABE is disabled by default.
- *Allow caching of share*—Enables or disables offline files. **Offline files**, also known as *client-side caching*, is a feature of shared folders that allows users to access the contents of shared folders when not connected to the network. If a file is opened in a share with caching enabled, it's downloaded to the client's local storage so that it can be accessed later, even if the client isn't

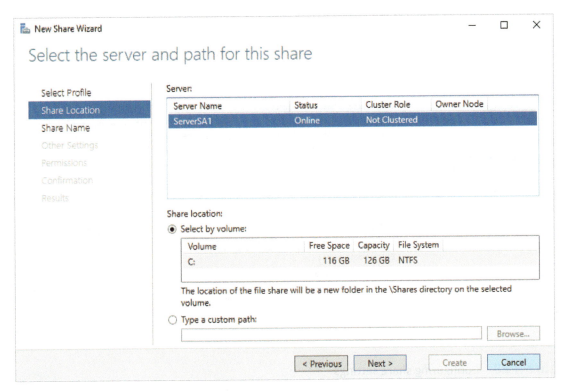

Figure 4-18   Specifying a share location

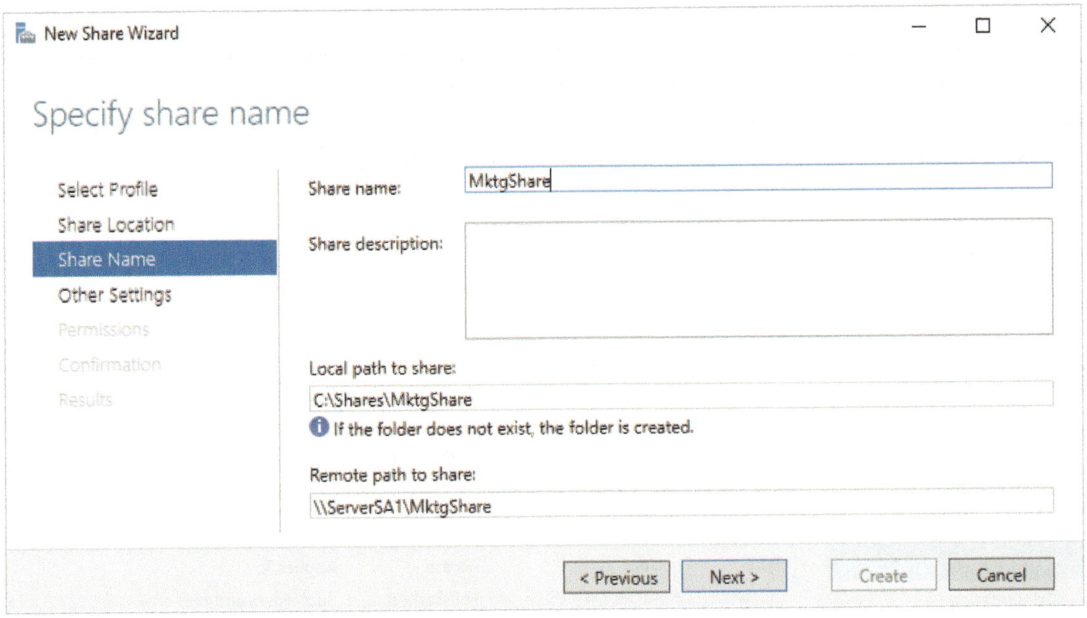

Figure 4-19   Specifying the share name

connected to the network. Later, when the client reconnects, the file is synchronized with the copy on the share. Clients have the capability to always use the locally cached version of files even when connected to the network. This feature can be enabled in Group Policy with the Configure slow-link mode policy setting. If caching is enabled and the BranchCache for Network Files role service is installed, the BranchCache feature can also be enabled on the share. BranchCache is discussed more in *MCSA Guide to Networking with Windows Server 2016, Exam 70-741* (Cengage, 2018).

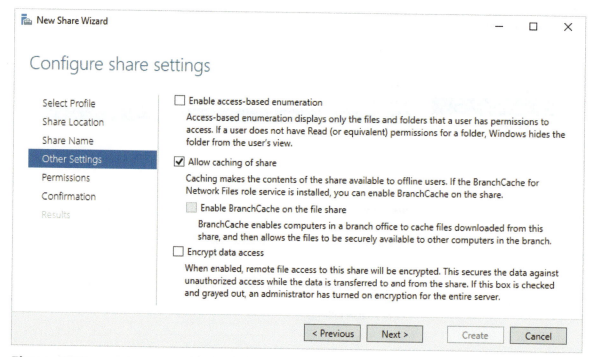

Figure 4-20   Configuring share settings

- *Encrypt data access*—When this feature is enabled, retrieving files from the share is encrypted to prevent someone from using a network sniffer to view the contents of files as they're transferred across the network.

You set permissions for the share in the next window (see Figure 4-21). By default, new share permissions are set to Read Only for Everyone, and file and folder permissions are inherited from the parent folder. If you click the Customize permissions button, you can edit permissions in the Advanced Security Settings dialog box. Because it's a shared folder, a new tab is added for managing share permissions.

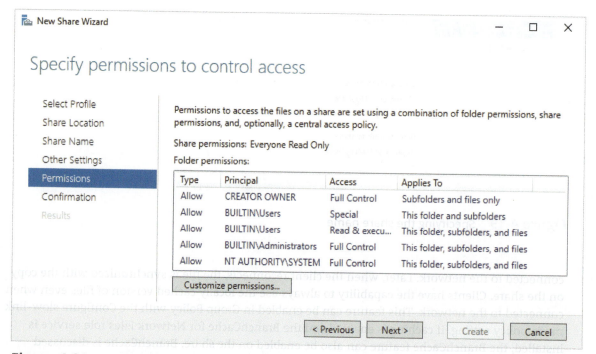

Figure 4-21   Setting permissions for the share

In the last window, you confirm your choices and create the share. When the new share is created, it's added to the list of shares in File and Storage Services. You can make changes to any settings configured in the New Share Wizard by right-clicking the share and clicking Properties.

Managing Shares with the Shared Folders Snap-In

You use the Shared Folders snap-in to create, delete, and monitor shares; view open files; and monitor and manage user connections or sessions. To open this snap-in, add it to an MMC or open the Computer Management MMC. The Shared Folders snap-in has the following subnodes:

- *Shares*—In the Shares node (shown in Figure 4-22), you can view all shares, their path on the local file system, and how many clients are currently connected to each share. You can also open the folder on the local file system, stop sharing a folder, and create new shares.

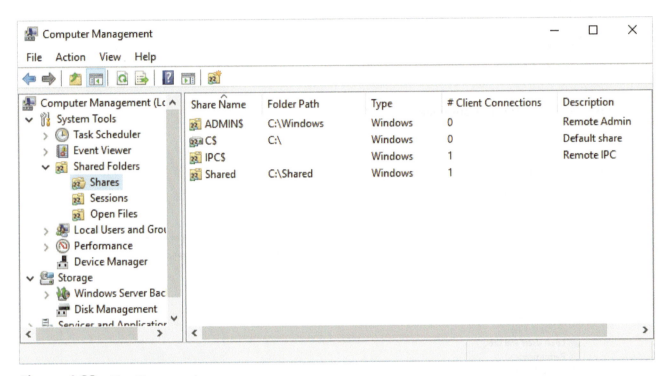

Figure 4-22   The Shares node

- *Sessions*—The Sessions node lists users who currently have a network connection to the server, which client computer they're connected from, how many files they have open, and how long they have been connected (see Figure 4-23). Administrators can select a user and close the session.
- *Open Files*—The Open Files node lists files that network users currently have open and which user has opened the file (see Figure 4-24).

The Shared Folders snap-in is useful for monitoring how much a server's shares are being used and by whom. You can also use this tool to see whether any files are being accessed over the network before shutting down the server or otherwise interrupting server access. You can also check the Idle Time column in the Sessions node to see whether a user is actively using shares on the server (a short idle time) or simply has a share open but hasn't accessed any files for a while (a longer idle time).

You can view and change a share's properties by double-clicking it in the Shares node. You can't change the share's name or the folder location, but you can change the user limit, offline settings, share permissions, and file and folder permissions. In addition, you can publish a share in Active Directory or change the publish options of a published share.

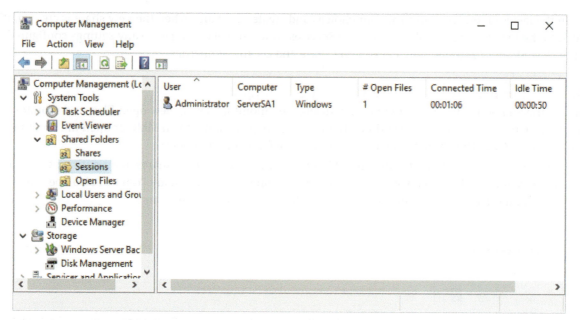

Figure 4-23   The Sessions node

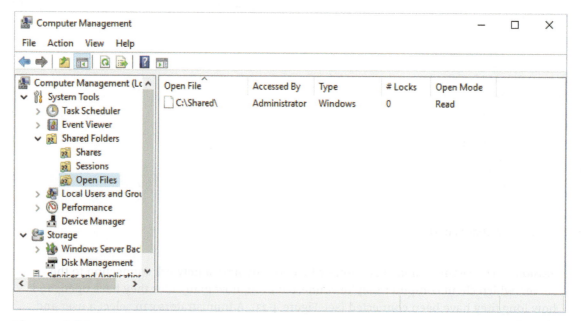

Figure 4-24   The Open Files node

Creating and Managing Shares at the Command Line

Shared folders can be created and managed at the command line with the `net share` command or PowerShell cmdlets. Take a look at the `net share` command first:

- `net share MyDocs=D:\Documents`—Creates a share named MyDocs using the D:\Documents folder
- `net share MyDocs`—Lists information about the MyDocs share
- `net share MyDocs /delete`—Deletes the MyDocs share
- `net share`—Lists shares on the computer

For more information and examples on using `net share`, type `net share /?` at a command prompt.

Managing and Creating Shares with PowerShell

Several dozen PowerShell cmdlets are available for working with file shares; Table 4-2 lists a few. For details on using a cmdlet, type `get-help` *cmdlet* `-detailed` at a PowerShell prompt. To see a list of all cmdlets related to Windows shares, type `get-command -Module SmbShare` at a PowerShell prompt.

Table 4-2 PowerShell cmdlets for working with file shares

PowerShell cmdlet	Description
New-SmbShare	Creates a share
Get-SmbShare	Lists shares on the computer
Remove-SmbShare	Deletes a share
Set-SmbShare	Changes a share's properties
Get-SmbShareAccess	Displays permissions for a share
Grant-SmbShareAccess	Adds a permission to a share
Close-SmbOpenFile	Closes a shared file that a client has open
Close-SmbSession	Closes a file share session
Get-SmbOpenFile	Displays information about currently open shared files
New-SmbMapping	Creates a drive letter mapping to a share
Remove-SmbMapping	Deletes a drive letter mapping
Set-SmbClientConfiguration	Sets the configuration of a file-sharing client
Set-SmbServerConfiguration	Sets the configuration of a file-sharing server

Take a look at a few examples:

- `New-SmbShare MyDocs D:\Documents`—Creates a share named MyDocs, using the D:\Documents folder
- `Get-SmbShare MyDocs | Format-List -Property *`—Lists detailed information about the MyDocs share
- `Remove-SmbShare MyDocs`—Deletes the MyDocs share
- `Get-SmbShare`—Lists shares on the computer

Default and Administrative Shares

Every Windows OS since Windows NT (excluding Windows 9x and Windows Me) includes **administrative shares**, which are hidden shares available only to members of the Administrators group. On computers that aren't domain controllers, these shares are as follows:

- *Admin$*—This share provides network access to the Windows folder on the boot volume (usually C:\Windows).
- *Drive$*—The *drive* represents the drive letter of a disk volume (for example, C$). The root of each disk volume (except removable disks, such as DVDs and floppy disks) is shared and accessible by using the drive letter followed by a dollar sign.
- *IPC$*—IPC means interprocess communications. This share is less an administrative share than a system share. It's used for temporary connections between clients and servers to provide communication between network programs.

Domain controllers have all the previous hidden administrative shares as well as the following default shares, which aren't hidden but are considered administrative shares:

- *NETLOGON*—Used for storing default user profiles as well as user logon scripts for pre-Windows 2000 clients.
- *SYSVOL*—Used by Active Directory for replication between DCs. Also contains group policy files that are downloaded and applied to Windows 2000 and later clients.

Windows creates administrative shares automatically, and permissions on these shares can't be changed. An administrator can disable sharing on the Admin$ share or a volume administrative share, but the share is re-created the next time the system starts or when the Server service is restarted. The IPC$ share can't be disabled.

> **Tip** ⓘ
>
> You can prevent Windows from creating administrative shares automatically by creating the Registry subkey HKEY_LOCAL_MACHINE\SYSTEM\CurrentControlSet\Services\LanmanServer\Parameters\AutoShareServer, setting the value to 0, and restarting the server.

The dollar sign at the end of a hidden share name prevents the share from being displayed in a network browse list. To access a hidden share, you must use the UNC path. For example, entering \\ServerSA1\C$ opens the root of the C drive on Server1. You can create your own hidden shares by simply placing a $ at the end of the share name. Sometimes administrators use hidden shares to prevent users from attempting to access shares for which they don't have permission.

Accessing File Shares from Client Computers

The discussion of file sharing so far has focused on how to create and manage shared resources. However, for shared resources to be useful, users must know how to access them. You have already seen some access methods in this chapter's activities. The following methods of accessing shared folders are among the most common:

- *UNC path*—The **UNC path**, which you've seen in examples and activities, uses the syntax *server**share*[*subfolder*][*file*]. The parameters in brackets are optional. In fact, the *share* parameter is optional if all you want to do is list shared resources on a server. Using *server* by itself in a File Explorer window lists all shared folders and printers (except hidden shares) on that server. The disadvantage of this method is that the user must know the server name and share name, and in a network with dozens or hundreds of servers and shares, that might be asking a lot.
- *Active Directory search*—The Active Directory search allows you to search by keyword or simply list all shared folders in the directory. With this method, users don't need to know the hosting server's name. However, shares aren't published to Active Directory automatically, so this method might not find all shared folders on the network.
- *Mapping a drive*—Administrators often set up a logon script or configure a group policy in which a drive letter is mapped to a network folder where users can store documents. Users can also map a drive letter to shared folders that they access often. Users tend to be more comfortable using drive letters to access files in a Windows environment because all their local resources (hard drives, DVD drives, and flash drives) are accessed in this manner. Drive letters can be mapped only to the root of the share, as in *server**share*, not to a subfolder of the share, as in *server**share**folder1*.
- *Browsing the network*—You can open the Network node in File Explorer and see a list of all computers found on the network. You can then browse each computer to find the share you want. This method has the advantage of not requiring you to know the server's name. However, starting with Windows Vista, you must enable the Network Discovery feature for your computer to see other computers and for your computer to be seen by other computers. You can enable this feature in the Network and Sharing Center by clicking *Change advanced sharing settings*. Browsing a network for shares might be convenient in a small network, but in a large network, you could be browsing for quite a while to find the right computer.

Activity 4-6: Sharing a Folder with Simple File Sharing

Time Required: 10 minutes

Objective: Create a test folder and then share it with simple file sharing.

Required Tools and Equipment: ServerSA1

Description: You understand that there are several ways to create shared folders. You decide to try simple file sharing to see how it sets permissions automatically. Before you create shares, you create a new volume that will be used for working with shared folders and permissions.

1. Sign in to ServerSA1 as **Administrator**, if necessary.
2. Open Disk Management and create a 5 GB volume named TestVol on the 20.0 GB disk formatted as NTFS. Assign the drive letter H:. Use defaults for all other parameters. (*Tip:* If you need help, review Activity 4-2 for instructions on creating a new volume.)
3. Open File Explorer, and create a folder named **TestShare1** on TestVol.
4. Open TestShare1's Properties dialog box, and click the **Security** tab. Make a note of the permissions assigned on this folder, and then close the Properties dialog box.
5. Right-click **TestShare1**, point to **Share with**, and click **Specific people** to open the File Sharing dialog box. Notice that the Administrator user and Administrators group already have access.
6. Click the list arrow next to the Add button, and click **TestUser** in the list. (You can also create a new user by clicking the *Create a new user* option.) Click the **Add** button. By default, the user has Read permission. Click the list arrow next to Read and click **Read/Write**.
7. Click **Share**. You see a message indicating the folder is shared. You can email links to the shared folder or copy the links to the Clipboard. You can also click the *Show me all the network shares on this computer* link to open the network browse window for your server. Click **Done**.
8. Open TestShare1's Properties dialog box. Click the **Sharing** tab, and then click **Advanced Sharing**.
9. Click **Permissions**. Notice that the Everyone group and Administrators group are assigned Full Control to the share, which is the default setting with simple file sharing. Permissions can be restricted by using file and folder permissions through the Security tab. Click **Cancel** twice.
10. In the TestShare1 folder's Properties dialog box, click the **Security** tab. Scroll through the users and groups in the top pane. Notice that TestUser and Administrator were added to the list and they have Full Control permissions. In addition, the CREATOR OWNER user has been removed. However, all other groups and users were maintained. In the real world, this may or may not be what you intended. Simple file sharing is just that—simple—but you might want to exert more control over file sharing.
11. Close all open windows and continue to the next activity.

Activity 4-7: Sharing a Folder with Advanced Sharing

Time Required: 15 minutes

Objective: Create a new folder and share it with advanced sharing.

Required Tools and Equipment: ServerSA1

Description: You're concerned that simple file sharing doesn't always have the results you want, so you decide to experiment with advanced sharing. You create a new folder, share it, and assign permissions. The permissions allow all members of the Users group to read files in the share, give all members of the Administrators group full control, and allow TestUser to create new files (with full control over them) and read files created by other users.

1. On ServerSA1, open **File Explorer**, and create a folder named **TestShare2** on TestVol. Open **TestShare2**'s Properties dialog box, and click the **Security** tab. Examine the new folder's default permissions. The Users group has Read & execute, List folder contents, and Read permissions. The Administrators group has Full Control permission, and the CREATOR OWNER special identity has advanced permissions that give any user who creates or owns a file full control over the file.

2. Click the **Sharing** tab, and then click **Advanced Sharing**. Click to select the **Share this folder** check box. Leave the share name as is, and then click **Permissions**. By default, the share permission is Allow Read for Everyone.

3. In this activity, you don't want Everyone to have Read permission, so click **Remove**. Click **Add**, type **Users**, click **Check Names**, and then click **OK**. Next, click **Add**, type **Administrators**, click **Check Names**, and then click **OK** to add the Administrators group.

4. Click **Users** and click the **Full Control** check box in the Allow column. Click **Administrators** and click the **Full Control** check box in the Allow column. Even though the Users group permission is set to Full Control, file and folder permissions will restrict them to Read and Read & execute. Click **OK** twice.

5. Click the **Security** tab. Notice that the permissions haven't changed as they did when you used simple file sharing. Click **Edit**, and then click **Add**. Type **TestUser** and click **Check Names**. Click **OK**.

6. Click **TestUser**. Notice that the permissions for TestUser are set to Read & execute, List folder contents, and Read. Click **Write** in the Allow column, which gives TestUser the ability to create and make changes to files. Click **OK** and then **Close**.

7. Later in this chapter, you will learn more about permissions and work with them. Close all open windows, and continue to the next activity.

Activity 4-8: Creating a Share with File and Storage Services

Time Required: 5 minutes

Objective: Create a share with File and Storage Services.

Required Tools and Equipment: ServerSA1

Description: You want to practice creating shares by using simple and advanced file sharing. In this activity, you use File and Storage Services to create a share.

1. Sign in to ServerSA1 as **Administrator**, if necessary.

2. In Server Manager, click **File and Storage Services**, and then click **Shares**.

3. Click the **Tasks** list box and click **New Share** to start the New Share Wizard. In the Select Profile window, click **SMB Share - Quick**, and then click **Next**.

4. In the Share Location window, click the **H:** volume in the Select by volume section, and then click **Next**.

5. In the Share Name window, type **NewShare1** in the Share name text box. By default, the local path to the share is set to H:\Shares\NewShare1. You can change the local path, but for now, leave it as is. Click **Next**.

6. In the Other Settings window, read the descriptions for the three options described previously. Leave the default settings and click **Next**.

7. In the Permissions window, review the default permissions. Note that the share permissions are Everyone Read Only, which means that only Read access to the share is allowed for all users. The Folder permissions lists the file and folder permissions. By default, Administrators have Full Control, and Users can read and create files when accessing the folder locally. Click the **Customize permissions** button to open the *Advanced Security Settings for NewShare1* dialog box where you can change the file and folder permissions and share permissions, if necessary. Click **Cancel**, and then click **Next**.

8. In the Confirmation window, review your choices, and then click **Create**. After the share is created successfully, click **Close**. You see the new share in the list of shares.

9. Close all windows and continue with the next activity.

Activity 4-9: Creating a Hidden Share and Monitoring Share Access

Time Required: 10 minutes

Objective: Create a hidden share and monitor access to shared folders.

Required Tools and Equipment: ServerSA1

Description: You want to be able to keep users from seeing certain shares on the network unless they type the UNC path for the share. You haven't worked with hidden shares yet, so you want to experiment with them. You create a new folder on TestVol and then share it with the Shared Folders snap-in. You append a $ to the share name so that it's hidden, verify that the share is hidden, and then open it by using the full UNC path. Then you use the Shared Folders snap-in to monitor access to the share.

1. On ServerSA1, open File Explorer and create a new folder on TestVol named **HideMe**.
2. Open Computer Management and click to expand **Shared Folders**. Right-click **Shares** and click **New Share** to start the Create a Shared Folder Wizard. Click **Next**.
3. In the Folder Path window, type **H:\HideMe** in the Folder path text box, and then click **Next**.
4. In the Name, Description, and Settings window, type **HideMe$** in the Share name text box, and then click **Next**.
5. In the Shared Folder Permissions window, click **Administrators have full access; other users have read-only access**, and then click **Finish**.
6. In the Sharing was Successful window, click **Finish**.
7. Right-click **Start**, click **Run**, type **\\ServerSA1**, and press **Enter**. A File Explorer window opens listing the shares on ServerSA1. The share you just created isn't listed because it's hidden. Close the File Explorer window.
8. Right-click **Start**, click **Run**, type **\\ServerSA1\HideMe$**, and press **Enter**. A window opens showing the share's contents. A hidden share is hidden only in network browse lists, but if you specify the share in a UNC path, it's available to all who have permission.
9. Minimize the File Explorer window, and open the Computer Management window. In the left pane, click **Shares**, and you see the HideMe$ share listed. The Client Connections column displays the number 1 because you currently have the share open.
10. Click **Sessions**, and you see that the Administrator account has one open file. Click **Open Files**, and you see the H:\HideMe folder listed as an open file. (Folders are considered files in Windows.) Close Computer Management and File Explorer.
11. Sign out or shut down ServerSA1 because you sign in as a different user in the next activity.

Activity 4-10: Mapping a Drive

Time Required: 10 minutes

Objective: Map a drive letter to a shared folder.

Required Tools and Equipment: ServerSA1

Description: In this activity, you use several methods to map a drive letter to a share. For testing purposes, you will map the drive on the same server as the share is located, but you would use the same procedure when accessing the share from another computer.

1. On ServerSA1, right-click **Start**, click **Run**, type **\\ServerSA1**, and press **Enter**.
2. Right-click the **NewShare1** share and click **Map network drive** to open the Map Network Drive dialog box (see Figure 4-25).
3. Click the **Drive** list arrow, and click **M:**. By default, the *Reconnect at sign-in* check box is selected, which is what you usually want in this situation. This option means the M drive always connects to this share when the user logs on. For this activity, click to clear the **Reconnect at sign-in** check box. You can also use a different user name to access this share, if necessary.

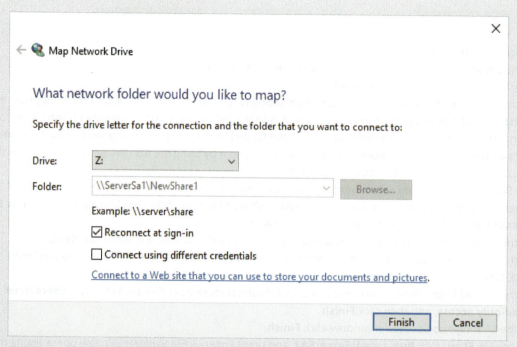

Figure 4-25 The Map Network Drive dialog box

4. Click **Finish**. A File Explorer window opens, showing the contents of the share. Close this window.

5. In the File Explorer window that's still open, click **This PC**. Notice that the M: drive is listed under Network Locations, below the Devices and drives section. Right-click the **M:** drive and click **Disconnect** to remove the drive mapping.

6. On the File Explorer menu bar, click **Computer**, and then click **Map network drive** on the ribbon to open the Map Network Drive window. Click the **M:** drive in the Drive list box. In the Folder text box, type **\\ServerSA1\NewShare1**, and then click **Finish**.

7. Disconnect the M: drive again as you did in Step 5.

8. Open a command prompt window. Type **net use m: \\ServerSA1\NewShare1** and press **Enter**. In File Explorer, verify that the drive has been mapped. The `net use` command is good to use in batch files for mapping drives.

9. At the command prompt, type **net use** and press **Enter** to see a list of mapped drives. Type **net use m: /delete** and press **Enter** to disconnect the M: drive again.

10. Close all open windows.

Network File System

Not every network is composed solely of computers running Windows. Some networks include Linux and UNIX computers that use the native file-sharing system, Network File System. NFS is a file-sharing protocol that allows users to access files and folders on other computers across a network. From a user's standpoint, NFS makes network resources seem to be part of the local file system, much like mapping a drive does for Windows file shares. NFS has both a client and a server component; both are installed by default on most Linux and UNIX systems.

Windows Server 2016 supports an NFS server component as a role service under the File and Storage Services role and an NFS client component as a feature. You can install either component or both. The Enterprise Edition of Windows 10 supports an NFS client but not the NFS server component.

Installing and Configuring Server for NFS

You install Server for NFS like any other role service by using the Add Roles and Features Wizard or the PowerShell cmdlet `Install-WindowsFeature`. After it's installed, the tab NFS Sharing is added to the Properties dialog box of folders.

The NFS Sharing tab shows the current status of NFS for the folder (whether or not the folder is shared by using NFS). Clicking the Manage NFS Sharing button opens the NFS Advanced Sharing dialog box shown in Figure 4-26. In the NFS Advanced Sharing dialog box, you can configure the following settings:

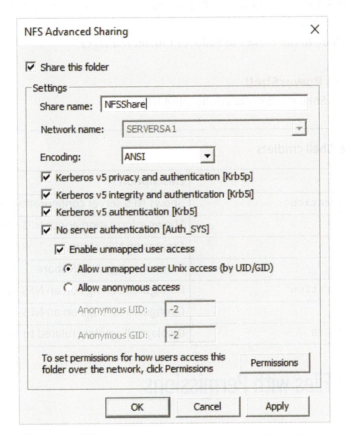

Figure 4-26   The NFS Advanced Sharing dialog box

- *Share this folder*—When this check box is selected, the folder is shared with NFS.
- *Share name*—Name the share; the default value is the name of the folder.
- *Encoding*—Choose the encoding method, which determines the characters that can be used in file and directory names.
- *Authentication*—Configure Kerberos authentication options and specify whether to allow unmapped user access and anonymous access. If you enable the No server authentication option, you can select Enable unmapped user access. Doing so allows users of Linux and UNIX systems to access the NFS share without authenticating through Active Directory. You can also allow anonymous access.
- *Permissions*—By default, all NFS client computers that request access to the share are allowed Read-Only access. You can change the default access to Read-Write or No Access. You can add client groups and assign each group different access.

You can also configure an NFS share using the New Share Wizard in File and Storage Services from Server Manager. If you configure an NFS share using File and Storage Services, the Server for NFS role is automatically installed.

Implementing an NFS Data Store

You can add fault tolerance and high availability to Server for NFS in Windows Server 2016 by allowing an NFS share to be configured on a Windows failover cluster. An NFS share on a Windows failover cluster is called an **NFS data store**, which provides a highly available storage solution for applications using NFS, such as VMware ESX Server and other Linux and UNIX applications. To implement an NFS data store, perform the following steps:

1. Install the File Services role, the Server for NFS role service, and the Failover Clustering feature.
2. Create a failover cluster (described in Chapter 9).
3. Configure the File Server role in Failover Cluster Manager, which is installed when the Failover Clustering feature is installed.
4. Add an NFS file share to the cluster in Failover Cluster Manager.

Configuring NFS with PowerShell

Table 4-3 lists some PowerShell cmdlets for configuring NFS.

Table 4-3   NFS PowerShell cmdlets

Cmdlet	Description
Get-NfsServerConfiguration	Shows NFS server configuration settings
Get-NfsShare	Shows information about NFS shares on a server
New-NfsShare	Creates an NFS share
Remove-NfsShare	Stops sharing an NFS share
Set-NfsClientConfiguration	Configures settings on an NFS client
Set-NfsShare	Configures settings on an NFS share
Get-Command -Module NFS	Displays all cmdlets related to the NFS service

Securing Access to Files with Permissions

 **Certification**

- **70-740 – Implement storage solutions:**
  Configure disks and volumes

Sharing files on a Windows server is a fairly straightforward process, but configuring permissions to secure shared files so that only authorized users can access them is a little more complex. There are two modes for accessing files on a networked computer: network (sometimes called *remote*) and interactive (sometimes called *local*). Similarly, there are two ways to secure files: share permissions and file and folder permissions. Share permissions are applied when a user attempts network access to shared files. File and folder permissions always apply whether file access is attempted interactively or remotely, through a share. That last statement might sound confusing, so take a closer look at how permissions work.

As discussed in Chapter 1, **permissions** specify which users can access a file system object (a file or folder) and what users can do with the object if they're granted access. Each file system object has permissions associated with it, and each permission can be set to Allow or Deny. Permissions can be viewed as a gatekeeper to control who has access to files. When you sign in to a computer or domain, you're issued a ticket containing information such as your user name and group memberships. If you attempt to access a file or a folder, the gatekeeper examines your ticket and compares your user name and group memberships to the file or folder's access list. If neither your user name nor your groups are on the list, you're denied access. If you or your groups *are* on the list, you're issued an access ticket that combines all your allowed permissions. You can then access the resource as specified by your access ticket.

That's how the process works when you're attempting interactive access to files. If you're attempting network access, there are two gatekeepers: one that checks your ticket against the share permissions access list and, if you're granted access by share permissions, another that checks your ticket against the file and folder permissions access list. The file and folder permissions gatekeeper is required to examine your ticket only if you get past the share gatekeeper. If you're granted access by share permissions, you're issued an access ticket. Then if you're granted access by file and folder permissions, you're allowed to keep the access ticket that gives you the lesser amount of permission of the two.

For example, Mike is granted Read access by share permissions and Read and Write access by file and folder permissions. Mike gets to keep only the Read access ticket because it's the lesser of the two permissions. As another example, neither Mike nor any of Mike's groups are on the share permissions access list. There's no need to even examine file and folder permissions because Mike is denied access at the share permissions gate. As a final example, Mike is granted Full Control access by share permissions and Modify access by file and folder permissions. Mike's access ticket gives him Modify permission because it allows less access than Full Control.

The general security rule for assigning permissions to resources is to give users the least access necessary for their job. This rule is often referred to as the *least privileges principle*. Unfortunately, this axiom can be at odds with another general rule: *Keep it simple.* Sometimes determining the least amount of access a user requires can lead to complex permission schemes. The more complex a permission scheme is, the more likely it will need troubleshooting, and the more troubleshooting that's needed, the more likely an administrator will assign overly permissive permissions out of frustration.

Note

Because FAT volumes don't have permissions, everybody who logs on locally to a computer with a FAT volume has full access to all files on that volume. If a folder is shared on a FAT volume, network users' access is determined solely by share permissions. Only the NTFS and ReFS file systems support file and folder permissions.

Security Principals

Three types of objects, called **security principals**, can be assigned permission to access the file system: users, groups, and computers. A file system object's security settings have three components that make up its **security descriptor**:

- *Discretionary access control list*—A list of security principals with permissions defining access to an object is called a **discretionary access control list (DACL)**. Each entry in the DACL is an **access control entry (ACE)**. A security principal or group not included in the DACL has no access to the object.
- *Object owner*—Usually the user account creating the object or a group or user who has been assigned ownership of the object is the **object owner**, which has special authority over the object. Most notably, even if the owner isn't in the object's DACL, the owner can still assign permissions to the object.
- *System access control list*—A **system access control list (SACL)** defines the settings for auditing access to an object.

How Permissions Are Assigned

Users can be assigned permission to an object in four different ways:

- The user creates the object. In this case, the user account is granted Full Control permission to the object and all descendant objects and is assigned as owner of the object.
- The user's account is added to the object's DACL. This method is called **explicit permission**.
- A group the user belongs to is added to the object's DACL. This method is also considered explicit permission.
- Permission is inherited from the DACL of a parent object the user or group account has been added to. This is **inherited permission**.

Effective Permissions

When a user has been assigned permission to an object through a combination of methods, the user's **effective permissions** are a combination of the assigned permissions. For example, if Joe Tech1's account has been added to an object's DACL and assigned the Allow Read permission, and a group that Joe Tech1 belongs to has been added to the same object's DACL and assigned the Allow Write permission, Joe Tech1 has both Read and Write permissions to the object. A user's effective permissions determine the user's effective access to an object.

Share Permissions

Share permissions apply to folders and files accessed across the network. Before a file can be accessed across the network, it must reside in a shared folder or a subfolder of a shared folder. Share permissions are configured on a shared folder and apply to all files and subfolders of the shared folder. These permissions can't be configured on files; file and folder permissions are used for that purpose. There are three share permissions levels (see Figure 4-27):

- *Read*—Users can view contents of files, copy files, run applications and script files, open folders and subfolders, and view file attributes.
- *Change*—All permissions granted by Read, plus create files and folders, change contents and attributes of files and folders, and delete files and folders.
- *Full Control*—All permissions granted by Change, plus change file and folder permissions as well as take ownership of files and folders. (File and folder permissions and ownership are available only on NTFS volumes.)

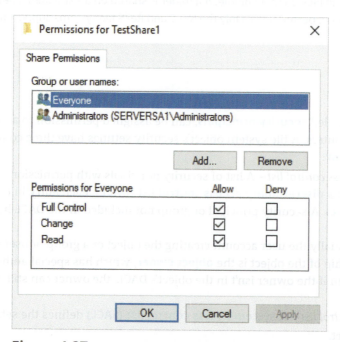

Figure 4-27 Share permissions levels

Windows assigns default permissions depending on how a folder is shared, as you have seen. Generally, the default share permission is Read for the Everyone special identity. On FAT volumes, share permissions are the only way to secure files accessed through the network. File and folder permissions protect file accesses via the network and those done interactively.

> **Note** 📎
>
> Users, groups, and special identity groups are discussed in detail in *MCSA Guide to Identity with Windows Server 2016, Exam 70-742* (Cengage, 2018).

File and Folder Permissions

File and folder permissions give both network users and interactive users fine-grained access control over folders and files. Unlike share permissions, which can be configured only on a shared folder, file and folder permissions can be configured on both folders and files. By default, when permissions are configured on a folder, subfolders and files in that folder inherit the permissions. However, inherited permissions can be changed when needed, making it possible to have different permission settings on files in a folder.

Permission inheritance defines how permissions are transmitted from a parent object to a child object. In a file system, parent objects can be a volume or folder, and child objects can be folders and files. For example, a folder can be the parent object, and any files it contains, including other folders, are considered child objects. All objects in a volume are child objects of the volume. So, if a user is assigned the Modify permission to a folder, all subfolders and files in the folder inherit the permission, and the user has Modify permission to these objects as well. Permission inheritance and how to change it are discussed later in the section "Permission Inheritance."

To view or edit permissions on a folder or file, you use the Security tab of the object's Properties dialog box. Unlike share permissions, which have only three permission levels, there are six basic permissions in the Security tab for folders and five permissions for files. Folders also have 14 advanced permissions, and files have 13. Advanced permissions aren't completely separate from basic permissions, however. Each basic permission is really a grouping of advanced permissions, as you will see later.

Basic permissions for folders and files are as follows (see Figure 4-28):

- *Read*—Users can view file contents, copy files, open folders and subfolders, and view file attributes and permissions. However, unlike the Read permission in share permissions, this permission doesn't allow users to run applications or scripts.
- *Read & execute*—This grants the same permissions as Read and includes the ability to run applications or scripts. When this permission is selected, List folder contents and Read are selected, too.
- *List folder contents*—This permission applies only to folders and grants the same permission as Read & execute. However, because it doesn't apply to files, Read & execute must also be set on the folder to allow users to open files in the folder.
- *Write*—Users can create and modify files and read file attributes and permissions. However, this permission doesn't allow users to read or delete files. In most cases, the Read or Read & execute permission should be given with the Write permission.
- *Modify*—Users can read, modify, delete, and create files. Users can't change permissions or take ownership. Selecting this permission automatically selects Read & execute, List folder contents, Read, and Write.
- *Full control*—Users can perform all actions given by the Modify permission with the addition of changing permissions and taking ownership. This permission is very powerful because it gives users complete control over who can access a file or folder as well as take ownership (discussed later in "File and Folder Ownership"). Full control should be assigned to nonadministrator users only sparingly. In most cases, the Modify permission gives users enough capabilities to interact with the file system.

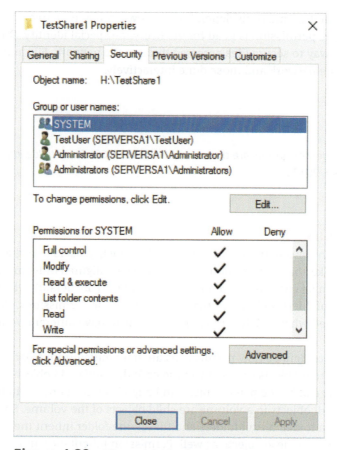

Figure 4-28   File and folder basic permissions

Basic permissions should work for most situations. Configuring advanced permissions should be reserved for special circumstances. The temptation to configure advanced permissions to follow the least privileges principle can lead to breaking the keep it simple rule and result in administrators' and users' frustration. However, if you look at the file and folder permissions that Windows sets by default on every volume, you see a few ACEs that use advanced permissions. So although you don't have to use them often, you need to understand them, particularly to figure out how initial volume permissions are set. Table 4-4 describes each advanced permission and lists which basic permissions include it.

Table 4-4   File and folder advanced permissions

Advanced permission	Description	Included in basic permission
Full control	Same as the standard Full control permission	Full control
Traverse folder/ execute file	For folders: Allows accessing files in folders or subfolders even if the user doesn't normally have access to the folder For files: Allows running program files	Full control, Modify, Read & execute, List folder contents
List folder/read data	For folders: Allows users to view subfolders and filenames in the folder For files: Allows users to view data in files	Full control, Modify, Read & execute, List folder contents, Read
Read attributes	Allows users to view file or folder attributes	Full control, Modify, Read & execute, List Folder Contents, Read

Table 4-4   File and folder advanced permissions *(continued)*

Advanced permission	Description	Included in basic permission
Read extended attributes	Allows users to view file or folder extended attributes	Full control, Modify, Read & execute, List folder contents, Read
Create files/write data	Allows users to create new files and modify the contents of existing files	Full control, Modify, Write
Create folders/ append data	Allows users to create new folders and add data to the end of existing files but not change existing data in a file	Full control, Modify, Write
Write attributes	Allows users to change file and folder attributes	Full control, Modify, Write
Write extended attributes	Allows users to change file and folder extended attributes	Full control, Modify, Write
Delete subfolders and files	Allows users to delete subfolders and files in the folder	Full control
Delete	Allows users to delete the folder or file	Full control, Modify
Read permissions	Allows users to read file and folder permissions of a folder or file	Full control, Modify, Read & execute, List folder contents, Read, Write
Take ownership	Allows users to take ownership of a folder or file, which gives the user implicit permission to change permissions on that file or folder	Full control

File and Folder Ownership

As mentioned, every file system object (files and folders) has an owner. An object owner is granted certain implicit permissions regardless of how permissions are set in the object's DACL: viewing and changing permissions for the object and transferring ownership to another user. So it's possible that users can be file owners but not be able to open the files they own. However, because owners can change permissions on files they own, they can grant themselves the permissions they want.

A user can become the owner of a file system object in three ways:

- *Create the file or folder*—The user who creates a file or folder is automatically the owner.
- *Take ownership of a file or folder*—User accounts with Full control permission or the Take ownership advanced permission for a file or folder can take ownership of the file or folder. Members of the Administrators group can take ownership of all files.
- *Assigned ownership*—An Administrator account can assign another user as the owner of a file or folder.

Permission Inheritance

On an NTFS or ReFS volume, permissions are first set at the root of a volume, and all folders and files in the volume inherit these settings unless configured otherwise.

Note

Windows changes the default inheritance settings on many folders created during installation so that they don't inherit all permissions from the root of the volume.

You can change how permission inheritance works by going to advanced settings in the Security tab of a file or folder's Shared Properties dialog box. When you select an ACE and click Edit, you see seven options for how permissions on a folder apply to other objects in the folder, as shown in Figure 4-29.

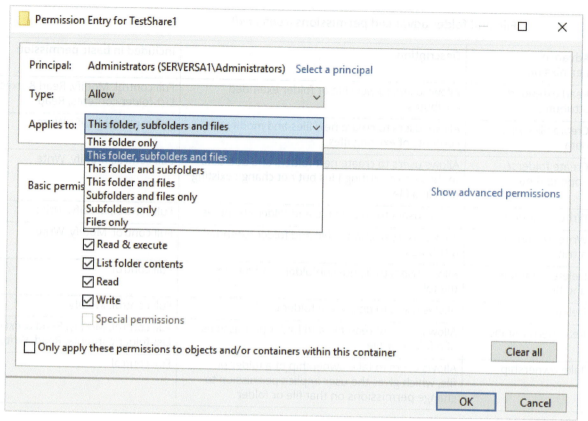

Figure 4-29   Configuring permission inheritance

All basic permissions have the Applies to option set to *This folder, subfolders and files*, but there might be reasons to change this default setting. For example, you might want users to be able to create and delete files in a folder but not delete the folder itself. To do this, you could set the standard Read & execute and Write permissions on the folder, and then set the Delete advanced permission to apply to subfolders and files only.

Subfolders and files are configured to inherit permissions by default; however, permission inheritance can be disabled. If you need to remove permissions from a file or folder, you must disable inheritance first. You can add new ACEs or add permissions to an existing ACE with inheritance enabled, but you can't remove inherited permissions. To disable permission inheritance, open the Advanced Security Settings dialog box for an object (see Figure 4-30) and click the Disable inheritance button. When you disable inheritance, you're prompted to convert the existing inherited permissions into explicit permissions or remove all inherited permissions. In most cases, converting the permissions is best so that you have a starting point from which to make changes. The *Replace all child object permission entries with inheritable permissions from this object* option forces the current folder's child objects to inherit applicable permissions. If a child object has inheritance disabled, this option re-enables it.

Effective Access

With all the variables involved in permissions, determining what access a user account has to a file or folder isn't always easy, but Windows has a tool called **effective access** to help sort out object access. As shown previously, the Advanced Security Settings dialog box has an Effective Access tab where you can select a user or group to see its access to a file or folder after taking into account sharing permission, file and folder permissions, and group memberships (see Figure 4-31). You can also see which permissions a user or group has, and for permissions that aren't granted, the Access limited by column specifies whether the limiting factor is share or file and folder permissions.

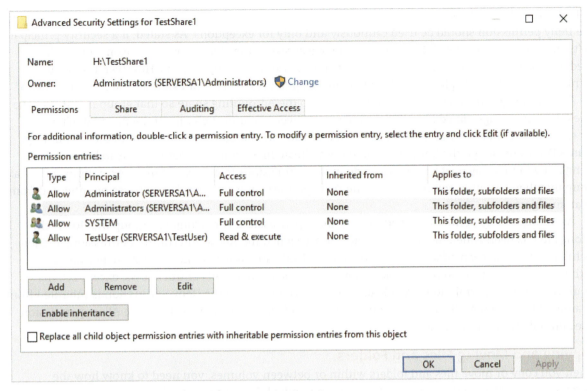

Figure 4-30   The Advanced Security Settings dialog box

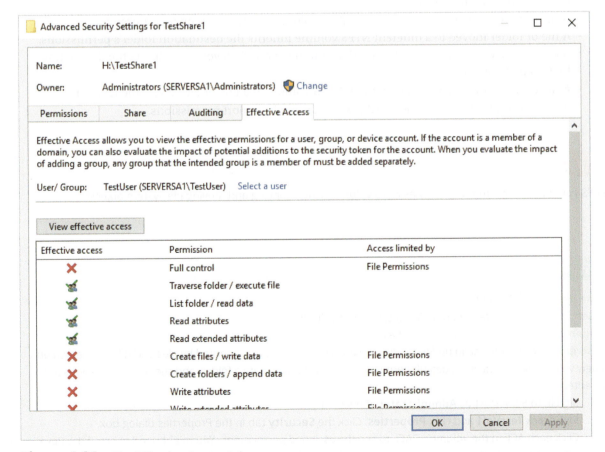

Figure 4-31   The Effective Access tab

Using Deny in an ACE

The Deny permission should be used cautiously and only for exceptions. As stated, if a security principal isn't represented in an object's DACL, it doesn't have access to the object. For this reason, you don't need to add Deny ACEs to every object to prevent users from accessing objects. However, the Deny permission does have its place, usually when an exception is needed. For example, Barb is a member of the Accounting group which has been given access to the Accounting share so that group members have access to accounting-related files. Barb is a new employee, so until she's fully trained, you don't want her to be able to make changes to files in the share. You can add Barb's user account to the Accounting share's DACL and assign the Deny Delete and Deny Create files/write data permissions to her account. Using Deny in this way enables you to assign broad permissions to groups yet make exceptions for certain group members. Another common use of the Deny permission is to override a permission inherited from a parent object.

As a rule, a Deny permission overrides an Allow permission. For example, a group that Joe Tech1 belongs to has been added to an object's DACL and assigned the Allow Full control permission, and Joe Tech1's account has been added to the same object's DACL and assigned the Deny Write permission. In this case, Joe Tech1 could perform all actions on the object that Full control allows, except actions requiring the Write permission. There's an exception to this rule: If the Deny permission is inherited from a parent object and the Allow permission is explicitly added to the object's DACL, the Allow permission takes precedence if there's a conflict.

Copying and Moving Files and Folders

When you copy or move files and folders within or between volumes, you need to know how the permissions assigned to those files and folders are handled. Here's a list of rules:

- A file or folder copied within the same NTFS volume or to a different NTFS volume inherits permissions from the destination folder. If the destination is the root of the volume, it inherits permissions from the root of the volume.
- A file or folder moved within the same NTFS volume retains its original permissions.
- A file or folder moved to a different NTFS volume inherits the destination folder's permissions.
- A file or folder moved from a FAT or FAT32 volume to an NTFS volume inherits the destination folder's permissions.
- A file or folder moved or copied from an NTFS volume to a FAT or FAT32 volume loses all permission settings because FAT/FAT32 volumes don't support permissions.

Note

ReFS volumes behave the same way as NTFS volumes when copying and moving file system objects.

Activity 4-11: Examining Default Settings for Volume Permissions

Time Required: 10 minutes
Objective: Examine default permission settings on a volume.
Required Tools and Equipment: ServerSA1
Description: You want a solid understanding of which permissions are inherited by files and folders created on a new volume, so you view the default permissions on a volume, create a folder, and see how permissions are inherited.

1. Sign in to ServerSA1 as **Administrator**, if necessary.
2. Right-click **TestVol1** and click **Properties**. Click the **Security** tab in the Properties dialog box.
3. Click each ACE in the volume's DACL to see the assigned permissions. You might need to scroll the Permission list box to see the Special permissions entry. (If there is a check in the Special permissions row, it means the account has been assigned one or more advanced permissions.)

4. Click the **Advanced** button. Notice that the Administrators group and SYSTEM and CREATOR OWNER special identities are granted Full control. Double-click the **CREATOR OWNER** entry. This special identity is given Full control but only over subfolders and files. This entry ensures that any user who creates a file or folder is granted Full control permission for that object. A user must have at least the Write basic permission to create files and folders. Click **Cancel**.

5. Double-click the **Users** entry with Create files/write data in the Access column. This entry and the Users entry above it allow users to create folders and files, but files can be created only in subfolders. This permission prevents users from creating files in the root of the volume. Click **Cancel**.

6. Double-click the **Everyone** entry. This set of permissions allows the Everyone special identity to read and execute files and view a list of files and folders in the root of the volume. The *Applies to* setting "This folder only" prevents child objects from inheriting these permissions. Click **Cancel** three times.

7. Create a folder in the root of the TestVol volume named **TestPerm**.

8. Open the TestPerm folder's Properties dialog box, and click the **Security** tab. Click any ACE in the Group or user names list box. Permissions for the entries are grayed out, meaning you can't change them because they are inherited. Click **Cancel**.

9. Create a text file in the TestPerm folder named **Permfile1**.

10. Open the `Permfile1` file's Properties dialog box, and click the **Security** tab. Notice that the file inherits the TestPerm folder's permissions except the CREATOR OWNER special identity, which is assigned only to folders, not files.

11. Close all open windows and continue to the next activity.

Activity 4-12: Experimenting with File and Folder Permissions

Time Required: 20 minutes
Objective: Experiment with file and folder permissions.
Required Tools and Equipment: ServerSA1
Description: You're somewhat confused about file and folder permissions, so you create some files to use in a variety of permission experiments.

1. Sign in to ServerSA1 as **Administrator**, if necessary.

2. Open **File Explorer**, and navigate to the **TestPerm** folder you created on the TestVol volume.

3. First, you want to be able to view file extensions in File Explorer so that you can create batch files easily. Click **View** on the toolbar, and then click the box next to **File name extensions**. You can now see the `.txt` extension on the `Permfile1` file you created previously.

4. Create a text file called **TestBatch.bat** in the TestPerm folder. When asked whether you want to change the file extension, click **Yes**.

5. Right-click **TestBatch.bat** and click **Edit**. Type **@ Echo This is a test batch file** and press **Enter**. On the next line, type **@ Pause**. Save the file, and then exit Notepad. To test your batch file, double-click it. A command prompt window opens, and you see "This is a test batch file. Press any key to continue . . . ." Press the **spacebar** or **Enter** to close the command prompt window.

6. Open the Properties dialog box for TestBatch.bat, click the **Security** tab, and then click **Advanced**. Click the **Disable inheritance** button. In the message box that opens, click **Convert inherited permissions into explicit permissions on this object**. Notice that the three permissions entries now indicate None in the Inherited from column (see Figure 4-32). Click **OK**.

7. On the Security tab for TestBatch.bat, click **Edit**. Click **Users** in the Group or user names list box. In the Permissions for Users list box, click to clear the **Read & execute** check box in the Allow column and leave the **Read** check box selected. Click **OK** twice.

8. Sign out and sign in as **TestUser** with **Password01**. In File Explorer, browse to the **TestPerm** folder on the TestVol volume. Double-click the **TestBatch.bat** file. Read the error message. The error message indicates that you cannot access the file. This is because you are trying to run (execute) the batch file and you no longer have the Read & execute permission. Click **OK**.

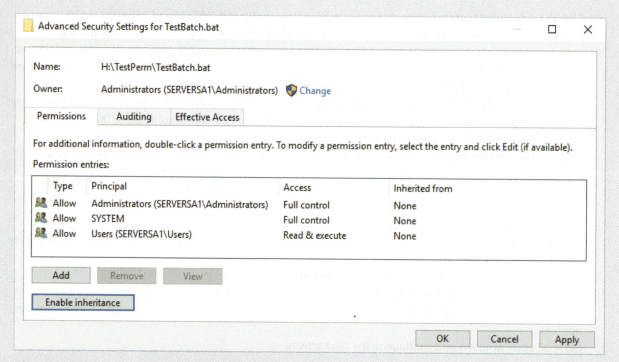

Figure 4-32 Permissions after removing inheritance

9. Right-click **TestBatch.bat** and click **Edit**. Notice that you can still open this file because you have Read permission. Click **File**, and then click **Save**. A dialog box opens asking you to save the file. Click **Save**. When prompted to replace the file, click **Yes**. You see a message indicating that access is denied because you don't have write permission to the file. Click **OK** and exit Notepad.

10. In File Explorer, right-click the right pane and point to **New**. Strangely, the right-click New menu and the Quick Access toolbar menu offer only Folder as an option. However, you can save a file you create in Notepad in this folder.

11. Right-click **TestBatch.bat** and click **Edit**. Click **File**, **Save As** from the menu. In the Save As dialog box, type **NewBatch.bat** and click **Save**. Exit Notepad.

12. Open the Properties dialog box for NewBatch, and click the **Security** tab. Click **TestUser**. This user has been assigned Full control of the file because of the CREATOR OWNER Full control permission on the parent folder. Click **Advanced**. You see TestUser next to Owner. Notice that you can change the owner if you click the Change link.

13. Disable permission inheritance and convert the existing permissions. (Refer back to Step 6, if necessary.) Click **OK** until you get back to the Security tab of the NewBatch file's Properties dialog box.

14. Click **Edit**. Click **TestUser**, and then click **Remove**. Click the **Users** entry, and then click **Remove**. Only SYSTEM and Administrators are left in the DACL. Click **OK** twice.

15. Double-click **NewBatch**. You see a message indicating that access is denied because you no longer have permission to open or execute this file. Click **OK**. Although you no longer have access to this file, you're still the file owner and, therefore, can assign yourself permissions.

16. Open the Properties dialog box for NewBatch, click the **Security** tab, and then click **Edit**. Click **Add**. Type **TestUser**, click **Check Names**, and then click **OK**. Click **Full control** in the Allow column in the Permissions for TestUser list box. Click **OK** twice. Double-click **NewBatch** to verify that you can open and execute the file.

17. Sign out from the system, and continue to the next activity.

Activity 4-13: Restricting Access to Subfolders of Shares

Time Required: 20 minutes
Objective: Restrict access to a subfolder of a share.
Required Tools and Equipment: ServerSA1
Description: The Sales Department wants a subfolder of the Marketing share to store sensitive documents that should be available only to users in the Sales Department because some Marketing and Advertising users tend to leak information before it should be discussed outside the company. You could create a new share, but the Sales Department users prefer a subfolder of the existing share. To do this activity, you need to create a couple of groups and some users to put in the groups.

1. Sign in to ServerSA1 as **Administrator**.
2. Right-click **Start** and click **Computer Management**. You'll create two users named **Marketing1** and **Sales1**.
3. Click to expand **Local Users and Groups** and then click the **Users** folder. In the Actions pane, click **More Actions** and click **New User**.
4. Type **Marketing1** in the User name text box. Type **Password01** in the Password and Confirm password text boxes. Click to clear **User must change password at next logon** and click **Create**. Repeat this step, replacing Marketing1 with **Sales1**. Click **Close** when finished.
5. In the left pane, right-click **Groups** and click **New Group**. In the Group name text box, type **MarketingG**.
6. Next, users in the Marketing and Sales departments should be added to the MarketingG group. To do this, click **Add**. In the Select Users dialog box, type **Marketing1; Sales1**, click **Check Names**, and then click **OK**. Click **Create** and then **Close**.
7. Create a group named **SalesG** and add the **Sales1** user to the group. Close **Computer Management**.
8. Open File Explorer. On TestVol, create a folder named **MktgDocs**. In the MktgDocs folder, create a subfolder named **SalesOnly**.
9. Open the Properties dialog box for MktgDocs and click **Sharing**. Click **Advanced Sharing**, and then click **Share this folder**. Click **Permissions**, and then remove **Everyone** from the DACL.
10. Add the **Users** group to the DACL and give the group Full Control to the share. You limit access to files and subfolders by using file and folder permissions. Click **OK** until you're back to the MktgDocs Properties dialog box.
11. Click the **Security** tab. Currently, the Users group has Read permission to the folder and the Administrators group has Full Control. Click **Advanced**. Click **Disable Inheritance**, and then click the **Convert** option. Click **OK**.
12. Click **Edit**, click **Users**, and click **Remove**.
13. Add both the **MarketingG** and **SalesG** groups to the DACL. Click **MarketingG**, and click the **Write** check box in the Allow column so that MarketingG has Read & execute, List folder contents, Read, and Write permissions to the folder. Repeat for **SalesG**. Click **OK** and then **Close**.
14. In File Explorer, open the **MktgDocs** folder, and then open the Properties dialog box for the **SalesOnly** folder. Click the **Security** tab. The SalesOnly folder has inherited permissions from the MktgDocs folder.
15. Disable inheritance on the SalesOnly folder, being sure to convert existing permissions. In the Security tab, click **Edit**. Click **MarketingG**, and then click **Remove**. Click **OK** twice.
16. Sign out from ServerSA1 and log back on as **Sales1**. Open the MktgDocs share by right-clicking **Start**, clicking **Run**, typing **\\ServerSA1\MktgDocs**, and pressing **Enter**. Create a text file in MktgDocs named **Mktg1**.
17. Open the **SalesOnly** folder and create a text file named **SalesDoc**. You have verified that you can create files while signed in as a member of the SalesG group. Open the Properties dialog box for SalesDoc and click the **Security** tab. Note that SalesG and Sales1 are in the DACL. Click **SalesG**, and notice that SalesG has Read & execute, Read, and Write permissions. Click **Sales1**, and notice that Sales1 has Full control because it's the file owner.

18. Sign out from ServerSA1 and sign back in as **Marketing1**. Open the MktgDocs share by right-clicking **Start**, clicking **Run**, typing **\\ServerSA1\MktgDocs**, and pressing **Enter**. Create a text file in MktgDocs named **Mktg2**. You have verified that members of the MarketingG group can create files in the MktgDocs share.

19. Try to delete the `Mktg1` file that Sales1 created. You can't because you have only Write permission to the file, which doesn't allow you to delete files.

20. Double-click the **SalesOnly** folder. You see a network error message because the Marketing1 user doesn't have access to the SalesOnly folder. Click **Close**.

21. Shut down ServerSA1.

Chapter Summary

- *Storage* is any digital media that data can be written to and later retrieved from. Long-term storage includes USB drives, SD cards, CDs/DVDs, magnetic tape, SSDs, and HDDs.

- All computers require at least some storage, but servers usually require more than client computers. Server storage is needed for OS files, page files, log files, virtual machines, database files, and user documents, among others.

- The main methods of storage access are local, DAS, NAS, and SAN. Local and DAS are similar, but DAS can also be a separate unit attached through an external interface. NAS is a standalone storage device with a network interface. A SAN is the most complex storage device, using high-speed networking technologies to provide shared storage.

- Configuration of local disks can be divided into two broad categories: physical disk properties and logical disk properties. Physical disk properties include disk capacity, rotation speed, and the disk interface technology. SATA and SAS are the most common disk interfaces on servers.

- Disk types include basic disks and dynamic disks. Partitioning types include MBR and GPT. Volume types are simple, spanned, striped, mirrored, and RAID-5. File systems include FAT, NTFS, and ReFS.

- Windows Server 2016 can mount virtual disks and use them like regular volumes. Virtual disks are stored as files with a .vhd or .vhdx extension.

- The File Server role service is required to share folders. You can install this role service in Server Manager, or you can simply share a folder to have it installed automatically. The SMB protocol is used to access Windows file shares, but Windows also supports NFS.

- There are two types of permissions to restrict access to files and folders: share and NTFS. Share permissions restrict network access to files and folders, and NTFS permissions restrict both interactive/local and network access.

- There are several ways for client computers to access shared folders: using the UNC path, doing an Active Directory search, mapping a drive, and browsing the network.

- Every recent Windows OS includes administrative shares, which are hidden shares available only to members of the Administrators group. They include Admin$, Drive$, and IPC$, and on domain controllers, the NETLOGON and SYSVOL shares are added.

- Network File System (NFS) is a file-sharing protocol that allows users to access files and folders on other computers across a network. Windows Server 2016 supports an NFS server component as a role service under the File and Storage Services role and an NFS client component as a feature.

- Three types of objects can be assigned permission to access the file system: users, groups, and computers. These object types are referred to as *security principals*.

- Permissions are assigned in four ways: user creates an object, user account is added to the DACL, a group the user belongs to is added to the DACL, and permission is inherited. Effective permissions are the combination of assigned permissions.

- There are three share permissions: Read, Change, and Full Control. There are six basic file and folder permissions: Read, Read & execute, List folder contents, Write, Modify, and Full control. On an NTFS or ReFS volume, permissions are set at the root of a volume first, and all folders and files in that volume inherit these settings unless configured otherwise.

Key Terms

access-based enumeration (ABE)	inherited permission	security principal
access control entry (ACE)	local storage	Serial ATA (SATA)
administrative shares	logical unit number (LUN)	serial attached SCSI (SAS)
backplane	Master Boot Record (MBR)	Server Message Block (SMB)
basic disk	mirrored volume	share permissions
boot volume	network-attached storage (NAS)	simple volume
direct-attached storage (DAS)	Network File System (NFS)	small computer system
discretionary access control	NFS data store	interface (SCSI)
list (DACL)	object owner	solid state drive (SSD)
disk drive	offline files	spanned volume
dynamic disk	page file	storage appliance
effective access	partition	storage area network (SAN)
effective permissions	permission inheritance	striped volume
explicit permission	permissions	system access control list (SACL)
extended partition	primary partition	system volume
file and folder permissions	RAID-5 volume	UNC path
file system	redundant array of independent	virtual hard disk (VHD)
formatting	disks (RAID)	volume
GUID Partitioning Table (GPT)	security descriptor	

Review Questions

1. Which of the following is an example of long-term storage? (Choose all that apply.)
   a. Magnetic tape
   b. CPU cache
   c. SSD
   d. RAM

2. Which of the following is true about an SSD?
   a. Uses magnetic platters
   b. Has no moving parts
   c. Uses a proprietary interface
   d. Uses EPROM

3. Which of the following is an example of what a server uses storage for? (Choose all that apply.)
   a. Page file
   b. Virtual machines
   c. Working memory
   d. Documents

4. Which of the following is true about a page file?
   a. It should be stored on a separate disk from the Windows folder.
   b. It's usually stored in fast random access memory.
   c. Windows stores frequently accessed drivers in it.
   d. The page file is usually smaller than 50 MB.

5. Local storage is rarely direct-attached storage. True or False?

6. You want shared network storage that's easy to set up and geared toward file sharing with several file-sharing protocols, but you don't want the device to be dedicated to a single computer. What should you consider buying?
   a. SAN
   b. DAS
   c. NAS
   d. LAS

7. What type of interface are you likely to find on a DAS device for connecting the device to the server that uses it?
   a. SATA
   b. IDE
   c. PATA
   d. eSATA

8. You have four servers that need access to shared storage because you're configuring them in a cluster. Which storage solution should you consider for this application?
   a. NAS
   b. SAN
   c. SCSI
   d. DAS

9. Which of the following is defined as a physical component with a disk interface connector?
   a. Format
   b. Partition
   c. Volume
   d. Disk drive

10. You have installed a new disk and created a volume on it. What should you do before you can store files on it?
    a. Format it.
    b. Partition it.
    c. Initialize it.
    d. Erase it.

11. Which disk interface technology transfers data over a parallel bus?
    a. SATA
    b. USB
    c. SAS
    d. SCSI

12. What's created automatically when you install Windows Server 2016 on a system with a disk drive that has never had an OS installed on it before?
    a. System volume
    b. Dynamic disk
    c. GPT
    d. Extended partition

13. What type of volumes or partitions can be created on a basic disk? (Choose all that apply.)
    a. Spanned volume
    b. Striped partition
    c. Extended partition
    d. Simple volume

14. Which of the following is true about GPT disks?
    a. They support a maximum volume size of 2 TB.
    b. GPT is the default when initializing a disk in Disk Management.
    c. They use CRC protection for the partition table.
    d. You can't convert a GPT disk to MBR.

15. You have a server with Windows Server 2016 installed on Disk 0, a basic disk. You're using the server to store users' documents. You have two more disks that you can install in the server. What should you do if you want to provide fault tolerance for users' documents?
    a. Convert Disk 0 to dynamic. Create a striped volume using Disk 0, Disk 1, and Disk 2.
    b. Create a RAID 1 volume from Disk 1 and Disk 2.
    c. Convert the new disks to GPT. Create a spanned volume using Disk 1 and Disk 2.
    d. Create a RAID-5 volume from Disk 0, Disk 1, and Disk 2.

16. You need a disk system that provides the best performance for a new application that frequently reads and writes data to the disk. You aren't concerned about disk fault tolerance because the data will be backed up each day; performance is the main concern. What type of volume arrangement should you use?
    a. Spanned volume
    b. RAID 1 volume
    c. RAID 0 volume
    d. RAID-5 volume

17. You need to protect sensitive files from unauthorized users even if the disk is stolen. What feature should you use and on what file system?
    a. EFS, NTFS
    b. Disk compression, ReFS
    c. Quotas, NTFS
    d. Shadow copies, ReFS

18. Which of the following PowerShell cmdlets will allow you to view a list of disks?
    a. List-Disk
    b. Set-Disk
    c. View-Disk
    d. Get-Disk

19. You come across a file with a .vhd extension on your server's hard disk. What should you do to see this file's contents?
    a. Right-click the file and click Open.
    b. Open the file in Notepad.
    c. Burn the file to a DVD.
    d. Mount the file.

20. Which of the following virtual disk formats supports virtual disks up to 2 TB and allows backward compatibility with Windows Server 2008?
    a. VHD
    b. ReFS
    c. VHDX
    d. FAT

21. Which type of virtual disk would you create if you needed to use the virtual disk in a production environment that required fast disk performance?
    a. Dynamically expanding
    b. Thin provisioned
    c. Fixed size
    d. VHD

22. Which of the following is a UNIX native file-sharing protocol that is supported by Windows Server 2016 File and Storage Services role?
    a. SMB
    b. FTP
    c. TFTP
    d. NFS

23. Which of the following Windows Server 2016 role services is required to share folders?
    a. File Server
    b. Storage Server
    c. DHCP Server
    d. Hyper-V Server

24. Which of the following can be used to create shares? (Choose all that apply.)
    a. Advanced sharing
    b. Disk Management
    c. Simple file sharing
    d. File and Storage Services

25. Which SMB share option should you enable if you don't want users to see files they don't have at least Read permission to?
    a. Offline files
    b. Hidden shares
    c. BranchCache
    d. Access-based enumeration

26. Which of the following commands or cmdlets can be used to list the shares on the computer? (Choose all that apply.)
    a. `New-SmbShare`
    b. `Net Share`
    c. `Get-SmbShare`
    d. `Net Disk`

27. Which administrative share does Active Directory use for replication?
    a. NETLOGON
    b. SYSVOL
    c. Admin$
    d. IPC$

28. You need a highly available file-sharing system that accommodates the native Linux and UNIX file-sharing protocol. What do you need to configure?
    a. A Network File System data store
    b. A round-robin SMB file share
    c. A SAN using the iSNS protocol
    d. A server cluster using SMB

29. Which of the following is part of a file system object's security settings and defines the settings for auditing access to an object?
    a. DACL   c. ACL
    b. ACE   d. SACL

30. Which of the following is *not* a basic file and folder permission?
    a. Read & execute
    b. Change
    c. Write
    d. List folder contents

31. In which of the following ways can a user become a file's owner? (Choose all that apply.)
    a. Take ownership of the file.
    b. Create the file.
    c. Belong to the File Owner special identity.
    d. Be assigned as the owner by an administrator.

32. Which of the following file and folder permissions allows a user to read, modify, delete, and create files but does not allow the user to change a file's permissions?
    a. Read & execute   c. Write
    b. Modify   d. Full control

Critical Thinking

The following activities give you critical thinking challenges. Case Projects offer a scenario with a problem to solve for which you supply a written solution.

Case Project 4-1: Dealing with a Disk Crash

Last week, a disk containing CSM Tech Publishing's current project manuscripts crashed. Fortunately, there was a backup, but all files that had been added or changed that day were lost. A new disk had to be purchased for overnight delivery, and the data had to be restored. Several days of work time were lost. The owner of CSM Tech wants to know what can be done to prevent the loss of data and time if a disk crashes in the future. The server currently has two disks installed: one for the Windows boot and system volumes and one for manuscript files. The disk used for manuscript files is about one-third full. There's enough money in the budget to purchase up to two new drives if needed. What solution do you recommend, and why?

Case Project 4-2: Creating a Shared Folder Structure

CSM Tech Publishing has asked you to develop a file-sharing system for the company's departments, which include Management, Marketing, Sales, Development, and Editorial. The following are some requirements for the file-sharing solution:

- Management must be able to access all files in all the shares unless stated otherwise and must be able to create, delete, and change files.
- The Management Department must have a share that only it can access, and each member of the department must be able to create, delete, and change files in the share.
- Marketing and Sales should have one common folder that both departments' users have access to. Members of both departments should be able to create new files, have full control over files they create, and view and change files created by other group members. They should not be able to delete files created by other members.
- Sales should have its own share that only Sales and Management have access to. The Sales users must have full control over all files in the share.
- Development and Editorial have their own shares that only these departments and Management have access to. The users from these two departments must have full control over all files in their department shares.

- There should be a public share in which users in the Management Department can create, change, and delete documents, and all other users have the ability only to read the documents.
- There should be a share available to management that no other users can see in a browse list. It contains confidential documents that only selected users in the Management Department have access to.
- Users must be able to restore files they accidentally delete or restore an earlier version of a file without having to use a backup program.
- Sales users must be able to access the files in the Sales share when they're traveling whether they have an Internet connection or not. When Sales users are back in the office, any changed files should synchronize with their mobile devices automatically. All Sales users have a Windows 8.1 laptop or tablet computer running Windows RT 8.1.
- All users except Management users should be limited to 10 GB of space on the volume housing shares. Management users should be limited to 50 GB.

Given these requirements, perform the following tasks and answer the following questions:

1. Design the folder structure and include information about the permissions (sharing and NTFS) you plan to assign to each share and group of users. Name each share appropriately.
2. What tool will you use to create the shares? Why?
3. What protocols and technologies (including file system) will be used to set up these shared folders? Explain the reason for using each protocol or technology.

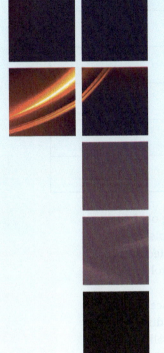

CHAPTER 5

CONFIGURING ADVANCED STORAGE SOLUTIONS

After reading this chapter and completing the exercises, you will be able to:

Work with Storage Spaces

Configure iSCSI

Implement data deduplication

Implement Storage Replica

You have learned how to configure basic storage solutions with direct attached storage. Many applications require advanced storage solutions to provide fault tolerance and high performance. This chapter discusses a variety of methods for creating and configuring advanced storage solutions that provide flexibility, high availability, high performance, and fault tolerance. You'll learn how to implement Storage Spaces, a technology based on virtual disks, configure shared storage for high-availability applications such as server clusters, and implement data deduplication and Storage Replica. Data deduplication helps reduce storage requirements by eliminating duplicated data, whereas Storage Replica provides server-to-server and cluster-to-cluster volume replication for high-availability applications.

Using Storage Spaces

 **Certification**

- **70-740 – Implement storage solutions:**
  Implement server storage

Table 5-1 describes what you need to do the hands-on activities in this chapter.

Table 5-1   Activity requirements

Activity	Requirements	Notes
Activity 5-1: Creating a Storage Space with File and Storage Spaces	ServerSA1	There must be three unallocated disks installed on ServerSA1.
Activity 5-2: Cleaning Up Storage Spaces	ServerSA1	
Activity 5-3: Creating a Storage Space with PowerShell	ServerSA1	
Activity 5-4: Installing the iSCSI Target Server Role Service and Creating an iSCSI Virtual Disk	ServerDC1, ServerDM1, ServerDM2	
Activity 5-5: Configuring an iSCSI Initiator	ServerDC1, ServerDM1, ServerDM2	
Activity 5-6: Removing an iSCSI Target and Virtual Disk	ServerDC1, ServerDM1, ServerDM2	
Activity 5-7: Installing and Configuring Data Deduplication	ServerDC1, ServerDM1	

Storage Spaces, first introduced in Windows Server 2012, provides flexible provisioning of virtual storage. It uses the flexibility available with virtual disks to create volumes from storage pools. A **storage pool** is a collection of physical disks from which virtual disks and volumes are created and assigned dynamically. Volumes created from storage pools can be simple volumes, striped volumes, or fault-tolerant RAID volumes.

Unlike traditional physical disks and volumes created in Disk Management, Storage Spaces can allocate storage by using thin provisioning. **Thin provisioning** uses dynamically expanding disks so that you can provision a large volume, even if you have the physical storage for a volume only half the size. Later, you can add physical disks to the disk pool, and Storage Spaces expands into the additional storage as needed. If the disk pool becomes full, Windows takes it offline to alert you that you need to add physical storage to the pool.

Storage Spaces uses the concept of **just a bunch of disks (JBOD)** in which two or more disks are abstracted to appear as a single disk to the OS but aren't arranged in a specific RAID configuration. JBOD gives you more flexibility because you can simply add a physical disk to a storage pool, and existing volumes can grow into the new space as needed. You can even add external disks to a pool via an external bus architecture, such as SAS or eSATA. If you use an external disk system, it should be a certified JBOD system, preferably using a SAS disk controller. You can find JBOD systems that are certified specifically for Storage Spaces.

Note

Using slower external bus architectures, such as USB, adversely affects your storage solution's overall performance and isn't recommended.

Storage Spaces brings storage flexibility to a Windows server for a fraction of the cost of a traditional storage area network (SAN), which before Storage Spaces was the best way to achieve similar storage features and performance. Storage Spaces offers the following features that are usually found only in traditional SAN-based storage arrays:

- *Disk pooling*—A collection of physical disks viewed as a single storage space from which volumes can be provisioned for the server's use.

- *Data deduplication*—A feature that finds data that exists on a volume multiple times and reduces it to a single instance, thereby reducing space used on the volume. Data deduplication is a role service that can be installed and then enabled on volumes separately. Data deduplication is discussed in more detail later in this chapter in the section "Implementing Data Deduplication."
- *Flexible storage layouts*—Storage Spaces has three storage options, called **storage layouts**:
  - Simple space: A **simple space** is a simple volume with no fault tolerance or **resilience**, as Storage Spaces calls storage that can recover from disk failure. A simple space can use disk striping (RAID 0) if two or more physical disks are available, which provides better performance than a volume on a single disk or a spanned volume. Figure 5-1 shows a simple space using disk striping across two disks. It also shows two files, F1 and F2. F1 is spread across both disks in two parts (F1-a and F1-b). F2 is spread across both disks in four parts (F2-a, F2-b, F2-c, and F2-d).

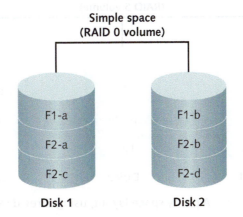

Figure 5-1   A simple space layout, using two disks

  - Mirror space: A **mirror space** is a resilient storage layout configured as a two-way or three-way mirrored volume. A two-way mirror (RAID 1) requires at least two disks in the storage pool, and a **three-way mirror** requires at least five disks. This resilient storage layout maintains data if one disk (two-way mirror) fails or two disks (three-way mirror) fail. Mirror spaces are recommended for all storage applications that require resiliency. Figure 5-2 shows a mirror space with two disks. However, all parts of both files, F1 and F2, are on both Disk 1 and Disk 2, so if one disk fails, the other disk has a complete copy of all the data.

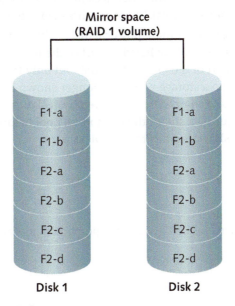

Figure 5-2   A mirror space layout, using two disks

- Parity space: A **parity space** is similar to a RAID 5 volume and can be configured for single parity or dual parity. At least three disks are required for a single parity space, and seven disks are required for a dual parity space. A **dual parity space** can recover from simultaneous failure of two disks. Parity spaces are recommended for archival storage, not standard storage workloads, because calculating parity data decreases performance somewhat. Figure 5-3 shows a parity space with three disks. The same two files are represented in this figure with the files striped across two disks and parity information written to the third disk. The parity information is spread across all three disks. If any disk fails, the parity information on the remaining disks is used to reconstruct missing data from the failed disk.

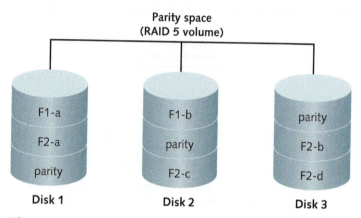

Figure 5-3 A parity space layout, using three disks

- *Storage tiering*—Storage tiering combines the speed of solid state drives (SSDs) with the low cost and high capacity of hard disk drives (HDDs). You can add SSDs to a storage pool with HDDs, and Windows keeps the most frequently accessed data on the faster SSD disks and moves less frequently accessed data to HDDs. This scheme improves performance substantially without the expense of moving all storage to costly SSDs.

Creating Storage Spaces

Storage Spaces is configured with File and Storage Services in Server Manager or PowerShell cmdlets (more than 70 for working with Storage Spaces). There are three components of a storage space:

- *Storage pool*—This consists of one or more physical disks with unallocated space. Physical disks available for adding to a storage pool are listed as part of the **primordial pool**. If a disk already has a volume on it, it's still part of the primordial pool, but only the unallocated space is used for a storage pool. A disk added to a storage pool is no longer shown in Disk Management unless it contains a traditional volume. You need two or more physical disks in a pool if you want to create a resilient storage space. Figure 5-4 shows the primordial pool before any storage pools have been created. Available disks are shown in the Physical Disks pane.

 Note

A disk that has been converted to dynamic isn't listed in the primordial pool and can't be a member of a storage pool.

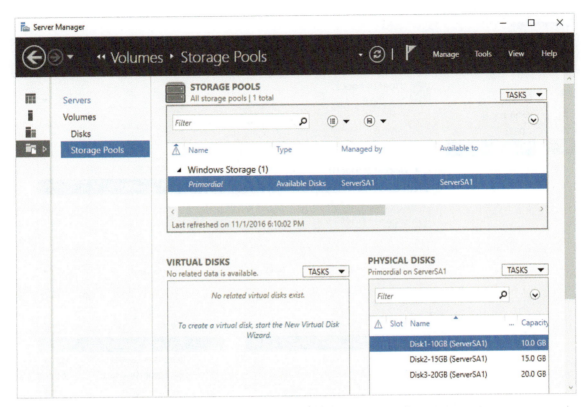

Figure 5-4   The primordial pool

- *Virtual disks*—You create virtual disks from storage pools and choose the storage layout: simple, mirror, or parity. If you choose a storage layout your pool can't support (for example, a parity layout when you have only two disks in the pool), Storage Spaces prompts you to choose another one. Next, you select the provisioning type: thin provisioning (described previously) or **fixed provisioning**, which allocates all space for the virtual disk from the storage pool immediately. Then you specify the disk size. After a virtual disk is created, it's available in Disk Management like any other disk, and you can perform the usual operations on it. Storage Spaces creates the virtual disk as a GUID partition table (GPT) disk. Figure 5-5 shows a new storage pool with three member disks and a virtual disk that's been created. The virtual disk is thin provisioned and uses a parity layout.

Note
You might hear the term *LUN* associated with virtual disks in Storage Spaces. As defined in Chapter 4, a LUN is a logical reference to a unit of storage that could be composed of part of a physical disk or an entire array of disks, which is exactly what a virtual disk is.

- *Volumes*—After you create a virtual disk, you create volumes. Every volume you create on the disk uses the virtual disk's storage layout and provisioning type. For example, if you create two volumes on a virtual disk with a parity layout, both volumes are parity (RAID 5) volumes. You create a

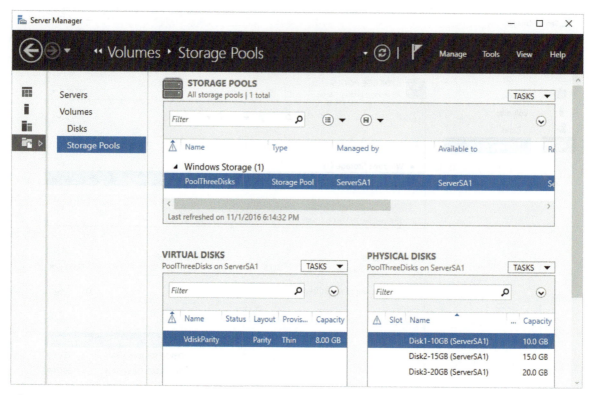

Figure 5-5 A new storage pool and virtual disk

volume on a virtual disk in much the same way as on a traditional disk. You can use File and Storage Services or Disk Management. After a volume is formatted, it's ready to use like any other volume you create. The new volume is available in File Explorer, File and Storage Services, and Disk Management.

Figure 5-6 is a logical view of how these components work. You start with one or more disks that are part of the primordial pool. Next, you create storage pools from one or more of the disks in the primordial pool. In the figure, Pool1 is composed of two disks, and Pool2 is made up of three disks. After a disk is assigned to a pool, it's no longer part of the primordial pool. Two disks labeled "unused" remain part of the primordial pool after Pool1 and Pool2 are created. Two types of virtual disk layouts can be created from Pool1—simple and mirror—because you need at least two disks to create a mirror layout, and a simple layout can be created from any number of disks. You can create any of the three virtual disk layouts from Pool2 because a parity layout requires at least three disks. It's important to understand that you can create more than one virtual disk of any type supported from a pool until you run out of physical disk space in the pool. If you do, you can add disks from the primordial pool to make the pool larger.

From the virtual disks, you create volumes (not shown in Figure 5-6). As mentioned, the volumes you create match the virtual disk's layout. You can create multiple volumes from a single virtual disk as you can with physical disks.

Creating a Storage Pool and Volume with PowerShell

You use the New-StoragePool cmdlet to create a new Storage Pool in PowerShell. First, you'll need to get information about the physical disks you can add to the pool because this information is needed when you run the New-StoragePool cmdlet. For example, if you want to add all disks that are available for pooling, use the following cmdlet:

```
$PoolDisks = Get-PhysicalDisk -CanPool $true
```

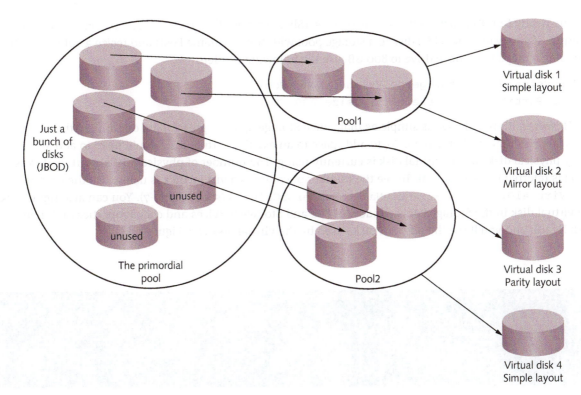

Figure 5-6   Storage Spaces from primordial pool to virtual disk

This command stores the list of disks available for pooling in a variable named $PoolDisks. Next, you want to use that variable in the New-StoragePool cmdlet to create a pool named Pool1 and add the disks contained in the $PoolDisks variable to the pool. The New-StoragePool cmdlet requires the -StorageSubSystemFriendlyName parameter that for local storage you can use "Windows*":

```
New-StoragePool -FriendlyName Pool1 -PhysicalDisks
    $PoolDisks -StorageSubSystemFriendlyName "Windows*"
```

Now that your storage pool is created, you can create a virtual disk and a new volume. To create a virtual disk on Pool1, use the New-Volume cmdlet. When you create a new volume on a storage pool, a virtual disk is automatically created to match the volume name, size, and resiliency setting. The following cmdlet creates a volume named Vol1 with size 500 GB and assigns drive letter V:

```
New-Volume -StoragePoolFriendlyName Pool1 -FriendlyName Vol1 -Size 500 GB
    -DriveLetter V
```

By default, the New-Volume cmdlet creates a fixed size virtual disk configured as a mirror and formatted with NTFS. If you have only one disk in the pool, you must specify a resiliency setting of "Simple" as in -ResiliencySettingName Simple. To specify a thin provisioned disk, use the -ProvisioningType Thin parameter.

Expanding a Storage Pool

One of the advantages of Storage Spaces versus traditional storage is the ability to easily expand the amount of storage available for your virtual disks. Consider that you are using thin provisioning and the maximum size of all of your virtual disks is 300 GB, but they reside on physical disks that total only 250 GB. You find that your virtual disks are approaching the limit of your physical disks and need to expand. A simple solution is to attach a new physical disk to your server, right-click the pool in Server Manager, and click Add Physical Disk (or use the Add-PhysicalDisk PowerShell cmdlet). Once a physical disk is added, you can go to Disk Management, File and Storage Services, or PowerShell and expand any volumes that are nearly full. To expand a volume using PowerShell, you use the `Resize-Partition` cmdlet. For example, if you wanted to add a disk to a storage pool with friendly name Pool1 and resize a volume in the pool that is mapped to the V: drive to 800 GB, use the following cmdlets:

```
Add-PhysicalDisk -StoragePoolFriendlyName Pool1
Resize-Partition -DriveLetter V -size 800 GB
```

However, it's not always as simple as that, since Storage Spaces spreads data out among the physical disks that are in the pool. So, to add space to an existing virtual disk, you'll need to add as many physical disks as the virtual disk is currently using. The number of physical disks a virtual disk is using is referred to as a **column**. To see the number of columns a virtual disk is using, use the cmdlet `Get-VirtualDisk | ft FriendlyName, NumberOfColumns` (see Figure 5-7). You can also right-click the virtual disk in the Storage Pools window of File and Storage Services and click Properties and then click Health and you'll see the physical disks used by the virtual disk (see Figure 5-8).

```
PS C:\Users\Administrator> Get-VirtualDisk | ft FriendlyName, NumberOfColumns

FriendlyName NumberOfColumns
------------ ---------------
Vdisk1                     4
Vdisk2                     3
Vdisk3                     2
```

Figure 5-7   Command to show the number of columns a virtual disk is using

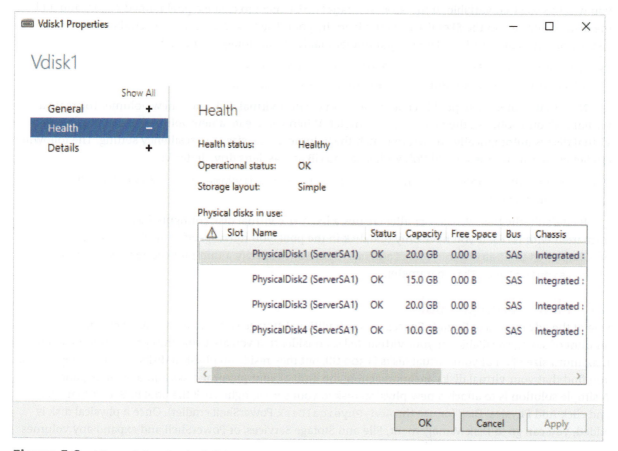

Figure 5-8   View of the physical disks in use by a virtual disk

Once you know how many physical disks a virtual disk is using, you'll want to add the same number of physical disks to the pool before you can expand the size of the virtual disk and then the volume.

> **Note** 📎
>
> When a mirror space is involved, the number of columns doesn't always equal the number of physical disks. To calculate the number of physical disks needed to expand a mirror, multiply the NumberOfColumns value times the NumberOfDataCopies value. You can see these values using the `Get-VirtualDisk | fl` command. A mirror space created with two or three disks will typically have one column and two data copies, requiring two disks to expand it. A mirror space created with four or five disks will typically have two columns and two data copies, requiring four disks to expand it.

Replacing a Failed Physical Disk in a Storage Pool

If you are using a mirror or parity space, your volumes can survive a physical disk failure. However, if one of the disks in a storage pool fails or is failing, you'll want to replace it as soon as possible because your system's performance and reliability will be compromised until you do. To replace a failed or failing physical disk from a storage pool, follow these steps:

1. Identify the problem disk. You may need to check the Windows System event log to find the disk ID, or your disk system may have LED indicators to show you that a disk has failed.

2. Replace the failed physical disk.

3. Add the replacement disk to the pool using File and Storage Services or the PowerShell cmdlet `Add-PhysicalDisk`. Make sure the new disk has at least as much space as the disk it is replacing.

4. Retire the old disk. If a disk fails entirely, Storage Spaces will retire it automatically, but if the disk is in the process of failing (read and write errors on a disk indicate imminent failure), you may need to retire it manually. You can view the health of a disk in File and Storage Services by going to Storage Pools, right-clicking the disk, clicking Properties, and then clicking Health. Or, in PowerShell, type `Get-PhysicalDisk` and look at the `HealthStatus` column. To retire a disk, use the command `Set-PhysicalDisk -FriendlyName DiskName -Usage Retired`. Alternatively, you can select the physical disk that isn't healthy and use that in the `Set-PhysicalDisk` command as follows:

```
$BadDisk = Get-PhysicalDisk -HealthStatus Unhealthy
$BadDisk | Set-PhysicalDisk -Usage Retired
```

> **Note** 📎
>
> Other values for -HealthStatus include Healthy, Unknown, and Warning.

5. Next, you repair the storage pool and all the virtual disk in it:

```
Get-StoragePool -FriendlyName Pool1 | Get-VirtualDisk | RepairVirtualDisk
```

6. Finally, you remove the disk from the storage pool. In the following command, the `$BadDisk` variable was created in Step 4:

```
Remove-PhysicalDisk -StoragePoolFriendlyName Pool1 -PhysicalDisks $BadDisk
```

Depending on how your storage pool is allocated, you may not always need to replace a physical disk that has failed. If your storage pool still has sufficient unallocated space on the remaining disks equivalent to the space used on the failed disk, Storage Spaces will use that space to make up for the missing disk. For example, suppose you have a storage pool that has three identical physical disks (Disk1, Disk2, and Disk3) and a virtual disk that uses the mirror layout with Disk1 and Disk2. If Disk1 fails, the virtual disk will automatically use Disk3 to repair the mirror if Disk3 has sufficient unallocated space to make up for Disk1. The pool and virtual disk will still have a degraded health status until you retire and remove the failed disk from the pool, but the virtual disk will be operational.

Disk Allocation Options

When you add a physical disk to a storage space, you have three options for how that physical disk can be used, which Storage Spaces refers to as the allocation type (see Figure 5-9):

- *Automatic*—An **automatic disk** will be used as Storage Spaces sees fit when a virtual disk is created. With Automatic allocation, Storage Spaces will attempt to use the optimal number of physical disks (columns) when creating a virtual disk. For example, if you have four physical disks in the pool all set to Automatic and you create a simple volume, Storage Spaces will stripe the data across all four physical disks. A disk with Automatic allocation may also be used to automatically repair a resilient volume in the event another disk fails. This is in contrast to Manual allocation as you see.

- *Hot Spare*—A **hot spare disk** will sit idle until it is needed to repair a volume due to disk failure. If a disk in the pool fails, an appropriate hot spare will automatically be put into service without administrator intervention. When that occurs, the Hot Spare disk will be changed to Automatic allocation.

- *Manual*—With **manual disk** allocation, the administrator chooses which disks will be used when creating a virtual disk. For example, if you have four physical disks in the pool set to Manual allocation when you create a virtual disk with a simple layout, you must choose which disks Storage Spaces should use to create the virtual disk. So, you can choose one disk, two, three, or all four. If you are creating a mirror layout virtual disk, you must choose at least two disks, and if you are creating a parity layout virtual disk, you must choose at least three disks. This option is not recommended if the pool also has disks that use Automatic allocation.

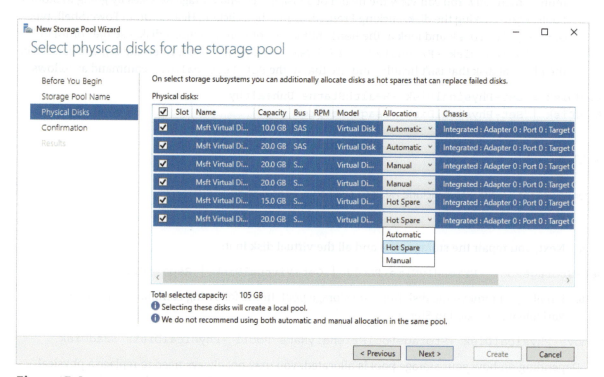

Figure 5-9   Selecting physical disk allocation type

While you can have different disks in the same pool that are allocated as Automatic or Manual (as you saw in Figure 5-9, plus two set as Hot Spare), you can create virtual disks only from physical disks that have the same allocation type. An example is having two physical disks in a pool that are allocated as Automatic and two that are allocated as Manual; when you create a virtual disk, you will have to choose which allocation type to use, and you are presented with only the disks of that allocation type (see Figure 5-10). So, even though you might have four usable disks in the pool, as shown previously in Figure 5-9, you can use only those of the allocation type chosen for any one virtual disk.

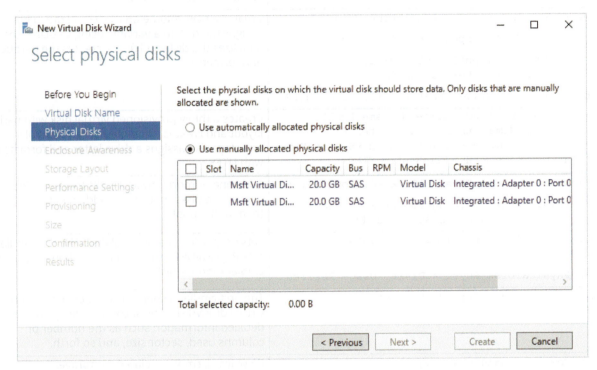

Figure 5-10   Choosing the allocation type to use for a virtual disk

Configuring Enclosure Awareness

As mentioned, you can attach external disk enclosures to a server to expand the amount of storage available and to create additional Storage Spaces. Windows Server 2016 contains a feature called **enclosure awareness** in which Storage Spaces can place copies of data on separate enclosures ensuring that if an entire disk enclosure fails, the data is maintained. To use enclosure awareness, you must enable it during the process of creating a virtual disk (by clicking a simple check box when using the New Virtual Disk Wizard or in PowerShell by using the `-IsEnclosureAware $true` parameter in the `New-VirtualDisk` cmdlet). Enclosure awareness is relevant only if you are using a resilient space such as a mirror space or parity space. You need at least three enclosures, and the allocation mode of all disks in each enclosure must be set to Automatic and the enclosures must be Storage Spaces certified.

Using PowerShell to Manage Storage Spaces

As you have seen, many PowerShell cmdlets are available to work with Storage Spaces. Table 5-2 lists the most common ones.

Table 5-2   PowerShell cmdlets for working with Storage Spaces

PowerShell cmdlet	Function

`$PoolDisks = Get-PhysicalDisk -CanPool $true`
 	
`New-StoragePool -FriendlyName`
`    Pool1 -PhysicalDisks $PoolDisks`
`    -StorageSubSystemFriendlyName "Windows*"`
	Creates a storage pool: first, gets an array of physical disks that can be pooled; then creates the pool.

`New-VirtualDisk Pool1 -FriendlyName Vdisk1` `    -Size 100GB -ProvisioningType Thin`	Creates a thinly provisioned virtual disk named Vdisk1 from storage pool Pool1. By default, resiliency is set to "mirror."

`$NewDisk = Get-Disk -FriendlyName Vdisk1`
 	
`Initialize-Disk -InputObject $NewDisk`
 	
`New-Partition -InputObject $NewDisk`
`    -AssignDriveLetter -UseMaximumSize`
 	
`Format-Volume -DriveLetter F -FileSystem NTFS`
	Creates a new volume on the virtual disk. First, assigns the disk to a variable using Get-Disk, then initializes the disk, and finally creates the partition and formats it.

`New-Volume -StoragePoolFriendlyName Pool1`
`    -FriendlyName NewVol -DriveLetter F:`
`    -ProvisioningType Thin ResiliencySettingName`
`    Parity -Size 50GB -FileSystem NTFS`
	Creates a thinly provisioned virtual disk with parity layout and creates a volume named NewVol in one step; also assigns a drive letter and formats it with NTFS.

`$DisksToAdd = Get-PhysicalDisk -CanPool $True`
 	
`Add-PhysicalDisk -StoragePoolFriendlyName`
`    Pool1 -PhysicalDisks $DisksToAdd`
	Adds one or more physical disks to a pool. First, gets all the disks that can be added and then adds them to the pool.

`Set-PhysicalDisk PhysicalDisk6 -Usage`
`    ManualSelect`
 	
`Set-PhysicalDisk PhysicalDisk6 -Usage Retired`
	Sets properties of a physical disk. The first cmdlet sets PhysicalDisk5 to Manual allocation. The second cmdlet retires a disk.

`Get-VirtualDisk -FriendlyName Vdisk1`	The first cmdlet displays basic information about virtual disk Vdisk1.The second cmdlet provides detailed information such as the number of columns used, sector size, and so forth.
`Get-Command -Module Storage`	Displays all cmdlets related to storage.

Configuring Tiered Storage

Tiered storage was introduced in Storage Spaces in Windows Server 2012 R2. To configure tiered storage, you must have at least one SSD and one HDD as part of a Storage Spaces storage spool. You specify tiered storage when you create a virtual disk with the New Virtual Disk Wizard in Storage Spaces. In the Virtual Disk Name window, click the *Create storage tiers on this virtual disk* check box, as shown in Figure 5-11. If Storage Spaces doesn't recognize a disk as an SSD, you can configure it as one with the following PowerShell cmdlet after the disk has been added to a storage pool:

`Set-PhysicalDisk *diskname* -MediaType SSD`

Note

If you use that PowerShell cmdlet to change the media type of a disk, you might need to press the Refresh button in Server Manager before the disk will be properly recognized as an SSD.

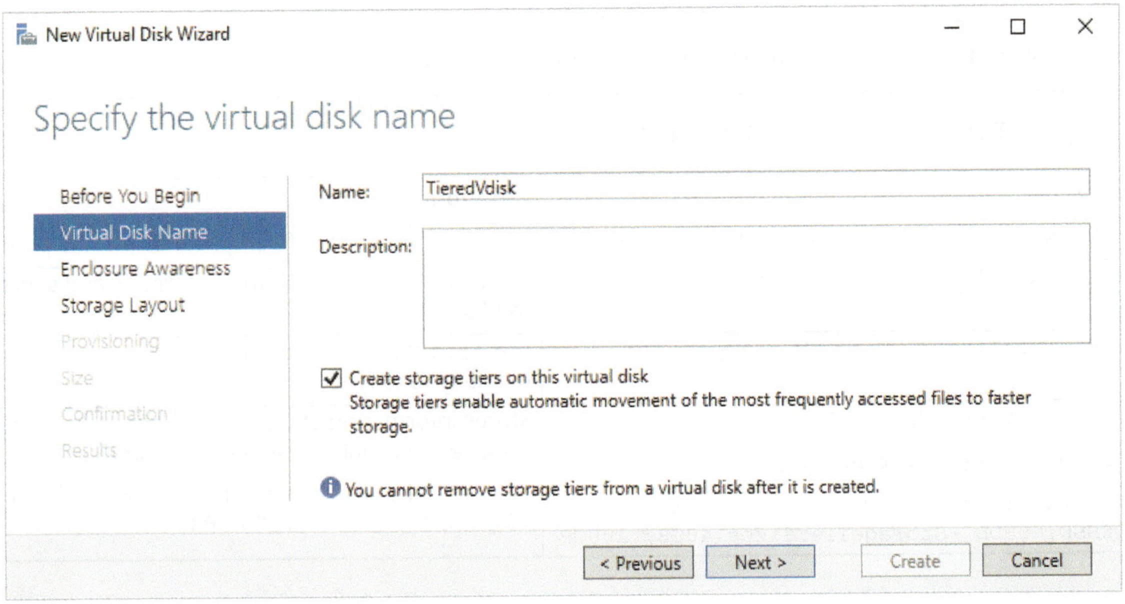

Figure 5-11   Creating a storage tier

After you select the storage layout and provisioning type (storage tiers require fixed provisioning so you can't use thin provisioning), you configure the size of the virtual disk and how you want to use the SSDs and HDDs in the tier (see Figure 5-12). Normally, the amount of space you allocate from SSDs is considerably smaller than that from HDDs. A typical ratio of HDD space to SSD space might be 4 to 1, 5 to 1, or higher. If you need to create more than one virtual disk, you can distribute space from a single SSD among several virtual disks.

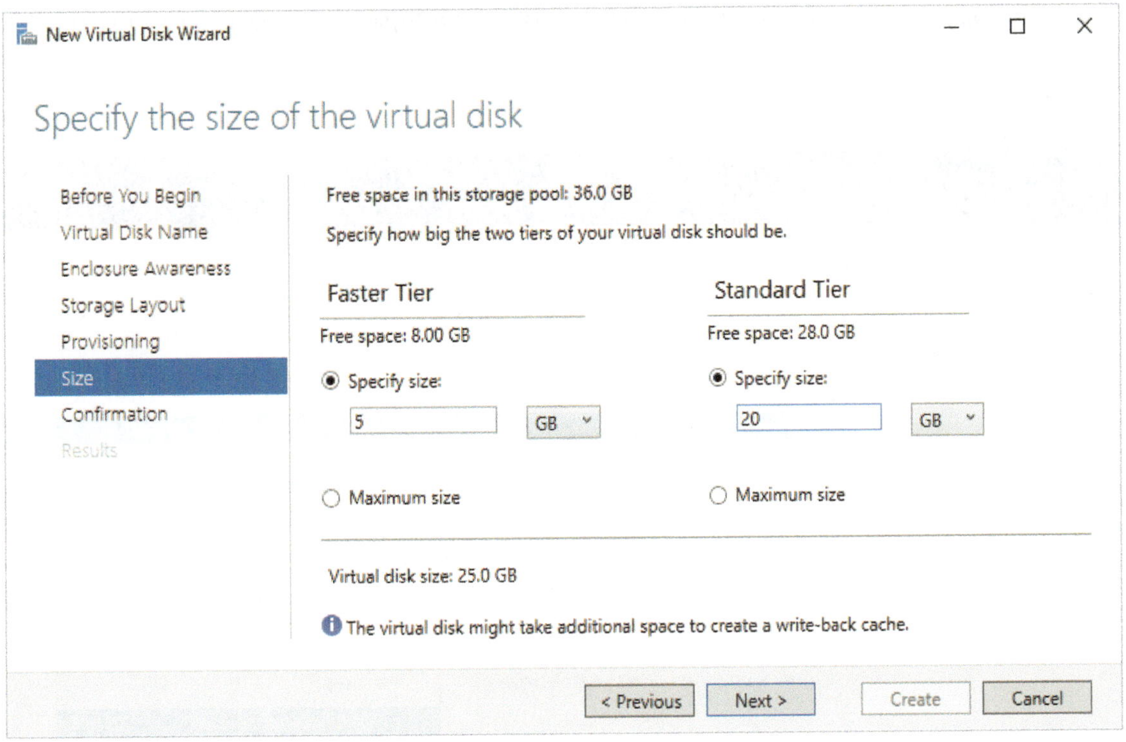

Figure 5-12   Configuring the size of storage tiers

Configuring Tiered Storage with PowerShell

Table 5-3 list some common commands for configuring tiered storage.

Table 5-3	Tiered storage PowerShell cmdlets
Cmdlet	**Description**
`Set-PhysicalDisk diskname -MediaType SSD`	Sets the media type of a physical disk in the pool to SSD
`New-StorageTier SSDTier -MediaType SSD`	Creates a storage tier named `SSDTier` and sets the media type to SSD
`New-StorageTier HDDTier -MediaType HDD`	Creates a storage tier named `HDDTier` and sets the media type to HDD

`$SSD=Get-StorageTier SSDTier`
 	
`$HDD=Get-StorageTier HDDTier`
 	
`New-VirtualDisk diskname -StorageTiers`
`    $SSD, $HDD -StorageTierSizes 40GB, 200GB`
	Stores information about storage tiers `SSDTier` and `HDDTier` in variables named `$SSD` and `$HDD`
	
	Creates a virtual disk named `diskname` and assigns 40 GB to `SSDTier` and 200 GB to `HDDTier`

Activity 5-1: Creating a Storage Space with File and Storage Services

Time Required: 20 minutes

Objective: Create a storage pool, virtual disk, and volume with Storage Spaces.

Required Tools and Equipment: ServerSA1 with three unallocated disks installed

Description: In this activity, you create a storage pool, virtual disk, and volume with Storage Spaces. You also see how Disk Management displays physical disks that have been added to a storage pool.

1. Start ServerSA1, and sign in as **Administrator**, if necessary.
2. In Server Manager, click **File and Storage Services**, and then click **Storage Pools**. Click the **Refresh** icon so that the disks are inventoried and displayed correctly. After the screen refreshes (which might take a minute or so), you see the primordial pool and three disks in the Physical Disks pane, similar to Figure 5-13.

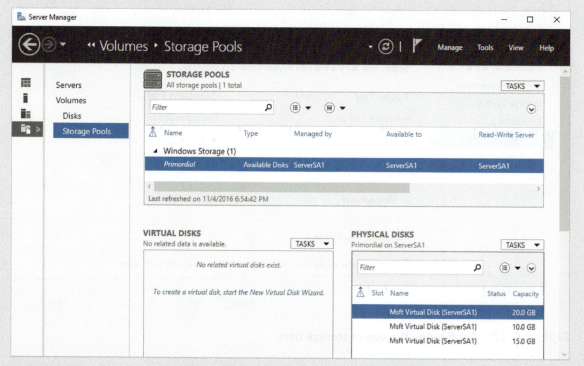

Figure 5-13   The primordial pool with three disks

Note

If you are using Hyper-V virtual machines, the physical disks will be named Msft Virtual Disk (ServerSA1). If you are using another virtualization platform, the virtual disks will be named something else.

3. Right-click the **Primordial** pool and click **New Storage Pool**. In the Before You Begin window of the New Storage Pool Wizard, read the information and click **Next**.

4. In the Storage Pool Name window, type **Pool1** in the Name text box, and then click **Next**.

5. In the Physical Disks window, click all three check boxes (see Figure 5-14). At the bottom of the window is the total capacity of the selected disks. Notice that this is where you can change the allocation type from Automatic to Manual or Hot Spare. Click **Next**.

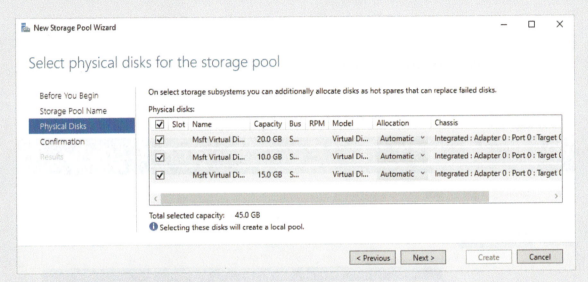

Figure 5-14   Selecting physical disks for a storage pool

6. In the Confirmation window, click **Create**. After the new pool is created, click **Close**. In the Storage Pools window, click **Pool1**. You see the members of the pool in the Physical Disks pane. You no longer see the primordial pool because you don't have more disks available to add to a pool.

7. Open Disk Management, and notice that Disk 1, Disk 2, and Disk 3 are no longer shown because they're part of a storage pool. Close Disk Management.

8. In Server Manager, right-click **Pool1** and click **New Virtual Disk**.

9. The Storage Pool window lists only one pool, so click **OK**. Read the information in the Before You Begin window, and then click **Next**. In the Virtual Disk Name window, type **Vdisk1** in the Name text box. The check box for creating storage tiers is grayed out because an SSD isn't part of the pool. Click **Next**.

10. In the Enclosure Awareness window, the option to enable closure awareness is grayed out since you don't have a Storage Spaces certified enclosure attached to the server. Click **Next**.

11. In the Storage Layout window (see Figure 5-15), notice that the default option is Mirror. Click each option and read the description. Click **Mirror** in the Layout list box, and then click **Next**.

12. In the Provisioning window, click the **Thin** option button, and then click **Next**.

13. In the Size window, type **10** to create a 10 GB virtual disk, and then click **Next**.

14. In the Confirmation window, verify your choices, and then click **Create**. Creating the virtual disk might take a few minutes. Click to clear the **Create a volume when this wizard closes** check box. Click **Close**. The new virtual disk is listed in the Virtual Disks pane (see Figure 5-16).

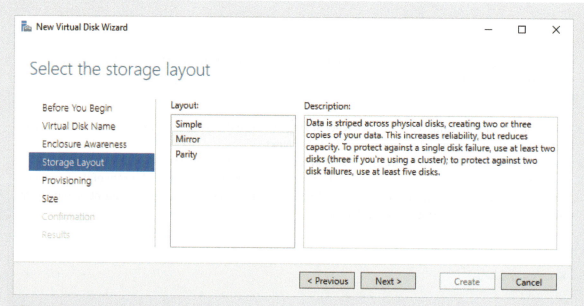

Figure 5-15   Selecting a storage layout

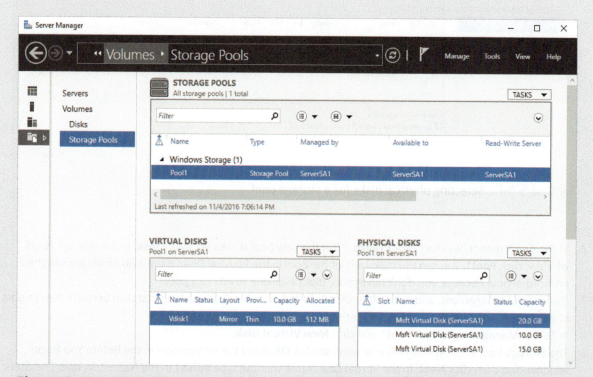

Figure 5-16   A new virtual disk

15. Open Disk Management to see that the new virtual disk is available. Close Disk Management. At this point, you don't need to create a new volume, but to do so, you follow the same procedure as in earlier activities using either File and Storage Services or Disk Management.
16. In File and Storage Services, right-click **Vdisk1** and click **Properties**. In the Vdisk1 Properties window, click **Health**. You see that all three physical disks are in use.
17. Continue to the next activity.

Activity 5-2: Cleaning Up Storage Spaces

Time Required: 20 minutes

Objective: Delete the virtual disk and storage pool created in the previous activity.

Required Tools and Equipment: ServerSA1

Description: You delete the storage space you created in the previous activity.

1. On ServerSA1, open Server Manager, if necessary.
2. In Server Manager, click **File and Storage Services**, and then click **Storage Pools**. In the Virtual Disks section, right-click **Vdisk1** and click **Delete Virtual Disk**. When prompted to continue, click **Yes**.
3. In the Storage Pools section, right-click **Pool1** and click **Delete Storage Pool**. When prompted to delete the pool, click **OK**. The disks are returned to the primordial pool.
4. Continue to the next activity.

Activity 5-3: Creating a Storage Space with PowerShell

Time Required: 20 minutes

Objective: Create a storage pool, virtual disk, and volume using PowerShell.

Required Tools and Equipment: ServerSA1 with three unallocated disks installed

Description: In this activity, you create a storage pool, virtual disk, and volume with PowerShell.

1. On ServerSA1, open a PowerShell window as follows: Click the **search icon** next to Start, type **power**, and then click **Windows PowerShell** in the search results.
2. You will add all available disks to the pool using the default allocation type of Automatic. Type **$PoolDisks=Get-PhysicalDisk -CanPool $True** and press **Enter**.
3. To create a new pool, type **New-StoragePool -FriendlyName Pool1 -PhysicalDisks $PoolDisks -StorageSubSystemFriendlyName "Windows*"** and press **Enter**.
4. To create a new volume and parity layout virtual disk, format the volume, and assign a drive letter, type **New-Volume -StoragePoolFriendlyName Pool1 -FriendlyName NewVol -DriveLetter V -ProvisioningType Thin ResiliencySettingName Parity -Size 10GB** and press **Enter**. Note that it was not necessary to specify the format since NTFS is selected by default. When the command is completed, you see output showing information about the new volume.
5. To see information about the new virtual disk, type **Get-VirtualDisk** and press **Enter**. To see more details about the virtual disk displayed in list format, type **Get-VirtualDisk | FL** and press **Enter**. Look for the NumberOfColumns row and see that it uses three columns. Type **Get-VirtualDisk | FT FriendlyName, Size, NumberOfColumns** and press **Enter**. This command shows only specific properties of the virtual disk displayed in table format.
6. Type **Get-VirtualDisk | Where-Object -Property OperationalStatus -eq OK** and press **Enter**. Use this cmdlet to see virtual disks according to their operational status. Some of the possible operational status values include OK, Detached, Degraded, Lost Communication, and Suboptimal. Next, type **Get-VirtualDisk -HealthStatus Healthy** and press **Enter**. The other possible health status values are Unhealthy, Warning, and Unknown.
7. Now, you will delete the volume, virtual disk, and storage pool. Type **Remove-VirtualDisk NewVol** and press **Enter**. Press **Enter** to confirm. Both the volume and virtual disk are deleted. Type **Remove-StoragePool Pool1** and press **Enter**. Press **Enter** to confirm.
8. Verify that the three disks in Pool1 were returned to the primordial pool and are once again available to be placed in a pool. Type **Get-PhysicalDisk -CanPool $True** and press **Enter**.
9. Shut down ServerSA1.

Configuring iSCSI

Certification

- 70-740 – Implement storage solutions:
  Implement server storage

Up to now, we have focused on working with local storage in which a single Windows server manages locally attached disks and virtual disks. However, some advanced functions such as server clusters and virtual machine live migration require shared storage in which multiple servers can access storage devices through a SAN. This section discusses how to implement a SAN using the Internet Small Computer System Interface (iSCSI) protocol.

Implementing a SAN with iSCSI

A SAN is a storage system that uses high-speed networking technologies to give servers fast access to large amounts of shared disk storage. The storage on a SAN appears to the server OS as though it's physically attached to the server. You can set up a SAN with Windows servers by using the iSCSI protocol, which carries SCSI device commands over an IP network. There are two main components in a Windows Server 2016 iSCSI SAN solution:

- *iSCSI target*—An **iSCSI target** is a logical storage space made available to iSCSI clients by a server running the iSCSI Target Server role service. The iSCSI target consists of one or more virtual disks on the iSCSI target server.

- *iSCSI initiator*—An **iSCSI initiator** is the iSCSI client that sends iSCSI commands to the iSCSI target. Each iSCSI initiator is assigned an **iSCSI qualified name (IQN)** that the iSCSI target uses to give it access to iSCSI storage. The IQN is an identifier that iSCSI targets and initiators use to identify the iSCSI device in an iSCSI connection. An IQN—for example, `iqn.1991-05.com.microsoft:ServerDM1.MCSA2016.local`—follows this format:

  - The literal string `iqn` followed by a period.
  - The date the naming authority took ownership of the domain in the format *yyyy-mm* followed by a period. On Microsoft iSCSI devices, the date is always 1991-05.
  - The reverse domain name of the authority followed by a colon. On Microsoft iSCSI devices, it's `com.microsoft:`.
  - The name of the iSCSI target or initiator.

Windows Server 2016 includes both the iSCSI initiator, which is preinstalled, and the iSCSI target, which is installed as a role service under File and Storage Services. Figure 5-17 shows a SAN and the relationship between an iSCSI target and iSCSI initiators. In the figure, the iSCSI target server makes storage available to iSCSI initiators as **block-level storage**, which the storage client sees as a local drive. The storage can be formatted and volumes can be created like any other local storage device. Conversely, **file-level storage** is storage the client has access to only as files and folders. A Windows file share is file-level storage.

The iSCSI target makes storage available to iSCSI initiators as an iSCSI virtual disk, also called an **iSCSI logical unit number (LUN)**. An iSCSI LUN is a reference ID to a logical drive the iSCSI initiator uses when accessing storage on the iSCSI target server. An iSCSI target can contain one or more iSCSI LUNs, depending on how many virtual disks are associated with the iSCSI target.

Note 📎

The iSCSI initiator is also available in Windows client OSs such as Windows 10 from the Administrative Tools menu in Control Panel.

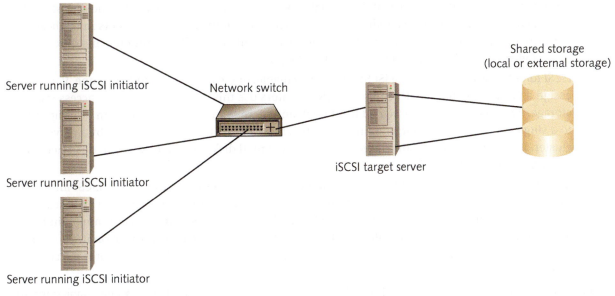

Figure 5-17   A SAN with iSCSI

Configuring an iSCSI Target

An iSCSI target is installed on the server hosting storage for the SAN. The storage can be internal hard drives or external disk enclosures connected through a high-speed bus, such as e-SATA or SAS. An iSCSI target allows servers running the iSCSI initiator to access shared storage by using the iSCSI protocol over standard network technologies, such as Ethernet. From the viewpoint of an iSCSI initiator, the storage appears as a local volume.

Two components make up the iSCSI target software in Windows Server 2016:

- *iSCSI target server*—This required component gives iSCSI initiators access to shared storage.
- *iSCSI target storage provider*—Although this component isn't required, it provides Virtual Disk Service (VDS) and Volume Shadow Copy Service (VSS) support to applications needing these services.

The general steps for configuring an iSCSI target are as follows:

1. Install the iSCSI Target Server role service and, optionally, the iSCSI Target Storage Provider role service.
2. Create an iSCSI virtual disk.
3. Create an iSCSI target and assign one or more iSCSI virtual disks to the target.

Steps 2 and 3 are combined when you use the iSCSI Virtual Disk Wizard described in the next section.

Creating an iSCSI Virtual Disk

You create an iSCSI virtual disk with the iSCSI Virtual Disk Wizard accessed via File and Storage Services. This wizard walks you through the process as you provide the following information:

1. *Virtual disk location*—Select the server and volume for storing the virtual disk. By default, it's stored in a folder named iSCSIVirtualDisks that the wizard creates in the root of the selected volume. You can also specify a custom path, such as V:\iSCSI\disks.
2. *Virtual disk name*—Assign a name and optional description to the virtual disk. The name, in VHDX virtual disk format, is the name of the virtual disk file. For example, if you accepted the default folder location on volume V and assigned the name Vdisk1, the virtual disk is stored in V:\iSCSIVirtualDisks\Vdisk1.vhdx.

3. *Virtual disk size*—Specify the size of the virtual disk. You can also specify whether the disk should be a fixed size, dynamically expanding, or differencing disk. A fixed size disk results in the best performance. A differencing disk requires a path to a parent virtual disk. A differencing disk is a type of virtual disk that you will learn about in Chapter 7.

4. *iSCSI target*—Specify an existing iSCSI target, if available, or create one. If you create one, you assign a name and optional description. iSCSI initiators use this descriptive name to access the storage. Every virtual disk is assigned to a target, and more than one virtual disk can be assigned to a single target. A sample target name might be Cluster1 if the target is to be used by a server cluster. If you specify an existing target, creating the virtual disk is complete, so you don't need to perform Steps 5 and 6.

5. *Identify iSCSI initiators*—Specify the iSCSI initiators that can access the virtual disk. iSCSI initiators that have been given access to the virtual disk can discover and connect to the target. They can be identified by IQN, DNS name, IP address, or MAC address. If an iSCSI initiator is running Windows Server 2012 or later and you have already started the iSCSI initiator client software on it, you can query the initiator computer for its ID. You can identify more than one iSCSI initiator if the storage will be used in a server cluster.

6. *Select authentication*—Challenge-Handshake Authentication Protocol (CHAP) can be enabled for an iSCSI initiator to authenticate to the iSCSI target and reverse CHAP can be enabled for the target to authenticate to the initiator. Authentication is optional and in most cases, you don't need to enable it. If you need a secure connection to the iSCSI target, you can configure IPsec after the virtual disk is created.

Configuring an iSCSI Initiator

The iSCSI initiator is built into Windows Server 2012 and Windows 8 and later. In Windows Server, you access it from the Tools menu in Server Manager or by using PowerShell. The first time you run the iSCSI initiator configuration software, you're asked whether you want to start the Microsoft iSCSI service now and each time Windows starts. If you want the computer to connect to the iSCSI target automatically each time Windows starts, click Yes; otherwise, you can click No and start the service manually in the Services console.

When you open the iSCSI initiator for the first time and start the service, the iSCSI Initiator Properties dialog box opens. It is where you specify a target to connect with by entering the server's fully qualified domain name. The initiator software queries the server to see whether it hosts any targets the initiator has been granted permission to access. An iSCSI target server might be hosting more than one target, so a dialog box opens with a list of all targets discovered. Select the target and click Connect. (If only one target is listed, you're connected automatically.) Any virtual disks associated with the target are available to the client computer. You have to bring the disks online, initialize them, and format them in Disk Management before connecting to them for the first time.

The iSCSI initiator doesn't reconnect to a target automatically each time Windows starts unless you configure it to do so. In the Volume and Devices tab of the iSCSI Initiator Properties dialog box, you can configure specific devices or all available devices to reconnect automatically at Windows startup.

The steps for configuring the iSCSI Initiator in PowerShell are as follows:

1. Create a new iSCSI Target portal using the `New-IscsiTargetPortal -TargetPortal` `ServerName` cmdlet where `ServerName` is the name of the server hosting the iSCSI virtual hard disk.

2. View the available iSCSI targets (there could be more than one) using the `Get-IscsiTarget` cmdlet.

3. Connect to the iSCSI targets with `Get-IscsiTarget | Connect-IscsiTarget`.

4. To see the current iSCSI connections, use `Get-IscsiConnection`, and to see current sessions, use `Get-IscsiSession`.

5. To see available iSCSI disks, use `Get-IscsiSession | Get-Disk`.

Table 5-4 lists some commands for configuring iSCSI.

Table 5-4   iSCSI PowerShell cmdlets

Cmdlet	Description
`Get-IscsiServerTarget`	Shows information about an iSCSI target
`Get-IscsiVirtualDisk`	Shows information about an iSCSI virtual disk
`New-IscsiServerTarget`	Creates an iSCSI target
`New-IscsiVirtualDisk`	Creates an iSCSI virtual disk
`Set-IscsiServerTarget`	Configures settings of an iSCSI target
`Set-IscsiVirtualDisk`	Configures settings of an iSCSI virtual disk
`Get-Command -Module IscsiTarget`	Displays all cmdlets related to iSCSI targets
iSCSI initiator cmdlets	**Description**
`Connect-IscsiTarget`	Connects an initiator to a target
`New- IscsiServerTargetPortal`	Creates a portal from an iSCSI initiator to an iSCSI server target
`Disconnect-IscsiTarget`	Disconnects an initiator from a target
`Get-IscsiTarget`	Shows information about all currently connected targets
`Get-IscsiConnection`	Shows the current iSCSI connection
`Get-IscsiSession`	Shows current iSCSI sessions
`Get-Command -Module iSCSI`	Displays all cmdlets related to iSCSI initiators

Activity 5-4: Installing the iSCSI Target Server Role Service and Creating an iSCSI Virtual Disk

Time Required: 15 minutes
Objective: Install the iSCSI Target Server role service and create an iSCSI virtual disk.
Required Tools and Equipment: ServerDC1, ServerDM1, ServerDM2
Description: In this activity, you install the iSCSI Target Server role service and then create a 10 GB iSCSI virtual disk and assign it to an iSCSI target.

1. Start ServerDC1 and ServerDM1. Sign in to ServerDM1 as the domain administrator. (*Note:* Be sure you sign in to ServerDM1 as the domain administrator MCSA2016\administrator, not the local administrator).

2. On ServerDM1, open a PowerShell window. To install the iSCSI Target Server and iSCSI Target Storage Provider role services, type **Install-WindowsFeature FS-iSCSITarget-Server, iSCSITarget-VSS-VDS** and press **Enter**. Close PowerShell after the installation is complete.

3. Sign in to ServerDM2 as the domain **Administrator**. If you are prompted to enter your password for Administrator, press **Esc** to switch users, then press **Esc** again, and select **Other user**. Type **mcsa2016\administrator**, press **Tab**, type the password, and then press **Enter**.

4. Type **PowerShell**, press **Enter**, and then type **Start-Service msiSCSI** and press **Enter** to start the iSCSI initiator service on ServerDM2.

5. Switch to **ServerDM1**, and in the left pane of Server Manager, click **File and Storage Services**. Click **iSCSI**.

6. In the right pane, click the **To create an iSCSI virtual disk, click the New iSCSI Virtual Disk Wizard** link.
7. In the iSCSI Virtual Disk Location window, ensure that the **Select by volume** option button is selected. By default the C: volume is selected as the location to store the iSCSI virtual disks as shown in Figure 5-18. Click **Next**.
8. In the iSCSI Virtual Disk Name window, type **Vdisk1** in the Name text box, and click **Next**.
9. In the iSCSI Virtual Disk Size window, type **10** in the Size text box, click the **Dynamically expanding** option button (see Figure 5-19), and then click **Next**.

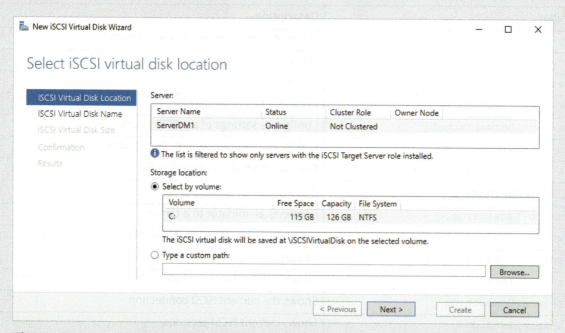

Figure 5-18 Specifying the iSCSI virtual disk location

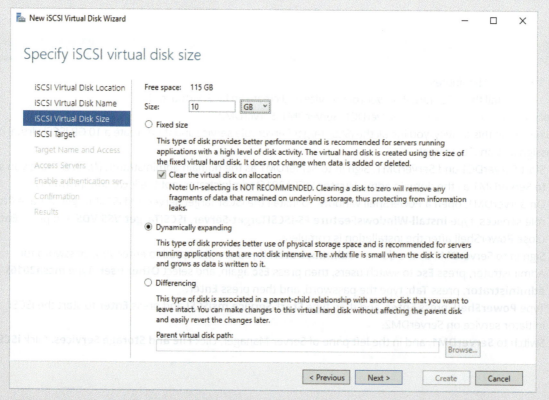

Figure 5-19 Specifying the size and type of virtual disk

10. In the iSCSI Target window, because there are no existing targets, accept the default option **New iSCSI target** and click **Next**.

11. In the Target Name and Access window, type **ServerDM1target** and click **Next**.

12. In the Access Servers window, click **Add**. In the Add initiator ID dialog box, click the **Query initiator computer for ID** option button, if necessary, and type **ServerDM2.MCSA2016.local** in the text box (see Figure 5-20). This step allows ServerDM2 to access to the iSCSI target. Click **OK**.

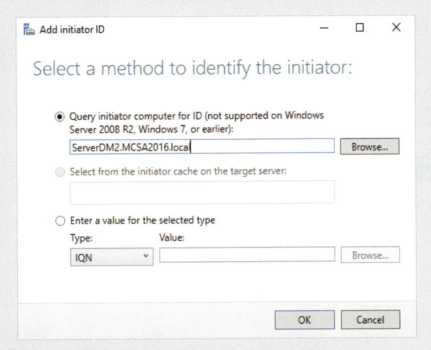

Figure 5-20   Adding an iSCSI initiator to the target

13. The server queries ServerDM2 to get its IQN (see Figure 5-21), which is why you started the iSCSI service on ServerDM2 first. If you were configuring shared storage for use by a server cluster, you could add more initiators. Click **Next**.

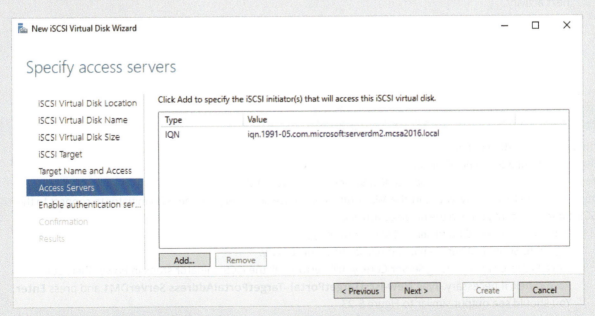

Figure 5-21   The Access Servers window after adding an iSCSI initiator to the target

14. In the Enable authentication service window, click **Next** since you will use Active Directory for authentication. In the Confirmation window (see Figure 5-22), verify the settings and click **Create**. After the iSCSI virtual disk is created, click **Close**.

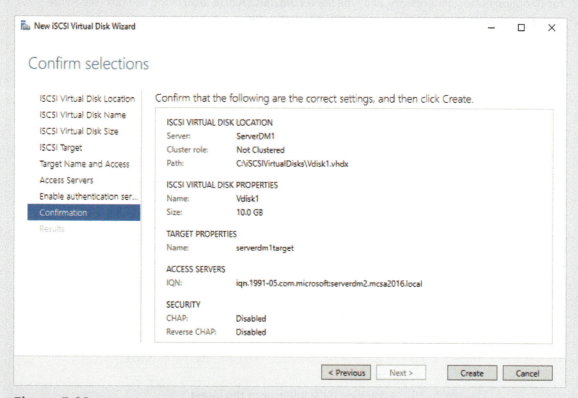

Figure 5-22   Confirming the new iSCSI virtual disk

15. In File and Storage Services, you see the new virtual disk and the iSCSI target. If you need to make changes to either, you can right-click it and click Properties. Stay signed in to both servers and continue to the next activity.

Activity 5-5: Configuring an iSCSI Initiator

Time Required: 10 minutes
Objective: Configure an iSCSI initiator.
Required Tools and Equipment: ServerDC1, ServerDM1, ServerDM2
Description: In this activity, you start the Microsoft iSCSI service and configure the iSCSI initiator to connect to the iSCSI target you configured in the previous activity.

1. Make sure ServerDC1 and ServerDM1 are running.
2. Sign in to ServerDM2 as domain administrator, if necessary.
3. Since ServerDM2 is running Server Core, you'll perform all the iSCSI Initiator steps in PowerShell. Start PowerShell, if necessary. Type **New-IscsiTargetPortal -TargetPortalAddress ServerDM1** and press **Enter**. You should see output similar to Figure 5-23.

```
PS C:\Users\administrator.MCSA2016> New-IscsiTargetPortal -TargetPortalAddress serverdm1


InitiatorInstanceName  :
InitiatorPortalAddress :
IsDataDigest           : False
IsHeaderDigest         : False
TargetPortalAddress    : serverdm1
TargetPortalPortNumber : 3260
PSComputerName         :
```

Figure 5-23   Creating a new iSCSI target portal

4. Next, type **Get-IscsiTarget** and press **Enter**. You'll see the IQN for ServerDM1 in the output.
5. Type **Get-IscsiTarget | Connect-IscsiTarget** and press **Enter** to connect to the target. You see output similar to that in Figure 5-24, which shows you the iSCSI session details. Now that you are connected, you can see the session details by typing Get-iSCSISession.

```
PS C:\Users\administrator.MCSA2016> Get-IscsiTarget | Connect-IscsiTarget


AuthenticationType    : NONE
InitiatorInstanceName : ROOT\ISCSIPRT\0000_0
InitiatorNodeAddress  : iqn.1991-05.com.microsoft:serverdm2.mcsa2016.local
InitiatorPortalAddress : 0.0.0.0
InitiatorSideIdentifier : 400001370000
IsConnected           : True
IsDataDigest          : False
IsDiscovered          : False
IsHeaderDigest        : False
IsPersistent          : False
NumberOfConnections   : 1
SessionIdentifier     : ffff930fbbb70010-4000013700000002
TargetNodeAddress     : iqn.1991-05.com.microsoft:serverdm1-serverdm1target-target
TargetSideIdentifier  : 0100
PSComputerName        :
```

Figure 5-24   Connecting to an iSCSI target

6. To see the disks available, type **Get-iSCSISession | Get-Disk** and press **Enter**. You see output similar to that in Figure 5-25. You see the iSCSI disk that you created on ServerDM1. Note the disk number as you will use it in later steps. In Figure 5-25, the disk number is 5.

```
PS C:\Users\administrator.MCSA2016> Get-IscsiSession | Get-Disk

Number Friendly Name Serial Number              HealthStatus     OperationalStatus    Total Size Partition
                                                                                                 Style
------ ------------- -------------              ------------     -----------------    ---------- ---------
5      MSFT Virtu... 0D8554F7-98EF-423A-9868-05766... Healthy     Offline                 10 GB RAW
```

Figure 5-25   Listing available iSCSI disks on the target

7. Type **Get-Disk** and press **Enter** to list local disks. You see the 10 GB iSCSI disk from the previous step because from ServerDM2's perspective, the iSCSI disk is local storage. You can now manage the disk like you would a locally attached disk.
8. Since the iSCSI disk is offline, you need to bring it online and initialize it. In the following two commands, be sure the disk number corresponds with the disk number you saw in Step 6. Type

Set-Disk -Number 5 -IsOffline $False and press **Enter**. To initialize it, type **Initialize-Disk -Number 5** and press **Enter**. You can now create a volume and format the disk as you would any other disk.

9. Go to ServerDM1 and click **File and Storage Services**, and then click **iSCSI**, if necessary. Click the **Refresh** button to refresh the display. In the iSCSI Virtual Disks section, you see that the virtual disk's status is Connected, and in the iSCSI Targets section, you see that the target status is Connected (see Figure 5-26).

Figure 5-26   The status of iSCSI devices on the iSCSI target server

10. Continue to the next activity.

Activity 5-6: Removing an iSCSI Target and Virtual Disk

Time Required: 10 minutes

Objective: Remove iSCSI.

Required Tools and Equipment: ServerDC1, ServerDM1, ServerDM2

Description: In this activity, you disconnect the iSCSI target and stop the iSCSI initiator service and then remove the target.

1. Make sure ServerDC1 and ServerDM1 are running.
2. Sign in to ServerDM2 as domain administrator, if necessary.
3. Start PowerShell, if necessary. Type **Get-iSCSITarget | Disconnect-iSCSITarget** and press **Enter**. Pres **Enter** to confirm.
4. Type **Get-Disk** and press **Enter** to verify that the disk is no longer connected to ServerDM1.
5. Type **Stop-Service msiSCSI** and press **Enter** to stop the iSCSI initiator service.
6. On ServerDM1, in the iSCSI section of File and Storage Services, press the **Refresh** button and you will see ServerDM2 is no longer connected.
7. Right-click the iSCSI virtual disk and click **Remove iSCSI Virtual Disk**. In the Remove iSCSI Virtual Disk dialog box, click the check box next to **Delete the iSCSI virtual disk file from the disk** and click **OK.**
8. Shut down all servers.

The Internet Storage Name Service

The **Internet Storage Name Service (iSNS)** is an IP-based protocol used to communicate between iSNS clients and servers. An iSNS client is an iSCSI initiator running the iSNS protocol that discovers iSCSI targets. An iSNS server provides a management platform for iSCSI devices similar to those in a Fibre Channel SAN. The iSNS protocol can actually be used in networks running Fibre Channel SANs, but the Microsoft iSNS server supports only iSCSI devices.

iSNS is essentially a central storage location for iSCSI devices, so iSCSI can be managed centrally when you have many servers providing iSCSI targets. iSNS offers the following benefits for iSCSI SANs on large networks:

- *Scalability*—Setting up iSCSI SANs on larger IP networks is easier.
- *Manageability*—Management of iSCSI targets, initiators, and management nodes can be centralized.
- *Monitoring*—You can monitor the status of iSCSI devices and receive change notifications.

iSCSI initiators use iSNS by sending queries to the iSNS server to discover iSCSI targets and receive notifications about new iSCSI targets or targets that are no longer available. iSCSI targets use iSNS by registering with the iSNS server so that their status is available to iSCSI initiators.

Implementing iSNS

To implement iSNS in Windows Server 2016, install the iSNS Server Service feature with the Add Roles and Features Wizard or PowerShell. After the feature is installed, configure it by opening iSNS Server from the Tools menu in Server Manager (see Figure 5-27). The General tab of the Properties dialog box shows the currently registered iSCSI devices.

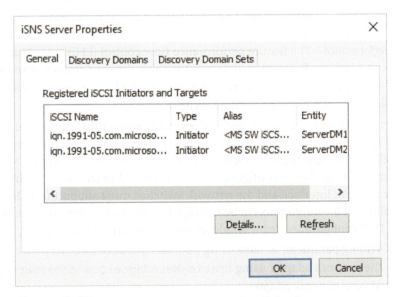

Figure 5-27   The iSNS Server Properties dialog box

You must configure an iSCSI initiator to register with the iSNS server. To register an iSCSI initiator, add an iSNS server in the Discovery tab of the iSCSI Initiator Properties dialog box. The Discovery Domains tab of the iSNS Server Properties dialog box is where you create groups of iSCSI devices to partition iSCSI resources. Creating discovery domains lets you limit which targets iSCSI initiators can discover and connect to. A discovery domain named *Default DD* is created automatically, and all registered iSCSI devices are added to it. You can create additional domains and move devices to them as needed to group devices together. An iSCSI target can be discovered by an initiator only if the two are in the same discovery domain.

> **Note**
>
> To register a server running Server Core with an iSNS server, you can use the `iSCSIcli.exe` command from a command prompt. Type `iscsicli` and press Enter. First, you must create a firewall exception for iSNS. Type `FirewallExemptiSNSServer` and press Enter. Then add the iSNS server; for example, type `AddiSNSServer ServerDM1` and press Enter.

You can further partition devices by creating discovery domain sets, which consist of one or more discovery domains. A discovery domain set named *Default DDS* is created automatically and contains Default DD. Discovery domain sets can be enabled or disabled. iSCSI targets in disabled discovery domain sets can't be discovered by an iSCSI initiator.

Configuring Data Center Bridging

Data center bridging (DCB) is an enhancement to Ethernet that provides additional features for use in enterprise data centers, in particular where server clustering and SANs are in use. As it pertains to SANs and iSCSI, Ethernet by itself has some problems. Ethernet is a *best-effort* delivery system that doesn't guarantee delivery of frames. Lost frames can be tolerated by many applications because network protocols like TCP detect missing data and retransmit it. However, storage is less forgiving of lost data even if that data will eventually be retransmitted. Storage input/output cannot easily tolerate delays, so DCB was designed specifically to prevent delays in delivery of data in iSCSI applications and create what is referred to as a *lossless* environment, meaning a network environment in which data delivery is guaranteed without undue delays. DCB improves performance in iSCSI deployments in the following ways:

- *Quality of Service (QoS)*—Bandwidth can be allocated on a per protocol basis, ensuring that iSCSI traffic gets a minimum of network bandwidth.
- *Deterministic performance*—The feature performance flow control (PFC) ensures a consistent stream of data, providing a lossless Ethernet environment with no dropped frames or retransmissions.
- *DCB Exchange*—This provides automatic configuration of iSCSI parameters between DCB-enabled network interfaces and DCB-enabled network switches.

Windows Server 2016 supports DCB as an installable feature using the Add Roles and Features Wizard in Server Manager or the `Install-WindowsFeature Data-Center-Bridging` PowerShell cmdlet. You can list the PowerShell cmdlets specific to configuring DCB using the `Get-Command -Module DCBQoS` cmdlet. Although there are a number of configuration settings possible with DCB, it's important to understand that your network interface and the network switches must support DCB. By default, network interfaces are set to allow DCB configuration to be managed by the switch the interface is connected to. If you want to manage DCB configuration from Windows Server, perform these steps:

- Turn the DCBX Willing parameter to false using `Set-NetQoSDcbxSetting -Willing 0`.
- Enable DCB on the network adapter using `Enable-NetAdapterQos Ethernet` replacing *Ethernet* with the name of your network adapter.

Configuring Multipath IO (MPIO)

Multipath IO (MPIO) provides fault tolerance for Windows storage networks, including iSCSI SANs. As the name implies, MPIO provides a storage server, for example, an iSCSI server, with multiple paths between the server and the actual storage. Microsoft MPIO supports Fibre Channel, iSCSI, and SAS interfaces. The primary requirement is that the server must have at least two interfaces with a connection to the storage network. For example, iSCSI SANs work over Ethernet networks so two network interfaces must have access to the iSCSI network. For serial attached SCSI (SAS) shared storage, there must be two or more SAS adapters with a physical connection to the storage array.

MPIO is an installable feature that can be installed using the Add Roles and Features Wizard or using PowerShell with `Install-WindowsFeature Multipath-IO`. Once installed, the tool MPIO is added to

Server Manager where you can install support for the type of storage device you need, for example, iSCSI or SAS (see Figure 5-28). If Windows detects devices that are MPIO compliant, they will be listed. After you add devices, you must restart the computer.

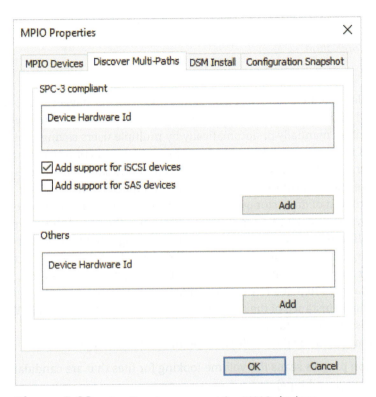

Figure 5-28   Configuring support for MPIO devices

After a reboot, supported MPIO devices will be listed on the General tab of the MPIO Properties dialog box. On your iSCSI Initiator computers, you enable the MPIO to the target from the Targets tab by clicking Properties from the Targets tab, clicking Add session, and then clicking Enable multi-path (see Figure 5-29). Using PowerShell, just add the `-IsMultipathEnabled $True` argument in the `Connect-IscsiTarget` cmdlet.

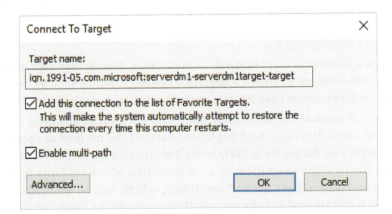

Figure 5-29   Configuring MPIO on an iSCSI Initiator

With MPIO enabled, if one of the network interfaces loses connection to the iSCSI target, the other interface will automatically take over the iSCSI connection, assuming that the other interface has a path to the iSCSI target. MPIO's primary applications are with highly available failover clusters that use iSCSI SANs and when deploying clustered Storage Spaces.

Implementing Data Deduplication

 **Certification**

- **70-740 – Implement storage solutions:**
  Implement data deduplication

The sheer number of files and the quantity of data stored on servers is staggering. To make matters worse, much of the data stored in those files is duplicated. Data duplication comes from multiple versions of the same file being saved either manually or automatically by multiple users saving copies of shared files and from multiple copies of the same email (including attachments such as photos) being sent to dozens, or even thousands, of users. In addition, virtual disks that contain the same operating systems can be up to 95% identical. These are just some of the many ways data is duplicated on servers.

To cope with the amount of data, storage systems have gotten bigger and more complex, and developers of storage systems seek to find methods to maximize the use of those systems. One of those methods is data deduplication. **Data deduplication** is a technology that reduces the amount of storage necessary to store an organization's data. Data deduplication (or dedup, for short) actually consists of multiple techniques for reducing storage requirements, including data compression, which transforms a series of repeated data bytes to just a few bytes, and deduplication, which reduces multiple copies of a file or data block to a single instance of the file or data block. Data deduplication in Windows Server 2016 combines both compression and data deduplication.

Windows Server 2016 performs data deduplication in a series of steps:

1. The deduplication process scans the volume looking for files that are candidates for deduplication (based on the file age and type).
2. Files are organized into variable-size chunks.
3. Duplicate chunks are identified.
4. A single instance of each duplicate chunk is placed into a chunk store and optionally compressed.
5. The original file chunk in the file system is replaced with a pointer to the chunk in the chunk store (called a **reparse point**).
6. When a reparse point is encountered during file access, the deduplication system redirects the file access to the appropriate chunk in the chunk store.

When to Use Data Deduplication

As mentioned, there are a number of ways that data is duplicated. You can use data deduplication for a variety of applications, but it cannot be used on operating system volumes such as the Windows boot or system volume. Some of the common uses for data deduplication include the following:

- *File servers*—General-purpose file servers that store user documents including multimedia files such as video and music files often hold duplicated data. As the number of users increases, the amount of duplicated data there is likely to be. This may be particularly true when many users work with copies of the same file such as in education where students access and often save assignment and lesson files such as PowerPoints, syllabi, and so forth. Also, if Shadow Copies for shared folders is enabled where multiple versions of the same file are kept so users can access previous versions, the volumes those shared files reside on are good candidates for data deduplication.
- *Backup servers*—Backup sets can have a lot of duplicated data, especially when multiple versions of full backups are kept or with virtualized backups using Microsoft Data Protection Manager, a component of Microsoft System Center.

- *Virtualization servers*—As mentioned, most of the volume that is used to store the OS is identical among multiple virtual machines. Although you can't run deduplication on the OS volume on the system on which the deduplication feature is installed, you can run deduplication on virtual disks that contain the OS for virtual machines. Data deduplication for virtual desktop infrastructures (VDIs) is particularly useful because the virtual disks used by VMs that users access in a VDI environment typically have the same OS and same applications installed.

There are likely many other applications for data deduplication, but it isn't for every situation. For example, database servers such as SQL servers might or might not benefit from data deduplication, depending on the nature of the data stored. If you are unsure of whether a particular storage scenario would benefit from data deduplication, you can perform a test using a tool included when you install data deduplication but before you actually enable it on your volume. The tool, DDPEval.exe, will evaluate any volumes or network shares you specify. This tool should be run on a test dataset; for example, you can restore a backup of a volume that you are considering for data deduplication to a test server or virtual machine and run the DDPEval.exe tool on the test system. The DDPEval.exe tool generates a report providing information about the amount of data that can be saved if data deduplication is deployed.

Like any optimization tool, there is some overhead with data deduplication. Data deduplication runs periodically and requires server resources, so it might not be a good solution on servers that have a high utilization rate all day, every day. It works best on servers that have some idle time such as late at night or on weekends or on servers that are consistently busy but processor and disk utilization is moderate.

Implementing Data Deduplication

Data deduplication can be installed on both physical servers and virtual machines. Once you have identified candidates for data deduplication, install the Data Deduplication role service under File and Storage Services (see Figure 5-30).

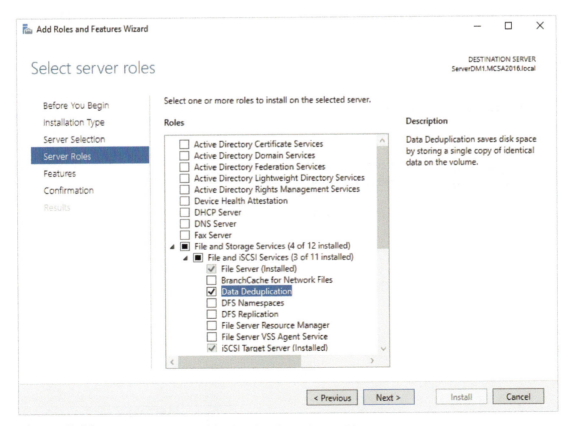

Figure 5-30   Installing Data Deduplication from Server Manager

The requirements and limitations of data deduplication are as follows:

- A physical or virtual machine running Windows Server 2012 or higher with at least one volume that does not contain the operating system is required. For satisfactory performance, at least 4 GB of RAM is recommended.
- The volume can be partitioned using MBR or GPT but must be formatted using NTFS. Volumes larger than 64 TB are not supported.
- Volumes running deduplication should have at least 10% free space.
- The volume can be local storage or part of a Fibre Channel or iSCSI SAN but cannot be a remote volume accessed through Windows file sharing (i.e., a mapped drive). Removable media are not supported. Cluster Shared Volumes (CSVs) are not supported.
- Encrypted files and files smaller than 32 KB are not processed by deduplication. Files up to 1 TB in size can be processed by deduplication.

Once installed, data deduplication must be enabled on selected volumes. You can enable data deduplication from File and Storage Services in Server Manager or using PowerShell. From File and Storage Services, right-click the volume and click Configure Data Deduplication (see Figure 5-31). In the Deduplication Settings window shown in Figure 5-31, you must choose a usage type for this volume. There are three usage types:

- *General purpose file server*—Data deduplication is optimized for general-purpose files such as documents, graphic files, video files, and so forth.
- *Virtual Desktop Infrastructure (VDI) server*—Data deduplication is optimized for virtual machine files such as virtual disks that are used in VDI.
- *Virtualized Backup Server*—Data deduplication is optimized for files used in virtualized backup applications.

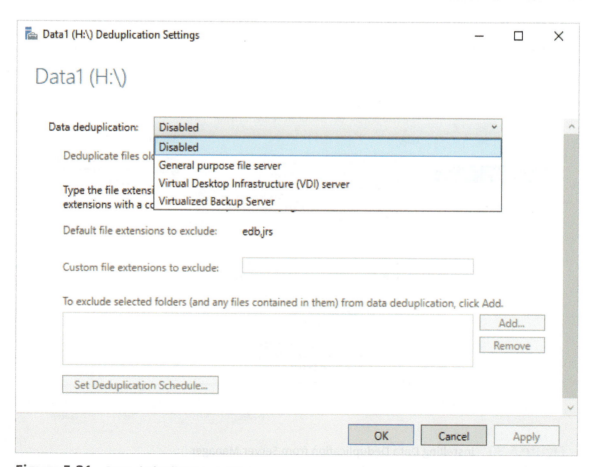

Figure 5-31   Data deduplication settings

After you select the usage type, you choose the age (in days) of files that should be considered for optimization. Only files older than the specified number of days are scanned for duplicate data. The default value is 3 days. A value of zero will cause deduplication to process all files, regardless of their age. By default, files with certain extensions are excluded from deduplication, depending on which usage type you choose. The default extensions are listed and you can add additional extensions, if desired. In addition, you can select folders that should be excluded from deduplication. By default, the entire volume is included.

Last, you choose the schedule and priority on which you wish deduplication to run (see Figure 5-32).

By default, deduplication runs in the background on an hourly basis at a low priority and pauses when the system is busy. If you choose *Enable throughput optimization*, deduplication runs at a normal priority on the schedule you specify. You can also create a second normal priority schedule, if desired. For example, one schedule can run weekdays starting after midnight while the other can run weekends starting in the morning. You can specify how many hours you would like the optimization process to run. You can have both the background optimization and the regular priority optimization schedules active, if desired.

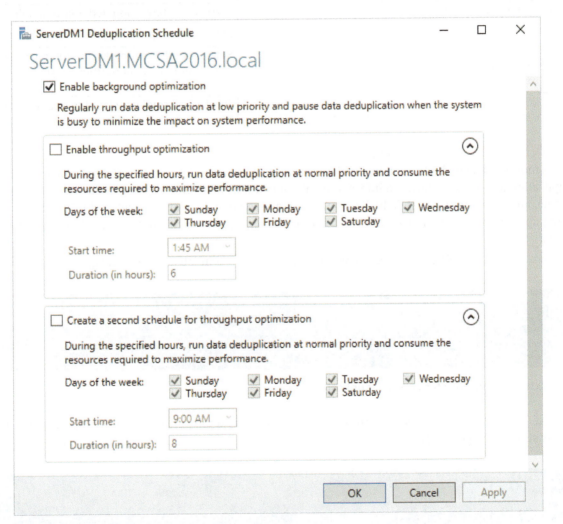

Figure 5-32   Configuring a data deduplication schedule

Configuring Data Deduplication with PowerShell

Configuring data deduplication with PowerShell involves the following two steps for default deduplication configuration:

- Install data deduplication: `Install-WindowsFeature FS-Data-Deduplication`
- Enable data deduplication on volume H: with the default usage type of General purpose file server:
  `Enable-DedupVolume -Volume H:`

Table 5-5 shows examples of various PowerShell cmdlets to configure different deduplication settings.

Table 5-5   PowerShell cmdlets for configuring data deduplication

PowerShell cmdlet	Function
`Enable-DedupVolume -Volume H: -UsageType HyperV`	Enables deduplication for Hyper-V usage.
`Enable-DedupVolume -Volume H: -UsageType Backup`	Enables deduplication for backup usage.
`Enable-DedupVolume -Volume H: -UsageType Default`	Enables deduplication for general file server usage.
`Set-DedupVolume H: -MinimumFileAgeDays 10`	Sets the minimum age of files that should be deduplicated to 10; a value of 0 means all files are processed.
`Start-DedupJob H: Optimization` `Stop-DedupJob H:`	Starts an optimization deduplication job. Stops all deduplication jobs on the volume.

`Set-DedupSchedule -Name "WeekendDedup" -Type`
`    Optimization -Start 9:00 -Duration 6 -Days`
`    Saturday,Sunday`
	Sets a schedule for deduplication on weekends to last for 6 hours at normal priority.

`Get-Command -Module Deduplication`	Displays all cmdlets related to deduplication.

Monitoring Data Deduplication

You can monitor data deduplication in a variety of ways. You can check the status of a running data deduplication job, get deduplication information about deduplicated volumes, look at the deduplication schedule, and view the status of deduplication, which gives you an idea of how well deduplication is keeping up with the data on the volume. Data deduplication is performed with the following PowerShell cmdlets:

- `Get-DedupJob`—Checks the status of a running deduplication job as shown in Figure 5-33.

```
PS C:\Users\administrator.MCSA2016> get-dedupjob

Type            ScheduleType      StartTime       Progress    State        Volume
----            ------------      ---------       --------    -----        ------
Optimization    Manual            6:20 PM         6 %         Running      h:
```

Figure 5-33   Get the status of a deduplication job

- `Get-DedupVolume`—Shows the amount of saved space and the percentage of savings on a volume as shown in Figure 5-34.

```
PS C:\Users\administrator.MCSA2016> Get-DedupVolume

Enabled     UsageType       SavedSpace      SavingsRate     Volume
-------     ---------       ----------      -----------     ------
True        Default         4.07 GB         69 %            H:
```

Figure 5-34   Get information about deduplication on a volume

- `Get-DedupSchedule`—Shows the current deduplication schedule as shown in Figure 5-35. There are three types of deduplication job: Optimization, Garbage Collection, and Scrubbing. Optimization scans files and deduplicates data and typically runs each hour. Garbage collection frees disk space by removing chunks from the chunk store that are no longer referenced by files. Scrubbing jobs analyze the chunk store log files to look for signs of corruption and make repairs when possible.

```
PS C:\Users\administrator.MCSA2016> Get-DedupSchedule

Enabled    Type               StartTime        Days          Name
-------    ----               ---------        ----          ----
False      Optimization                                      BackgroundOptimization
True       GarbageCollection  2:45 AM          Saturday      WeeklyGarbageCollection
True       Scrubbing          3:45 AM          Saturday      WeeklyScrubbing
```

Figure 5-35   Get the current deduplication schedule

- `Get-DedupStatus`—Shows the status of deduplication as shown in Figure 5-36. You can get an idea of how well deduplication is keeping up with the data on a volume by comparing the OptimizedFiles number with the InPolicyFiles number. The InPolicy files number is the number of files that need to be scanned for optimization and the OptimizedFiles number is the number already optimized. If the InPolicyFiles number is rising much faster than the OptimizedFiles number, then you may need to run additional optimization jobs to keep up with the workload.

```
PS C:\Users\administrator.MCSA2016> Get-DedupStatus

FreeSpace    SavedSpace    OptimizedFiles    InPolicyFiles    Volume
---------    ----------    --------------    -------------    ------
18.12 GB     4.07 GB       11580             11580            H:
```

Figure 5-36   Get the deduplication status

Backing Up and Restoring with Data Deduplication

Data deduplication provides features for backup applications to perform optimized backup and restore operations on volumes that have deduplication enabled. Optimized backups copy optimized files and the chunk store from shadow copies of the volume, therefore minimizing the backup size and the backup time. A non optimized backup copies the data on the volume as if data deduplication had not occurred, making the backup much larger and taking much longer. Optimized backups offer backup applications the option to perform full or incremental backups. Note that optimized backups can themselves be stored on optimized volumes, further reducing the space needed to store the backups.

Volume restores from optimized backups essentially reverse the process of an optimized backup. Restores can be full volume restores or selective restores. Both full volume restores and selective restores should be performed to a newly formatted volume.

Activity 5-7: Installing and Configuring Data Deduplication

Time Required: 10 minutes
Objective: Configure data deduplication.
Required Tools and Equipment: ServerDC1, ServerDM1
Description: In this activity, you install the Data Deduplication role service and then create a new volume on ServerDM1 and enable data deduplication on it.

1. Make sure ServerDC1 is running. Start ServerDM1 and sign in as **domain administrator**.
2. Open a PowerShell window. Type **Install-WindowsFeature FS-Data-Deduplication** and press **Enter**.
3. Open **Disk Management**. On the 20 GB disk, create a new volume named **DataVol**, formatted with NTFS, and assigned the **H:** drive letter. Use defaults for all other options.
4. In PowerShell, change to the H: drive by typing **h:** and pressing **Enter**. Next, you'll create two folders to store some duplicate files. Type **md data1** and press **Enter**. Type **md data2** and press **Enter**.
5. Next, copy a bunch of files to the data1 folder. Type **copy C:\windows\system32*.exe data1** and press **Enter**. Copy the same files to the data2 folder. Type **copy C:\windows\system32*.exe data2** and press

Enter. The files you copied take about 580 MB of space. You can verify this in File Explorer or by typing **Get-Volume h | fl** and pressing **Enter**. Subtract the SizeRemaining value from the Size value to get the amount of used space.

6. Now, enable disk deduplication on the volume. Type **Enable-DedupVolume -Volume H: -UsageType Default** and press **Enter**.

7. Set the minimum age for deduplication to 0 days. Type **Set-DedupVolume h: -MinimumFileAgeDays 0** and press **Enter**.

8. Start a deduplication job. Type **Start-DedupJob -Volume h: Optimization** and press **Enter**.

9. Check the status of the deduplication job by typing **Get-DedupJob** and pressing **Enter**. If there is no output, it means the job has already completed.

10. Check the status of deduplication by typing **Get-DedupStatus** and pressing **Enter**. You should see output showing how much space was saved and how many files were optimized. Type **Get-DedupVolume** and press **Enter** to see deduplication by volume. The output shows the type of optimization, the amount of saved space, and the percentage of savings.

11. Close PowerShell and using Disk Management, delete the H: volume. Shut down all servers.

Storage Replica

 **Certification**

- **70-740: Implement storage solutions:**
  Implement server storage

Storage Replica is a Windows Server feature that provides block-level file replication between storage devices, primarily for the purpose of fault tolerance and disaster recovery. The idea of Storage Replica seems to be at odds with the Data Deduplication service. Although data deduplication strives to eliminate duplicate data to free up disk space, the Storage Replica feature creates duplicates of data and uses more disk space. Whereas Data Deduplication's target is to reduce duplicated data within a single file system, Storage Replica's primary goal is to copy data from one server or storage system to another server or storage system for the purposes of fault tolerance and disaster recovery. Storage Replica can be used to replicate data between servers and between server clusters no matter whether those servers are in the same room, different buildings, or even different countries.

Block-level replication means that individual data blocks on the disk are copied as they change as opposed to file-level replication, which replicates entire files as they change. With block-level replication, if the contents of a file change, only the parts of the file that changed are replicated rather than the entire file. Storage Replica supports local storage such as SAS or SATA disks, and iSCSI or Fibre Channel–based SAN storage. To ensure consistent data between storage sites, Storage Replica uses log files that are used to back out changes if a failure occurs.

Storage Replica Use Scenarios

Storage Replica supports three primary use scenarios:

- *Server-to-server*—Replication occurs between two servers. Storage can be a Storage Spaces volume with shared SAS storage, locally attached storage, or an iSCSI or Fibre Channel SAN. Replication is configured and managed using PowerShell only.

- *Cluster-to-cluster*—Replication occurs between two clusters. Storage can be a Storage Spaces volume with shared SAS storage, an iSCSI or Fibre Channel SAN, or a Storage Spaces Direct volume. Replication can be configured using PowerShell or Failover Cluster Manager.

- *Stretch cluster*—Replication occurs between two clusters configured as a stretch cluster. A **stretch cluster** is a cluster in which the cluster members are located in different geographical locations. A stretch cluster is primarily used in disaster recovery scenarios such as when one location is subject to a natural disaster such as flood or hurricane, so the other location assumes its workload.

Installing and Configuring Storage Replica

Before you implement Storage Replica, you should verify that your servers meet the minimum requirements:

- 4 GB of RAM in each server
- Two CPU cores; or on virtual machines, two virtual processors must be assigned to each server
- Servers should be domain members for automatic Kerberos authentication
- 1 Gbps network connection
- Replication volume must be NTFS or ReFS formatted with GPT partitioning
- A log volume with at least 8 GB free space; NTFS or ReFS with GPT partitioning; an SSD disk is highly recommended for the log volume
- Both the replication volume and log volume on each server must have identical sector sizes
- Replication and log volumes cannot be used to store OS components including the paging file

Storage Replica is a Windows Server 2016 feature you can install with Server Manager or PowerShell. To install Storage Replica with PowerShell, use the following cmdlet:

```
Install-WindowsFeature Storage-Replica -IncludeManagementTools
```

Be sure to add the `-IncludeManagementTools` option or the PowerShell cmdlets necessary to configure Storage Replica won't be installed. Before implementing Storage Replica, you can test the configuration of your servers using the following cmdlet:

```
Test-SRTopology -SourceComputerName ServerDM1 -SourceVolumeName R:
   -SourceLogVolumeName L: -DestinationComputerName ServerDM2 -DestinationVolumeName R:
   -DestinationLogVolumeName L: -DurationInMinutes 30 -ResultPath C:\temp
```

This cmdlet tests Storage Replica between two servers, ServerDM1 and ServerDM2. The volume to be replicated is the R: drive and the log volume is the L: drive. The test is run for 30 minutes and an HTML report is generated and saved in C:\temp.

> **Tip** ⓘ
>
> In order to get useful results from `Test-SRTopology`, you should introduce a load on the source storage volume. You can download a utility called `Diskspd.exe` from Microsoft TechNet (*technet.microsoft.com*).

To begin replication, you create a partnership between the source and destination computers:

```
New-SRPartnership -SourceComputerName ServerDM1 -SourceVolumeName R:
   -SourceLogVolumeName L: -SourceRGName RG01 -DestinationComputerName ServerDM2
   -DestinationVolumeName R: -DestinationLogVolumeName L: -DestinationRGName RG02
```

As part of that command, you assign a replication group number using the `-SourceRGName` and `-DestinationRGName` parameters. To check the status of the replication, use the following cmdlet:

`Get-SrGroup`—Shows the status of all running replication groups as shown in Figure 5-37.

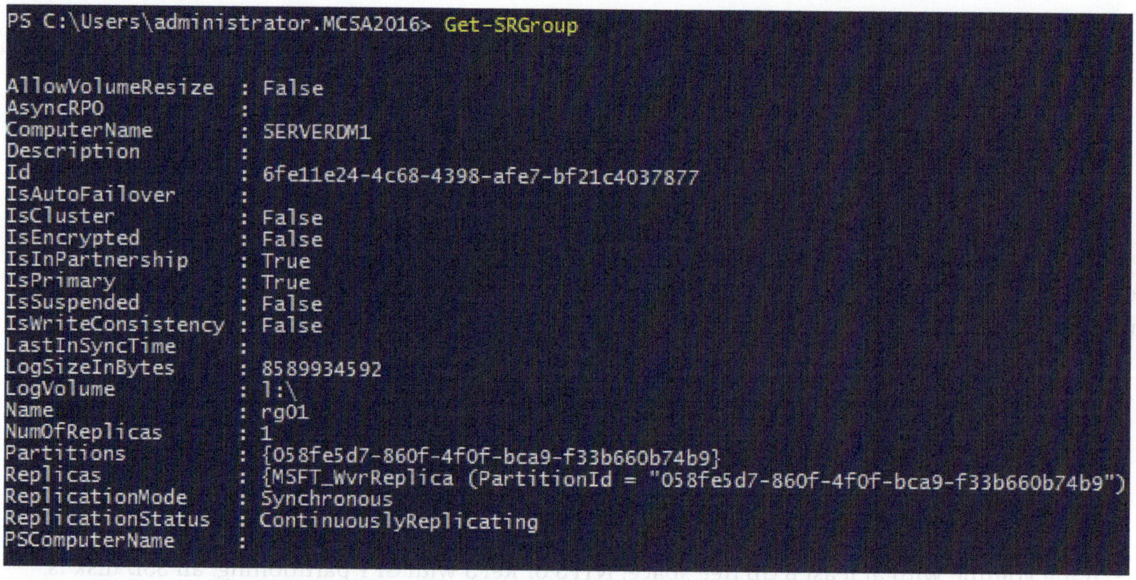

```
PS C:\Users\administrator.MCSA2016> Get-SRGroup

AllowVolumeResize   : False
AsyncRPO            :
ComputerName        : SERVERDM1
Description         :
Id                  : 6fe11e24-4c68-4398-afe7-bf21c4037877
IsAutoFailover      :
IsCluster           : False
IsEncrypted         : False
IsInPartnership     : True
IsPrimary           : True
IsSuspended         : False
IsWriteConsistency  : False
LastInSyncTime      :
LogSizeInBytes      : 8589934592
LogVolume           : l:\
Name                : rg01
NumOfReplicas       : 1
Partitions          : {058fe5d7-860f-4f0f-bca9-f33b660b74b9}
Replicas            : {MSFT_WvrReplica (PartitionId = "058fe5d7-860f-4f0f-bca9-f33b660b74b9")
ReplicationMode     : Synchronous
ReplicationStatus   : ContinuouslyReplicating
PSComputerName      :
```

Figure 5-37 Output of Get-SRGroup

`Get-SRPartnership`—Shows information about the Storage Replica partnership. To remove replication, run the following cmdlets:

`Get-SRPartnership | Remove-SRPartnership`—Run this cmdlet only on the source computer.

`Get-SRGroup | Remove-SRGroup`—Run this cmdlet on the source and destination computers.

One-Way Replication

It's important to understand that Storage Replica is one-way replication: from a source volume to a destination volume. Only the source volume is available during replication. The destination volume is taken offline during replication and the data is unavailable to applications. In the event of a failure, you must remove the partnership to bring the destination volume back online using the `Remove-SRPartnership` cmdlet. Alternatively, in the event of a planned failover, you can reverse replication so the destination volume becomes the source and vice versa using the `Set-SRPartnership` cmdlet.

Synchronous and Asynchronous Replication

Storage Replica supports two modes of replication:

- *Synchronous replication*—With synchronous replication, an application writes data to the source volume, and while the source volume log file is updated, data is written (replicated) to the destination volume; then the destination log file is updated. Only after the destination data has been written and the destination log file has been updated is an acknowledgment sent to the application. This ensures that the data remains in synch with zero data loss in the event of a failure at the source site. Synchronous replication requires a very low latency network connection between source and destination with a connection of 10 Gbps recommended, and 1 Gbps required.

- *Asynchronous replication*—Replicates data between sites over slower, high-latency networks. With asynchronous replication, there is no guarantee that data will be identical when a failure occurs; however, the amount of unsynchronized data is dependent on the latency of the network. Storage Replica runs continuously, so changes are still replicated as soon as they occur.

Chapter Summary

- Storage Spaces provides flexible provisioning of virtualized storage by using storage pools. A storage pool is a collection of physical disks from which virtual disks and volumes are created and assigned dynamically.

- A storage space is a collection of physical disks from which virtual disks and volumes are created and assigned dynamically. Storage Spaces can allocate storage by using thin provisioning.

- Storage Spaces uses the concept of just a bunch of disks (JBOD) in which two or more disks are abstracted to appear as a single disk to the OS but aren't arranged in a specific RAID configuration.

- Storage Spaces brings storage flexibility to a Windows server. Storage Spaces has three storage options: simple space, mirror space, and parity space. Storage Spaces can be configured with File and Storage Services in Server Manager or PowerShell cmdlets.

- An advantage of Storage Spaces versus traditional storage is the ability to easily expand the amount of storage available for your virtual disks. Storage Spaces also allows you to replace a failed physical disk in a storage pool.

- Storage Spaces allows you to choose three different allocation types when you add a physical disk to a storage space. You can choose automatic disk, hot spare disk, or manual disk.

- Windows Server 2016 contains a feature called *enclosure awareness* in which Storage Spaces can place copies of data on separate enclosures, ensuring that if an entire disk enclosure fails, the data is maintained.

- Tiered storage was introduced in Storage Spaces in Windows Server 2012 R2. Tiered storage combines the speed of solid state drives (SSDs) with the low cost and high capacity of hard disk drives (HDDs).

- A storage area network (SAN) uses high-speed networking technologies to give servers fast access to large amounts of shared disk storage. You can set up a SAN with Windows servers by using the iSCSI protocol. The iSCSI protocol carries SCSI device commands over an IP network.

- An iSCSI target is a logical storage space made available to iSCSI clients by a server running the iSCSI Target Server role service. An iSCSI initiator is the iSCSI client that sends iSCSI commands to the iSCSI target.

- The Internet Storage Name Service (iSNS) is an IP-based protocol used to communicate between iSNS clients and servers. iSNS offers these benefits for iSCSI SANs on large networks: scalability, manageability, and monitoring.

- Data center bridging (DCB) is an enhancement to Ethernet that provides additional features for use in enterprise data centers where server clustering and SANs are in use.

- Windows Server 2016 supports DCB as an installable feature using the Add Roles and Features Wizard in Server Manager or via a PowerShell cmdlet. You can list the PowerShell cmdlets specific to configuring DCB using the `Get-Command -Module DCBQoS` cmdlet.

- Multipath IO (MPIO) provides fault tolerance for Windows storage networks, including iSCSI SANs. MPIO provides a storage server with multiple paths between the server and the actual storage.

- Data deduplication is a technology, utilizing multiple techniques, that reduces the amount of storage necessary to store an organization's data. Data deduplication can be installed on both physical servers and virtual machines.

- Data deduplication provides features for backup applications to perform optimized backup and restore operations on volumes that have deduplication enabled. Optimized backups copy optimized files and the chunk store from shadow copies of the volume, therefore minimizing the backup size and the backup time.

- Storage Replica is a Windows Server feature that provides block-level file replication between storage devices, primarily for fault tolerance and disaster recovery.

Key Terms

automatic disk
block-level replication
block-level storage
column
data center bridging
   (DCB)
data deduplication
dual parity space
enclosure awareness
file-level storage
fixed provisioning
hot spare disk

Internet Storage Name
   Service (iSNS)
iSCSI initiator
iSCSI logical unit number (LUN)
iSCSI qualified name (IQN)
iSCSI target
just a bunch of disks (JBOD)
manual disk
mirror space
Multipath IO (MPIO)
parity space
primordial pool

reparse point
resilience
simple space
storage layouts
storage pool
Storage Replica
Storage Spaces
stretch cluster
thin provisioning
three-way mirror
tiered storage

Review Questions

1. You see something named *primordial* in File and Storage Services. What can you do with it?
   a. Create a storage pool
   b. Create a virtual disk
   c. Format it
   d. Create a new volume

2. What type of storage layout does Storage Spaces support? (Choose all that apply.)
   a. Simple space
   b. Mirror space
   c. Parity space
   d. Striped space

3. Which of the following is a feature in Windows Server 2016 that combines the speed of SSDs with the low cost and high capacity of HDDs?
   a. JBOD
   b. Thin provisioning
   c. Storage tiering
   d. Resilient spaces

4. Which feature in Storage Spaces finds data on a volume that exists multiple times and reduces it to a single instance?
   a. Disk quotas
   b. Storage tiering
   c. Fixed provisioning
   d. Data deduplication

5. Which of the following uses dynamically expanding storage?
   a. Thin provisioning
   b. Primordial pools
   c. Parity volumes
   d. Resilient File System

6. Which of the following refers to the number of physical disks that a virtual disk is using and must be considered when you add space to an existing virtual disk?
   a. Sectors
   b. Columns
   c. Volumes
   d. Virtual disk

7. Which of the following PowerShell cmdlets will allow an administrator to replace a failed disk in a storage pool?
   a. `Get-PhysicalDisk`
   b. `Include-VirtualDisk`
   c. `Add-VirtualDisk`
   d. `Add-PhysicalDisk`

8. When you add a physical disk to a storage space, which of the following are allocation types that will determine how the new disk will be used? (Choose all that apply.)
   a. Automatic
   b. Manual
   c. Virtual
   d. Hot Spare

9. What feature in Windows Server 2016 will allow Storage Spaces to place copies of data on separate enclosures ensuring that if an entire disk enclosure fails the data is maintained?
   a. Secondary volumes
   b. Enclosure awareness
   c. Disk awareness
   d. Virtual replacement

10. Which of the following physical disk arrangements will allow you to set up a tiered storage configuration?
    a. Two SSDs
    b. Three SSDs
    c. Two HDDs
    d. One SSD & One HDD

11. Which of the following is a valid disk provisioning option when configuring storage tiers?
    a. Virtual provisioning
    b. Thin provisioning
    c. Fixed provisioning
    d. Set provisioning

12. Which of the following is a logical storage space consisting of one or more virtual disks in an iSCSI system?
    a. iSCSI qualified name
    b. iSCSI target
    c. iSCSI initiator
    d. iSNS server

13. What does iSCSI use to reference a logical drive provided by the iSCSI target?
    a. iSCSI LUN
    b. IQN value
    c. iSNS ID
    d. Target ID

14. If you enable authentication on an iSCSI target, what authentication protocol is used?
    a. PAP
    b. CHAP
    c. EAP
    d. PEAP

15. When looking over an iSCSI configuration, you see the string iqn.1991-05.com.microsoft:SAN. domain1.local. What are you looking at?
    a. iSCSI initiator handle
    b. iSNS target name
    c. Internet Storage Name
    d. iSCSI qualified name

16. You want to be able to group iSCSI devices and manage them from a central server. What should you install?
    a. iSCSI LUN
    b. iSCSI Management Service
    c. iSNS Server
    d. iSCSI Target Server

17. Which of the following is an enhancement to Ethernet that provides additional features for use in enterprise data centers where server clustering and storage area networks (SANs) are in use?
    a. Server bridging
    b. Data clustering
    c. Data center bridging
    d. Virtual data clustering

18. In iSCSI deployments, which of the following allows bandwidth to be allocated on a per protocol basis, guaranteeing that iSCSI traffic gets a minimum of network bandwidth?
    a. Quality of Service
    b. Deterministic performance
    c. Protocol priority
    d. DCB Exchange

19. Which of the following will allow a server with two or more interfaces to provide fault tolerance for Windows storage networks, including iSCSI SANs?
    a. Single-path IO
    b. Multipath IO
    c. Multipath SCSI
    d. Dual Virtual IO

20. With respect to data deduplication, where does Windows Server 2016 place a single instance of duplicated data?
    a. Chunk store
    b. Disk store
    c. Deduplication file
    d. Dedup folder

21. After installing data deduplication, which of the following tools will allow you to run a test to determine whether a specific storage scenario would benefit from data deduplication without enabling it on your volume?
    a. DDVol.exe
    b. File manager
    c. DDPEval.exe
    d. SYSEval.exe

22. Which of the following files will *not* be processed by data deduplication? (Choose all that apply.)
    a. A 500 MB file
    b. An encrypted file
    c. A 16 KB file
    d. A video file

23. Which of the following PowerShell cmdlets allows you to view the amount of saved space and the percentage of savings on a volume when utilizing data deduplication?
    a. `Get-DedupSchedule`
    b. `Get-DedupStatus`
    c. `Get-DedupJob`
    d. `Get-DedupVolume`

24. Which of the following means that individual data blocks on the disk are copied as they change as opposed to file-level replication, which replicates entire files as they change?
    a. Volume replication
    b. Storage Replica
    c. Block-level replication
    d. File-level replication

25. Which of the following use scenarios is supported by Storage Replica? (Choose all that apply.)
    a. Stretch cluster
    b. Server-to-server
    c. Cluster-to-server
    d. Cluster-to-cluster

Critical Thinking

The following activities give you critical thinking challenges. Case Projects offer a scenario with a problem to solve and for which you supply a written solution.

Case Project 5-1: Creating Flexible Storage

It's been 6 months since the disk crash at CSM Tech Publishing, and the owner is breathing a little easier because you installed a fault-tolerant solution to prevent loss of time and data if a disk crashes in the future. Business is good, and the current solution is starting to get low on disk space. In addition, the owner has some other needs that might require more disk space, and he wants to keep the data on separate volumes. He wants a flexible solution in which drives and volumes aren't restricted in their configuration. He also wants to be able to add storage space to existing volumes easily without having to reconfigure existing drives. He has the budget to add a storage enclosure system that can contain up to 10 HDDs. Which Windows feature can accommodate these needs, and how does it work?

Case Project 5-2: Using Advanced File and Storage Features

You're the IT administrator for CSM Tech Publishing. You've just had a meeting with the general manager about some data storage problems the company has been having. You've been asked to find solutions for the following problems:

- You have a database application that has been exhibiting poor performance caused by latency from the drives it uses for storage. The storage system uses Storage Spaces and consists of four 1 TB HDDs. You have been asked to see what you can do to improve the performance of the storage used by the database application. You have a limited budget for the project—certainly not enough for a new server but probably enough for some new components.

- You have a file server that is used to store user documents. Many of the documents stored by users are related to projects that several users collaborate on and on which many users keep their own copies of the files. In addition, you use Shadow Copies for shared folders so users can easily revert files to previous editions. You also know that many users keep copies of training videos and other multimedia files. You want to reduce the amount of storage being used on your file server without making users change the way they work and store files.

What solutions do you propose for these two file and storage problems? Include implementation details.

CHAPTER 6

IMPLEMENTING VIRTUALIZATION WITH HYPER-V: PART 1

After reading this chapter and completing the exercises, you will be able to:

Install the Hyper-V server role

Create and use virtual machines

Manage and configure virtual machines

Virtualization has become a mainstream technology in both small and large networks. Server virtualization can be used to achieve a variety of goals, including consolidating servers, increasing server availability, creating virtual desktops, isolating applications for testing, and more. For these reasons and more, the Hyper-V role is likely to be a part of most Windows Server 2016 deployments.

This chapter focuses on how to use the Hyper-V server role for a virtualization platform. You learn the requirements for installing Hyper-V and how to install and configure the Hyper-V role. You'll learn how to manage Hyper-V both locally and remotely, create virtual machines, and manage and optimize virtual machines. In Chapter 7, you'll learn how to work with Hyper-V virtual disks and Hyper-V virtual networks.

Installing Hyper-V

 Certification

- **70-740 – Implement Hyper-V:**
  Install and configure Hyper-V

- **70-740 – Install Windows Servers in host and compute environments:**
  Create, manage, and maintain images for deployment

Table 6-1 describes what you need for the hands-on activities in this chapter.

Table 6-1 Activity requirements

Activity	Requirements	Notes
Activity 6-1: Resetting Your Virtual Environment	ServerHyperV	
Activity 6-2: Creating a Virtual Machine	ServerHyperV	
Activity 6-3: Working with Virtual Machines in Hyper-V Manager	ServerHyperV, ServerVM1 virtual machine	
Activity 6-4: Exporting and Importing a VM	ServerHyperV, InstallCore virtual machine	
Activity 6-5: Enabling Enhanced Session Mode	ServerHyperV, ServerVM1 virtual machine	
Activity 6-6: Managing a VM with PowerShell Direct	ServerHyperV, ServerVM1	

Note 📎

The Hyper-V role is supported on a virtual machine running on a Windows Server 2016 Hyper-V host (referred to as nested virtualization) if the host requirements are met. It's also possible to install and use the Hyper-V role on a virtual machine running in VMware Workstation 9 and later, but additional configuration steps are necessary. See the lab setup guide in the Before You Begin section of the Introduction to this book for details for using Hyper-V in a nested virtualization scenario. Nested virtualization is also covered in Chapter 7.

As you learned in Chapter 1, virtualization creates a software environment to emulate a computer's hardware and BIOS, allowing multiple operating systems to run on the same physical computer at the same time. In Windows Server 2016, you use the Hyper-V server role to create this environment. Before jumping into installing Hyper-V, review the following virtualization terms:

- A *virtual machine (VM)* is the virtual environment that emulates a physical computer's hardware and BIOS.
- A *guest OS* is an operating system installed in a VM in the same way that you install an operating system on a physical computer. Hyper-V supports a wide variety of guest OSs, as discussed later in "Creating Virtual Machines in Hyper-V."
- A *host computer* is the computer on which VMs run, and a host OS is the operating system running on the host.
- *Virtualization software* is the software for creating and managing VMs and creating the virtual environment in which a guest OS is installed. Examples are VMware Workstation, Oracle VirtualBox, and, of course, Hyper-V.
- The *hypervisor* is the virtualization software component that creates and monitors the virtual hardware environment, which allows multiple VMs to share physical hardware resources. The hypervisor on a host computer acts somewhat like an OS kernel, but instead of scheduling processes for access to the CPU and other devices, it schedules VMs. It's sometimes called the *virtual machine monitor (VMM)*.

- A **virtual disk** consists of files on the host computer that represent a virtual machine's hard disk.
- A **virtual network** is a network configuration created by virtualization software and used by virtual machines for physical and virtual network communication.
- A **checkpoint** is a partial copy of a VM made at a particular moment; it contains changes made since the VM was created or since the last checkpoint and can be used to restore the VM to its state when the checkpoint was taken. A checkpoint is also referred to as a *snapshot*.

As a type 1 hypervisor, the Hyper-V virtualization environment sits between the hardware and virtual machines. Each virtual machine is a child partition on the system, and Windows Server 2016 with Hyper-V installed is the parent or management partition. The Hyper-V management console runs on Windows Server 2016 in the parent partition and serves as an interface for managing the VMs running in child partitions, as shown in Figure 6-1.

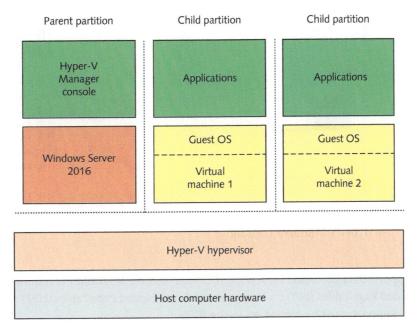

Figure 6-1   The Hyper-V architecture

Note 📎

Hyper-V Server, a free download, can be installed on a server without having Windows Server 2016 installed. Hyper-V is then managed by another server running Windows Server 2016.

Figure 6-2 shows the Hyper-V Manager console in Windows Server 2016 with four VMs running. At the bottom of the middle pane is a thumbnail of the currently selected VM, named 740-ServerDC1. You can double-click the thumbnail to connect to the VM and use it like a physical computer.

Hyper-V is a server role that's installed like any server role in Windows Server 2016 by using the Add Roles and Features Wizard in Server Manager or the `Install-WindowsFeature` PowerShell cmdlet. However, unlike some other roles you can install, your system must meet a few prerequisites to install and use Hyper-V:

- Windows Server 2016 Standard or Datacenter Edition installed
- A 1.4 GHz or faster 64-bit CPU with virtualization extensions (AMD-V or Intel-VT)

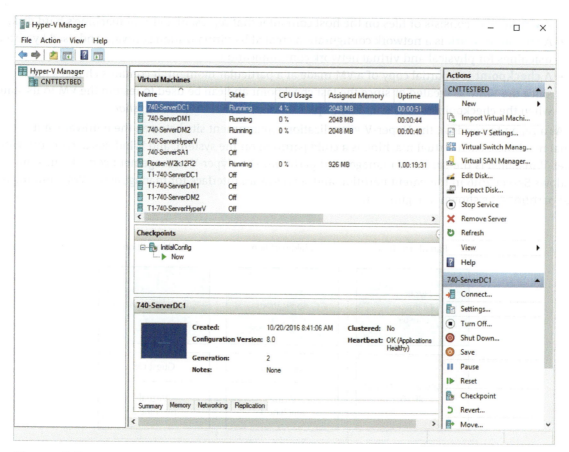

Figure 6-2 The Hyper-V Manager console

- A CPU that supports Data Execution Prevention (DEP) and second-level address translation (SLAT). SLAT is called Extended Page Tables (EPT) on Intel processors and Nested Page Tables (NPT) on AMD processors
- Virtualization support must be turned on in the BIOS
- Free disk space at least equal to the minimum requirement for the OS you're going to install as a virtual machine

Note

Remember that the amount of space required by a guest OS is no different from the space required of an OS installed on physical hardware.

- RAM at least equal to the minimum amount required for Windows Server 2016 plus the minimum amount required for the OS you're installing

Note

For example, the minimum amount of RAM required by Windows Server 2016 is 512 MB. If you plan to install a Windows Server 2016 guest OS, you need another 512 MB for the guest for a total of 1 GB. For all practical purposes, however, 2 to 4 GB of RAM should be considered the minimum amount on a Hyper-V host machine.

After you have an adequately configured system running a 64-bit version of Windows Server 2016, you can install the Hyper-V role. Although you can install Hyper-V on Windows Server 2016 running as a virtual machine, you need to perform some additional tasks as outlined in Chapter 7 in the section "Nested Virtualization."

> **Note** 📎
>
> To check whether your system meets the requirements for Hyper-V, type `systeminfo` at a command prompt and scroll down to the bottom to the section labeled Hyper-V Requirements. You'll see the requirements listed and whether your system meets them.

Installing the Hyper-V Role and Management Tools

When you install the Hyper-V role from Server Manager, you are prompted to install the management tools, which you should do if you will be managing Hyper-V from the same server that is running Hyper-V. To install the Hyper-V role from PowerShell, including management tools, use the cmdlet `Install-WindowsFeature Hyper-V -IncludeManagementTools`. If you will be managing Hyper-V remotely, you can install just the management tools on the management computer: `Install-WindowsFeature RSAT-Hyper-V-Tools` installs both the GUI and the PowerShell Hyper-V module for PowerShell. The cmdlet `Install-WindowsFeature Hyper-V-Powershell` installs only the Hyper-V module for PowerShell.

Managing Hyper-V Remotely

A server running Hyper-V is likely to be resource intensive, especially if it is running several VMs, so you might want to consider managing the server remotely so that the management tasks are offloaded to another computer. In addition, you can install Hyper-V in a Nano Server deployment, which requires remote management. As mentioned, you can install the Hyper-V management tools on a computer that is not running the Hyper-V role. Once the management tools are installed, you can use them to manage Hyper-V remotely. If you installed the GUI management tools, you can run Hyper-V Manager and then click the Hyper-V Manager node in the left pane, and click Connect to Server in the Actions pane. Then specify the name of the server running the Hyper-V role. Both the Hyper-V host and the management computer must be configured for remote management as discussed in Chapter 3. As a reminder, you can enable remote management through Server Manager by clicking Local Server and then clicking Remote management or using the PowerShell cmdlet `Configure-SMRemoting`.

To remotely manage Hyper-V using PowerShell, PowerShell remoting must be enabled. By default, PowerShell remoting is enabled on Windows Server 2012 and later, but if it becomes disabled, use the PowerShell cmdlet `Enable-PSRemoting` on the computer you wish to manage. With PowerShell remoting enabled, you open a PowerShell prompt from the management computer and type `Enter-PSSession ServerHyperV` (or whatever the name of the remote server is). If both computers are in the same domain, you will not have to enter credentials. If the remote server is not in a domain or in a different domain, use the cmdlet `Enter-PSSession ServerHyperV Credential (Get-Credential)` and you will be prompted for the credentials to sign in to the remote server. However, the remote server must be added to the TrustedHosts list on the management server first as discussed in Chapter 3. Once you are connected to the remote server, your PowerShell prompt changes by the addition of [ServerHyperV] at the beginning of the prompt. From there on, every PowerShell cmdlet you enter is executed on the remote server. To exit the remote PowerShell session, simply type `exit`.

> **Note** 📎
>
> Remote management with PowerShell is not limited to Hyper-V, of course. Once you are connected to the remote server with `Enter-PSSession`, you can manage all aspects of the remote server with PowerShell cmdlets.

Hyper-V Licensing

When you install a guest OS in a virtual machine, you must have a valid license for the guest OS. Windows Server 2016 with Hyper-V includes licenses for **virtual instances** of Windows Server 2016 with the Standard and Datacenter editions:

- Standard Edition includes two licenses for virtual instances of Windows Server 2016 on a fully licensed host computer, which means you can install Windows Server 2016 as a guest OS on up to two VMs without having to purchase an additional Windows Server 2016 license.
- Datacenter Edition includes licenses for unlimited virtual instances of Windows Server 2016.

Upgrading to Hyper-V on Windows Server 2016

If you have VMs from Hyper-V running in Windows Server 2012 or Windows Server 2008, you need to upgrade the VM configuration version to take advantage of new features in Windows Server 2016. The VM configuration version can be seen in Hyper-V Manager by selecting the VM and looking at the summary in the bottom pane as shown in Figure 6-3. From PowerShell, use the cmdlet `Get-VM | ft Name, Version`. The configuration version for Windows Server 2016 Hyper-V is 8.0. If the version of the VM is less than that, you'll see the Upgrade Configuration option (the VM must be turned off) in Hyper-V Manager in the Actions pane. If the Upgrade Configuration option isn't available, the VM is already at the highest configuration level. To perform the upgrade, simply click Upgrade Configuration. In PowerShell use the cmdlet `Update-VMVersion VMName` where *VMName* is the name of the virtual machine.

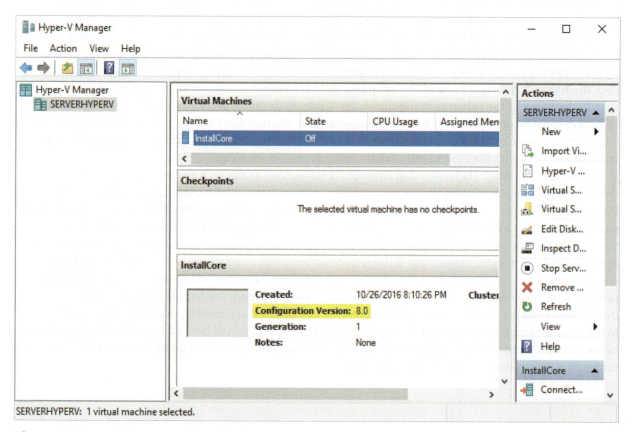

Figure 6-3   Finding the configuration version

Creating Virtual Machines in Hyper-V

 **Certification**

- **70-740 – Implement Hyper-V:**
  Configure virtual machine (VM) settings

With Hyper-V installed, the Hyper-V Manager console is available in Server Manager's Tools menu. You use it to create and manage virtual machines, configure virtual networks, and configure the Hyper-V server. In addition, there are a number of PowerShell cmdlets for creating and configuring VMs, discussed later in this section.

To use virtualization, you must create a virtual machine first. In Hyper-V Manager, all tasks related to configuring the Hyper-V server and creating and managing virtual machines are listed in the Actions pane.

Hyper-V VMs consist of these files stored on the Hyper-V server:

- *Configuration file*—This XML file containing the details of a VM's virtual hardware configuration is stored by default in the Virtual Machines folder in *%systemroot%*\ProgramData\Microsoft\Windows\Hyper-V. Each checkpoint created for a VM also has an XML configuration file associated with it that is stored by default in the same path in the Snapshots folder. These files have an .xml extension. You can change the path where these files are stored when you create the virtual machine, and you can also change the default path in Hyper-V Settings.
- *Virtual hard disk files*—Each virtual hard disk assigned to a VM has an associated VHD or VHDX file that holds the hard disk's contents. By default, these files are stored in C:\Users\Public Documents\Hyper-V\Virtual hard disks\; they have a .vhd or .vhdx extension. VHDX is the newer and preferred virtual hard disk format. VHDX disks provide better performance than VHD disks do and have a 64 TB capacity compared with 2 TB for VHD disks.

In addition, you might also find the following types of files associated with a VM:

- *Differencing or checkpoint files*—These files are similar to virtual hard disk files, but they're associated with a parent VHD or VHDX file and are created when you create a differencing disk or checkpoint. Differencing disks are discussed in Chapter 7, and checkpoints are discussed in the "Managing Checkpoints" section later in this chapter. These files have an .avhd or .avhdx extension, depending on whether they're associated with a VHD or VHDX virtual hard disk.
- *Saved state files*—If you save a VM's state, two files are created. A file with a .bin extension contains the contents of the saved VM's memory, and a file with a .vsv extension contains the saved state of the VM's devices. Both files are in a folder named with the GUID of the VM located where the VM's configuration file is stored.

The process of creating a VM involves just a few general steps:

1. Start the New Virtual Machine Wizard in Hyper-V Manager.
2. Give the new VM a descriptive name.
3. Choose a location for the VM. Storing VMs on a hard disk that's separate from your Windows Server 2016 installation is usually best. In data center applications, VMs are often stored on storage area networks (SANs) for enhanced reliability and management. With this setup, if a host server goes down or is taken out of service for maintenance, another Hyper-V host can be assigned to run its VMs without having to physically move VM files.
4. Choose a generation 1 or generation 2 virtual machine. A generation 1 virtual machine creates a virtual hardware environment compatible with Hyper-V versions before Windows Server 2012. A generation 2 virtual machine requires at least a Windows Server 2012 or Windows 8 guest OS and supports features such as secure boot, PXE boot, and SCSI boot.
5. Assign the amount of memory the VM requires. Memory requirements for VMs are typically the same as requirements for installing the OS on a physical computer. With Hyper-V, you can take advantage of dynamic memory allocation in which the hypervisor allocates only as much memory

as the VM needs, up to the maximum specified. The amount of memory assigned to a VM can be changed later, but the VM must be turned off.

6. Configure networking. You have the choice of connecting with an external switch, which uses one of the host network adapters by using a private switch or an internal switch or by leaving the VM disconnected from the network. There are no virtual switches until you create one, which you can do during Hyper-V installation or after installation is complete using Hyper-V Manager or PowerShell. You can change the network connection for a VM at any time, including while the VM is running.

7. Create a virtual hard disk. You can give the virtual disk a name or accept the default, and you can choose the virtual disk's size and location. Putting virtual disk files on a drive separate from the Windows Server 2016 host's boot drive results in the best performance. You can also use an existing virtual hard disk or attach a hard disk later.

8. Install an OS. In this step, you can install an OS from media inserted in the host's physical CD/DVD drive (generation 1 VM only), from a CD/DVD image file (an `.iso` file), from a boot floppy disk image (generation 1 VM only), or over the network by using PXE boot. You can also install an OS later.

Basic Virtual Machine Management with Hyper-V Manager

With Hyper-V, a virtual machine runs in the background until you connect to it in Hyper-V Manager. A running VM doesn't require using Hyper-V Manager, nor does it require anyone to be signed in to the server. Furthermore, you can configure a VM to start and shut down automatically when the host server starts and shuts down. In addition, like any OS, you can manage a VM remotely by using tools such as Remote Desktop and MMCs if the VM is configured to communicate with the host network.

Hyper-V Manager provides a graphical interface for creating, managing, and interacting with VMs. The middle pane shows all installed VMs at the top (see Figure 6-4) and displays each VM's name, state, CPU use, assigned memory, uptime, and status. Normally, the Status column doesn't display anything unless you perform a task such as exporting a VM or creating a checkpoint. When you select a VM, the Checkpoints section shows a list of checkpoints created for it. If you click the VM's name in this section, you see a screenshot of the VM at the time the checkpoint was taken along with the time and date it was taken. The bottom section shows a real-time screenshot of a running VM. When a running VM's screen changes, the screenshot in Hyper-V Manager reflects the change with a slight delay.

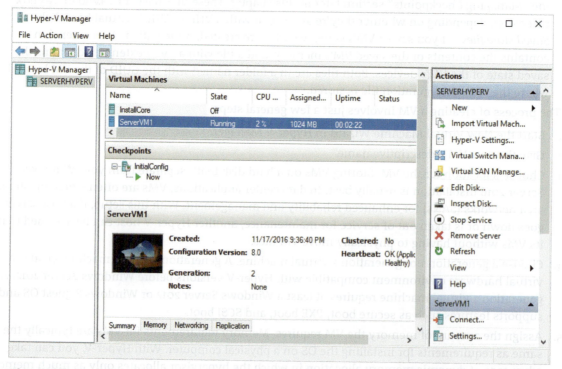

Figure 6-4   Hyper-V Manager showing a virtual machine

Connecting to a virtual machine opens a window that serves as the user interface to the VM and looks similar to a Remote Desktop connection. You can connect to a VM by using any of the following methods:

- Right-click the VM and click Connect.
- Double-click the VM.
- Select the VM and double-click its screenshot in the bottom section.
- Select the VM and click Connect in the Action menu or Actions pane.

After you're connected, you see the Virtual Machine Connection console, shown in Figure 6-5. The toolbar icons from left to right are as follows:

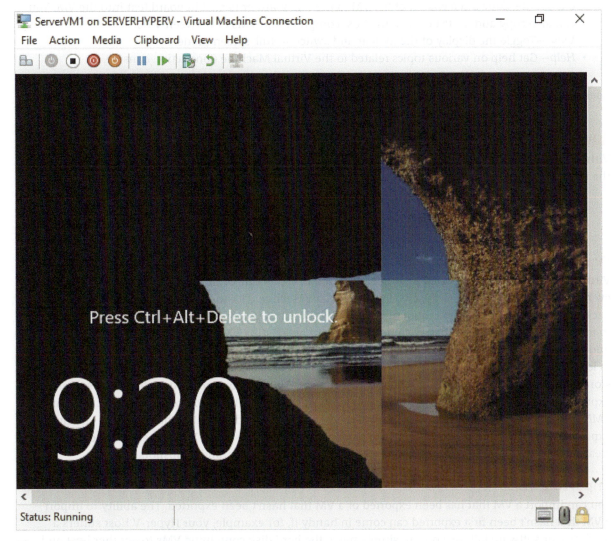

Figure 6-5   The Virtual Machine Connection console

- Ctrl+Alt+Delete (sends a Ctrl+Alt+Delete keystroke to the VM)
- Start (starts the VM)
- Turn Off (turns off the VM)
- Shut Down (sends a signal to the OS to perform a shutdown)
- Save (saves the VM's state, similar to Windows hibernation mode)
- Pause (pauses the VM, similar to Windows sleep mode)
- Reset (resets the VM)
- Checkpoint (creates a checkpoint of a VM)
- Revert (reverts to a VM's checkpoint)
- Enhanced session (changes the session mode to enhanced)

Most of the options on the toolbar are self-explanatory, but checkpoints are discussed later in the chapter in the "Managing Virtual Machines" section and the enhanced session mode is discussed in the "Enhanced Session Mode" section. You can access all these toolbar options from the Action menu, too. The following list summarizes some tasks you can perform with other menus:

- *File*—Access the VM's settings and exit the VM.
- *Action*—Perform all the actions on the toolbar.
- *Media*—Specify a CD/DVD drive that the VM should connect to, specify an .iso file that the VM mounts as a virtual CD/DVD drive, or specify a floppy disk image that can be mounted as a virtual floppy disk.
- *Clipboard*—Copy a screenshot of the VM to the Clipboard or paste Clipboard text into the VM. You can also copy and paste between the host computer and VMs or between VMs.
- *View*—Toggle the display of the toolbar and switch to full-screen mode.
- *Help*—Get help on various topics related to the Virtual Machine Connection console.

If you want to disconnect from a VM, which closes the Virtual Machine Connection console but doesn't shut down the VM, simply click File, Exit from the menu or close the window.

Advanced VM Creation Methods

Virtual machines can be created by using methods other than the New Virtual Machine Wizard, including the following:

- Importing an exported VM
- Copying the virtual disk
- Converting a physical machine to a virtual machine

Exporting VMs

Virtual machines can be exported and then imported to create one or more virtual machines. You can even export a running VM. Because you can export a VM while it's running, this feature allows you to back up a VM by exporting it without first shutting it down. You can use an exported VM as a backup, to move a VM to a different host, or to make a copy of an existing VM. When you choose the Export option for a VM, you're prompted to enter a path for storing the exported VM. You can export the VM to local storage or enter a path to a network share. After a VM is exported, it can be moved to archival storage as a backup, imported on another server running Hyper-V, or imported on the same server. To export a VM using PowerShell, use the Export-VM *VMName* -Path *C:\ExportVMs* cmdlet replacing *VMName* and *C:\ExportVMs* with the name of the VM to export and the path where the files should be exported. When you export a VM, it creates a folder with the name of the VM in the specified path and creates three subfolders named Virtual Machines, Virtual Hard Disks, and Snapshots.

Importing VMs

You can import a VM that has been exported or a VM that hasn't been exported. The ability to import a VM that hasn't been first exported can come in handy if, for example, your Hyper-V host suffers a hardware or software failure; you can simply move the hard disk containing VMs to another host and import them in place. When you import a VM, you have three options for the type of import:

- *Register the virtual machine in place (use the existing unique ID)*—This option registers the exported VM in Hyper-V from its current location. No copy of the exported VM is made. Use this option only if you're restoring a failed or corrupt VM or rebuilding a Hyper-V host and the files are already where you want them. The advantage of this option is that the import process is fast. Note that you can't import a VM that already exists in Hyper-V. If you need to import a VM that is already in Hyper-V (for example, if it is corrupt or will no longer boot for some reason), you must first delete that VM in Hyper-V Manager or use the Restore the virtual machine option discussed next.
- *Restore the virtual machine (use the existing unique ID)*—This option is usually best for restoring VMs from an export intended as a backup. It copies the VM files to their original location on the host,

leaving the exported files unchanged and available for future restoration if needed. You can't use this option if the original exported VM is already running on the Hyper-V host, so you must shut it down.

- *Copy the virtual machine (create a new unique ID)*—Use this option to make a copy or clone of a VM and register it in Hyper-V. For example, use this option if you want to use a VM as a template for additional VMs that you can run on the same Hyper-V host or another Hyper-V host. Because a new unique ID is created, the VMs can run on the same Hyper-V host as the exported VM.

> **Caution** ⚠
>
> If you import a VM in which the original VM is a member of a domain, you must run Sysprep on the guest OS before you can make it a member of the same domain as the exported VM. For example, you are running a domain named MCSA2016.local and you create a VM named ServerDM1 and export that VM. You then join ServerDM1 to the domain. Next, you import ServerDM1 using the copy option. Next, you change its computer name and try to join it to the MCSA2016.local domain. You will get an error indicating that the VM is already a member of the domain. You must first run Sysprep on the imported VM since Sysprep will change the necessary security identifiers within Windows.

To import a VM using PowerShell, use the `Import-VM -ImportType -Path PathtoVM` cmdlet where `-ImportType` is either `-Register` to register the VM in place or `-Copy` to restore the VM and use the existing unique ID. Use `-Copy -GenerateNewId` to copy the VM and create a new unique ID. *PathtoVM* is the path of the VM configuration file. You need the file name of the configuration file, which includes the VM's GUID. The GUID is the unique identifier for the VM and is 128 bits in length or 32 hexadecimal digits, which is rather cumbersome to type. However, there is a shortcut as long as there is only one configuration file in the path from which you are importing. First, find out the name of the configuration file by looking in the Virtual Machines folder where you exported the VM. Make a note of the first character of the file name (it will be a hexadecimal number). Then, when you type the `Import-VM` cmdlet, type the path to the configuration file and then type only the first character of the file name and press Tab. PowerShell will complete the file name for you. You will see this in action in an activity.

> **Note** 📎
>
> By default, when you import a VM with the copy option, it will copy it to the default location specified in the Hyper-V settings for virtual machines and virtual hard disks. You can override this using the `-VirtualMachinePath` and `-VhdDestinationPath` parameters.

Copying a Virtual Disk

Copying a virtual disk doesn't actually create a new VM, but doing so means you don't have to install a guest OS on a new VM you create. The result isn't much different from an export operation followed by an import with the *Copy the virtual machine (create a new unique ID)* option, but the procedure is different:

1. Copy the virtual hard disk from an existing VM to a new folder. Hyper-V virtual hard disks have the extension `.vhdx` and are usually placed in the location you select when you create a virtual hard disk in the New Virtual Machine Wizard. The VM that's currently using the virtual disk must be shut down before you copy it.

2. Create a virtual machine with the New Virtual Machine Wizard, but in the Connect Virtual Hard Disk window, select the *Use an existing virtual hard disk* option, and browse to the copied virtual hard disk. With PowerShell, use the `New-VM` cmdlet, include the `-VHDPath` parameter and specify the path to the copied VHD.

Because the guest OS is on the virtual hard disk, you have a new VM with the same guest OS as the virtual hard disk. The only real difference between this method and the export/import method is that in this method, you must create the VM and can change the VM's name and configuration in the New Virtual Machine Wizard.

Converting a Physical Machine to a Virtual Machine

Hyper-V has no built-in tools to create a VM from a physical computer, but other tools are available for this task. One comes with the Microsoft System Center Virtual Machine Manager (SCVMM), which is a tool for managing multiple Hyper-V hosts. It has the Convert Physical Server Wizard that walks you through the conversion process.

A less expensive and less complex option is to download the free `disk2vhd` utility from *http://technet.microsoft.com/sysinternals/*. This utility runs on the physical computer you wish to convert and creates a virtual hard disk file from the disk on the physical server. You can then create a Hyper-V VM and use the option to use an existing virtual disk. Be aware that the OS on the physical disk was originally meant for a particular hardware configuration, so you might have to change other settings. The original physical disk is unaltered and can be used as always.

> **Tip** ⓘ
>
> You can create a virtual disk by copying the contents of one of the host machine's physical disks. In Hyper-V Manager, just click New, Hard Disk and then in the Configure Disk window, select the *Copy the contents of the specified physical disk* option. If you remove a computer's OS disk and install it in the Hyper-V host machine, you can create a new virtual disk from it and attach it to a VM. You can do this with data disks as well. Using the `disk2vhd` utility is usually an easier solution, however.

Summary of PowerShell Cmdlets for Working with VMs

You can also create and manage VMs with PowerShell cmdlets and create PowerShell scripts to automate VM management. Table 6-2 describes the cmdlets you use most often when working with VMs. To see all cmdlets that work with VMs, use the `Get-Command *-VM*` cmdlet. To see all Hyper-V related cmdlets, use the `Get-Command -Module Hyper-V` cmdlet. There are over 200 of them.

Table 6-2 PowerShell cmdlets for working with VMs

Cmdlet	Use	Example

New-VM	Create a virtual machine.	To create a VM named VMTest1 with 2 GB RAM and a blank virtual disk named `VMTest1.vhdx` stored in the V:\ VMs\VMTest1 folder, enter:
		
		`New-VM -Name VMTest1 -MemoryStartupBytes`
		`  2GB -NewVHDPath V:\VMs\VMTest1\VMTest1.vhdx`

Start-VM	Start a VM.	To start all VMs with a name starting with "VMTest," enter: `Start-VM -Name VMTest*`
Stop-VM	Shut down a VM. Use the `-Force` option to force the shutdown even if running applications have unsaved data or the screen is locked. Loss of data can result if a running application doesn't automatically save data.	To shut down all VMs with a name starting with "VMTest," enter: `Stop-VM -Name VMTest*`

Table 6-2   PowerShell cmdlets for working with VMs *(continued)*

Cmdlet	Use	Example
Get-VM	Display information about a VM. This can also be used to pipe information to other cmdlets.	To display a list of running VMs, enter: `Get-VM	Where-Object {$_.State -eq 'Running'}`
Suspend-VM	Pause a running VM.	`Suspend-VM -Name VMTest1`
Save-VM	Save the state of a VM.	`Save-VM -Name VMTest1`
Restart-VM	Shut down and restart a VM.	`Restart-VM -Name VMTest1`
Checkpoint-VM	Create a VM checkpoint (snapshot).	To create a checkpoint for VMTest1 named "BeforeInstallingAD," enter: `Checkpoint-VM -Name "VMTest1" -SnapshotName "BeforeInstallingAD"`
Restore-VMSnapshot	Restore a VM to a previous checkpoint.	To restore the VMTest1 VM to a snapshot named "BeforeInstallingAD," enter: `Restore-VMSnapshot -Name "BeforeInstallingAD" -VMName VMTest1`
Export-VM	Export a VM.	To export the VMTest1 VM to the V:\VMExport folder, enter: `Export-VM -Name VMTest1 -Path V:\VMExport`
Import-VM	Import a VM.	To import the previously exported VMTest1 with the copy and create new ID option, enter: `Import-VM -Path "V:\VMExport\VMTest1" -Copy -GenerateNewID`

Generation 1 and Generation 2 VMs

When you create a VM with the New Virtual Machine Wizard or the New-VM PowerShell cmdlet, you have the option of creating a generation 1 or generation 2 VM. Generation 2 VMs are based on revised virtual hardware specifications, so they have enhanced VM capabilities and support for newer standards:

- *Unified Extensible Firmware Interface (UEFI) firmware instead of traditional PC BIOS*—Enhances the VM's hardware environment and removes the 2.2 TB partition limit for the boot volume. Also supports PXE boot with synthetic device drivers as well as booting from a SCSI virtual disk. The guest OS must be a 64-bit OS.
- *Device support*—Removes support for legacy network adapters, IDE controllers, legacy keyboards, and floppy disk controllers. Adds support for booting from software-based devices, using virtual machine bus (VMBus), SCSI devices, and a new software-based DVD drive. Generation 2 VMs don't support booting from a physical DVD device; you must use an ISO file or a network boot to start an installation.
- *Network boot with IPv6*—Generation 1 VMs could network boot only with IPv4.
- *VHDX-only support*—Generation 2 VMs support only VHDX hard disk files, but you can convert a VHD file to VHDX with the Convert-VHD PowerShell cmdlet.
- *GPT boot*—Generation 2 VMs can boot to a boot disk that uses a GUID Partitioning Table (GPT) partitioning scheme.
- *Disk expansion*—A VHDX disk can be expanded while the VM is online, including the boot volume.
- *Reduced attack surface*—By removing legacy devices and adding the secure boot feature, security is improved for generation 2 VMs.
- *Secure boot*—Prevents unauthorized code from running during a system boot.

There are other changes, but this list contains the most important improvements. Converting a generation 1 VM to generation 2 is possible, but you can't use a generation 2 VM on Hyper-V versions before Windows Server 2012 R2. In addition, generation 2 VMs support only Windows 8 or Windows Server 2012 and later guest OSs.

Activity 6-1: Resetting Your Virtual Environment

Time Required: 5 minutes

Objective: Reset your virtual environment by applying the InitialConfig checkpoint or snapshot.

Required Tools and Equipment: ServerHyperV

Description: Apply the InitialConfig checkpoint or snapshot to ServerHyperV.

1. Be sure that ServerHyperV is shut down. In your virtualization program, apply the InitialConfig checkpoint or snapshot to ServerHyperV.
2. Close your virtual machine environment.

Activity 6-2: Creating a Virtual Machine

Time Required: 10 minutes

Objective: Create a new virtual machine using PowerShell.

Required Tools and Equipment: ServerHyperV

Description: The Hyper-V role is installed on your server and you are ready to create a virtual machine. In Chapter 2, you created a virtual machine using Hyper-V Manager. In this activity, you create a VM using PowerShell.

1. Sign in to ServerHyperV as **Administrator**.
2. Open a PowerShell window. You will create a new virtual machine named VMTest1 with 1 GB of RAM and a 40 GB virtual hard disk located in C:\VMs\VMTest1.
3. In PowerShell, type **New-VM VMTest1 -MemoryStartupBytes 1GB -NewVHDPath C:\VMs\VMTest1\ VMTest1.vhdx -NewVHDSizeBytes 40GB** and press **Enter**. By default, a generation 1 VM is created unless you specify otherwise using the -Generation 2 parameter. In addition, a network adapter is created, but it is not connected to a virtual switch.
4. Next, you connect the network adapter to the virtual switch named PrivateNet. Type **Connect-NetworkAdapter VMTest1 -Name "Network Adapter" -SwitchName PrivateNet**, and press **Enter**.
5. You need to point the virtual DVD to an ISO file if you want to install an OS on it. You point the DVD drive to an ISO file on the host at path C:\isos\w2k16.iso. Type **SetVMDvdDrive VMTest1 -Path C:\isos\w2k16.iso** and press **Enter**.
6. To see information about the new VM, type **Get-VM VMTest1** and press **Enter**. You see just a summary of the VM. To see more details, type **Get-VM VMTest1 | fl *** and press **Enter**. That command tells PowerShell to show all the properties of the VM in a list format (`fl` means Format-List, and the asterisk * means all properties). You can also see the VM and its settings in Hyper-V Manager. Open Hyper-V Manager, if desired, and verify that your VM can be seen and managed there.
7. One of the nice things about using PowerShell to manage VMs is that you can get detailed information about VMs and create scripts for a number of management functions. For example, you can start all VMs that are currently turned off. Type **Get-VM | Where-Object {$_.State -eq "Off"} | Start-VM** and press **Enter**. All VMs that are currently off are started. You can access most of the properties of a VM by using the syntax `&_.PropertyName`. For example, in the cmdlet you just entered the *PropertyName* is `State`.
8. Next, you can stop all the running VMs. Type **Get-VM | Where-Object {$_.State -eq "Running"} | Stop-VM -Force** and press **Enter**. The `-Force` parameter causes the VM to be turned off even if the OS is locked or there is no OS installed.
9. You will delete this VM since you will use the premade VMs named ServerVM1 and ServerVM2 for the remainder of the Hyper-V activities. Type **Remove-VM VMTest1 -Force** and press **Enter**. Removing a VM doesn't delete the virtual disk it was using. To delete the virtual disk, just use the `del` command. Type **del C:\ VMs\VMTest1\VMTest1.vhdx** and press **Enter**.
10. Stay signed in to ServerHyperV and continue to the next activity.

Activity 6-3: Working with Virtual Machines in Hyper-V Manager

Time Required: 25 minutes
Objective: Explore Hyper-V Manager.
Required Tools and Equipment: ServerHyperV, ServerVM1 virtual machine
Description: In this activity, you work with Hyper-V Manager to become familiar with managing virtual machines in Windows Server 2016. You create a checkpoint, make some changes to the OS, and revert to the checkpoint.

1. Sign in to ServerHyperV as **Administrator**, if necessary.
2. Open Server Manager, and click **Tools, Hyper-V Manager** from the menu.
3. Right-click the **ServerVM1** virtual machine and click **Connect**.
4. Power on ServerVM1 by clicking the **Start** toolbar icon or clicking **Action, Start** from the menu. While Windows is booting, close the Virtual Machine Connection console. Notice that in Hyper-V Manager, the VM's CPU use changes as Windows boots, and the VM's screenshot in the bottom pane changes periodically.
5. Double-click the VM's screenshot at the bottom of Hyper-V Manager to open the Virtual Machine Connection console for the VM. After Windows finishes booting, click the **Ctrl+Alt+Delete** toolbar icon (the leftmost icon) to send a Ctrl+Alt+Delete keystroke to the VM, and sign in as **Administrator**.

> **Tip** ⓘ
>
> To see a description of any toolbar icon, hover your mouse pointer over it.

6. Start Notepad, and type your name in a new text document. Don't close Notepad or save the file yet. In the Virtual Machine Connection console menu, click the **Save** toolbar icon or click **Action, Save**.
7. Close the Virtual Machine Connection console. In Hyper-V Manager, notice that the State column for the VM shows Saved (or Saving if it hasn't finished saving). After it has finished saving, open the Virtual Machine Connection console by double-clicking **ServerVM1**. Start the VM by clicking the **Start** toolbar icon. You're right where you left off in Notepad.
8. Save the Notepad file to your desktop as **file1.txt**, and then exit Notepad.
9. Click the **Checkpoint** toolbar icon or click **Action, Checkpoint** from the menu. When you're prompted to enter a name, type **BeforeDeletingFile1**, and then click **Yes**. You see a message titled "Production checkpoint created." Read the information in the message, which informs you that the running application state was not included in the checkpoint. Production checkpoints are a new feature in Windows Server 2016 and are discussed later in this chapter. Click **OK**.
10. After the checkpoint is finished, minimize the VM, and note in Hyper-V Manager that the checkpoint is listed in the Checkpoints section. Maximize the VM, and delete file1 from your desktop. Empty the Recycle Bin so that you know the file is really gone.
11. Click the **Revert** toolbar icon or click **Action, Revert** from the menu.
12. Click **Revert** when prompted. The VM displays a message that it's reverting and the VM is turned off. Start the VM and sign in. When the desktop is displayed again, you should see the Notepad file back on the desktop. Close the Virtual Machine Connection console.

> **Note** 📎
>
> The VM was turned off when you reverted the checkpoint because it is a Production checkpoint that doesn't save the running state of the VM. If it had been a regular checkpoint, the VM would have stayed on and you would have been returned to the running state when you took the checkpoint.

13. In Hyper-V Manager, right-click **ServerVM1** and click **Shutdown**. When prompted, click the **Shut Down** button. The Status column displays Shutting Down Virtual Machine. Close the Virtual Machine Connection console.

14. After the VM state changes to Off, delete the checkpoint by right-clicking **BeforeDeletingFile1** in the Checkpoints section and clicking **Delete Checkpoint**. Click **Delete** to confirm.

15. Stay signed in to ServerHyperV if you're continuing to the next activity.

Activity 6-4: Exporting and Importing a VM

Time Required: 30 minutes

Objective: Export a VM and then import it using PowerShell.

Required Tools and Equipment: ServerHyperV

Description: In this activity, you practice exporting and importing a VM using PowerShell. You will work with the VM named InstallCore because it takes much less time to export and import it, and it takes less disk space.

1. On ServerHyperV, open a PowerShell window.

2. Type **Export-VM InstallCore -Path C:\ExportVMs** and press **Enter**. PowerShell will create the ExportVMs folder for you.

3. When the export has completed, type **dir C:\ExportVMs** and press **Enter**. You see a folder named InstallCore. Type **dir C:\ExportVMs\InstallCore** and press **Enter**. You see the three folders that contain the exported VM. Type **dir "C:\ExportVMs\InstallCore\Virtual Machines"** and press **Enter**. Be sure to include the quotation marks (") since there is a space in the path. You see the two files that have the configuration information of your exported VM. Make a note of the first character of the file name (both file names are the same except for the extension).

4. Now, you will import the VM using the following cmdlet. In the path parameter, be sure to use quotation marks, type the first character of the configuration file name in place of the *X*, and press the Tab key where it says <Tab> so that PowerShell will finish the path with the configuration file name. Type **Import-VM -Copy -GenerateNewID -Path "C:\ExportVMs\InstallCore\VirtualMachines\X<Tab>** and press **Enter**. Note that had you not included the `GenerateNewID` option, you would have received an error about a duplicate identifier.

Tip ⓘ

You can use the Tab key in any path when typing PowerShell cmdlets or command prompt commands. Windows will always display the first file or folder name it finds that starts with the character or characters you type. For example, if you type dir c:\ex<Tab>, Windows will complete that part of the path with C:\ExportVMs\, assuming a folder with that name exists.

5. Verify the new virtual machine by typing **Get-VM** and pressing **Enter**. Note that there are now two VMs with the name InstallCore. The next thing you would do is rename the imported VM. To do that in PowerShell, you'd need to use the virtual machine ID since you can't distinguish them by name. For now, open **Hyper-V Manager**.

6. The VM you just imported will be listed second since it has a later creation date. To verify, click each VM and look in the bottom pane where the creation date is shown. Delete the second virtual machine named **InstallCore** by right-clicking it and clicking **Delete**. Click **Delete** to confirm. Note that deleting the VM in Hyper-V only deletes the configuration file, not the virtual hard disk.

7. Stay signed in and continue to the next activity.

Managing Virtual Machines

 **Certification**

- **70-740 – Implement Hyper-V:**
  Configure virtual machine (VM) settings

Now that you have a general understanding of how Hyper-V works and how to configure virtual networks and virtual hard disks, this section covers additional features you can use to manage and configure the virtual environment. In particular, you examine the following:

- Virtual machine hardware settings
- Integration Services
- Checkpoints
- Automatic start and stop actions
- Resource metering
- Enhanced Session mode

Virtual Machine Hardware Settings

Virtual machines have a number of hardware settings that can be configured. Chapter 7 covers working with virtual hard disks and virtual network settings in more detail. In this section, you look at options for changing BIOS settings, modifying the amount of memory allocated to a VM, and configuring virtual processor settings. Most settings can't be changed unless the VM is powered off. All these settings are accessed by right-clicking a VM and clicking Settings.

BIOS and Firmware Settings

The BIOS settings for a generation 1 VM enable you to change the order in which the VM's BIOS searches for boot devices (see Figure 6-6). To do this, click a device in the Startup order list box and click the up or down arrow to change its order. For example, if you already have an OS installed on the VM's hard disk, you might want to set the boot order to list the IDE disk first so that the VM doesn't attempt to boot from a CD.

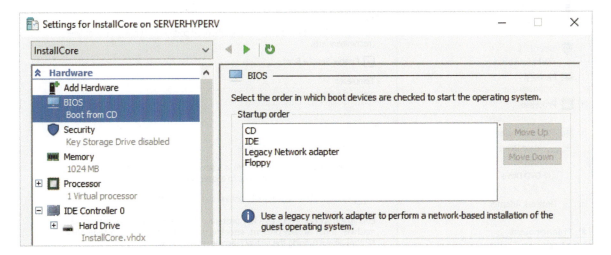

Figure 6-6   BIOS settings for a generation 1 VM

On a generation 2 VM, the hardware category is Firmware instead of BIOS (see Figure 6-7). As with generation 1 VM, you can set the boot order. By default, a generation 2 VM is set to boot from the network adapter using PXE boot or from the DVD drive if you specified an ISO file to connect to the DVD drive. After Windows is installed, the first entry in the boot order is set to a file that is the Windows boot manager file. Secure Boot is enabled by default and is recommended because it prevents unauthorized code from running at startup. On generation 2 VMs, the disk controllers are SCSI only, IDE, and CD; IDE drives are no longer supported.

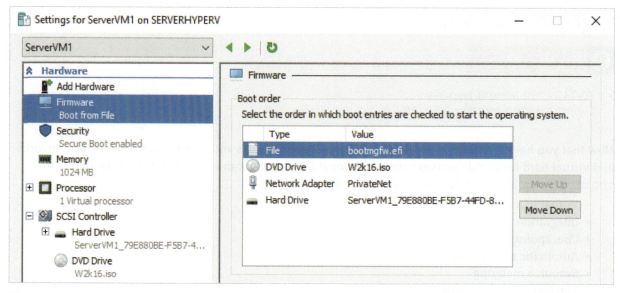

Figure 6-7 Firmware settings for a generation 2 VM

Security

In the Security settings of a VM (see Figure 6-8), you can enable or disable Secure Boot (generation 2 VMs only) and enable encryption support, which allows you to encrypt the virtual hard disks. A new feature in Windows Server 2016 is Shielded VMs. If you enable shielding, Secure Boot and encryption are automatically enabled. Shielding prevents a compromised or malicious administrator from accessing the data on a VM and allows only specific hosts to run the VM. Specifically, you must deploy the Host

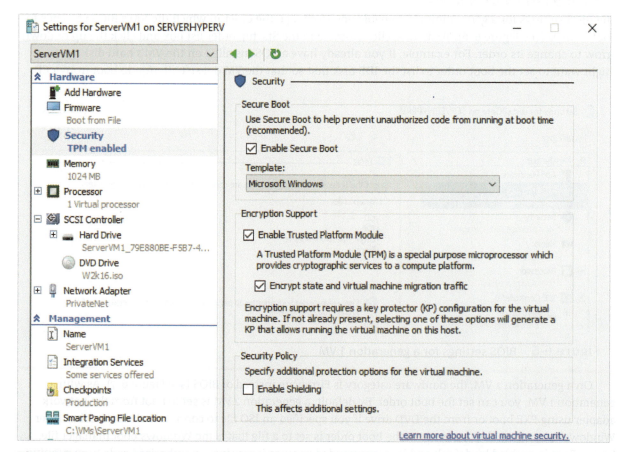

Figure 6-8 Virtual machine security settings

Guardian Service (HGS), which sets up a trust relationship between the host and the VM, disallowing other hosts from running the VM and preventing the host from running untrusted VMs. Shielded VMs and the Host Guardian Service are beyond the scope of this book and these topics are covered in Exam 70-744: Securing Windows Server 2016.

Memory Allocation

When you create a VM, you can configure the amount of memory it has allocated from the host computer, and you can change this amount at any time later while the VM is turned off. The amount of memory you allocate must take into account other VMs running simultaneously and have enough memory left over for the host server. Windows Server 2016 running Hyper-V needs about 800 MB RAM (512 MB for Windows Server 2016 and 300 MB for Hyper-V) plus 32 MB for each running VM that has been assigned up to 1 GB RAM. For example, if you plan to run three virtual machines, each with 1 GB RAM, you need 3 × 1 GB for the VMs plus 32 MB × 3 plus 800 MB for the host, for a total of a little less than 4 GB. If the VMs are allocated more than 1 GB, add 8 MB to the host for each additional GB.

Dynamic Memory

Dynamic Memory allows an administrator to set startup, minimum, and maximum memory allocation values for each VM. Hyper-V adjusts the memory allocation for a VM up or down, based on its actual memory needs, between the minimum and maximum value you specify. Dynamic Memory isn't enabled by default; you enable it by choosing Memory in the VM's settings (see Figure 6-9). The following list describes the settings for this feature:

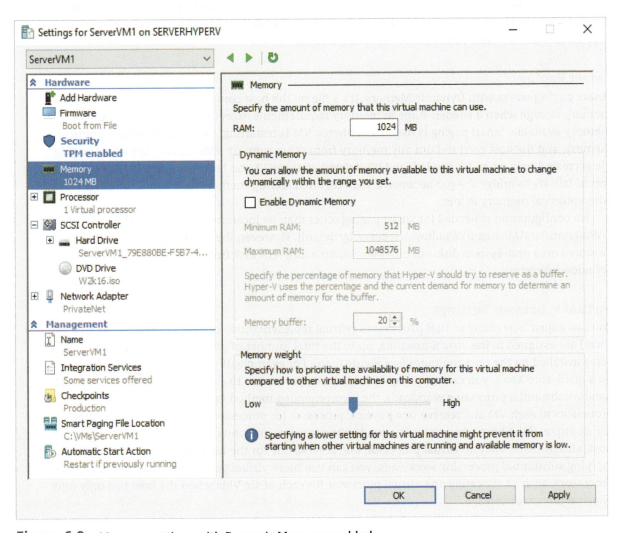

Figure 6-9   Memory settings with Dynamic Memory enabled

- *RAM*—This setting specifies the amount of RAM allocated to a VM when it starts. When a computer starts, it often consumes more RAM because of all the processes loaded into memory and started. Some processes look for a minimum amount of available RAM when they're started, and if this amount isn't available, they don't start. After all the initial processes have started, the system might require less than the startup RAM.
- *Minimum RAM*—The least amount of RAM the VM can ever be allocated.
- *Maximum RAM*—The most amount of RAM the VM can ever be allocated.
- *Memory buffer*—The amount of extra memory Hyper-V attempts to assign to a VM above the VM's current requirements. For example, if the memory buffer is set to 20% and the VM currently needs 1 GB RAM, Hyper-V attempts to allocate 1 GB plus 20%, or 1.2 GB. The memory buffer amount is allocated to a VM only if there's enough physical memory to support the requested amount.
- *Memory weight*—This slider represents a priority. If there's not enough physical memory to allocate the requested amount of RAM to all VMs, the VMs with the highest memory weight are given the highest priority. By default, the memory weight slider is set in the middle of the scale.

Hot Add Memory

Hyper-V in Windows Server 2016 adds the ability to hot add and remove memory, which is the addition of memory or removal of memory while the VM is running. This feature is supported only on VMs running Windows 10 or Windows Server 2016 guest OSs and some distributions of Linux. Furthermore, the VM configuration version must be version 8 or higher, so VMs created in earlier versions of Hyper-V will not support this feature until you upgrade the configuration.

Smart Paging

Smart paging works with Dynamic Memory. It's a file on the host computer used for temporary memory storage when a sudden surge in memory requirements exceeds the physical amount of memory available. Smart paging is used only when a VM is restarting, there's no available physical memory, and the host can't reclaim any memory from other running VMs. In fact, the smart paging file is created only when it's needed, and it's deleted after the VM no longer needs it. So, this file is a sort of failsafe to bridge the gap between a VM's required startup memory and its minimum memory when physical memory is low.

No configuration is needed for smart paging other than its location on the host, which is C:\ProgramData\Microsoft\Windows\Hyper-V by default. However, the smart paging file should be stored on a non-system disk—in other words, on a different disk from the one holding the \Windows directory.

Virtual Processor Settings

You can adjust how many **virtual processors** (virtual representations of physical processors or processor cores) are assigned to the virtual machine, up to the total number of physical processors or processor cores installed on the host computer (see Figure 6-10). For example, if you're running a Hyper-V server on a quad-core Xeon, you can assign up to four virtual processors to each VM. However, if your VMs handle substantial processing workloads, the recommended method is to assign one or more virtual processors to each VM and reserve one physical processor (or processor core) for the host computer. For example, if the host computer has a quad-core processor and you're running three VMs on the host, allocate each VM one virtual processor, and reserve one for the host computer. If your VMs aren't carrying substantial processing workloads, you can use more virtual processors than there are physical processors, such as allocating one virtual processor for each of six VMs when the host has only four physical processor cores.

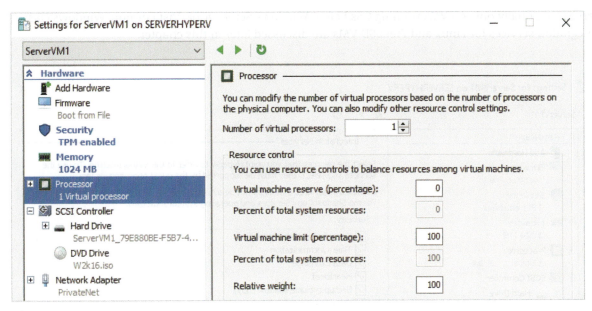

Figure 6-10   Virtual processor settings

The *Resource control* section specifies how host resources are allocated to the VM. In this example, the host has four processors, and the VM has been assigned two:

- *Virtual machine reserve (percentage)*—This setting specifies what percentage of the total processing resources allocated to the VM is guaranteed to be available. The default setting is 0. If you change this setting, the percent of total system resources value changes to reflect what percentage of the total host processing power that is in reserve for the VM. For example, if the VM has been assigned two virtual processors on a host with four processors and you reserve 50% for the VM, 25% of the total host system resources are held in reserve for the VM.
- *Virtual machine limit (percentage)*—This value specifies what percentage of the assigned processing power the VM can use. The default value is 100. If you assign two processors to the VM on a host with four processors, the VM can use 100% of the processing power of two processors, which sets the percent of total system resources at 50. That leaves 50% of the total processing power available for other workloads.
- *Relative weight*—This setting assigns a priority to the VM's access to processing resources when more than one VM is competing for the same resource. The value can be from 1 to 10,000; the higher the value, the higher the VM's priority. The default value is 100. If multiple VMs have the same relative weight value, they get an equal share of the available resources.

Note

Storage controllers, virtual disks, and network adapters are discussed in Chapter 7. This discussion about managing virtual machines continues in the next section, "Integration Services."

Integration Services

The Integration Services section of a VM's settings (see Figure 6-11) indicates which integration services are enabled on a VM. On Windows VMs starting with Windows Server 2008 and Vista, all the services shown in Figure 6-11, except Guest services, are installed by default. You need to install integration services manually only on VMs running OSs before Windows Server 2008/Vista or non-Windows OSs. Integration services for Linux and FreeBSD VMs are discussed later in this chapter.

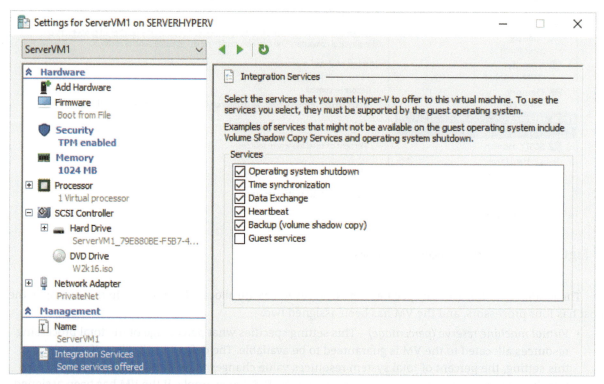

Figure 6-11   Integration Services settings

Note

Hyper-V versions prior to Windows Server 2016 had an option in the Virtual Machine Connection Action menu to install integration services. Performing this action was a good idea, even on OSs that have integration services already installed because you got the most current version and bug fixes. Starting with Windows Server 2016, updates to integration services are delivered via Windows Update.

Integration Services provides enhanced drivers for the guest OS and improves performance and functionality for IDE and SCSI storage devices, network interfaces, and mouse and video devices. The storage controller and network interface drivers included in Integration Services are called **synthetic drivers**, and they're optimized for use in the Hyper-V environment. **Emulated drivers**, which are used when Integration Services isn't installed, are also referred to as *legacy drivers*.

Enhanced video and mouse drivers in Integration Services make using a guest OS's user interface easier. Without integration services installed, the VM captures the mouse when you click inside the VM window, and you must press Ctrl+Alt+left arrow to release the mouse back to the host OS. With Integration Services installed, however, you can move the mouse from guest to host freely. Furthermore, if you access the guest OS through Remote Desktop, the mouse isn't functional in the guest OS at all unless Integration Services is installed.

Aside from enhanced drivers, Integration Services offers these additional services that you can enable or disable in the VM's settings:

- *Operating system shutdown*—Allows you to shut down the VM by clicking the Shutdown button in the Virtual Machine Connection console or in Hyper-V Manager.

- *Time synchronization*—Allows you to synchronize the VM's time with the host. If the VM is a Windows domain controller, however, you shouldn't use this option because domain controllers have their own time synchronization mechanism.
- *Data exchange*—Allows the VM and host to exchange information by using Registry keys.
- *Heartbeat*—Allows the host machine to detect when the VM has locked up or crashed. The host sends heartbeat messages to the guest VM periodically, and the heartbeat service on the guest VM responds. If it fails to respond, the host machine logs an event.
- *Backup (volume shadow copy)*—Allows host backup programs to use Volume Shadow Copy Service (VSS) to back up VM hard disk files.
- *Guest services*—Allows copying files to a running VM "out of band," meaning without using a virtual network connection. Guest services uses the Hyper-V VMBus that all VMs are connected internally through Hyper-V. By default, guest services is disabled, but after it is enabled, you can use the PowerShell cmdlet `Copy-VMFile` on the host computer to copy files from the host to the VM.

Checkpoints

Checkpoints, as you have seen, allow you to save the state of a VM and return to that state at a later time. In previous versions of Hyper-V, the only configuration option for checkpoints was specifying the path where they are stored. Starting with Windows Server 2016, Hyper-V now has two types of checkpoint (see Figure 6-12):

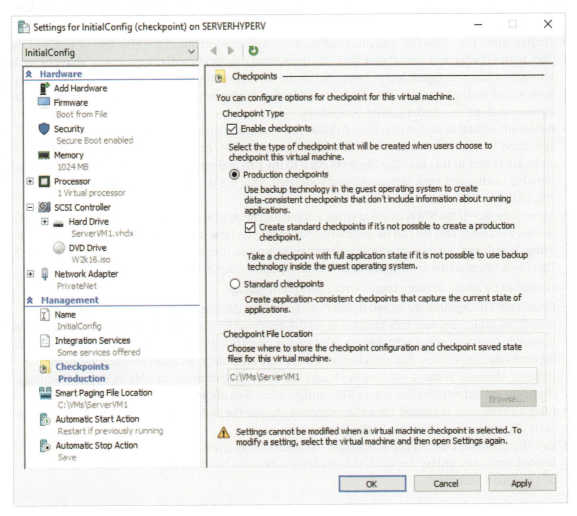

Figure 6-12   Configuring checkpoints

- *Standard checkpoint*—This is the original type of checkpoint that captures the state of a VM, including the running state, if desired. Standard checkpoints should only be used in development and testing, not on production VMs. They are particularly useful if you need to capture the running state of a VM for troubleshooting purposes and for performing what-if scenarios in a lab environment.
- *Production checkpoint*—This new type of checkpoint is supported for production VMs and uses backup technology in the guest OS to create the checkpoint. Production checkpoints do not save the running state of a VM, but they can be created while the VM is running. If you apply a production checkpoint to a running VM, the VM will be shut down and you must restart it. Production checkpoints can be created only on a VM running a supported OS. If you try to create a production checkpoint on a VM that does not support it, a standard checkpoint will be created instead. Production checkpoints are available only on VMs running on a Windows 10 or Windows Server 2016 Hyper-V host.

Managing Checkpoints

Checkpoints make working with VMs more flexible than working with physical machines. You can use them to revert a VM to a previous state, which allows you to explore what-if situations and recover from installations and configurations that have gone wrong. You can create up to 50 checkpoints per VM and revert a VM to any saved checkpoint. This feature is particularly useful in testing and lab environments because you can reset a VM to its original state with the click of a button. With production checkpoints, they can also be safely used on production VMs as well.

When you create a checkpoint, either two or three files are created, depending on whether the VM is running at the time:

- *Configuration file*—This file contains configuration information about the checkpoint (such as the path to the checkpoint virtual disk file) and the virtual machine configuration. Any changes to the virtual machine configuration are recorded in the configuration file, including network, memory, device, and storage settings. This file is stored in the checkpoint file location path specified for the virtual machine in a folder named Snapshots.
- *Automatic virtual hard disk (AVHD or AVHDX) file*—A virtual disk file with the `.avhd` or `.avhdx` extension is created for each virtual disk attached to the VM. All changes made to any of the virtual disks are stored in this file. The file links back to the original virtual disk (VHD or VHDX), which remains unchanged until the checkpoint is deleted. This file is stored in the same folder as the original virtual hard disk file.
- *Saved state file*—If the VM is running when a standard checkpoint is created, the contents of the VM's memory is saved. This file can be quite large, depending on how much memory the VM is currently using. This doesn't apply to production checkpoints because they do not save the running state of a VM. This file is stored in the same location as the checkpoint configuration file.

You need to be aware of some issues with checkpoint storage:

- By default, checkpoints are stored in the C:\ProgramData\Microsoft\Windows\Hyper-V\ Snapshots folder. Because this location is on the host's system volume (where the C:\Windows folder is stored), however, you might want to relocate the checkpoints folder to a different disk if possible for performance reasons. You can change the checkpoint storage location for each VM in the Hyper-V Manager Settings window or change the default location for all VMs in Hyper-V Settings by changing the default location where VM configuration files are stored.
- After a checkpoint is created for a VM, you can't change the checkpoint location for that VM, but each VM can have a different checkpoint location.
- You should always use Hyper-V Manager to delete checkpoints. Checkpoint files shouldn't be deleted manually unless the VM has been deleted because the files must be merged with the original hard disk file.

- If you create a standard checkpoint while a VM is running, the amount of space required for the checkpoint includes the amount of memory allocated to the VM (much like a hibernate file), which substantially increases the total amount of space the checkpoint needs. Ideally, create checkpoints while the VM is shut down to reduce the disk space used.

Some additional cautions regarding checkpoints:

- Checkpoints decrease a VM's disk performance, so use them only as necessary and delete checkpoints that are no longer needed.
- Checkpoints must be deleted before expanding a disk.
- Checkpoints can't be used with pass-through or differencing disks. Pass-through and differencing disks are discussed in Chapter 7.

Reverting to and Applying Checkpoints

There are two ways to use a saved checkpoint: revert and apply. Reverting to a checkpoint returns the VM to its state when the *most recent* checkpoint was taken. The Revert option is available in the Actions pane of Hyper-V Manager when a VM is selected and no checkpoints are currently selected. If you click the Revert option in the Actions pane, the VM is reverted to the last checkpoint made.

The Apply option is available when a checkpoint is selected in the Checkpoints section. Selecting the most recent checkpoint and applying it has the same effect as using the Revert option. However, if you select an earlier checkpoint and apply it, a new checkpoint subtree is created, as shown in Figure 6-13. Checkpoint3 was applied, and the VM is now in the state it was in when Checkpoint3 was taken, as indicated by the Now arrow. Checkpoint2 and Checkpoint4 are still available, but they represent a different checkpoint subtree than Checkpoint3. Because Hyper-V allows you to skip back and forth in time, so to speak, you can test several application scenarios with the ability to return to an initial state or any one of several configurations. Just be aware that the more checkpoints and checkpoint subtrees a VM has, the more resources used by the host computer, so be sure to delete checkpoints and checkpoint subtrees when they are no longer needed.

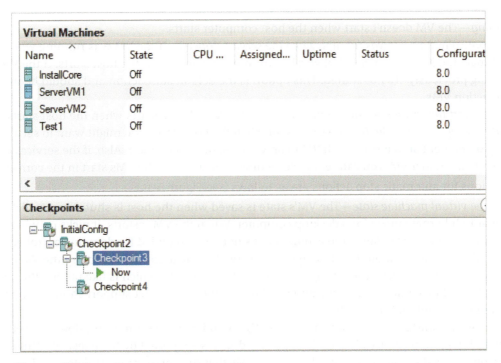

Figure 6-13   After applying a checkpoint

Automatic Start and Stop Actions

You use automatic start actions and automatic stop actions to specify how a VM should behave when the host computer starts and shuts down. The options for automatic start actions are as follows (see Figure 6-14):

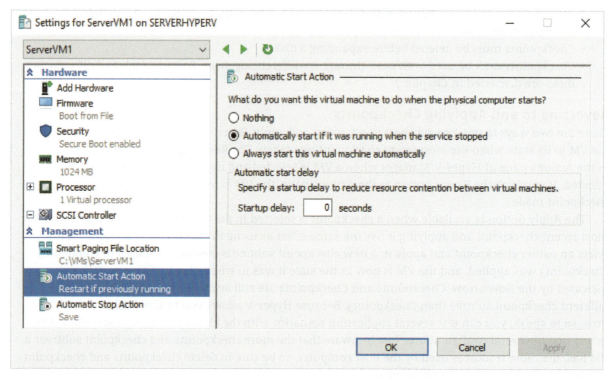

Figure 6-14 Automatic Start Action settings

- *Nothing*—The VM doesn't start when the host computer starts.
- *Automatically start if it was running when the service stopped*—If the VM was running when the host machine (or Hyper-V service) was last running, it starts when the host starts. If the VM wasn't running previously, it's not started. This option is the default start action and should be used with production VMs.
- *Always start this virtual machine automatically*—The VM always starts when the host starts.
- *Startup delay*—If multiple VMs are set to start when the host starts, you might want to set a startup delay of different amounts for each VM to prevent resource contention. Also, if the services of one VM depend on another VM, you can set the delay time to ensure that the VMs start in the correct order.

The options for automatic stop actions are as follows (see Figure 6-15):

- *Save the virtual machine state*—The VM's state is saved when the host is shut down, which is similar to hibernate mode for a desktop computer. When the VM restarts, it picks up where it left off. This option is the default stop action, but it's not recommended for domain controllers. Be aware that the same amount of disk space is reserved as the amount of memory the VM uses.
- *Turn off the virtual machine*—This option powers down the VM, which is like pulling the power cord on a physical machine. It's not recommended unless the VM doesn't support shutdown, but even then, the save option is preferable.
- *Shut down the guest operating system*—The VM's OS undergoes a normal shutdown procedure as long as Integration Services is installed and shutdown is supported by the guest OS. This option is recommended for domain controllers, other VMs that run server roles, and applications that synchronize with other servers.

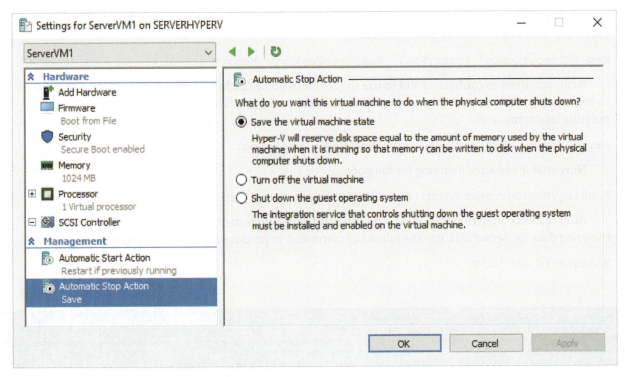

Figure 6-15   Automatic Stop Action settings

Resource Metering

Resource metering is a Hyper-V feature that allows vendors of large-scale virtualization to measure customer use of VM resources for billing purposes. Resource metering is enabled and configured by using PowerShell cmdlets on the Hyper-V host and can measure the following resource metrics on a virtual machine:

- Average CPU use
- Incoming and outgoing network traffic per network adapter
- Minimum, maximum, and average physical memory use
- Maximum disk space allocated

To enable resource metering, enter the following command at a PowerShell prompt on the Hyper-V host:

```
Enable-VMResourceMetering -VMName VirtualMachine
```

Resource metering can be enabled on an entire VM with this command, but you might also want to measure use for particular metrics. For example, you might want to measure disk use only for virtual hard disks, memory, or network. To target specific metrics, you create a resource pool for one or more metrics and then enable resource metering for the resource pool. You can create resource pools of the following types:

- *Memory*—Measures physical memory use
- *Processor*—Measures CPU use
- *Ethernet*—Measures network traffic
- *VHD*—Measures virtual hard disk use
- *ISO*—Measures CD/DVD usage
- *VFD*—Measures virtual floppy disk use
- *FibreChannelPort*—Measures use of a virtual Fibre Channel port

For example, to create a resource pool named MemoryPool to measure memory use, enter the following command at a PowerShell prompt:

```
New-VMResourcePool MemoryPool -ResourcePoolType Memory
```

Next, you need to configure a VM to use the resource pool. The following command tells ServerVM1 to begin using resource pool MemoryPool to measure memory use. The VM must be shut down before entering this command:

```
Set-VMMemory ServerVM1 -ResourcePoolName MemoryPool
```

Now enable resource metering for the pool:

```
Enable-VMResourceMetering -ResourcePoolName MemoryPool
```

After resource metering is enabled, you can display resource-metering data. To display all resource-metering data for ServerVM1, use the following command to produce the output in Figure 6-16:

```
Measure-VM ServerVM1
```

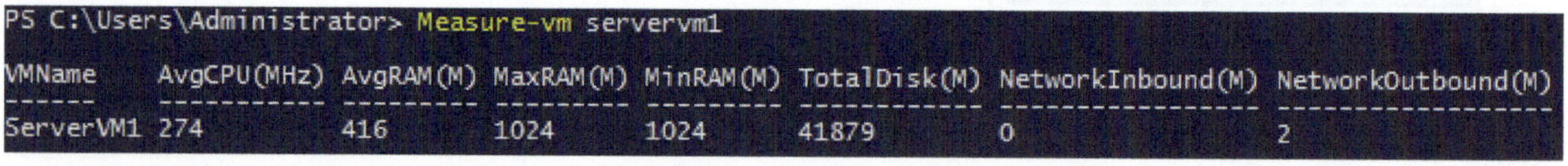

```
PS C:\Users\Administrator> Measure-vm servervm1

VMName      AvgCPU(MHz)  AvgRAM(M)  MaxRAM(M)  MinRAM(M)  TotalDisk(M)  NetworkInbound(M)  NetworkOutbound(M)
------      -----------  ---------  ---------  ---------  ------------  -----------------  ------------------
ServerVM1   274          416        1024       1024       41879         0                  2
```

Figure 6-16　Output from the `Measure-VM` **cmdlet**

To view the data for a resource pool, use the following command to get output similar to that in Figure 6-17:

```
Measure-VMResourcePool MemoryPool
```

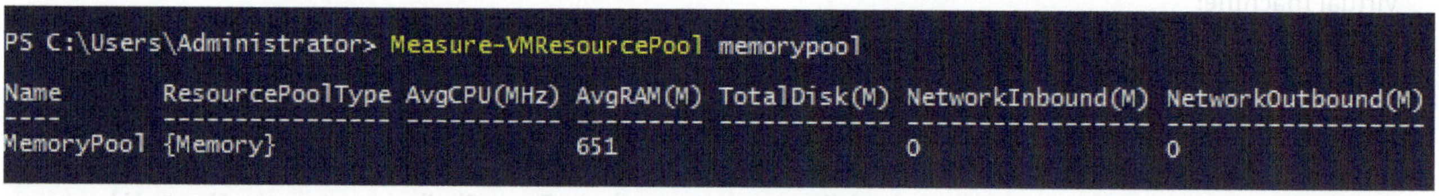

```
PS C:\Users\Administrator> Measure-VMResourcePool memorypool

Name         ResourcePoolType  AvgCPU(MHz)  AvgRAM(M)  TotalDisk(M)  NetworkInbound(M)  NetworkOutbound(M)
----         ----------------  -----------  ---------  ------------  -----------------  ------------------
MemoryPool   {Memory}                       651                      0                  0
```

Figure 6-17　Output from the `Measure-VMResourcePool` **cmdlet**

You can create PowerShell scripts for enabling and disabling resource metering, collecting results, and formatting and saving the results to report files for convenient review.

Enhanced Session Mode

Enhanced Session mode is a feature that improves interaction and device redirection between the host computer and the Virtual Machine Connection console. It's supported by Windows Server 2012 R2 and Windows 8.1 Pro and Enterprise and later guest OSs. It provides much the same functions as a Remote Desktop connection without the need for a network connection to the guest OS.

A regular session, called a *basic session* in Hyper-V, redirects only screen, mouse, and keyboard I/O from the guest to the Virtual Machine Connection console. An enhanced session offers these additional redirected resources and features:

- Audio redirection
- Printer redirection
- USB devices and smart cards

- Drives
- Some plug-and-play devices
- Display configuration
- Copy and paste of Clipboard data, files, and folders

With Enhanced Session mode enabled, the first thing you notice is that when you try to connect to a Virtual Machine Connection console, a message box prompts you to select the display configuration. If you click the Show Options button, you see the dialog box shown in Figure 6-18.

Figure 6-18   Enhanced Session mode settings

You can click the Local Resources tab to choose which resources from the VM should be redirected to the host computer. For example, you can print to a printer connected to the host computer from the guest OS or play audio files on the guest through the host computer's speakers. You also have access to the Clipboard so that you can copy and paste text and files between the host and the guest.

 Note

To copy and paste files between the host and the guest, you must use the copy-and-paste method; you can't drag and drop files between the host and the guest.

You can also redirect drives so that files on the host computer are available to the VM. If you do, a new drive icon is displayed in File Explorer on the guest OS. For example, if you redirect the C drive on the ServerHyperV host, a new icon named *C on ServerHyperV* is listed under Devices and drives in File Explorer on the guest OS. The VM now has access to files on the C drive of the host computer.

Enabling Enhanced Session Mode

To use Enhanced Session mode, you must enable it in Hyper-V Manager and on the guest OS. By default, Enhanced Session mode is enabled on guest OSs that support it. However, verify the following:

- Remote Desktop Services must be running on the guest OS. This service is running by default, but you can verify it or start it, if necessary, in the Services MMC. Selecting the *Allow remote connections to this computer* option in the System Properties dialog box isn't necessary.
- You must sign in to the guest OS with an account that's a member of the local Administrators or remote Desktop Users group.

To enable Enhanced Session mode, in Hyper-V Manager, click Hyper-V Settings and then click Enhanced Session Mode Policy. In the right pane, click Allow enhanced session mode (see Figure 6-19). To configure Virtual Machine Connection to use Enhanced Session mode, click Enhanced Session Mode in the left pane under User and click Use enhanced session mode, which is enabled by default. To enable it on the VM, start the VM and when prompted, click Connect. On the Hyper-V connect window, you'll see that the Session mode icon is now enabled and the VM is running in Enhanced Session mode. Click the Session mode icon between enhanced and basic session modes. To enable Enhanced Session mode using PowerShell, use the `Set-VMHost -EnableEnhancedSessionMode $true` cmdlet on the Hyper-V host.

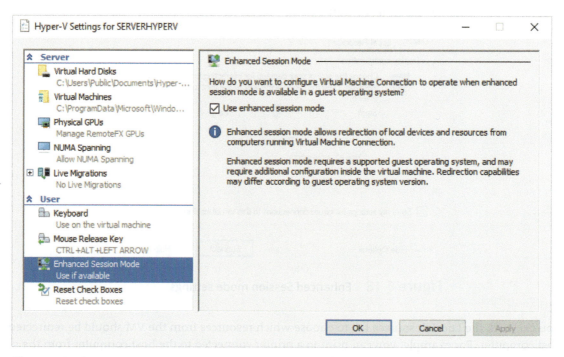

Figure 6-19   Enabling Enhanced Session mode in Hyper-V Manager

Non-Uniform Memory Access Support

Non-Uniform Memory Access (NUMA) is a system memory architecture used in multiprocessor systems that allows processors to more efficiently share memory. On multiprocessor systems, there are multiple banks of memory that are assigned to each processor. Consider a system that has two physical processors, CPU-A and CPU-B. The motherboard has 64 GB of RAM, and 32 GB is assigned to CPU-A and 32 GB is assigned to CPU-B. The memory assigned to CPU-A is considered local memory from CPU-A's perspective, and the memory assigned to CPU-B is considered remote from CPU-A's perspective. CPU-A can access both its local memory and the remote memory assigned to CPU-B, but access to the local memory is considerably faster. You can look at it like a computer that is accessing disk storage that is local versus storage that is remote, located on another server across the network. The computer can access both the local and remote storage, but access to the local storage is faster.

NUMA divides the memory and processors into groups called *NUMA nodes*. Memory in the same node as the processor is local memory, and memory in a different node is remote memory. An operating system that supports NUMA attempts to run processes and applications using a processor and memory that are located in the same node, so those processes have faster access to their allocated memory.

Hyper-V and Hyper-V VMs support NUMA, so when a VM starts, the memory required by the VM is allocated from a single NUMA node, if possible, and from the same NUMA node as the virtual processor. If more memory is needed than can be allocated from a single NUMA node, additional memory is allocated from another NUMA node. This is referred to as **NUMA spanning**. Although NUMA spanning allows a VM to run when not enough resources exist in a single NUMA node, performance is decreased because some memory access will be to a remote NUMA node.

Configuring NUMA

By default, NUMA spanning is enabled in Hyper-V, but it can be disabled. To change the setting in Hyper-V Manager, click Hyper-V Settings and click NUMA Spanning. Click the check box (see Figure 6-20) to enable or disable NUMA spanning. This setting affects all VMs on the Hyper-V host.

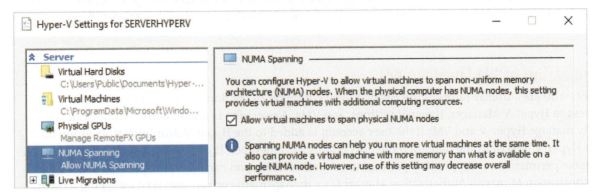

Figure 6-20   Enabling or disabling NUMA spanning

NUMA can be configured on individual VMs (see Figure 6-21). In most cases, the Use Hardware Topology setting should be used for optimal performance because the virtual NUMA settings will match the host computer's NUMA architecture. However, if the VM will be moved or migrated between multiple Hyper-V hosts that have different NUMA architectures, the VM should be configured with the lowest values available among all the hosts that might run the VM. For example, if one host has a maximum number of processors value of 2 and maximum amount of memory value of 4096, and another host has a maximum processors value of 4 and a maximum amount of memory value of 8192, the VM's NUMA settings should be set to the lower of the two.

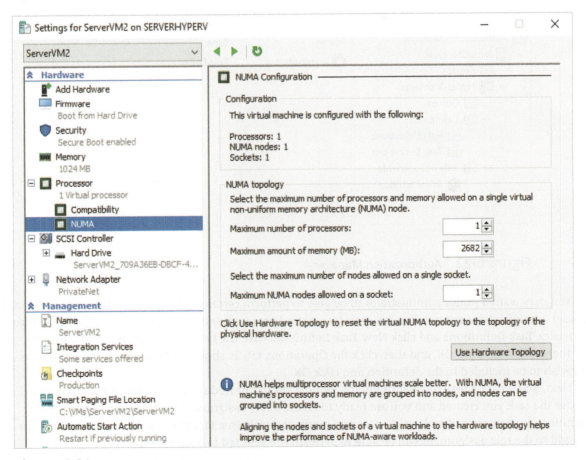

Figure 6-21   Configuring NUMA on a VM

Note

NUMA settings will have no effect on a VM that has Dynamic Memory enabled. A VM with Dynamic Memory enabled will be allocated resources only from a single NUMA node irrespective of the NUMA settings. Also, note that VMs that don't have memory requirements sufficient to use more than one NUMA node will not benefit from NUMA.

Delegation of VM Management

Users who are administrators of the Hyper-V host computer or are domain administrators have full access to Hyper-V Manager, Hyper-V settings, and VMs. A user who is not an administrator can still fully manage Hyper-V and VMs if the user account is added to the Hyper-V Administrators group on the Hyper-V host or in the domain if the host is a domain member. If you want a user or group of users to have permissions in Hyper-V to perform only specific tasks, you can fine-tune permissions using Authorization Manager. Authorization Manager is a management console you start by typing AzMan. msc from a run dialog box or from the search feature on the taskbar. From the Authorization Manager console, right-click Authorization Manager and click Open Authorization Store. Click Browse, and browse to C:\ProgramData\Windows\Hyper-V\InitialStore.XML (see Figure 6-22). You can define roles and tasks. By default, there is one role defined, that of Administrator, and that role can perform all tasks in Hyper-V on all VMs. Both the Administrators group and the Hyper-V Administrators group are assigned to the Administrator role.

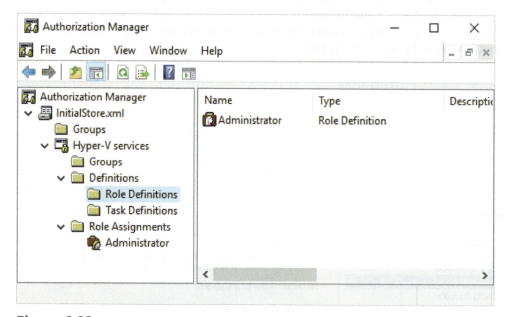

Figure 6-22   Authorization Manager

You may want a junior administrator to be able to perform certain tasks in Hyper-V Manager without broader administrative control. You can start by creating new task definitions. In Authorization Manager, right-click Task Definitions and click New Task Definition. Give the task a name such as Manage VMs, and then click Add. Click OK, and then click the Operations tab as shown in Figure 6-23. Click the tasks you wish to be included in the definition and click OK.

Next, you create a new role definition following a similar procedure as in adding a task definition. Choose the task you created and you are ready to create a role assignment where you can add the role definition you just created and assign user and group accounts (see Figure 6-24). The users and groups you add to the role assignment will be able to perform the selected tasks you assigned.

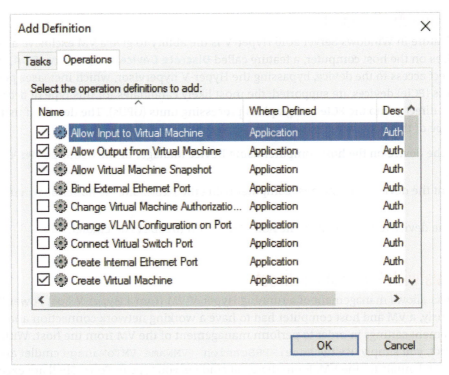

Figure 6-23   Creating a new task definition

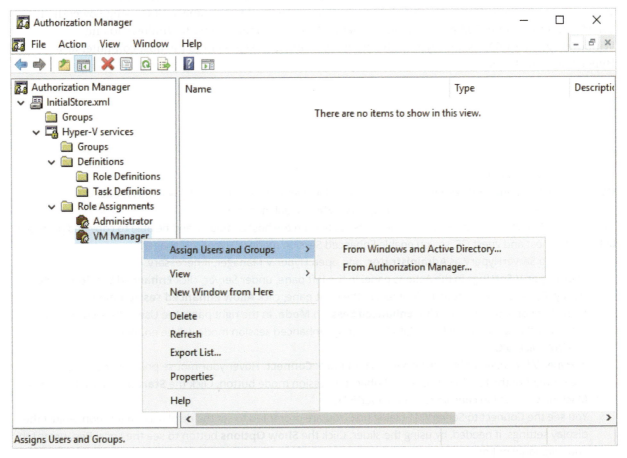

Figure 6-24   Creating a role assignment

Discrete Device Assignment

Another new feature in Windows Server 2016 Hyper-V is the ability to give a VM exclusive access to hardware devices on the host computer, a feature called **Discrete Device Assignment (DDA)**. With DDA, the VM has direct access to the device, bypassing the Hyper-V hypervisor, which increases performance. Only PCI Express (PCIe) devices are supported; the most likely candidates for this type of access are SSD drives that plug directly into the PCIe and graphics processing units (GPUs). The details of using DDA are beyond the scope of this book, but the basic steps are as follows:

1. Disable the device on the host computer using Device Manager or the `Disable-PnPDevice` cmdlet.
2. Dismount the device from the host computer using the `Dismount-VMHostAssignableDevice` cmdlet.
3. Attach the device to the VM using the `Add-VMAssignableDevice` cmdlet.

Managing VMs with PowerShell Direct

PowerShell Direct allows management of a running Hyper-V VM from a Hyper-V host PowerShell prompt. Previously, a VM and host computer had to have a working network connection and valid remote management settings in order to perform management of the VM from the host. With PowerShell Direct, you simply use the `Enter-PSSession -VMName VMToManage` cmdlet and provide proper credentials for the VM. From there, all cmdlets you type in PowerShell are executed on the VM. To exit to the host PowerShell session, type `Exit-PSSession`. You can also run a PowerShell script that is located on the host. For example, if you have a script named VMScript.ps1, you can run it on a VM named *VMServer1* from the Hyper-V host using `Invoke-Command -VMName VMServer1 -FilePath C:\Scripts\VMScript.ps1`. The ability to manage VMs using PowerShell Direct greatly simplifies VM management. PowerShell Direct works only with Windows 10 and Windows Server 2016 VMs and Hyper-V hosts, and you must be signed in to the host computer as a Hyper-V administrator.

Activity 6-5: Enabling Enhanced Session Mode

Time Required: 10 minutes
Objective: Enable Enhanced Session mode in Hyper-V Manager and connect to a VM with this mode.
Required Tools and Equipment: ServerHyperV, ServerVM1 virtual machine
Description: You want your guest OS to have access to files on the host computer and be able to copy and paste files between the host and guest OS, so you enable Enhanced Session mode in Hyper-V Manager.

1. Sign in to ServerHyperV as **Administrator**, and open Hyper-V Manager, if necessary.
2. Click **Hyper-V Settings** in the Actions pane. In the left pane, under Server, click **Enhanced Session Mode Policy**. By default, this mode is disabled. In the right pane, click **Allow enhanced session mode**.
3. In the left pane, under User, click **Enhanced Session Mode**. In the right pane, the Use enhanced session mode checkbox is on by default. With this setting, enhanced session mode will be enabled when you connect to a VM. Click **OK**.
4. In Hyper-V Manager, right-click **ServerVM1** and click **Connect**. Hover your mouse point over the icon on the far right of the tool bar. This is the Enhanced Session mode button. Click the **Start** button in the Virtual Machine Connection console to start ServerVM1.
5. You see the Connect to ServerVM1 dialog box. You are prompted to set the display configuration. Adjust the display settings, if needed, by using the slider. Click the **Show Options** button to see the Local Resources tab and additional options.

6. Click the **Local Resources** tab, and then click the **More** button. Click to expand **Drives**, click **Local Disk (C:)**, and click **OK**. Click **Connect**.

7. Sign in to ServerVM1 as **Administrator**. Open File Explorer, click **This PC** in the left pane, and click the **C on ServerHyperV** icon. You see the contents of the C drive on ServerHyperV.

8. Next, you'll copy and paste a file from the ServerHyperV host to the ServerVM1 VM. On ServerHyperV, right-click the desktop, point to **New** and click **Text Document**. Right-click the file and click **Copy**.

9. On ServerVM1, right-click the desktop and click **Paste** to copy the file from ServerHyperV to ServerVM1.

10. Shut down ServerVM1 and close the connection window. Now, disable Enhanced Session mode using PowerShell. On ServerHyperV, open a PowerShell prompt and type **Set-VMHost -EnableEnhancedSessionMode $false** and press **Enter**.

11. Close the PowerShell window and continue to the next activity.

Activity 6-6: Managing a VM with PowerShell Direct

Time Required: 10 minutes
Objective: Manage a VM with PowerShell Direct.
Required Tools and Equipment: ServerHyperV, ServerVM1
Description: You open a PowerShell prompt on ServerHyperV and establish a PowerShell Direct connection to a VM and perform some configuration tasks on the VM.

1. Open a PowerShell prompt on ServerHyperV.

2. To manage a VM with PowerShell Direct, first start the VM you wish to manage. Type **Start-VM ServerVM1** and press **Enter**. Type **Get-VM ServerVM1** and press **Enter** to see that the state is Running.

3. Type **Enter-PSSession -VMName ServerVM1** and press **Enter**. You are prompted for credentials for the virtual machine. Log on as **Administrator**. You see the PowerShell prompt changes by the addition of `[ServerVM1]:` to the beginning of the prompt. Any commands, both PowerShell and command prompt, that you enter will be executed on the VM.

4. Type **Get-Disk** and press **Enter**. Type **Get-NetIPAddress** and press **Enter**. You see that the output of both cmdlets reflects the settings of ServerVM1.

5. Type **Stop-Computer** and press **Enter**. Interestingly, this cmdlet does not work to shut down the VM; however, the command prompt command shutdown does. Type **shutdown /s /t 0** and press **Enter**. There is no output from the command, but you can check the status of the VM in Hyper-V Manager. Press **Enter**, and you will see that the prompt changes back to the host computer because ServerVM1 is shut down.

6. Close the PowerShell window and shut down ServerHyperV.

Chapter Summary

- The Hyper-V virtualization environment sits between the hardware and virtual machines. Each virtual machine is a child partition on the system, and Windows Server 2016 with Hyper-V installed is the parent or management partition. The Hyper-V management console runs on Windows Server 2016 in the parent partition and serves as an interface for managing the VMs running in child partitions.

- You can install Hyper-V in a Nano Server deployment; the Nano Server will require remote management. You can also install the Hyper-V management tools on a computer that is not running the Hyper-V role. Once the management tools are installed, you can use them to manage Hyper-V remotely.

- Hyper-V is installed as a server role in Windows Server 2016 64-bit versions of Standard and Datacenter editions. The CPU on the host machine must be 64-bit and support virtualization extensions, such as AMD-V or Intel-VT. Standard Edition includes a license for two virtual instances of Windows Server 2016, and Datacenter Edition includes unlimited virtual instances of Windows Server 2016.

- Virtual machines from Hyper-V running in Windows Server 2012 or Windows Server 2008 must have an upgraded VM configuration version to take advantage of new features in Windows Server 2016. The VM configuration version can be seen in Hyper-V Manager.

- Hyper-V allows a virtual machine to run in the background until you connect to it in Hyper-V Manager. A running VM doesn't require using Hyper-V Manager, nor does it require anyone to be signed in to the server. You can manage a VM remotely by using tools such as Remote Desktop and MMCs if the VM is configured to communicate with the host network.

- Virtual machines can be exported and then imported to create one or more virtual machines. You can even export a running VM. You can import a VM that has been exported or a VM that hasn't been exported first.

- Virtual machines created with the new Virtual Machine Wizard have the option of creating a generation 1 or generation 2 VM. Generation 2 VMs are based on revised virtual hardware specifications; they have enhanced VM capabilities and support for newer standards.

- Many aspects of a VM's physical environment can be configured, including BIOS settings, memory allocation, and virtual processor settings. Hyper-V in Windows Server 2016 adds the ability to hot add and remove memory, which is the addition of memory or removal of memory while the VM is running.

- Checkpoints allow you to save the state of a VM and return to that state later. Standard checkpoints enable you to revert a VM to a previous state; they should not be used on production VMs. Production checkpoints are a new type of checkpoint that supports production virtual machines and uses backup technology in the guest OS to create the checkpoint.

- A VM's software environment can be enhanced by installing Integration Services, which includes enhanced drivers for disk, network, display, and mouse devices. Automatic start and stop actions can be configured to determine what actions the VM should perform when the host computer is shut down and started.

- Resource metering allows vendors providing large-scale virtualization to measure customer use of VM resources for billing purposes. Enhanced Session mode is a feature that improves interaction and device redirection between the host computer and the Virtual Machine Connection console.

- Non-Uniform Memory Access (NUMA) is a system memory architecture used in multiprocessor systems that allow processors to efficiently share memory. The allocation of additional memory from another NUMA node is referred to as *NUMA spanning*.

- Administrators of the Hyper-V host computer or domain administrators have full access to Hyper-V Manager. However, they can use Authorization Manager to allow a user or group of users to have permissions in Hyper-V to perform only specific tasks.

- Discrete Device Assignment (DDA) and PowerShell Direct are new features in Windows Server 2016 Hyper-V. Discrete Device Assignment allows a VM exclusive access to hardware devices on the host computer. PowerShell Direct allows the management of a running Hyper-V VM from a Hyper-V host PowerShell prompt.

Key Terms

checkpoint	Non-Uniform Memory Access	standard checkpoint
Discrete Device Assignment (DDA)	(NUMA)	synthetic driver
Dynamic Memory	NUMA spanning	virtual disk
emulated drivers	production checkpoint	virtual instance
Enhanced Session mode	resource metering	virtual network
Integration Services	smart paging	virtual processor

Review Questions

1. Which of the following is described as a partial copy of a VM made at a specific moment?
   a. Virtual instance
   b. Differencing disk
   c. Hypervisor
   d. Checkpoint

2. You have just purchased and installed Windows Server 2016 Standard Edition. How many virtual instances of Windows Server 2016 can you run on a fully licensed host computer without purchasing an additional Windows Server 2016 license?
   a. One virtual instance
   b. Two virtual instances
   c. Three virtual instances
   d. Unlimited virtual instances

3. You have just placed a new Windows Server 2016 with Hyper-V server into production; this server is the management partition. Which of the following best describes a new virtual machine installed on this system?
   a. Parent partition
   b. Secondary partition
   c. Child partition
   d. Virtual partition

4. You have just purchased a server with Windows Server 2016 Datacenter Edition installed. The server has 4 GB RAM, a 200 GB hard disk, and an Intel 1.6 GHz Xeon processor with Intel-VT. You plan to install the Hyper-V server role on this server and run two Windows Server 2016 VMs, each with a 2 GB RAM allocation. You have discovered that this server does not work for this purpose. What should you do?
   a. Install more RAM
   b. Install a bigger hard disk
   c. Install Standard Edition
   d. Upgrade the processor

5. When you install the Hyper-V role from Server Manager, you will be prompted to install the management tools. You should install these management tools if you need to do which of the following?
   a. Manage Hyper-V on a remote management computer
   b. Manage Hyper-V from the same server that is running Hyper-V
   c. Manage Hyper-V from any remote computer
   d. Manage Hyper-V utilizing a VPN connection

6. If you choose to install Hyper-V in a Nano Server deployment, what type of server management must be implemented to manage Hyper-V?
   a. Remote server management
   b. Local server management
   c. Virtual server management
   d. Local host server management

7. You created a VM running Windows Server 2016 and some applications. You want to create a second VM quickly that has the same configuration options and installed applications as the first one. You plan to use this second VM on the same Hyper-V server as the first. You want good disk performance from both VMs. What should you do?
   a. Create a VM with a differencing disk. Assign the first VM's virtual disk as the parent disk; the first VM will continue to use its original virtual disk.
   b. Export the first VM, and import it with the *Copy the virtual machine* option to create the second VM.
   c. Create a VM. Create a checkpoint of the first VM. Copy and rename the checkpoint file and use it for the second VM's virtual hard disk.
   d. Export the first VM and import it using the *Register the virtual machine in place* option. Use the imported VM as the second virtual server.

8. You have an old server running Windows Server 2016 that has had intermittent hardware failures in the past few months that cause the server to shut down. You haven't been able to isolate the problem, but you suspect that the hard disks are beginning to fail, and the server is no longer under warranty. You have been using a Hyper-V server for about a year with two VMs running on it. This quad-core server has plenty of disk space and ample processing power and memory. Which of the following might be a good solution for the ailing server that requires the least amount of cost and administrative effort?

   a. Purchase a new machine. Remove the hard disk from the old server, and install it in the new server.

   b. Create a VM on your Hyper-V server. Remove the hard disk from the old machine, and install it in the Hyper-V server. Set the disk offline and use it as a pass-through disk for the new VM.

   c. Create a VM on your Hyper-V server. On the old server, run a physical-to-virtual conversion. Use the resulting virtual hard disk file as the virtual disk for the new VM. Take the old server offline.

   d. Create a VM on your Hyper-V server. Install Windows Server 2016 as the guest OS. Carefully configure the guest OS to match the old server's configuration, and take the old server offline.

9. To remotely manage Hyper-V using PowerShell, PowerShell remoting must be enabled. By default, PowerShell remoting is enabled on Windows Server 2012 and later. However, if it becomes disabled, which of the following PowerShell cmdlets will allow you to remotely manage Hyper-V using PowerShell?

   a. `Configure-PSRemoting`

   b. `Enable-PSRemoting`

   c. `Enable-SMRemoting`

   d. `Configure-SMRemoting`

10. You are creating a new VM in Hyper-V on a Windows Server 2016 server. Your new VM will use Windows 10 and support the use of PXE boot. Which hardware generation type should you select during the new VM's creation process?

    a. Generation 1

    b. Generation 1 or generation 2

    c. Generation 2

    d. Generation 3

11. Which of the following Hyper-V guest virtual machine configurations would allow you the ability to hot add and remove memory? (Choose all that apply.)

    a. Windows Server 2016 with Hyper-V, running a Windows 8.1 VM

    b. Windows Server 2012 R2 with Hyper-V, running a Windows 10 VM

    c. Windows Server 2016 with Hyper-V, running a Windows 10 VM

    d. Windows Server 2016 with Hyper-V, running a Windows Server 2016 VM

12. Your network has had long power outages that have caused Hyper-V servers to shut down after the UPS battery is drained. When power returns, the Hyper-V servers restart automatically, but the VMs don't start. You need to make sure the VMs start when the host starts. What should you do?

    a. Change the VMs' BIOS settings

    b. Write a script on the host that starts the VMs automatically when the host starts

    c. Reinstall Integration Services

    d. Change the automatic start action setting on the VMs

13. Checkpoints for your test VMs are taking up too much space on the host's system disk. You have two test VMs running, each with one checkpoint to represent the baseline testing environment. You're finished with your current testing and are ready for another round of testing, but you want to make sure your checkpoints are stored on another volume. What should you do?

    a. In Hyper-V Manager, change the checkpoints' path in the Settings window to point to the other volume; the checkpoints are moved automatically.

    b. Use File Explorer to move the checkpoint files from their current location to the other volume.

    c. Shut down the VMs. Apply the checkpoint to each VM, and delete all checkpoints in Hyper-V Manager. Change the path of the checkpoint files to the other volume, and create a new checkpoint for each VM.

    d. In each VM's settings, change the checkpoint path. Apply the checkpoint, and then create a new checkpoint for each VM. Delete the old checkpoints in File Explorer.

14. Which of the following is true if you enable shielding and create a shielded VM in Windows Server 2016? (Choose all that apply.)

    a. Secure Boot is automatically disabled.

    b. Secure Boot is automatically enabled.

    c. Encryption is automatically enabled.

    d. Encryption is automatically disabled.

15. You have four checkpoints of a VM. You want to return the VM to its state when the second checkpoint was taken. Which checkpoint option should you use?
    - **a.** Apply
    - **b.** Save
    - **c.** Select
    - **d.** Revert

16. You're working with a Windows Server 2003 VM in Hyper-V. Every time you click the mouse in the VM window, it's captured, and you must press Ctrl+Alt+left arrow to use the mouse on the host OS, which is getting annoying. What can you do to make using the VM easier?
    - **a.** Install a new mouse on the host system that supports Hyper-V
    - **b.** Install Integration Services on the host computer
    - **c.** Install Integration Services on the VM
    - **d.** Install emulated mouse drivers on the VM

17. You are configuring four VMs on a Hyper-V server. One of the virtual machines needs to be assigned a new relative weight value to allow it to have priority to the shared processing resources between the four VMs. All four VMs are currently set to the default relative weight of 100. What relative weight value can you use to configure the VM that needs priority to the shared processing resources?
    - **a.** 1
    - **b.** 200
    - **c.** 99
    - **d.** 0

18. You want to allow your VM the ability to copy files to a running VM without using a virtual network connection. Which of the following integration services should you enable in the VM's settings?
    - **a.** Guest services
    - **b.** Data exchange
    - **c.** Heartbeat
    - **d.** Time synchronization

19. You solved the problem with VMs not starting when the host restarts, but now you notice that VMs take a long time to start when the host starts. On some hosts, you have as many as six VMs. You also find that the VM running an application server can't initialize correctly because the VM running DNS isn't available immediately. What can you do to improve VMs' startup times and solve the application server problem?
    - **a.** Set a virtual machine priority in Hyper-V's Settings window
    - **b.** Set a startup delay for each VM, making sure the delay for the DNS server is lower than the application servers
    - **c.** Change the BIOS settings of the DNS server to use the Quick Boot option
    - **d.** Assign more virtual processors to the VMs you want to start faster

20. Which of the following resource metrics can be measured when you enable the Hyper-V feature resource metering? (Choose all that apply.)
    - **a.** Average physical memory use
    - **b.** Maximum disk space allocation
    - **c.** Minimum, maximum, and average CPU use
    - **d.** Outgoing network traffic per network adapter

21. You currently have four VMs running on a Hyper-V server. You need to increase the amount of memory to VM4 so that you can install a new application. You're running low on physical memory. You tried to allocate less memory to the other three VMs to free up memory, but after you did so, they wouldn't start. What can you do that doesn't involve installing additional physical memory on the host or changing the configuration of the guest OSs?
    - **a.** Enable Dynamic Memory on all the VMs, and set the startup memory higher than the minimum memory
    - **b.** Configure resource metering on all four VMs
    - **c.** Uninstall server roles on the guest OSs until you have enough free memory for VM4
    - **d.** Enable memory Quality of Service (QoS) on the other three VMs and set a maximum IOPS for their memory use

22. You're using a VM with a Windows 8.1 Pro guest OS to run applications that you want isolated from the host computer and the LAN. However, you want to be able to print from the VM to the printer connected to your host and copy files between the host and guest OS. What can you enable to accomplish this task?
    - **a.** Enable Enhanced Session mode in Hyper-V, and verify that Remote Desktop Services is running on the guest
    - **b.** Create shares on the host and VM to transfer files back and forth, and install a printer driver on the guest OS
    - **c.** Connect the VM running Windows 8.1 to an external virtual switch
    - **d.** Install Integration Services on the Windows 8.1 guest OS and enable the device-sharing and file-sharing options

23. Which of the following is a system memory architecture used in multiprocessor systems that allow processors to share memory more efficiently?
    a. Non-Uniform Memory Access
    b. Uniform ROM Access
    c. Uniform Memory Access
    d. Shared Memory Access

24. You have decided that you would like a junior administrator to have the ability to perform limited tasks in Hyper-V Manager. However, you do not want the junior administrator to have broader administrative control over your system. What management console will specifically allow you to configure your Hyper-V permissions to accomplish this task?
    a. Virtual Device Manager
    b. Authorization Manager
    c. Hyper-V Manager
    d. System Management Console

25. You currently have an application server VM running on your Windows Server 2016 Hyper-V server. Your application server VM's performance would benefit greatly if the host machine's SSD drives could be accessed by allowing the application server VM to bypass the Hyper-V hypervisor. What feature in Windows Server 2016 Hyper-V can give your application server VM exclusive access to hardware devices on the host computer?
    a. Hyper-V Manager
    b. Authorization Manager
    c. Virtual Device Assignment
    d. Discrete Device Assignment

26. Which of the following Powershell cmdlets will allow the management of a running Hyper-V VM named VMTestServer from a Hyper-V host PowerShell prompt?
    a. `Get-PSSession  -VMName VMTestServer`
    b. `Enter-Session  -VM VMTestServer`
    c. `Enter-PSSession  -VMName VMTestServer`
    d. `Enter-PSSession  -VM VMTestServer`

Critical Thinking

The following activities give you critical thinking challenges. Case Projects offer a scenario with a problem to solve for which you supply a written solution.

Case Project 6-1: Devising a Hyper-V Solution

You want to optimize your datacenter using Hyper-V virtualization. You have targeted four servers with dual-core processors that are old and taking up quite a bit of space. You want to implement the functions of these four servers using virtual machines. Two servers are running Windows Server 2012 R2, and two are running Windows Server 2016. Each of the four servers has two disks, one for the Windows OS and the other for data storage. The OS volume is using about 100 GB of space on each server, and the data volume is a 250 GB volume with each server using about half the available space. You need to devise a plan to deploy each of the four servers as a virtual machine. Create a plan that details the host server hardware and software configuration (what edition of Windows Server 2016 should be installed, what server roles, etc.) and the virtual machine configuration. What are some of the considerations that must be taken into account to implement your plan? What are some of the options for transferring the function of each server to a virtual machine?

Case Project 6-2: Choosing Checkpoints

Your network has four Hyper-V hosts, which are running three domain controllers and about 10 member servers. Three of the member servers named HR1, HR2, and HR3 are running on a Windows Server 2012 R2 Hyper-V host; the others are running on Windows Server 2016 Hyper-V hosts. All VMs are running Windows Server 2016. You are currently running an enterprise human resources application on the HR1, HR2, and HR3 servers. You are considering upgrading this application to a new version that was recently released. Before you proceed with the upgrade, you set up a test environment consisting of a Windows Server 2016 Hyper-V host and three VMs. You haven't been using checkpoints on any of your VMs, but you want to start doing so as an extra form of disaster recovery in the event of VM corruption or errors introduced by updates. On your test environment, you want to use checkpoints while you are testing the new application. What type of checkpoints should you use throughout your live network and test network? Explain.

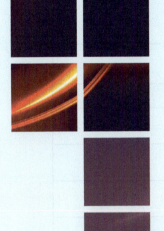

IMPLEMENTING VIRTUALIZATION WITH HYPER-V: PART 2

After reading this chapter and completing the exercises, you will be able to:

Work with virtual hard disks

Configure virtual networks

Configure nested virtualization

Implement Linux and FreeBSD virtual machines

Continuing with our discussion of Hyper-V and virtualization, this chapter covers virtual hard disks including dynamically expanding, fixed, differencing, and pass-through disks. We also look at shared VHDX files, which are also covered in more detail in Chapter 9. Next, we examine the three types of virtual switch and deployment scenarios for each. Along with configuring virtual switches, you'll learn about configuring virtual network adapters including hardware acceleration and advanced features such as MAC address spoofing, protected network, and port mirroring. You'll also learn how to create and configure NIC teaming both on the host server and in a virtual machine.

Virtualization is a big topic, and configuring a testing lab is critical to being able to understand its features and options. Windows Server 2016 helps you along by introducing nested virtualization, which allows you to install Hyper-V and run a VM within another VM. You'll learn how to properly configure your Hyper-V host to enable nested virtualization. Finally, we'll briefly look at deploying Linux and FreeBSD VMs in Hyper-V.

Working with Virtual Hard Disks

 **Certification**

- **70-740 – Implement Hyper-V:**
  Configure Hyper-V storage

Table 7-1 describes what you need for the hands-on activities in this chapter.

Table 7-1   Activity requirements

Activity	Requirements	Notes
Activity 7-1: Resetting Your Virtual Environment	ServerHyperV	
Activity 7-2: Creating a Dynamically Expanding Virtual Disk	ServerHyperV, ServerVM1 virtual machine	
Activity 7-3: Editing a Virtual Disk	ServerHyperV, ServerVM1 virtual machine	
Activity 7-4: Working with External Virtual Switches	ServerHyperV, ServerVM1 and ServerVM2 virtual machines	
Activity 7-5: Working with Internal Virtual Networks	ServerHyperV, ServerVM1 and ServerVM2 virtual machines	

As you've learned, a virtual hard disk is a file on the host computer with the `.vhd` or `.vhdx` extension. From a VM's standpoint, a virtual hard disk is no different from a physical hard disk. However, from the perspective of an IT manager using Hyper-V, virtual hard disks are more flexible than physical disks. Virtual hard disks can be one of three types:

- *Fixed size*—The full amount of space required for a fixed-size disk, as the name implies, is allocated on the host's storage when the virtual disk is created. **Fixed-size disks** are recommended when the VM needs to run disk-intensive (many disk I/O operations) applications because performance is slightly better than with dynamically expanding disks because it is not necessary to perform the extra step of expanding the size of the disk when disk writes are performed.
- *Dynamically expanding*—As data is written to it, the virtual hard disk file grows up to the size you specify when the disk is created. The dynamic aspect of this type of disk goes only one way; the file doesn't shrink when data is deleted from the virtual disk. This option saves host disk space until the disk grows to its maximum size but at the expense of performance. **Dynamically expanding disks** are somewhat slower than fixed-size disks, and there are some concerns about host disk fragmentation when using them. However, with the VHDX format, Microsoft has made strides toward performance parity between fixed-size and dynamically expanding disks. Unless the VM is running disk-intensive applications, dynamically expanding disks are a good choice. Additionally, VMs that use dynamic disks can be backed up faster because VHDX files are usually smaller than fixed-disk files.

Note

Although dynamically expanding virtual disks do not dynamically shrink as data is deleted, you can edit the disk and compact it to reclaim host disk space. Editing virtual disks is discussed in the next section.

- *Differencing*—A **differencing disk** uses a parent/child relationship. A parent disk is a dynamically expanding or fixed-size disk with an OS installed, possibly with some applications and data. It becomes the baseline for one or more child (differencing) disks. A VM with a differencing disk operates normally, but any changes made to its hard disk are made only to the differencing disk, leaving the parent disk unaltered. The parent disk shouldn't be connected to a VM because it must not be changed in any way. With differencing disks, several VMs can be created by using the parent disk as the baseline but using only the additional host disk space of the differencing disk. Differencing disks are an ideal way to provision (make available) several VMs quickly without having to install an OS and applications or copy an entire virtual disk. Differencing disks work like dynamically expanding disks in that both start very small and grow as data is written to them. All child disks must use the same format (VHD or VHDX) as the parent disk.

Creating and Modifying Virtual Disks

Virtual disks can be created when a VM is created or with the New Virtual Hard Disk Wizard. During VM creation, the disk is created as a dynamically expanding disk, but you can change it to a fixed-size disk later. When you use the wizard, the first thing you do is choose the disk format for which you have the following options (see Figure 7-1):

- *VHD*—This is the original virtual disk format and provides backward compatibility with virtual machines created in OSs prior to Windows Server 2012. The VHD format supports virtual disks up to 2 TB in size.
- *VHDX*—This is the default option, supporting virtual disks up to 64 TB. The VHDX format also provides resiliency to problems that might occur due to unexpected power failures or host system crashes. They can be used only on VMs created in Windows Server 2012 or later.
- *VHD Set*—A new feature starting with Hyper-V in Windows 10 and Windows Server 2016, a **VHD set** is a shared virtual hard disk used with VM cluster configurations when multiple VMs have access to the same virtual hard disk for fault tolerance and load-balancing applications. Shared VHDX format virtual hard disks are supported in earlier versions of Hyper-V, but they cannot be resized or migrated to other hosts. In addition, backups of VMs using shared VHDX files are not supported. VHD sets remove these limitations of shared VHDX files. Shared virtual disks are discussed in more detail later in this chapter.

After you select the format of a virtual disk, you choose the disk type as shown in Figure 7-2 and discussed earlier. Dynamically expanding is the default choice and recommended for most applications.

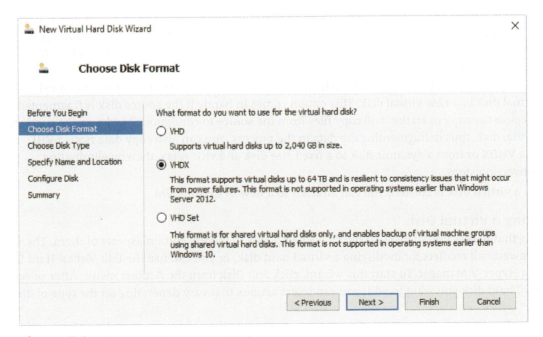

Figure 7-1   Choosing the virtual disk format

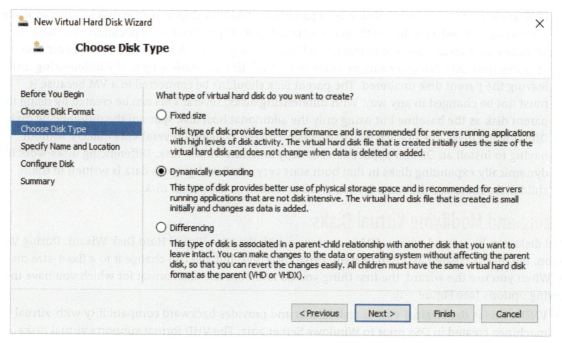

Figure 7-2 Choosing the virtual disk type

The next step is to specify a name for the virtual disk file and the location on the host where it is stored. Virtual disks are created in a default location (C:\Users\Public Documents\Hyper-V\Virtual hard disks\) unless you specify a different path or change the default location in Hyper-V settings. You can view and change the default location by clicking Hyper-V Settings in the Actions pane in Hyper-V Manager. You can also specify a shared folder to store the virtual disk using the UNC path of the share.

The last step is to specify the size of the virtual disk as shown in Figure 7-3. On this screen, you can choose one of three options:

- *Create a new blank virtual disk*—With this option, simply specify the size of the virtual disk in gigabytes (GB).
- *Copy the contents of a specified physical disk*—With this option, you can convert a physical disk to a virtual disk. This option comes in handy when you want to convert the disks on a physical computer to virtual disks. To do so, attach the physical disk from the computer you wish to convert to the Hyper-V host computer and select this option.
- *Copy the contents of a specified virtual hard disk*—This option copies the contents of an existing virtual disk to a new virtual disk. This option comes in handy if the source disk is fragmented because the copy operation will copy files from the source to contiguous blocks on the destination virtual disk, thus defragmenting the data in the process. You can also copy data from a VHD to a VHDX or from a dynamic disk to a fixed size disk and vice versa, thereby eliminating conversion steps.

After a virtual disk is created, you can attach it to a new or existing VM.

Modifying a Virtual Disk

One thing that makes virtual disks so flexible is being able to modify certain aspects of them. There are several PowerShell cmdlets for modifying a virtual hard disk, or you can use the Edit Virtual Hard Disk Wizard in Hyper-V Manager. To start this wizard, click Edit Disk from the Actions menu. After selecting the virtual hard disk you want to edit, you can select actions that vary depending on the type of disk you

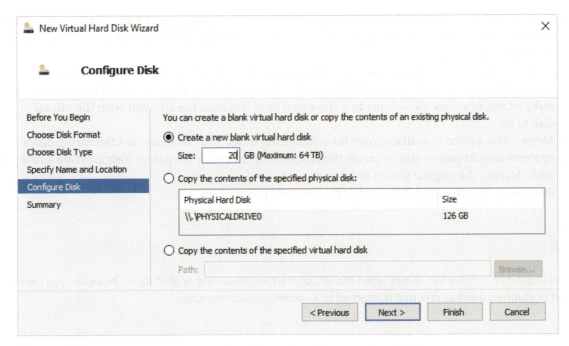

Figure 7-3   Specifying the size and configuration of a new virtual disk

select. Figure 7-4 shows the options for dynamically expanding and fixed-size disks. These three options, as well as three additional disk editing options, are described here:

- *Compact*—Reduces the size of a dynamically expanding disk by eliminating the space used by deleted files.
- *Convert*—Converts a dynamically expanding disk to a fixed-size disk and vice versa. You can also change the format from VHD to VHDX and vice versa. Note that converting a disk creates a new virtual disk and does not delete the original disk.

Figure 7-4   Selecting an edit action for a dynamically expanding disk

- *Expand*—Allows you to make a fixed-size or dynamically expanding disk larger. After you expand the disk, you can use Disk Management or diskpart.exe in Windows to extend the volume to use the additional space.
- *Shrink*—Allows you to make a fixed-size or dynamically expanding disk smaller. Before you can shrink a virtual disk, you must first use the Shrink Volume feature in Disk Management or diskpart.exe to shrink the volume to a size equal to or less than the size you wish the virtual disk to be.
- *Merge*—This option is available only for differencing disks. You can merge a differencing disk's contents into its parent disk or merge the differencing disk with the parent disk to create a new disk while leaving the original parent disk unchanged.
- *Reconnect*—Reconnects a differencing disk with its parent disk.

Tip ⓘ

You can expand or shrink a virtual disk when the virtual machine is running or shut down; however, you cannot convert or compact a virtual disk that is attached to a running virtual machine.

A little explanation is needed for a few of these disk-editing tasks. When you convert a dynamic disk to a fixed-size disk, a new fixed-size virtual disk is created, and you supply a new name. After the conversion is finished, you disconnect the original dynamic disk from the VM and connect the new fixed-size disk. Alternatively, you can rename the dynamic disk (or delete it) and then rename the new fixed-size disk the same as the original dynamic disk. With this method, the VM connects to the new fixed-size disk automatically when you restart it. For example, if the original dynamically expanding disk is named `ServerVM1.vhdx` you can name the new fixed-size disk `ServerVM1fixed.vhdx` when you do the conversion. When the conversion is finished, rename `ServerVM1.vhdx` as `ServerVM1dyn.vhdx` and rename `ServerVM1fixed.vhdx` as `ServerVM1.vhdx`.

Tip ⓘ

If you rename the fixed-size disk instead of connecting the new fixed-size disk in the VM's settings, you must make sure the VM has at least Modify permissions to the new virtual hard disk. In most cases, the Authenticated Users group is assigned the Modify permission automatically, which is adequate, but if the VM fails to start and displays an *Access denied* error, check the permissions for the `.vhdx` file.

An important consideration to keep in mind before you edit a disk that is connected to a VM is that no checkpoints can be associated with the VM attached to the virtual disk you're expanding.

Pass-Through Disks

A **pass-through disk** isn't a virtual disk; it's a physical disk in the offline state that's attached to the host. It can be connected to a VM only if it has been set to offline status. If you have an offline physical disk on the host, you can attach it to a VM in the VM's Settings window (see Figure 7-5). If the disk already has data on it, the data is retained and available to the VM.

From the VM's standpoint, a pass-through disk works just like a virtual disk except you can't use any of the disk-editing options on it, you can't take checkpoints, and you can't use a differencing disk with it. A pass-through disk has modest performance advantages over virtual disks, but unless you really need the extra bit of performance, a pass-through disk's lack of flexibility makes it less attractive as a VM storage option. Pass-through disks do have an advantage over VHD disks because VHD disks

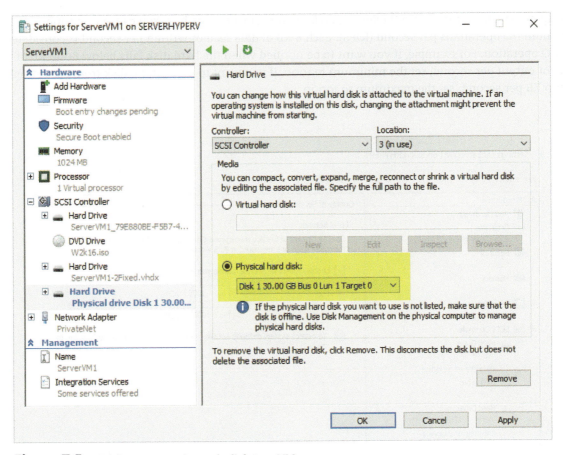

Figure 7-5   Adding a pass-through disk to a VM

are limited to 2 TB. However, the VHDX format doesn't have the 2 TB limitation, so using pass-through disks is a benefit only when direct access to the physical drive improves performance. Some applications that might benefit from the VM using a pass-through disk include SQL servers and high-performance cluster servers.

> **Note**
>
> For high-performance disk storage, many administrators prefer using storage area network (SAN) through Fibre Channel or iSCSI instead of pass-through disks.

Storage Quality of Service

Storage Quality of Service (QoS) enables administrators to specify minimum and maximum performance values for virtual hard disks. The maximum specified value actually limits a VM's access to a virtual hard disk to prevent it from consuming too many storage resources, which can affect other VMs' access to storage. Setting a minimum specified value generates a notification if access to a virtual hard disk falls below the specified threshold.

Storage QoS can be set on IDE and SCSI virtual hard disks. In Hyper-V Manager, open a VM's Settings window, click to expand the hard disk where you want to set QoS, and click Quality of Service (see Figure 7-6). Click the *Enable Quality of Service management* check box. You can set minimum and maximum I/O operations per second (IOPS). Each 8 KB of data read or written per second is considered one I/O operation. For example, if you want to be notified when the hard disk falls below 8000 KB of input or output per second, set the minimum to 1000. If you want to prevent the disk from exceeding 80,000 KB per second, set the maximum to 10000.

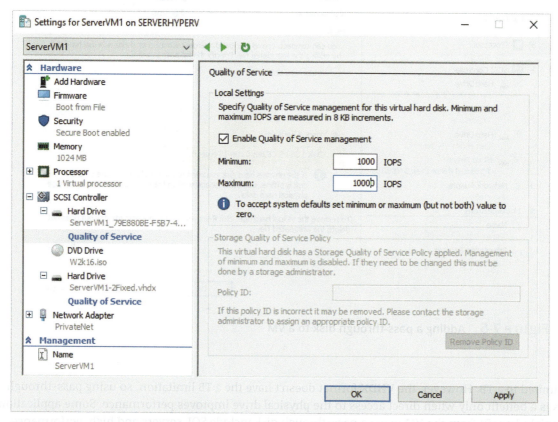

Figure 7-6 Enabling storage QoS

In addition, with Storage QoS enabled, you can monitor storage performance of VMs stored on a Scale-Out File Server cluster. Multiple VMs can be monitored this way from a central location.

Storage QoS Requirements

Storage QoS is used in cluster environments where VM storage is shared. These include the following scenarios:

- *Hyper-V is used in a Scale-Out File Server*—In this scenario, the VM storage is located on a Scale-Out File Server cluster and Hyper-V is installed on at least one server in a compute cluster.
- *Hyper-V is used with Cluster Shared Volumes*—In this scenario, Hyper-V is running in a failover cluster and is using Cluster Shared Volumes for VM storage.

Note

Scale-Out File Server and Cluster Shared Volumes are discussed more in Chapter 9.

Storage QoS Policies

Storage QoS policies can be created and applied to individual virtual disk files or to multiple virtual disk files. Two types of policies exist: Aggregated policies and Dedicated policies. An **Aggregated policy** applies the minimum and maximum IOPS values to a set of virtual disks working as a whole. In other words, if you apply an Aggregated policy that specifies a minimum 1000 IOPS and maximum 5000 IOPS to five virtual disks, the policy guarantees that the combined minimum of all five virtual disks will be 1000 IOPS and the combined maximum will be 5000. This means that if all five disks have similar I/O requirements, they will get an average of 200 IOPS each at minimum and up to 1000 IOPS each at maximum.

A **Dedicated policy** applies the minimum and maximum values to each virtual disk that the policy is applied to, so if a Dedicated policy with the same limits is applied to five virtual disks, each disk is guaranteed the respective minimum and maximum IOPS values.

Storage QoS policies can be created using PowerShell; for example, the following cmdlet creates a policy with the minimum and maximum IOPS values of 1000 and 5000, respectively:

```
New-StorageQoSPolicy -Name FileServer -PolicyType Aggregated -MinimumIOPS
1000 -MaximumIOPS 5000
```

Once the policy is created, use the `Get-StorageQoSPolicy` cmdlet to display the policy ID number and then use the `Set-VMHardDiskDrive -QoSPolicyID` *PolicyIDNumber* cmdlet to apply it to a virtual disk.

Activity 7-1: Resetting Your Virtual Environment

Time Required: 5 minutes
Objective: Reset your virtual environment by applying the InitialConfig checkpoint or snapshot.
Required Tools and Equipment: ServerHyperV
Description: Apply the InitialConfig checkpoint or snapshot to ServerHyperV.

1. Be sure ServerHyperV is shut down. In your virtualization program, apply the InitialConfig checkpoint or snapshot to ServerHyperV.
2. Close your virtual machine environment.

Activity 7-2: Creating a Dynamically Expanding Virtual Disk

Time Required: 20 minutes
Objective: Create a dynamically expanding virtual disk and attach it to a VM.
Required Tools and Equipment: ServerHyperV with the ServerVM1 virtual machine
Description: Your VM needs a new virtual hard disk where you can store data files, so you create a dynamically expanding virtual disk, attach it to ServerVM1, and then create a new volume on the disk.

1. Sign in to ServerHyperV as **Administrator** and open Hyper-V Manager.
2. In the Actions pane, click **New** and then **Hard Disk**. In the Before You Begin window, click **Next**.
3. In the Choose Disk Format window, accept the default setting **VHDX** and click **Next**.
4. In the Choose Disk Type window, accept the default setting **Dynamically expanding** and click **Next**.
5. In the Specify Name and Location window, type **ServerVM1-2.vhdx**. (Although the name isn't critical, you will be attaching this new virtual disk to ServerVM1, and the -2 in the name indicates it's the second disk.) Leave the location as is and click **Next**.
6. In the Configure Disk window, type **5** in the **Size** text box. You're creating a small 5 GB virtual disk because you convert it to a fixed-size disk later; the larger the disk, the longer it takes to convert and the more storage on the host it takes. Notice that you can copy the contents of an existing physical disk or virtual disk instead of creating a blank disk, if needed. Click **Next**.

7. In the Summary window, review the options for the new disk, and click **Finish**.

8. Next, you connect ServerVM1 to the new virtual disk. In Hyper-V Manager right-click **ServerVM1** and click **Settings**.

9. In the Settings for ServerVM1 window, click **SCSI Controller**, and click **Add** to add a hard drive. Notice that you can create a new virtual disk at this time, but because the disk you want is already created, click **Browse**. Click **ServerVM1-2** and click **Open**. Click **OK**.

10. In Hyper-V Manager, double-click **ServerVM1** and click the **Start** icon. Sign in to **ServerVM1**, open File Explorer, and click **This PC**. The new virtual disk isn't shown because you need to initialize it and create a new volume first.

11. On ServerVM1, right-click **Start** and click **Disk Management**. Right-click **Disk 1** and click **Online** to bring the disk online. Right-click it again and click **Initialize Disk**. Click **OK**.

12. Right-click the **Unallocated** box next to Disk 1 and click **New Simple Volume**. Finish the New Simple Volume Wizard by naming the volume **TestVol** and accepting the defaults for the other options. After the disk is finished formatting, close Disk Management.

13. In File Explorer, you should see the new volume with drive letter E assigned. (If you see a message stating that you need to format the disk, click **Cancel**.) Create a folder on the E drive, and create a text file in this folder.

14. Shut down ServerVM1. Stay signed in to ServerHyperV and continue to the next activity.

Activity 7-3: Editing a Virtual Disk

Time Required: 15 minutes

Objective: Edit a virtual disk with Hyper-V Manager.

Required Tools and Equipment: ServerHyperV with the ServerVM1 virtual machine

Description: In this activity, you convert a dynamically expanding disk to a fixed-size disk and expand and shrink the disk.

1. Sign in to ServerHyperV as **Administrator**, and open Hyper-V Manager, if necessary.

2. Right-click **ServerVM1** and click **Settings**. In the left pane, click the **ServerVM1-2.vhdx** hard disk under SCSI Controller, and in the right pane, click **Edit**.

3. In the Locate Disk window, read the information about editing virtual hard disks. Note that editing differencing disks, disks with checkpoints, and disks involved in replication might result in data loss. Click **Next**.

4. In the Choose Action window, click the **Convert** option button, and then click **Next**. In the Choose Disk Format window, accept the default **VHDX**, and click **Next**.

5. In the Choose Disk Type window, click **Fixed size**, and then click **Next**. In the Configure Disk window, leave the current path, and type **ServerVM1-2Fixed** at the end of it (the .vhdx extension will be added automatically). Click **Next**.

6. In the Summary window, click **Finish**. The conversion takes a few minutes.

7. When the conversion is finished, click **Browse** in the Settings for ServerVM1 window. The fixed-size disk is shown with the size of about 5 GB. Click **ServerVM1-2Fixed** and click **Open** to attach this disk to ServerVM1. Click **OK**.

8. In Hyper-V Manager, double-click **ServerVM1** and click the **Start** icon. Sign in to ServerVM1, and open File Explorer. Explore the E drive to verify that the files you created in the previous activity are still there.

9. Close File Explorer and open Disk Management by right-clicking **Start** and clicking **Disk Management**. Notice that there is no unallocated space on Disk 1.

10. In Hyper-V Manager, right-click **ServerVM1** and click **Settings**. Click **Hard Drive ServerVM1-Fixed** under SCSI Controller and click **Edit** in the right pane to open the Edit Virtual Hard Disk Wizard.

11. In the Locate Virtual Hard Disk window, click **Next**. In the Choose Action window, the only option is Expand since you can't convert a virtual disk that is attached to a running VM. Click **Next**.

12. In the Configure Disk window, type **7** in the New size box and click **Next**. In the Summary window, click **Finish**.

13. In the Settings window, click **OK**. Open the ServerVM1 connection window. Disk Management should still be open. You see that there is now 2 GB of unallocated space on Disk 1.

14. Right-click **TestVol** and click **Extend Volume**. Accept the default options to extend the volume to the maximum size of about 7 GB. You have successfully expanded the virtual disk and extended the volume to occupy the additional space.

15. Now, you'll shrink the volume and then shrink the virtual disk. Right-click **TestVol** and click **Shrink Volume**. In the Enter the amount of space to shrink in MB box, type **5000** to shrink the volume by 5 GB. Click **Shrink**.
16. In Hyper-V Manager, open the Settings window for ServerVM1, click the hard drive and click **Edit**. Click **Next**.
17. Since the volume is not occupying all the available space on the virtual disk, you now have the option to Shrink the virtual disk to reclaim disk space on the host. Click **Shrink** and click **Next**. The minimum size you can shrink the volume is 3 GB, so type **3** in the New size box and click **Next**. Click **Finish**.
18. Click **OK** to close the Settings window. Continue to the next activity.

Hyper-V Virtual Networks

- **70-740 – Implement Hyper-V:**
  Configure Hyper-V networking

Hyper-V virtual machines are used for a variety of reasons, and how a particular VM is used usually dictates how you configure the VM's network connection. VMs are connected to a virtual network through a Hyper-V virtual switch created in Hyper-V Manager or with a PowerShell cmdlet. Each virtual switch you create is a separate virtual network. You can create three types of virtual switches and, by extension, virtual networks: external, internal, and private.

To create, delete, and modify virtual switches in Hyper-V, click Virtual Switch Manager in the Actions pane or use the PowerShell cmdlets listed when you enter `Command *-VMSwitch*`. The following sections describe the types of virtual networks you can create.

> **Note**
>
> Another option is to not connect a VM to a virtual switch at all, but most server functions require an active network connection.

External Virtual Switches

An **external virtual switch** binds a virtual switch to one of the host's physical network adapters, allowing VMs to access a LAN connected to the host. During installation of the Hyper-V role, you have the option of creating an external virtual switch by binding one or more of the host's physical adapters to a virtual switch. Only one external switch can be created per physical network adapter. When a VM is connected to an external switch, it acts like any other device on the LAN. For example, the VM can get an IP address from a DHCP server on the external network and use the network's default gateway to access other networks and the Internet.

You use an external virtual switch when external computers must have direct access to the VM or when the VM must have access to external network resources, such as when a VM is configured as a web server, DNS server, or domain controller.

> **Note**
>
> You can use a wired or wireless NIC to bind to an external switch. However, when you bind a wireless NIC, Hyper-V creates an additional network bridge adapter on the host computer.

If you're using external virtual switches, having more than one physical NIC installed on the host computer is highly recommended. This way, you can dedicate one of the NICs to host communication, and the other NIC or NICs can be bound to external virtual switches.

When a NIC is designated for use in an external virtual switch, Windows binds the Hyper-V Extensible Virtual Switch protocol to the physical NIC and unbinds all other protocols. This process creates a virtual switch through which VMs and the host can communicate with the physical network and each other. A new virtual network adapter (virtual NIC) is created on the host computer that has all the usual protocol bindings enabled. The VMs configured to use the external virtual switch are bound to the virtual NIC, which communicates through the virtual switch.

To help you understand virtual networks better, Figure 7-7 shows a host computer without any virtual networks configured, and Figure 7-8 shows the host and VMs connected to an external virtual network. In Figure 7-8, the host's physical NIC is bound only to the Hyper-V Extensible Virtual Switch protocol and has a physical connection to the external network. The host's physical NIC has a virtual connection to the virtual switch and facilitates communication between VMs and the external network. The new virtual NIC created on the host has all the usual network protocol bindings (Client for Microsoft Networks, File and Printer Sharing for Microsoft Networks, TCP/IP, and so forth), allowing host applications and protocols to communicate through the virtual switch to the external network and VMs.

Figure 7-7 A host computer with no virtual networks configured

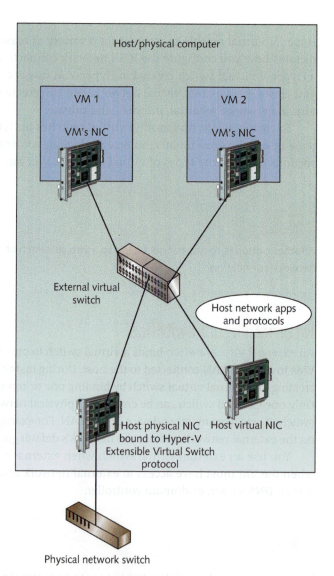

Figure 7-8 A host and VM connected through an external virtual network

Internal Virtual Switches

An **internal virtual switch** allows VMs and the host computer to communicate with one another but doesn't give VMs access to the physical network. An internal switch isn't bound to any of the host's physical NICs. When an internal virtual switch is created, a new virtual NIC is created on the host computer that's bound to the name of the new internal virtual switch. The new virtual NIC allows the host computer to communicate with the VMs on that internal switch. A virtual switch is created, but it's internal to Hyper-V and, therefore, can't be seen on the host computer. By default, the new virtual NIC attempts to get an address via DHCP, but because it doesn't have a connection to the physical network, it's assigned an APIPA address. Any VMs connected to the internal switch are also assigned an APIPA address if you don't assign a static IP address. Figure 7-9 shows how an internal virtual switch works. The difference between an external and internal virtual switch is that the host virtual NIC doesn't have a connection to the physical network switch, which prevents VMs from communicating with the physical network. In addition, the host physical NIC and host virtual NIC have all the normal bindings, allowing network applications and protocols to communicate with both NICs. Only the host can communicate with the VMs.

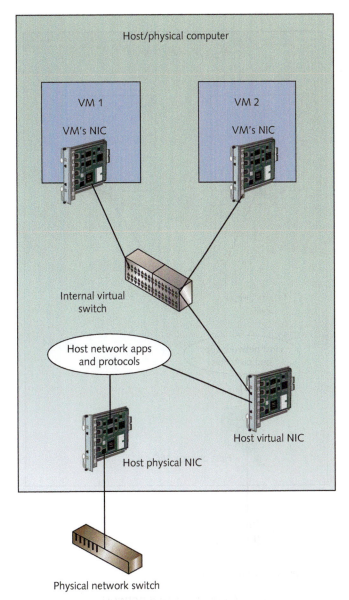

Figure 7-9   **An internal virtual network**

An internal virtual switch is used when devices on the physical network don't need direct access to the VMs and vice versa. Examples include test and lab environments where you want VMs to be isolated from the physical network but still want to communicate with VMs from the host. You can also use an internal virtual switch to isolate applications from the external network but allow communication between the networks by using a VM configured as a router. This configuration is discussed later in the section "Communicating between Hyper-V Switches."

Private Virtual Switches

A **private virtual switch** isn't much different from an internal virtual switch except that the VMs connected to the private virtual switch can't communicate with the host computer. Creating a private virtual switch doesn't create a network connection on the host computer because there's no connection between the host computer and the VMs. Figure 7-10 shows this configuration. Notice that there's no virtual NIC on the host in this configuration because there's no communication between the host and the VMs.

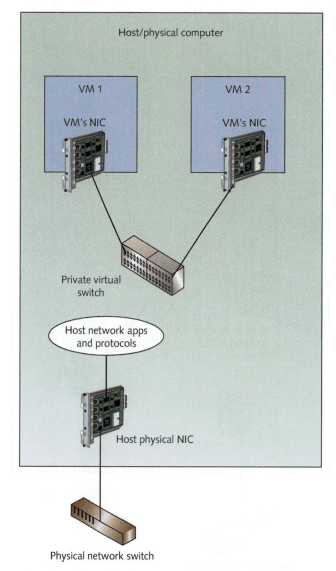

Figure 7-10   A private virtual network

A private virtual switch is used when you want to isolate the VMs connected to the network from all outside communication. You might use this setup as a domain testing environment or a development network in which you need to isolate virtual network traffic.

Communicating between Hyper-V Switches

What if you want to isolate VMs in their own private network, but you want them to be able to access other private networks or an external network? With a physical network, you do this by creating subnets and using a router to route traffic between them. Hyper-V virtual networks are no different. You can do this in two different ways:

- Create an external and a private virtual switch, and then configure one VM with two NICs and have one NIC connected to each virtual switch (see Figure 7-11). You can configure a Windows server as a network router by installing the Remote Access role and installing the Routing role service. This VM can route packets between the private switch and the external switch.
- Create an internal virtual switch and enable routing on the host machine so that it routes between the internal and physical switches (see Figure 7-12).

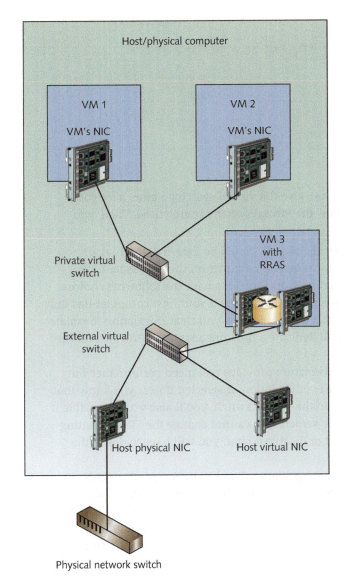

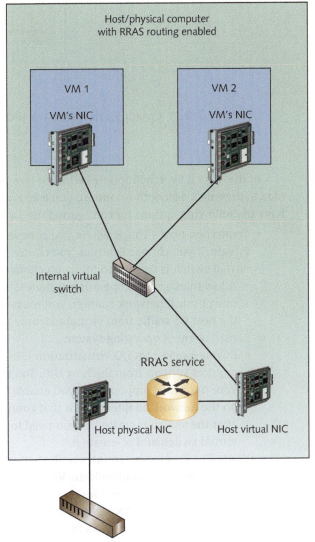

Figure 7-11   Routing between a private and an external virtual switch

Figure 7-12   Routing between an internal network and the physical network

Creating a Virtual Switch

You create a virtual switch in Hyper-V Manager by clicking Virtual Switch Manager in the Actions pane. From this window, you can edit an existing virtual switch or create a new virtual switch. Choose External, Internal, or Private and click Create (see Figure 7-13). It doesn't matter too much what you choose here because you'll be able to change it on the next screen.

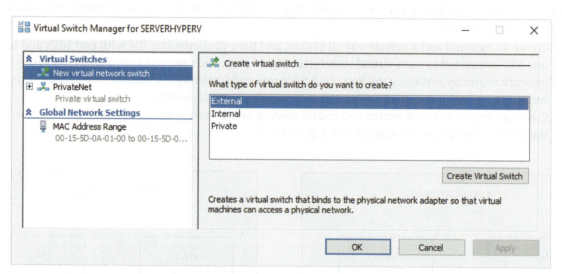

Figure 7-13 Creating a new virtual switch

In the Virtual Switch Properties window (see Figure 7-14), give the virtual switch a name. It's a good idea to provide a descriptive name so you'll know later how the virtual switch is being used. Then, you have the following options for configuring the switch:

- *Connection type*—This is where you choose whether the switch should be External, Internal, or Private. If you choose External, you choose the physical network adapter on the host system the virtual switch is connected to. If you choose External network, you also have the following choices:
  - Allow management operating system to share this network adapter: If your host computer has only one physical network adapter, you must choose this option. Ideally, you clear this option to isolate the host OS traffic from virtual machine traffic and dedicate a network adapter on the host for the management operating system.
  - Enable single-root I/O virtualization (SR-IOV): This feature provides enhanced performance but requires support from the host NIC. You should leave this option unselected unless you know that your hardware supports it. If you enable SR-IOV on the virtual switch, you'll also want to enable it on the network adapter of VMs that connect to the switch. You cannot change the SR-IOV setting after the switch is created. If you need to enable it or disable it later, you will have to delete the virtual switch and re-create it.
- *VLAN ID*—This setting isolates traffic between the management OS and VMs. You set the VLAN identifier to correspond with the VLAN identifier configured on the physical switch. The host machine's virtual NIC used for management is placed on the specified VLAN, but VM traffic is not affected. Enabling VLAN identification is available for external or internal networks but not private networks. Configuring VLANs for VMs is discussed in the section "Adding and Removing Virtual Network Interface Cards" later in this chapter.

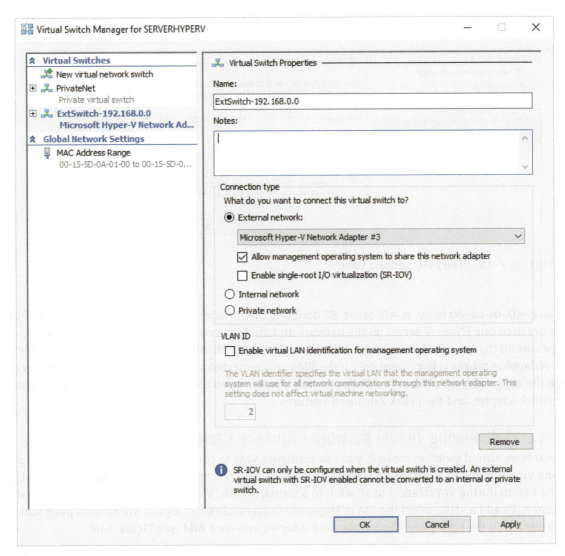

Figure 7-14 Virtual switch properties

Configuring MAC Addresses

Every network adapter must have a unique MAC address on the network, and the network adapters on VMs are no different. Because the network adapter on a VM is virtual and, therefore, can't have a true burned-in address, Hyper-V must assign a MAC address to each network adapter connected to a virtual network, using a pool of addresses it maintains. When a new network adapter is connected to a virtual network, a MAC address is assigned dynamically to the adapter from the pool. The MAC address pool contains 256 addresses by default, but this number can be changed. To view or change the MAC address pool in Hyper-V Manager, click Virtual Switch Manager, and then click MAC Address Range in the left pane (see Figure 7-15).

If you want to expand or change the pool, be aware that the first three bytes are the organizationally unique identifier (OUI) assigned to Microsoft and shouldn't be changed. The fourth and fifth bytes are the hexadecimal equivalent of the last two octets of the MAC address of the server's physical NIC. To expand the pool, changing the second to last byte of the maximum address is best. For example, in Figure 7-15, if you change the 02 to 03 in the Maximum text boxes, your range of available addresses is

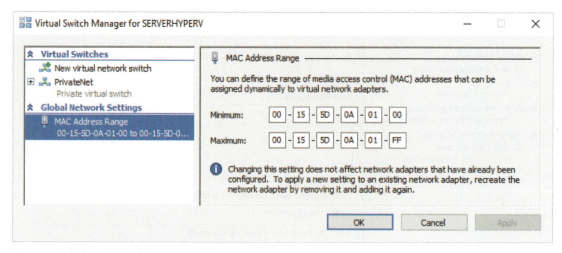

Figure 7-15   The MAC address pool

now 00-15-5D-01-02-00 to 00-15-5D-01-03-FF, doubling the number of addresses from 256 to 512. If you have more than one Hyper-V server on the network and are connecting VMs to an external network, you must be careful that you don't overlap the MAC address range with another server's range. The problem with overlapping ranges is important only if the VMs are connected to the external network. To view or change the assigned MAC address to a VM's network adapter, open the VM's settings and click to expand the network adapter, and then click Advanced Features.

Adding and Removing Virtual Network Interface Cards

Once you have virtual switches created, you can configure VMs to connect to them. To do so, you need at least one virtual network interface card (vNIC) on a VM. A vNIC is created when you create a VM and you have the option during VM creation to attach it to a virtual switch. You can also add a vNIC to a VM after it is created. To add a vNIC, select the VM in Hyper-V Manager, click Settings in the Actions pane and click Add Hardware. In the right pane, choose Network Adapter and click Add (see Figure 7-16).

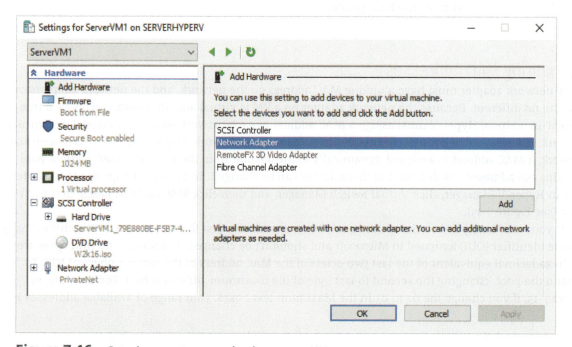

Figure 7-16   Creating a new network adapter or vNIC

When you create a new vNIC, you have the following options (see Figure 7-17):

- *Virtual switch*—Specify the virtual switch this vNIC should be connected to. You can also leave the vNIC not connected to any network.
- *VLAN ID*—If you choose the Enable virtual LAN identification option, the vNIC will be configured for the specified virtual LAN (VLAN). VLANs enable you to create subnets, or broadcast domains, on a single external virtual switch. Each VLAN effectively creates an isolated network, much like a private virtual switch. The physical NIC on the host must support VLANs (also called *VLAN tagging*) for this option to work. When you enable VLAN identification, you choose an ID number that is the VLAN identifier configured on the physical network switch. All VMs that share a VLAN ID can communicate with one another as though they were on the same subnet. The machines sharing a VLAN ID must be configured with IP addresses that have a common network ID. Machines with different VLAN IDs can't communicate directly with one another but can communicate if a router is configured to route between the VLANs. The primary reason for configuring VLANs on VMs is to allow VMs that are connected to the same virtual switch to be isolated from one another on separate broadcast domains. You configure a router to route between VLANs just as you configure one to route between separate virtual networks, as discussed earlier in this chapter.
- *Bandwidth Management*—If you enable bandwidth management, you can specify the minimum and maximum bandwidth (in Mbps) available to the vNIC. For example, if you have three VMs connected to an external virtual switch that is mapped to a 100 Mbps physical NIC on the host, you could configure the maximum bandwidth on each VM to about 33 Mbps so that each VM has equal bandwidth but no VM can monopolize the link. Or if one VM must always have at least 20 Mbps of bandwidth available, set the minimum bandwidth for this VM to 20 and leave the maximum bandwidth at 0; a 0 value means unrestricted.

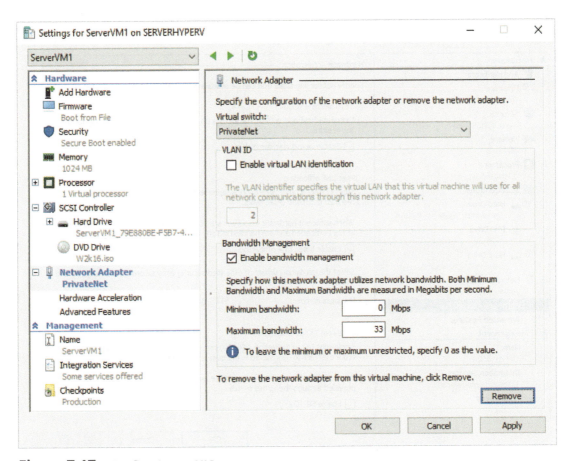

Figure 7-17   Configuring a vNIC

Tip ⓘ

The terms *virtual network interface card (vNIC)* and *virtual network adapter* are equivalent. Microsoft uses the term *virtual network adapter* in many of its commands and management consoles but uses the term *vNIC* in much of its documentation.

Advanced Virtual Network Configuration

Certification

- **70-740 – Implement Hyper-V:**
  Configure Hyper-V networking

Aside from connecting a VM's network adapter to a virtual switch, you might need to perform other configuration tasks related to a VM's network connections. The following sections cover these advanced configuration tasks: hardware acceleration on vNICs, advanced vNIC features, NIC teaming, synthetic versus legacy network adapters, and Fibre Channel adapters.

Virtual NIC Hardware Acceleration

There are three hardware acceleration features for vNICs as shown in Figure 7-18 and described here:

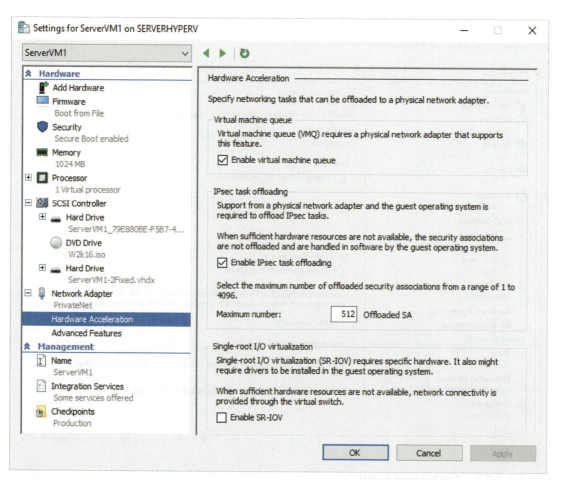

Figure 7-18   Hardware acceleration options for virtual NICs

- *Virtual machine queue*—**Virtual machine queue (VMQ)** accelerates vNIC performance by delivering packets from the external network directly to the vNIC, bypassing the management operating system. VMQ is enabled or disabled on each vNIC. When VMQ is enabled, a dedicated queue is created for the vNIC on the physical NIC. When packets arrive on the physical interface for the vNIC, they are delivered directly to the VM. In contrast, when VMQ is not enabled, packets are placed in a common queue and distributed to the destination vNIC on a first-come, first-served basis. VMQ is enabled by default but must be supported by the physical NIC on the host computer.

- *IPsec task offloading*—With this option (the default setting) enabled, the physical NIC handles much of the processing required to handle IPsec security associations. If sufficient resources are not available on the physical NIC, IPsec security associations are handled by the guest OS. To configure IPsec task offloading with PowerShell, use `Set-VMNetworkAdapter -IpsecOffloadMaximumSecurityAssociation` *Max* where *Max* is the maximum number of associations that can be offloaded to the physical NIC. If *Max* is set to zero, IPsec task offloading is disabled.

- *Single-root I/O virtualization (SR-IOV)*—**Single-root I/O virtualization (SR-IOV)** enhances the virtual network adapter's performance by allowing a virtual adapter to bypass the virtual switch software on the parent partition (the Hyper-V host) and communicate directly with the physical hardware, thereby lowering overhead and improving performance. The performance advantage is most obvious on high-speed NICs, such as 10 GB Ethernet and higher. SR-IOV must be supported by a PCI Express NIC installed on the host, and installing drivers on the guest OS might be necessary. If you enable SR-IOV but resources to support it aren't available, the virtual network adapter connects by using the virtual switch as usual. You must also enable SR-IOV in the Virtual Switch Manager when you create the external virtual switch. If you enable SR-IOV and it's supported, you can check Device Manager on the VM and see the actual NIC make and model listed under network adapters. For adapters with SR-IOV not enabled or not supported, you see only the Microsoft Hyper-V network adapter.

Configuring vNICs with Advanced Features

In the Advanced Features dialog box for a network adapter (see Figure 7-19), you can configure the following features and security options:

- *MAC address*—By default, network adapters are assigned a MAC address dynamically, but you can assign a static MAC address, if necessary. You must be careful not to duplicate a MAC address, and changing the OUI portion of the address isn't recommended. If you do change it, make sure bit 2 of the first byte is set, indicating that the address is locally administered and doesn't contain an OUI. For example, you can change the first byte to 02. You might want to use a static MAC address if the VM moves between host computers, and you want its MAC address to remain the same. For example, if you're using DHCP reservations, the reservation is based on the MAC address, so the VM's MAC address must stay the same for the reservation to work.

- *Enable MAC address spoofing*—If this option is enabled, the VM can change the source MAC address on outgoing packets, and the virtual switch is allowed to "learn" addresses other than the one assigned to the virtual adapter. This feature makes the virtual network less secure, but it might be necessary for network load balancing and clustering.

- *DHCP guard*—This option prevents a VM from acting as a DHCP server. With this option enabled, if the VM sends a DHCP server message on the specified interface, the virtual switch will drop the packet. This option is most useful when your Hyper-V servers are operating in a multitenant environment in which multiple clients are using VMs hosted on your servers and you have little control over what services they may install. Essentially, it prevents a VM from becoming a rogue DHCP server. It is recommended that this option be enabled on all VMs except actual DHCP servers. To enable the option on all adapters on all VMs running on a host, use the following PowerShell cmdlet on the Hyper-V host:

```
Get-VM | Set-VMNetworkAdapter -DhcpGuard On
```

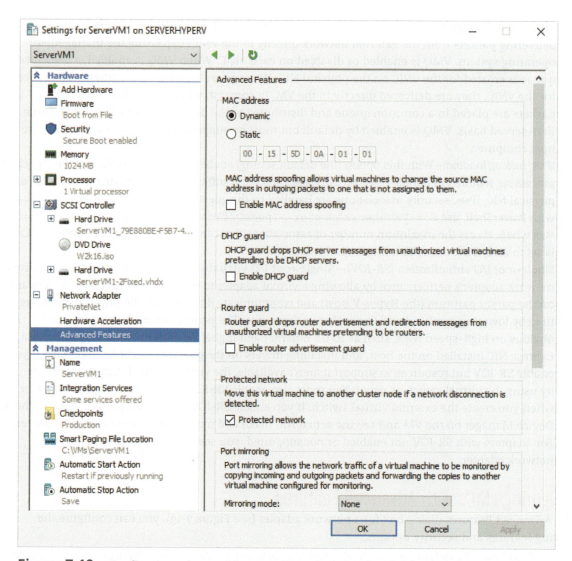

Figure 7-19   Configuring advanced features for a virtual network adapter

To allow DHCP packets to be transmitted from a VM named MyDHCPServer that is a legitimate DHCP server, use the following cmdlet:

```
Set-VMNetworkAdapter -VMName MyDHCPServer -DhcpGuard Off
```

- *Router guard*—Similar to the DHCP guard option, it prevents a VM from sending router advertisements and redirection messages to other VMs. Enable and disable this feature using PowerShell in a similar manner as for DHCP guard:

```
Get-VM | Set-VMNetworkAdapter -RouterGuard On
```

- *Protected network*—This feature is enabled by default. If Hyper-V detects that the VM's network adapter becomes disconnected from the network, it attempts to move the VM to another server where the network is available. This option is applicable only on Hyper-V failover clusters. Uncheck this option if you don't want a VM to be moved automatically to another cluster node if the network connection fails.
- *Port mirroring*—Traffic from the virtual switch port to which the adapter is connected is copied and sent to another VM's virtual switch port for the purposes of monitoring and capturing network traffic. Port mirroring can be configured as None, Source, or Destination. The None setting disables

port mirroring on the vNIC. Use the Source setting if you want incoming and outgoing network traffic to be monitored. Use the Destination setting if you want monitored traffic to be sent to the vNIC. Typically, you would have a network monitoring or protocol analyzer application running on the VM that is configured as Destination.

- *Device naming*—This option (not shown in Figure 7-19 but shown later in Figure 7-22) allows the name of the virtual network adapter to be available to the guest OS. When you create a network adapter using PowerShell, you can assign it a descriptive name because the default name is just Network Adapter. This name is usually available only on the host machine in Hyper-V Manager or in PowerShell cmdlets. However, with Device naming enabled, the name is available in the guest OS using the `Get-NetAdapterAdvancedProperty` cmdlet or from the Advanced tab of the adapter's properties in Network Connections. This feature allows you to better correlate the network adapter you see from the host computer with the network adapter in the guest OS.

Configuring NIC Teaming

NIC teaming allows multiple network interfaces to work in tandem to provide increased bandwidth, load balancing, and fault tolerance. Another term for this is **load balancing and failover (LBFO).** You can create a NIC team with a single network interface, but most of the utility of a NIC team comes from having more than one in the team. Windows Server 2016 supports up to 32 NICs in a team.

Let's consider how NIC teaming provides load balancing. **Load balancing** distributes traffic between two or more interfaces, providing an increase in overall network throughput that a server is able to maintain. A basic example illustrates the concept. Suppose each of two client stations is transferring a 100 MB file to a share on a Windows server. A server with a single NIC operating at 100 Mbps could transfer both files in about 20 seconds (10 seconds for each file). A server with a two-NIC team will load balance the data from the two clients with each NIC able to transfer data at 100 Mbps, totaling 200 Mbps, cutting the total transfer time in half.

Here's an example of how to use NIC teaming for fault tolerance, or failover. **Failover** in this context is the ability of a server to recover from network hardware failure by having redundant hardware that can immediately take over for a device failure. Suppose you have a server that must be highly available. A server with a single NIC that is connected to a switch becomes unavailable if the switch or the NIC fails. However, with a NIC team configured to provide failover, you can connect one NIC to one switch and the other NIC to another switch. If one NIC or switch fails, the other NIC takes over, maintaining server availability.

You can configure NIC teaming on a Hyper-V host server and allow the VMs running on the host to benefit from the NIC team, or you can configure NIC teaming in the guest OS of a VM to provide a dedicated NIC team for that particular VM.

You configure NIC teaming using Server Manager or PowerShell. The process is the same whether you configure it on a physical computer or a VM; however, there are additional considerations when you configure NIC teaming on a VM as described later. From Server Manager, click on Local Server. In the left-hand column of the Properties page, you'll see a link for NIC Teaming, which is disabled by default. Clicking the link brings you to the NIC Teaming configuration page, as shown in Figure 7-20.

In Figure 7-20, you see three panes, which have the following functions:

- *Servers*—This pane shows the available servers for which you can manage NIC teaming. You add servers to this list in a manner similar to adding servers to Server Manager by clicking Tasks and Add Servers. The Servers pane also shows you whether the server is a physical or virtual server and the number of NIC teams defined.
- *Teams*—This pane lists the current NIC teams, their mode and status, and which network adapters are part of the team. You can create or delete a NIC team by clicking Tasks.
- *Adapters and Interfaces*—This pane shows you the list of network adapters available to be added to a NIC team. You can add an interface to an existing team or add an adapter to a new team.

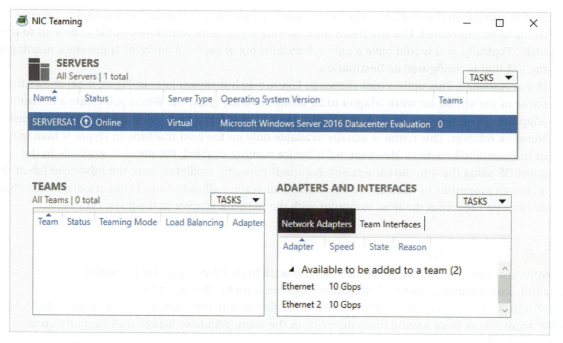

Figure 7-20 NIC Teaming configuration

From PowerShell, you can list, create, remove, rename, and set properties of a team using the following commands:

- `Get-NetLbfoTeam`—Shows a list of NIC teams on the server.
- `New-NetLbfoTeam`—Creates a new NIC team and adds network adapters to the team; you can optionally set the properties of the team.
- `Remove-NetLbfoTeam`—Deletes a team.
- `Rename-NetLbfoTeam`—Renames a team.
- `Set-NetLbfoTeam`—Sets the properties of an existing team.

To get help on using any of these PowerShell commands, from a PowerShell prompt, type `get-help` followed by the command.

NIC Teaming Modes

When you create a new NIC Team, you can configure the teaming mode and the load-balancing mode (see Figure 7-21):

- *Teaming mode*—There are three teaming modes:
  - Switch Independent: This is the default mode and the only mode available for VMs. Using Switch Independent mode, you connect the NICs in a team to separate switches for fault tolerance. The switches are unaware that a connected NIC is part of a team; the server provides all the teaming functions. You can also connect the NICs to the same switch. Switch Independent mode allows you to configure fault tolerance in one of two ways: Active or Standby. Active makes all NICs active, which means that you get the benefit of the bandwidth from all NICs in the team. If one NIC fails, the others continue to run. Standby lets you choose an adapter that remains in standby mode until there is a failure. Upon failure, the NIC in standby mode becomes active. The default setting is Active.
  - Static Teaming: This mode, also called *switch dependent mode*, is primarily used for load balancing. All NICs are connected to one switch and the switch participates in the NIC teaming process. You must use a switch that supports IEEE 802.3ad, which is a standard that defines link aggregation. The switch must be manually configured to identify ports to which members of a switch team are connected. The switch load balances network traffic between the switches.

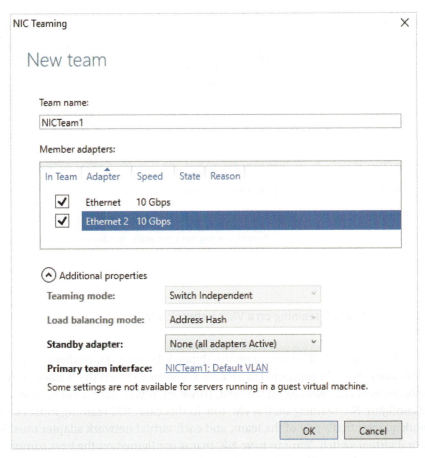

Figure 7-21   Configure NIC Teaming modes

- Link Aggregation Control Protocol (LACP): LACP, defined in IEEE 802.1ax, allows a switch to automatically identify ports to which a team member is connected and dynamically create a team. You must use a switch that supports LACP and enable the protocol before it can be used.
- *Load-balancing mode*—The load-balancing mode determines how the server load balances outgoing data packets among the NICs in the team. There are three options:
  - Address Hash: This mode uses an algorithm based on properties of the outgoing packet to create a hash value. The hash value is then used to assign the packet for delivery using one of the NICs in the team. This is the only load-balancing mode available when configuring NIC teaming on a VM.
  - Hyper-V Port: This method is used when the team members are connected to a Hyper-V switch. Each virtual NIC is associated with only one team member at system startup. This method works well if there are a number of VMs running to evenly distribute the load among NICs in the team.
  - Dynamic: This is the default mode on physical computers. In this mode, traffic is evenly distributed among all team members, including from virtual NICs. A potential problem with the Address Hash and Hyper-V Port modes is that a NIC in the team could be overwhelmed when there are very large traffic flows involving a single NIC, even if the other NICs had unused capacity. This mode balances large flows of traffic over multiple NICs, thereby providing even distribution of traffic among all team members.

NIC Teaming on Virtual Machines

As mentioned, you can configure NIC teaming on VMs as well as physical computers. On VMs, you use the same procedure as on physical computers, but for the most reliability, you should enable the feature first in the network adapter's Advanced Features dialog box (shown in Figure 7-22). If you don't enable it, you can still create a NIC team in the VM's guest OS, but if one of the physical NICs in the team fails, the team stops working instead of providing failover protection. NIC teaming can be configured only on vNICs connected to an external virtual switch.

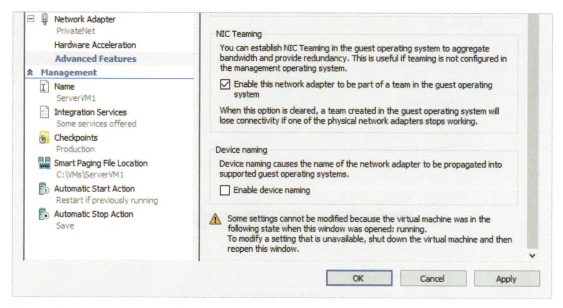

Figure 7-22　Enabling NIC teaming on a VM's network adapter

If you have already configured NIC teaming on the Hyper-V host server, configuring it on VMs running on the host isn't necessary. Any VM connected to an external virtual switch that's mapped to the host's NIC team gets the benefits of NIC teaming on the host. However, if you want a VM to have a dedicated NIC team, you should configure NIC teaming on the VM, too. In this case, NIC teaming must be enabled on each virtual network adapter that's part of the team, and each virtual network adapter must be connected to a separate external virtual switch. You can have NIC teams configured on the host computer and on VMs, but they must use separate physical NICs. That is, the NICs on the host that are part of a NIC team can't be used in a NIC team on a VM and vice versa. Likewise, an external virtual switch can be mapped only to a NIC team on the host or to a physical NIC on the host; it can't be mapped to a NIC that's a member of a NIC team. You must plan physical and virtual network configurations carefully to be sure you have enough physical NICs to accommodate the host's physical network needs and the virtual network needs.

Note

Although NIC teaming on physical computers can use up to 32 NICs in a team, Microsoft supports VM NIC teams with only two team members. You can create a team with more members, but it's not officially supported.

Implementing Switch Embedded Teaming

Switch Embedded Teaming (SET) is a new feature in Windows Server 2016 that allows up to eight identical physical adapters on the host system to be configured as a team and mapped to a virtual switch. The virtual switch can control all the physical adapters simultaneously, providing fault tolerance and load balancing. SET is targeted for enterprise servers with very fast NICs, 10 GB and faster. The physical NICs can be connected to the same or different physical switches providing additional fault tolerance. To configure SET, you simply create a new virtual switch and specify the network adapters that should be members as in the following cmdlet:

```
New-VMSwitch -Name SETSwitch1 -NetAdapter Ethernet1,Ethernet2
  -EnableEmbeddedTeaming $true
```

Next, you add the virtual network adapters that will communicate through the SET-enabled switch:

```
Add-VMNetworkAdapter -SwitchName SETSwitch1 -Name Adapter1
```

SET supports remote direct memory access (RDMA) on virtual network adapters, which provides additional performance benefits. You must enable RDMA on the virtual network adapter created on the host system. The adapter will always be named vEthernet (*VirtualAdapterName*) where *VirtualAdapterName* is the name assigned when you created the virtual network adapter.

```
Enable-NetAdapterRDMA "vEthernet (Adapter1)"
```

Synthetic versus Legacy Network Adapters

On generation 1 VMs, you have the option of using synthetic network adapters or legacy network adapters. **Synthetic network adapters** (network adapters that use synthetic drivers in Hyper-V) are available on generation 1 VMs only if Integration Services is installed. On generation 2 VMs, legacy network adapters have been deprecated, and you must have Integration Services installed to add a network adapter.

In general, you should always use synthetic network adapters (shown as just Network Adapters in the Add Hardware section of the Settings window for a VM) because they produce much better performance than legacy adapters do. However, with a generation 1 VM, you should use a legacy network adapter in the following situations:

- The guest OS doesn't support synthetic network adapters, such as some non-Windows OSs that don't support Integration Services.
- You need to PXE boot, or the VM needs to access the network for some other reason before the OS starts. Synthetic network adapters on Generation 1 VMs do not support PXE boot and do not function before the OS starts.

Note that generation 2 VMs don't support legacy network adapters, and the synthetic adapters on generation 2 VMs do support PXE boot, so there's no reason to use a legacy adapter. However, generation 2 VMs support only Windows Server 2012/R2 and later and 64-bit versions of Windows 8/8.1 and later. So, for older VMs, you might want to install a legacy network adapter on the VM for PXE boot and then replace it with a synthetic network adapter after the OS is installed.

Configuring Fibre Channel Adapters

A Fibre Channel adapter allows a VM to access Fibre Channel storage directly. For example, a VM can access a Fibre Channel SAN to gain access to large amounts of high-performance storage. Access to shared Fibre Channel storage also enables administrators to cluster VMs to provide application and node-level fault tolerance across multiple Hyper-V servers.

To use Fibre Channel on a VM to connect to a SAN, you must first create a virtual Fibre Channel SAN in Hyper-V Manager. To do so, click Virtual SAN Manager in the Actions pane. In the Virtual SAN Manager, click Create to add a virtual Fibre Channel SAN (see Figure 7-23).

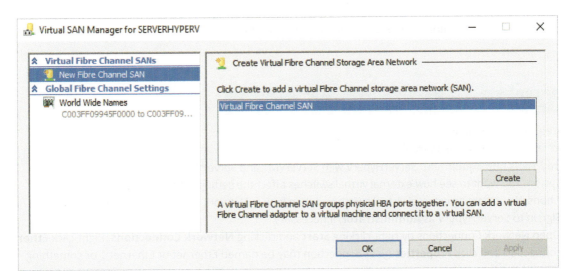

Figure 7-23   Adding a virtual Fibre Channel SAN

Before you can add a virtual Fibre Channel SAN, the host computer must have the necessary Fibre Channel host bus adapters and drivers installed and configured. After creating a virtual Fibre Channel SAN, you add a Fibre Channel adapter to the VM by using the Add Hardware option in the VM's Settings window. In the Fibre Channel Adapter dialog box (see Figure 7-24), you connect the adapter to the virtual SAN you created in the Virtual SAN Manager and configure additional options. Configuring Fibre Channel SANs is beyond the scope of this book, but you should know about this option for VMs if Fibre Channel SANs are already part of your storage configuration.

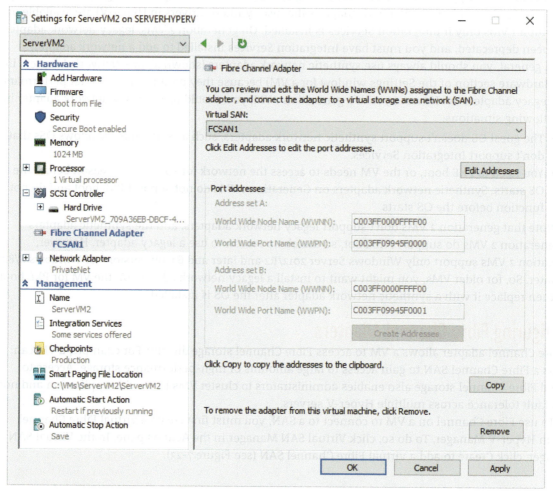

Figure 7-24 Adding a Fibre Channel adapter to a VM

Activity 7-4: Working with External Virtual Switches

Time Required: 20 minutes
Objective: Create an external virtual switch.
Required Tools and Equipment: ServerHyperV with ServerVM1 and ServerVM2
Description: You want to see how external virtual switches affect the settings of the host computer's network connections. You create an external virtual switch and then look in Network Connections to see the results.

1. Sign in to ServerHyperV as **Administrator**, if necessary.
2. Open Network Connections by right-clicking **Start** and clicking **Network Connections**. Right-click **Ethernet** connection and click **Properties** (your connection may be named Ethernet or Ethernet 1 or something

similar). Scroll through the properties until you see the Hyper-V Extensible Virtual Switch protocol. The protocol is installed but isn't checked, which means it isn't bound to the adapter. (*Note:* If a protocol is bound to an adapter, that means it is enabled.) Close the **Properties** dialog box.

3. Open Hyper-V Manager, click **Virtual Switch Manager** in the Actions pane. In the left pane, click **New virtual network switch**, if necessary. Click **External** in the right pane, and then click **Create Virtual Switch** to create an external virtual network.

4. Type **External-192.168.0** in the Name text box. Examine the other setting options. Notice that under External network, you can select which NIC on the host computer the switch should be connected to. Click **OK** and click **Yes** in the Apply Networking Changes message box.

5. Open the Network Connections window. You see a new connection named vEthernet (External-192.168.0). Next, open the Properties dialog box for the Ethernet connection (not the vEthernet connection). Notice that only the Hyper-V Extensible Virtual Switch protocol is checked, which means that it is now bound to the adapter. This is the physical NIC that creates the virtual switch for the external network. Click **Cancel**.

6. Open the Properties dialog box for the vEthernet connection. Most of the protocols are selected except Hyper-V Extensible Virtual Switch and Microsoft Network Adapter Multiplexor Protocol. This is the virtual NIC that VMs and the host computer use to communicate with the virtual switch and, therefore, the physical network. Figure 7-25 shows both network connections side by side. Click **Cancel** to close the Ethernet Properties dialog box.

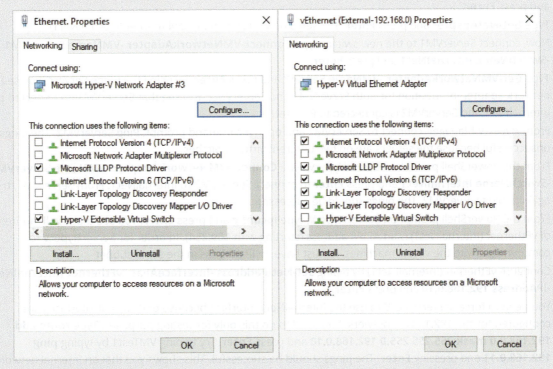

Figure 7-25   The physical NIC bound to the Hyper-V Extensible Virtual Switch protocol (left) and the new virtual NIC (right)

7. In Hyper-V Manager, right-click **ServerVM1** and click **Settings**.

8. In the Settings for ServerVM1 window, click **Network Adapter** in the left pane under **Hardware**. In the right pane, click the **Virtual switch** list arrow and click **External-192.168.0**. Click **OK**. Follow the same procedure for ServerVM2.

9. Start and connect to both **ServerVM1** and **ServerVM2**. Open a command prompt on ServerVM1 and type **ping 192.168.0.12** and press **Enter** (192.168.0.12 should be the IP address of ServerVM2). The pings should be successful. (If your pings are not successful, you may need to disable the firewall on ServerVM1 and ServerVM2 or configure a firewall rule to allow ICMP packets).

10. Close the Virtual Machine Connection consoles. In Hyper-V Manager, reconnect ServerVM1 and ServerVM2 back to the PrivateNet virtual switch.

11. Continue to the next activity.

Activity 7-5: Working with Internal Virtual Networks

Time Required: 20 minutes

Objective: Create an internal virtual switch using PowerShell and connect a VM to it.

Required Tools and Equipment: ServerHyperV with ServerVM1 and ServerVM2

Description: You want to see how internal virtual networks affect communication between VMs and the host computer, so you create an internal virtual network and connect one of the VMs to this network.

1. On ServerHyperV, open a PowerShell window. Type **New-VMSwitch InternalNet1 -SwitchType Internal** and press **Enter**.

2. Type **Get-NetAdapter** and press **Enter**. You see a new adapter named vEthernet (InternalNet1).

3. Now, connect ServerVM1 to the new switch. Type **Connect-VMNetworkAdapter -VMName ServerVM1 -SwitchName InternalNet1** and press **Enter**.

4. Type **Get-VMNetworkAdapter -VMName Server*** and press **Enter**. By using the name Server*, you see the network adapter information for both ServerVM1 and ServerVM2. You see that ServerVM1 is connected to InternalNet1 and ServerVM2 is connected to PrivateNet.

5. From Hyper-V Manager, connect to ServerVM1 and open a command prompt. Ping ServerVM2. The pings are unsuccessful because the servers are on two different virtual switches.

6. From the PowerShell prompt on ServerHyperV, type **Connect-VMNetworkAdapter -VMName ServerVM2 -SwitchName InternalNet1** and press **Enter** to connect ServerVM2 to InternalNet1. From ServerVM1, try again to ping ServerVM2. The pings should be successful.

7. From the PowerShell prompt on ServerHyperV, type **ipconfig** and press **Enter**. You see that the IP address of vEthernet (InternalNet1) is an APIPA address (starting with 169.254). In order for ServerHyperV to communicate with the virtual machines, it must have an IP address in the same subnet.

8. Configure vEthernet (InternallNet1) by typing **Set-NetIPaddress -InterfaceAlias "vEthernet (InternalNet1)" -IPAddress 192.168.0.10** and press **Enter**.

9. You need to force ServerHyperV to use the InternalNet1 interface because both virtual interfaces are configured for the 192.168.0.0 network. You need to do this only for testing purposes. Type **route add 192.168.0.0 mask 255.255.255.0 192.168.0.10** and press **Enter**. Try to ping VMTest1 by typing **ping 192.168.0.11** and pressing **Enter**. The pings should be successful. This shows you that an internal network allows communication between the host and the virtual machines.

10. Delete the route you just created by typing **route delete 192.168.0.0 mask 255.255.255.0 192.168.0.10** and pressing **Enter**. Reconnect ServerVM1 and ServerVM2 to PrivateNet by typing **Connect-VMNetworkAdapter -VMName ServerVM1,ServerVM2 -SwitchName PrivateNet** and pressing **Enter**.

11. Next, delete the virtual switches you created by typing **Remove-VMSwitch InternalNet1** and pressing **Enter**. Press **Enter** to confirm. Type **Remove-VMSwitch External-192.168.0** and press **Enter**. Press **Enter** to confirm.

12. Close all windows on ServerHyperV and shut down ServerVM1 and ServerVM2.

Nested Virtualization

- **70-740 – Implement Hyper-V:**
  Install and configure Hyper-V

If you've been doing the activities in Chapter 6 and this chapter, chances are that you are using nested virtualization. Nested virtualization provides the ability to run a hypervisor inside another hypervisor. For example, if you have a physical server running Hyper-V and you install a VM in Hyper-V and then install Hyper-V on the VM, you are running nested virtualization. You are not limited to Hyper-V; for example, nested virtualization can be implemented with VMware and other virtualization platforms. However, this discussion focuses on implementing nested virtualization in Hyper-V on Windows Server 2016. Nested virtualization in Hyper-V is supported only in Windows 10 and Windows Server 2016 and later. Both the host machine and the VM must be running Windows 10 or Windows Server 2016. To configure nested virtualization, take the following steps:

1. Install Hyper-V on Windows Server 2016 or Windows 10 (you can also use Hyper-V Server 2016).
   - The host computer must have an Intel processor that includes the VT-x virtualization extensions and extended page tables (EPT) technology (also known as *second level address translation [SLAT]*).
2. Create a VM and install Windows 10 or Windows Server 2016. Turn off the VM.
3. On the physical Hyper-V host, run this cmdlet: `Set-VMProcessor -VMName VirtualMachine -ExposeVirtualizationExtensions $true` where *VirtualMachine* is the name of the VM you created in Step 2.
4. Configure MAC address spoofing on the virtual NIC of the physical Hyper-V host. You can do that in Hyper-V Manager or with the following cmdlet: `Set-VMNetworkAdapter -VMName HyperVHost -MacAddressSpoofing On`.
5. Start the virtual machine and install Hyper-V. Now you can create VMs in Hyper-V running in the VM.

There are a few caveats regarding nested virtualization that you should be aware of. The VM that is running Hyper-V cannot use dynamic memory while Hyper-V is running. You can enable dynamic memory, but it will have no effect; you must turn off the VM to adjust its memory. Therefore, you should disable dynamic memory on the Hyper-V VM. In addition, you cannot live migrate a VM that is running Hyper-V. Live migration is a feature that allows you to move a running VM to another Hyper-V host with no downtime.

Implementing Linux and FreeBSD Virtual Machines

- **70-740 – Install Windows Servers in host and compute environments:**
  Create, manage, and maintain images for deployment

Hyper-V supports Linux and FreeBSD VMs with no special configuration if you use emulated device drivers. However, recall that emulated drivers provide inferior performance compared to synthetic drivers. For the best performance of Linux and FreeBSD VMs, you need to install Linux Integration Services (LIS) or FreeBSD Integration Services (BIS). Some of the newer Linux kernels include support for integration services, but if the distribution you wish to install doesn't include them, you can download them from the Microsoft download center by searching for "Linux Integration Services." Once downloaded, you can install them in the Linux VM. FreeBSD releases beginning with version 10 provide built-in support for integration services; for older versions, download and install the integration services from the Microsoft download center.

Chapter Summary

- A virtual hard disk is a file on the host computer with the `.vhd` or `.vhdx` extension. Virtual hard disks are more flexible than physical disks. Three types of virtual hard disks can be created: dynamically expanding, fixed size, and differencing. A fourth type of hard disk, called a pass-through disk, can be attached to a VM. It is an offline physical disk attached to the host. Storage Quality of Service (QoS) is a feature in Windows Server 2016 that enables administrators to specify minimum and maximum performance values for virtual hard disks.

- Virtual disks can be created when a VM is created or with the New Virtual Hard Disk Wizard. During VM creation, the disk is created as a dynamically expanding disk, but you can change it to a fixed-size disk later. When you use the wizard, the first thing you do is choose the disk format. The virtual disk can be formatted as a VHD, VHDX, or a VHD set.

- There are three types of virtual networks: external, internal, and private. External networks connect the VM to the host's physical network, and internal networks allow VMs to communicate only with one another and the host. Private networks allow communication only between the VMs connected to them. More than one private and internal network can be created on a host.

- You create a virtual switch in Hyper-V Manager by clicking Virtual Switch Manager in the Actions pane. From this window, you can edit an existing virtual switch or create a new virtual switch. Choose External, Internal, or Private. Then you can configure the switch with the following options: Connection type, Allow management operating system to share this network adapter, Enable single-root I/O virtualization, and VLAN ID.

- A network adapter on a VM is virtual and cannot have a true burned-in address, and Hyper-V must assign a MAC address to each network adapter connected to a virtual network, using a pool of addresses that it maintains. When a new network adapter is connected to a virtual network, a MAC address is assigned dynamically to the adapter from the pool. The MAC address pool contains 256 addresses by default.

- There are three hardware acceleration features for vNICs: virtual machine queue (VMQ), IPsec task offloading, and Single-root I/O virtualization (SR-IOV). In the Advanced Features dialog box for a network adapter, you can configure the following features and security options: MAC address, Enable MAC address spoofing, DHCP guard, Protected network, Port mirroring, and Device naming.

- NIC teaming allows multiple network interfaces to work in tandem to provide increased bandwidth, load balancing, and fault tolerance. You can create a NIC team with a single network interface, but most of the utility of a NIC team comes from having more than one in the team. Windows Server 2016 supports up to 32 NICs in a team. There are three teaming modes: Switch Independent, Static Teaming, and LACP.

- Load balancing distributes traffic between two or more interfaces, providing an increase in overall network throughput a server is able to maintain. The load-balancing mode determines how the server load balances outgoing data packets among the NICs in the team. There are three options: Address Hash, Hyper-V Port, and Dynamic.

- When using generation 1 VMs, you have the option of using synthetic network adapters or legacy network adapters. Generation 2 VMs don't support legacy network adapters, and the synthetic adapters on generation 2 VMs do support PXE boot, so there's no reason to use a legacy adapter.

- A Fibre Channel adapter allows a VM to access Fibre Channel storage directly from a VM. Before you can add a virtual Fibre Channel SAN, the host computer must have the necessary Fibre Channel host bus adapters and drivers installed and configured.

- Nested virtualization is the ability to run a hypervisor inside another hypervisor. Nested virtualization in Hyper-V is supported only in Windows 10 and Windows Server 2016 and later.

- Hyper-V supports Linux and FreeBSD VMs with no special configuration if you use emulated device drivers. For the best performance of Linux and FreeBSD VMs, you need to install Linux Integration Services (LIS) or FreeBSD Integration Services (BIS).

Key Terms

Aggregated policy
Dedicated policy
differencing disk
dynamically expanding disk
external virtual switch
failover
fixed-size disk

internal virtual switch
load balancing
load balancing and failover (LBFO)
NIC teaming
pass-through disk
private virtual switch

single-root I/O virtualization (SR-IOV)
storage Quality of Service (QoS)
synthetic network adapter
VHD set
virtual machine queue (VMQ)

Review Questions

1. Windows 2016 Hyper-V will allow you to utilize three different types of virtual disks. Which of the following is *not* a virtual disk type found in Windows 2016?
   a. Dynamically expanding
   b. Fixed size
   c. Differencing
   d. Checkpoint

2. Which of the following virtual disk formats is a shared virtual hard disk used with virtual machine cluster configurations when multiple VMs have access to the same virtual hard disk for fault tolerance and load-balancing applications?
   a. VHD
   b. VHDX
   c. VHD set
   d. VHDX set

3. What virtual disk option can be selected to allow a differencing disk's contents to be incorporated into its parent disk or combine the differencing disk with the parent disk to create a new disk while allowing the original disk to be unchanged?
   a. Compact
   b. Convert
   c. Shrink
   d. Merge

4. A system administrator needs to create a high-performance SQL server. What type of disk configuration will allow the administrator to connect an offline physical disk that is connected to the host machine to a VM to maximize a VM's performance?
   a. Pass-through disk
   b. Expanded disk
   c. Fixed-size disk
   d. Differencing disk

5. As a system administrator, you have been assigned the task of setting up a new server cluster where the VM storage will be shared. You

will need the ability to specify the minimum and maximum performance values for the virtual hard disks. Which of the following features available on Windows Server 2016 can be utilized to accomplish this task?
   a. Performance monitoring
   b. Storage Quality of Service
   c. Dedicated storage
   d. Pass-through disks

6. A virtual switch with the host's physical NIC bound to the Hyper-V Extensible Virtual Switch protocol is called which of the following?
   a. External virtual switch
   b. Private virtual switch
   c. Hosted virtual switch
   d. Internal virtual switch

7. You have three VMs that must communicate with one another and with the host computer but not be able to access the physical network directly. What type of virtual network should you create?
   a. Private
   b. Internal
   c. Hosted
   d. External

8. You're installing a new VM in Hyper-V that requires excellent disk performance for the installed applications to perform well. The applications require a virtual disk of about 200 GB. The host has two drives: one used as the Windows system drive and the other as a data drive of 500 GB. It's currently running a VM that uses a virtual disk stored on the host's data drive. This VM requires little disk access, uses only 20 GB of the host's data drive, and will max out at 40 GB. What type of disk should you use for the new VM you're installing?
   a. Differencing disk
   b. Dynamically expanding disk
   c. Pass-through disk
   d. Fixed-size disk

9. Your Hyper-V server has a single disk of 300 GB being used as the system disk and to host a dynamically expanding disk for a Windows Server 2016 VM. The VM's virtual disk has a maximum size of 200 GB and is currently 80 GB and growing. You have only about 30 GB free space on the host disk. You have noticed disk contention with the host OS, and the constant need for the virtual disk to expand is causing performance problems. You also have plans to install at least one more VM. You have installed a new 500 GB hard disk on the host and want to make sure that the VM doesn't contend for the host's system disk, and the expansion process doesn't hamper disk performance. What should you do?

   a. Create a new fixed-size disk on the new drive. Use the Disk Management MMC on the VM to extend the current disk to the new fixed-size disk.

   b. Shut down the VM. Convert the dynamically expanding disk to a fixed-size disk, being sure to place the fixed-size disk on the new host drive. Connect the VM to the fixed-size disk in place of the dynamically expanding disk. Delete the old virtual disk.

   c. Shut down the VM. Create a new fixed-size disk on the new drive. Copy the contents of the dynamically expanding disk to the new fixed-size disk. Connect the VM to the fixed-size disk in place of the dynamically expanding disk. Delete the old virtual disk.

   d. Create a new fixed-size disk on the new drive. Add the fixed-size disk to the VM as a new disk. On the VM, create a new volume on the new disk, and begin saving files to the new volume.

10. You have five VMs that you have created for using in a testing environment. You need to isolate all five VMs so that they cannot communicate with the host computer and any other host on a different network. What type of virtual switch should you create?

    a. Isolated
    b. External
    c. Internal
    d. Private

11. You have been assigned the task of creating a virtual switch in Hyper-V Manager. After assigning the switch a name and utilizing the Virtual Switch Properties window, you are ready to continue configuring the virtual switch.

Which of the following options should you select because your host machine has only one physical network adapter?

    a. Set connection type to internal
    b. Allow management operating system to share this network adapter
    c. Enable single-root I/O virtualization
    d. Set a VLAN ID

12. A VM network adapter must have a unique MAC address on the network. You have decided that you need to expand the current MAC address pool that is available to a VM. However, you have more than one Hyper-V server on the network and are connecting VMs to an external network. What negative situation should you be aware of when you are expanding the current MAC address pool?

    a. Creating an entirely new unique MAC address
    b. Overlapping the IP address range with another server's range
    c. Overlapping the MAC address range with another server's range
    d. Overlapping the MAC address range with another network

13. Which of the following is true about using differencing disks?

    a. Checkpoints can be used with differencing disks, but performance is decreased.
    b. The parent disk must not be changed.
    c. The parent disk must always be connected to a running VM.
    d. Differencing disks are very similar to fixed-size disks.

14. When you create a new VM in Hyper-V, you need at least one virtual network interface card (vNIC) on the VM. When you configure a vNIC, you can choose to have it configured for a specific VLAN. If you choose to enable VLAN identification, which of the following options must you configure?

    a. ID number
    b. ID identifier
    c. Tag identifier
    d. QoS number

15. You're working with a Windows Server 2016 VM in Hyper-V. You have decided that you are going to accelerate the vNIC's performance by delivering packets from the external network directly to the vNIC. What virtual NIC feature would you enable?

    a. IPsec task offloading
    b. Virtual machine vNIC priority
    c. Virtual machine queue
    d. Single-root I/O virtualization

16. Which of the following vNIC configuration options will allow the VM to change the source MAC address on outgoing packets and allow the virtual switch to learn addresses other than the one assigned to the virtual adapter?
    a. DHCP guard
    b. Port mirroring
    c. Device Naming
    d. MAC address spoofing

17. You have just created a vNIC using PowerShell and assigned your vNIC a specific name. You have enabled the Device naming option in the Advanced Features dialog box when configuring the vNIC. What PowerShell cmdlet will allow you to view the virtual adapter's descriptive name in the guest OS?
    a. `DEnable-NetAdapterProperty`
    b. `Get-NetAdapterAdvancedProperty`
    c. `Add-NetAdapterAdvancedProperty`
    d. `Get-NetAdapterProperty`

18. You have just installed a VM named VM5 running an application that requires the best possible network performance when communicating with resources on the physical LAN. The host has four NICs. One NIC is dedicated to the host computer, and the other two are bound to two virtual switches used by four other VMs on the system. One of the NICs is currently unused. What network configuration should you use that wouldn't disturb the current VM's network configuration?
    a. Connect VM5 to an internal network, and run Routing and Remote Access Service (RRAS) on the host server.
    b. Connect the four existing VMs to a private network, create a NIC team on the host server, and bind the NIC team to a virtual switch for VM5 to use.
    c. In Virtual Switch Manager, bind the unused NIC to an external virtual switch and enable SR-IOV. Connect VM5's virtual network adapter to that virtual switch and enable SR-IOV on the virtual network adapter.
    d. Create a NIC team in VM5, using all four NICs on the host. Turn on virtual network adapter sharing so that the NICs can be used for both the team and the other two virtual switches.

19. You have created a VM and installed Windows Server 2008 R2 over the network, using PXE boot. When you start the VM, it doesn't attempt to boot from the network. What should you do?
    a. Install a legacy virtual network adapter
    b. Configure the VM as a generation 2 VM
    c. Install a synthetic virtual network adapter
    d. Enable PXE boot in the VM's BIOS settings

20. You currently have four VMs running on a Hyper-V server. You find that VM2 sometimes monopolizes disk I/O. You want to limit the amount of disk resources that VM2 can use so the other VMs have satisfactory disk performance. What should you do?
    a. Enable SR-IOV on VM2's virtual hard disk
    b. Enable virtual hard disk sharing on VM2
    c. Configure VM2's disk as a pass-through disk
    d. Enable storage QoS on VM2's virtual hard disk

21. You currently have four VMs running on a Hyper-V server. You would like to utilize NIC teaming. Which of the following NIC teaming modes can be utilized with your VMs?
    a. Switch Independent
    b. Static Teaming
    c. LACP
    d. Dynamic

22. Which of the following load-balancing modes available in Hyper-V allows each virtual NIC to be associated with only one team member at system startup?
    a. Hyper-V Port
    b. Static load balancing
    c. Dynamic
    d. Address Hash

23. Which of the following is a new feature in Windows Server 2016 that allows up to eight identical physical adapters on the host system to be configured as a team and mapped to a virtual switch?
    a. Switch Teaming
    b. Switch Embedded Teaming
    c. Hyper-V Port
    d. Static adapter Teaming

24. You would like to utilize a VM to access Fibre Channel storage utilizing a Fibre Channel adapter directly from a VM. Which of the following components must be installed on the VM's host computer before you can add a virtual Fibre Channel SAN? (Choose all that apply.)
    a. Additional NIC
    b. Drivers
    c. Host bus adapter
    d. Fibre Channel adapter

25. Which of the following operating systems are currently supported when utilizing nested virtualization in Windows Server 2016? (Choose all that apply.)
    a. Windows Server 2012/R2
    b. Windows Server 10
    c. Windows Server 2016
    d. Windows Server 8.1

26. You would like to utilize Hyper-V to emulate a Linux desktop and a FreeBSD server for testing purposes in a computer lab. You do not wish to use any special configurations, and you do not need these VMs to be optimized for performance. You have also decided that you do not want to utilize any additional

services when creating these test VMs. What type of drivers will you use for these VMs?
a. Linux and FreeBSD drivers
b. Synthetic drivers
c. Host devices drivers
d. Emulated device drivers

Critical Thinking

The following activities give you critical thinking challenges. Case Projects offer a scenario with a problem to solve for which you supply a written solution.

Case Project 7-1: Choosing a Virtual Disk Configuration

You have two Windows Server 2016 computers with the Hyper-V role installed. Both computers have two hard drives, one for the system volume and the other for data. One server, HyperVTest, is going to be used mainly for testing and what-if scenarios, and its data drive is 250 GB. You estimate that you might have 8 or 10 VMs configured on HyperVTest with two or three running at the same time. Each test VM has disk requirements ranging from about 30 GB to 50 GB. The other server, HyperVApp, runs in the data center with production VMs installed. Its data drive is 500 GB. You expect two VMs to run on HyperVApp, each needing about 150 GB to 200 GB of disk space. Both are expected to run fairly disk-intensive applications. Given this environment, describe how you would configure the virtual disks for the VMs on both servers.

Case Project 7-2: Choosing a Virtual Network Configuration

You're setting up a test environment that involves two subnets with three Windows Server 2016 servers on each subnet. The servers are running broadcast-based network services, such as DHCP. The host computer is attached to the production network, so you must prevent any conflicts. You want the two subnets to be able to communicate with each other. The test environment consists of a single Windows Server 2016 machine running Hyper-V. Describe how you plan to configure the virtual network.

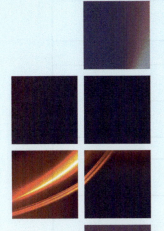

CHAPTER 8

IMPLEMENTING HIGH AVAILABILITY: SERVER CLUSTERS

After reading this chapter and completing the exercises, you will be able to:

Configure network load balancing

Configure a failover cluster

Businesses depend on their networks and network data more than ever before. If network servers aren't available, productivity can come to a grinding halt. The importance of server high availability can't be overstated, so Windows Server 2016 has several high-availability server options to ensure that productivity continues even if one server fails. This chapter discusses two high-availability options in Windows Server 2016: network load balancing and failover clustering.

Configuring Network Load Balancing

 **Certification**

- 70-740 – Implement high availability:
  Implement Network Load Balancing (NLB)

The Windows Server 2016 **network load balancing (NLB)** feature uses server clusters to provide both scalability and fault tolerance. A **server cluster** is a group of servers configured to respond to a single virtual IP address. Based on an internal algorithm, the servers decide which server should respond to each incoming client request. To provide scalability, the servers in an NLB cluster share the load of incoming requests based on rules you can define. To provide fault tolerance, a failed server can be removed from the cluster, and another server can take its place and begin servicing client requests that were handled by the failed server. Although NLB does provide some fault tolerance, its main function is to handle a large volume of client traffic efficiently.

Table 8-1 lists what you need for hands-on activities in this chapter.

TABLE 8-1 Activity requirements

Activity	Requirements	Notes
Activity 8-1: Resetting Your Virtual Environment	ServerDC1, ServerDM1, ServerDM2	
Activity 8-2: Installing the Network Load Balancing Feature	ServerDC1, ServerDM1, ServerDM2	
Activity 8-3: Creating an NLB Cluster	ServerDC1, ServerDM1, ServerDM2	
Activity 8-4: Resetting Your Virtual Environment	ServerDC1, ServerDM1, ServerDM2	
Activity 8-5: Configuring Shared Storage for Failover Clustering	ServerDC1, ServerDM1, ServerDM2	
Activity 8-6: Configuring the iSCSI Initiators	ServerDC1, ServerDM1, ServerDM2	
Activity 8-7: Installing the Failover Clustering Feature and Validating a Cluster Configuration	ServerDC1, ServerDM1, ServerDM2	
Activity 8-8: Creating a Failover Cluster	ServerDC1, ServerDM1, ServerDM2	
Activity 8-9: Creating a File Server Failover Cluster	ServerDC1, ServerDM1, ServerDM2	

From a client computer's perspective, a server cluster appears on the network as a single device with a single name and IP address. A cluster is assigned a name and an IP address. Client computers connect to the cluster instead of to the servers that make up the cluster. Figure 8-1 shows an NLB cluster with three

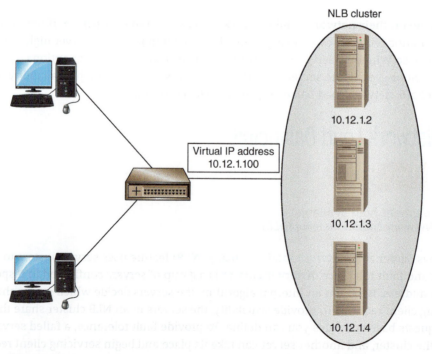

Figure 8-1 A logical depiction of network load balancing

servers participating. The clients use a single virtual IP address—in this example, 10.12.1.100—to access the cluster. The NLB software running on the servers responds to the virtual IP address and decides which of the three servers should respond to each client request.

NLB is well suited to TCP/IP-based applications, such as web servers and streaming media servers where the data can be replicated easily between participating servers and isn't changed by users. NLB clusters are also effective in distributing the load among virtual private network (VPN) servers and remote desktop server farms.

> **Caution** ⚠
>
> NLB isn't advisable if the data being accessed on the servers requires exclusive access as with some database, file and print, and email applications. Failover clusters, discussed later in this chapter, are a better fit for these types of applications.

Installing Network Load Balancing

NLB clusters don't have any special hardware requirements, but it's important that each server in the cluster is configured with the same OS version and updates are consistent on all servers. Typically, servers participating in an NLB cluster shouldn't provide services other than the ones the cluster is providing. For example, using a domain controller as a cluster server isn't recommended.

NLB must be installed on each server in the cluster, and the networking services to be load balanced must be installed and configured identically. NLB doesn't provide data replication, so the cluster administrator must make sure the data provided by cluster servers is consistent among all servers.

Ideally, the servers in an NLB cluster should be configured with two NICs. One NIC is used for communication with network clients that request cluster services, and the other NIC is dedicated for communication among cluster members. Figure 8-2 shows this arrangement. The second NIC can be configured to operate on a separate logical IP network as this figure shows, or it can be configured for the same IP network as NLB clients.

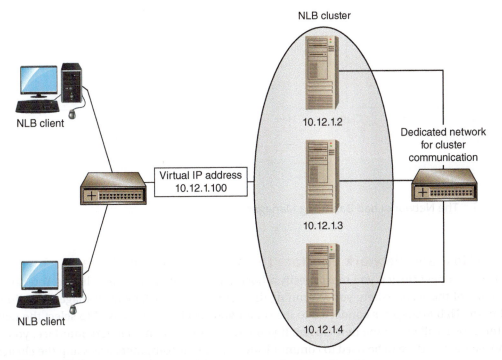

Figure 8-2   An NLB cluster with a separate cluster network

NLB is installed as a feature in Server Manager or using the `Install-WindowsFeature NLB` cmdlet. After it's installed, NLB is configured for all participating servers in the Network Load Balancing Manager. An NLB cluster can be configured on any server running the NLB Manager.

Creating a Network Load Balancing Cluster

After NLB is installed on each server, you can create a load balancing cluster and configure load balancing options. Creating an NLB cluster involves the following tasks:

- Create a new cluster.
- Select a host and network interface to participate in the cluster.
- Configure the host priority and host ID.
- Set the cluster IP address.
- Set the cluster name and operation mode.
- Configure port rules.
- Add servers to the cluster.

Additional configuration of the cluster can be done later if you want to change how traffic is distributed between servers. You take a closer look at each task before you configure an NLB cluster in Activity 8-3.

Creating a New Cluster

To create an NLB cluster, open the Network Load Balancing Manager from the Tools menu in Server Manager on one of the servers with the NLB feature installed. You have the option of creating a new cluster or connecting to an existing cluster (see Figure 8-3).

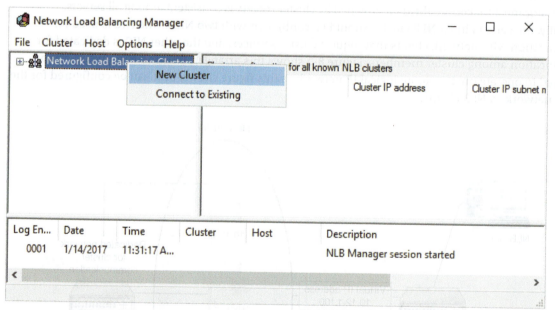

Figure 8-3 The Network Load Balancing Manager

Selecting a Host and Network Interface to Participate in the Cluster

When you create a new cluster, you must specify a host to participate in the new cluster. You can enter the name of the server where you're running the Network Load Balancing Manager or a different server. After the NLB Manager is connected to the server you specify, you're asked to select the network interface the server will use in the new cluster. If you have more than one network interface, you should choose the interface to be used to communicate with client computers accessing the cluster. In Figure 8-4, the Ethernet interface is selected as the NLB interface. The Ethernet 2 interface will be used for cluster communication and management communication. If you have only one NIC, it's used for both cluster communication and client communication.

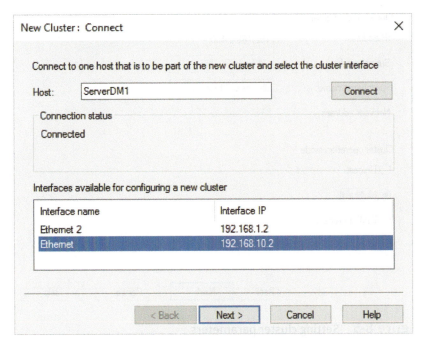

Figure 8-4   Configuring an NLB host and selecting an interface

Configuring the Host Priority and Host ID

Each host participating in an NLB cluster is assigned a unique host ID, which is also the host's priority in the cluster. You can have up to 32 servers in an NLB cluster, so you can choose a priority value from 1 to 32. The cluster member with the lowest priority (ID) handles all cluster traffic that isn't associated with a port rule. This behavior can be overridden by defining specific port rules (discussed later in the section "Configuring Port Rules"). Every server in a cluster must have a unique priority value.

Setting the Cluster IP Address

The cluster IP address, or **virtual IP address**, is the address network clients use to access the networking services provided by the cluster. A DNS host record should exist for the cluster name mapped to this address. If you're using a single NIC configuration for NLB servers, the cluster IP address is added to the NIC's TCP/IP properties, although, depending on your NIC, you might have to add this address manually. If you're using two NICs, the cluster address replaces the current address assigned to the NLB NIC, assuming you removed the dedicated IP address on the NLB NIC. You can use IPv4 or IPv6 addresses.

Setting the Cluster Name and Operation Mode

The cluster name and operation mode are set in the Cluster Parameters dialog box shown in Figure 8-5. The cluster name is the fully qualified domain name (FQDN) that clients use to access the cluster and is specified in the *Full Internet name* text box in the figure. The name should have a corresponding DNS host record entry associated with the cluster IP address. So in this figure, you need a DNS zone named MCSA2016.local with an A record for host nlb with the IP address 192.168.0.100.

Note You must have DNS set up correctly for NLB to work. You need to configure a zone for the FQDN specified for the cluster name and A records for each server. In addition, you must create an A record for the cluster name and cluster virtual IP address (NLB and 192.168.0.100 in Figure 8-5).

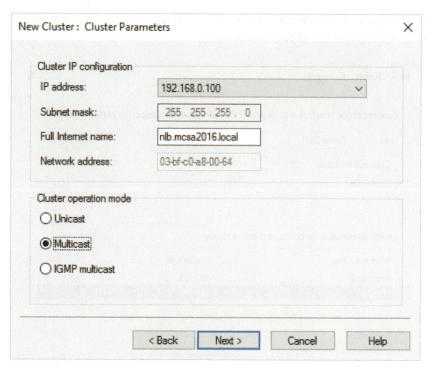

Figure 8-5   Setting cluster parameters

The **cluster operation mode** specifies the type of network addressing used to access the cluster: Unicast, Multicast, or IGMP multicast. The default option is Unicast. The multicast options can make network communication more efficient, but multicast support must be available and configured on your routers. If you're using only one NIC on cluster servers, Multicast mode is the best option. Using Unicast mode with a single NIC has some limitations: Regular (non-NLB) network traffic among cluster hosts isn't supported, so regular network traffic directed to one of the cluster hosts causes additional network overhead for all cluster hosts, and you can't manage other NLB hosts by using the Network Load Balancing Manager from another NLB host. If you must use Unicast mode, it's preferable to install two NICs so that one can be assigned to the NLB cluster and the other dedicated to regular traffic.

 Tip ⓘ

If NLB hosts are Hyper-V virtual machines and you configure Unicast mode with a single NIC, you must enable MAC address spoofing in the NIC properties of the virtual machine.

Defining Port Rules

The last step in the initial configuration of an NLB cluster is defining port rules. A **port rule** specifies which type of TCP or UDP traffic the cluster should respond to and how the traffic is distributed among cluster members. The default port rule, shown in Figure 8-6, specifies that all TCP and UDP traffic on all ports are balanced across cluster members according to each member's load weight. Each cluster member can be assigned a **load weight**, with the traffic distributed proportionally based on the load weight of other members. The higher the load weight, the more traffic that member handles. Port rules can be modified at any time if you want to change the cluster's default behavior. Port rules and other cluster configuration options are discussed later in the section "Configuring an NLB Cluster."

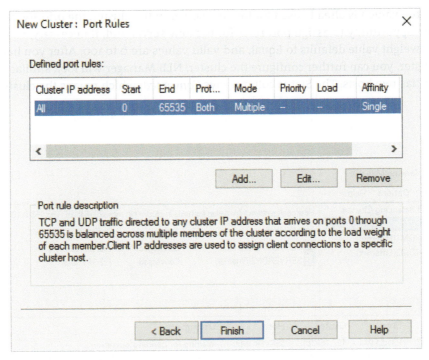

Figure 8-6   The default port rule

Adding Servers to the Cluster

After the cluster is created, you can add servers to it in the Network Load Balancing Manager by right-clicking the cluster and clicking Add Host to Cluster (see Figure 8-7). However, the Network Load Balancing feature must be installed on the server you want to add to the cluster. Again, you must select the network interface that the server will use for communication with clients, and you must assign a

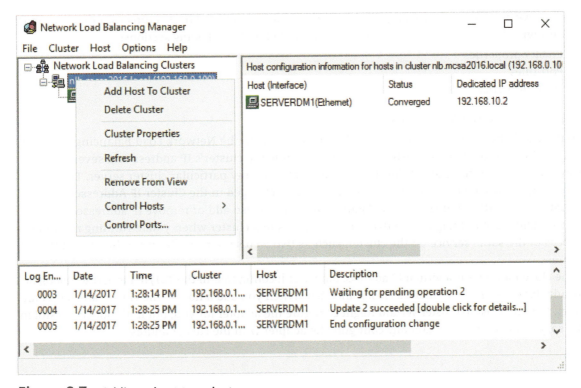

Figure 8-7   Adding a host to a cluster

priority. Because the value 1 is already used for the first server in the cluster, the priority value defaults to 2. You have the opportunity to assign port rules for the new server and, if necessary, change the load weight. The load weight value defaults to Equal, and valid values are 0 to 100. After you have at least two servers in the cluster, you can further configure the cluster. NLB Manager will look similar to Figure 8-8 when the cluster has two hosts. The Status column says *Converged*, which means the cluster is in good working order.

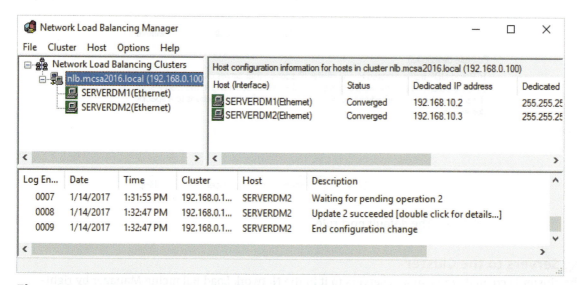

Figure 8-8   NLB Manager with two hosts—a converged cluster

Configuring an NLB Cluster

After you have a running NLB cluster, you can configure the cluster and host settings. Configuring an NLB cluster is divided into three categories, which are discussed in the following sections:

- Cluster properties
- Port rules
- Host properties

Configuring Cluster Properties

To configure cluster properties, right-click the cluster name in the Network Load Balancing Manager and click Cluster Properties. A cluster's properties include the cluster's IP address and several cluster parameters. These settings affect the cluster as a whole, not any particular cluster server. The cluster IP address is set when you create the cluster and can be changed in the Cluster IP Addresses tab of the cluster's Properties dialog box (see Figure 8-9). You can also add or remove IP addresses in this tab. You might want to assign more than one IP address to a cluster when you're running multiple instances of the same service on the cluster, such as two web servers, each responding to a different IP address.

The cluster address is a virtual IP address, but it's still configured in the TCP/IP Properties dialog box of an adapter on each server that's a cluster member. When you add a host to the cluster and select an adapter, the Add Host to Cluster Wizard might configure the adapter for you, but if it's not successful in doing so, you might have to manually configure the adapter with the cluster address.

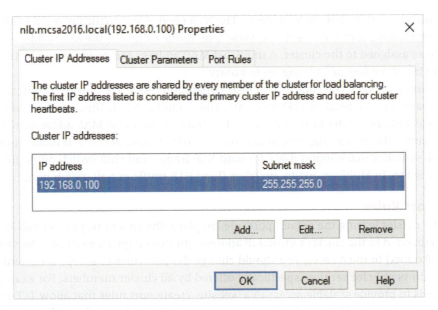

Figure 8-9   The Cluster IP Addresses tab

Cluster parameters are configured in the Cluster Parameters tab of the cluster's Properties dialog box (see Figure 8-10) and consist of the following:

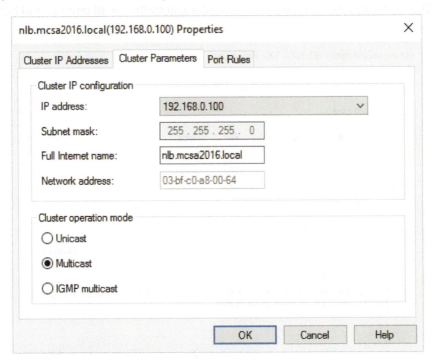

Figure 8-10   The Cluster Parameters tab

- *IP address*—Select the cluster's primary IP address. If more than one IP address is configured for the cluster, you can choose the primary address in the list box.
- *Subnet mask*—The subnet mask for the specified IP address. If you need to change this setting, you must do so in the Cluster IP Addresses tab.
- *Full Internet name*—This is the fully qualified domain name (FQDN) assigned to the cluster. This name must have an entry in DNS that resolves to the cluster's primary IP address.
- *Network address*—This is the cluster's MAC address. In Unicast operation mode, this address is configured on the cluster adapter on each server in the cluster. The NICs on your servers must

support changing the built-in MAC address. The NLB service automatically makes this change to the selected cluster adapter on each host server. In Multicast mode, the MAC address is a multicast MAC address assigned to the cluster. A multicast MAC address can be identified by the least significant bit of the first octet being set to binary 1.

- *Cluster operation mode*—The choices for cluster operation mode are Unicast, Multicast, and Internet Group Management Protocol (IGMP) multicast. The default mode is Unicast. If either multicast mode is selected, the cluster MAC address is changed to a multicast MAC address. In addition, in Multicast mode, the server adapter can also use its built-in MAC address. If IGMP multicast mode is selected, switches that support IGMP forward NLB frames only out switch ports that NLB servers are connected to. In Multicast mode, switches flood NLB traffic out all switch ports.

Configuring Port Rules

If you created the cluster leaving the default port rules in place, the cluster responds to all IP communication directed to the cluster's virtual IP address. (In this chapter's example, the virtual IP address is 192.168.0.100.) In most cases, you should change the port rules to accept communication on the cluster address only for services specifically offered by all cluster members. For example, if the cluster's purpose is to provide scalable access to a website, create port rules that allow TCP port 80 and possibly port 443 (for secure HTTP) yet disallow all other ports. Port rules apply to all hosts in a cluster and are configured in the Port Rules tab of the cluster's Properties dialog box. In Figure 8-11, three port rules were created. The first rule instructs the cluster to discard all traffic directed to the cluster in which the TCP or UDP ports are in the range 0 to 22. The second rule instructs the cluster to accept traffic that arrives on TCP port 23. The third rule instructs the cluster to discard all traffic for all ports 24 and higher.

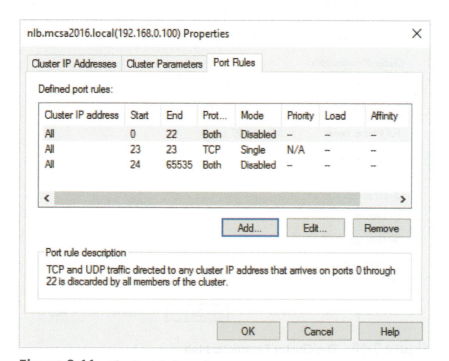

Figure 8-11   The Port Rules tab

To create or edit a rule, click Edit or Add in the Port Rules tab of the cluster's Properties dialog box to open the Add/Edit Port Rule dialog box shown in Figure 8-12. The port rule properties are as follows:

- *Cluster IP address*—The port rule can apply to all cluster IP addresses (the default), or you can select an address if more than one IP address is assigned to the cluster.
- *Port range*—You specify the port range from 0 to 65535. To select a single port, make the From and To values the same.
- *Protocols*—You can specify TCP or UDP or Both.

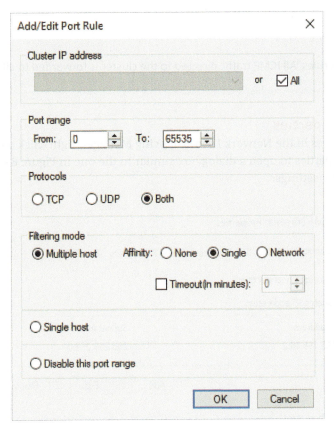

Figure 8-12   The Add/Edit Port Rule dialog box

- *Filtering mode*—The options for **filtering mode** are Multiple host or Single host. Multiple host is the default and provides scalability so that network traffic on the specified hosts is load balanced between all cluster hosts, according to each cluster host's assigned weight value. If Single host is selected, the host with the highest priority handles all traffic on the specified ports. If the host with the highest priority doesn't respond, the host with the next highest priority responds. The Single host option provides a level of fault tolerance but not scalability. In Multiple host mode, you select a **client affinity value** of one of the following:
  - None: With this option, any cluster member can respond to any client request, even multiple requests from the same client. For example, if the cluster is serving a website, a client can request multiple web pages or multiple elements of a single web page. In addition, one cluster member might handle one of the page requests, and another cluster member could handle another request. This option works well with the TCP protocol only, and only when the content being served is fairly static and stateless.
  - Single: This default affinity setting for port rules specifies that multiple requests from the same client are directed to the same cluster host. It must be used if the application has some level of dynamic data or if the client state must be maintained—for example, if the client must authenticate or establish an encrypted session.
  - Network: This affinity setting ensures that a single cluster host responds to client connections coming from a specific IP network, assuming a /24 prefix. This setting is used when clients access the cluster from behind multiple proxy servers, which might cause the client's source address to appear different on subsequent requests. This setting assumes that all proxy servers are in the same /24 subnet.
- *Timeout (in minutes)*—Set the amount of time to extend single or network affinity, which preserves the affinity configuration if the NLB cluster is changed while a client is connected.
- *Disable this port range*—Select this option when you want the cluster to discard packets matching the specified protocol and ports.

Note

ICMP isn't affected by port rules. All ICMP traffic directed to the cluster is forwarded to all cluster hosts.

Configuring Host Properties

To configure host properties in the Network Load Balancing Manager, right-click a host under the cluster name and click Host Properties to open a dialog box similar to the one in Figure 8-13. The Host Parameters tab contains the following settings:

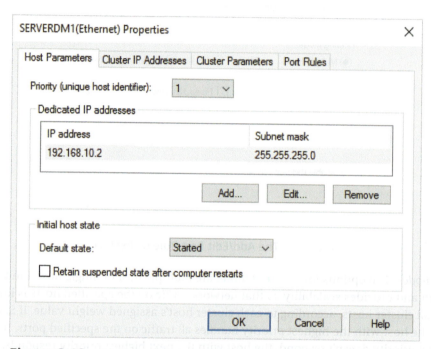

Figure 8-13 Configuring host properties

- *Priority (unique host identifier)*—This property, as discussed earlier, serves two purposes: as an identifier for each host so that no two hosts can be assigned the same value and as a priority value specifying that the host with the lowest value handles all traffic not covered by a port rule directed toward the cluster.
- *Dedicated IP addresses*—This setting is one or more IP addresses configured on the host's cluster adapter used for noncluster (dedicated) communication. If a second NIC is used for noncluster communication, this list can be empty because the second adapter's IP address is used automatically as the dedicated IP address.
- *Initial host state*—This property controls how the NLB service behaves when the OS boots. It has three options: Started, Stopped, and Suspended. The default option is Started, specifying that the host should join the cluster when the OS starts. If Stopped is selected, the host doesn't join the NLB cluster until it's started manually. If Suspended is selected, the host doesn't join the cluster when the OS starts and doesn't respond to remote NLB commands until it's resumed.
- *Retain suspended state after computer restarts*—If this check box is selected, the cluster host remains suspended if the host restarts while in a suspended state regardless of the default state option that's selected.

The Cluster IP Addresses tab shows the cluster's IP addresses. The Cluster Parameters tab shows you the cluster parameters shown earlier in Figure 8-10, but you can't change these parameters in this tab; you need to open the cluster's Properties dialog box to change values in this tab. You use the Port Rules tab to edit port rules that aren't set to the Disabled mode. Port rules for each host can be configured as follows (see Figure 8-14):

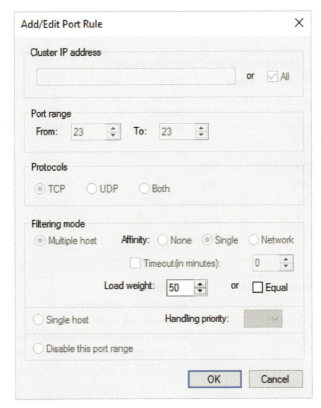

Figure 8-14   Changing the load weight or handling priority for a host

- *Multiple host filtering mode*—If the port rule filtering mode is set to Multiple host, a load weight can be assigned to the host for that port rule. By default, all hosts have equal weight, but if you want certain hosts to handle more traffic than others, you can set the load weight on each host. The load weight should be looked at as a percentage and can be set from 0 to 100. The total weight of all hosts should equal 100.
- *Single host filtering mode*—If the port rule filtering mode is set to Single host, the Handling priority value can be set. The host with the highest **handling priority** handles all traffic meeting the port rules' criteria. This value overrides the host priority value and allows you to assign different hosts to handle different types of traffic.

Managing an NLB Cluster

You might need to perform maintenance tasks on cluster servers as you would on any network server. To that end, you can change the state of hosts or the cluster as a whole. Figure 8-15 shows the options for controlling hosts that are cluster members. To control all hosts, right-click the cluster node and click Control Hosts. To control a single host, right-click the host and click Control Host. Then select one of these options:

- *Start*—Starts the NLB service on the host and causes the host to join the cluster and begin handling NLB traffic.
- *Stop*—Stops the NLB service so that the host doesn't handle any NLB traffic.
- *Drainstop*—The host completes any active NLB sessions and stops taking new sessions. Use this option instead of Stop if the host is actively serving clients. After using this option, the host is in the Stop state and must be started when you're ready for it to begin handling NLB traffic again.

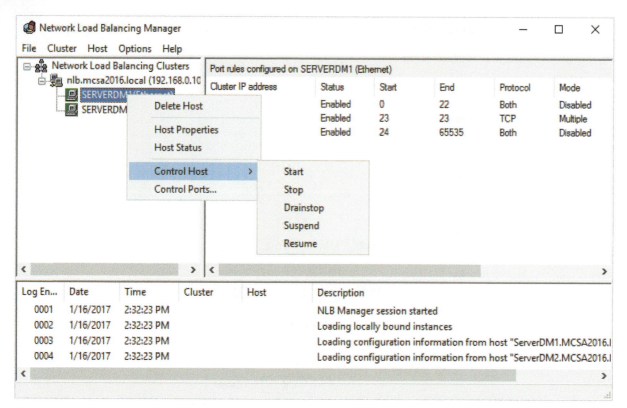

Figure 8-15 Controlling hosts

- *Suspend*—This option places the host in the Suspend state, which prevents it from handling new NLB traffic as well as NLB control commands except for Resume.
- *Resume*—Resumes a suspended host but places it in the Stop state. The host can take NLB commands and must be started before it can resume handling NLB traffic.

Upgrading an NLB Cluster

You can upgrade an NLB cluster to a new version of Windows Server by taking all the cluster hosts offline, upgrading each host, and then bringing the cluster back online. You can also use a **rolling upgrade**, which involves taking each cluster node offline, upgrading the host, and then bringing the node back online. A rolling upgrade maintains uninterrupted access to cluster services, but not all NLB applications support it. Before you perform an NLB cluster upgrade, you should keep the following in mind:

- Verify that all cluster services are supported on the new version of the OS you're upgrading to.
- Use the Drainstop option on each host before you begin the upgrade, and set the initial host state to Stop.
- After finishing the upgrade, verify that all services using NLB work correctly before bringing the host back into the cluster.

Using PowerShell to Configure NLB Clusters

Table 8-2 shows some PowerShell cmdlets you can use to configure NLB clusters. To see the full list of NLB-related PowerShell cmdlets, enter `Get-Command *nlb*`.

Table 8-2   PowerShell cmdlets for configuring NLB clusters

Cmdlet	Description
`Add-NlbClusterNode`	Adds a host to an existing NLB cluster
`Add-NlbClusterNodeDip`	Adds a dedicated IP address to an NLB cluster
`Add-NlbClusterPortRule`	Adds a port rule to an NLB cluster
`Add-NlbClusterVip`	Adds a virtual IP address to an NLB cluster
`Disable-NlbClusterPortRule`	Disables a port rule on an NLB cluster or host
`Enable-NlbClusterPortRule`	Enables a port rule on an NLB cluster or host
`Get-NlbCluster`	Gets information about an NLB cluster object
`Get-NlbClusterDriverInfo`	Gets information about an NLB driver
`Get-NlbClusterNode`	Gets information about an NLB cluster node object
`Get-NlbClusterNodeDip`	Gets the dedicated IP address of a cluster node
`Get-NlbClusterNodeNetworkInterface`	Gets information about network interface on a cluster node
`Get-NlbClusterPortRule`	Gets information about an NLB port rule
`Get-NlbClusterVip`	Gets the virtual IP address of a cluster
`New-NlbCluster`	Creates an NLB cluster
`New-NlbClusterIpv6Address`	Creates an IPv6 address for an NLB cluster
`Remove-NlbCluster`	Deletes an NLB cluster
`Remove-NlbClusterNode`	Removes a host from an NLB cluster
`Remove-NlbClusterNodeDip`	Removes a dedicated IP address from an NLB cluster
`Remove-NlbClusterPortRule`	Removes a port rule from an NLB cluster
`Remove-NlbClusterVip`	Removes a virtual IP address from an NLB cluster
`Resume-NlbCluster`	Resumes all hosts in an NLB cluster
`Resume-NlbClusterNode`	Resumes a suspended host in an NLB cluster
`Set-NlbCluster`	Edits the configuration of an NLB cluster
`Set-NlbClusterNode`	Changes settings of an NLB host
`Set-NlbClusterNodeDip`	Changes the dedicated IP address of an NLB cluster node
`Set-NlbClusterPortRule`	Edits the port rules for an NLB cluster
`Set-NlbClusterPortRuleNodeHandlingPriority`	Sets the host priority of a port rule for an NLB host
`Set-NlbClusterPortRuleNodeWeight`	Sets the load weight of a port rule for an NLB host
`Set-NlbClusterVip`	Changes the virtual IP address of an NLB cluster
`Start-NlbCluster`	Starts all hosts in an NLB cluster
`Start-NlbClusterNode`	Starts an NLB cluster host
`Stop-NlbCluster`	Stops all hosts in an NLB cluster
`Stop-NlbClusterNode`	Stops a host in an NLB cluster
`Suspend-NlbCluster`	Suspends all hosts in an NLB cluster
`Suspend-NlbClusterNode`	Suspends a single host in an NLB cluster

Activity 8-1: Resetting Your Virtual Environment

Time Required: 5 minutes
Objective: Reset your virtual environment by applying the InitialConfig checkpoint or snapshot.
Required Tools and Equipment: ServerDC1, ServerDM1, and ServerDM2
Description: Apply the InitialConfig checkpoint or snapshot to ServerDC1, ServerDM1, and ServerDM2.

1. Be sure that all three servers are shut down. In your virtualization program, apply the InitialConfig checkpoint or snapshot to ServerDC1, ServerDM1, and ServerDM2.
2. When the snapshot or checkpoint has finished being applied, continue to the next activity.

Activity 8-2: Installing the Network Load Balancing Feature

Time Required: 5 minutes
Objective: Install the network load balancing feature.
Required Tools and Equipment: ServerDC1, ServerDM1, and ServerDM2
Description: In this activity, you install the NLB feature on ServerDM1 and ServerDM2. ServerDC1 is the domain controller (DC) for the network and should be running during this activity.

1. Start ServerDC1. Start ServerDM1, and sign in to the domain as **Administrator**.
2. On ServerDM1, install **Network Load Balancing** by using the Add Roles and Features Wizard in Server Manager or the PowerShell cmdlet `Install-WindowsFeature NLB -IncludeManagementTools`.
3. Start ServerDM2, and sign in to the domain as **Administrator**. Install the **Network Load Balancing** feature. You will be managing the NLB cluster from ServerDM1, so there is no need to install the management tools.
4. Stay signed in to both servers for the next activity and leave ServerDC1 running.

Activity 8-3: Creating an NLB Cluster

Time Required: 15 minutes
Objective: Create an NLB cluster.
Required Tools and Equipment: ServerDC1, ServerDM1, and ServerDM2
Description: In this activity, you configure DNS for the NLB cluster and then configure the NLB cluster. You configure the NLB cluster hosts with two NICs using Multicast mode. The topology looks like Figure 8-16 except that you don't have NLB clients in your network.

1. First, you need to create the DNS record for the NLB cluster. Sign in to ServerDC1 as **Administrator**. Open a PowerShell window and type **Add-DnsServerResourceRecordA -Name NLB -ZoneName MCSA2016.local -IPv4Address 192.168.0.100** and press **Enter**. Verify the records in the zone by typing **Get-DnsServerResourceRecord -ZoneName MCSA2016.local** and pressing **Enter**. You will see several records, but verify that you see the NLB, ServerDC1, ServerDM1, and ServerDM2 records.
2. On ServerDM1, open Server Manager, and click **Tools**, **Network Load Balancing Manager** from the menu.
3. Right-click **Network Load Balancing Clusters** and click **New Cluster**. Type **ServerDM1** in the Host text box, and click **Connect**. After you're connected, the New Cluster: Connect dialog box shows the available interfaces for ServerDM1 (see Figure 8-17). Click **Ethernet** (the adapter with address 192.168.0.2) to choose the adapter you want to use for NLB traffic. The other interface will be used strictly for cluster communication between cluster servers. Click **Next**.

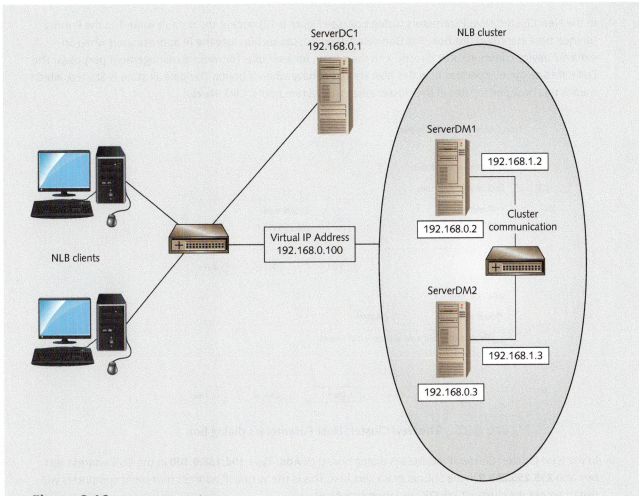

Figure 8-16   The NLB topology

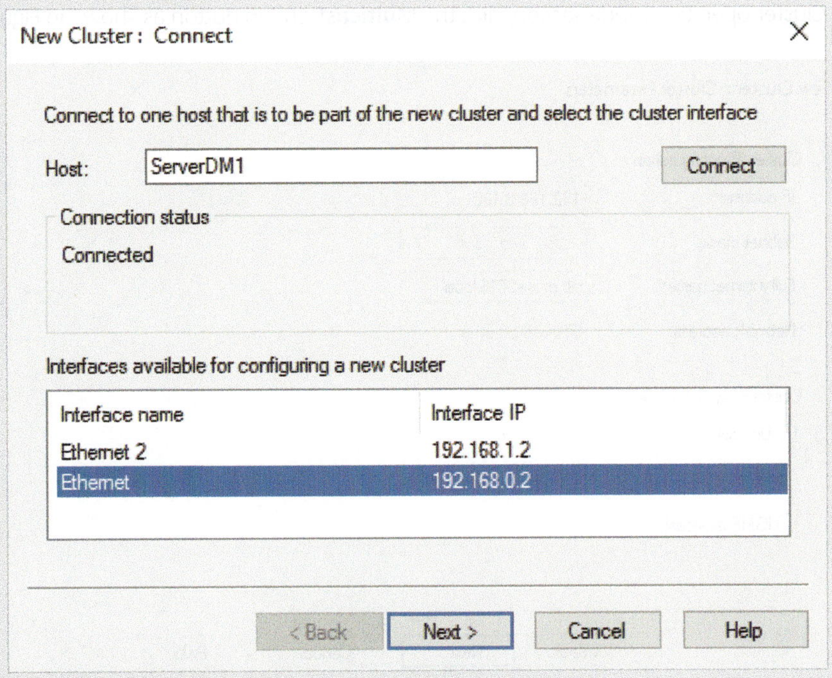

Figure 8-17   The New Cluster: Connect dialog box

4. In the New Cluster: Host Parameters dialog box (see Figure 8-18), accept the default value **1** in the Priority (unique host identifier) text box. The Dedicated IP addresses section lists the IP address used when an external device communicates directly with the server, for example, for remote management purposes. The Default state option specifies how this host should behave when it boots. The default state is Started, which means this host participates in the cluster when the system boots. Click **Next**.

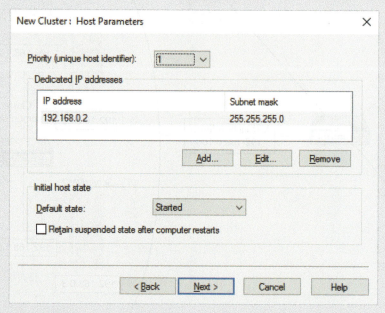

Figure 8-18   The New Cluster: Host Parameters dialog box

5. In the New Cluster: Cluster IP Addresses dialog box, click **Add**. Type **192.168.0.100** in the IPv4 address text box and **255.255.255.0** in the Subnet mask text box. This is the virtual IP address that client computers will use to access the cluster. Click **OK**, and then click **Next**.

6. In the New Cluster: Cluster Parameters dialog box, type **nlb.mcsa2016.local** in the Full Internet name text box. This is the name client that computers use to access the cluster and corresponds to the DNS record you created in Step 1. In the Cluster operation mode section, click the **Multicast** option button as shown in Figure 8-19. Click **Next**.

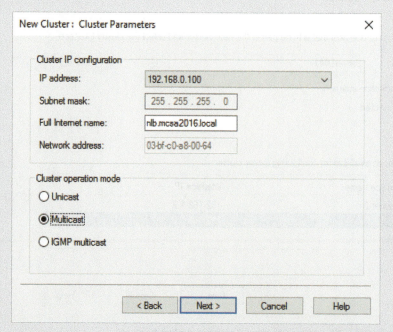

Figure 8-19   The New Cluster: Cluster Parameters dialog box

7. In the New Cluster: Port Rules dialog box, read the port rule description for the default port rule, and then click **Finish**.

8. If you don't see any error messages in the Network Load Balancing Manager, go on to Step 9. If you see an error stating "The bind operation was successful but NLB is not responding to queries," you have to set the cluster IP address manually on the network interface. To do so, open the Properties dialog box for the Ethernet connection, double-click **Internet Protocol Version 4 (TCP/IPv4)**, and click **Advanced**. Click **Add** in the IP addresses section. Type **192.168.0.100** for the IP address and **255.255.0.0** for the subnet mask, and then click **Add**. Click **OK** until you see the Network Connections window. Shut down and restart ServerDM1, and then open the Network Load Balancing Manager.

9. To add ServerDM2 as a second cluster host, right-click **nlb.mcsa2016.local** and click **Add Host To Cluster**.

10. Type **ServerDM2** in the Host text box, and click **Connect**. After the Ethernet interface is listed in the Interfaces available for configuring the cluster list box, click the interface with address **192.168.0.3** and click **Next**.

11. In the Add Host to Cluster: Host Parameters dialog box, leave the Priority setting at the default value of **2**, and click **Next**.

12. In the Add Host to Cluster: Port Rules dialog box, click **Finish**. You might have to add the cluster IP address (192.168.0.100) as a second IP address to the Ethernet adapter on ServerDM2 if you get the error message mentioned in Step 8. A correctly configured and working NLB cluster shows the status of both servers as Converged, and both servers are outlined in green, as shown in Figure 8-20.

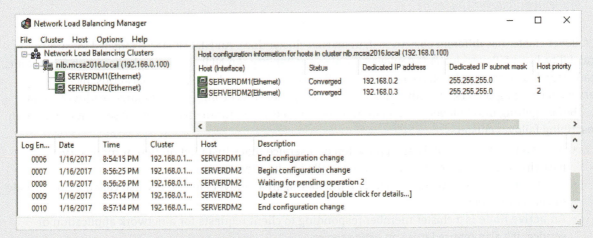

Figure 8-20   A correctly configured and working NLB cluster

13. To test that the cluster is working correctly, open a command prompt window on ServerDC1. Type **ping nlb** and press **Enter**. You should get successful ping replies. The first ping might time out, but this is normal. Type **arp -a** and press **Enter** to see the ARP table. You should see an entry for 192.168.0.100 with a MAC address that begins with 03, which is a multicast MAC address.

14. Stay signed in to all three servers if you're continuing to the next activity.

> **Note** 📎
>
> Configuring an NLB cluster can be complex, and much can go wrong. DNS must be set up correctly, NICs must be capable of dynamic MAC address changes, and the IP configuration must be correct. If you believe you have everything set correctly but the NLB Manager still reports errors, shut down both servers and restart them. Open the NLB Manager after both servers have restarted to see whether the problem has been solved.

Activity 8-4: Resetting Your Virtual Environment

Time Required: 5 minutes
Objective: Reset your virtual environment by applying the InitialConfig checkpoint or snapshot.
Required Tools and Equipment: ServerDC1, ServerDM1, and ServerDM2
Description: You are finished using NLB and will install Failover Clustering next. NLB and Failover Clustering cannot be installed on the same server, so you will apply the InitialConfig checkpoint or snapshot to ServerDC1, ServerDM1, and ServerDM2 to reset your environment. Alternatively, you could uninstall the NLB feature from ServerDM1 and ServerDM2, delete the secondary IP address from ServerDM1 and ServerDM2, and remove the NLB record from DNS.

1. Be sure that all three servers are shut down. In your virtualization program, apply the InitialConfig checkpoint or snapshot to ServerDC1, ServerDM1, and ServerDM2.
2. When the snapshot or checkpoint has finished being applied, continue to the next activity.

Failover Clusters

Certification

- 70-740 – Implement high availability:
  Implement failover clustering

A failover cluster has different objectives than an NLB cluster does. An NLB cluster is targeted toward scalability, but a failover cluster is deployed for **high availability**. An NLB cluster works best with fairly static, read-only data access, and a failover cluster is well suited to back-end database applications, file-sharing servers, messaging servers, and other mission-critical applications dealing with dynamic read/write data.

Before getting into failover clusters in more detail, take a few moments to review some terms used in describing failover clusters:

- A **clustered application** is an application or a service that's installed on two or more servers participating in a failover cluster. It's also called a *clustered service*.
- A **cluster server** is a Windows server participating in a failover cluster. It's also called a *cluster node* or *cluster member*.
- An **active node** is a cluster member responding to client requests for a network application or service. It's also referred to as an *active server*.
- A **passive node**, also called a *passive server*, is a cluster member that's not responding to client requests for a clustered application but is in standby to do so if the active node fails.
- **Standby mode** describes a cluster node that isn't active.
- A **quorum** is a database containing cluster configuration information about the status of each node (active or passive) for clustered applications. It's also used, in a server or communication failure, to determine whether the cluster is to remain online and which servers should continue participating in the cluster.
- The **cluster heartbeat** is communication between cluster nodes that provides the status of each node to the cluster quorum. The cluster heartbeat, or lack of it, informs the cluster when a server is no longer communicating.
- A **witness disk** is shared storage used to store cluster configuration data and help determine the cluster quorum.

A **failover cluster** consists of two or more servers, usually of identical configuration, that access common storage media. Typically, storage is in the form of a storage area network (SAN), which is external storage that can be shared among several servers that see SAN volumes as locally attached storage. The servers are connected to the SAN device through a secondary high-speed network connection, such as iSCSI (discussed in Chapter 5). One server in a failover cluster is considered the active server, and the other servers are considered passive. The active server handles all client requests for the clustered application, and passive servers wait in a type of standby mode. If the active server fails and stops responding, one of the passive servers becomes active and begins handling client requests as shown in Figure 8-21. In this diagram, Server1 is initially the active server, and Server2 is passive.

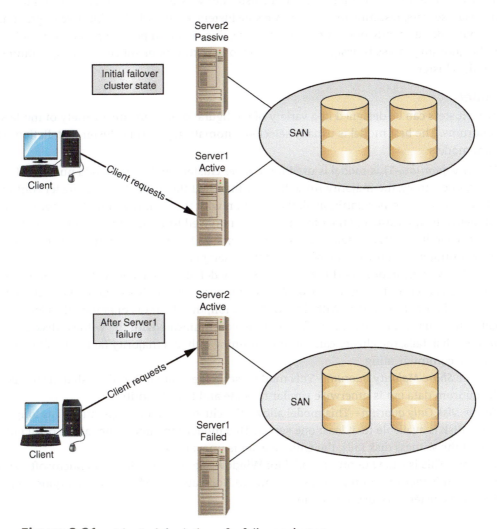

Figure 8-21   **A logical depiction of a failover cluster**

You might think that setting up a failover cluster wastes a lot of resources and money if only one server in a cluster is actually doing anything. Keep in mind, however, that you're providing high availability for an application or a service. If you need high availability for several services or applications, you can design clusters so that each server is active for a particular application or service and in standby mode for the services or applications the other servers are handling. That way, each server is active, just not for the same application or service.

How a Failover Cluster Works

Failover clusters work by using two or more servers and shared storage to provide fault tolerance and high availability. Like an NLB cluster, client computers see the failover cluster as a single entity that can be accessed by a single name or IP address. All servers have access to the application data so that if the active server fails, another server can take over the clustered application. So how do passive servers know when the active server is no longer able to serve client requests? They do so by using the quorum process. As mentioned earlier, a quorum is a database containing cluster configuration information.

This database defines the role of each cluster member and specifies which server should be active and which should be passive. Each cluster member must have the same configuration information for the cluster to operate correctly. If a cluster server can't access the quorum data, it can't participate in the cluster.

A failover cluster can operate correctly only if all cluster members can communicate with one another so that they have access to the same quorum data. A cluster network is **partitioned** if communication fails between cluster servers, resulting in two or more subclusters, each with the objective of providing the clustered service. Because only one server can be active, this situation poses a problem. To solve this problem, the quorum process is designed so that only one partition, or subcluster, can continue participating in the cluster.

Quorum Models

Because failover clusters can be designed in a variety of configurations, there are a variety of models for maintaining quorums. The best model is usually selected automatically during cluster installation. There are four quorum models:

- *Node Majority quorum*—This model is used for failover clusters that have an odd number of members. Quite simply, the majority rules. If fewer than half the nodes fail, the cluster continues to run. If the cluster becomes partitioned, the partition with the majority of nodes (more than half the total) owns the quorum, and the other nodes are removed from the cluster. For example, in a five-node cluster, if two servers fail or become partitioned, they're removed from the cluster, and the cluster continues to run with the remaining three servers.
- *Node and Disk Majority quorum*—This model is used by default on clusters with an even number of cluster nodes and uses the witness disk. The cluster quorum data is stored on the witness disk, which is shared among all nodes. With this configuration, the cluster is operational as long as at least half of the cluster members are online and can communicate with the witness disk. However, if the witness disk fails, the cluster can continue running only if a majority (at least half plus one) of servers are communicating.
- *Node and File Share Majority quorum*—This model uses a file share rather than shared storage to store the quorum data but is otherwise similar to Node and Disk Majority.
- *No Majority: Disk Only quorum*—This model allows the cluster to remain operational as long as the witness disk is available to at least one server. This model can endure the failure of all but one server, but if the witness disk fails, the entire cluster is unavailable.
- *Cloud witness*—This is a new quorum model for Windows Server 2016 that uses Microsoft Azure cloud storage; this type of quorum works similarly to Node and File Share Majority quorum and is used in stretch clusters, discussed in Chapter 9.

Requirements for a Failover Cluster

The first requirement for a Windows Server 2016 failover cluster is that all cluster servers must have Windows Server 2016 Standard or Datacenter Edition installed. Either edition supports up to 64 cluster members. Also, be aware that the application you want to cluster might limit the total number of cluster members.

Aside from the Windows Server edition, a few other hardware and software requirements must be met before you can build a failover cluster:

- Identical or nearly identical server components.
- Identical CPU architecture.
- Components should meet the "Certified for Windows Server 2016" logo requirements.
- Separate adapters for shared storage communication and network client communication.
- A supported cluster-compatible storage technology that meets the following requirements:
  - Serial Attached SCSI (SAS), Fibre Channel, or iSCSI storage technology should be used. SATA is acceptable but not recommended. Parallel SCSI for cluster storage is not supported.

- For iSCSI, you must use a separate network adapter that's dedicated to cluster storage.
- For cluster configurations that use a disk witness, the minimum is two volumes, one of which serves as the witness disk for the cluster.
- Cluster servers must run the same edition of Windows Server 2016. New in Windows Server 2016, a cluster can have servers running Windows Server 2012/R2 and Windows Server 2016; however, this operational mode should be transitory only while the cluster is being upgraded from Windows Server 2012/R2 to Windows Server 2016.
- All clustered applications or services must be the same version, and all cluster servers should have the same updates and service packs installed.

Cluster Storage Requirements

The storage requirements for a failover cluster are unique in that, in most configurations, the clustered application's data must be available to all cluster members, even though only one cluster member at a time accesses it. If the currently active cluster server fails, another cluster member must have access to the same data so that it can begin serving client requests. Shared storage is required on clusters using the Disk Majority and No Majority: Disk Only quorum models. Most clustered applications use these models. In addition, all components of the storage system should be Windows Server 2016 certified and use digitally signed device drivers.

Failover Cluster Installation

The failover cluster function on Windows Server 2016 is installed as a feature in Server Manager. The procedure for installing and creating a failover cluster is generally as follows:

1. Install the Failover Clustering feature on all servers.
2. Verify the cluster server network and shared storage access.
3. Run the cluster validation wizard.
4. Create the cluster.

Installing the Failover Clustering Feature

The first step simply involves using the Add Roles and Features Wizard in Server Manager or the `Install-WindowsFeature Failover-Clustering` PowerShell cmdlet on all servers in the cluster. Note that you shouldn't configure failover clustering and network load balancing on the same server.

Verifying the Cluster Server Network and Shared Storage Access

You can actually perform this step before installing the Failover Clustering feature, but just make sure this step is complete before moving on to the next step. The procedure you use to do this depends on the type of shared storage you're using for the cluster and the configuration of your network. In short, verify that all the servers can communicate with computers on the client network and that shared storage is visible in Disk Management.

Running the Cluster Validation Wizard

Before you create a new cluster, you should run the Validate a Configuration Wizard in the Failover Cluster Manager as shown in Figure 8-22. The Failover Cluster Manager is added to the Tools menu in Server Manager after you install the Failover Clustering feature.

You can run the Validate a Configuration Wizard as many times as you need until the cluster configuration is validated correctly. You should even run this wizard periodically on an active cluster to make sure the configuration is still in good working order. In the first window of the wizard, you're prompted to enter the names of servers to participate in the cluster. If you're running the wizard on an existing cluster, you can enter the cluster name instead.

Next, you choose the testing options you want. The choices are to run all tests or only selected tests. When you're validating a cluster configuration for the first time, you should run all tests. If you're validating an existing cluster, you can limit the tests to suspected problem areas. The selected tests run, and then a summary report is displayed. If any errors are listed in the report, you should have enough

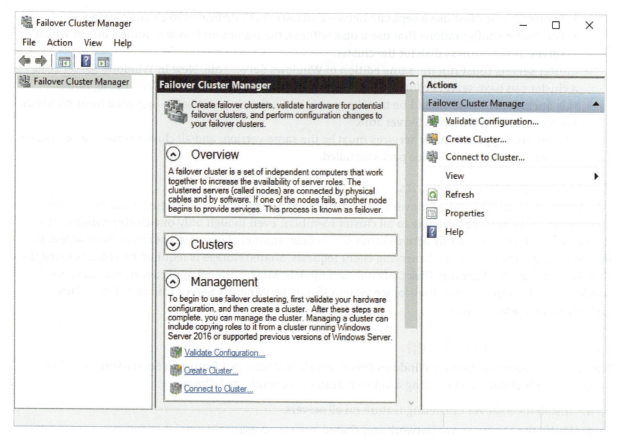

Figure 8-22 The Failover Cluster Manager

information to solve the problems. If there are no errors, the report indicates that the configuration is suitable for clustering.

Creating the Cluster

After your network and servers are validated, you can create a new failover cluster. The process is similar to the processes for validating the configuration and for creating an NLB cluster and is explained in Activity 8-7. During the process of creating the cluster, you're asked to enter a name for the cluster in the Access Point for Administering the Cluster window. You're also asked to provide an IP address. This name and address are used for accessing the cluster to administer it. The name and IP address are added to DNS as a host record. In addition, for domain-based clusters, a new computer object is created in Active Directory with the name of the cluster. The IP address is assigned to the network adapter selected for handling cluster clients on one of the servers. If this server becomes unavailable, the address is assigned to the other cluster server.

Configuring Failover Clustering

After a cluster is created, a number of configuration tasks should be performed, including the following:

- Configure the cluster networks.
- Configure the quorum model.
- Configure cluster storage.
- Configure a cluster role.

Configuring the Cluster Networks

The networks in a cluster are the critical link between clients and clustered applications and between cluster nodes and their shared storage. Cluster networks are used for the following types of communication:

- *Client access*—The network that clients use to access clustered services
- *Cluster communication*—Heartbeat and quorum vote communication and other cluster management communication
- *Storage network*—Access to shared storage, such as an iSCSI or a Fibre Channel SAN

Ideally, you should have at least two separate networks, one for client access to the cluster nodes and another for the storage network. Having three networks is even better with one for each type of cluster communication. Each network adapter should be connected to a different subnet, and network adapters should be renamed to reflect the network function. For example, you could name one adapter FOCAdapter (for Failover Cluster Adapter) and another StorageAdapter. In the Failover Cluster Manager, the networks are simply named Cluster Network 1, Cluster Network 2, and so forth. You should rename them to reflect the network's purpose. To do so, in the Failover Cluster Manager, click the Networks node in the left pane and then in the middle pane, right-click a cluster network, click Properties, and then enter a new name for the network. If you have a network dedicated to cluster communication, you should uncheck the option that allows clients to connect through the network (see Figure 8-23). On a cluster with only one network, you can leave the default settings.

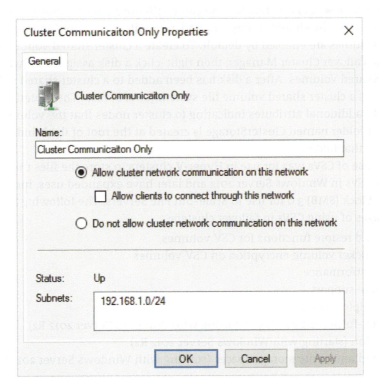

Figure 8-23   Viewing cluster network properties

Configuring the Quorum Model

If the quorum model selected by the Create Cluster process isn't suitable for your environment, you can change it. In the Failover Cluster Manager, click the name of the cluster in the left pane; in the Actions pane, click More Actions, and then click Configure Cluster Quorum Settings. The Configure Cluster Quorum Wizard walks you through changing the model (discussed earlier in the section "How a Failover Cluster Works"). In this wizard, you have the following options:

- *Use the default quorum configuration*—With this option, the cluster determines the quorum model to use and selects the witness disk. If you're unsure of how to configure the quorum, use this option.

- *Select the quorum witness*—You select the quorum witness disk, but the cluster determines other quorum options.
- *Advanced quorum configuration*—You select all quorum options. If you choose this option, you must select which of the servers vote in the quorum and select the witness disk or choose a file share witness.

Configuring Cluster Storage

During the cluster creation process, Windows detects shared storage that's available for use in the cluster and assigns one of the cluster nodes as the owner. If more than one shared disk is available, one is usually assigned as the witness disk for the quorum. If there are other shared disks that aren't recognized by the cluster, you can add them for use by the entire cluster by clicking Add Disk in the Actions pane. You can also add storage to a particular clustered service or application after one has been configured.

> **Note**
>
> Dynamic disks can't be used in a failover cluster; only basic disks can be added to a failover cluster.

By default, each cluster disk is owned by one cluster node, and all other cluster nodes see the disk as offline. Starting in Windows Server 2008 R2, you can configure a **cluster shared volume** in which all cluster nodes have access to the shared storage for read and write access. In Windows Server 2012 and later, cluster shared volumes are enabled by default. To create a cluster shared volume (CSV), click Disks in the left pane of the Failover Cluster Manager, then right-click a disk assigned to Available Storage, and click Add to Cluster Shared Volumes. After a disk has been added to a cluster shared volume, it appears in Disk Management as a cluster shared volume file system (CSVFS) disk. The underlying format is still NTFS or ReFS but with additional attributes indicating to cluster nodes that the volume is a CSV. When you configure a CSV, a folder named ClusterStorage is created at the root of the Windows OS drive, and the CSV is mounted in that folder.

The original purpose of CSVs was for use in Hyper-V clusters to store the files that compose virtual machines (VMs), but CSVs in Windows Server 2012 and later have expanded uses, including file sharing with Server Message Block (SMB) 3.0 for use in Scale-out File Servers. The following list includes some features and advantages of using CSVs in failover clusters:

- Better backup and restore functions for CSV volumes
- Support for BitLocker volume encryption on CSV volumes
- Improved CSV performance
- SMB 3.0 file share support
- Support for multiple subnets
- Support for ReFS-formatted volumes (starting with Windows Server 2012 R2)
- Data deduplication (starting with Windows Server 2012 R2)
- Support for tiered and parity storage spaces (starting with Windows Server 2012 R2)

Optimizing Cluster Storage

Fast and fault-tolerant access to cluster storage is critical to overall cluster performance. Because CSVs allow simultaneous read/write access to multiple cluster nodes, it's even more critical that the network access to the storage is optimized. Here are some considerations to keep in mind when configuring the cluster network for CSV access:

- Use multiple cluster networks to access CSV traffic. Consider using teamed network adapters for fault tolerance.
- Disable cluster network communication on cluster networks that carry CSV traffic. To do so, open the properties of a cluster network and click the *Do not allow cluster network communication on this network* option.

- Make sure that Client for Microsoft Networks and File and Printer Sharing for Microsoft Networks are enabled on the adapters that carry cluster communication.
- Configure a minimum bandwidth policy and a QoS priority policy for network traffic to each node using Group Policy in a domain-based environment or using local policies on nondomain-joined cluster members.

Configuring a Cluster Role

To configure a server role to use failover clustering, right-click Roles in the left pane of the Failover Cluster Manager and click Configure Role to start the High Availability Wizard. A number of Windows Server 2016 roles and features can be configured for failover clustering, as shown in Figure 8-24.

In most cases, before you run the High Availability Wizard, you must install the role or feature on each server in the cluster. This procedure is shown in Activity 8-9 with the File Server role. During the configuration of a service, you're prompted to enter a name that clients use when accessing it, called the **client access point**. For example, if you configure the File Server role on the Failover1 cluster, you might

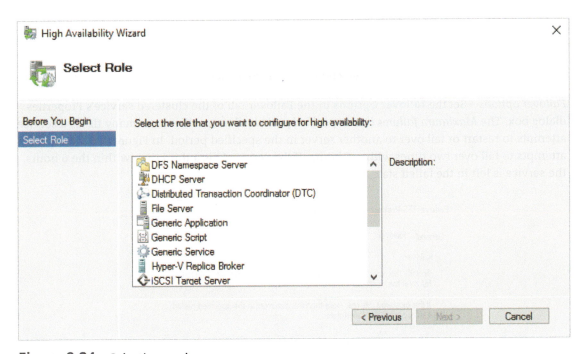

Figure 8-24   Selecting a role

name the client access point Failover1FS. You're also prompted for the IP address that clients use to access this cluster service. As with the access point for administering the cluster, a host record is created in DNS, and a new computer object is created in Active Directory (for domain-based clusters).

After the service is configured, you can configure other high-availability options, including the following:

- *Preferred owner*—The **preferred owner** is the server selected as the active server for the service or application. To configure the preferred owner, right-click the role and click Properties. The available servers are listed, and you can click the check box next to the servers to specify the preferred owner. By default, there's no preferred owner. If you select more than one preferred server, the most preferred server is at the top (see Figure 8-25).

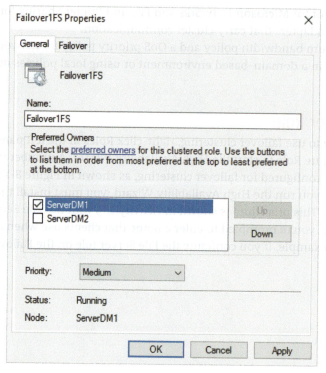

Figure 8-25 Selecting a preferred owner

- *Failover options*—Set the **failover options** in the Failover tab of the clustered service's Properties dialog box. The *Maximum failures in the specified period* value specifies how many times a service attempts to restart or fail over to another server in the specified period. In Figure 8-26, the service attempts to fail over two times within 6 hours. If the service fails a third time within the 6 hours, the service is left in the failed state.

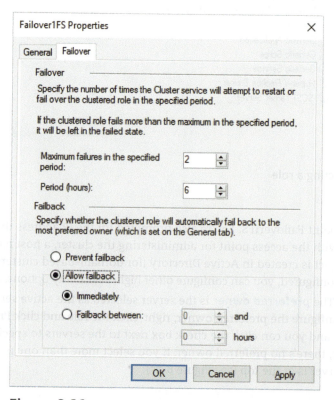

Figure 8-26 Failover and failback options

• *Failback options*—**Failback options** are also set in the Failover tab of the clustered service's Properties dialog box. If a preferred owner is specified, you have the option to revert to the most preferred owner when that server is available again. The failback can occur immediately or between certain hours of the day. The default option is to prevent failback.

Cluster-Aware Updating

Cluster-Aware Updating (CAU) is a failover cluster feature that automates software updates on cluster servers while maintaining cluster service availability. With this feature, you can control how the nodes in a cluster handle updates from Windows Update so that the cluster can continue providing services while updates take place. To enable CAU, right-click a cluster in Failover Cluster Management, click More Actions, and click Cluster-Aware Updating. The Cluster-Aware Updating window (see Figure 8-27) lists cluster nodes, and you can choose from the following actions:

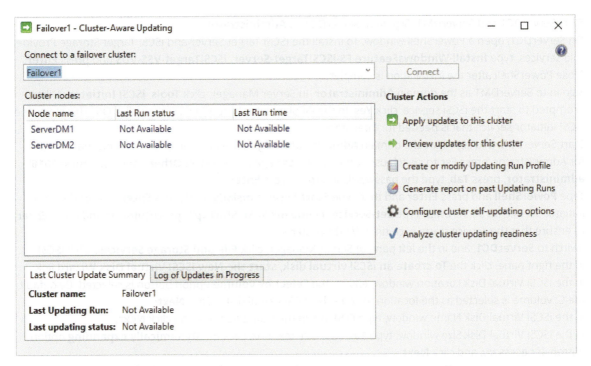

Figure 8-27   The Cluster-Aware Updating window

• *Apply updates to this cluster*—Configure and start a software update on the cluster.
• *Preview updates for this cluster*—See which updates each node in the cluster receives. You should choose this action before applying an update.
• *Create or modify Updating Run Profile*—Create an update profile to control updates.
• *Generate report on past Updating Runs*—Create a report showing update runs that have already occurred along with their status.
• *Configure cluster self-updating options*—Schedule updates, including the frequency and time of day that updates occur. You can also specify the order in which nodes are updated, run a script before or after updates occur, and specify retry and failure options.
• *Analyze cluster updating readiness*—Generate a report on whether the cluster is prepared for using CAU. The analyzer checks for cluster availability whether remote management is enabled on cluster nodes, firewall settings, and other CAU requirements.

Activity 8-5: Configuring Shared Storage for Failover Clustering

Time Required: 15 minutes
Objective: Install the iSCSI Target Server role service and create shared iSCSI virtual disks for a failover cluster.
Required Tools and Equipment: ServerDC1, ServerDM1, and ServerDM2
Description: In this activity, you install the iSCSI Target Server role service and then create two 10 GB iSCSI virtual disks and assign them to iSCSI targets.

> **Note** 📎
>
> These instructions are largely the same as those from Activities 5-4 and 5-5 except that the iSCSI Target Server is ServerDC1 and both ServerDM1 and ServerDM2 will be configured as iSCSI Initiators.

1. Start ServerDC1 and ServerDM1. Sign in to ServerDC1 as **Administrator**.
2. On ServerDC1, open a PowerShell window. To install the iSCSI Target Server and iSCSI Target Storage Provider role services, type **Install-WindowsFeature FS-iSCSITarget-Server**, **iSCSITarget-VSS-VDS** and press **Enter**. Close PowerShell after the installation is complete.
3. Sign in to ServerDM1 as the domain **Administrator**. In Server Manager, click **Tools**, **iSCSI Initiator**. When prompted to start the iSCSI service, click **Yes**. In the iSCSI Initiator Properties window, click **OK**. This starts the iSCSI initiator service that is needed for later steps.
4. Start ServerDM2 and sign in as the domain **Administrator**. If you are prompted to enter your password for Administrator, press **Esc** to switch users, then press **Esc** again, and select **Other user**. Type **mcsa2016\administrator**, press **Tab**, type the password, and then press **Enter**.
5. Type **PowerShell** and press **Enter** and then type **Start-Service msiSCSI** and press **Enter** to start the iSCSI initiator service on ServerDM2. Type **Set-Service -Name msiSCSI -StartupType Automatic** and press **Enter** to ensure that the service starts each time Windows starts.
6. Switch to **ServerDC1**, and in the left pane of Server Manager, click **File and Storage Services**. Click **iSCSI**.
7. In the right pane, click the **To create an iSCSI virtual disk, start the New iSCSI Virtual Disk Wizard** link.
8. In the iSCSI Virtual Disk Location window, ensure the **Select by volume** option button is selected. By default, the C: volume is selected as the location to store the iSCSI virtual disks. Click **Next**.
9. In the iSCSI Virtual Disk Name window, type **FOdisk1** in the Name text box and click **Next**.
10. In the iSCSI Virtual Disk Size window, type **10** in the Size text box, click the **Dynamically expanding** option button, if necessary, and click **Next**.
11. Because there are no existing targets, accept the default option **New iSCSI target** in the iSCSI Target window and click **Next**.
12. In the Target Name and Access window, type **ServerDC1target** and click **Next**.
13. In the Access Servers window, click **Add**. In the Add initiator ID dialog box, click the **Query initiator computer for ID** option button, if necessary, and type **ServerDM1.MCSA2016.local** in the text box. This step allows ServerDM1 to access to the iSCSI target. Click **OK**.
14. The server queries ServerDM1 to get its IQN, which is why you started the iSCSI service on ServerDM1 first. Repeat Step 13, replacing ServerDM1 with **ServerDM2**. When you have finished, the Access Servers window should look like the one in Figure 8-28. Click **Next**.
15. In the Enable authentication service window, click **Next** because you will use Active Directory for authentication. In the Confirmation window, verify the settings, and click **Create**. After the iSCSI virtual disk is created, click **Close**.
16. In File and Storage Services, you see the new virtual disk and the iSCSI target. If you need to make changes to either, you can right-click it and click Properties. Next, you'll create another virtual disk that will be used as the disk witness. In the right pane of File and Storage Services, right-click in the empty space and click **New iSCSI Virtual Disk**.
17. In the iSCSI Virtual Disk Location window, ensure that the **Select by volume** option button is selected. Click **Next**.

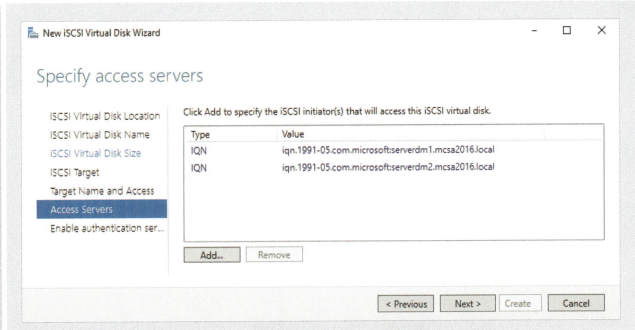

Figure 8-28   The Access Servers window after adding iSCSI initiators to the target

18. In the iSCSI Virtual Disk Name window, type **FOdisk2** in the Name text box, and click **Next**.
19. In the iSCSI Virtual Disk Size window, type **10** in the Size text box, click the **Dynamically expanding** option button, if necessary, and click **Next**.
20. Because you already have a target defined and have assigned initiators, just click **Next** in the iSCSI Target window. Click **Create**. After the iSCSI virtual disk is created, click **Close**.
21. Stay signed in to all servers and continue to the next activity.

Activity 8-6: Configuring the iSCSI Initiators

Time Required: 10 minutes
Objective: Configure the iSCSI initiators to access the virtual disks shared by ServerDC1.
Required Tools and Equipment: ServerDC1, ServerDM1, and ServerDM2
Description: In this activity, you start the Microsoft iSCSI service and configure the iSCSI initiator to connect to the iSCSI target that you configured in the previous activity.

1. Make sure ServerDC1, ServerDM1, and ServerDM2 are running.
2. Sign in to ServerDM1 as domain **Administrator**, if necessary, and open Server Manager.
3. Click **Tools, iSCSI Initiator**. In the iSCSI Initiator Properties window, type **ServerDC1.mcsa2016.local** in the Target text box. Click **Quick Connect**. In the Quick Connect box, you see the iqn for ServerDC1 (see Figure 8-29). Click **Done**.
4. The iSCSI Initiator Properties window Targets tab shows the target as Connected. Click the **Volumes and Devices** tab and click **Auto Configure** to automatically connect to all available devices. The two volumes are listed in the Volume List box (see Figure 8-30).
5. Click the other tabs in the iSCSI Initiator Properties window to see other configuration options. Click **OK** when you have finished.
6. Now, you must configure the iSCSI Initiator on ServerDM2. Because ServerDM2 is running Server Core, you'll perform all the iSCSI Initiator steps in PowerShell. Switch to **ServerDM2**. Start PowerShell, if necessary. Type **New-IscsiTargetPortal -TargetPortalAddress ServerDC1** and press **Enter**.
7. Next, type **Get-IscsiTarget** and press **Enter**. You'll see the iqn for ServerDC1 in the output.

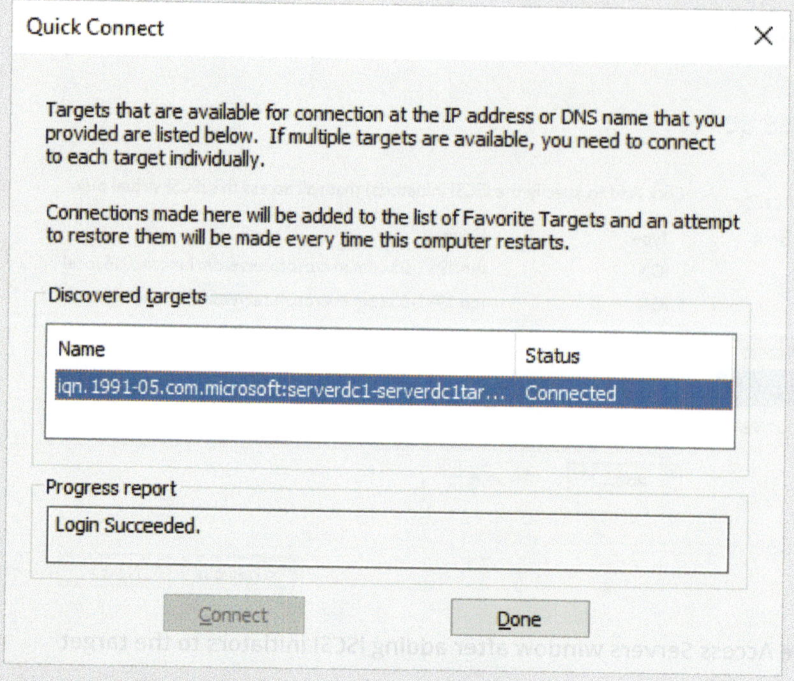

Figure 8-29 Connecting to an iSCSI target

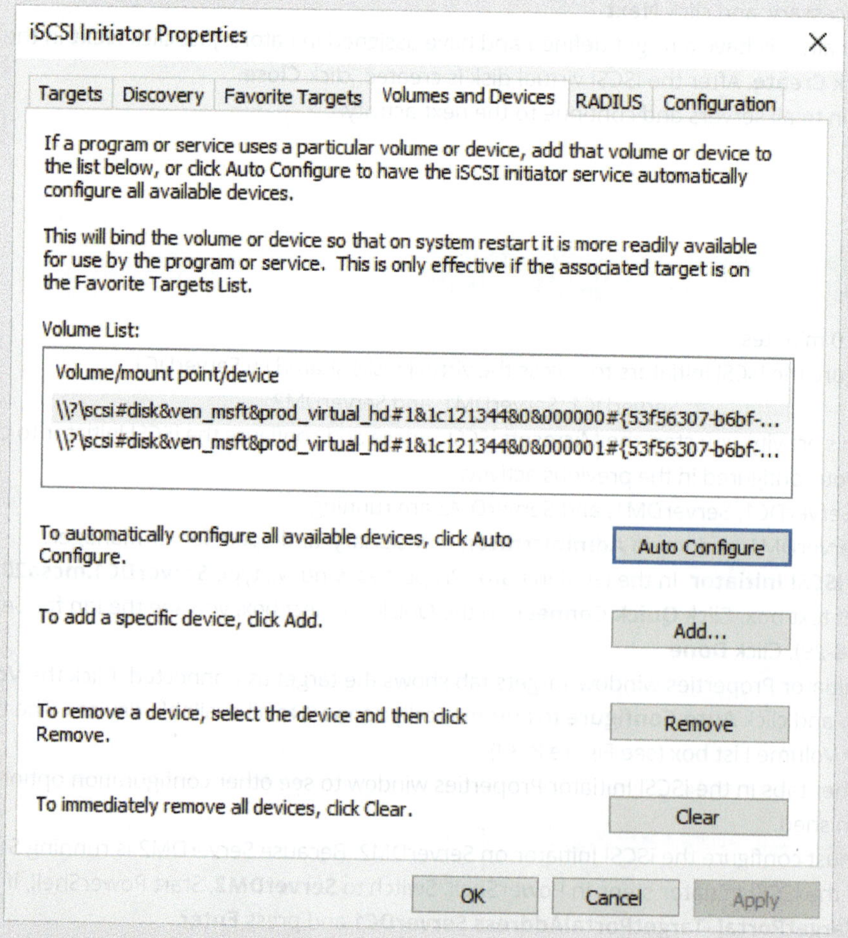

Figure 8-30 Connecting to volumes on the iSCSI target

8. Type **Get-IscsiTarget | Connect-IscsiTarget -IsPersistent $True** and press **Enter** to connect to the target. The -IsPersistent parameter ensures that the iSCSI client will connect to the target each time it restarts. Now that you are connected, you can view the session details. Type **Get-iSCSISession** and press **Enter**.

9. To see the disks available, type **Get-iSCSISession | Get-Disk** and press **Enter**. You see the virtual disks you created on ServerDC1. Take note of the disk numbers as you will use them in the next step.

10. Because the iSCSI disks are offline, you need to bring them online and initialize them. In the following two commands, be sure that the disk numbers correspond with the disk numbers you saw in Step 9. Type **Set-Disk -Number 4 -IsOffline $false** and press **Enter**. To initialize it, type **Initialize-Disk -Number 4** and press **Enter**. Repeat these two commands, replacing the disk number with the number of the second disk from Step 9 (see Figure 8-31).

```
PS C:\Users\administrator.MCSA2016> Get-IscsiSession | Get-Disk

Number Friendly Name Serial Number                      HealthStatus   OperationalStatus   Total Size Partition
                                                                                                      Style
------ ------------- -------------                      ------------   -----------------   ---------- ---------
4      MSFT Virtu... D355283F-D87C-4268-A664-BB479...   Healthy        Offline                 10 GB  RAW
5      MSFT Virtu... 7269C17A-2F41-4643-AE31-67087...   Healthy        Offline                 10 GB  RAW


PS C:\Users\administrator.MCSA2016> get-disk

Number Friendly Name Serial Number                      HealthStatus   OperationalStatus   Total Size Partition
                                                                                                      Style
------ ------------- -------------                      ------------   -----------------   ---------- ---------
0      Msft Virtu...                                    Healthy        Online                 127 GB  GPT
1      Msft Virtu...                                    Healthy        Offline                 20 GB  GPT
2      Msft Virtu...                                    Healthy        Offline                 15 GB  GPT
3      Msft Virtu...                                    Healthy        Offline                 10 GB  GPT
4      MSFT Virtu... D355283F-D87C-4268-A664-BB479...   Healthy        Offline                 10 GB  RAW
5      MSFT Virtu... 7269C17A-2F41-4643-AE31-67087...   Healthy        Offline                 10 GB  RAW


PS C:\Users\administrator.MCSA2016> Set-Disk -Number 4 -IsOffline $false
PS C:\Users\administrator.MCSA2016> Initialize-Disk -Number 4
PS C:\Users\administrator.MCSA2016> Set-Disk -Number 5 -IsOffline $false
PS C:\Users\administrator.MCSA2016> Initialize-Disk -Number 5
```

Figure 8-31   Initializing iSCSI disks with PowerShell

11. Switch to **ServerDM1** and open Server Manager, if necessary. Click **File and Storage Services**, and then click **Disks**. Look for the two iSCSI disks (shown in the Bus Type column). Right-click each disk and click **Bring Online** (see Figure 8-32). Click **Yes** when prompted.

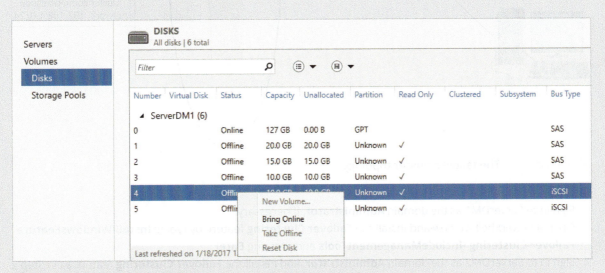

Figure 8-32   Bringing the iSCSI disks online in Server Manager

12. Right-click the first iSCSI disk and click **New Volume**. Follow the New Volume Wizard and assign drive letter **G**: to the first volume and give it the volume label **Cluster1**. Leave all other settings at the default. Repeat the process for the second iSCSI disk, assigning drive letter **H**: and volume label of **Cluster2**. Click **Close** when you have finished.

13. Leave all three servers running and continue to the next activity.

Activity 8-7: Installing the Failover Clustering Feature and Validating a Cluster Configuration

Time Required: 15 minutes
Objective: Install the Failover Clustering feature on two servers and validate a cluster configuration.
Required Tools and Equipment: ServerDC1, ServerDM1, and ServerDM2
Description: The topology for this cluster configuration is shown in Figure 8-33. In this topology, ServerDC1 is the iSCSI target, which has iSCSI shared storage for ServerDM1 and ServerDM2, the cluster servers. The clients in the figure are not part of the activity. You'll install the Failover Clustering feature on ServerDM1 and ServerDM2, and after the feature is installed, you'll validate the configuration.

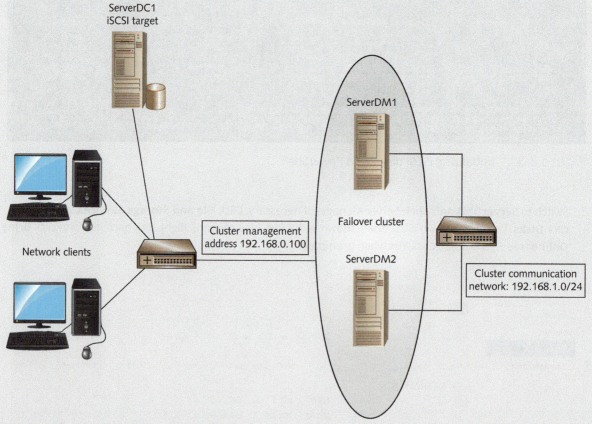

Figure 8-33 The failover cluster topology

1. Sign in to ServerDM1 as the domain **Administrator**, if necessary.
2. Open a PowerShell window and install the **Failover Clustering** feature by typing **Install-WindowsFeature Failover-Clustering -IncludeManagementTools** and pressing **Enter**.
3. Sign in to ServerDM2 as the domain **Administrator**, and install the **Failover Clustering** feature as in Step 2 without the -IncludeManagementTools option.

4. Switch to ServerDM1, open Server Manager, and click **Tools**, **Failover Cluster Manager** from the menu.
5. Click **Validate Configuration** in the Actions pane to start the Validate a Configuration Wizard. Read the information in the Before You Begin window, and then click **Next**.
6. In the Select Servers or a Cluster window, type **ServerDM1**, and click **Add**. Then type **ServerDM2**, and click **Add** again (see Figure 8-34). Click **Next**.

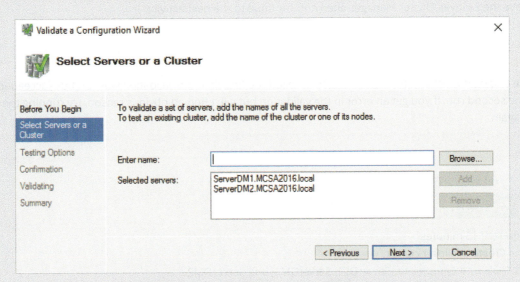

Figure 8-34   Selecting servers to validate a cluster configuration

7. In the Testing Options window, leave the default option **Run all tests (recommended)** selected, and click **Next**.
8. In the Confirmation window, review your validation settings, and then click **Next**.
9. The validation test runs, and each test reports results as it runs. The Summary window (see Figure 8-35) has a button that you can click to review the validation report when the tests are finished. If errors or warnings are reported in this window, click **View Report** to get additional information. You are likely to see a warning

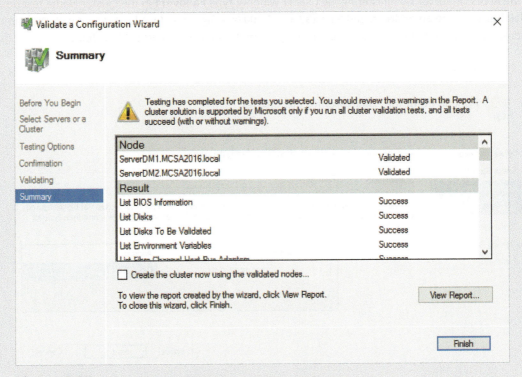

Figure 8-35   The cluster validation Summary window

about the operating system installation option because one server is installed with Desktop Experience and the other is Server Core. In addition, if Windows Update is disabled, you will see a warning. Warnings are usually okay. If there are errors, try to solve any problems and run the validation wizard again. Be sure the **Create the cluster now using the validated nodes** option is cleared. You will create the cluster in the next activity. Click **Finish**.

10. Leave the Failover Cluster Manager open and continue to the next activity.

> **Note**
>
> While testing this activity, the networking tests failed the first time the validation was run but succeeded on the second run. If you get an error in the validation but can't find an obvious reason, try running the test again.

Activity 8-8: Creating a Failover Cluster

Time Required: 15 minutes

Objective: Create a failover cluster.

Required Tools and Equipment: ServerDC1, ServerDM1, and ServerDM2

Description: Your cluster servers and network environment have been validated, so it's time to create the failover cluster.

1. Sign in to ServerDM1 as the domain **Administrator**, if necessary.
2. Open the Failover Cluster Manager, if necessary.
3. Click **Create Cluster** in the Actions pane to start the wizard. Read the information in the Before You Begin window, and then click **Next**.
4. In the Select Servers window, type **ServerDM1**, and click **Add**. Then type **ServerDM2**, and click **Add**. Click **Next**.
5. In the Access Point for Administering the Cluster window, type **Failover1** in the Cluster Name text box. Click **Click here to type an address**, and type **192.168.0.100** (see Figure 8-36). A host record with the name and address is added to DNS, and an Active Directory computer object is created. Click **Next**.

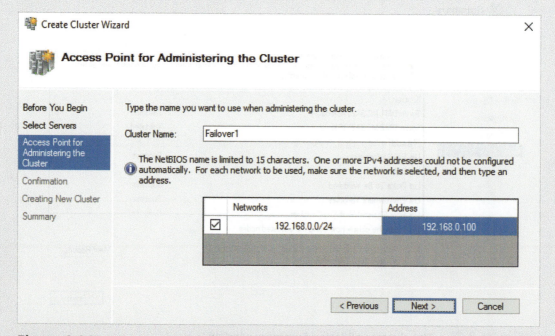

Figure 8-36 Entering the cluster name and address

6. The Confirmation window shows the settings for creating the cluster, which include the cluster name, IP address, and the nodes (servers) in the cluster. Also, be sure that the **Add all eligible storage to the cluster** option is checked. Click **Next**.

7. If errors or warnings are reported in the Summary window, click **View Report** to get additional information. If the cluster was created successfully, you see that the quorum mode of Node and Disk Majority was selected automatically (see Figure 8-37). Click **Finish**.

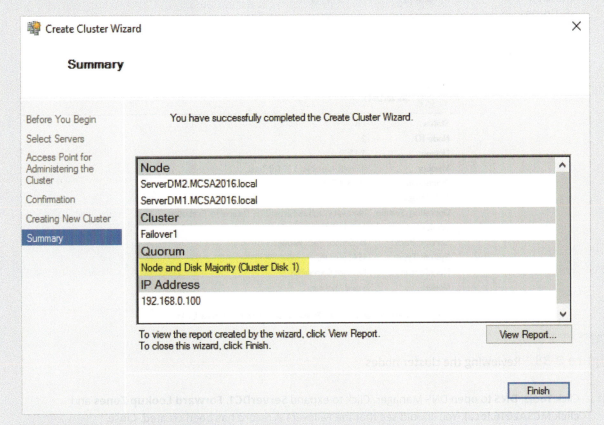

Figure 8-37   The Summary window showing the quorum mode

8. The next step is to review the cluster configuration in the Failover Cluster Manager. In the middle pane, review the cluster summary. In the left pane, click to expand the cluster name (**Failover1.MCSSA2016.local**), and then click **Nodes** to view the servers and their status in the middle pane. Click **ServerDM1** in the middle pane to see more details about this node (see Figure 8-38).

9. In the left pane, click to expand **Storage** and then click **Disks** to see the disks that are available for the cluster. The disks listed are shared storage from the iSCSI SAN. Notice that Cluster Disk 1 has been assigned as Disk Witness in Quorum. Also notice the Owner Node column, indicating which cluster server is currently owner of the storage.

10. In the left pane, click **Networks** to review the cluster networks. You see two networks listed. Cluster Network 1 is listed as Cluster and Client. Cluster Network 2 is listed as Cluster Only. Click each network to see the network address information in the bottom pane. Close the Failover Cluster Manager.

11. Sign in to ServerDC1 as **Administrator** and open **Server Manager**. Click **Tools**, **Active Directory Users and Computers**. Click the **Computers** folder. You should see the new computer account created for the cluster named Failover1. Close Active Directory Users and Computers.

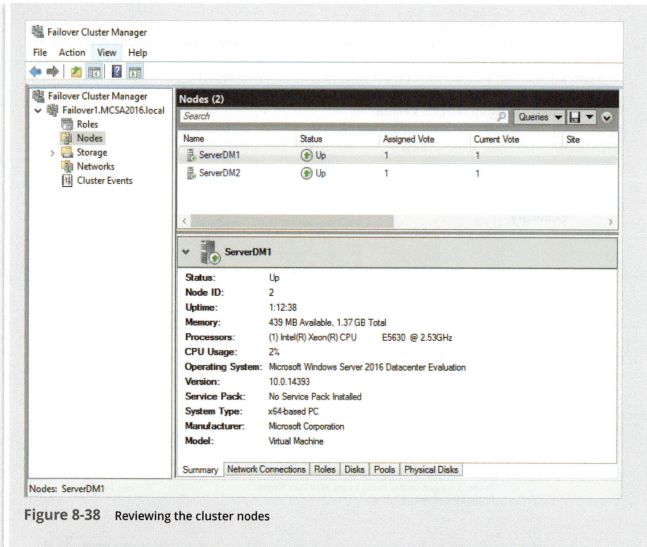

Figure 8-38 Reviewing the cluster nodes

12. Click **Tools**, **DNS** to open DNS Manager. Click to expand **ServerDC1**, **Forward Lookup Zones** and click **MCSA2016.local**. You should see that the Failover1 A record has been created. Close DNS Manager.

13. Stay signed in to all servers if you're continuing to the next activity.

Activity 8-9: Creating a File Server Failover Cluster

Time Required: 15 minutes

Objective: Configure the File Server role on the failover cluster.

Required Tools and Equipment: ServerDC1, ServerDM1, and ServerDM2

Description: Your cluster is up and running, so now it's time to configure a role for high availability. You will install the File Server role and then configure it in the failover cluster.

1. You need to install the File Server role on ServerDM1 and ServerDM2 so they can participate in the cluster role. Sign in to ServerDM1 as the domain **Administrator**, if necessary. Open a PowerShell window, if necessary, and then type **Install-WindowsFeature FS-FileServer** and press **Enter**. After the role is installed, close the PowerShell window. Repeat the process for ServerDM2.

2. Switch to ServerDM1 and open the Failover Cluster Manager, if necessary.

3. Click to expand **Failover1.MCSA2016.local** in the left pane. Right-click **Roles** and click **Configure Role** to start the High Availability Wizard.

4. Read the information in the Before You Begin window, and then click **Next**.

5. In the Select Role window, click **File Server**, and then click **Next**. In the File Server Type window, leave the default option **File Server for general use** selected. Notice that you also have the option to create a Scale-Out File Server. Click **Next**.

6. In the Client Access Point window, type **Failover1FS** in the Name text box, and then click **Click here to type an address**. Type **192.168.0.101** for the address of this cluster service, and then click **Next**.

7. In the Select Storage window, you select the storage volume you want to use. These servers were set up to share two iSCSI volumes, and one of them is used as the witness disk. Click the check box next to the cluster disk (probably named **Cluster Disk 2**), and then click **Next**.

8. Review the information in the Confirmation window, and then click **Next**.

9. If any errors or warnings were generated, click **View Report** in the Summary window and try to correct the problems; otherwise, click **Finish**.

10. In the Failover Cluster Manager, click **Roles** and then **Failover1FS** to review the summary information for the clustered service. Notice that one of the servers is designated as the current owner. The other server is in passive or standby mode.

11. Click the **Shares** tab at the bottom of the Roles window. Notice that a default administrative share is created. You can create new shared folders on the shared volume by using Share and Storage Management or the Add File Share link in the Actions pane. Click the **Summary** tab.

12. To test the failover configuration, click Roles in the left pane, right-click **Failover1FS** in the middle pane, point to **Move**, and click **Select Node**. In the Move Clustered Role dialog box, click **ServerDM2** or **ServerDM1**, whichever is listed, and then click **OK**. The Summary window shows the new owner of the service.

13. Close the Failover Cluster Manager.

Note

Chapter 9 continues coverage of failover quotas and you will need the current configuration on ServerDC1, ServerDM1, and ServerDM2, so do not revert the servers to an earlier snapshot.

Chapter Summary

- Network load balancing (NLB) uses server clusters to provide scalability and fault tolerance. A server cluster is a group of servers configured to respond to a single virtual IP address. To provide scalability, the servers in an NLB cluster share the load of incoming requests based on rules you can define. To provide fault tolerance, a failed server can be removed from the cluster, and another server can take its place and begin servicing client requests that were handled by the failed server.

- NLB is a feature available in Windows Server 2016 Datacenter and Standard editions. NLB clusters do not have any special hardware requirements, but it's important that each server in the cluster is

- configured with the same OS version, and updates are consistent on all servers. NLB is installed as a feature in Server Manager or using the `Install-WindowsFeature NLB` cmdlet.

- Creating an NLB cluster involves creating the cluster, selecting host and network interfaces, configuring the host ID, setting the cluster IP address, setting the cluster name and operation mode, configuring port rules, and adding servers to the cluster.

- Cluster configuration involves setting cluster properties, port rules, and host properties.

- You can control NLB cluster hosts with the following commands: start, stop, drainstop, suspend, and resume.

- An NLB cluster can be upgraded to Windows Server 2016 by taking all cluster hosts offline, upgrading each host, and then bringing the cluster back online. You can also use a rolling upgrade, which involves taking each cluster node offline, upgrading the host, and then bringing it back online.

- A failover cluster is deployed for high availability. It's well suited to back-end database applications, file-sharing servers, messaging servers, and other applications that are both mission critical and deal with dynamic read/write data.

- Failover clusters consist of two or more servers, usually of identical configuration, that access common storage media. Typically, storage is in the form of a SAN. One server in a failover cluster is considered the active server while one or more other servers are passive. The active server handles all client requests for the clustered application, and passive servers wait in a type of standby mode.

- Failover clusters provide fault tolerance and high availability. Like an NLB cluster, client computers see the failover cluster as a single entity that can be accessed by a single name or IP address.

- All failover cluster servers have access to the application data so that if the active server fails, another server can take over the clustered application. The passive servers know when the active server is no longer able to serve client requests using a process called a *quorum*. A quorum is a consensus among the cluster elements of the status of the cluster.

- The first requirement for a Windows Server 2016 failover cluster is that all cluster servers must have Windows Server 2016 Standard or Datacenter Edition installed. Except for the Windows Server edition, additional hardware and software requirements must be met before you can build a failover cluster.

- The failover cluster function on Windows Server 2016 is installed as a feature in Server Manager or by using the `Install-WindowsFeature Failover-Clustering` PowerShell cmdlet.

- The networks in a cluster are the critical link between clients and clustered applications and between cluster nodes and their shared storage. Cluster networks are used for client access, cluster communication, and storage network access. You should have at least two separate networks: one for client access to the cluster nodes and another for the storage network.

- Fast and fault-tolerant access to cluster storage is critical to overall cluster performance. Cluster shared volumes (CSV) allow multiple cluster nodes simultaneous read/write access; it's even more critical that the network access to the storage is optimized.

- Cluster-Aware Updating is a failover feature that allows updating failover cluster nodes with Windows updates while maintaining high availability. This feature allows you to control how the nodes in a cluster handle updates from Windows Update so that the cluster can continue providing services while updates take place.

Key Terms

active node	failback options	passive node
client access point	failover cluster	port rule
client affinity value	failover options	preferred owner
Cluster-Aware Updating (CAU)	filtering mode	quorum
cluster heartbeat	handling priority	rolling upgrade
cluster operation mode	high availability	server cluster
cluster server	load weight	standby mode
cluster shared volume	network load balancing (NLB)	virtual IP address
clustered application	partitioned	witness disk

Review Questions

1. Which of the following best describes a server cluster?
   a. A group of servers that can function independently
   b. A single server that has multiple virtual IP addresses
   c. A set of servers configured to respond to the same virtual IP address
   d. A group of servers that provide separate services

2. How does an NLB cluster provide fault tolerance?
   a. Based on an internal algorithm, the servers decide which server should respond to each incoming client request.
   b. A failed server can be removed from the cluster and another server can take its place.
   c. DNS records are changed to point clients to a different server if one fails.
   d. RAID and multiple NICs are used.

3. You have a website serving mostly static content, and the current server is unable to handle the traffic load. You think that you need three servers to handle the traffic load adequately, but you want to be able to prioritize how much traffic each server handles. Which high-availability solution makes the most sense?
   a. Create a round-robin load balancing configuration by using DNS.
   b. Use the failover cluster feature in Windows Server 2016.
   c. Create a distributed web server cluster utilizing Windows Server 2016.
   d. Use the network load balancing feature in Windows Server 2016.

4. Which of the following is *not* a step in creating and configuring an NLB cluster?
   a. Configuring the host priority
   b. Setting the cluster IP address
   c. Configuring port rules
   d. Configuring a preferred owner

5. Which of the following is a valid NLB cluster operation mode?
   a. Single host
   b. Network
   c. Multicast
   d. Suspended

6. Which filtering mode should you use when you want to provide scalability for several servers in an NLB cluster?
   a. Multiple host
   b. Failback immediate
   c. IGMP multicast
   d. Node majority

7. Under which circumstances should you use the None option when setting the client affinity value?
   a. When you want multiple requests from the same client to be directed to the same cluster host
   b. When clients access the cluster from behind multiple proxy servers
   c. When the content being served is fairly static and stateless
   d. When you want the cluster to discard packets matching the specified protocol and ports

8. Which of the following serves as an NLB cluster server identifier and determines which server will handle traffic not covered by a port rule?
   a. Dedicated IP address
   b. Port range
   c. Priority
   d. Affinity value

9. You manage an NLB cluster composed of three servers: Server1, Server2, and Server3. Your maintenance schedule indicates that Server1 is due for cleaning maintenance, which involves vacuuming dust and reseating all components. The NLB cluster is in constant use, so you don't want to interrupt any clients currently being served by Server1. Which option should you use to take Server1 temporarily offline yet allow it to complete active client requests?
   a. Stop
   b. Suspend
   c. Resume
   d. Drainstop

10. Which of the following is a failover cluster server that doesn't respond to client requests but is available to do so if the active server fails?
    a. Passive node
    b. Quorum node
    c. Active node
    d. Suspended node

11. Which of the following describes a cluster that has been divided into two or more subclusters because of lack of communication?
    a. Quorum
    b. Partitioned
    c. No majority
    d. Sanctioned

12. Which of the following is a valid quorum model? (Choose all that apply.)
    a. Node Majority
    b. Cloud witness
    c. Node and Disk Majority
    d. File Share and Disk Majority

13. Which of the following is a requirement for creating a Windows Server 2016 failover cluster? (Choose all that apply.)
    a. Two or more standalone servers
    b. Two or more quad-core CPUs
    c. Windows Server 2016 Standard or Datacenter Edition
    d. Identical CPU architecture

14. You're configuring a failover cluster and want a quorum configuration that can endure the failure of all but one server and remain operational. Which quorum configuration should you choose?
    a. Node Majority
    b. No Majority: Disk Only
    c. Node and File Share Majority
    d. Node and Disk Majority

15. Which of the following is created in Active Directory for domain-based clusters during the failover cluster creation process?
    a. A computer object with the name of the cluster
    b. A SAN object with the name of the witness disk
    c. An A record with the name and IP address of the cluster
    d. A cluster object containing the names of all the cluster servers

16. Which of the following is true about the network configuration of failover clusters?
    a. The shared storage should be on the same subnet as cluster clients.
    b. Cluster servers require a minimum of three NICs.
    c. The iSCSI storage server should be on a separate subnet from cluster clients.
    d. All NICs on each server must be configured on the same subnet.

17. Which of the following failover cluster options specifies how many times a clustered service can restart or fail to another server in a certain period before the service is left in the failed state?
    a. Preferred owner
    b. Failover options
    c. Affinity value
    d. Failback options

18. Which cluster storage option in Windows Server 2016 grants all cluster nodes read/write access to shared storage and is enabled by default?
    a. Cluster shared volume
    b. Volume pool
    c. Affinity storage system
    d. Mirrored storage volume

19. Which of the following is the name assigned to a clustered service?
    a. Network cluster name
    b. Cluster DNS name
    c. Cluster service name
    d. Client access point

20. Which failover cluster feature do you use to configure cluster self-updating options?
    a. NLB
    b. CAU
    c. CSV
    d. SAS

Critical Thinking

The following activities give you critical thinking challenges. Case Projects offer a scenario with a problem to solve and for which you supply a written solution.

Case Project 8-1: Choosing a High-Availability Solution

You have been hired to set up the network and servers for a new company using Windows Server 2016. The company is investing in an application critical to the company's business that all employees will use daily. This application uses a back-end database and is highly transaction oriented, so data is read and written frequently. To simplify maintenance of the front-end application, users will run it on remote desktop servers. The owner has explained that the back-end database must be highly available, and the remote desktop servers must be highly scalable to handle hundreds of simultaneous sessions. What high-availability technologies do you recommend for the back-end database server and the remote desktop servers? Explain your answer.

Case Project 8-2: Server Requirements for a Failover Cluster

You're setting up the application discussed in Case Project 8-1. Because the company is new, there are no servers—you're setting everything up from scratch. Describe the minimum requirements for this solution, including the number of servers and what they will be used for, the editions of Windows Server 2016, the basic network configuration, and any other devices you might need. Make a drawing of the network.

IMPLEMENTING HIGH AVAILABILITY: ADVANCED FAILOVER AND VIRTUAL MACHINES

After reading this chapter and completing the exercises, you will be able to:

Configure advanced failover clusters

Configure highly available virtual machines

Configure virtual machine movement

Failover clusters have some advanced configuration options to accommodate different cluster configurations. In this chapter, you learn about several of these options, such as quorum configuration and Active Directory–detached clusters. Because virtualization is a common technology used in data centers, it's only natural to want to make virtual machines highly available. You can configure high availability at the Hyper-V host level, referred to as *highly available* or *clustered* virtual machines, at the guest OS level, called *guest clustering*, or both. One advantage of using virtual machines (VMs) is their portability, and in this chapter, you learn several methods for moving VMs and their storage.

Advanced Failover Clusters

 Certification

- **70-740 – Implement high availability:**
  Manage failover clustering

In Chapter 8, you learned how to create a failover cluster and configure basic failover cluster settings. This chapter explores additional failover cluster settings and shows you how to configure roles for high availability. In addition, you learn how to back up and restore a failover cluster configuration. In this section, you look at the following advanced failover cluster configuration topics:

- Managing a failover cluster
- Configuring advanced quorum settings
- Configuring roles for high availability

- Upgrading a failover cluster
- Creating Active Directory–detached clusters
- Creating workgroup and multi-domain clusters
- Deploying clustered storage spaces
- Implementing Storage Replica with failover clusters
- Backing up and restoring cluster configurations

Table 9-1 lists what you need for the hands-on activities in this chapter.

Table 9-1   Activity requirements

Activity	Requirements	Notes
Activity 9-1: Exploring Failover Cluster Management Options	ServerDC1, ServerDM1, ServerDM2	
Activity 9-2: Configuring Advanced Quorum Settings	ServerDC1, ServerDM1, ServerDM2	
Activity 9-3: Performing a Live Migration	ServerDC1, ServerDM1, ServerHyperV	
Activity 9-4: Destroying a Failover Cluster	ServerDC1, ServerDM1, ServerDM2	
Activity 9-5: Removing the iSCSI Configuration	ServerDC1, ServerDM1, ServerDM2	

Managing a Failover Cluster

After a cluster has been created, you might need to perform some management tasks, including validating the cluster, adding nodes to it, or shutting down or destroying a cluster. You might also need to move cluster roles or resources from one cluster to another. In this section, you look at the following failover cluster management tasks:

- Validating a configuration
- Adding and removing a cluster node
- Shutting down and restarting a cluster
- Removing a cluster role and destroying a cluster
- Copying cluster roles
- Moving core cluster resources

Validating a Configuration

Before you create a cluster or add servers to an existing cluster, you can validate the cluster's configuration or the servers to be added to it. To validate a configuration, right-click the Failover Cluster Manager node in the Failover Cluster Manager console and click Validate Configuration. The Validate a Configuration Wizard starts, and you're prompted to select the servers or clusters you want to validate. If you select a server that's already a member of a cluster, all the cluster members are validated. If you select a server that isn't currently a member of a cluster, the server is validated for its suitability to be added to a cluster.

You can run all tests or selected tests. If you're validating a single server, the tests check for a suitable storage and network configuration as well as a valid system configuration. If it's a Hyper-V cluster, the Hyper-V configuration is validated. System configuration tests check for signed drivers, a valid OS edition, processor architecture, and so forth.

The Validate a Configuration Wizard creates a report and warns of any configuration parameters that might be a problem. The Summary window reports whether the cluster is valid or the server is suitable for clustering. A warning does not necessarily mean that the cluster configuration is invalid, but you should review the report and investigate any warnings reported. Any errors must be resolved before the configuration can be configured as a cluster. An error reported on an existing cluster should be investigated and resolved immediately.

You can also validate an existing cluster by right-clicking the cluster name in Failover Cluster Manager and clicking Validate Cluster. This action is the same as Validate a Configuration except that you don't need to enter a server name or cluster name. The Validate Cluster wizard automatically checks all servers that are members of the cluster (see Figure 9-1).

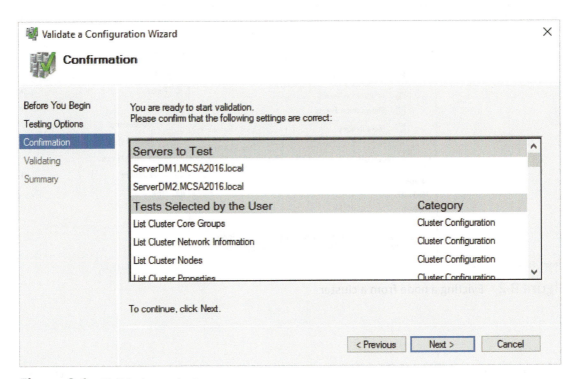

Figure 9-1   Validating a cluster

Adding and Removing a Cluster Node

To add a node to a cluster, right-click a cluster and click Add Node to start the Add Node Wizard. Then enter the server name in the Select Servers window. The selected server must have the Failover Clustering feature already installed. The Add Node Wizard validates the server for use in the cluster if it hasn't already been validated; however, running the Validate a Configuration Wizard on the server and the cluster before adding a node to the cluster is recommended. If the server is successfully validated, the server is added to the cluster, and the quorum settings are updated, if necessary.

To remove a node from a cluster, right-click the node, point to More Actions, and click Evict (see Figure 9-2). You can add the cluster node back to the cluster by using the Add Node Wizard.

Shutting Down and Restarting a Cluster

If you need to take a cluster offline, you can shut down the entire cluster, which stops all clustered roles and the cluster service on all nodes in the cluster. This approach is preferable to stopping the cluster service separately on each node. To shut down a cluster, right-click the cluster name in the Failover Cluster Manager, point to More Actions, and click Shut Down Cluster (see Figure 9-3). This action doesn't shut down Windows on the cluster nodes, but all cluster activities are stopped. To restart a cluster that has been shut down, right-click the cluster and click Start Cluster.

You can also stop and start the cluster service on a single cluster node. To do so, click Nodes in the Failover Cluster Manager, right-click the node, point to More Actions, and click Stop Cluster Service or Start Cluster Service.

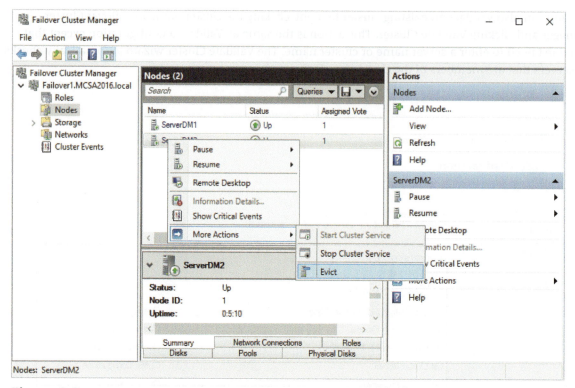

Figure 9-2 Evicting a node from a cluster

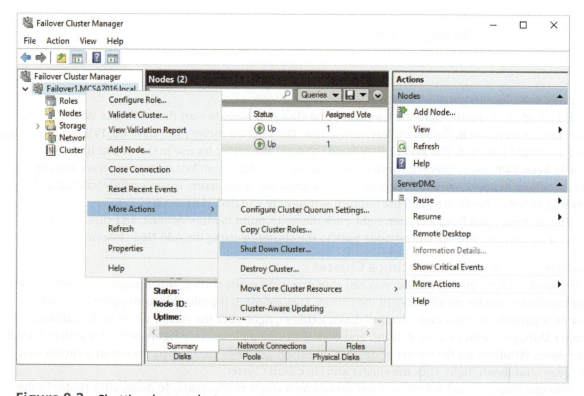

Figure 9-3 Shutting down a cluster

Removing a Cluster Role and Destroying a Cluster

To remove a clustered role, click the Roles node, right-click the role, and click Remove (see Figure 9-4). When you remove cluster roles, the corresponding computer accounts in Active Directory are disabled, and the DNS entries for the cluster roles are deleted. To destroy a cluster, right-click it, click More Actions, and click Destroy Cluster. If any clustered roles are configured, you need to delete the roles from the cluster before you can destroy it. The Destroy Cluster option deletes the cluster permanently, and the servers in the cluster can be used in other clusters, if needed. Also, the corresponding computer account in Active Directory is disabled, and the DNS entry for the cluster is deleted.

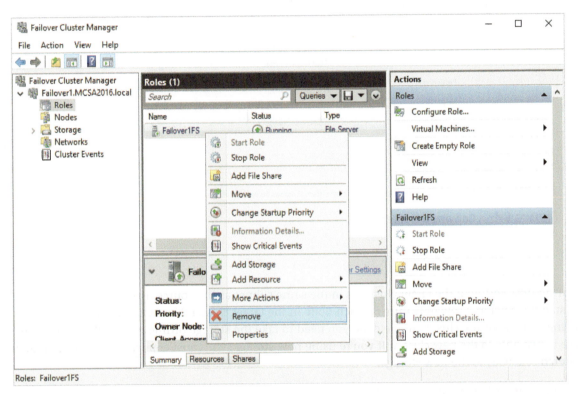

Figure 9-4   Removing a cluster role

Copying Cluster Roles

If you need to migrate clustered services and applications from one cluster to another, you can use the Copy Cluster Roles Wizard. However, the following roles can't be migrated by using this wizard:

- Microsoft SQL Server
- Microsoft Exchange Server
- Volume Shadow Copy Service tasks
- Task Scheduler tasks
- Cluster Aware Updating settings

You must ensure that the target cluster has been configured correctly for network and storage settings before migrating roles. To copy cluster roles, open the Failover Cluster Manager from a node in the target cluster (the cluster to which you are moving the role). Right-click the cluster, click More Actions, and click Copy Cluster Roles (see Figure 9-5). In the Copy Cluster Wizard, specify the source cluster and roles you want to copy. (The source cluster can't be the cluster from which you are running the Copy Cluster Roles Wizard.) The Copy Cluster Wizard copies the clustered role configuration

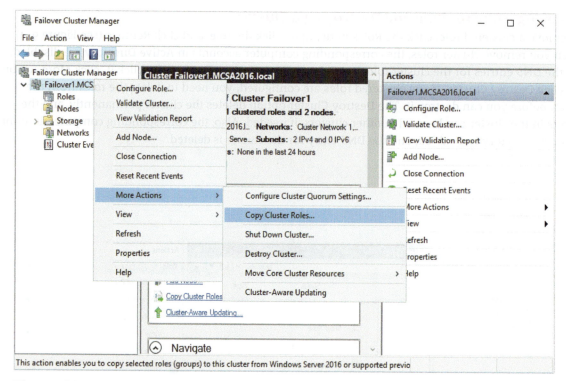

Figure 9-5 Copying a cluster role

and IP address setting if the target cluster is in the same subnet as the source. However, you still need to install the clustered role or feature on each node in the target cluster. In addition, if you're using existing storage for the clustered role data, you need to take the storage offline on the old cluster and make it available to the new cluster. If you're using new storage, you must copy any folders and data the clustered role uses to the new storage.

Moving Core Cluster Resources

If you need to perform maintenance operations on a cluster node, you should move any cluster resources from that node to another node in the cluster. **Core cluster resources** include the quorum resource, which is usually the witness disk or witness share; the IP address resource that provides the cluster IP address; and the network name resource that provides the cluster name. This command can also be used to simulate a failover if the server providing core resources fails. To move core cluster resources, right-click the cluster, point to More Actions, point to Move Core Cluster Resources, and click Best Possible Node or Select Node. If you choose Select Node, you can choose which server to transfer the core cluster resources to. To see which server currently owns the cluster core resources, click the cluster name in the left pane to see its summary in the middle pane, including the current host server of the cluster resources. In the bottom of the middle pane is a list of cluster core resources (see Figure 9-6).

Managing a Cluster with PowerShell

Table 9-2 lists PowerShell cmdlets you can use to manage failover clusters. To see a list of all commands related to failover clusters, enter `Get-Command -Module FailoverClusters` at a PowerShell prompt.

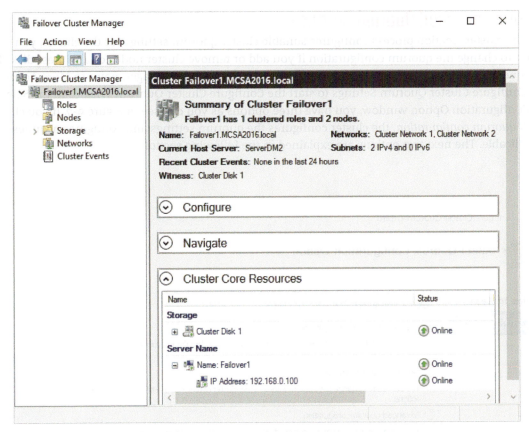

Figure 9-6 Cluster core resources

Table 9-2	PowerShell cmdlets for managing failover clusters

Cmdlet	Description
Test-Cluster	Runs validation tests on a cluster, nodes in a cluster, or a server that's not yet a member of a cluster
Get-Cluster	Displays information about a cluster
Get-ClusterGroup	Displays the owner and status of a cluster group
Add-ClusterNode	Adds a server to a failover cluster
Stop-Cluster	Shuts down a cluster
Start-Cluster	Starts the cluster service on all nodes in a cluster
Stop-ClusterNode	Shuts down the cluster service on a node in a cluster
Start-ClusterNode	Starts the cluster service on a node in a cluster
Remove-ClusterGroup	Removes a clustered role from a cluster
Remove-Cluster	Destroys a cluster
Remove-ClusterNode	Removes (evicts) a cluster node from the cluster
Move-ClusterGroup	Moves (copies) a cluster role from one cluster to another cluster or moves core cluster resources from one node to another

Configuring Advanced Quorum Settings

Although the cluster creation process configures suitable cluster quorum settings for the cluster, you might want to change the quorum configuration if you add or remove cluster nodes or a witness disk. To configure quorum settings, right-click the cluster in the Failover Cluster Manager, point to More Actions, and click Configure Cluster Quorum Settings to start the Configure Cluster Quorum Wizard. In the Select Quorum Configuration Option window, you have three options as you can see in Figure 9-7. If you choose *Use default quorum configuration*, the cluster configures the quorum settings and configures a witness disk, if applicable. The next two options are explained in the following sections.

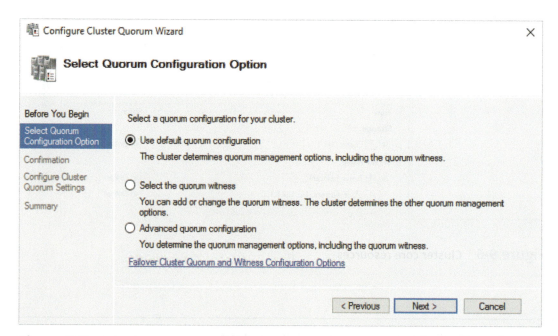

Figure 9-7   Selecting quorum configuration options

Selecting the Quorum Witness

If you choose the *Select the quorum witness* option, you can specify how you want the quorum witness to be configured, and the cluster determines the other quorum options. There are four options for configuring the quorum witness (see Figure 9-8):

- *Configure a disk witness*—If you choose this option, you're prompted to select a volume to act as the disk witness. The volume must be available to all cluster nodes through the cluster shared storage network.
- *Configure a file share witness*—With this option, you provide the path to a file share hosted on a server that's not in the cluster. The administrator configuring the file share witness must have Full Control permission to the file share. A file share witness should be used only if there's no shared storage between cluster nodes to create a disk witness as might be the case in a multisite or stretch cluster. In addition, the server hosting the file share should be in a site separate from any of the cluster nodes using the file share witness.
- *Configure a cloud witness*—With this option, you use Microsoft Azure cloud services as the cluster witness. You must provide an Azure storage account name and account key as well as specify an Azure service endpoint that defaults to core.windows.net (see Figure 9-9).

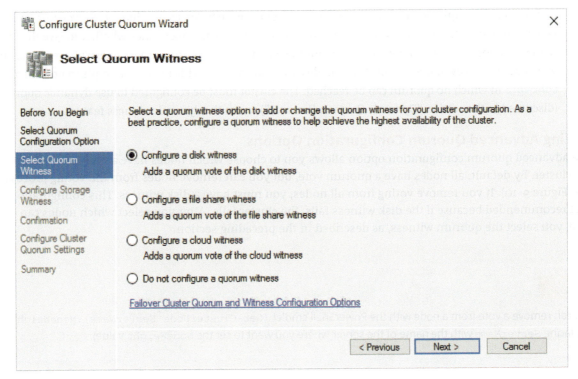

Figure 9-8   Selecting a quorum witness option

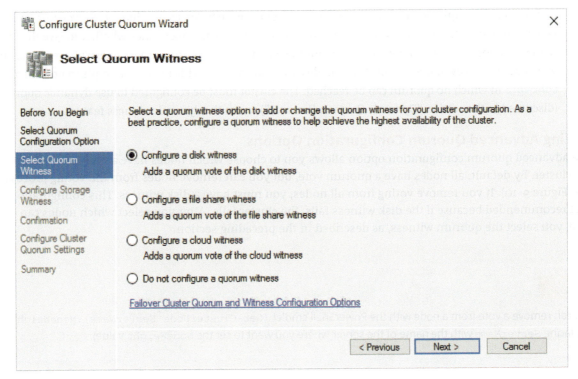

Figure 9-9   Configuring the cloud witness

- *Do not configure a quorum witness*—This option is not recommended as of Windows Server 2012 R2, which has added the **dynamic witness** feature in which the cluster determines whether to give the witness a quorum vote. If there are an odd number of cluster nodes, the witness doesn't have a quorum vote, but with an even number of cluster nodes, the witness does. This feature attempts to prevent a **split vote** in which no quorum can be reached. The cluster must be configured to use dynamic quorum (discussed in the section "Dynamic Quorum Features") to use the dynamic witness feature.

Setting Advanced Quorum Configuration Options

The advanced quorum configuration option allows you to choose which nodes have a quorum vote in the cluster. By default, all nodes have a quorum vote, but you can remove nodes from the voting process (see Figure 9-10). If you remove voting from all nodes, you must have a disk witness. This configuration isn't recommended because if the disk witness fails, the cluster fails. After you select which nodes can vote, you select the quorum witness, as described in the preceding section.

Note

You can remove a vote from a node with the PowerShell cmdlet `(Get-ClusterNode ServerName).NodeWeight=0` (replacing `ServerName` with the name of the server where you want to set the `NodeWeight` value).

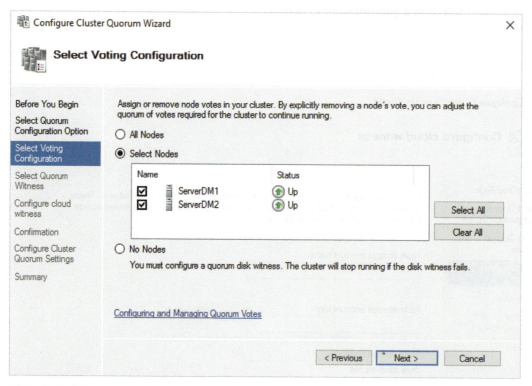

Figure 9-10 Selecting nodes for voting

Dynamic Quorum Features

Starting in Windows Server 2012, failover clusters have a feature called **dynamic quorum**, which is enabled by default. This feature assigns a cluster node vote dynamically depending on whether the node is an active member of the cluster. If a node is no longer active in the cluster, its vote is removed. In earlier versions of Windows Server, the number of node votes was static based on the initial cluster configuration. So if a cluster lost more than half its members, it stopped operating. With dynamic quorum, a cluster can continue running with only one active node because the number of votes needed to reach a quorum is adjusted dynamically. Therefore, it's not advisable to remove a node's vote manually because the cluster manager can't assign a node vote dynamically if it's manually overridden.

Another dynamic quorum feature introduced in Windows Server 2012 R2 is the capability to change node votes dynamically to create a **tie breaker for 50% node split**. For example, say you have a cluster consisting of four nodes and a file share witness. Two nodes are in Site1, and the other two nodes are in Site2. The file share witness is on a server in Site3. The quorum consists of a total of five votes. The link to Site3 goes down, and you're left with a total of four votes. The goal in a cluster quorum is always having an odd number of votes to prevent a tie. In this case, the cluster picks one of the four nodes and removes its vote, leaving a total of three votes. With three votes, two votes are required to reach a quorum. If one of the nodes in Site1 is selected to have its vote removed, Site1 has one vote, and Site2 has two votes. If the link between Site1 and Site2 goes down, the Site1 cluster partition goes offline, leaving the cluster partition in Site2 operational. You can also determine which cluster site will continue running in the event of a 50% node split by looking at a cluster property called *LowerQuorumPriorityNodeID*. You set this property to the ID of a node in the site that should go down if there's a 50% node split. To do so, run the PowerShell cmdlet `(Get-Cluster).LowerQuorumPriorityNodeID=X` (replacing *X* with the node ID). To get a node's ID, use the PowerShell cmdlet `Get-ClusterNode` *ServerName* `| Format-List -Property Id`, replacing *ServerName* with the name of the node for which you want to get an ID.

> **Note** 📎
>
> Dynamic quorum can be disabled by using the PowerShell cmdlet `(Get-Cluster).DynamicQuorum=0`. The LowerQuorumPriorityNodeID property still exists in Windows Server 2016 but has been deprecated in favor of dynamic quorum.

Configuring Cloud Witness

Cloud witness is a new quorum witness option introduced in Windows Server 2016. It allows you to specify a resource in Microsoft Azure to act as the cluster witness. The witness in this case is what Microsoft Azure refers to as a *file blob*, which is essentially a special file that bears the name of the cluster GUID. To use cloud witness, you must first create a Microsoft Azure Storage Account. As part of the account creation, an access key that is used during cloud witness configuration is generated (refer back to Figure 9-9). Microsoft recommends using cloud witness for all failover cluster quorum configurations when all the cluster nodes have reliable access to the Internet. Although cloud witness can be used for any failover cluster configuration, it is particularly useful in the following cluster configuration scenarios:

- Multisite or stretch cluster configurations (discussed later in this chapter in the section "Implementing Stretch Clusters")
- Clusters running as VMs in Microsoft Azure or other cloud providers
- Storage clusters
- Clusters without shared storage

The first step in using cloud witness is to create a Microsoft Azure Storage Account. If you don't already have a Microsoft Azure Account, you can sign up for a one-month free trial. You create a Microsoft Azure Storage Account using the Microsoft Azure management portal. From the management portal dashboard, click Storage accounts in the left pane (see Figure 9-11), and then click New to add a storage account.

In the Create storage account pane, fill in the following fields (see Figure 9-12):

- *Name*—This is the name of the storage account that must be unique within Microsoft Azure and must contain 3–24 characters of numbers and lowercase letters only.
- *Deployment model*—You can leave the default of Resource manager unless you have existing applications deployed using the Classic model.
- *Account kind*—Leave the default value of General purpose, which allows for different types of files including blob files.

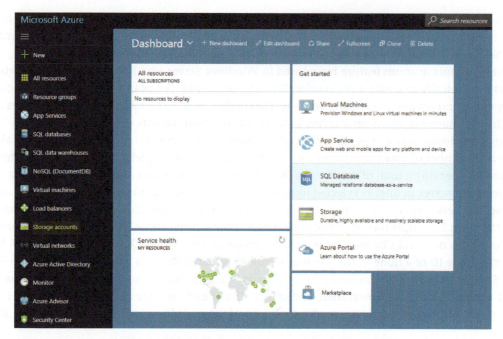

Figure 9-11 The Microsoft Azure Dashboard

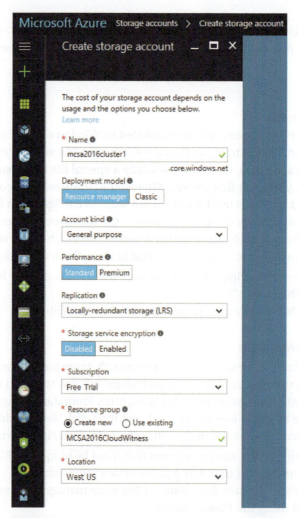

Figure 9-12 Create a storage account with Microsoft Azure

- *Performance*—Leave the default value of Standard because cloud witness doesn't require high performance storage.
- *Replication*—Choose Locally-redundant storage (LRS).
- *Storage service encryption*—Leave the default value of Disabled because no personal data is stored in a cloud witness blob file.
- *Subscription*—Choose your subscription if you have more than one.
- *Resource group*—Choose Create new unless you already have created a resource group. Give the resource group a name such as the name of your company and the purpose of the resource group. If you have more than one cluster using cloud witness, you can use the same resource group for each witness.
- *Location*—Choose the location for the resource group. You typically choose a location that is nearest to the datacenters that house the clusters.

Click Create, and Azure will create the new resource group and create the account. It may take a short while before the deployment is complete. Click the Refresh button on the Storage accounts screen to see the new account (see Figure 9-13).

Next, you need the access keys that you will use to configure cloud witness using Failover Manager. Click the new storage account in the Storage accounts window in Microsoft Azure and then click Access keys (see Figure 9-14). Two keys are generated, and either key can be used for configuring cloud witness. You'll need the Storage account name and the access keys to enter into the Configure cloud witness dialog box in Failover Manager.

Now, you can configure a cloud witness on your failover cluster. Use Failover Manager to configure cluster quorum settings described earlier under "Selecting Quorum Witness." After selecting the Configure a cloud witness option, fill in the Azure storage account name and Azure storage account key using the information for Microsoft Azure as shown in Figure 9-15. You can copy and paste the key from the Azure Access keys window (from Figure 9-14).

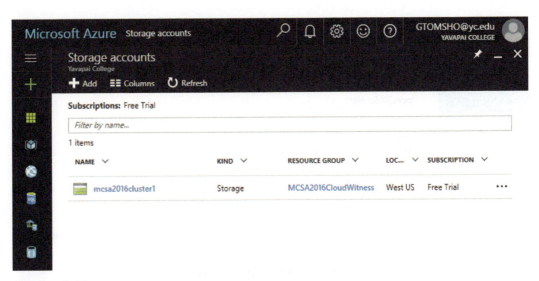

Figure 9-13   A new Microsoft Azure Storage account

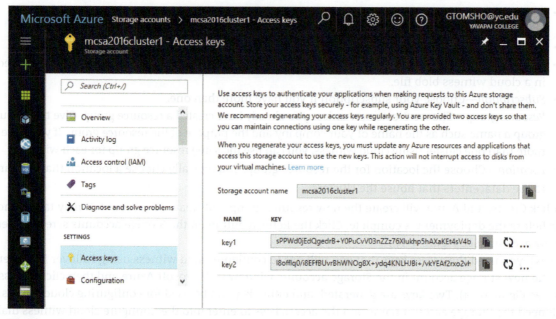

Figure 9-14   Access keys for accessing the Azure Storage account

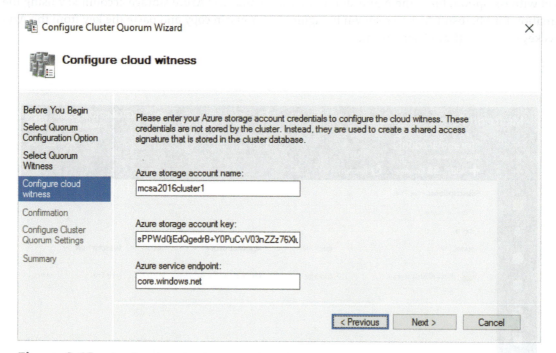

Figure 9-15   Configuring cloud witness for a failover cluster

Continue through the Configure Cluster Quorum Wizard. You can verify that cloud witness is being used as the cluster quorum witness by looking at the Cluster Core Resources (see Figure 9-16).

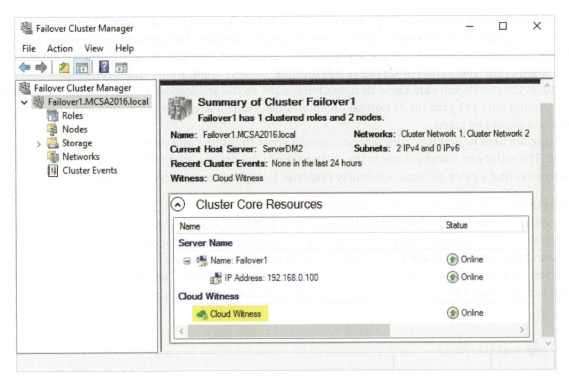

Figure 9-16   Verifying the cloud witness in Cluster Core Resources

Configuring Roles for High Availability

In Chapter 8, you configured the File Server role to use failover clustering. In this section, you take a closer look at the roles you can configure to use failover clustering and examine the File Server role in more detail.

When you configure an application or service for high availability, there are two broad categories: cluster-aware and generic. A cluster-aware service or application is designed to work with the failover clustering feature. A generic cluster application or service might be able to work in a clustered environment, but additional configuration tasks might be necessary for it to work correctly in a cluster. The cluster-aware roles in Windows Server 2016 include the following:

- DFS Namespace Server
- DHCP Server
- Distributed Transaction Coordinator (DTC)
- File Server
- Hyper-V Replica Broker
- iSCSI Target Server
- iSNS Server
- Message Queuing
- Virtual Machine
- WINS Server

One other role called *Other Server* provides a client access point and storage for an application you install later that can use the access point and storage.

Three categories of generic applications or services can be deployed in a failover cluster: Generic Application, Generic Script, and Generic Service. Applications, scripts, and services deployed with the

Generic failover cluster option are not cluster aware and, therefore, might not respond to a failover situation as quickly or in the same way that a cluster-aware role does. With generic applications and services, the cluster software starts the application or service and then periodically queries Windows to check whether the application or service is still running. Generic applications and services have fewer ways to let the cluster software know its operational state, so the application or service might still appear to be running but can't perform its normal function. In this case, the cluster software doesn't know that this action should be taken.

Using the Generic Script option, you can create a script that starts and monitors an application or service. The script can communicate to the cluster service the precise state of the application or service, thereby ensuring a more accurate and timely response to application or service problems.

Configuring Continuously Available Shares

There are two main options for configuring continuously available shares by using the File Server role (see Figure 9-17). The default option is *File Server for general use*, which supports standard Windows SMB shares and Network File System (NFS) shares and role services such as data deduplication, Distributed File System (DFS) replication, and File Service Resource Manager (FSRM). The ideal application for this option is a centralized share containing files that are created, opened, and closed frequently.

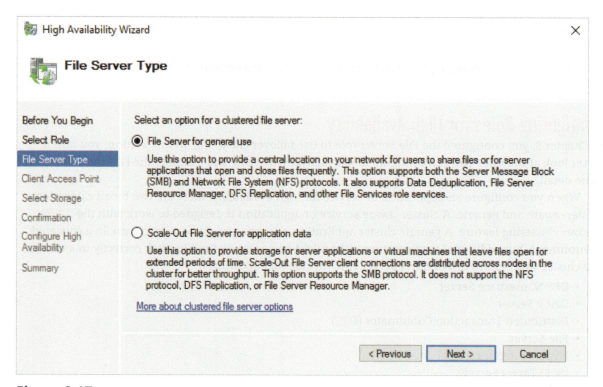

Figure 9-17   Selecting a File Server role option

The *Scale-Out File Server for application data* option is used for applications that leave files open for extended periods and file system operations such as creating, opening, and closing files are infrequent. A common use of this option is for a Hyper-V server where virtual machine files are stored on a file share. When using this option for virtual machine storage, performance and reliability are on par with typical SAN storage. With a **scale-out file server (SoFS)**, you have the reliability of failover clusters and the load distribution of an NLB because client connections are distributed among all nodes in the cluster. This option is recommended for Hyper-V deployments that use SMB shares for VM storage and for SQL deployments that use SMB. It doesn't support NFS, FSRM, or DFS replication. Up to eight nodes are supported in a scale-out file server cluster.

Note

Scale-out file server requires SMB 3.0, which is supported by Windows Server 2012 and higher, so you cannot create a SoFS cluster using Windows Server 2008 and earlier.

After you configure the File Server role in Failover Manager, you can create continuously available shares in File and Storage Services from Server Manager. To do so in Server Manager, click File and Storage Services, and then click Shares. Click New Share in the Tasks menu to start the New Share Wizard. Continue the wizard until you get to the Configure share settings window (see Figure 9-18). Ensure that the *Enable continuous availability* option is checked, and the share will be available to clients with failover capability. On this window, you can also configure other share options such as caching and encryption.

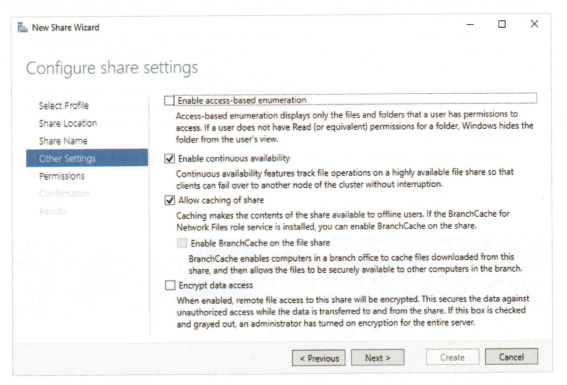

Figure 9-18   Configuring a continuously available share

Upgrading a Failover Cluster

If you're running a Windows Server 2012 failover cluster and want to migrate to a Windows Server 2016 cluster, you have a few options. One option is to add two nodes running Windows Server 2016 to the existing cluster and then transfer the roles and resources to the new nodes. After the resources and roles have been transferred, you can evict (remove) the older Windows Server 2012 nodes from the cluster. To evict a node from a cluster, right-click the node in Failover Cluster Manager, point to More Actions, and click Evict.

This option might not be feasible if you don't have extra servers available, however. Another option is to perform an in-place upgrade in which you evict one of the nodes running Windows Server 2012 from the cluster, upgrade the server to Windows Server 2016, and then add the node back to the cluster. After the node is rejoined to the cluster, transfer resources and roles to the new Windows Server 2016 node and evict another node running Windows Server 2012. Upgrade this node, and then rejoin it to the cluster. Perform this process until all nodes have been upgraded to Windows Server 2016. You should then validate the configuration to make sure the upgraded cluster is in good working order.

A third option is to build a new cluster with nodes running Windows Server 2016 and run the Copy Cluster Roles Wizard from one of the nodes in the new cluster. Then you can destroy the old Windows Server 2012 cluster. The Copy Cluster Roles Wizard was described earlier in the section "Copying Cluster Roles."

Implement Cluster Operating System Rolling Upgrade

The cluster upgrade options just discussed also work if you want to upgrade the cluster OS from Server 2008 to Server 2012. A drawback of these methods is that you must stop the cluster workloads while the upgrade process proceeds. If downtime of the failover cluster is not acceptable, Windows Server 2016 offers another cluster OS upgrade option called *Cluster Operating System Rolling Upgrade*. With **Cluster Operating System Rolling Upgrade**, you can upgrade a Windows Server 2012 R2 cluster to a Windows Server 2016 cluster without taking the workloads offline. This option is available only for SoFS and Hyper-V cluster configurations; other workloads running on the cluster will be unavailable for a short period of time while a node is being upgraded. With this cluster upgrade option, you upgrade one server at a time from Windows Server 2012 R2 to Windows Server 2016 without having to stop the cluster.

The cluster can actually operate with both Windows Server 2012 R2 nodes and Windows Server 2016 nodes in a cluster mode called *mixed-OS mode*. This is accomplished by having the Windows Server 2016 nodes operate in Windows Server 2012 R2 compatibility mode until all servers have been upgraded to Windows Server 2016. In addition, until all nodes are upgraded to Windows Server 2016, you can reverse the process, removing the Windows Server 2016 nodes and replacing them with Windows Server 2012 R2 nodes, if necessary. Once you are certain that the cluster works properly with all Windows Server 2016 servers, you run the `Update-ClusterFunctionalLevel` PowerShell cmdlet, which sets the operational mode of the cluster to Windows Server 2016 permanently, at which point you can no longer revert to Windows Server 2012 R2 nodes.

To see the cluster functional level of all clusters running on a server, use the following PowerShell cmdlet (see Figure 9-19):

```
Get-Cluster | Select Name,ClusterFunctionalLevel
```

```
PS C:\Users\administrator.MCSA2016> Get-Cluster | select Name,ClusterFunctionalLevel

Name        ClusterFunctionalLevel
----        ----------------------
Failover1                        9
```

Figure 9-19   Getting the cluster functional level

A value of 9 indicates that the cluster is running in Windows Server 2016 functional level; a value of 8 indicates a functional level of Windows Server 2012 R2, which means at least one server in the cluster is running Windows Server 2012 R2. So, a functional level of 8 can also mean that there is one or more server running Windows Server 2016.

Here are the basic steps you should follow to perform a rolling upgrade:

1. Back up the cluster database (backing up the database is discussed later in "Backing Up and Restoring Cluster Configuration").

2. Back up server data.

3. Stop Cluster-Aware Updating (CAU), if necessary. CAU was discussed in Chapter 8. If updating is currently occurring, click the Cancel Updating Run button to stop it. This is necessary so CAU doesn't pause the cluster during the upgrade. You can also run the PowerShell cmdlet `Stop-CauRun`, and it will stop updating if it is currently in progress.

4. Pause and drain roles on a node to be upgraded. You can use Failover Manager or `Suspend-ClusterNode` *NameofNode* `-Drain` where *NameofNode* is the name of the cluster node. This action moves the resources from that cluster node to another cluster node. You can also specify the `-TargetNode` parameter to specify a node where resources should be transferred.

5. Evict the node from the cluster.

6. Perform a clean install of Windows Server 2016 on the target node (or you can use a new machine if you will be retiring the old one). Configure the server appropriately for the cluster networks and storage.

7. Install and configure the cluster roles.

8. Install the Failover Clustering feature.

9. Join the node to the failover cluster (this needs to be done from a Windows Server 2016 server).

10. Move any resources to the new upgraded cluster node, if necessary.

11. Upgrade the rest of the cluster nodes to Windows Server 2016 using the preceding steps.

12. After verifying good cluster functionality, upgrade the cluster functional level.

Creating Active Directory–Detached Clusters

A feature first added in Windows Server 2012 R2 was the capability to deploy a failover cluster without needing Active Directory for network name management. As you know, when you create a failover cluster, a computer account is created in Active Directory for the cluster and any clustered roles you configure, and DNS entries are created for the cluster and cluster roles. An **Active Directory–detached cluster** still creates the DNS entries for name resolution, but computer accounts aren't created in Active Directory. This option for creating clusters allows someone who doesn't have permission to create computer objects in Active Directory to create a failover cluster.

> **Note**
>
> The nodes in an Active Directory–detached cluster must still be members of an Active Directory domain.

To create an Active Directory–detached cluster, all cluster nodes must be running Windows Server 2012 R2 or higher and be joined to the same domain. The cluster must be created with the following PowerShell cmdlet; it can't be created in the Failover Cluster Manager console:

```
New-Cluster ClusterName -Node Server1,Server2
  -AdministrativeAccessPoint DNS
```

The important parameter in this command is `-AdministrativeAccessPoint DNS`, which tells the cluster service that the cluster should be created without creating Active Directory computer accounts.

Creating Workgroup and Multi-Domain Clusters

With traditional clusters as well as Active Directory–detached clusters, all cluster members must still be members of the same domain (single-domain clusters). Windows Server 2016 failover clusters offers the ability to create clusters with non-domain members (Workgroup computers) or members of different domains (multi-domain clusters). Workgroup clusters and multi-domain clusters have the same requirements:

- Must meet the same requirements as single-domain clusters except for being members of the same domain.
- Must have all nodes running Windows Server 2016.
- Must have a local user account with the same name and password that is a member of the local Administrators group created on each cluster node. You can use the built-in Administrator account for this; however, it's preferable to use a different account. If you don't use the built-in Administrator account, be sure you open PowerShell as Administrator when you use PowerShell to manage the cluster.

- Have a cluster that must be created as an Active Directory–detached cluster, which means you need to use the `AdministrativeAccessPoint DNS` option when creating the cluster with PowerShell. If you use Failover Cluster Manager, it automatically detects that you are not creating a single-domain cluster and sets the access point as DNS only.
- Must have each cluster node configured with a primary DNS suffix so it can create and find DNS records for the cluster. You set this from System Properties, Computer Name tab, clicking Change, and clicking More (see Figure 9-20). In multi-domain clusters, the primary DNS suffix will already be set, but for workgroup clusters, it must be set manually.

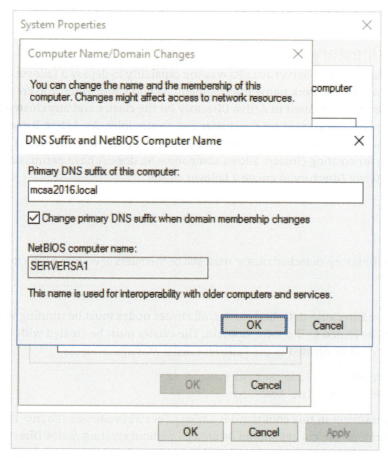

Figure 9-20   Configuring the primary DNS suffix

Once the requirements are met, you can create and configure a workgroup or multi-domain cluster normally with a couple caveats: Only cloud witness and disk witness quorum modes are supported; you cannot use a file share witness. In addition, not all workloads are supported: Workgroup and multi-domain clusters support only SQL Server, File Server, and Hyper-V; however, File Server and Hyper-V are not recommended.

Note

In a workgroup cluster, Failover Cluster Manager may not connect to the cluster automatically. To connect to the cluster, click Connect to Cluster in the Management pane of Failover Cluster Manager or right-click the Failover Cluster Manager node in the left pane and click Connect to Cluster.

Deploying Clustered Storage Spaces

You learned about Storage Spaces in Chapter 5. This section describes the steps for deploying a clustered storage space using a shared SAS storage enclosure. Before you can create a clustered storage space, your cluster and storage configuration must meet the following prerequisites:

- All servers must be running at least Windows Server 2016.
- You must have at least three disks that haven't had any volumes allocated on them.
- Disk controllers must be serially attached SCSI (SAS) and must not have RAID functionality enabled.
- Use a Windows Server 2016–certified just a bunch of disks (JBOD) storage enclosure that has an SAS connection for each cluster node. The Windows Server Catalog lists available certified enclosures.
- The disks used for the clustered storage pool must be dedicated to that pool.

There are two main methods for deploying a clustered storage space:

- Create a storage space before you create the failover cluster, and then add the storage to the failover cluster when running the Create Cluster Wizard.
- Create the failover cluster, and then create a clustered storage space in the Failover Cluster Manager.

After the prerequisites are met, perform the following steps. Steps 1 through 4 are used for the first method, and Steps 1, 2, 4, and 5 are used for the second method:

1. Install the Multipath I/O (MPIO) feature on all cluster nodes if there are redundant paths to the storage enclosure.
2. Verify that the shared disks are available in Disk Management and File and Storage Services or are using the `Get-PhysicalDisks` cmdlet. All servers should have access to all the shared disks.
3. Create the storage spaces by using File and Storage Services or PowerShell. (Skip this step for Method 2.)
4. Create a failover cluster.
5. *Don't do this step for the first method*—Create storage spaces in the Failover Cluster Manager instead of using File and Storage Services or PowerShell. To do so, expand the Storage node in the Failover Cluster Manager, click Pools, and click New Storage Pool in the Actions pane. This starts the New Storage Pool wizard.

You can then add a clustered storage space volume to a cluster shared volume (CSV) if you're using CSVs.

Implementing Storage Replica with Failover Clusters

We first visited Storage Replica in Chapter 5. This section aims to provide instructions for implementing Storage Replica in a cluster-to-cluster scenario. As discussed in Chapter 5, Storage Replica can be used for server-to-server, cluster-to-cluster, and stretch cluster data replication scenarios. The configuration of Storage Replica for cluster-to-cluster replication follows the same procedure as with server-to-server replication (discussed in Chapter 5) with a few important differences. Assume you have two clusters named ClusterA and ClusterB, each of which has two servers. ClusterA has servers Server1A and Server2A and ClusterB has servers Server1B and Server2B. Follow these steps to enable Storage Replica between the clusters:

- Each cluster must grant access to the other cluster to enable replication. On any node on ClusterA, use the following PowerShell cmdlet:

```
Grant-SRAccess -Cluster ClusterB
```

- On any node on ClusterB, use the following PowerShell cmdlet:

```
Grant-SRAccess -Cluster ClusterA
```

- Configure replication between the clusters. Note that for the `-SourceComputerName` and `-DestinationComputerName` parameters, you use the cluster name instead of server names.

```
New-SRPartnership -SourceComputerName ClusterA -SourceVolumeName R:
  -SourceLogVolumeName f: -SourceRGName RG01 -DestinationComputerName ClusterB
  -DestinationVolumeName R: -DestinationLogVolumeName f: -DestinationRGName RG02
```

Configuring Storage Replica between two servers in a failover cluster is the same as configuring it between two servers that are not in a failover cluster. However, if the servers are in the same failover cluster, you can use Failover Cluster Manager instead of PowerShell. Note that you can use this method to configure Storage Replica in a failover cluster in which the cluster nodes are located in the same datacenter or a stretch cluster in which the nodes are located in different sites. The most common scenario is to use Storage Replica for stretch clusters in which the nodes located in different sites use two sets of storage. If a site goes offline, the nodes operating in the other site can continue to operate without data loss. Only synchronous replication is supported. The requirements are the same as for other Storage Replica scenarios: two equal size volumes (one is the source and one is the destination) and two log disks in which all disks use GPT partitioning.

To configure Storage Replica using Failover Cluster Manager, under the cluster name, click Storage and then Disks. Then right-click the source volume, point to Replication, and click Enable. The Configure Storage Replica wizard begins (see Figure 9-21). You provide the same information to the wizard as when you use the `New-SRPartnership` PowerShell cmdlet.

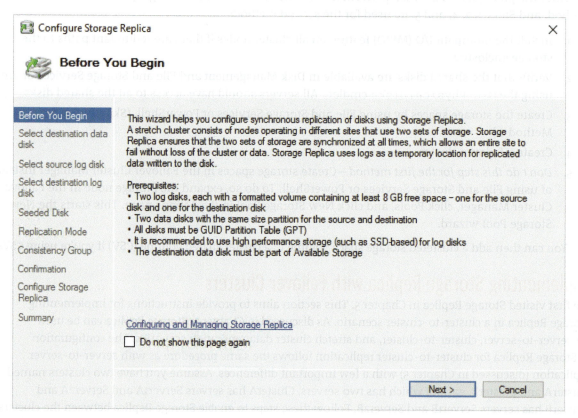

Figure 9-21   Configure Storage Replica wizard

Backing Up and Restoring Cluster Configuration

You can see by now that configuring a failover cluster can be complex. After you have created and configured a failover cluster, you don't want to lose all your hard work if disaster strikes. You can get some peace of mind by using Windows Server Backup to back up a failover cluster configuration. First, you need to install the Windows Server Backup feature on at least one node in the cluster by using the Add Roles and Features Wizard or PowerShell. Before backing up the cluster configuration, verify that the cluster node where you're doing the backup is active in the cluster, the cluster is running, and it has a quorum.

Any Windows Server Backup that allows a system recovery includes the cluster configuration data, such as a full server backup or a custom backup incorporating the system state. Because the witness disk also includes cluster configuration data, it's a good idea to include it in the backup. You should also back up the data on clustered disks. Only disks that are online and owned by the node where you're performing the backup can be backed up, so you might need to do a backup on more than one server to make sure all the cluster data is backed up.

Restoring a Failover Cluster Configuration

Cluster configuration data is replicated automatically to all cluster nodes and the witness disk, if present. If you need to restore the cluster configuration on a single cluster node, you have two options:

- *Authoritative restore*—In this case, the configuration contained in the backup is replicated to all cluster nodes after the backup is finished. You use this type of restore when you need to roll back the cluster configuration to an earlier point, perhaps because of an administrative error made when changing the cluster configuration. You must use the `wbadmin.exe` program to perform an authoritative restore.
- *Nonauthoritative restore*—In this case, you restore a node from the system state backup, and it rejoins the cluster. Then the current cluster configuration stored on the other cluster nodes is replicated to it.

Activity 9-1: Exploring Failover Cluster Management Options

 Note

The activities in this chapter require that you have completed the activities from Chapter 8 and that the shared storage and failover cluster on ServerDC1, ServerDM1, and ServerDM2 are in good working order.

Time Required: 15 minutes

Objective: Explore failover cluster management options.

Required Tools and Equipment: ServerDC1, ServerDM1, and ServerDM2

Description: In this activity, you explore failover cluster management options. First, you run the Validate a Configuration Wizard to verify that your cluster is still in good operational order. Next, you use some PowerShell cmdlets to stop and start a cluster. Finally, you move cluster resources from one node to another and verify the results with a PowerShell cmdlet.

1. Start ServerDC1, ServerDM1, and ServerDM2. On ServerDM1, sign in to the domain as **Administrator**.
2. On ServerDM1, open Server Manager, and start the Failover Cluster Manager. In the left pane, right-click **Failover1.MCSA2016.local** (the cluster node) and click **Validate Cluster** to start the Validate a Configuration Wizard. It verifies that the cluster is still in good working order.
3. In the Before You Begin window, read the information, and then click **Next**.
4. In the Testing Options window, leave the default option **Run all tests** selected, and then click **Next**.
5. In the Confirmation window, review the tests to be performed, and then click **Next** to start the validation tests.
6. Watch the progress of the tests. You might get warnings, but you probably need to attend only to errors. When the tests are finished, click **View Report**. An Internet Explorer window opens and displays the tests by category.
7. Click any test categories with warnings or errors. There shouldn't be any errors, but if there are, review the suggested steps to fix any errors. When you're finished, close Internet Explorer and click **Finish** in the Summary window.
8. Next, you shut down and then restart a cluster. In the Failover Cluster Manager, right-click **Failover1.MCSA2016.local**, point to **More Actions**, and click **Shut Down Cluster**. In the Shutdown Cluster dialog box, click **Yes**.

9. To start the cluster, open a PowerShell window. Type **Start-Cluster** and press **Enter**. (You can also start the cluster from Failover Cluster Manager, but this gives you practice using PowerShell to manage a cluster.)

10. To see all information about the cluster, type **Get-Cluster | fl –Property *** and press **Enter**.

11. In Failover Cluster Manager, verify that the cluster is started. To see which server owns cluster core resources, click **Failover1.MCSA2016.local**. The Summary section in the middle pane shows that the server listed after Current Host Server owns the core resources.

12. To view the core resources, scroll down until you see Cluster Core Resources. Click to expand the **Server Name** resource and then the **Storage** resource. The disk listed under Cluster Disk 1 is the witness disk.

13. To change the owner of the cluster core resources, right-click **Failover1.MCSA2016.local**, point to **More Actions**, point to **Move Core Cluster Resources**, and click **Select Node**. Click the node shown (which is ServerDM1 or ServerDM2, depending on which node currently doesn't own the cluster core resources). Click **OK**. In the Summary section of the Failover Cluster Manager, you should see that the Current Host Server has changed, indicating the new owner of the cluster core resources.

14. In the PowerShell window, type **Get-ClusterGroup "Cluster Group"** and press **Enter** to display the current owner of the core cluster resources. Type **Move-ClusterGroup "Cluster Group"** and press **Enter** to move the core cluster resources to the best possible node, which is the node that doesn't currently own the resources. The output of the cmdlet shows the current owner of the resources. Close the PowerShell window.

15. Leave all servers running for the next activity.

Activity 9-2: Configuring Advanced Quorum Settings

Time Required: 15 minutes
Objective: Configure advanced quorum settings.
Required Tools and Equipment: ServerDC1, ServerDM1, and ServerDM2
Description: In this activity, you configure advanced quorum settings with the Configure Cluster Quorum Wizard and PowerShell cmdlets.

1. On ServerDM1, open Server Manager, and start the Failover Cluster Manager, if necessary. In the left pane, right-click **Failover1.MCSA2016.local**, point to **More Actions**, and click **Configure Cluster Quorum Settings** to start the Configure Cluster Quorum Wizard.

2. In the Before You Begin window, read the information, and then click **Next**.

3. In the Select Quorum Configuration Option window, click the **Advanced quorum configuration** option button, and then click **Next**.

4. In the Select Voting Configuration window, All Nodes is selected by default. You can deselect nodes by clicking Select Nodes or No Nodes, as shown previously in Figure 9-10. Recall that removing all votes from nodes requires a disk witness, which represents a single point of failure. Click **Next**.

5. In the Select Quorum Witness window, you can configure a disk witness, a file share witness, or no witness. Configuring a witness is always recommended, so leave the default option **Configure a disk witness**, and then click **Next**.

6. In the Configure Storage Witness window, you can choose the storage device that should be the witness. Accept the default, and then click **Next**.

7. In the Confirmation window, review the selected options. You aren't making any changes, so click **Cancel**.

8. Open a PowerShell window. Type **Get-ClusterNode ServerDM1 | fl –Property NodeWeight** and press **Enter**. The value of `NodeWeight` is 1, which means that ServerDM1 has a quorum vote.

9. Type **(Get-ClusterNode ServerDM1).NodeWeight=0** and press **Enter**. Type **Get-ClusterNode ServerDM1 | fl –Property NodeWeight** and press **Enter**. The value of `NodeWeight` is now 0, meaning that ServerDM1 no longer has a quorum vote.

10. In the Failover Cluster Manager, click **Nodes** in the left pane. Look in the Assigned Vote and Current Vote columns to see that ServerDM1 doesn't have a vote. You can restore ServerDM1's vote using the Configure Quorum Settings wizard, but it's simpler to use PowerShell. From the PowerShell prompt, type **(Get-ClusterNode ServerDM1).NodeWeight=1** and press **Enter**.

11. In the PowerShell window, type **Get-Cluster | fl -Property DynamicQuorum** and press **Enter**. The value is 1, indicating that the dynamic quorum feature is enabled.

12. Type **Get-Cluster | fl -Property LowerQuorumPriorityNodeID** and press **Enter**. The default value is 0, indicating that no nodes have a lower quorum priority.

13. To get the ID of a node, type **Get-ClusterNode ServerDM1 | fl -Property Id** and press **Enter**. You can use the ID value if you want to set the `LowerQuorumPriorityNodeID` property discussed previously in "Configuring Advanced Quorum Settings."

14. Close the PowerShell window. Leave all servers running for the next activity.

Implementing Stretch Clusters

 **Certification**

- 70-740 – Implement high availability:
  Manage failover clustering

Earlier in the chapter, we discussed how to configure a failover cluster when the cluster nodes are in different physical sites (otherwise known as *multisite* or *stretch clusters*) using features such as Storage Replica and Cloud Witness. This section expands on stretch clusters configuration and explains the requirements for a stretch cluster, quorum configurations, the network configuration, data replication settings, and heartbeat settings to best support a stretch cluster. We'll also discuss a new feature in Windows Server 2016 called *site-aware failover clusters*.

- *Stretch cluster requirements*—The computer and software requirements for a stretch cluster are the same as for any failover cluster. The main consideration is the investment in physical servers and the infrastructure to support the servers and network. You should use similar server hardware for the cluster nodes in all sites, and you need to be sure that the network infrastructure in all sites supports the shared storage scheme you're using. In addition, if you decide to use a file share witness, you need a third physical site for the share, so cloud witness is recommended in lieu of file share witness.

- *Stretch cluster node and quorum configuration*—Stretch clusters work best if there's an even number of cluster nodes with a cloud witness quorum configuration. However, if you choose to use a file share witness, the file share should be in a third site, not in the same site as any of the cluster nodes. That way, if one site goes down, the file share is still available for the quorum as shown in Figure 9-22. Site 1 is the primary site with active cluster nodes providing services. Site 2 is the failover, or hot backup, site with cluster nodes in standby. The cluster storage at Site 1 is configured as read/write and is replicated to Site 2's storage, which is configured as read only. Site 3 contains the file share witness that is accessible to both sites. If Site 1 becomes inaccessible, Site 2 becomes active, and the storage becomes read/write. The use of cloud witness is similar except that you don't have to maintain a third site. Of course, your clusters must be able to access the Internet and Azure storage.

    If you can't configure the cluster with a cloud witness or file share witness at a neutral site, configure the quorum as node majority, being sure to have an odd number of nodes. The primary site has an odd number of servers, and the failover site has an even number of nodes. As discussed earlier, Windows Server 2012 and later support dynamic quorum, which is enabled by default. This feature recalculates quorum votes automatically if a cluster node leaves or returns to the cluster. In addition, Windows Server 2012 R2 and later support dynamic witness, which guarantees an odd number of votes by allowing the witness vote to be ignored if the total number of votes, including the witness, is an even number.

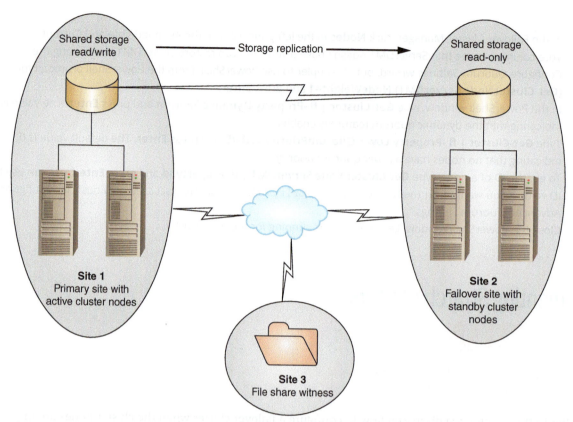

Figure 9-22 Multisite failover cluster configuration

- *Multisite cluster network configuration*—When configuring a multisite cluster, your network design probably includes multiple IP subnets, at least one per physical site. Support for multisubnet clusters has been included in Windows failover clusters since Windows Server 2008. However, client computers must be able to discover network services on another subnet when a site failover occurs. The problem lies mainly with DNS because the cluster name's IP address changes. So the effectiveness of a multisite, multisubnet cluster partially depends on how fast DNS entries are replicated between DNS servers and how quickly these entries are reported to the client. You should also consider multisite/multisubnet Hyper-V clusters. If the VMs use static IP addresses, when failover occurs, their addresses need to be configured manually for the new subnet. Using DHCP addresses for VMs solves this problem, however. Another option to consider is configuring the network with VLANs so that the cluster nodes on each site are in the same IP subnet.

- *Data replication options*—As discussed, Windows Server 2016 offers Storage Replica to replicate cluster data between sites, allowing the storage to be local to the cluster nodes.

- *Heartbeat settings*—The **heartbeat** is a signal sent between cluster nodes to inform them that a node is up and running. If a cluster node fails to send a heartbeat signal in a specific time, the node is considered unavailable. A stretch cluster might miss heartbeats sent between cluster nodes because of varying network conditions, and a cluster node might be mistakenly considered down. By default, heartbeat frequency is one per second (1000 ms) for nodes in the same subnet. If 10 heartbeats in a row are missed, failover to another cluster node occurs. You can specify heartbeat settings differently for each node, depending on whether cluster nodes are in the same or a different subnet. There are six different heartbeat settings that can be configured:

  - SameSubnetDelay: Specifies the heartbeat frequency for nodes in the same subnet. Default value is 1000 ms; range is 250 to 2000 ms.

- SameSubnetThreshold: Specifies the number of missed heartbeats for nodes in the same subnet before a failover occurs. Default value is 10 (5 for Windows Server 2012 R2); range is 3 to 120.
- CrossSubnetDelay: Specifies the heartbeat frequency for nodes in different subnets. Default value is 1000 ms; range is 250 to 4000 ms.
- CrossSubnetThreshold: Specifies the number of missed heartbeats for nodes in different subnets before a failover occurs. Default value is 20 (5 for Windows Server 2012 R2); range is 3 to 120.
- CrossSiteDelay: Specifies the heartbeat frequency for nodes in different sites. Default value is 1000 ms; range is 250 to 4000 ms. This value applies only to Windows Server 2016 and later.
- CrossSiteThreshold: Specifies the number of missed heartbeats for nodes in different sites before a failover occurs. Default value is 20; range is 3 to 120. This value applies only to Windows Server 2016 and later.

> **Note** 📎
>
> The heartbeat values for CrossSiteDelay and CrossSiteThreshold are new for Windows Server 2016 and are valid only on Windows Server 2016 clusters that have been configured for site awareness, discussed in the next section.

The delay values are configured with the `Get-Cluster` PowerShell cmdlet. Heartbeat values take place immediately, and they are set for the entire cluster at one time. The following example sets the CrossSiteDelay value to 2000 ms (2 seconds). To set any of the other five values, simply replace CrossSiteDelay with the appropriate key word from the list of heartbeat settings described above.

```
(Get-Cluster).CrossSiteDelay = 2000
```

Site-Aware Failover Clusters

Features such as dynamic quorum, the ability to set heartbeat settings based on subnets, and Storage Replica have made stretch clusters easier to manage and more reliable. However, a cluster cannot distinguish between nodes located in one city versus another, especially when virtual LANs (VLANs) are used and nodes in Pittsburgh reside on the same subnet as nodes in Phoenix. What is really needed, is a way to group nodes based on their physical location, regardless of IP address settings: enter site-aware clusters.

A **site-aware cluster** is a new feature in Windows Server 2016 that allows an administrator to assign a name to a physical location (site) and assign cluster nodes to each location. These are called *fault domains*. A **fault domain** is a property of a cluster that has name, type, description, and location values. You create a fault domain with the `New-ClusterFaultDomain` cmdlet and then assign cluster nodes to the domain. For example, if you have a stretch cluster with two cluster nodes in Pittsburgh (named PitClustServer1 and PitClustServer2) and two cluster nodes in Phoenix (named PhxClustServer1 and PhxClustServer2), you might use the following set of cmdlets to create fault domains and assign nodes to each site:

- First, create the fault domains named Pittsburgh and Phoenix:

```
New-ClusterFaultDomain -Name Pittsburgh -Type Site -Description "Active Site"
  -Location "Pittsburgh, PA USA"
New-ClusterFaultDomain -Name Phoenix -Type Site -Description "Standby Site"
  -Location "Phoenix, AZ USA"
```

- Next, assign cluster nodes to the fault domains.

```
Set-ClusterFaultDomain -Name PitClustServer1 -Parent Pittsburgh
Set-ClusterFaultDomain -Name PitClustServer2 -Parent Pittsburgh
Set-ClusterFaultDomain -Name PhxClustServer1 -Parent Phoenix
Set-ClusterFaultDomain -Name PhxClustServer2 -Parent Phoenix
```

With fault domain created, you have the following advantages that nonsite-aware clusters don't have:

- Failover will occur to a node in the same site before failing over to a node in a different site. If a node in Pittsburgh fails, clustered services will failover to a node in Pittsburgh, if possible. This is called **failover affinity**. This applies to both node failure and node drain in which nodes are taken offline manually for maintenance purposes.
- CSVs are load balanced across nodes in the same site.
- For Hyper-V clusters, VMs are kept on nodes in the same site as their storage when live migration occurs.
- Heartbeat values can be configured for cross-site scenarios using the CrossSiteDelay and CrossSiteThreshold parameters discussed in the previous section.
- You can set a preferred site where cluster services will reside when the cluster is initialized. For example, if you want the nodes in the Pittsburgh site to own the cluster resources, use the following cmdlet: (Get-Cluster).PreferredSite = Pittsburgh.
- If you use the PreferredSite option, dynamic quorum gives preference to the preferred site in the event of a 50% quorum split with no witness. The preferred site always wins quorum in this case.

Fault domains aren't limited to sites. Other fault domain types are Chassis and Rack, which are set using the -Type parameter with the New-ClusterFaultDomain cmdlet. In this way, fault domains are hierarchical. You can assign a cluster node to a chassis, a chassis to a rack, and a rack to a site, for example, using the -Parent parameter of the Set-ClusterFaultDomain cmdlet. This way, you can prioritize failover based on different location scopes. For example, if you have cluster nodes in one datacenter but located in different server racks, you can prioritize the nodes in one rack over the other, perhaps based on the rack's network connectivity or fault tolerance. The following sets of cmdlets create two rack fault domains and assign them to a site.

```
New-ClusterFaultDomain -Name Rack1Pit -Type Rack -Description "Rack 1 — Pittsburgh"
New-ClusterFaultDomain -Name Rack2Pit -Type Rack -Description "Rack 2 — Pittsburgh"
Set-ClusterFaultDomain -Name Rack1Pit -Parent Pittsburgh
Set-ClusterFaultDomain -Name Rack2Pit -Parent Pittsburgh
```

Figure 9-23 shows two nodes in Failover Cluster Manager after creating rack and site fault domains and adding the nodes to rack.

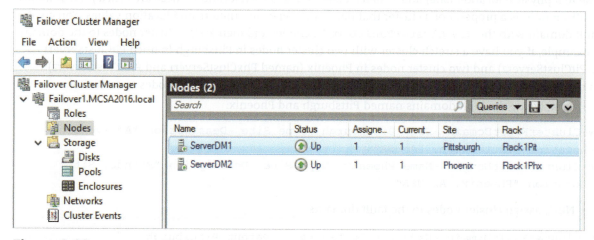

Figure 9-23 Two nodes assigned to fault domains

Implementing High Availability in Hyper-V

- **70-740 – Implement high availability:**
  Implement high availability and disaster recovery options in Hyper-V

The use of virtual machines has become standard practice in both small and large organizations. Because so many organizations depend on virtual servers for enterprise applications, being able to provide high availability to the Hyper-V hosts that run them has become paramount. This section describes the steps for configuring high availability and disaster recovery options in Hyper-V and configuring monitoring on highly available virtual machines. Later in the section "Configuring Guest Clustering," you will look at configuring a guest cluster and virtual machine movement when you learn how to move VMs easily from one Hyper-V server to another.

Configuring Highly Available Virtual Machines

A **highly available virtual machine** (also known as a *clustered virtual machine*) allows you to make applications and services highly available simply by installing them on a VM residing on a Hyper-V server configured for high availability. In other words, configuring each application or service for high availability isn't necessary because the VM it's running on is highly available. To configure a highly available VM, you need to create a failover cluster on two or more host computers running the Hyper-V role. In addition, it's best to use CSVs to store the highly available VMs because multiple VMs hosted by different Hyper-V servers can be put on the same CSV. If you use traditional shared storage, each node in the cluster requires a separate volume for its hosted VMs. Before creating a highly available VM, you should perform the following tasks:

- Verify that you have two host computers that meet requirements for the Hyper-V role and the Failover Clustering feature.
- Be sure all host computers are members of the same domain.
- Install the Hyper-V role and Failover Clustering feature on all servers participating in the failover cluster.
- Configure the shared storage the failover cluster will use.
- In Hyper-V Manager, configure the virtual networks the VMs will use.
- Validate the failover cluster configuration by running the Validate a Configuration Wizard in the Failover Cluster Manager.
- Create the failover cluster.
- Add storage to a cluster shared volume if you're using CSVs (recommended).

Creating a Highly Available VM

You can create a highly available VM directly in the Failover Cluster Manager, which configures a VM for high availability automatically. In the Failover Cluster Manager, click the Roles node, and in the Actions pane, click Virtual Machines and then New Virtual Machine to start the New Virtual Machine Wizard. The first window prompts you to choose the target cluster node to host the VM (see Figure 9-24). From that point, the New Virtual Machine Wizard runs normally as though you had started it in Hyper-V Manager.

In the Specify Name and Location window, you must select the option, *Store the virtual machine in a different location*. If you're using a CSV, select one of the virtual disk volumes in the C:\ClusterStorage folder (see Figure 9-25). If you're using traditional shared storage, specify the shared storage currently owned by the target cluster node you selected.

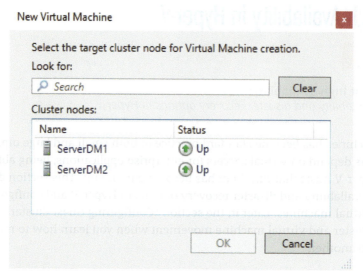

Figure 9-24   Choosing a target cluster node

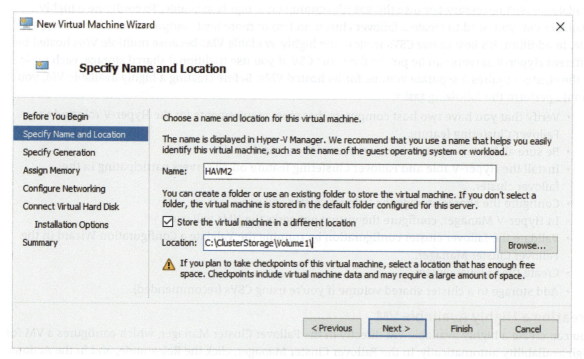

Figure 9-25   Choosing shared storage for the VM

After you specify the location, continue with the New Virtual Machine Wizard as usual. You need to select the following options for the new VM:

- *Specify the generation*—You can choose generation 1 or 2. Generation 2 VMs offer some advanced features and are recommended.
- *Assign memory*—Choose the right amount of memory for applications the VM will run.
- *Configure networking*—You should have created the virtual switches earlier; select one from the available choices.

- *Configure the virtual hard disk*—Be sure the path to the virtual hard disk points to the shared storage location—for example, C:\ClusterStorage\Volume1 if you're using CSVs. You can also attach a hard disk later or use an existing virtual hard disk. In any case, the virtual disk must be on shared storage.
- *Install an operating system*—You can specify a path to installation media or install an OS later.

The wizard creates the VM and configures it for high availability automatically. A report is generated so that you can see whether there are any errors or warnings in configuring the VM for high availability. The Roles node in the Failover Cluster Manager shows the highly available VM and its current status (see Figure 9-26). If you click the VM, you can manage it in the Failover Cluster Manager. You can test failover by using the Move option in the Actions pane, which enables you to choose Live Migration, Quick Migration, or Virtual Machine Storage. To test failover of a running VM, choose Live Migration. You can specify which node to fail over to, or you can select Best Possible Node to have the cluster service choose for you. The status of the live migration process is shown in the middle pane of the Failover Cluster Manager. Live Migration and other virtual machine movement options are discussed later in the section "Configuring Virtual Machine Movement." If the live migration is successful, you have a highly available VM.

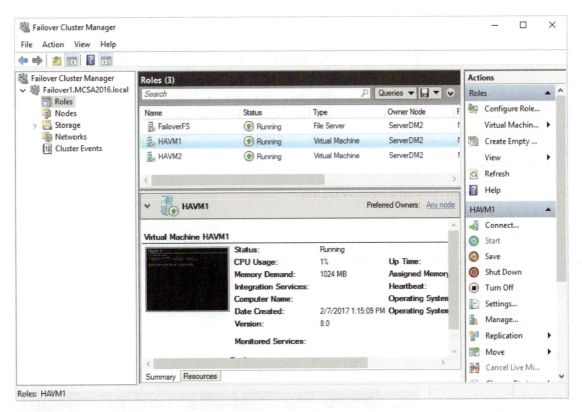

Figure 9-26   Two highly available VMs in Failover Cluster Manager

Configuring an Existing VM for High Availability

If the VM you want to configure for high availability already exists, you can move it to shared storage (with the Move option in Hyper-V Manager) and configure it for high availability in the Failover Cluster Manager. Click Configure Role in the Actions pane to start the High Availability Wizard. In the Select Role window, click Virtual Machine. You see a list of VMs you can configure for high availability. Select one or more of the VMs and continue with the High Availability Wizard.

Using Drain on Shutdown

What happens if you shut down a Hyper-V host that's configured in a cluster hosting one or more VMs? The best way to shut down a node in a Hyper-V cluster is to place it in maintenance mode by pausing it and selecting Drain Roles. Doing so signals the cluster that the host is going to be unavailable and the VMs are live-migrated automatically to another node in the cluster. To pause a node, right-click it in the Failover Cluster Manager, point to Pause, and click Drain Roles (see Figure 9-27). Then you can take the node offline for maintenance and so forth. When you resume the node, you can choose Fail Roles Back if you want the VMs (and any other clustered roles that were running on the server when it was paused) to be migrated back to that node.

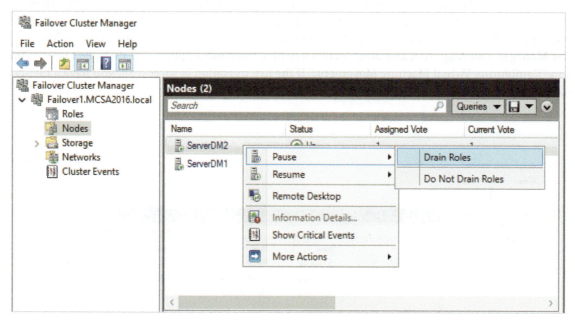

Figure 9-27   Drain roles on a Hyper-V cluster

Look back at Figure 9-26 where both VMs were running on ServerDM2. In Figure 9-27, ServerDM2 is paused and the roles are drained. Now, take a look at Figure 9-28 where both VMs were automatically live migrated to ServerDM1.

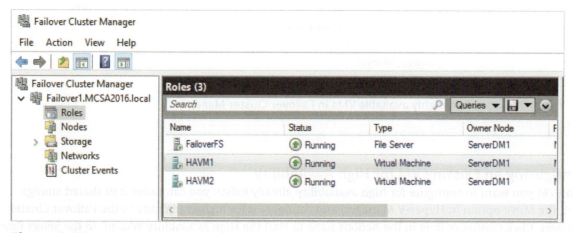

Figure 9-28   VMs were live-migrated to ServerDM1

Suppose, however, that you simply shut down a clustered Hyper-V server without pausing it first. In Windows Server 2012, the state of running VMs is saved, the VMs are moved, and then the VMs are resumed on another cluster node. This process results in downtime for VMs that are moved. Windows Server 2012 R2 introduced the **drain on shutdown** feature, which drains roles automatically and live-migrates the VMs to another cluster node before the Hyper-V server shuts down. Drain on shutdown is enabled by default on Windows Server 2012 R2 and later.

Implement Node Fairness

Node fairness is a new failover cluster feature in Windows Server 2016 that helps optimize usage of failover cluster node members. VMs hosted on clustered Hyper-V servers can move from node to node based on system reboots and maintenance operations, resulting in unbalanced distribution of VMs throughout the cluster. Node fairness attempts to identify Hyper-V nodes that are hosting a disproportionate number of VMs and redistribute VMs to other nodes that are underutilized. Live migration is used for VM movement, so no down time is incurred. Node fairness works with other failover tuning features such as fault domains. The two most important factors used for evaluating a node's load are:

- CPU utilization
- Memory utilization

Node fairness is enabled by default and can be configured using Failover Cluster Manager from the Balancer tab of the Properties page of the cluster (see Figure 9-29). As you can see from the figure, there are two Modes and three Aggressiveness levels. You can configure load balancing to load balance only when a node initially joins the cluster, or configure it to always load balance (the default value).

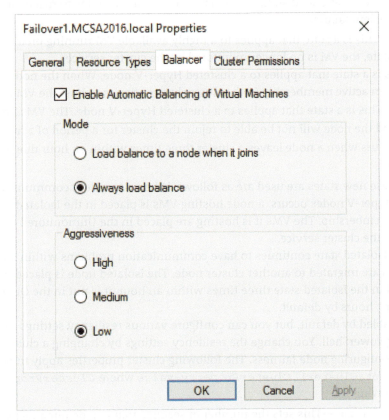

Figure 9-29   The Balancer tab of a cluster's Properties page

To configure this setting with PowerShell, you modify the `AutoBalancerMode` property of the cluster. The `AutoBalancerMode` property can have three possible values: 0 = Automatic load balancing is disabled, 1 = Load balance to a node when it joins, and 2 = Always load balance (the default). To configure the `AutoBalancerMode` property, use the following PowerShell cmdlet where *value* is 0, 1, or 2:

```
(Get-Cluster).AutoBalancerMode = value
```

The three Aggressiveness settings are described as follows:

- *Low*—Nodes are moved when the host is 80% or higher loaded. This is the default setting.
- *Medium*—Nodes are moved when the host is 70% or higher loaded.
- *High*—Nodes are moved when the host is 60% or higher loaded.

Using PowerShell, the Aggressiveness setting is configured with the `AutoBalancerLevel` property of a cluster. The `AutoBalancerLevel` property can have three possible values that determine the Aggressiveness setting: 1 = Low, 2 = Medium, and 3 = High.

To configure the `AutoBalancerLevel` property, use the following PowerShell cmdlet where *value* is 1, 2, or 3:

```
(Get-Cluster).AutoBalancerLevel = value
```

Implementing VM Resiliency

Many of the features of a failover cluster are designed to prevent or reduce downtime in the event of a catastrophic failure; however, sometimes failures are transient and short lived. Aggressive reaction to such failures sometimes causes more harm than good. Many of the failures are due to problems with communication between cluster nodes. When cluster nodes fail to communicate, the cluster takes action, assuming a node has failed or gone offline. If the communication failure is temporary, it might be better to simply wait until the problem is resolved rather than have the cluster go into failover mode. To this end, Windows Server 2016 has added additional cluster node and VM states to make highly available VMs more resilient to transient failures:

- *Unmonitored*—This is a state that applies to a highly available VM running on a clustered Hyper-V host. In this state, the VM is no longer monitored by the cluster service.
- *Isolated*—This is a state that applies to a clustered Hyper-V node. When the node is in this state, it is removed from active membership in the cluster but continues to host the VM role.
- *Quarantined*—This is a state that applies to a clustered Hyper-V node. The VMs hosted by the node are drained and the node will not be able to rejoin the cluster for a period of 2 hours by default. Quarantine occurs when a node leaves a cluster three times within an hour due to communication or other failure.

The way that these new states are used are as follows: When a transient communication failure between clustered Hyper-V nodes occurs, a node hosting VMs is placed in the Isolated state and removed from active cluster membership. The VMs it is hosting are placed in the Unmonitored state and are no longer monitored by the cluster service.

If a node in the Isolated state continues to have communication problems within 4 minutes (by default), the VMs are migrated to another cluster node. The isolated node is placed in the Down state. If the node is placed in the Isolated state three times within an hour, it is put in the Quarantined state where it remains for 2 hours by default.

Resiliency is enabled by default, but you can configure various resiliency settings to change the default values using PowerShell. You change the resiliency settings by changing a cluster property in a similar manner to configuring node fairness. The following cluster properties apply to resiliency and are changed using the `(Get-Cluster).ClusterProperty=value` where *ClusterProperty* is the setting described in the following list:

- `QuarantineDuration`—This sets the number of seconds that a node remains in quarantine. The default is 7200 (2 hours). The range is 0 to 0xffffffff. A value of 0xffffffff (or -1) means the node will remain in quarantine indefinitely until brought online manually.

- `QuarantineThreshold`—This determines the number of failures within a 1-hour period before a node is placed in the Quarantined state. The range is 0 to 3.
- `ResiliencyLevel`—A value of 2 is the default and specifies that resiliency is always used in the event of node failure. A value of 1 specifies that resiliency is used only when the cause of the failure is known. The range is 1 to 2.
- `ResiliencyDefaultPeriod`—This specifies the number of seconds nodes can remain in the Isolated state. The default value is 240 (4 minutes). The range is 0 to 0xffffffff. This setting applies to all nodes in a cluster. A value of 0 means the node will not go into Isolated state.
- `ResiliencyPeriod`—This is similar to ResiliencyDefaultPeriod but applies to a particular cluster node instead of all nodes in the cluster. Use `(Get-Cluster "Node Name")` `.ResiliencyPeriod=value` to set this property.

Another aspect of VM resiliency is VM storage resiliency. In previous versions of Windows Server, if a highly available VM lost access to its storage, it would crash. In Windows Server 2016, a highly available VM that loses access to its storage will be placed in a Paused-Critical state. If the problem is resolved within 30 minutes, the VM resumes running from the same state it was in before being paused. This feature requires that the VM's storage is on a CSV. You can configure storage resiliency using PowerShell cmdlets. To enable storage resiliency use the following:

```
Set-VM VMName -AutomaticCriticalErrorAction Pause
```

To disable storage resiliency replace `Pause` with `None` in the preceding cmdlet.

The following cmdlet specifies the amount of time a VM can remain in the Paused-Critical state before being powered off. A value of 0 powers off the VM immediately, and the maximum is 24 hours (1440 minutes).

```
Set-VM VMName -AutomaticCriticalErrorActionTimeout Minutes
```

Configuring Virtual Machine Monitoring

Virtual machine monitoring enables you to monitor resources, applications, and services running on highly available VMs. If a resource fails, the cluster node can take actions to recover, such as attempting to restart a service or moving the resource to another cluster node. VM monitoring has the following prerequisites:

- The guest OS and Hyper-V host must be running at least Windows Server 2012.
- The guest OS must be a member of the same domain as the Hyper-V host.
- The user running managing the cluster must be a member of the local Administrators group in the VM's guest OS.

To configure VM monitoring, you need to enable the Virtual Machine Monitoring firewall rule on each guest to be monitored. To do so, open Windows Firewall from Control Panel and click *Allow an app or feature through Windows Firewall*. Then click to select the Virtual Machine Monitoring rule, making sure the Domain check box is selected (see Figure 9-30).

In the Failover Cluster Manager on a VM's host machine, click Roles, right-click the VM you want to monitor (the guest OS must be running), point to More Actions, and click Configure Monitoring. In the list of services that's displayed, click to select each one you want to monitor.

If a service being monitored is determined to have failed, a service restart is attempted up to two times by default. If the service fails to start after the second restart attempt, an event with ID 1250 is generated in the System log, and the VM is restarted. If another failure occurs, the VM is moved to another cluster node and started. This behavior is the default action for a failed service. You can change the failure response policy by selecting the VM in the Failover Cluster Manager and clicking the Resource tab at the bottom of the Roles pane. Then right-click the VM and click Properties to open the VM's Properties dialog box. In the Policies tab (see Figure 9-31), you can choose whether to perform a restart and specify the time between restart attempts. In the Advanced Policies tab, you can select which cluster hosts can be owners of the resource and the resource health check intervals. Use the Settings tab to determine the actions to take if the virtual machine stops and whether automatic recovery is enabled for the virtual machine.

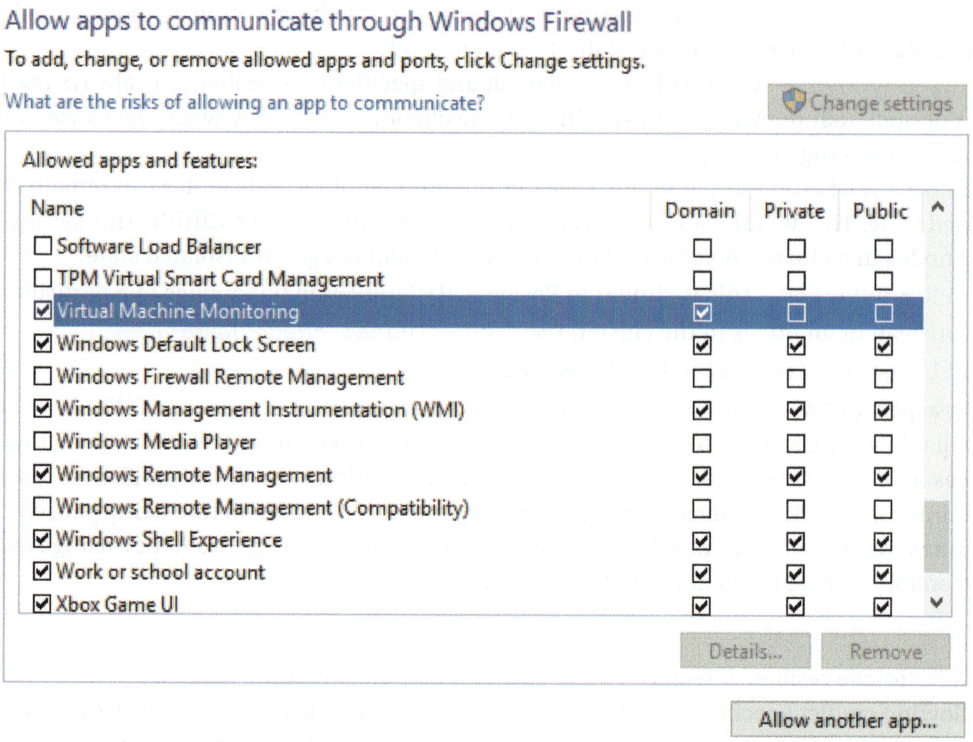

Figure 9-30 Enabling the Virtual Machine Monitoring firewall rule

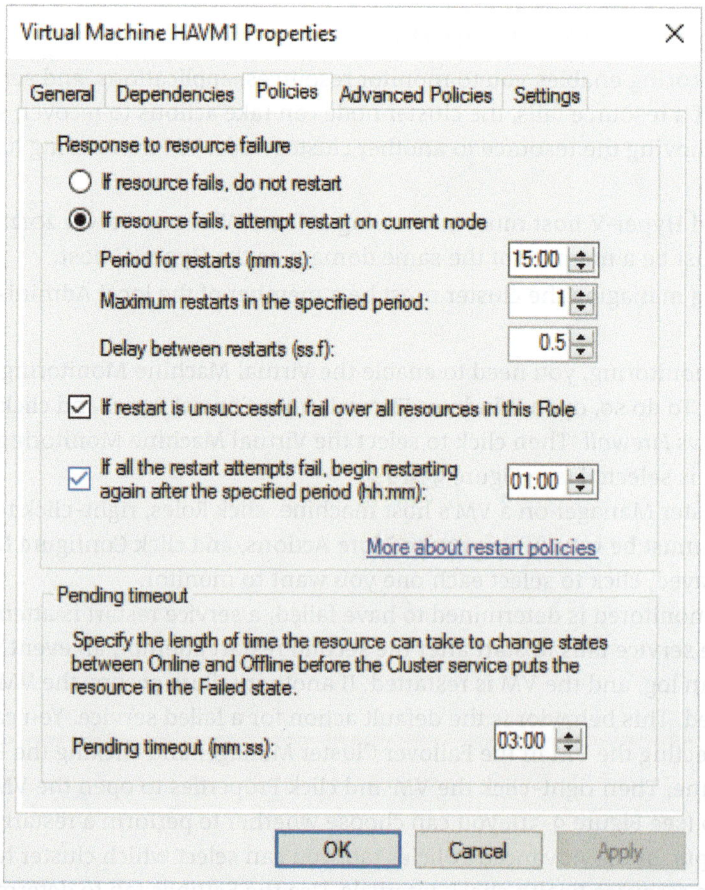

Figure 9-31 Configuring VM failure response policies

Configuring Guest Clustering

Guest clustering is different from a highly available or clustered VM in that it requires two or more VMs with a guest OS installed and configured for failover clustering. A highly available VM requires configuring the Hyper-V host server with the Failover Clustering feature, but in a guest cluster, the failover clustering occurs in the VM's guest OS. Each application requiring high availability must be configured in the guest OS by using the Failover Cluster Manager. The benefits of using guest clustering versus a clustered VM are as follows:

- *Monitoring clustered resources in the guest OS*—A clustered VM can fail over only to another Hyper-V server if the entire VM or host OS fails, but a guest cluster monitors each clustered resource, such as applications and services, network, and storage, and can initiate recovery or failover if a failure is detected.
- *Hyper-V host optimization*—VMs participating in a guest cluster can be moved easily between Hyper-V hosts to optimize Hyper-V host resource use.
- *Host failure protection*—VMs participating in a guest cluster can reside on multiple Hyper-V hosts so that clustered applications and services are protected from VM failure as well as host failure. In addition, the Hyper-V hosts can be configured in a failover cluster, adding resiliency for highly available applications.

Ideally, the VMs in a guest cluster are on separate Hyper-V servers so that if the Hyper-V host fails, the cluster can continue to function. However, you can run a guest cluster on a single Hyper-V cluster to provide some fault tolerance and for testing purposes. If you choose a single Hyper-V server to host the cluster, each cluster node should be connected to a separate virtual network assigned to its own physical NIC. In addition, each VM participating in the cluster should be stored on a separate physical disk on the host or on a shared virtual hard disk (described later). These measures provide cluster fault tolerance in case of component failure on the Hyper-V host.

To create a guest cluster, you follow the same basic procedure as for creating a failover cluster with physical hosts, and the same prerequisites apply. For example, for domain-based clusters, all the guest OSs must belong to the same Active Directory domain, and shared storage must be available to all cluster nodes. Shared storage can be provided by a SAN using iSCSI or Fibre Channel as with a physical host cluster. Starting in Windows Server 2012 R2, a guest cluster can use a shared virtual hard disk instead of traditional SAN storage.

The steps for configuring a two-node guest cluster running Windows Server 2016 and using a two-node Hyper-V failover cluster are as follows:

1. Configure the Hyper-V failover cluster as described earlier in the section "Configuring Highly Available Virtual Machines." The Hyper-V failover cluster can use a CSV or a scale-out file server for shared storage.
2. Create two highly available virtual machines.
3. Install Windows Server 2016 on both virtual machines.
4. Join each VM to an Active Directory domain.
5. Install the Failover Clustering feature on both VMs.
6. Make sure both VMs have access to the shared storage.
7. Create the failover cluster and add both VMs to the cluster.

Configuring a Shared Virtual Hard Disk

You can avoid having to configure traditional SAN storage for the guest cluster by using a **shared virtual hard disk (shared VHDX)**, which is a virtual disk created in shared storage on the Hyper-V cluster (see Figure 9-32). Using a shared VHDX is a good solution for applications running on the guest cluster, such as file sharing and database applications. In these applications, the shared folders or database files are stored on the shared VHDX. In Figure 9-32, two Hyper-V nodes make a cluster using a Cluster Shared Volume (CSV). A VM runs on each Hyper-V node, making a guest cluster using a shared VHDX for shared storage.

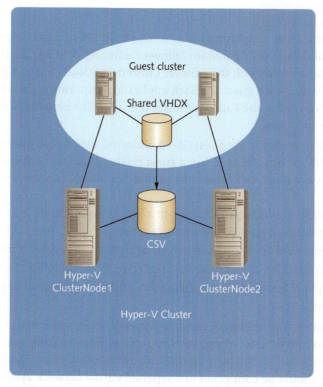

Figure 9-32 A guest cluster using a shared VHDX for cluster storage

To use a shared VHDX for a guest cluster, you need to make sure the following requirements are met:

- You have configured a Hyper-V failover cluster as described earlier in "Configuring Highly Available Virtual Machines." The Hyper-V hosts must be running Windows Server 2012 R2 or higher.
- You're using CSVs or a share on a scale-out file server to store the virtual hard disk.
- The guest OS on all cluster nodes must be running Windows Server 2012 or higher. If Windows Server 2012 is used, the guest must be updated with Windows Server 2012 R2 Integration Services.
- The shared VHDX must be connected to a virtual SCSI controller and be in the VHDX format. The shared VHDX can be a fixed-size or dynamically expanding disk but not a differencing disk.

To create a shared VHDX for a guest cluster, configure the VM from Failover Manager by clicking the Roles node, clicking the VM, and then clicking Settings. Click SCSI Controller, click Shared Drive, and then click Add (see Figure 9-33). In the Shared Drive dialog box, click New to start the New Virtual Hard Disk Wizard.

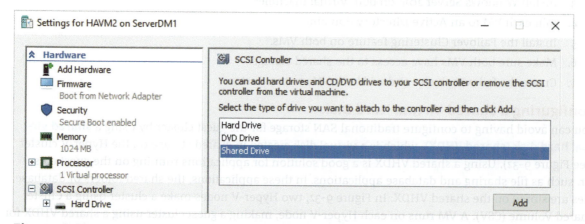

Figure 9-33 Adding a shared drive to a VM in a guest cluster

Follow the wizard as usual except that on the Choose Disk Format window, you have the option to use VHDX or VHD Set. **VHD Set** is a new option and is designed specifically for shared virtual hard disks. It enables backup of virtual machine groups and online disk resizing. VHD Set is the default option, but you can choose VHDX for backward compatibility with Windows Server 2012/R2 VMs (see Figure 9-34). In the Specify Name and Location dialog box, be sure to navigate to C:\ClusterStorage\Volume1 (or the appropriate CSV) so that the shared VHDX is stored on the CSV on the host. After you have created a shared VHDX on one VM, you can add the shared VHDX to other VMs in the guest cluster.

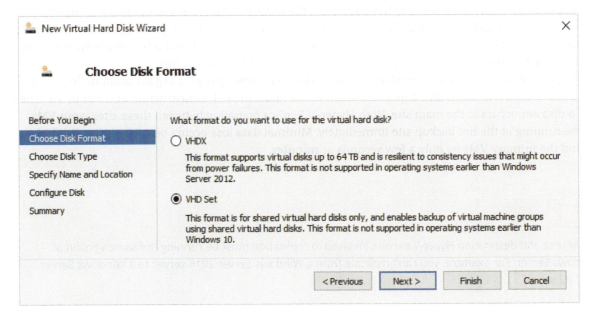

Figure 9-34   Selecting the disk format for a shared VHDX

Configuring Virtual Machine Movement

 **Certification**

- 70-740 – Implement high availability:
  Implement high availability and disaster recovery options in Hyper-V

A big advantage of using a virtual machine is making efficient use of computer and network resources. You can put multiple VMs to work on a single host server to concentrate workloads or distribute VMs among multiple hosts to spread out the workload. As you've seen, you have more resiliency with highly available VMs by using Hyper-V failover clusters, creating guest clusters, or combining both functions to have multilevel fault tolerance.

To get the most out of VMs using multiple Hyper-V hosts, you need to be able to move VMs and VM storage quickly and easily from one host to another with limited service disruption. There are several methods for moving a virtual machine, depending on why you want to move it and how your VMs and Hyper-V hosts are configured:

- Hyper-V Replica
- Live migration
- Quick migration
- Storage migration
- VM import and export

Configuring Hyper-V Replica

Hyper-V Replica periodically replicates changes in a VM to a mirror VM hosted on another Hyper-V server. It works over a regular IP network and can be enabled on standalone servers or servers in a failover cluster. There are no domain requirements, so the Hyper-V servers might or might not be members of a domain or can even be members of different domains. In addition, the Hyper-V servers can be at the same site or at different sites, so you can continue VM operation easily if a single server goes down or an entire site suffers a catastrophic failure. There are no shared storage requirements, so there's no need to configure a SAN or cluster. In fact, a VM with a shared VHDX cannot be replicated.

Replication occurs asynchronously, so although the replica VM is always in operational condition, its state might lag behind the original VM by a few seconds to a few minutes, depending on the settings and connection speed between hosts. You can configure encryption so that the data transfer between hosts is secure, and you can configure compression to reduce bandwidth requirements.

Hyper-V Replica can also be used for site-level disaster recovery if your organization maintains a **hot backup site**, a location that duplicates much of the main site's IT infrastructure and can be switched to if a disaster occurs at the main site. With Hyper-V Replica operating between these sites, your VMs can be running at the hot backup site immediately. Minimal data loss occurs because the replica VMs lag behind the primary VMs by only a few seconds or minutes.

> **Note** 📎
>
> The source and destination Hyper-V servers involved in replication must be running the same version of Windows Server. For example, you can't replicate from a Windows Server 2016 server to a Windows Server 2012 R2 server.

To configure Hyper-V Replica, follow these steps:

1. Enable replication on the Hyper-V server to receive replicated VMs. In the Settings window of Hyper-V Manager, click Replication Configuration in the left pane, and click *Enable this computer as a Replica server* (see Figure 9-35). The Hyper-V server on which you enable replication is called the **replica server**. Note that if the Hyper-V server is a member of a failover cluster, the option to enable replication in Hyper-V Manager is disabled; you need to configure replication settings in the Failover Cluster Manager console.

2. Select the authentication method. You can select Kerberos authentication (using port 80 by default, but you can change the port), but data transfers aren't encrypted with this authentication method. You can also select certificate-based authentication, which encrypts data transfers over HTTPS. You should choose certificate-based authentication if the two Hyper-V servers aren't members of the same forest.

3. Specify servers that can replicate to this server and the storage location. You can allow any server that authenticates to replicate to this server or select specific servers. If you select specific servers, you can specify a different storage location for each one. After you finish configuring replication, you're prompted to configure the firewall.

4. Configure firewall rules to allow replication. Create a new inbound firewall rule on the replication server that enables the predefined Hyper-V Replica HTTP Listener (TCP-In) rule.

5. Configure each VM you want to replicate on one or more source servers that you want to replicate to the replica server. These steps are explained in the next section.

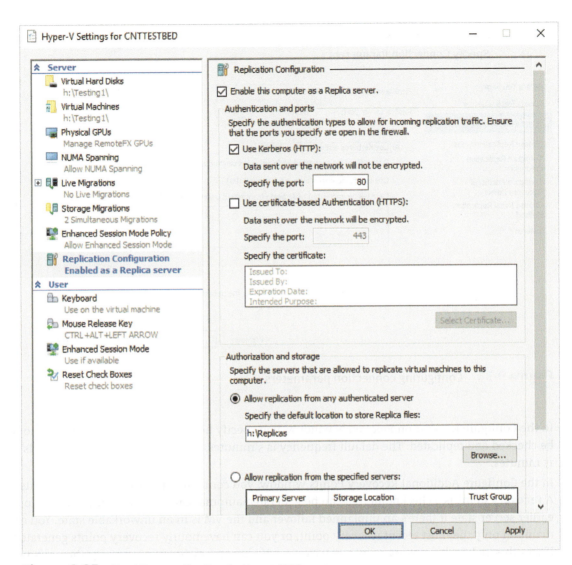

Figure 9-35   Enabling replication in Hyper-V Manager

Enabling Replication on a Virtual Machine

Before a VM can be replicated to the replica server, replication must be configured in the VM's settings. To do so, follow these steps:

1. In Hyper-V Manager, click the VM you want to enable replication for, and in the Actions pane, click Enable Replication. The Enable Replication Wizard begins.

2. In the Specify Replica Server window, type the name of the replica server or click Browse to select one.

3. In the Specify Connection Parameters window, you choose the authentication method and whether to compress network data (see Figure 9-36). The authentication method must match the authentication method on the replica server.

4. In the Choose Replication VHDs window, exclude the virtual disks that shouldn't be replicated. By default, all virtual disks are replicated, but you can deselect any that shouldn't be.

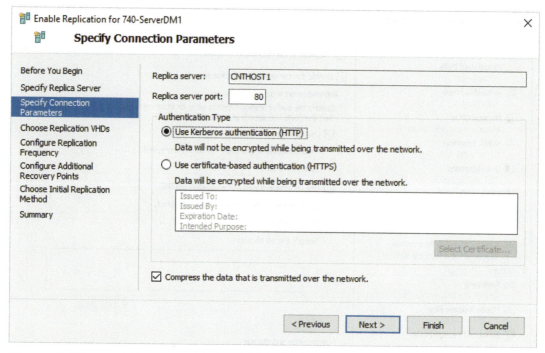

Figure 9-36 Configuring connection parameters

5. In the Configure Replication Frequency window, you specify how often changes to the VM should be checked and replicated. The default frequency is 5 minutes, and you can choose 30 seconds or 15 minutes.

6. In the Configure Additional Recovery Points window, you configure options for recovery points. A **recovery point** is a checkpoint that can be generated automatically so that you can revert to an earlier server state if there's an unplanned failover and the VM is in an unworkable state. You can maintain only the most recent recovery point, or you can have hourly recovery points generated. If you choose hourly recovery points, you can specify how many hours of coverage (how many hourly recovery points to maintain), as shown in Figure 9-37.

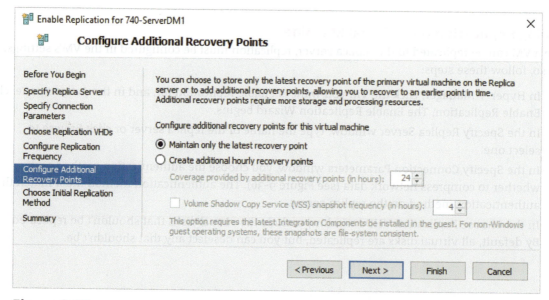

Figure 9-37 Configuring recovery points

7. In the Choose Initial Replication Method window, you can send the initial replica over the network or export a copy of the VM to external media. If the VM is very large or the replica server is located across a low bandwidth link, using external media might be the best option. The initial replica copy requires the most bandwidth; from then on, only changes are replicated. You can also start the replication immediately or at a scheduled date and time (see Figure 9-38).

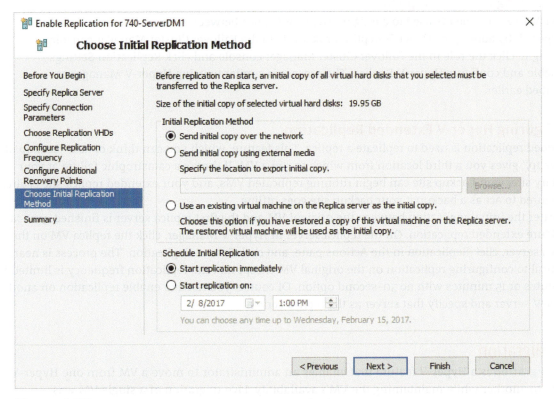

Figure 9-38   Specifying the initial replication method

8. When you have finished configuration and replication begins, you're prompted to configure the network connection settings on the replicated VM if the virtual networks on the source and destination Hyper-V server don't match. When replication begins, check the status by clicking the VM, and in the Actions pane, click Replication, View Replication Health. The following are other options on the Replication menu in the Actions pane from the replica VM side (not the original VM):

- Failover: This option should be used when the primary VM fails. If the primary VM is still running, this option won't work.
- Test Failover: Verify the replica's health so that you know it will work in an actual failover. The original VM continues to work normally.
- Pause Replication: Pause the replication process.
- Extend Replication: This option is discussed later in Configuring Hyper-V Extended Replication.
- Import Initial Replica: This option is available only if you specified using external media for initial replication.
- Remove Replication: This option stops replication but doesn't delete the replica VM.

From the source Hyper-V server, the replication actions you can perform on a replicated VM include the Pause Replication, Remove Replication, and View Replication Health options already discussed. In addition, you have the Planned Failover option. A planned failover is initiated only on the source Hyper-V server. It should be used when you need to take the source server down for maintenance or when you know a service outage is imminent, such as a planned power outage or a coming storm.

Configuring Hyper-V Replica Broker

Hyper-V Replica Broker is used to configure Hyper-V Replica between failover cluster nodes. You configure it by adding the Hyper-V Replica Broker role in the Failover Cluster Manager console. Then right-click the role in the Failover Cluster Manager console and click Replication Settings to enable and configure Hyper-V Replica. The process is similar to using Hyper-V Manager as described earlier.

Configuring Hyper-V Extended Replication

Extended replication is used to replicate a replica. This feature, which you can think of as a "backup of a backup," gives you a third location from which to run a VM. If there's a catastrophic failure at your primary site, your backup site can begin running replicated VMs, and your extended replica site is already configured to act as a backup if your backup site goes offline.

After the initial replication between the original VM and the first replica server is finished, you can configure extended replication. On the replica server in Hyper-V Manager, click the replica VM on the replica server, click Replication in the Actions pane, and click Extend Replication. The process is nearly identical to configuring replication on the original VM except that the replication frequency is limited to 5 minutes or 15 minutes with no 30-second option. Of course, you need to enable replication on another Hyper-V server and specify that server as the replica server.

Live Migration

Live migration is a Hyper-V feature that enables an administrator to move a VM from one Hyper-V server to another while maintaining the VM's availability. Live migration of a single VM was introduced in Windows Server 2008 R2, and Windows Server 2012 added the capability to live-migrate multiple VMs simultaneously. Before you can use live migration, the environment must meet these prerequisites:

- Two or more servers running the Hyper-V role or Hyper-V server.
- The same processor manufacturer. For example, both servers must be running Intel processors or AMD processors. You can't live-migrate between Hyper-V servers with processors from different manufacturers.
- The name of the virtual switches used by the VMs must be the same on each Hyper-V server.
- The VM to be migrated must be using virtual hard disks, not pass-through disks.

Live migration is enabled by default on clustered Hyper-V servers but not on nonclustered servers. In addition, the initial live migration setting allows you to perform two simultaneous live migrations. You can enable or disable live migrations or change the limit in Hyper-V Manager by opening the Hyper-V Settings window and clicking Live Migrations in the left pane (see Figure 9-39). The Live Migrations dialog box is also where you can specify which IP addresses can be used to perform migrations. If you have multiple NICs, for example, you can specify a network to use.

Figure 9-39   Changing live migration settings

Virtual machines can be live-migrated in different ways, depending on the virtual environment configuration. The preceding prerequisites apply to all live migration methods. Specific live migration settings might have additional requirements. The following types of live migrations are discussed in this section:

- Cluster live migration
- Live migration with SMB shares
- Shared-nothing live migration
- Cross-version live migration

Cluster Live Migrations

VM live migrations between two Hyper-V servers configured in a cluster are usually very fast. Because the VM files are stored on shared storage, ownership of the VM transfers between the cluster nodes quickly, and then the memory state of the running VM must be transferred. A typical clustered live migration generally occurs in seconds rather than minutes. Additional requirements for clustered live migrations include the following:

- Two or more Hyper-V servers configured in a failover cluster.
- Shared storage set up with CSVs or SMB shares.

To perform a cluster live migration, select a virtual machine in the Failover Cluster Manager, click Move in the Actions pane, point to Live Migration, and then click Best Possible Node if you want the Failover Cluster Manager to select the node to migrate to, or click Select Node if you want to choose the node. The live migration starts, and its status is shown in the Information column for the VM in the middle pane.

Live Migrations with SMB Shares

You can perform live migration between two Hyper-V servers that aren't clustered if the VMs are stored on an SMB share and the Hyper-V hosts are members of the same domain or are in trusted domains. In this case, the VM's configuration files and virtual hard disks are in a file share accessible by both Hyper-V servers. The permissions on the share must grant access to both Hyper-V server computer accounts. When you create the VMs, you must use the share's UNC path to specify the VM's location and its virtual disk location.

In addition, you must sign in to the source Hyper-V server (the one currently running the VM) to perform the migration or configure constrained delegation. By default, live migration uses the Credential Security Support Provider (CredSSP) authentication protocol, which is suitable if you perform the migration from the source Hyper-V server. If you want to use remote management with PowerShell or Remote Desktop to perform the migration, you must use the Kerberos protocol and configure constrained delegation. You can configure the authentication protocol in Hyper-V Manager by clicking Advanced Features under the Live Migrations settings shown previously in Figure 9-39.

Shared-Nothing Live Migrations

Another option for performing live migrations between nonclustered Hyper-V servers is **shared-nothing live migration**. As the name implies, the live migration is done between Hyper-V servers that have no common storage. The VM's files are stored in local storage on the Hyper-V server. This type of live migration takes the longest because all the VM's files must be copied across the network to the destination Hyper-V server. The virtual machine storage is copied from the source Hyper-V server while it continues to run, and then the configuration files and the running VM's memory contents are copied. The VM remains available to clients throughout the operation. To perform shared-nothing live migration, follow these steps:

1. Verify that all prerequisites for live migration discussed earlier have been met.
2. Enable live migrations on all Hyper-V servers.
3. Sign in to the source Hyper-V server, and open Hyper-V Manager.
4. Select the VM to be migrated and click Move in the Actions pane.
5. In the Choose Move Type window, click Move the virtual machine. (You also have the option to move just the VM's storage, but for a live migration, you must move the entire VM.)
6. Specify the name of the destination Hyper-V server.
7. Choose whether to move the VM's data and configuration file to a single location or specify the location of each item. Moving the VM's data and configuration file to a single location is easiest, but you can specify different locations for the configuration file, virtual disks, snapshot files, and paging file, if necessary.
8. Select the locations on the destination server.

You can also use shared-nothing live migration to move VMs between servers that are members of different clusters. To do so, first remove the VM from the cluster in the Failover Cluster Manager. Next, use Hyper-V to move the VM to the destination Hyper-V server that's a member of a different cluster, using the shared-nothing live migration procedure described previously. Finally, add the VM to the cluster in the Failover Cluster Manager. You don't need to shut down a VM to remove it from or add it to a cluster.

Cross-Version Live Migrations

You can move a VM running on a Windows Server 2012 R2 server to a Windows Server 2016 server, but the reverse isn't possible. The VM configuration must be at least version 5 (the Windows Server 2012 R2 version). This option allows you to upgrade Hyper-V servers to Windows Server 2016 without any VM downtime. All the live migration methods discussed in this section are available.

Quick Migration

Quick migration is a migration option available only between Hyper-V servers in a failover cluster. The advantage is that it's available in Windows Server 2008 Hyper-V servers and later. Unlike live migration in which there's no downtime for the migrated VM, a quick migration usually results in a minute or more of downtime, depending on how much memory the VM uses. Quick migration involves copying the VM data to the destination Hyper-V node, saving the VM's state on the source node, and then copying the machine state to the destination Hyper-V node and resuming the servers. To perform a quick migration, select the VM you want to use in the Failover Cluster Manager, click Move in the Actions pane, and click Quick Migration. Like a live migration, you can choose the node you want to move the VM to, or you can let the Failover Cluster Manager select the best possible node. You can use quick migration in the following situations:

- Your Hyper-V servers are running Windows Server 2008. (Live migration wasn't available until Window Server 2008 R2.)
- You want to distribute VMs to different cluster nodes during off hours and don't require live migrations.
- You need to perform maintenance on the current host server.

Storage Migration

A **storage migration** is usually used when you simply need to move a VM's storage from one volume to another without actually moving the VM to another Hyper-V server. You can perform a storage migration while the VM is still running or when it's shut down. You might want to do a storage migration for the following reasons:

- The current storage location is running low on free space, and you have added new storage.
- You want to move the VM's virtual disks from local storage to shared storage in preparation for making the VM highly available.
- You want to move VM storage to a temporary location while the server's storage system is upgraded.
- You want to move the VM's virtual disks to higher performing storage, such as an SSD.

You can perform a storage migration on a Hyper-V cluster or a standalone Hyper-V server. In the Failover Cluster Manager, select the VM, click Move in the Actions pane, and then click Virtual Machine Storage. You can choose some or all of the VM's data files, including the virtual hard disks, checkpoints, paging file, and configuration files. You see a list of available shared storage as the destination, or you can add an SMB share to the list of destinations.

On a standalone Hyper-V server, select the VM, and click Move in the Actions pane. In the Move Wizard, you can choose between moving the entire VM or just the VM storage. You can move all storage items to the same location, choose different locations for each item, or just move the machine's virtual hard disks.

VM Export and Import

The virtual machine movement options discussed earlier simply move a VM, its data, or both to a different location on the same server, within a cluster, or on different servers. Virtual machine export creates a copy of an existing VM, and virtual machine import creates a new VM. To export or import a VM on a Hyper-V cluster, use the PowerShell cmdlets `Export-VM` and `Import-VM` from any node in the cluster. To easily move the VM among cluster nodes, you can specify shared storage as the destination. The following list describes a situation in which you might want to use VM exporting and importing:

- *Export a virtual machine to create a backup*—The VM can later be imported on the same Hyper-V host to replace an existing VM that became corrupted or on another Hyper-V host if the original host fails or is being replaced.
- *Export a virtual machine to create a copy*—After you export the VM, you can import it into a new VM, thereby saving the time needed to install the OS.
- *Export a VM to be moved to another host*—The virtual machine move or live migration options discussed earlier are generally preferable to performing an export and then an import, but circumstances might prevent you from using the other options, such as a failure on the original host or the target Hyper-V server not being on the same network as the original.

> **Note**
>
> More details on exporting and importing VMs can be found in Chapter 6.

Configuring Virtual Machine Network Health Protection

Virtual machine network health protection is a feature that automatically moves a VM from one cluster node to another if a network disconnection is detected. Virtual machine network health protection is configured on the network interface on each VM and is enabled by default. To enable or disable the feature, open the settings for a VM in Hyper-V Manager or the Failover Cluster Manager, click to expand the network adapter you want to change, and click Advanced Features. Click to enable or disable the *Protected network* check box. To enable or disable network protection using PowerShell, you need to set the `NotMonitoredInCluster` property of the VM's network adapter. To enable network protection (the default setting), set the value of the property to `$false`, and to disable it, set the value to `$true` as follows:

```
Get-VM VMName | Set-VMNetworkAdapter -NotMonitoredInCluster $true
```

Activity 9-3: Performing a Live Migration

Time Required: 35 minutes

Objective: Perform a live migration.

Required Tools and Equipment: ServerDC1, ServerDM1, and ServerHyperV

Description: In this activity, you install the Hyper-V role on ServerDM1. You'll also join ServerHyperV to the domain. You then configure live migration on both servers and migrate the VM from ServerHyperV to ServerDM1. Because you won't be using shared storage for this migration, this is referred to as a *shared-nothing live migration*.

1. Start ServerDC1, ServerDM1, and ServerHyperV, if necessary. On ServerDM1, sign in to the domain as **Administrator**.
2. On ServerDM1, open a PowerShell window and type **Install-WindowsFeature Hyper-V IncludeManagementTools –Restart** and press **Enter**. Hyper-V is installed and the computer restarts.
3. While Hyper-V is installing on ServerDM1, sign in to ServerHyperV as **Administrator**. You will add ServerHyperV to the domain. Open a PowerShell prompt and type **Add-Computer –DomainName mcsa2016.local –Restart** and press **Enter**. When prompted for credentials, type **administrator** and **Password01**. ServerHyperV restarts and is now a member of the MCSA2016.local domain.
4. On ServerHyperV, sign in to the domain as **Administrator**. (From the sign-in screen, click **Other user** and type **mcsa2016\administrator and Password01**). Open **Hyper-V Manager**.
5. In the left pane of Hyper-V Manager, click **ServerHyperV**, if necessary. In the Actions pane, click **Hyper-V Settings**.
6. In the left pane, click **Live Migrations** and in the right pane, click **Enable incoming and outgoing live migrations**, if necessary.
7. Click **Use any available network for live migration** and click **OK**. Sign out of ServerHyperV; this is necessary for the type of live migration authentication you are using (CredSSP).
8. Sign in to ServerDM1 and open Hyper-V Manager. Click **ServerDM1** in the left pane, and click **Hyper-V Settings** in the Actions pane.
9. Click **Live Migrations** and click **Enable incoming and outgoing live migrations**, if necessary. Click **Use any available network for live migration** and click **OK**.
10. You need to create a virtual switch that the migrated VM will use when it is moved to this Hyper-V host. Click **Virtual Switch Manager**, click **Private**, and click **Create Virtual Switch**. In the Name box, type **PrivateNet**. Click **OK**. PrivateNet is the name of the virtual switch on ServerHyperV.

11. Sign in to ServerHyperV and open Hyper-V Manager. Start **ServerVM1**. Once ServerVM1 is started, right-click it, and click **Move** to start the wizard. Click **Next**.

12. In the Choose Move Type window, accept the default option of **Move the virtual machine** and click **Next**. Notice the other option is to move only the virtual machine's storage (a storage migration).

13. In the Specify Destination window, type **ServerDM1** and click **Next**.

14. In the Choose Move Options window, accept the default of **Move the virtual machine's data to a single location** and click **Next**.

15. In the Virtual Machine window, type **C:\VMs** and click **Next**. The folder C:\VMs will be created during the migration process. Click **Finish**.

16. The move takes some time because it has to move the virtual machine files and virtual hard disk to the other server. If the VM was stored on shared storage such as a Scale Out File Server or CSV, the move would occur much faster. When the move is finished, go to ServerDM1, open Hyper-V Manager, and verify the VM is there and running.

17. Shut down ServerHyperV but leave the other machines running for the next activity.

Activity 9-4: Destroying a Failover Cluster

> **Note** 📎
>
> In the next two activities, you destroy the failover cluster and shared iSCSI storage. If you think you will want to work more with failover clusters, it is advisable to shut down the servers and create a snapshot with a name such as FailoverClusters so that you can revisit failover clusters if desired.

Time Required: 15 minutes

Objective: Destroy a failover cluster.

Required Tools and Equipment: ServerDC1, ServerDM1, and ServerDM2

Description: You're finished working with failover clusters, so in this activity, you remove the Failover1FS role, evict ServerDM2 from the cluster, and then destroy the cluster. Although evicting nodes from the cluster first isn't necessary, you do it for practice.

1. Start ServerDC1, ServerDM1, and ServerDM2, if necessary. On ServerDM1, sign in to the domain as **Administrator**.

2. On ServerDM1, open Server Manager, and start the Failover Cluster Manager, if necessary. In the left pane, click to expand **Failover1.MCSA2016.local**, and then click **Roles**.

3. In the middle pane, right-click **Failover1FS** and click **Remove**. In the Remove File Server message box, click **Yes**.

4. Next, you evict ServerDM2; however, you can't evict a node that causes the cluster to lose a quorum. So first you need to give ServerDM1 its quorum vote back that you removed in Activity 9-2. Open a PowerShell window, and then type **(Get-ClusterNode ServerDM1).NodeWeight=1** and press **Enter**. Close the PowerShell window.

5. In the left pane of the Failover Cluster Manager, click **Nodes**. ServerDM1 has its vote restored. In the middle pane, right-click **ServerDM2**, point to **More Actions**, and click **Evict**. In the Evict node ServerDM2 message box, click **Yes**.

6. In the left pane of the Failover Cluster Manager, right-click **Failover1.MCSA2016.local**, point to **More Actions**, and click **Destroy Cluster**. In the Destroy Cluster message box, click **Yes**. Close the Failover Cluster Manager.

7. Leave all servers running for the next activity.

Activity 9-5: Removing the iSCSI Configuration

Time Required: 15 minutes
Objective: Remove the iSCSI configuration.
Required Tools and Equipment: ServerDC1, ServerDM1, and ServerDM2
Description: You're finished working with iSCSI, so in this activity, you disconnect the iSCSI volumes, delete the iSCSI targets, and then delete the volume on the second disk on ServerDC1.

1. Start ServerDC1, ServerDM1, and ServerDM2, if necessary. On ServerDM1, sign in to the domain as **Administrator**.
2. On ServerDM1, open Server Manager, if necessary, and click **Tools, iSCSI Initiator** from the menu. Click the **Targets** tab, if necessary. Click the target in the Discovered targets list box, and click **Disconnect**. In the Disconnect From All Sessions message box, click **Yes**. Click **OK**.
3. On ServerDM2, sign in to the domain as **Administrator**. This needs to be changed for PowerShell.
4. On ServerDC1, sign in as **Administrator**. Open Server Manager, if necessary. Click **File and Storage Services**, and then click **iSCSI**.
5. In the middle pane, scroll down until you see the iSCSI Targets section. Right-click the target and click **Remove Target**. In the Remove Target message box, click **Yes**.
6. Scroll up to the iSCSI Virtual Disks section, and then right-click **vdisk1** and click **Remove iSCSI Virtual Disk**. In the Remove iSCSI Virtual Disk message box, click the **Delete the iSCSI virtual disk file from the disk** check box, and click **OK**. Repeat this step for **vdisk2**.
7. Shut down all servers.

Implementing Storage Spaces Direct

 Certification

- 70-740 – Implement high availability:
  Implement Storage Spaces Direct

You learned about Storage Spaces in Chapter 4. **Storage Spaces Direct (S2D)** is a new feature in Windows Server 2016 that extends the storage pool concept on a single server to multiple servers in a failover cluster. In other words, storage pools can be distributed among all the nodes in a failover cluster and as new nodes are added, their storage can be automatically added to the storage pools. Storage Spaces Direct is available only with the Datacenter edition of Windows Server 2016 and can be implemented on the Desktop Experience, Server Core, or Nano Server installation options.

The target application for Storage Spaces Direct is to provide storage in the form of a Cluster Shared Volume for highly available VMs in a Hyper-V failover cluster. Although S2D is not limited to that application, it is the scenario we'll focus on. With that in mind, the implementation of Storage Spaces Direct has the following requirements and recommendations:

- *Two to 16 servers*—All servers must be running the Datacenter edition of Windows Server 2016 and must meet the requirements for a failover cluster.
- *High-speed 10 GB Ethernet adapters that use RDMA (recommended)*—Microsoft also recommends two NICs for fault tolerance and performance. A lower-performance network can be used, particularly for lab and testing purposes, but should not be used in production environments.
- *Each server with at least four locally attached drives via SATA, SAS, or Non-Volatile Memory Express (NVMe)*—A minimum of six drives is recommended with at least two of the drives being SSD or NVMe. (Note that if S2D is deployed using VMs or virtualized storage, only two virtual drives, in addition to the OS drive, per server are required). All servers in the cluster must have the same type and number of drives and firmware versions must match.
- *RAID HBA controllers, MPIO-enabled storage, and SAN devices are not supported.*

There are two ways to deploy Storage Spaces Direct: hyper-converged and disaggregated. Hyper-converged S2D places Hyper-V and Storage Spaces Direct on the same cluster, whereas disaggregated S2D uses two clusters, a Storage Spaces Direct cluster and a Hyper-V cluster. The details of these two deployments are discussed later. Regardless of the deployment scenario, the basic setup is the same.

Enabling Storage Spaces Direct

To begin using Storage Spaces Direct, build a failover cluster that meets the requirements. You should not configure an iSCSI SAN because shared storage will be provided by S2D. In fact, when you create the cluster, you should specify that the cluster does not add available storage to the cluster. You should, of course, validate the cluster configuration before you create the cluster. Because you don't set up shared storage beforehand, the cluster validation will warn you about not having suitable storage. Alternatively, you can run the validation to test specifically for Storage Spaces Direct and exclude the normal storage tests using the following cmdlet:

```
Test-Cluster -Node ClusServer1,ClusServer2,ClusServer3 -Include
   "Inventory","Network","System Configuration", "Storage Spaces Direct"
```

By default, the cluster creation process searches for available storage and adds the storage to the cluster. In this case, you don't want that to occur. To create a cluster so that the cluster does not automatically add storage, use the following PowerShell cmdlet, being sure to include the -NoStorage option:

```
New-Cluster S2DCluster -node ClusServer1,ClusServer2,ClusServer3 -NoStorage
```

Storage Spaces Direct is enabled on an entire cluster using PowerShell or System Center Virtual Machine Manager (SCVMM), an add-on product for Windows Server 2016. To enable S2D with PowerShell, use the following cmdlet on any of the cluster nodes:

```
Enable-ClusterS2D
```

That's it; pretty simple. This cmdlet enables S2D, locates all available storage on all cluster nodes and creates a new S2D storage pool that is available to all cluster nodes. If SSD or NVMe disks are available, the pool is created using storage tiers so that the fastest storage is used for disk caching.

> Just as with Storage Spaces, it's important that the disks used for S2D are online and initialized, but no partitions or volumes have been created prior to enabling S2D.

The default name of the storage pool created is "S2D on *ClusterName*" where *ClusterName* is the name of the cluster created with the New-Cluster cmdlet, in this case, S2DCluster. You can specify a storage pool name if desired by adding the -S2DPoolFriendlyName *PoolName* parameter to the Enable-ClusterS2D cmdlet where *PoolName* is the name you would like to use.

Creating the Virtual Disks and Volumes

The next step is to create virtual disk volumes from the new S2D pool. The easiest way to do this is by using the New-Volume PowerShell cmdlet from any cluster node. The following cmdlet creates a 1 TB volume named ClusVol1 in the S2DPool storage pool and uses the CSVFS_ReFS file system. CSVFS_ReFS is specifically used for Cluster Shared Volumes and formats the volumes with ReFS. You can also use CSVFS_NTFS. If your application doesn't use CSVs, you can use NTFS or ReFS. By default, S2D creates two-way mirrored volumes on two-server clusters or three-way mirrored volumes on three-server clusters. If you have four or more servers, you can create parity volumes using the -ResiliencySettingName Parity parameter.

```
New-Volume -StoragePoolFriendlyName S2DPool -FriendlyName
   ClusVol1 -FileSystem CSVFS_ReFS -Size 1TB
```

You can also create volumes in which you specify tiered storage. Storage Spaces Direct has predefined tier templates called *Performance and Capacity* that can be used in the New-Volume cmdlet. The Performance template uses mirror resiliency, and the Capacity template uses parity resiliency. For example, if you want to create the same volume as specified in the previous cmdlet except that you want 200 GB of storage to use the Performance template and 800 GB to use the Capacity template, you can use the following cmdlet:

```
New-Volume -StoragePoolFriendlyName S2DPool -FriendlyName
   ClusVol1 -FileSystem CSVFS_ReFS -StorageTiersFriendlyNames
   Performance,Capacity -StorageTierSizes 200GB,800GB
```

It may seem strange that both mirrored and parity resiliency are being used on a single volume, but that's a new feature in Windows Server 2016 when tiers are used. Data is first written to the faster, mirrored part of the volume and later moved to the higher capacity parity portion of the volume.

Implementing Hyper-Converged Storage Spaces Direct

In a **hyper-converged Storage Spaces Direct deployment**, the storage and the Hyper-V role are part of the same cluster. All cluster nodes have Hyper-V installed, and all nodes have S2D enabled. The advantage of this model is that there is only one cluster to manage and less network traffic because there is no cross-cluster network traffic. The disadvantage is that scaling cluster resources is an all-or-nothing proposition. If you need more storage, you need to add another cluster node that includes both S2D and Hyper-V; if you need only more Hyper-V resources, you need to add another cluster node that includes Hyper-V and S2D with the required amount of storage. This deployment scenario is best for small and medium-sized deployments. In this scenario, you add the Storage Spaces volumes you create to CSV storage using Cluster Failover Manager (or PowerShell), which Hyper-V uses for VM storage (see Figure 9-40). In the figure, you would likely have more servers than depicted. A typical Storage Spaces Direct solution uses four servers for optimal fault tolerance.

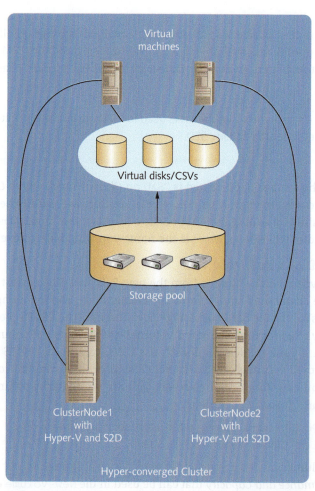

Figure 9-40   A hyper-converged Storages Spaces Direct implementation

Implementing Disaggregated Storage Spaces Direct

In a **disaggregated Storage Spaces Direct deployment**, there are two separate clusters: an S2D cluster and a Hyper-V cluster. Using this scenario, the Hyper-V cluster can be scaled independently of the storage cluster and vice versa. For example, you can have a Hyper-V cluster composed of three nodes and an S2D cluster composed of four nodes. Later, if you need more storage, you can add a node to the S2D cluster without affecting the Hyper-V cluster. A disaggregated S2D deployment uses Scale-out File Servers to offer the CSVs used by the Hyper-V hosts for VM storage (Figure 9-41). In that figure, the Hyper-V cluster uses storage provided by the S2D cluster for VM storage.

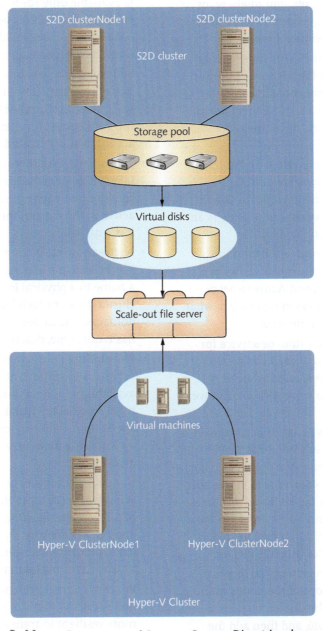

Figure 9-41   A disaggregated Storage Spaces Direct implementation

Chapter Summary

- After a cluster has been created, you might need to perform some management tasks, including validating the cluster, adding nodes to it, or shutting it down or destroying it. You might also need to move cluster roles or resources from one cluster to another.

- Although the cluster creation process configures suitable cluster quorum settings, you might want to change the quorum configuration if you add or remove cluster nodes or a witness disk.

- Dynamic witness is a feature in which the cluster determines whether to give the witness a quorum vote. If there are an odd number of cluster nodes, the witness doesn't have a vote, but if there are an even number of cluster nodes, the witness does have a quorum vote.

- Failover clusters have a feature called dynamic quorum, which is enabled by default. With dynamic quorum, a cluster node vote is assigned dynamically, depending on whether the node is an active member of the cluster.

- Cloud witness is a new quorum witness option introduced in Windows Server 2016. It allows you to specify a resource in Microsoft Azure to act as the cluster witness. The witness in this case is what Microsoft Azure refers to as a file blob.

- When you configure an application or service for high availability, there are two broad categories: cluster-aware and generic. A cluster-aware service or application is designed to work with the Failover Clustering feature.

- If you're running a Windows Server 2012 R2 failover cluster and want to migrate to a Windows Server 2016 cluster, you have a few options. One option is to add two nodes running Windows Server 2016 to the existing cluster and then transfer the roles and resources to the new nodes. After the resources and roles have been transferred, you can evict (remove) the older Windows Server 2012 R2 nodes from the cluster.

- Another upgrade option is to perform an in-place upgrade in which you evict one of the nodes running Windows Server 2012 from the cluster, upgrade the server to Windows Server 2016, and then add the node back to the cluster. After the node is rejoined to the cluster, transfer resources and roles to the new Windows Server 2016 node and evict another node running Windows Server 2012. Upgrade this node, and then rejoin it to the cluster.

- Windows Server 2016 offers an additional cluster OS upgrade option called Cluster Operating System Rolling Upgrade. With Cluster Operating System Rolling Upgrade, you can upgrade a Windows Server 2012 R2 cluster to a Windows Server 2016 cluster without taking the workloads offline. This option is available only for SoFS and Hyper-V cluster configurations; other workloads running on the cluster will be unavailable for a short period while a node is being upgraded.

- You can deploy a failover cluster without needing Active Directory for network name management. An Active Directory–detached cluster still creates the DNS entries for name resolution, but computer accounts aren't created in Active Directory.

- You can use Windows Server Backup to back up the failover cluster configuration. First, verify that the cluster node you're performing the backup from is active in the cluster, the cluster is running, and it has a quorum.

- A site-aware cluster is a new feature in Windows Server 2016 that allows an administrator to assign a name to a physical location (site) and assign cluster nodes to each location. These are called fault domains. A fault domain is a property of a cluster that has name, type, description, and location values.

- The ability to provide high availability to virtual servers is as important as the ability to provide high availability to the physical hosts that run them. A highly available virtual machine allows you to make applications and services highly available simply by installing them on a VM configured for high availability.

- Node fairness is a new failover cluster feature in Windows Server 2016 that helps optimize usage of failover cluster node members. Node fairness attempts to identify Hyper-V nodes that are hosting a disproportionate number of VMs and redistribute VMs to other nodes that are underutilized.

- Windows Server 2016 has added additional cluster node and VM states to make highly available VMs more resilient to transient failures. Three new VM states are unmonitored, isolated, and quarantined.

- Virtual machine monitoring allows you to monitor resources, applications, and services running in highly available VMs. If a resource fails, the cluster node can take actions to recover.

- Guest clustering is different from a highly available or clustered VM in that a guest cluster requires two or more VMs with a guest OS installed and configured for failover clustering.

- A big advantage of using virtual machines is the ability to make efficient use of computer and network resources. You can put multiple VMs to work on a single host server to concentrate workloads, or you can distribute VMs among multiple hosts to spread out the workload.

- Live migration is a Hyper-V feature that allows an administrator to move a virtual machine from one Hyper-V server to another while maintaining the availability of the VM.

- Quick migration is a migration option available only between Hyper-V servers in a failover cluster. The advantage of quick migration is that it's available in Windows Server 2008 Hyper-V servers and later.

- A storage migration is usually used when you simply need to move a VM's storage from one volume to another without moving the VM to another Hyper-V server. You can perform a storage migration while the VM is still running or when it's shut down.

- Virtual machine network health protection is a feature that automatically moves a VM from one cluster node to another if a network disconnection is detected. Virtual machine network health protection is configured on the network interface on each VM and is enabled by default.

- Storage Spaces Direct (S2D) is a new feature in Windows Server 2016 that extends the storage pool concept on a single server to multiple servers in a failover cluster. In other words, storage pools can be distributed among all the nodes in a failover cluster, and as new nodes are added, their storage can be automatically added to the storage pools.

- In a hyper-converged Storage Spaces Direct deployment, the storage and the Hyper-V role are part of the same cluster. All cluster nodes have Hyper-V installed, and all nodes have S2D enabled. In a disaggregated Storage Spaces Direct deployment, there are two separate clusters: an S2D cluster and a Hyper-V cluster. Using this scenario, the Hyper-V cluster can be scaled independently of the storage cluster and vice versa.

Key Terms

Active Directory–detached cluster
cloud witness
Cluster Operating System Rolling
   Upgrade
core cluster resources
disaggregated Storage Spaces
   Direct deployment
drain on shutdown
dynamic quorum
dynamic witness
failover affinity
fault domain
guest clustering

heartbeat
highly available virtual machine
hot backup site
hyper-converged Storage Spaces
   Direct deployment
Hyper-V Replica
live migration
node fairness
quick migration
recovery point
replica server
scale-out file server (SoFS)
shared-nothing live migration

shared virtual hard disk
   (shared VHDX)
site-aware cluster
split vote
storage migration
Storage Spaces Direct (S2D)
tie breaker for 50% node split
VHD Set
virtual machine monitoring
virtual machine network health
   protection

Review Questions

1. Before you create a cluster, what task should you perform in the Failover Cluster Manager?
   a. Connect to the cluster
   b. Live-migrate one or more servers
   c. Validate a configuration
   d. Configure cluster quorum settings

2. When you add a node to an existing cluster, which of the following can take place?
   a. Quorum settings are updated.
   b. A new iSCSI target is created.
   c. A new DNS record is created.
   d. An existing cluster node is disabled.

3. You need to perform maintenance on a cluster and must take the entire cluster offline. Which of the following is the best approach?

   a. For each node, right-click the node, point to More Actions, and click Stop Cluster Service.

   b. Right-click the cluster name, point to More Actions, and click Shut Down Cluster.

   c. Use the Windows shutdown procedure on each cluster node.

   d. Click the cluster name, and then click Close Connection in the Actions pane.

4. Which of the following is true about copying cluster roles?

   a. You should run the Copy Cluster Wizard from the source cluster.

   b. You need to install the clustered role on the nodes in the target cluster.

   c. Storage used by the current clustered role must remain online during the copy.

   d. Data is copied automatically to new cluster storage.

5. Which of the following is considered a core cluster resource?

   a. Cluster node

   b. Central processor

   c. CSV data disk

   d. Witness disk

6. Which cmdlet displays a list of all PowerShell cmdlets related to failover clusters?

   a. `Show-All -Commands FailoverCl*`

   b. `Get-Module -Name Failover`

   c. `Get-Command -Module FailoverClusters`

   d. `Show-Module -Display Cluster*`

7. Which of the following is *not* a quorum witness configuration option?

   a. Configure a local disk witness

   b. Configure a file share witness

   c. Configure a cloud witness

   d. Configure a disk witness

8. What feature is found in Windows Server 2016 that attempts to prevent a split vote from occurring?

   a. Cluster shared volume

   b. Node majority quorum

   c. Witness share

   d. Dynamic witness

9. In Windows Server 2016 failover clusters, why isn't it advisable to remove a node's vote manually?

   a. The dynamic quorum won't work.

   b. The node will go offline.

   c. Quorum can never be reached.

   d. The witness disk will be disabled.

10. You have six cluster nodes split evenly between SiteA and SiteB and no witness. The link between the sites goes down, leaving two separate cluster partitions. The SiteA cluster continues to function, and the SiteB cluster goes offline. All nodes are running Windows Server 2016. Why did this problem occur?

    a. A node in SiteA was given an extra vote.

    b. A witness share was created in SiteB.

    c. Dynamic quorum removed a vote from SiteB.

    d. SiteA was assigned a disk witness automatically.

11. Which of the following quorum witness options introduced in Windows Server 2016 will allow you to declare a resource in Microsoft Azure to act as a cluster witness?

    a. Cloud witness

    b. File share witness

    c. Azure witness

    d. Disk witness

12. Why is it better to use cluster-aware roles instead of generic applications or services for high-availability applications?

    a. The cluster might not know whether the generic application failed.

    b. Generic services can't access witness disks.

    c. A client access point can't be configured for a generic application.

    d. Dynamic quorum is disabled on generic services.

13. Which configuration results in the best performance and reliability for a Hyper-V failover cluster with VMs stored on a file share?

    a. SMB share

    b. Scale-out file server

    c. NFS share

    d. DFS replication

14. You need to upgrade a two-node cluster that has Windows Server 2012 servers. You have added two Windows Server 2016 servers to the cluster and transferred the roles and resources to the new servers. What should you do next?

    a. Live-migrate the new servers.

    b. Restart the cluster service on the new servers.

    c. Put the cluster in maintenance mode.

    d. Evict the Windows Server 2012 nodes.

15. You're preparing to upgrade a Windows Server 2012 R2 Hyper-V cluster to a Windows Server 2016 Hyper-V cluster, and you cannot allow any server downtime when performing the upgrade. Which

of the following Windows Server 2016 options will allow you to perform this task?

a. Operating System Rolling Upgrade

b. Cluster Rollback

c. Cluster Operating System Rolling Upgrade

d. In-place upgrade

16. You're configuring a new failover cluster but don't want to create new accounts in Active Directory. What should you do?

a. In the New Cluster Wizard, choose the Active Directory–Detached option.

b. Run the `New-Cluster` cmdlet with the `-AdministrativeAccessPoint` parameter.

c. Don't join the cluster nodes to an Active Directory domain.

d. Use the NETBios option for resolving cluster and role names.

17. You have decided to configure a Windows Server 2016 failover cluster and incorporate several members from a different domain. After confirming that all the requirements have been met, you decide to create the multi-domain cluster. Which of the following quorum model options can be selected for your Windows Server 2016 multi-domain cluster? (Choose all that apply.)

a. Cloud witness

b. File-share witness

c. Do not configure a quorum witness

d. Disk witness

18. Which of the following is a prerequisite for deploying a clustered storage space?

a. All servers must be running Windows Server 2008 R2 or later.

b. RAID must be enabled on the SAS disk controller.

c. You need at least three unallocated disks.

d. A mirror space requires Windows Server 2012 R2.

19. Which of the following PowerShell cmdlets will allow you to configure Storage Replica between two different server clusters by granting access to the other cluster to enable replication?

a. `Add-Cluster`

b. `New-SRPartnership -Cluster`

c. `Grant-SRAccess -Cluster`

d. `Grant-SRPartnership`

20. There are two methods for deploying a clustered storage space. Which of the following steps is used in both methods?

a. Install the MPIO feature.

b. Create storage spaces with File and Storage Services.

c. Create a storage space in the Failover Cluster Manager.

d. Verify that none of the disks are shown in Disk Management.

21. Which of the following is a signal that is used by cluster nodes to verify that a node is up and operating?

a. Heartbeat

b. Node signal

c. Node delay

d. Threshold

22. Which of the following is a feature in Windows Server 2016 that permits an administrator to allocate a name to a physical location and delegate cluster nodes to each location?

a. Fault domain

b. Site-aware cluster

c. Assigned domain

d. Cluster allocation

23. Which of the following is true about a clustered virtual machine? (Choose all that apply.)

a. You need to have shared storage available to the VM's guest OS.

b. You need two or more host computers running Hyper-V.

c. All host computers should be members of the same domain.

d. CSVs aren't recommended for shared storage.

24. If you're using cluster shared volumes for highly available VMs, which of the following is a likely path for storing the VM files?

a. \\Server\SharedVM

b. D:\

c. C:\ClusterStorage

d. FTP:\\Server

25. After reviewing some system performance data, you have noticed that some of your virtual machines hosted on clustered Hyper-V servers are currently distributed throughout the cluster in an unbalanced configuration. What feature in Windows Server 2016 will allow you to optimize your cluster node members for better performance?

a. Node sync

b. Node fairness

c. Performance Cluster

d. Node balance

26. With respect to a clustered Hyper-V node, which of the following VM states allows the node to be removed from active membership in the cluster but continues to host the VM role?

a. Quarantined

b. Monitored

c. Isolated

d. Unmonitored

27. In Windows Server 2016 server, what specific state will a high availability VM be placed into if it has lost access to its storage?
    a. Paused-Critical
    b. Isolated
    c. Quarantined
    d. Paused

28. What feature in Windows Server 2016 causes a highly available VM to be live-migrated automatically if the host that it's running on is shut down?
    a. Cluster shared volume
    b. Authoritative restore
    c. Dynamic witness
    d. Drain on shutdown

29. Which option on a VM should you select if you want to enable virtual machine network health detection?
    a. Protected network
    b. Hardware acceleration
    c. Virtual machine queue
    d. NIC teaming

30. Which Windows Server 2016 feature will allow you to distribute Storage Pools between all nodes in a failover cluster and allow new nodes to add their storage automatically to storage pools?
    a. Distributed Storage
    b. Storage Cluster
    c. Storage Spaces Direct
    d. Clustered Storage

Critical Thinking

The following activities give you critical thinking challenges. Case Projects offer a scenario with a problem to solve and for which you supply a written solution.

Case Project 9-1: Choosing a Quorum Configuration

You're going to set up a high-availability share configuration with failover clusters. You have four sites, and three will have cluster nodes. Site1 has three cluster nodes, Site2 has four cluster nodes, Site3 has two cluster nodes, and Site4 has no cluster nodes. What quorum configuration should you choose for this configuration? Describe some quorum features that will make configuration easier and improve cluster availability.

Case Project 9-2: Setting Up a Guest Cluster

You have three Hyper-V servers, and you're currently running four VMs on each server for a total of 12 VMs. You want to be sure that if a Hyper-V server fails or you need to take one down for maintenance, the VMs will continue to run. Describe the configuration you plan to use, including options for shared storage.

CHAPTER 10

MAINTAINING SERVER INSTALLATIONS

After reading this chapter and completing the exercises, you will be able to:

Describe Windows Server Update Services (WSUS)

Install the WSUS role

Configure WSUS

Implement Windows Defender

Installing Windows on a number of desktop computers and servers can be a time-consuming task, but once the OS is installed, your work is not yet done. Hackers and malware designers are constantly looking for and finding vulnerabilities in operating systems. When a vulnerability is discovered through malicious activities or by Microsoft's own software engineers, a patch is developed and made available for users to update their computers. In addition, bugs are found and OS enhancements are made, and updates to address both are made available. This chapter discusses the Windows Update program for downloading and installing available updates. In large networks, you usually want to centralize and control the update process—enter Windows Server Update Services (WSUS). This chapter discusses how to install the WSUS role and then configure the role and the client computers using WSUS. Microsoft's solution to malware is Windows Defender. This chapter discusses how to configure Windows Defender using Group Policy and PowerShell and how to integrate WSUS with Windows Defender to ensure your anti-malware software and definitions are up to date on all computers throughout the enterprise.

An Overview of Windows Server Update Services

Table 10-1 summarizes what you need for the hands-on activities in this chapter.

Table 10-1	Activity requirements	
Activity	**Requirements**	**Notes**
Activity 10-1: Resetting Your Virtual Environment	ServerDC1, ServerDM1	
Activity 10-2: Installing the WSUS Role	ServerDC1, ServerDM1	
Activity 10-3: Performing WSUS Postinstallation Tasks	ServerDC1, ServerDM1	Internet connection required
Activity 10-4: Creating a Custom Computer Group	ServerDC1, ServerDM1	
Activity 10-5: Configuring Windows Update with Group Policy	ServerDC1, ServerDM1	
Activity 10-6: Configuring WSUS Synchronization and Approval Rules	ServerDC1, ServerDM1	

Windows Server Update Services (WSUS) is a server role that makes it possible for administrators to take control of Microsoft product updates on computers running Windows. Another term for this process is **patch management**. When patch management is done with WSUS, administrators can control which product updates are allowed as well as the source and timing of these updates. In a typical WSUS setup, the WSUS server downloads patches, security updates, bug fixes, and other updates from the Microsoft Update servers and then distributes these updates to Windows computers after they have been approved. This means that updates are downloaded from the Internet only once to the WSUS server instead of once for each computer needing the update.

You install WSUS on a Windows Server 2016 computer like any other server role. After it's installed and configured, you configure Windows clients to use the WSUS server for Windows updates. Ideally, clients are configured by using Group Policy, so your clients need to be domain members. The WSUS server can be a standalone server or a domain member, but installing WSUS on a domain controller isn't recommended. In most cases, you configure WSUS to download updates for all the products your clients are running. You can then approve which updates you want your clients to install. Some advantages of using WSUS for Windows updates include the following:

- Centralized control over Microsoft product updates
- Reduced Internet bandwidth usage
- Only approved updates are installed
- Ease in determining which patches and updates have been applied

Before you delve into the details of WSUS, it's useful to review how the Windows Update process works by default when no WSUS server is available.

Windows Update

Windows Update is a built-in function of all Windows OSs. When Windows is installed, one of the first things it does is to check for important updates that have been released since the current build. A **build** is a particular compilation of the operating system and it determines which updates have been incorporated into the OS installation. You can find the build of the OS by typing `systeminfo` from a command prompt. The `systeminfo` command also lists the hotfixes that have been installed. A **hotfix** is an update to Windows that fixes a bug that usually has a limited scope, affecting only specific usage scenarios.

In Windows Server 2016, Windows Update is enabled by default and Windows checks for updates and downloads and installs updates automatically (see Figure 10-1; highlighting added). If an update requires a computer restart, Windows will defer the restart until the computer is outside of active hours. You can change the default active hours by clicking Change active hours on the Windows Update settings page (see Figure 10-2). You can set a range of up to 12 hours. In addition, Windows will check to see if the computer is being used before restarting it.

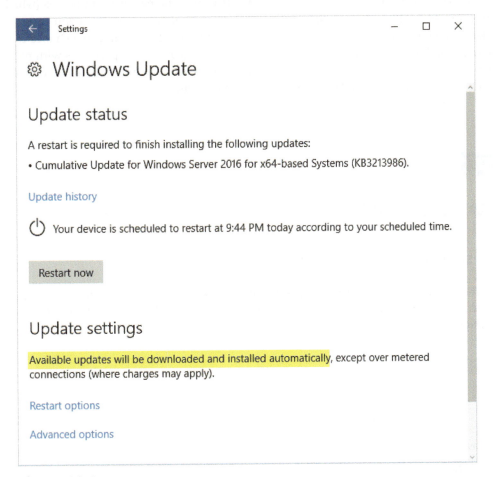

Figure 10-1   Windows Update settings

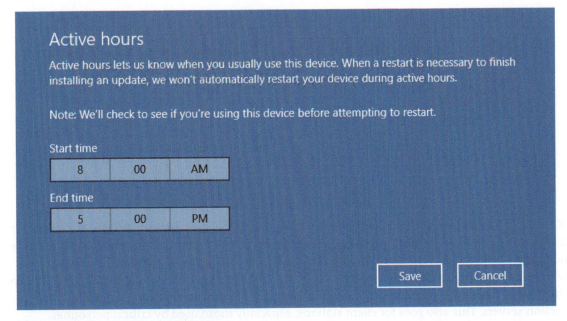

Figure 10-2   Change active hours

If a restart is pending for an installed update, you can choose a custom time for the restart to occur by clicking Restart options. You can choose a specific time and postpone the restart for up to 6 days (see Figure 10-3). If you click Advanced options, you can choose to get updates for other installed Microsoft products when Windows is updated. You also have the option to defer feature updates. A **feature update** adds new features or enhances existing features whereas regular updates (which Microsoft refers to as **quality updates**) fix software defects and enhance security. If you choose to defer feature updates, the new features won't be installed for several months, giving you a chance to install them on nonproduction servers in a test lab to ensure that they won't cause problems with production applications. If you want to see updates that have already been installed and updates that are pending a restart, click Update history in the Windows Update settings window.

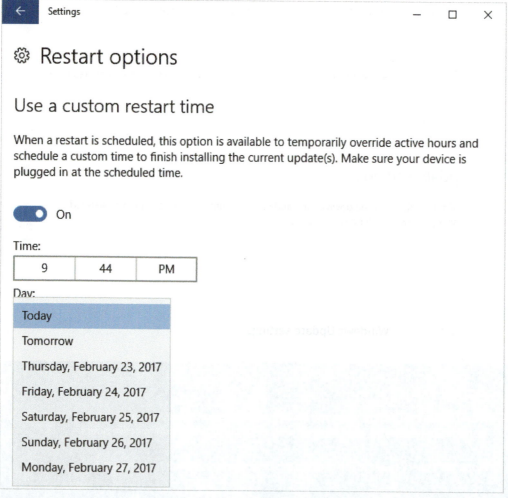

Figure 10-3 **Restart options**

Keeping your servers and client computers up to date with the latest security enhancements and bug fixes is obviously critical. However, updating production servers can have consequences. Updates have been known to cause problems, and although you can choose custom restart options, you might want more flexibility in handling how and when updates are installed than the manual settings provide. Most administrators want to be able to install and test all updates on test servers before deploying them to production servers. This also goes for client stations, especially those used by critical personnel.

It's also important to realize that if you have dozens or hundreds of computers that download updates automatically, you're likely to notice a substantial strain on the Internet connection because updates require computers to contact Microsoft Update servers.

This is where the WSUS role comes in. Between WSUS and Group Policy in an Active Directory environment, administrators have much more control over the updating process. And, instead of all your computers accessing Microsoft Update servers, you can designate one or a few servers as update servers that access the Internet to download updates from Microsoft Update servers.

> **Note** 🔗
>
> You can disable Windows Update by disabling the Windows Update service in the Services MMC. However, this is not recommended because your computer(s) will be exposed to security vulnerabilities that are resolved by updates to Windows. In addition, your computer(s) will not have the latest reliability enhancements. Also, doing so, whether by design or as a side effect of disabling the service, causes intermittent high CPU utilization.

Installing the WSUS Role

Certification

- **70-740 – Maintain and monitor server environments:**
  Maintain server installations

The WSUS role is installed by using Add Roles and Features in Server Manager or by using the PowerShell `Install-WindowsFeature` cmdlet. Some requirements for running the WSUS role on Windows Server 2016 are as follows:

- 1.4 GHz CPU
- 10 GB available disk space (40 GB recommended)
- 2 GB RAM
- 100 Mbps network interface

In addition to the hardware requirements, the server on which you install the WSUS role should be a member of an Active Directory domain and cannot run Remote Desktop Services. Although a domain environment is not required, client configuration is much easier if the WSUS server and all the client computers are domain members.

The disk requirements for the WSUS server vary depending on which products you need to update, how many updates you need to store locally, and how many clients will be served. In an environment with multiple client and server OS versions, disk requirements will probably be higher. In addition, as mentioned, the WSUS server shouldn't be installed on a domain controller.

WSUS Storage Requirements

WSUS has the following requirements for storage:

- *WSUS database*—This database stores the WSUS configuration data and update metadata along with information about WSUS client interactions. All WSUS servers require a WSUS database. The default database is the built-in Windows Internal Database (WID), which is essentially a light version of a SQL database with no management interface. You can configure WSUS to use a SQL Server Express or full SQL Server installation, too. The WID database provides the same performance as a SQL database. Using the WID database is recommended unless you're already running a SQL server for other applications or plan to deploy WSUS with network load balancing (NLB). The database requires a minimum of 2 GB free space on the volume where it's stored.

- *Local file system storage*—In most situations, you want to store the actual update files on storage available to the local WSUS server such as on a local drive or a network share and to configure clients to download updates from the WSUS server. This setup constitutes the bulk of the WSUS disk space requirement. However, when client computers have a faster connection to the Internet than to the WSUS server (perhaps in some branch office arrangements), you can opt to store only update metadata in the WSUS database and have clients download approved updates directly from the Microsoft Update servers.

Note

The database server and the WSUS server need not be the same computer, but if they're not, the database server does need to be in the same domain as the WSUS server or in a trusted domain. In addition, the database server cannot be a domain controller.

WSUS Deployment Options

WSUS can be installed as a single-server solution, supporting from a few dozen to several hundred clients at a single site or a multiple-server solution, providing update services to large multiple-site enterprises. In the single-server solution, the WSUS server is deployed in the company intranet and communicates directly with Microsoft Update servers. Client computers then contact the WSUS server to download and install approved updates (see Figure 10-4).

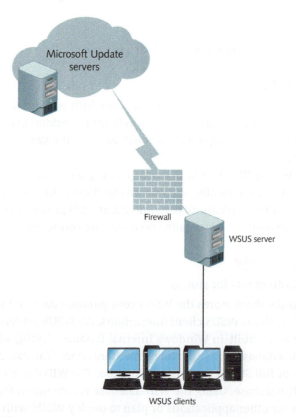

Figure 10-4 A single-server WSUS deployment

For a multiple-server solution (see Figure 10-5), a single WSUS server is configured to contact Microsoft Update servers to get updates and then distributes updates to additional WSUS servers located on different parts of the network. Client computers can then contact the nearest WSUS server to download updates.

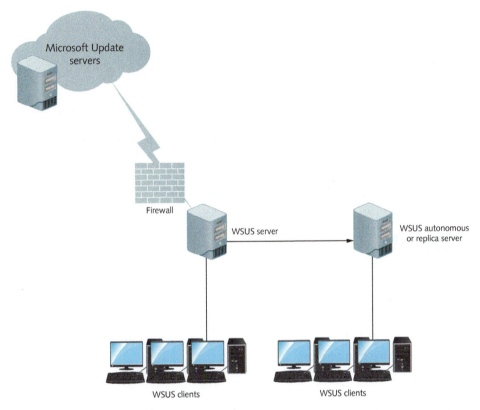

Figure 10-5 A multiple-server WSUS deployment

When using a multiple-server deployment, you have two WSUS administration options:

- *Autonomous mode*—**Autonomous mode** provides distributed administration and is the default option when you install WSUS. Using autonomous mode, an administrator for each WSUS server has the responsibility of approving updates and managing WSUS client groups (discussed later in this chapter).
- *Replica mode*—**Replica mode** provides centralized administration of update approvals and client groups. An administrator maintains client groups and approves updates on the server that connects to Microsoft Update servers and the information is inherited by downstream WSUS servers.

Regardless of the deployment, WSUS uses the HTTPS protocol on TCP port 443 by default to collect updates from Microsoft Update servers and between WSUS servers in a multiple-server deployment. You can change these ports, but be aware that the configured ports must be open on the relevant firewalls.

Installing WSUS

When you install WSUS using the Add Roles and Features Wizard in Server Manager, during installation you're prompted to install additional features that are required for WSUS. Next, you select role services. In the Role Services window shown in Figure 10-6, you see the following options:

- *WID Connectivity*—When this option is selected, WSUS uses the Windows Internal Database, which is adequate for most applications. This check box should be selected unless you plan to use SQL server.

- *WSUS Services*—This check box should be selected. This option installs a number of services that WSUS needs; you can see a list in the Description box in Figure 10-6.
- *SQL Server Connectivity*—This check box should be selected only if you aren't going to use the WID database. The wizard doesn't let you select both this check box and the WID Connectivity check box. If you select this check box, you need to enter the details of the database server you plan to use in a subsequent window.

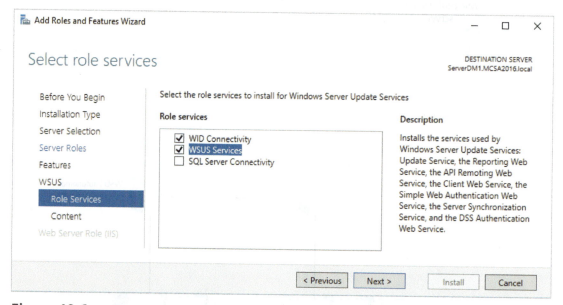

Figure 10-6   Selecting role services

After you select role services, you see a window where you can choose to store the update files on the local server along with the path (see Figure 10-7). The path can be a local drive letter and folder or a UNC path to a share on another server. If you decide not to store update files on the local server or a network share, the files are downloaded from the Microsoft Update servers as needed by clients. You can change whether updates should be stored locally and change the storage path after WSUS has been installed.

As part of the WSUS installation, the Web Server role and related role services are also installed. After you click Install in the Confirmation window, the WSUS installation begins. Installation can take quite a while because of the amount of software that must be installed. After WSUS is installed, you must perform some configuration tasks before you can begin using WSUS. When you first open the WSUS management console, a wizard guides you through these tasks:

- Choose the **upstream server**. Decide whether to get updates from the Microsoft Update servers on the Internet or another WSUS server. If this is the first WSUS server, you select Microsoft Update servers. If there's already one or more WSUS servers on your network, you can have the new server synchronize updates with an existing WSUS server.
- Configure network settings, such as whether WSUS should use a proxy server when synchronizing. During this step, your server will contact the Microsoft Update Servers to collect information. This step could take several minutes.
- Specify which languages the updates should include.
- Select the products the WSUS server should collect updates for.

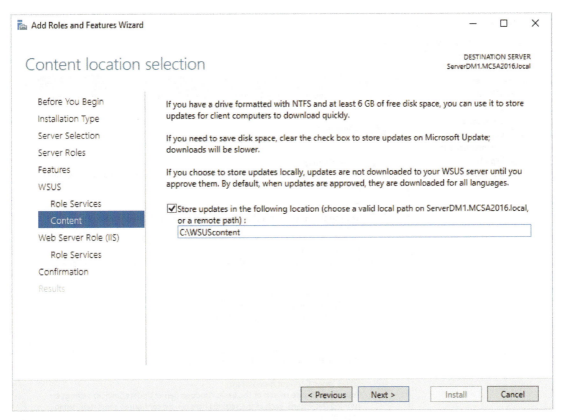

Figure 10-7   Selecting the content location

- Specify the update classifications that should be synchronized; for example, you can choose whether the server should get critical updates, security updates, definition updates, service packs, drivers, tools, and so forth.
- Configure the synchronization schedule to tell the WSUS server how often it should check for updates.

All the settings configured with the WSUS Configuration Wizard can be changed in the Update Services console by clicking Options (shown in Figure 10-8). You can also run the configuration wizard again by clicking Options and then WSUS Server Configuration Wizard.

You're almost ready to start using WSUS, but before clients can begin using the WSUS server for automatic updates, you must perform several configuration tasks, which are discussed in the next section.

Dealing with Multiple Windows Versions

If all your servers and clients are running the latest version of Windows, WSUS configuration and management would be fairly straightforward. However, most environments run multiple versions of Windows. Some things to be aware of when running mixed environments include the following:

- Group Policy settings for Windows Update vary depending on the version of Windows installed on a computer. Be sure to carefully inspect the policy setting details and description, paying particular attention to the Supported on field that tells you which versions of Windows the policy applies to.

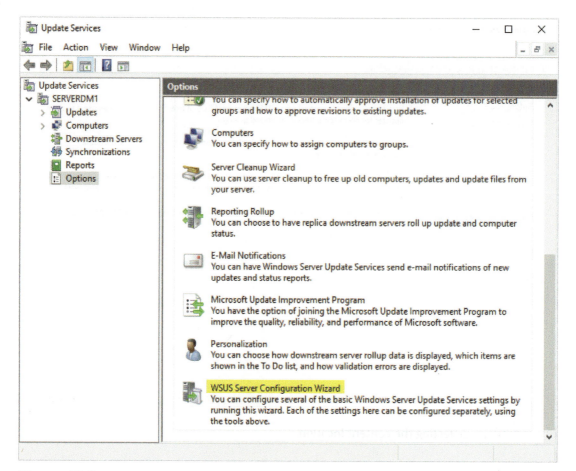

Figure 10-8 Options available in the Update Services console

- Be sure that the WSUS server is downloading updates for the appropriate versions of Windows that are running in your network. If new versions of Windows are added to your network, you need to ensure that WSUS is synchronizing that version with Microsoft Update servers. If older versions of Windows are retired, be sure to deselect those products. You do this in the Products and Classification dialog box in the Options screen of the Update Services console.
- Running more versions of Windows means more disk space is required on the WSUS server.

Activity 10-1: Resetting Your Virtual Environment

Time Required: 5 minutes
Objective: Reset your virtual environment by applying the InitialConfig checkpoint or snapshot.
Required Tools and Equipment: ServerDC1, ServerDM1
Description: Apply the InitialConfig checkpoint or snapshot to ServerDC1 and ServerDM1.

1. Be sure that the servers are shut down. In your virtualization program, apply the InitialConfig checkpoint or snapshot to ServerDC1 and ServerDM1.
2. When the snapshot or checkpoint has finished being applied, continue to the next activity.

Activity 10-2: Installing the WSUS Role

Time Required: 35 minutes

Objective: Install the WSUS role and required additional roles and features.

Required Tools and Equipment: ServerDC1, ServerDM1

Description: In this activity, you install the WSUS role and launch postinstallation tasks.

1. Start ServerDC1 and ServerDM1. Sign in to ServerDM1 as **Administrator**.
2. On ServerDM1, open Server Manager, click **Manage, Add Roles and Features** from the menu. In the Add Roles and Features Wizard, click **Next** until you get to the Server Roles window.
3. Scroll down the list of roles, and click the box next to **Windows Server Update Services**.
4. In the dialog box asking you to confirm the additional features needed for this role, click **Add Features**, and then click **Next**.
5. In the Features window, click **Next**. Read the window describing WSUS, and then click **Next**.
6. In the Role Services window, make sure the **WID Database** and **WSUS Services** check boxes are selected, and then click **Next**.
7. In the Content window, make sure the **Store updates in the following location** check box is selected, type **C:\WSUScontent** in the text box, and then click **Next**.
8. In the Web Server Role (IIS) window, read the information about IIS, and then click **Next**. In the Role Services window, click **Next**.
9. In the Confirmation window, click **Install**.
10. The next window shows the progress of the installation. (*Note:* You can close this window and view the progress later by clicking the Notifications flag on the command bar of Server Manager.) For now, wait until the installation is finished, which might take several minutes, and then click **Close**.
11. Click the Notifications flag in Server Manager, and then click **Launch Post-Installation tasks**. Additional configuration tasks are performed.
12. Stay signed in and continue to the next activity.

Activity 10-3: Performing WSUS Postinstallation Tasks

Time Required: 20 minutes or longer

Objective: Perform postinstallation tasks for the WSUS role.

Required Tools and Equipment: ServerDC1, ServerDM1, and an Internet connection

Description: You have just installed WSUS and related roles and features. Now you need to open the Update Services console and perform the initial configuration tasks.

1. In Server Manager, click **Tools, Windows Server Update Services** from the menu to start the Windows Server Update Services Configuration Wizard.
2. In the Before You Begin window, read the information, and then click **Next**.

> **Tip** ⓘ
>
> If you ever need to run the wizard again, you can do so in the Update Services console by clicking Options in the left pane.

3. In the Join the Microsoft Update Program window, click to clear the check box to decline joining the program, and then click **Next**.
4. In the Choose Upstream Server window (see Figure 10-9), make sure **Synchronize from Microsoft Update** is selected, and then click **Next**. Click **Next** in the Specify Proxy Server window.

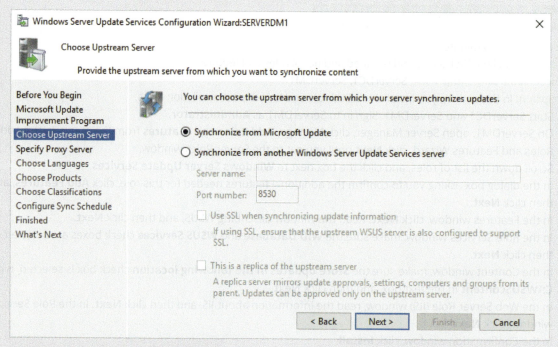

Figure 10-9 Choose the upstream server

5. In the Connect to Upstream Server window, click **Start Connecting** (see Figure 10-10). This step downloads information about the types of updates available, products that can be updated, and available languages. It requires the server to have a working Internet connection and might take several minutes to finish. Click **Next** when the Next button is available. (Note that you can cancel this step by clicking **Stop Connecting** if it is taking too long and then click **Cancel** to close the wizard.)

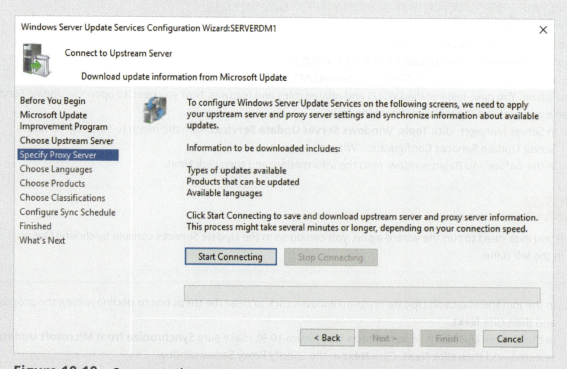

Figure 10-10 Connect to the upstream server

6. In the Choose Languages window, select the language or languages for your region, and then click **Next**.

7. In the Choose Products window, all Windows products are selected by default. Scroll down until you see the Windows check box. To reduce the download time and disk space used, click to clear the **Windows** check box, then click to select the **Windows Server 2016** check box (see Figure 10-11), and then click **Next**.

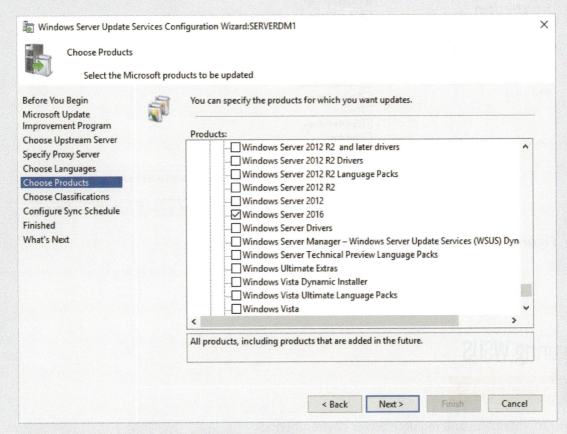

Figure 10-11   Choosing the products to update

8. In the Choose Classifications window (see Figure 10-12), accept the default selections (Critical Updates, Definition Updates, and Security Updates), and then click **Next**.

9. In the Configure Sync Schedule window, accept the default option, **Synchronize manually**. If you choose Synchronize automatically, you can select the time of day you would like to perform the first synchronization and how many synchronizations per day, up to 24. Click **Next**.

10. In the Finished window, you have the option to begin synchronizing with the Microsoft Update servers on the Internet. Accept the default option to not start synchronization now, and click **Next**.

11. The What's Next window shows additional tasks you might need to complete before using the WSUS server. Click **Finish**. The Update Services console opens and displays a summary of the update status of computers on the network. Close the Update Services console.

12. Continue to the next activity.

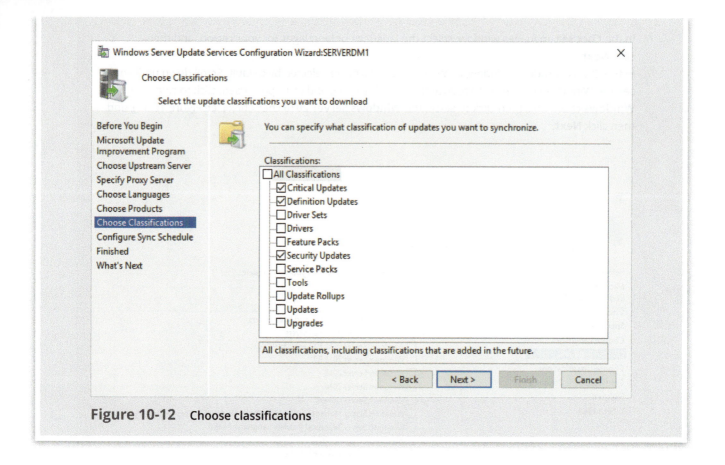

Figure 10-12 Choose classifications

Configuring WSUS

 **Certification**

• **70-740 – Maintain and monitor server environments:**
  Maintain server installations

Before the clients in your network can begin using WSUS for automatic updates, you need to perform a few configuration tasks on WSUS. Some of these tasks are done in the Update Services console, and others use Group Policy to configure WSUS clients remotely:

• Create computer groups
• Assign computers to groups
• Configure Windows Update on client computers
• Configure WSUS synchronization and approval rules

Creating Computer Groups

With computer groups, you can target specific computers for different types of updates. There are two default groups: All Computers and Unassigned Computers. When a client computer contacts the WSUS server, it's added to both groups by default. You can also create custom groups to meet your needs.

As the name implies, the Unassigned Computers group holds all computers you haven't assigned to a custom group. After you've created custom groups, you move computers from the Unassigned Computers group to your custom groups. The All Computers group always contains every computer that has contacted the WSUS server. Figure 10-13 shows the relationship between these groups.

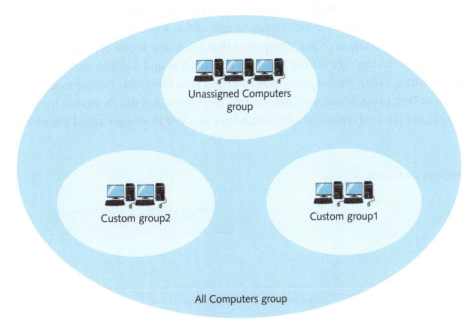

Figure 10-13   WSUS computer groups

Custom groups can be used to organize computers for targeting specific updates and to test updates on a limited number of computers before deploying updates to the rest of the network. Creating at least one custom group for update testing is recommended.

Assigning Computers to Groups

You select the method for assigning computers to groups in the Update Services console by clicking Options in the left pane and then Computers in the center pane. The Computers dialog box shown in Figure 10-14 opens with these options: Use the Update Services console (which specifies server-side targeting) and Use Group Policy or registry settings on computers (which specifies client-side targeting). These options are described in the following list.

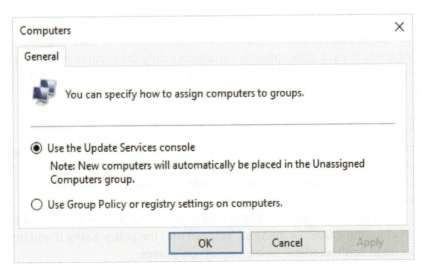

Figure 10-14   Specifying how computers are added to WSUS groups

- *Use the Update Services console*—This method is called **server-side targeting** because the action takes place at the WSUS server. Server-side targeting is enabled by default. After creating custom groups, simply move computer accounts from the Unassigned Computers group to the custom group.
- *Use Group Policy or registry settings on computers*—This method, **client-side targeting**, is the preferred one. To use it, you should have a domain controller in your network, and clients should be domain members. The term *client-side targeting* is used because the Group Policy setting changes the relevant Registry setting on client computers that are in the scope of the Group Policy in Active Directory. The affected Registry setting instructs the client to add itself to the specified group. The Group Policy setting called *Enable client-side targeting* is in Computer Configuration, Policies, Administrative Templates, Windows Components, Windows Update. As shown in Figure 10-15, this policy causes affected clients to add themselves to a WSUS group named MemberServers.

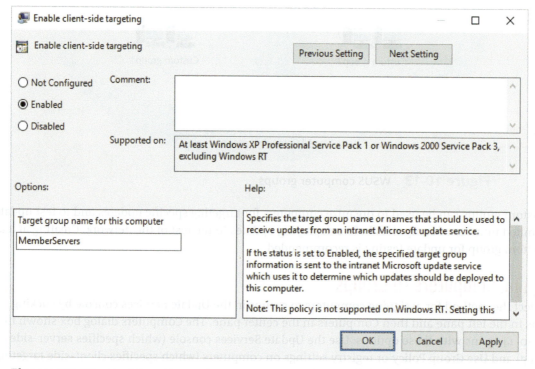

Figure 10-15   Enabling client-side targeting

If your clients are not domain members, you can still configure client-side targeting using the Local Group Policy Editor (`gpedit.msc`). This option is satisfactory only for small networks with no domain controller because you have to change the settings on every computer. The setting is the same as what's shown in Figure 10-15.

Configuring Windows Update on Client Computers

Before you can begin using the WSUS server, your clients must be told to use the WSUS server instead of the Microsoft Update servers on the Internet to find and download updates. If your computers are domain members, you can use Group Policy on a domain controller to configure Windows Update; otherwise, you can configure clients separately with the Local Group Policy Editor.

When you use Group Policy to configure WSUS clients, it's best to create one or more Group Policy Objects (GPOs) for configuring WSUS. By doing so, you can find the policy easily if you need to make adjustments later to client configurations for a group of computers.

If you have a lot of computers in your network, you can divide computer accounts into different Active Directory organizational units (OUs) and link a GPO with different WSUS parameters to each OU. For example, this tactic allows you to stagger the update schedule so that the computers in each OU attempt to download and install updates from the WSUS server at different times of the day.

The policy settings for Windows Update can be found in Computer Configuration, Policies, Administrative Templates, Windows Components, and Windows Update where you also find the setting for client-side targeting. Microsoft has drastically changed the Windows Update policies over the years, so you have to look at the details for each policy to see on which versions of Windows the policy is supported. For example, the Configure Automatic Updates policy no longer applies to Windows 10 and Windows Server 2016. You used to be able to turn automatic updates off using this policy, but you can no longer do so unless some of your client computers are running older versions of the OS.

The main settings for configuring your clients to access the WSUS server are the following (highlighted in Figure 10-16):

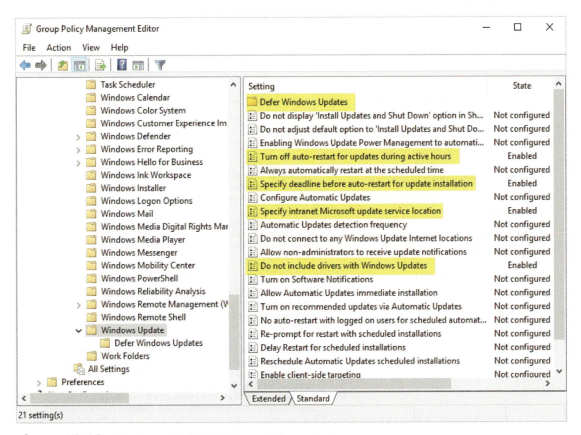

Figure 10-16   Windows Update settings in Group Policy

- *Defer Windows Updates*—This policy has several options for setting when updates are received that are discussed in more detail later.
- *Turn off auto-restart for updates during active hours*—If you enable this policy, WSUS clients will restart outside of active hours when an update requires a restart. You can configure the active hours within a 12-hour time frame. If you disable or don't configure this policy, users can select the active hours on their local machine.

- *Specify intranet Microsoft update service location*—It has the following settings (see Figure 10-17):
  - Not Configured, Enabled, Disabled: If this policy is enabled, client computers download approved updates from the specified WSUS server. If it's disabled or not configured, client computers download updates from the Microsoft Update servers on the Internet (unless automatic updates are disabled).
  - Set the intranet update service for detecting updates: You specify the URL to the WSUS server in the format *http://WSUSServer:8530; WSUSServer* is the name of the Windows Server 2016 server with the WSUS role installed and configured. You should also specify the port number 8530, the default port WSUS uses. If you're using HTTPS for updates, the default port is 8531.
- *Set the intranet statistics server*—Specify the server to collect update statistics from WSUS clients. You can use the same URL as for the update server in the previous setting, or you can specify a different server name.

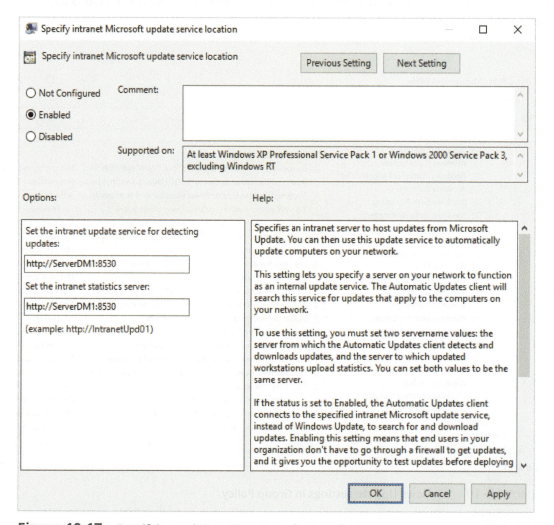

Figure 10-17   Specifying an intranet server to host updates

- *Specify deadline before auto-restart for update installation*—If this policy is enabled, a restart will occur after the specified number of days has elapsed (unless a restart was initiated by the user or for some other reason beforehand) (see Figure 10-18).

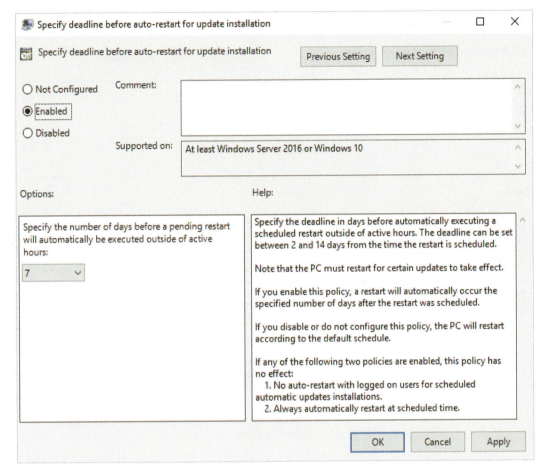

Figure 10-18   Specify the deadline before auto-restart for update installation

- *Do not include drivers with Windows Updates*—If this policy is enabled, device drivers will not be included with updates. This is important because changes to device drivers can have a significant effect on the operation and performance of the computer and driver updates should always be tested on nonproduction systems first.

There are two Windows Update policies that relate to Feature Updates, and they are found in the Defer Windows Updates folder (see Figure 10-16 shown previously):

- *Select when Feature Updates are received*—If you enable this policy, you can specify which type of feature updates to receive and when they are received (see Figure 10-19):
  - Current Branch: **Current Branch** causes WSUS clients to download and install feature updates as soon as they are available.
  - Current Branch for Business: **Current Branch for Business** causes WSUS clients to download and install feature updates after Microsoft has verified that the feature is suitable for enterprise installations.
  - Defer updates: You can defer feature updates for up to 180 days on either branch. Feature updates for the selected branch will not be installed until the number of days specified.
  - Pause feature updates: You can pause feature updates for 60 days by selecting this option. For example, if you defer updates for 90 days and select the Pause option, updates will be deferred for a total of 150 days. If you clear the Pause option, feature updates will occur on the chosen schedule.

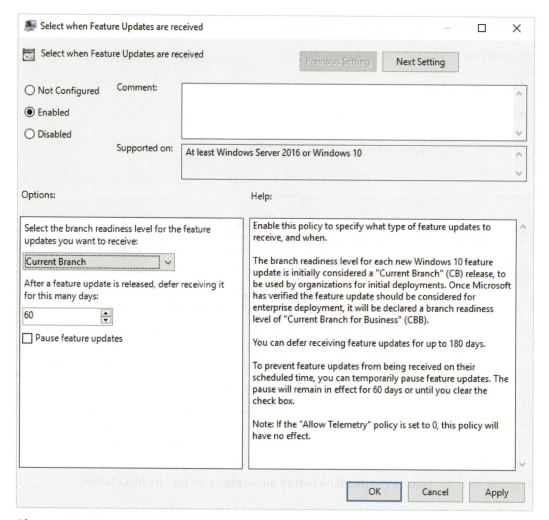

Figure 10-19 Select when feature updates are received

- *Select when Quality Updates are received*—If you enable this policy, you can defer quality updates for up to 30 days and pause them for an additional 35 days. This policy gives you a chance to test all updates thoroughly before deploying them to production servers. For example, you can configure quality updates to be received immediately on your test servers and clients while deferring them on production systems.

Note

There are many more Windows Update settings in Group Policy than are discussed here. You should open each policy and read which Windows versions it applies to and the description so you know what the Windows Update options are in your environment.

After you have configured automatic updates in a GPO, you can link it to the domain or an OU containing computer accounts. If you have several OUs containing computer accounts, you can create a GPO with different settings for each OU, if needed. If all computers require the same settings, the GPO can be linked to the domain. However, if it's linked at the domain level, the automatic update settings also affect servers and domain controllers (DCs). You might want different updates for servers, DCs, and critical client stations until you have thoroughly tested them.

> **Note** 📎
>
> When configuring Windows Update on client computers, you can use the Local Group Policy Editor to configure clients that aren't members of a domain. The policy settings are the same as in the domain-based GPO.

WSUS Synchronization and Approval Rules

WSUS clients can download and install only approved updates from the WSUS server. The administrator can configure automatic approval for certain types of updates and for particular groups of computers. Other updates can be approved manually. Updates that aren't approved are not downloaded and installed by WSUS clients. Before updates are approved, the WSUS server must synchronize with the Microsoft Update servers on the Internet.

Manual synchronization of updates is the default setting, but you have the option to configure automatic synchronization on a set schedule. To do this, in the Update Services console, click Options and then Synchronization Schedule. The Synchronization Schedule (shown in Figure 10-20) has two options:

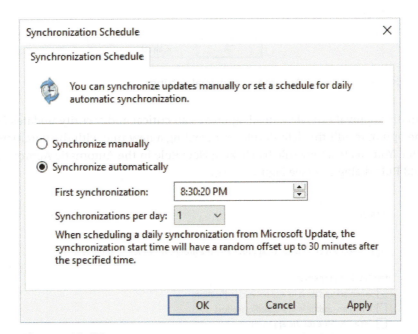

Figure 10-20   Configuring a synchronization schedule

- *Synchronize manually*—If this option is selected, the administrator must click Synchronizations in the left pane of the Update Services console and click Synchronize Now in the Actions pane. The WSUS server then attempts to contact a Microsoft Update server on the Internet. If you choose this option, manual synchronization should be done at least once a week to make sure your computers have the latest critical security updates.
- *Synchronize automatically*—If you select this option, you can configure what time of day the first synchronization should occur and the number of synchronizations per day. If you choose more than one synchronization per day, the WSUS server attempts to synchronize every $24/n$ hours, with n representing the number of synchronizations per day. The maximum synchronizations per day is 24.

Using Automatic Approvals

The Automatic Approvals option in WSUS enables you to approve specific types of updates for groups of computers automatically. After updates are approved, clients can download and install updates according to the settings of the Windows Updates client. You configure automatic approvals in the Update Services console by clicking Options and then Automatic Approvals to open the dialog box shown in Figure 10-21.

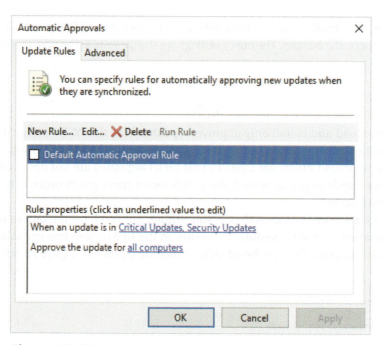

Figure 10-21   Automatic approval settings

A default automatic approval rule, if enabled, approves all critical and security updates for all computers. You have the option to edit the default rule, but creating a new rule with the parameters you want is usually better. You create a new rule by clicking New Rule in the Automatic Approvals dialog box, which opens the Add Rule dialog box (see Figure 10-22).

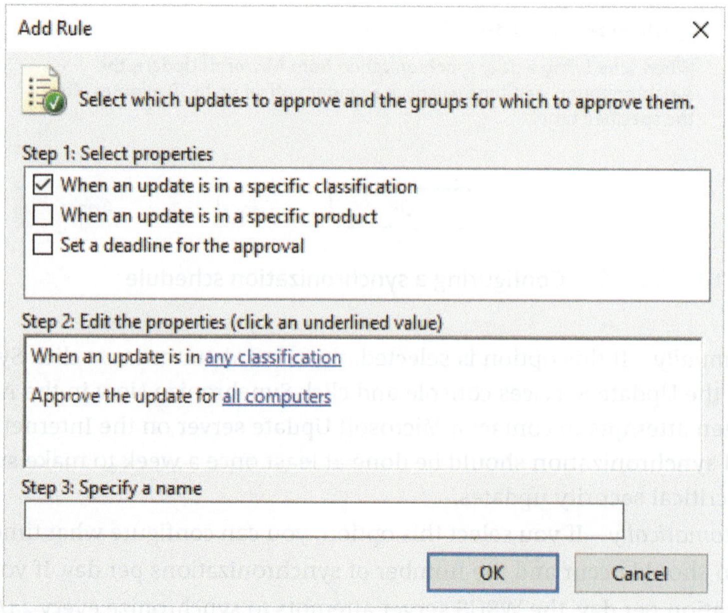

Figure 10-22   Creating a new approval rule

The rule can include one or more of the following criteria:

- *Update classification*—You choose one or more update classifications (shown in Figure 10-23).

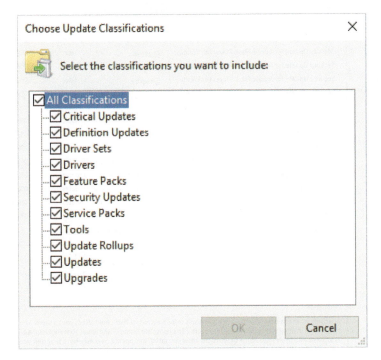

Figure 10-23   Update classifications for a new rule

- *Specific product*—You choose which products are included in the approval rule.
- *Approval deadline*—If you set a deadline, updates are installed automatically when the deadline expires even if a client computer is set to install updates manually instead of automatically.

By default, the All Computers group is the target of a new approval rule. You can change this setting by choosing one or more WSUS groups.

Configuring Manual Approval

You can approve updates manually in the Update Services console by clicking Updates and then clicking All Updates, Critical Updates, Security Updates, or WSUS Updates, as shown in Figure 10-24. You see a list of updates that have been synchronized with the Microsoft Update servers. Click an update to see its description in the lower pane. Right-click an update to see a shortcut menu (shown in Figure 10-24) you can use to approve or decline an update or get additional status information about it. You can also select more than one update in the list before right-clicking so that you can approve multiple updates at once.

Clicking Approve in the shortcut menu displays a list of WSUS groups. For each group, you can approve the update for installation or removal or choose not to approve a previously approved update (see Figure 10-25). If you approve the update for installation or removal, you can also set a deadline that forces the update even if the client is configured to install updates manually.

Having a test group for each OS and application configuration in your organization is recommended. This way, you can approve updates for test groups and verify that the updates don't cause any problems with the OS or installed applications before approving updates for production systems. This practice is particularly important for servers.

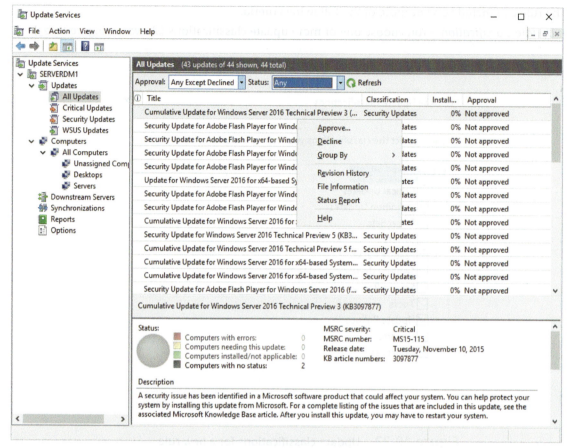

Figure 10-24   Viewing the list of synchronized updates

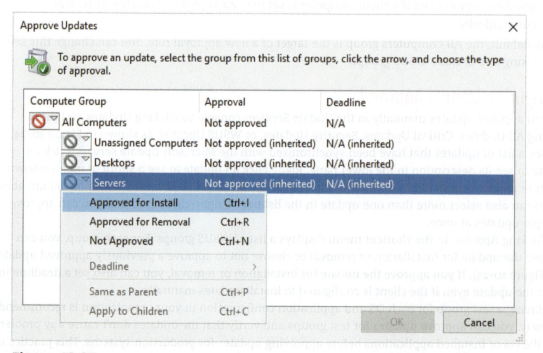

Figure 10-25   Approving updates

Configuring Update Sources and Proxy Servers

The update source for a WSUS server is the Microsoft Update servers or another WSUS server. If you need to change the current configuration, open the Update Services console, click Update Source and Proxy Server, and click the Update Source tab (see Figure 10-26). You have the following options in this dialog box:

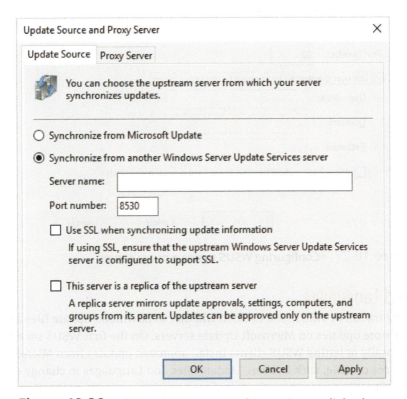

Figure 10-26   The Update Source and Proxy Server dialog box

- *Synchronize from Microsoft Update*—This is the default setting and the only option available if you have only one WSUS server in the network.
- *Synchronize from another Windows Server Update Services server*—This setting is available when you have a multiple-server WSUS deployment. If you choose this option, you specify the following:
  - Server name: Enter the upstream WSUS server name in this text box.
  - Port number: By default, port 8530 is used to communicate between WSUS servers. If you're using SSL, the port number is 8531 by default. The firewall on the WSUS servers must allow inbound traffic on these ports.
  - Use SSL when synchronizing update information: Choose this option if you want communication between WSUS servers to use SSL.
  - This server is a replica of the upstream server: Choose this option if the server should operate in replica mode. The default setting is autonomous mode.

Using a Proxy Server

If the firewall between a WSUS server and the update source (Microsoft Update servers or an upstream WSUS server) blocks the communication ports that WSUS uses to synchronize updates, you can configure the WSUS server to use a proxy server in the Proxy Server tab (see Figure 10-27). A proxy server uses port 80, which should be allowed by almost all firewalls. You specify the proxy server name and optionally a port number and user credentials, if needed, to connect to the proxy server. Configuring the proxy server is beyond the scope of this book.

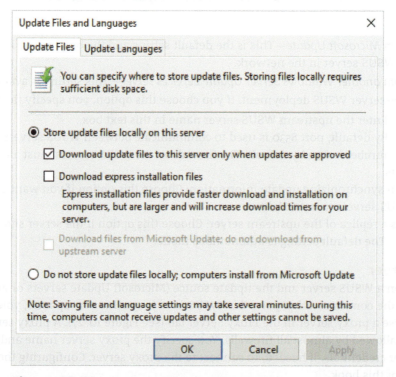

Figure 10-27 Configuring WSUS to use a proxy server

Updating Files and Languages

During the initial configuration of WSUS, you decided whether to download update files and store them on the WSUS server or store updates on Microsoft Update servers. On the first WSUS server, you have the choice of storing files locally or letting WSUS clients install approved updates from Microsoft Update servers. In the Update Services console, click Options, Update Files and Languages to change or refine these settings (see Figure 10-28).

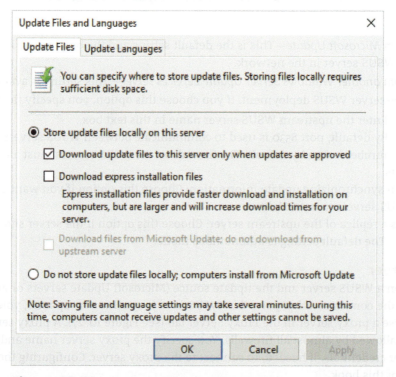

Figure 10-28 Updating files and languages

In this dialog box, you have two main options:

- *Store update files locally on this server*—If you select this option, you have three additional options:
  - Download update files to this server only when updates are approved: This is the default option. If you disable this option, all update files are downloaded whether they're approved or not.
  - Download express installation files: If this option is selected, the downloaded files are larger and take up more space on the server, but WSUS clients are able to download and install updates faster from the WSUS server.
  - Download files from Microsoft Update; do not download from an upstream server: This option is available only on a **downstream server** when you have a multiple-server WSUS deployment. By default, downstream servers get update files from upstream servers. If this option is selected, the server gets files directly from Microsoft Update servers.
- *Do not store update files locally; computers install from Microsoft Update*—If you select this option, update must still be approved before clients can install them, but approved updates are downloaded by clients directly from Microsoft Update servers, not stored on local servers.

If your organization uses Windows in several languages, click the Update Languages tab shown in Figure 10-28, and choose the languages you want to download updates for.

Changing the Update Files Location

After you have used WSUS for a while, you might need to move the location for update files because, for example, you're running out of space on the current volume or want to offload files to a different disk to improve performance. To do this, you use the command-line tool `wsusutil.exe` with the `movecontent` option to change the path and optionally copy existing update files to the new location. You use this command to manage aspects of your WSUS server from the command line, many of which you can't do with Update Services console. This command is in the folder where WSUS is installed, which is usually C:\Program Files\Update Services\Tools. So, to change the location from C:\WSUSContent to D:\WSUScontent, you do the following:

1. Create a new folder on the D: volume named WSUScontent.
2. Open a command prompt window and change to the C:\Program Files\Update Services\Tools directory.
3. Enter the command `wsusutil movecontent D:\WSUScontent`.

By default, `wsusutil.exe` copies the existing content to the new location. If you want to change the path but not copy existing content, add the `-skipcopy` option at the end of the command.

Configuring SSL

You can configure WSUS servers to use SSL for a more secure WSUS deployment. By using SSL, update metadata is encrypted and WSUS servers are authenticated. To configure SSL, follow these steps:

1. Install a certificate for the WSUS website. You can use the Active Directory Certificate Services role for this purpose.
2. Change the bindings on the WSUS website to use HTTPS.
3. Configure the WSUS website's virtual root to use SSL.
4. To tell WSUS to use SSL, issue the command `wsusutil.exe configuressl` *WSUSServerName* (replacing *WSUSServerName* with the name of the WSUS server configured on the installed certificate).
5. Finally, you configure clients to use SSL. Using Group Policy, configure the Microsoft update service location setting to use HTTPS in the URL instead of HTTP.

Creating WSUS Reports

You might want to periodically see the results of WSUS client updates and WSUS server synchronizations. WSUS has a built-in report generator to show you the following types of information (see Figure 10-29):

- *Update reports*—These reports show summary or detailed information about each update, including which computers received each update.

- *Computer reports*—These reports show summary or detailed information about each computer getting updates, including which updates were installed by each computer.
- *Synchronization reports*—This report shows the results of the last synchronization.

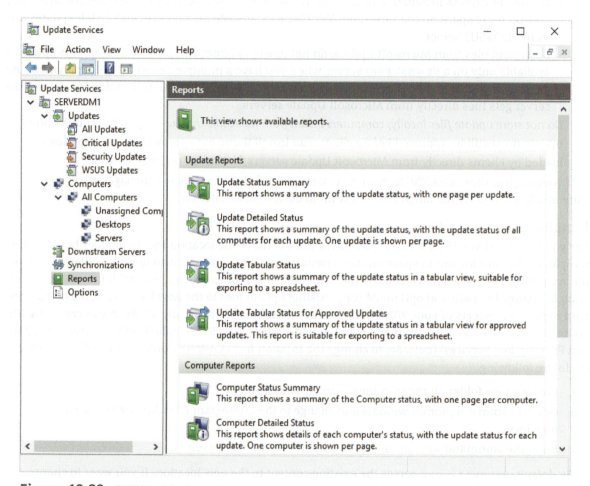

Figure 10-29 WSUS reports

The reports feature requires installing the Microsoft Report Viewer 2012 Redistributable before you can view reports. If you click a report in the Update Services console without installing this component, you're prompted to install the report viewer.

Configuring WSUS with PowerShell

As with most features in Windows Server 2016, WSUS has a bevy of PowerShell cmdlets for automating some configuration tasks. Table 10-2 lists many of the PowerShell cmdlets that you can use to configure most aspects of WSUS.

To see a full list of WSUS-related PowerShell cmdlets, type `Get-Command *-Wsus*` at a PowerShell prompt. For more information on a cmdlet, type `Get-Help` `CmdletName` (replacing `CmdletName` with the name of the cmdlet).

Some of these cmdlets are useful only when used with another command. For example, `Approve-WsusUpdate` should be used with `Get-WsusUpdate`. The following command uses `Get-WsusUpdate` to produce a list of updates that have the classification "Critical" and are currently

Table 10-2 PowerShell cmdlets for configuring WSUS

Cmdlet	Description
Add-WsusComputer	Adds a client computer to a WSUS group.
Approve-WsusUpdate	Approves an update.
Deny-WsusUpdate	Declines an update.
Get-WsusClassification	Shows a list of WSUS classifications.
Get-WsusComputer	Shows a list of WSUS client computers registered on the WSUS server.
Get-WsusProduct	Shows a list of all products by category currently available on WSUS.
Get-WsusServer	Shows the WSUS server.
Get-WsusUpdate	Shows a list of all updates currently available, including the classification and approval status of each update.
Invoke-WsusServerCleanup	Cleans up old update files on a WSUS server, including unused update files, old revisions, superseded updates, and inactive computer accounts.
Set-WsusClassification	Enables or disables an update classification for synchronization. For example, you can enable or disable drivers or service packs.
Set-WsusProduct	Enables or disables a product for synchronization.
Set-WsusServerSynchronization	Sets the source for WSUS synchronization: Microsoft Update or an upstream server. Also allows you to set the upstream server name, port number, and SSL.

not approved. This list is then piped to the `Approve-WsusUpdate` cmdlet, which approves each update for installation by all computers.

```
Get-WsusUpdate -Classification Critical -Approval
    Unapproved | Approve-WsusUpdate -Action Install
    -TargetGroupName "All Computers"
```

Remember, you can add the `-whatif` parameter to a command to see the results of the command without actually performing the action.

Activity 10-4: Creating a Custom Computer Group

Time Required: 25 minutes
Objective: Create a WSUS custom computer group after exploring the Update Services console.
Required Tools and Equipment: ServerDC1, ServerDM1
Description: In this activity, you explore the Update Services console and create a computer group.

1. On ServerDM1, in Server Manager, open the Update Services console.
2. In the left pane, click to expand **ServerDM1**, and then click **Updates**. This window shows an overview of the updates. Click to expand **Updates**, and then click **All Updates**. No updates are shown yet because you haven't synchronized with the Microsoft Update servers.
3. In the left pane, click to expand **Computers** and then **All Computers**. You see a group named Unassigned Computers, which contains all computers that haven't been assigned to another group. The All Computers group contains all computer groups and the computers in those groups.
4. Right-click **All Computers** and click **Add Computer Group**. Type **Desktops** for the name, and then click **Add**.

5. Repeat Step 4 to create a group named **Servers**. You now have two computer groups you can use to organize desktop computers and servers so that you can specify different update rules for them. You add computers to these groups later.

6. In the left pane, click **Downstream Servers**. If any servers were using this server as the update source, they would be listed here.

7. In the left pane, click **Synchronizations**. You see a history of synchronization attempts and the resulting status.

8. In the left pane, click **Reports**. You can generate a number of reports on updates with this option.

9. In the left pane, click **Options**. All the options you set with the Windows Server Update Services Configuration Wizard in the previous activity and more can be configured here. If you want to run the wizard again, for example, click the WSUS Server Configuration Wizard at the bottom of the Options pane.

10. You're using client-side targeting, which is enabled in the Update Services console and then configured with Group Policy. To enable client-side targeting, click **Options** in the left pane, and click **Computers** in the center pane. Click the **Use Group Policy or registry settings on computers** option button, and then click **OK**. Client-side targeting is now enabled.

11. The next step is to enable client computers to use this server for Windows Update, which you do in the next activity. Close the Update Services console and continue to the next activity.

Activity 10-5: Configuring Windows Update with Group Policy

Time Required: 10 minutes

Objective: Create a GPO to configure Windows Update on client computers.

Required Tools and Equipment: ServerDC1, ServerDM1

Description: Now that WSUS is configured, you need to configure clients to use the WSUS server for their updates. You also enable client-side targeting by using Group Policy on a domain controller. To use the new GPO you create, you create an OU in Active Directory, move a computer account to it, and link the GPO to the OU.

1. On ServerDC1 in Server Manager, click **Tools, Group Policy Management** from the menu.

2. In the left pane of Group Policy Management, click to expand **Domains** and click to expand **MCSA2016.local**. Right-click **Group Policy Objects** and click **New**.

3. In the New GPO dialog box, type **WSUS-Servers,** and then click **OK**. Right-click the GPO you just created and click **Edit**.

4. In the Group Policy Management Editor, navigate to Computer Configuration, Policies, Administrative Templates, Windows Components, Windows Update.

5. In the right pane, double-click **Enable client-side targeting**. In the Enable client-side targeting window click the **Enabled** option button. In the *Target group name for this computer* list box, type **Servers**, which is the name of the group you created in the previous activity, and then click **OK**.

6. Next, you tell clients the name of the WSUS server where they should download updates. In the right pane of the Group Policy Management Editor, double-click **Specify intranet Microsoft update service location**. Click the **Enabled** option button.

7. In the Options section, type **http://ServerDM1:8530** in both text boxes, and then click **OK**.

8. Double-click **Turn off auto-restart for updates during active hours**. Click the **Enabled** option button. Under Active Hours, change the **End** time to **8 PM** so that the policy now looks like Figure 10-30. Click **OK**.

9. Double-click **Defer Windows Updates**. Double-click **Select when Feature Updates are received**. Click the **Enabled** option button. In the Options box, change the days value to **10**. Click **OK**.

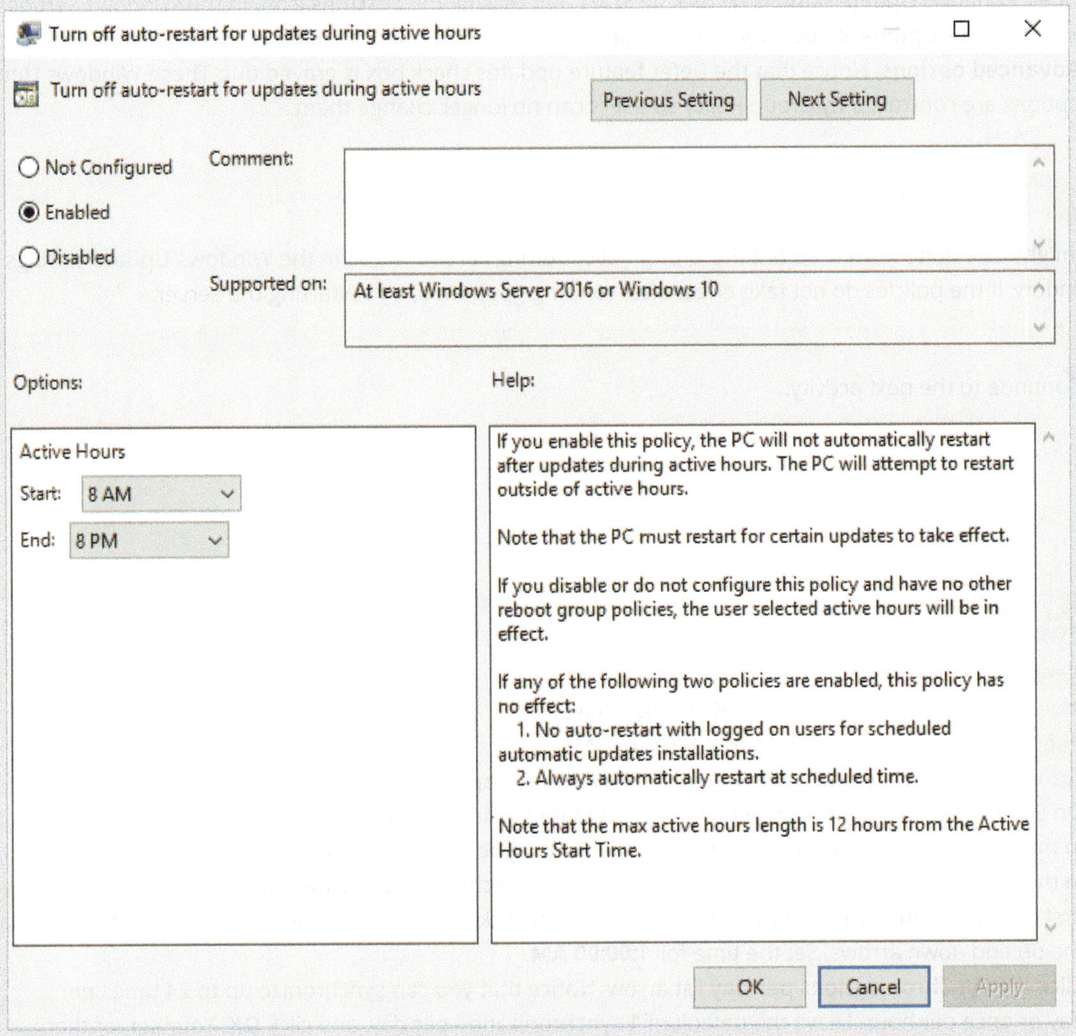

Figure 10-30   Turn off auto-restart for updates during active hours

10. Browse through the other policies available for Windows Update so that you know what you can configure with Group Policy. When you're finished, close the Group Policy Management Editor and Group Policy Management.

11. Next, you need to link the GPO to an OU containing the target computer accounts. Open Active Directory Users and Computers, and create an OU named **Servers**. Move the **ServerDM1** and **ServerDM2** computer accounts from the Computers folder to the Servers OU you just created. When asked if you are sure you wish to move the object, click **Yes**.

12. Open Group Policy Management, and then right-click the **Servers** OU and click **Link an Existing GPO**. In the Select GPO dialog box, click **WSUS-Servers**, and then click **OK**. Close Group Policy Management. Now, both ServerDM1 and ServerDM2 will be affected by the policies you just configured.

13. On ServerDM1, open a command prompt, type **gpupdate /force**, and press **Enter**. This command causes new policies to be downloaded from the server immediately. Close the command prompt.

14. Open Windows Update settings by clicking **Start** and clicking the **Settings** icon. In the Windows Settings window, click **Update & security**. Notice that the Change active hours option is no longer available. Click **Advanced options**. Notice that the Defer feature updates check box is grayed out. These Windows Update options are controlled by Group Policy so users can no longer change them.

> **Note** 🔗
>
> It might take quite a while before the Group Policy settings are reflected in the Windows Update settings window. If the policies do not take effect after running `gpupdate`, try restarting the server.

15. Continue to the next activity.

Activity 10-6: Configuring WSUS Synchronization and Approval Rules

Time Required: 15 minutes
Objective: Configure synchronization and approval rules.
Required Tools and Equipment: ServerDC1, ServerDM1
Description: In this activity, you configure synchronization and approval rules.

1. On ServerDM1, in Server Manager, open the Update Services console, if necessary.
2. In the left pane, click **Options**. In the right pane, click **Synchronization Schedule**.
3. In the Synchronization Schedule dialog box, click the **Synchronize automatically** option button. You set the first synchronization for the day by typing the time or clicking the hour, minute, second, or AM/PM and using the up and down arrows. Set the time for **1:00:00 AM.**
4. Click the **Synchronizations per day** list arrow. Notice that you can synchronize up to 24 times per day or once per hour. Leave the default of **1** synchronization per day, and click **OK**. Your server then synchronizes with Microsoft Update servers once a day at 1:00 a.m. (*Note:* If you don't want the server to synchronize automatically, change the setting back to Synchronize manually. Ask your instructor for guidance.)
5. In the right pane of the Update Services console, click **Automatic Approvals**. In the Rule properties list box, click the **all computers** link.
6. In the Choose Computer Groups dialog box, click to clear the **Unassigned computers** and **Desktops** check boxes so that only the **Servers** check box is selected. The automatic approval rule then applies only to computers in this group. Updates for all other computers and servers must be approved manually. Click **OK**.
7. Click the **Default Automatic Approval Rule** check box to enable the rule.
8. Click **New Rule** to see how you can create your own approval rules. You can approve rules by update classification (e.g., critical updates, security updates, and service packs) and for specific products (Windows 10, Office, etc.). You can also set an approval deadline. Click **Cancel**, and then click **OK** to close the Automatic Approvals dialog box.
9. Shut down all servers.

Implementing Windows Defender

- 70-740 – Maintain and monitor server environments:
  Maintain server installations

Windows Defender is the Windows anti-malware solution that is installed and enabled by default. Windows Defender monitors the system for various malware threats such as viruses, worms, and spyware. Because Windows Defender is installed by default, there is no requirement to configure it, but you may want to configure some options that are specific to your environment. In addition, you can configure WSUS to approve Windows Defender updates automatically. The following sections describe how to configure Windows Defender using Group Policy and PowerShell and how to configure WSUS to approve Windows Defender updates automatically.

Configuring Windows Defender with Group Policy

You can configure Windows Defender manually through the Windows Settings app (see Figure 10-31), but in an enterprise environment, it's impractical to configure it on each computer. In addition, by using Group Policy, you know that it's configured consistently throughout the enterprise and users cannot make changes to the configuration.

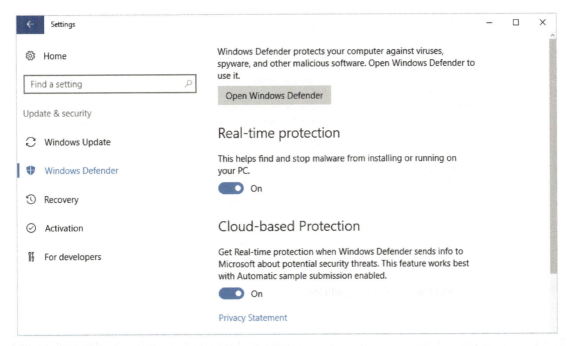

Figure 10-31   Windows Defender settings app

The Windows Defender policies (see Figure 10-32) are found in Group Policy under Computer Configuration, Policies, Administrative Templates, Windows Components, Windows Defender. As you can see, there are numerous settings you can configure, many more than you can with the Windows Settings app or with PowerShell. We'll look at a few of the more common settings you may want to utilize:

- *Turn off Windows Defender*—If this setting is enabled, Windows Defender will not run on the computers affected by this policy. You may want to enable this option if you are using a third-party anti-malware program.

- *Randomize scheduled task times*—Enable this setting to randomize the start time of scheduled tasks such as system scans and definition updates. This policy is useful on virtual machines running on the same host to distribute resource utilization on the host over a period of time. For example, it prevents several VMs from simultaneously running scans that can use considerable CPU and disk resources.
- *Exclusions*—The Exclusions folder contains settings to allow you to disable scanning and real-time protection for specific files or all files in specified folders. You can also exclude specific file extensions or processes from scanning.
- *Real-time Protection*—There are a number of policy settings in the Real-time Protection folder. Real-time protection is enabled by default, so files that are received by the network or opened are scanned immediately for malware. The Turn off real-time protection policy lets you disable real-time protection so malware is detected only when scheduled scans occur.
- *Scan*—The Scan folder has settings to configure when and how often to perform scans and which drives to scan such as whether to scan removable or network drives.

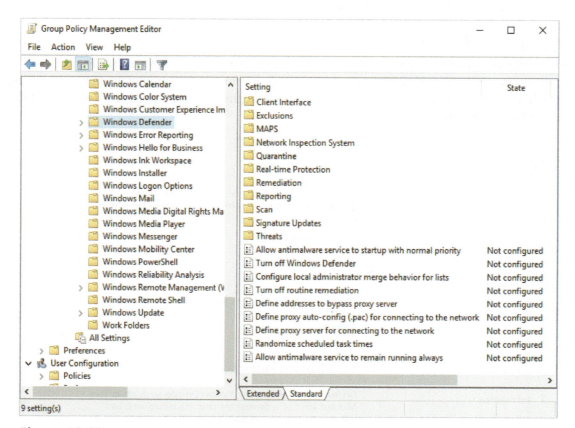

Figure 10-32   Windows Defender policies

This list is only a small number of Windows Defender settings you can configure with Group Policy. Browse through the settings in the Windows Defender folder in Group Policy to get the full picture of the many settings that can be configured.

Configuring Windows Defender with PowerShell

PowerShell gives you more control over Windows Defender on the local computer than the Windows Settings app, but it doesn't have the array of settings that Group Policy provides. To see a list of PowerShell cmdlets for Windows Defender, type `Get -Command -Module Defender` at a PowerShell prompt (see Figure 10-33).

To see what each of the cmdlets does and how to use them, type `Get-Help` *cmdletName* where *cmdletName* is the name of one of the cmdlets from Figure 10-33.

```
PS C:\Users\Administrator> Get-Command -Module Defender

CommandType     Name
-----------     ----
Function        Add-MpPreference
Function        Get-MpComputerStatus
Function        Get-MpPreference
Function        Get-MpThreat
Function        Get-MpThreatCatalog
Function        Get-MpThreatDetection
Function        Remove-MpPreference
Function        Remove-MpThreat
Function        Set-MpPreference
Function        Start-MpScan
Function        Start-MpWDOScan
Function        Update-MpSignature
```

Figure 10-33   Listing PowerShell cmdlets related to Windows Defender

Configuring WSUS for Windows Defender

Windows Defender works by comparing data patterns, called *signatures*, in files to signatures of known malware. When a signature match is made, Windows Defender flags the file as potential malware and takes action such as deleting or quarantining the file. In order for this method to be effective, Windows Defender's signature database must be kept up to date. Periodically, Windows Defender downloads updated signatures through Windows Update. If WSUS is implemented on the network, it is critical that these updates are approved and distributed to WSUS clients as soon as possible. An administrator can facilitate this process by configuring WSUS to auto-approve Windows Defender updates. To ensure that Windows Defender updates are included in WSUS and that they are automatically approved, perform the following steps on the WSUS server:

1. First, make sure Windows Defender and definitions are downloaded by WSUS:

    - Open the Update Services console, click Options, and click Products and Classifications.
    - On the Products tab, under Windows, find and select Windows Defender (highlighted in Figure 10-34).
    - On the Classifications tab, make sure Definition Updates is selected.

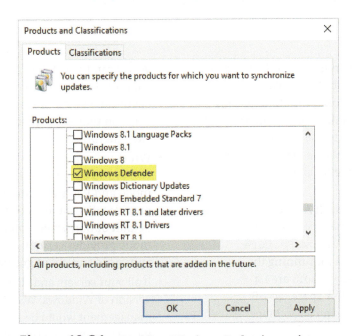

Figure 10-34   Enabling Windows Defender updates

2. Next, enable automatic approvals for Windows Defender:

- In Options, click Automatic Approvals and click New Rule. In the Add Rule dialog box, click the check box *When an update is in a specific classification*.
- Under Edit the properties, click any classification. In the Choose Update Classifications, uncheck all classifications except Definition Updates.
- Give a name to the rule such as DefUpdates. The rule should look like Figure 10-35. If necessary, you can narrow the update to specific computer groups or leave the default of all computers.

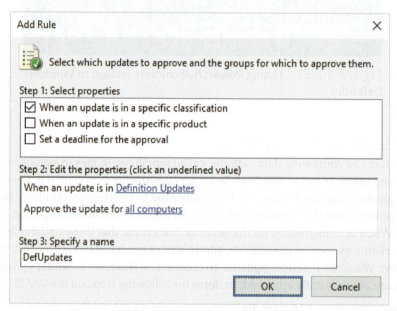

Figure 10-35   Creating a rule to automatically approve definition updates

Chapter Summary

- Windows Server Update Services (WSUS) is a server role that allows an administrator to take control of Microsoft product updates on computers running Windows OS. After it's installed and configured, you configure Windows clients to use the WSUS server for Windows updates. Clients are best configured with Group Policy, so your clients need to be domain members.

- The WSUS role is installed with Add Roles and Features in Server Manager or by using the PowerShell `Install-WindowsFeature` cmdlet. Some requirements for running the WSUS role on Windows Server 2016 are 1.4 GHz CPU, 10 GB available disk space (40 GB recommended), 2 GB RAM, and a 100 Mbps network interface.

- WSUS can be installed as a single-server solution supporting from a few dozen to several hundred clients at a single site or as a multiple-server solution providing update services to large multi-site enterprises.

- When using a multiple-server deployment, you have two WSUS administration options: Autonomous mode and Replica mode. The Autonomous mode provides distributed administration and is the default option when you install WSUS. Replica mode provides centralized administration of update approvals and client groups.

- If all your servers and clients are running the latest version of Windows, WSUS configuration and management would be straightforward. However, most environments run multiple versions of Windows.

- Some of the things to be aware of when running mixed OS environments include Group Policy settings for Windows Update; these settings vary depending on the version of Windows installed on a computer. You should also know that the Group Policy settings for Windows Update vary depending on the version of Windows installed on a computer. If older versions of Windows are retired, be sure to deselect those products.

- Before clients in a network can begin using WSUS for automatic updates, you need to perform some configuration tasks on WSUS: creating computer groups, assigning computers to groups, configuring Windows Update on client computers, and configuring WSUS synchronization and approval rules.

- To use WSUS server, your clients must be told to use the WSUS server instead of the Microsoft Update servers on the Internet to find and download updates. If your computers are domain members, you can use Group Policy on a domain controller to configure Windows Update; otherwise, you can configure clients separately with the Local Group Policy Editor.

- Other WSUS configuration tasks you might need to undertake include updating the source and proxy server, updating files and language settings, configuring SSL, upgrading a WSUS server, and creating WSUS reports.

- In Windows Server 2016, WSUS has several PowerShell cmdlets for automating some configuration tasks. To see a list of WSUS-related PowerShell cmdlets, type `Get-Command *-Wsus*` at a PowerShell prompt.

- Windows Defender is the Windows anti-malware solution that is installed and enabled by default. Windows Defender monitors the system for various malware threats such as viruses, worms, and spyware. You can configure WSUS to approve Windows Defender updates automatically.

- You can configure Windows Defender manually through the Windows Settings application. In an enterprise environment, you should use Group Policy to configure Windows Defender to ensure that your configurations are consistent throughout the enterprise environment and that users cannot make changes to the configuration.

Key Terms

autonomous mode
build
client-side targeting
Current Branch
Current Branch for Business

downstream server
feature update
hotfix
patch management
quality update

replica mode
server-side targeting
upstream server
Windows Server Update Services
   (WSUS)

Review Questions

1. How are client computers usually configured to access a WSUS server?
   a. Using the Windows Update Control Panel applet
   b. Using Group Policy in a domain environment
   c. Using WSUS discover mode
   d. Using regedit to configure Windows Update manually

2. Which of the following is true when using WSUS for Windows updates? (Choose all that apply.)
   a. It increases Internet bandwidth use.
   b. It centralizes control over product updates.
   c. Only approved updates are installed.
   d. It is easy to determine which updates have been applied.

3. Which of the following protocols is utilized by WSUS by default to collect updates from Microsoft Update servers and among WSUS servers in a multiple-server deployment?
   a. HTTPS
   b. FTP
   c. HTTP
   d. UDP

4. Which of the following is a reason to use WSUS in your network?
   a. No server is required.
   b. Client computers always get updates faster.
   c. It requires less Internet bandwidth.
   d. All updates are installed automatically.

5. Which of the following is a requirement for running the WSUS role in Windows Server 2016? (Choose all that apply.)
   a. Installed on a domain controller
   b. 10 GB available disk space
   c. 2 GB RAM
   d. Full SQL Server installation

6. Which WSUS server mode centralizes administration of update approvals and client groups?
   a. Replica mode
   b. Clone mode
   c. Autonomous mode
   d. Automatic mode

7. Which of the following is true about installing WSUS? (Choose all that apply.)
   a. You must install SQL Server before you install WSUS.
   b. Update files can be stored on a share on another server.
   c. The Web Server role is also installed.
   d. Clients can begin using WSUS as soon as it's installed.

8. Which of the following is an update classification that you can configure the WSUS server to synchronize with? (Choose all that apply.)
   a. Critical updates
   b. Service packs
   c. Information updates
   d. Security updates

9. You are currently administering a Windows environment that is utilizing multiple versions of Windows OS. Which WSUS considerations should be reviewed when using multiple versions of Windows in this environment? (Choose all that apply.)
   a. WSUS server downloads the correct updates based on the Windows versions operating in your network.
   b. WSUS is synchronizing any new versions of Windows you have recently added with Microsoft Update servers.
   c. Identify and deselect all older versions of Windows no longer in use on your network.
   d. Ensure that all security updates are compatible with the different Windows versions on your network.

10. What should you do if you want to target specific computers for different types of updates?
    a. Create custom groups
    b. Configure Windows Update on the client
    c. Install additional WSUS servers
    d. Put computers on separate networks

11. Which of the following is a method for adding computers to WSUS groups? (Choose all that apply.)
    a. Server-side targeting
    b. Local Group Policy
    c. Client-side targeting
    d. Windows Update configuration

12. Which of the following is a method for configuring clients to use a WSUS server?
    a. On the client, go to Control Panel, Windows Update
    b. Enable WSUS discovery on clients
    c. Use Group Policy for domain members
    d. Configure the client list in WSUS options

13. Which of the following default computer groups allow you to target specific computers for different types of updates? (Choose all that apply.)
    a. All Computers
    b. Assigned Computers
    c. Local Computers
    d. Unassigned Computers

14. You have decided to use a WSUS server to update a group of computers that are not part of a domain. What specific tool can you use to configure a client computer to use WSUS when it is not part of a domain?
    a. Client Policy Editor
    b. Local Group Policy Editor
    c. WSUS console
    d. Group Policy

15. If you configure a WSUS server for automatic synchronization twice per day, which of the following is true?
    a. Client computers are sent updates every 12 hours.
    b. The WSUS server contacts the Microsoft Update servers every 12 hours.
    c. Updates don't require approval before clients are updated.
    d. The second synchronization is attempted only if the first one fails.

16. Which of the following is true about automatic approvals? (Choose all that apply.)
    a. The default automatic approval rule is enabled by default.
    b. The default automatic approval rule applies only to unassigned computers.
    c. You can change the update classification of the default rule.
    d. You can set a deadline to force an update.

17. If you want WSUS clients to download and install updates faster from the WSUS server, which WSUS server option should you configure?
    a. Download express installation files
    b. Do not store update files locally
    c. Synchronize from another WSUS server
    d. Synchronize from Microsoft Update

18. Which of the following commands will allow WSUS to use SSL for implementing a more secure WSUS deployment?
    a. `wsusutil.exe ssl`
    b. `wsusutil.exe configuressl`
    c. `ssl wsusutil.exe`
    d. `wsusutil.exe enablessl`

19. A system administrator should occasionally view the results of WSUS client updates and WSUS server synchronizations. Using the WSUS built-in report generator, which report will allow you to view the updates that have been installed on each Windows computer in your network?
    a. Update reports
    b. Computer reports
    c. WSUS Summary reports
    d. Synchronization reports

20. Which of the following PowerShell cmdlets will allow you to decline a WSUS update?
    a. `Omit-WsusUpdate`
    b. `Decline-WsusUpdate`
    c. `Deny-Update`
    d. `Deny-WsusUpdate`

21. You have recently noticed that a specific host server running some critical VMs is using a concerning amount of CPU and disk resources. Each VM on this host is using Windows Defender, and you have noticed that the Windows Defender system scans have been operating at the same time. Which setting should be configured within Group Policy to mitigate these performance issues and still allow Windows Defender to operate?
    a. Scan
    b. Turn off Windows Defender
    c. Randomize scheduled task times
    d. Exclusions

Critical Thinking

The following activities give you critical thinking challenges. Case Projects offer a scenario with a problem to solve and for which you supply a written solution.

Case Project 10-1: Unable to Configure Windows Update

You have recently hired a server administrator to help maintain your servers and desktops in your Windows domain. She was working with a desktop computer and found that she couldn't configure Windows Update. Write a memo explaining why she was unable to configure Windows Update and point out four advantages of using WSUS.

Case Project 10-2: Designing a WSUS Deployment

You manage a network with four domain controllers running Windows Server 2016, seven member servers running Windows Server 2016, four member servers running Windows Server 2012 R2, 100 Windows 10 computers, and 35 Windows 8.1 computers. You need to maintain updates and patches on all these computers. Explain how you would set up WSUS to do so. Which WSUS features would you use? What method would you use to allow you to target specific computers with different types of updates? What method would you use to configure Windows Update on client computers?

CHAPTER 11

SERVER MONITORING AND BACKUP

After reading this chapter and completing the exercises, you will be able to:

Monitor Windows Server

Back up Windows Server

Recover Windows Server from backup

Back up and recover specific roles

Installing a server and never having to worry about performance would be great, but it isn't realistic. Server use changes when users are added and applications are installed, and problems with hardware and application updates can cause unexpected events. For these reasons, Windows Server 2016 includes several tools, such as Task Manager and Performance Monitor, to help you check and analyze server performance. In this chapter, you learn how to use these tools to troubleshoot problems and to evaluate performance to see whether and where changes to system configuration are needed.

The idea of a server going down or a hard disk crashing on a mission-critical server keeps IT administrators up at night, especially if they don't have procedures in place to recover from these events quickly. This chapter covers backup and restore features in Windows Server 2016 that can help IT administrators sleep better knowing they can recover a system from failure or data loss. You learn about Windows Server Backup and strategies for backing up server roles, including file servers, domain controllers, virtualization servers, and web servers.

Monitoring a Windows Server

- **70-740 – Maintain and monitor server environments:**
  Monitor server installations

Table 11-1 summarizes what you need for the hands-on activities in this chapter.

Table 11-1 Activity requirements

Activity	Requirements	Notes
Activity 11-1: Resetting Your Virtual Environment	ServerDC1, ServerDM1	
Activity 11-2: Creating a Custom View in Event Viewer	ServerDC1	
Activity 11-3: Creating an Event Subscription	ServerDC1, ServerDM1	
Activity 11-4: Exploring Task Manager	ServerDC1	
Activity 11-5: Using Performance Monitor	ServerDC1	
Activity 11-6: Creating a Performance Baseline Report with a Data Collector Set	ServerDC1	
Activity 11-7: Creating a Performance Alert	ServerDC1	
Activity 11-8: Installing Windows Server Backup and Scheduling a Backup	ServerDC1, ServerDM1	ServerDC1 is not used in the activity, but it is the domain controller for the domain in which ServerDM1 is a member, so it should be running.
Activity 11-9: Performing a One-Time Backup of Selected Files	ServerDC1, ServerDM1	ServerDC1 is not used in the activity, but it is the domain controller for the domain in which ServerDM1 is a member, so it should be running.
Activity 11-10: Recovering a File	ServerDC1, ServerDM1	ServerDC1 is not used in the activity, but it is the domain controller for the domain in which ServerDM1 is a member, so it should be running.

In networks, any number of things can go wrong or affect the performance and availability of servers and their resources, so network administrators should monitor which users are signed in, what they're doing, and what resources they're using. Some problems reveal themselves over time, so reviewing past data to detect trends is the best type of analysis to perform. If you're troubleshooting an ongoing problem or responding to a complaint about current performance, however, most likely you want to see what's happening on the system in real time instead of reviewing old log data. Luckily, Windows provides several types and sources of information on the health of a server and the network. The categories of information that you can monitor includes events occurring on the system, tasks running on the system, and resources being used. The following sections explore the available information and the tools you can use to collect and analyze this information.

Monitoring Events

As events occur on a Windows server, they're recorded in one of several event logs. Windows Server 2016 includes **Event Viewer**, an MMC snap-in, to review the events recorded in logs on your local computer as well as other computers on the network. You can also use Event Viewer to get more detailed information on a specific event. This tool is useful for tracking down system or application problems and investigating security violations. It can also react to events, so you can create a task that runs a program or script when a specific type of event occurs.

Viewing Events

After events have been logged, Event Viewer reads a log and formats the information in a form that's easy to read and interpret. You can start Event Viewer with the Computer Management console, the Tools menu in Server Manager, or the `eventvwr.msc` command. At startup, Event Viewer looks like Figure 11-1.

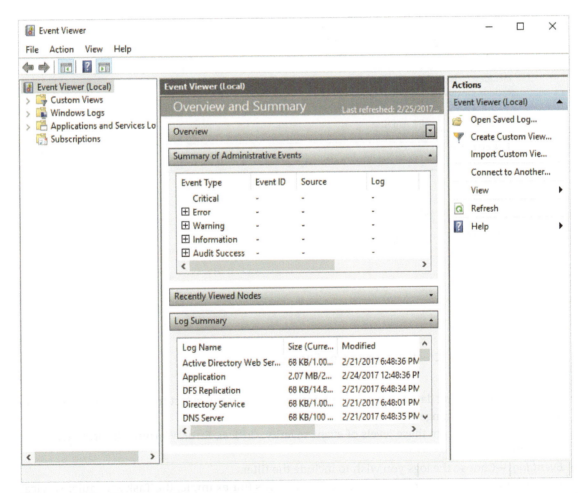

Figure 11-1   The Event Viewer main window

A busy system might log hundreds or even thousands of events, and if you're trying to isolate a particular problem, going through every item in an event log can be daunting. For this reason, Event Viewer offers several ways to search, filter, and sort event logs.

To search an event log, expand the log group that the event log belongs to (for example, Windows Logs), click the event log (such as Application) you want to find an event in, and then click Find in the

Actions pane. Basic search features are limited to text occurrences—using keywords such as "error" or phrases such as "did not start." For an event to be included in the search results, an exact text match is required. For example, "did start" doesn't match "did not start," and vice versa.

To create a filter, select a log in the left pane, and then click Filter Current Log in the Actions pane. Filters give you more flexibility in specifying criteria than the basic Find function does; however, they're limited to a single event log. Here are the criteria for filtering (see Figure 11-2):

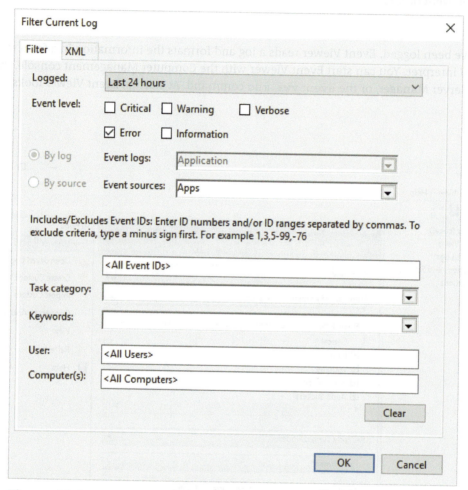

Figure 11-2   Creating an event log filter

- *Logged*—The time and date range an event occurred in. You can select from a list of several periods or specify a custom range.
- *Event level*—Select from these levels of event severity: Critical, Error, Warning, Information, and Verbose.
- *Event logs*—Choose the logs you wish to include the filter.
- *Event sources*—Select one or multiple sources of events (for example, the Task Scheduler service).
- *Event IDs*—You can enter a single ID or multiple IDs separated by commas. Placing a minus sign in front of an ID excludes it from the filter results.
- *Task category*—A list of categories becomes available only if you select an event source with corresponding tasks.
- *Keywords*—Select from a list of predefined keywords, such as Audit Failure or Audit Success.
- *User*—Use specific user accounts as filters. You can enter a single user or a list of users separated by commas.
- *Computer(s)*—Use a specific computer or groups of computers as filters. For multiple computers, separate the list items with commas.

Clicking a column header sorts an event log based on the column's contents. For example, clicking the Date and Time column header sorts the display from the earliest event to the latest. Click again to display the most recent event at the top. Sorting might take a while if the log is large. To return a list of events to its default order, right-click the column header and click Remove Sorting.

Each event has detailed information associated with it. When you click an event in the center pane, details are displayed in a pane under the list of events. For example, a user disconnecting a Remote Desktop session without logging off generates an information event with a specific code. Double-clicking the event opens a separate window showing details (see Figure 11-3), which is useful when you want to compare details of several events at once.

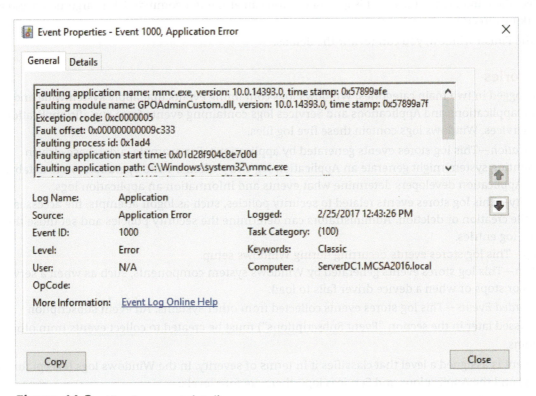

Figure 11-3   Viewing event details

Notice the two tabs in this window: General and Details. The General tab formats information about the event in an easy-to-read table format. The Details tab formats information in XML view or "friendly view" with the data in a tree structure and the event name bolded. You can save event log information in these formats: an event file that can be opened and displayed in Event Viewer; an XML file, similar to the XML view in the Details tab; and a tab-delimited or comma-delimited file.

Creating Tasks from Events

Responding to events manually can be time-consuming and inefficient because an administrator would have to review the logs constantly. However, you can create a task in Event Viewer that runs whenever a particular event is logged. Follow these steps:

1. Right-click an event in a log and click Attach Task To This Event to start the Create Basic Task Wizard.

2. You can enter a name for the task or use the name that's assigned automatically. The assigned name begins with the log name followed by the source and event ID.

3. The next window shows details about the type of event that triggers the task: log name, source, and event ID. This information can't be changed.

4. In the Action window, you select from these options: Start a program, Send an e-mail (deprecated), or Display a message (deprecated). To run a program or script, click the Start a program option button, and then click Next.

> **Note** 📎
>
> Sending an e-mail and displaying a message are deprecated options. They're still available, but they might be removed in later versions, so using them isn't recommended.

5. In the Start a Program window, type the program or script name you want to run (or browse to and select the name) when the event is generated. You can also enter command-line arguments and a working directory.

6. In the Finish window, you can review the details.

Log Categories

Events are logged in two main categories: Windows logs containing events that apply systemwide and events from applications and Applications and Services logs containing events from specific applications or system services. Windows logs contain these five log files:

- *Application*—This log stores events generated by applications. For example, a database-driven accounting system might generate an Application log entry when a write operation to the database fails. Application developers determine what events and information an application logs.
- *Security*—This log stores events related to security policies, such as logon attempts, file accesses, and file creation or deletion. Administrators can determine the security policies and set those that create log entries.
- *Setup*—This log stores events occurring during Windows setup.
- *System*—This log stores events generated by Windows system components, such as when a service starts or stops or when a device driver fails to load.
- *Forwarded Events*—This log stores events collected from other systems. An event subscription (discussed later in the section "Event Subscriptions") must be created to collect events from other systems.

Each event is assigned a level that classifies it in terms of severity. In the Windows logs (except for the Security log) and the Applications and Services logs, there are four levels:

- *Error*—A problem that can affect how the application or component logging the event functions.
- *Critical*—An unrecoverable failure in an application or a component.
- *Warning*—An issue that doesn't immediately affect operations but might cause future problems if not addressed.
- *Information*—Provision of information related to normal operations, such as a service starting or stopping normally.

The Security log has these two levels: Success Audit (a file or object was accessed successfully) and Failure Audit (a file or object was accessed unsuccessfully).

Although the basic information in Windows logs can be helpful in troubleshooting Windows system and application problems, the information in Applications and Services logs is usually more useful in troubleshooting. There are four subtypes of these logs: Admin, Operational, Analytic, and Debug.

The Admin subtype shows a problem and a solution with instructions on how to fix the problem. The detail and guidance it supplies make it a good source of troubleshooting information for users, administrators, and support staff. Operational logs aren't as straightforward, and determining solutions might require more analysis; typically, users don't have the knowledge or expertise to use an Operational log. Analytic logs record a series of events related to a problem. Because the volume of events logged can be quite high, sifting through information in Analytic logs requires more effort than with Admin or Operational logs. Debug logs contain events that software developers can evaluate to troubleshoot programs. By default, the Analytic and Debug logs are hidden and disabled. To make them visible, right-click the log category you want to enable, point to View, and click Show Analytic and Debug Logs.

Creating Custom Views

Now that you know where different types of events are stored, you might be thinking of situations in which grouping different types of events makes it easier to see relationships or simply have an overall view. The problem is that Event Viewer typically shows information from only one log at a time. So, how can you mix a variety of data from different logs? You can create custom views to pull data from multiple logs based on the criteria listed previously in "Viewing Events." Event logs are XML based, which enables you to construct XML queries, but the selections in the Filter tab allow you to create views that should answer most needs without requiring XML coding knowledge.

Event Subscriptions

Instead of going from system to system to check event logs, you can use the Forwarded Events log to view event information from remote computers in a single log, which can save a lot of time. To create this log, you need an event subscription. An **event subscription** specifies what server to collect events from, what events to collect, and the local event log to write them to. Activity 11-2 guides you through creating a custom view, and Activity 11-3 guides you through creating an event subscription.

Using Task Manager

Viewing what has happened on a system by looking at events that were generated is valuable but reactive; events have already happened, and you can only react to the results of these events. With **Task Manager**, a monitoring tool to view running processes and the resources they are consuming, you can see what's happening with processes running on the system in real time so that you can take action in a timely manner, if needed.

When you start Task Manager, you see a list of applications running in the foreground on the system. These are applications that have a window currently open. Clicking the More details arrow at the bottom expands the view to show more detailed information (see Figure 11-4). This view has five tabs: Processes, Performance, Users, Details, and Services. In the following sections, you will look at different tasks to see how you might use the data in these tabs.

Monitoring Processes

The Processes tab is an easy-to-read perspective of what processes are consuming which resources and the load generated on the server. There are three sections of the Processes tab: Apps, which are applications such as Notepad or Microsoft Management Console; Background processes, such as DNS Server; and Windows processes, such as Desktop Window Manager. By default, each section is sorted alphabetically. Clicking a column name sorts the display. The display is limited to two metrics—CPU and Memory—which makes it easy to see the system's CPU and memory use as a whole and for each process.

If more information for a process is available (indicated by the arrow to the left of the process name), you can expand the process to view the additional information, as shown for Microsoft Management Console in Figure 11-4. You can also expand background processes to see what services are running, which can be useful in troubleshooting. In previous versions of Task Manager, processes and services were shown separately, so seeing a relationship between them was more difficult. Right-clicking a service gives you the option to stop the service or open the service's control panel. Right-clicking a process gives you the option to end the task, go to that process in the Details tab, or go to the program file's location. The Details tab has more information on each process, including

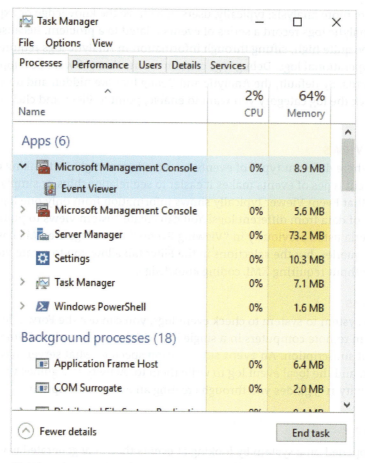

Figure 11-4   The Processes tab

the process ID (PID), the status of the process, what username it's running under, CPU and memory use for the process, and a brief description of the process.

Basic Performance Monitoring

Although there are many specialized tools you can use for performance monitoring, you can do basic monitoring in the Performance tab of Task Manager (see Figure 11-5) on three important performance components: CPU, memory, and network adapters (Ethernet in the figure). These components are listed on the left with basic current information. Under the CPU component on the left is the percentage currently being used and the processor speed. The graph on the right shows the percentage of the CPU used in the most recent 60-second period. Above the graph is the processor make, model, and speed. Under the graph on the right are the CPU's physical details, including maximum speed (in GHz), number of sockets, number of cores, number of logical processors, whether virtualization is enabled, and the size of the L1 and L2 caches.

 Note

Some systems include an L3 cache in addition to the L1 and L2 caches. On virtual machines, you may not see cache information.

The details on the left under the graph are more operational and include the current percentage utilization of the CPU, the current processor speed, how many processes are running, how many threads are in use, how many handles are in use, and the system's current uptime. A **thread** is the smallest piece

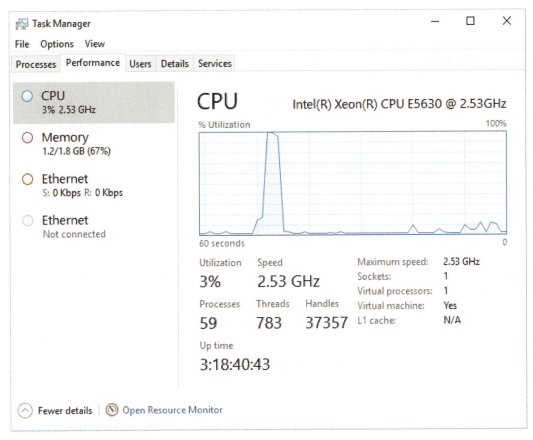

Figure 11-5   The CPU view of the Performance tab

of program code that Windows can schedule for execution. For example, Microsoft Word is an application and is listed in Task Manager in the Processes tab, but several threads can be scheduled to run within this larger process, such as the spell checking and autocorrect features. A **handle** is a reference to a resource on the computer. Handles are often associated with open files but can also be associated with a block of memory or other data structures an application is using. Handles help processes and the OS keep track of open and used resources.

Depending on the number of tasks a server is called on to perform, memory use can be a critical resource to monitor. Clicking Memory displays the view shown in Figure 11-6. In this view, you see statistics on how much memory is being used, how much is available, and what percentage of the total it represents. On the right are two graphs: Memory usage, which shows the memory use over a 60-second period, and Memory composition, which divides how the memory is being used into four categories:

- *In Use*—Memory used by the OS, applications, and other processes.
- *Modified*—Memory containing content that must be written to disk before being released for other purposes.
- *Standby*—Memory containing cached information.
- *Free*—Memory available for use.

Tip ⓘ

You have to hover your mouse over parts of the Memory composition graph to see the In use, Modified, Standby, and Free labels.

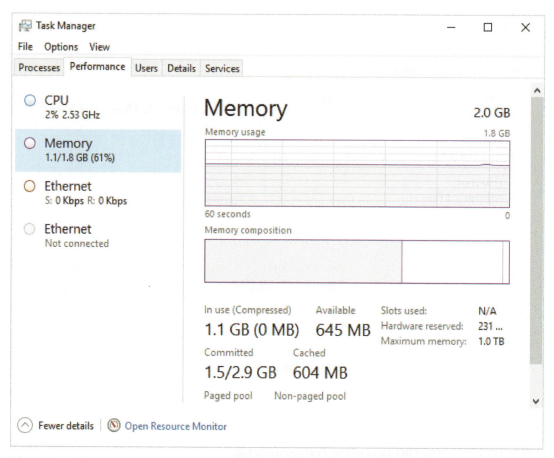

Figure 11-6 The Memory view of the Performance tab

Below the graphs on the right is hardware information, including the memory's speed, how many memory slots are being used, the form factor (indicating the type of memory), and how much memory is reserved for use by hardware. More data is available under the graphs, including the following:

- *In use*—Total amount of memory currently allocated by the OS and running processes.
- *Available*—The amount of physical memory that can be used by the system and running processes.
- *Committed*—A measure of the demand for virtual memory. As the amount of committed memory exceeds available physical memory, paging increases, and if it becomes excessive, it can have a serious effect on performance.
- *Cached*—The sum of modified and standby memory, described in the preceding list.
- *Paged pool*—The amount of memory currently required by the OS kernel and drivers that can be written to virtual memory.
- *Non-paged pool*—The amount of memory currently required by the OS kernel and drivers that must remain in physical memory.

A server usually handles a lot of network traffic. When the network adapter component is selected on the left, a graph on the right shows the network throughput over a 60-second period (see Figure 11-7). Above the graph, you see the type of network interface card (NIC). This graph makes it easy to see problems such as excessive network use. The information under the graph shows the network adapter name, connection type, and the IPv4 and IPv6 addresses. Right-clicking this graph gives you the option View network details, which displays real-time details about the network traffic, including percent utilization, bytes sent and received, and throughput (see Figure 11-8).

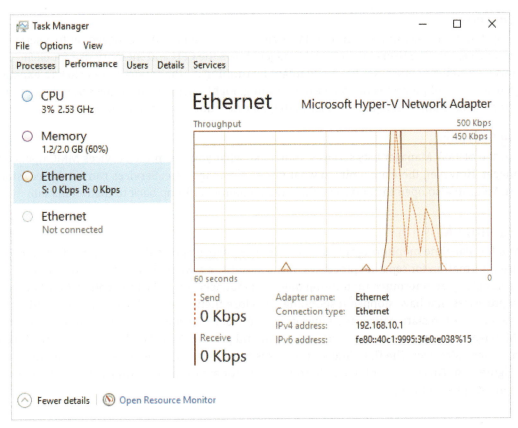

Figure 11-7 The network view of the Performance tab showing an Ethernet connection

Property	Ethernet	Ethernet
Network utilization	4.37%	0%
Link speed	10 Gbps	10 Gbps
State	Connected	Disconnected
Bytes sent throughput	0.07%	0%
Bytes received throughput	4.30%	0%
Bytes throughput	4.37%	0%
Bytes sent	8,349,548	0
Bytes received	461,967,551	0
Bytes	470,317,099	0
Bytes sent per interval	953,199	0
Bytes received per interval	54,625,284	0
Bytes per interval	55,578,483	0
Unicasts sent	319,070	0
Unicasts received	133,534	0
Unicasts	452,604	0
Unicasts sent per interval	15,777	0
Unicasts received per interval	37,593	0
Unicasts per interval	53,370	0
Nonunicasts sent	114	0

Figure 11-8 Viewing network details

Logged-On Users

Besides the system processes and background tasks running on a server, users logged on to a server consume resources, too. The Users tab in Task Manager shows the CPU and memory use for each logged-on user as well any processes he or she might be running on the server. If you click to expand the user, you see a list of processes the account is running. Right-clicking a user gives you the options of disconnecting the user and managing the user in the User Accounts control panel.

Managing Services

The Services tab of Task Manager lists services, much like what you see in the Services MMC opened via Server Manager. However, there are limits to what you can manage here. Services can be started, stopped, or restarted. You can also open the Services MMC, search online, or jump back to the Details tab.

Using Resource Monitor

Another tool for real-time monitoring is **Resource Monitor**, which shows CPU, memory, disk, and network use information for separate processes or the system as a whole in real time. You can go beyond the simple system resource monitoring that Task Manager offers. With Resource Monitor, you can review processes that have stopped responding and close them if needed; check a current file use by applications; and start, restart, pause, and end services. You start Resource Monitor from the Tools menu in Server Manager or by typing `resmon.exe` at a command prompt. You can also start it from a link at the bottom of Task Manager. The first time you start Resource Monitor, it defaults to the Overview tab shown in Figure 11-9. This tab and others in Resource Monitor are formatted similarly with data in tables on the left and graphs on the right.

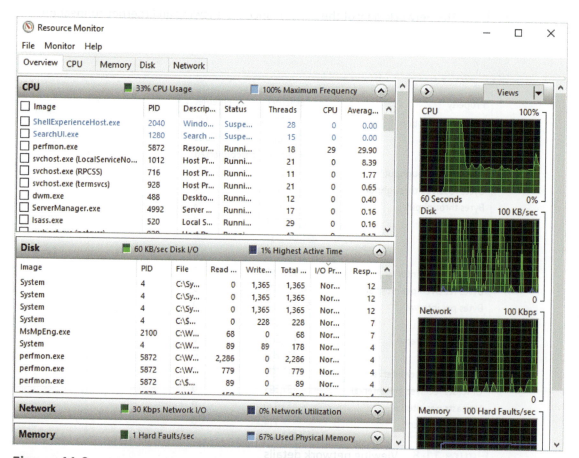

Figure 11-9   The Overview tab of Resource Monitor

The left side of the Overview tab is divided into four sections—CPU, Disk, Network, and Memory—that show current utilization and activity. Right-clicking a process in the CPU section gives you options to end, suspend, or resume it. If an application has stopped responding, for example, you can analyze the wait chain to see whether the application might be waiting on another process to release needed resources. If an application is consuming a lot of CPU or disk I/O resources, you could pause or end it to give other applications a chance to run. On the right are real-time graphs of CPU and memory use and disk and network activity. You can resize the graphs to small, medium, or large.

The CPU tab is divided into four sections: Processes, Services, Associated Handles, and Associated Modules (see Figure 11-10). The Processes section displays the name of the program executable file, the PID, a short description of the process, its status, the number of threads in use, the percentage of the CPU it's currently using, and an average of CPU use for the past 60 seconds. The Services section displays a service's name, PID, description, and status as well as the service group it belongs to, the current percentage of CPU being used, and the average CPU use. Right-click a service to start, stop, or restart it. The Associated Handles section shows the file handles in use by selected processes, and the Associated Modules section shows files, such as dynamic link libraries (DLLs), used by selected processes as part of their operation. When you click a check box next to a process name in the Processes section, the results in the lower sections are filtered. Only the services, file handles, and module names associated with this process are shown.

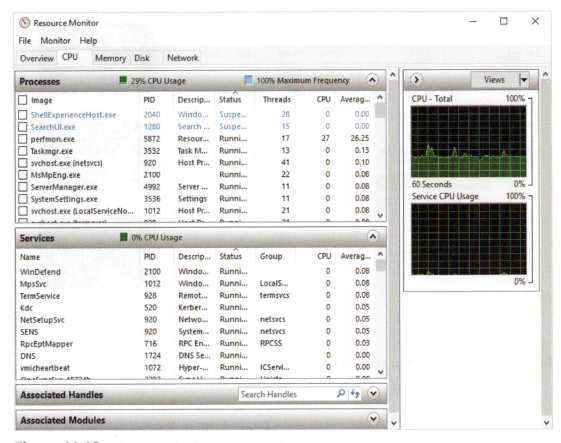

Figure 11-10   The CPU tab of Resource Monitor

Tip (i)

The PID is useful in linking the information in each section to a particular process or image.

In the Memory tab, the graphs on the right show overall memory use. The left side is divided into two sections: Processes and Physical Memory (see Figure 11-11). In the Processes section, each process's memory use is divided into these categories:

- *Hard Faults/sec*—The number of times the process must read memory written to the paging file.
- *Commit*—How much physical memory plus pages from the paging file the OS reserves for the process.
- *Working Set*—How much physical memory is currently in use.
- *Shareable*—How much physical memory is in use and shared with other processes.
- *Private*—How much physical memory is in use and not shared with other processes, which is a fairly close indication of the amount of memory this process requires to run.

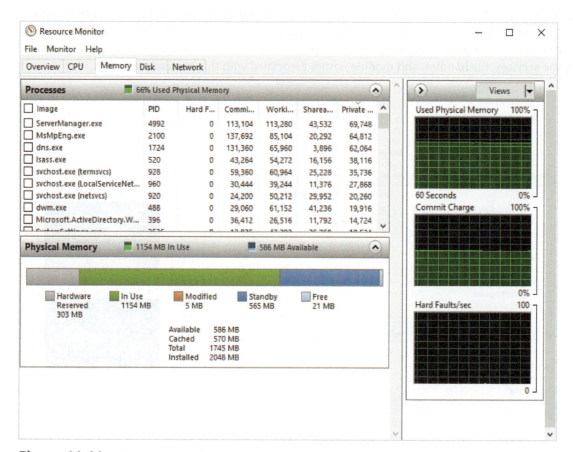

Figure 11-11 The Memory tab of Resource Monitor

The Physical Memory section has a color-coded bar graph of overall memory allocation divided into these sections:

- *Hardware Reserved*—Memory reserved by hardware components, such as buses, video cards, and sound cards, used to communicate with the OS.
- *In Use*—Memory used by OS processes, drivers, and other processes.
- *Modified*—Pages of modified memory that haven't been accessed for some time.
- *Standby*—Memory still linked to a process but available for reuse.
- *Free*—Memory not in use by any processes or released when a process ended.

The totals under the graph in this section show available, cached, total, and installed memory. The total memory is the amount installed minus the amount of hardware reserved memory (because this memory isn't part of the available pool). If you're troubleshooting performance problems, especially when there's a heavy load on a server, the graphs and displays in the Memory tab can be particularly useful. Watch for frequent periods of high levels of hard faults, which can indicate a problem with how memory is being used. (Keep in mind, however, that some hard faults are normal and don't reflect a problem.) If a lot of memory is consistently in use (shown by the size of the green bar), you might want to consider adding memory. Remember to examine the actual values as well the percentages; if a large amount of physical memory is present, there may still be sufficient memory for the system to perform adequately even at high percentages of utilization.

In the Disk tab (see Figure 11-12), graphs on the right show overall disk activity and the queue length for each disk. The left side includes three sections: Processes with Disk Activity, Disk Activity, and Storage. For each process, the Disk Activity section shows the files in use (one per line), read activity, write activity, total activity (read + write), priority, and response time. To filter the display, you can click the check box next to a process. The Storage section shows logical disks with their physical drive numbers. Several metrics in both sections can help you troubleshoot performance problems. For example, in the Storage section, a consistently high value in the Active time column (showing the percentage of time a disk is actually servicing requests) can indicate a bottleneck, and adding disk storage and distributing the load could alleviate this problem. In the Disk Activity section, response times consistently higher than 20 milliseconds (ms) warrant attention, and consistent response times higher than 50 ms indicate a serious problem.

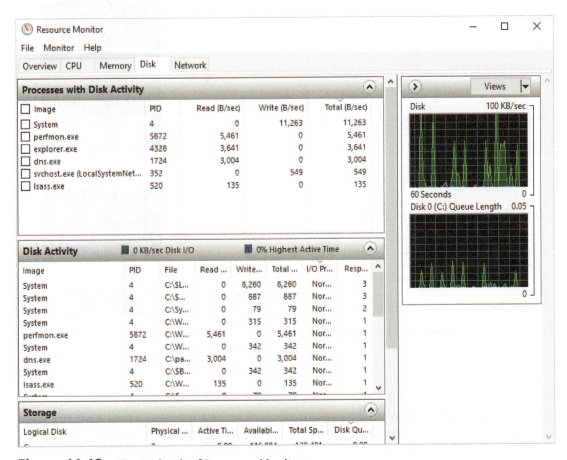

Figure 11-12   The Disk tab of Resource Monitor

In the Network tab, graphs on the right show overall network bandwidth use over the past 60 seconds, the number of TCP connections, and the current utilization of Ethernet connections (determined by the number of NICs) (see Figure 11-13). The left side is divided into these sections: Processes with Network Activity, which shows the processes currently accessing the network and how much data is being sent and received; Network Activity, which lists the amount of data processes are sending and receiving as well as their network addresses; TCP Connections, which lists local and remote addresses and ports associated with programs (executable images) accessing the network; and Listening Ports, which lists all ports currently listening. To filter the display, you can click the check box next to a process. Metrics in this tab that are especially useful for troubleshooting include Ethernet connection use graphs. Watch for consistent utilization higher than 40%, which can indicate a network bottleneck that might be improved with some changes to the network layout (such as adding subnets). Consistent utilization in the 60% to 70% range is a good indicator that you should reexamine the network layout. If you're seeing utilization consistently higher than 90%, there's definitely a problem that should be solved as soon as possible.

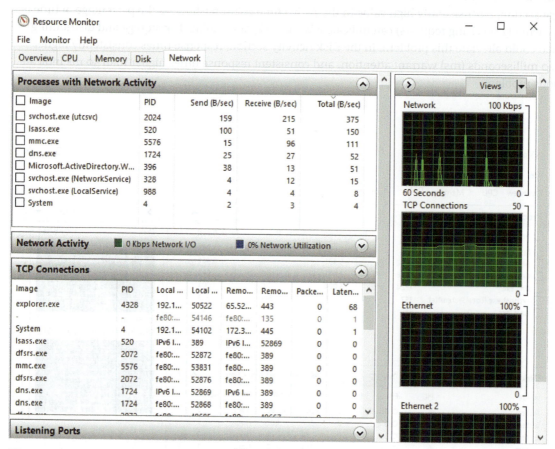

Figure 11-13 The Network tab of Resource Monitor

Using Performance Monitor

Although general data can point you in the right direction, more detailed metrics are helpful in identifying a specific problem. **Performance Monitor** is a performance monitoring tool that uses a variety of data sources to examine how roles, services, and applications affect the performance of a computer. Data can be examined in real time or logged for later analysis. To access Performance Monitor, open Computer Management and click Performance or run `perfmon.msc` (see Figure 11-14). Performance Monitor can collect and combine data from three sources:

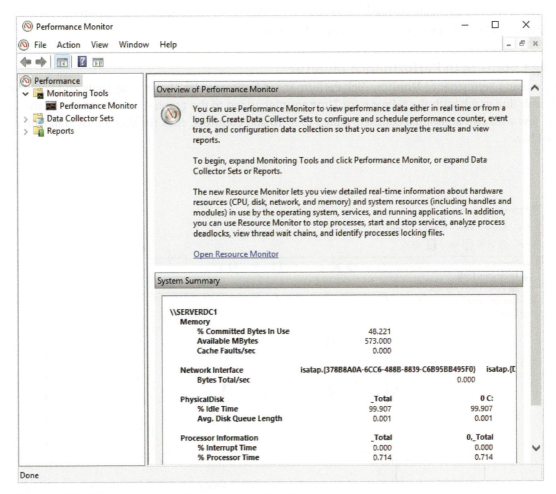

Figure 11-14 Overview of Performance Monitor

- *Performance counters*—A **performance counter** is a performance metric from OS components and applications. Depending on what is being reported, these can be counts (e.g., physical disk reads per seconds) or percentages (e.g., CPU utilization).
- *Configuration information*—Changes to values of Windows Registry keys. A data collector set (covered later in this section) is used to determine which keys are monitored.
- *Event trace data*—Log files created by applications and device drivers that incorporate Event Tracing for Windows (ETW). This data is different from events shown in Event Viewer and is usually used only by software developers.

Performance Monitor can monitor real-time activity and review logs for historical information, and you can customize the data that's collected in logs. You can also trigger alerts and tasks based on user-defined thresholds and generate a variety of reports. Access to this tool is determined by what groups a user belongs to. Administrators can access all features, and other groups have access but with certain limits:

- *Users*—This group can view log files and modify display properties but can't access real-time data and can't create or modify data collector sets.

- *Performance Monitor Users*—This group can view log files and real-time data and modify display properties but can't create or modify data collector sets.
- *Performance Log Users*—This group can use all features available to the other two groups. If this group is given the *Log on as a batch user* right, members can create and modify data collector sets; however, data collector sets must run under their own credentials. This group can't use the Windows Kernel Trace provider in data collector sets.

Adding Counters to Performance Monitor

To begin using Performance Monitor, click Performance Monitor under Monitoring Tools and you'll see the default line graph with the %Processor Time counter added to the graph. Figure 11-15 shows the line graph view with two additional counters added to it. To add counters, click the green plus sign icon on the tool bar.

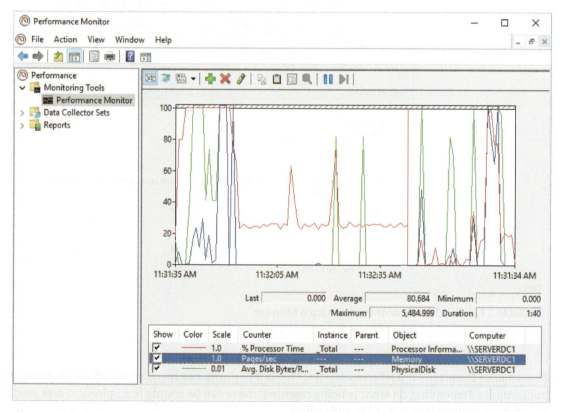

Figure 11-15   The Performance Monitor line graph

In the Add Counters dialog box, you can choose which computer you wish to monitor or leave the default of the local computer. You can then choose from dozens of categories of counters, listed in alphabetical order. Click to expand a counter category and choose a counter from that category (see Figure 11-16), or you can choose to add all counters from the category. In Figure 11-16, the PhysicalDisk category is selected and the Avg Disk Bytes/Read counter is selected for monitoring. After you have selected counters, you can check out the real-time graph data again.

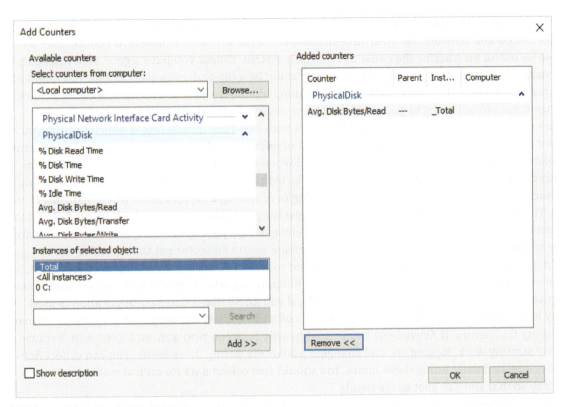

Figure 11-16   Adding counters

To customize a view, you can open the Performance Monitor Properties dialog box by right-clicking the graph and clicking Properties. There are five tabs with options for customizing the display:

- *General*—Control display elements, such as the legend explaining graphs, the value bar (showing the last, average, minimum, and maximum values for a selected metric), and the length of time the graph covers. You can also decide whether to display the minimum, maximum, or average value for the graph's duration and specify how often samples of data are taken and how long to display data.
- *Source*—Specify whether to display current activity on the system, which is good for troubleshooting an immediate problem or activity from log files or a database, which is a good option when you're looking for trends or a recurring problem. With log files and databases, you can also set a time range for viewing data.
- *Data*—Select which performance counters to display and configure line or bar color, scale, and style for each counter. With the scale setting, you can show both smaller and larger numbers on the same graph (for example, CPU and memory use).
- *Graph*—Select the type of view (Line Chart, Histogram, or Report) and do some customizing, if you like. For example, you can configure scrolling and wrapping for a line graph or add vertical and horizontal grids to a histogram.
- *Appearance*—Control colors for the graph background, control background (the area around the graph), text labels, and grid lines. You can also change the font for text labels and add a border.

Viewing performance data in real time is helpful if you want to see the impact that certain actions have on selected counters. For example, you might want to see whether Active Directory replication results in unacceptably high CPU and network use. After adding the necessary counters, you can force replication to occur or make a change to Active Directory to trigger automatic replication and observe the changes in CPU and network use. Real-time monitoring of performance counters in Performance Monitor can also be useful for tracking the cause of a sluggish system. Unless you have a good idea what part of the system to examine, however, finding the cause could be a hit-and-miss proposition. You might have better results checking the graphs in Resource Monitor, which give you an overall view of the resources being used instead of having to guess which ones to observe in Performance Monitor.

One reason tracking causes of poor performance with real-time monitoring is difficult is that you have no point of reference for comparing data. This point of reference, called a performance baseline or simply a **baseline**, is a record of performance data gathered when a system is performing well under normal operating conditions. Generally, baseline data is collected shortly after a system is put into service and then again each time changes are made, such as installing or removing a server role or when many users are added. The baseline data collected during normal operating conditions can then be compared with data collected during peak resource demands to give you insight into your system's capabilities and limitations.

To create a baseline of performance data, you create a **data collector set** that specifies the performance counters you want to collect, how often to collect them, and how long to collect them. You can create multiple data collector sets that capture different aspects of system performance and measure performance during different periods. For example, if you know that a database application is used heavily between 10:00 a.m. and 3:00 p.m., you can collect CPU, disk, memory, and network performance data during that period. If Active Directory is used heavily between 7:00 a.m. and 10:00 a.m. because users are starting work, logging on, and changing passwords during these hours, you can collect Active Directory—related data during these hours. You should also collect data for critical resources over an entire day so that you can spot usage trends.

A data collector set can contain a variety of types of information collected and displayed as a graph or report. Information types in a data collector set include the following:

- *Performance counters*—These system performance indicators used to view real-time data are also used in data collector sets.
- *Counter alerts*—Events generated when a counter falls below or exceeds a specified threshold. For example, you can create an alert to log an entry in the Application log if the % Processor Time counter exceeds 90%.
- *Event traces*—Logs information based on system or application events.
- *System configuration*—Monitors and records changes to Registry keys.

Predefined data collector sets can be run as they are or used as templates to create user-defined data collector sets. These data collector sets include Active Directory Diagnostics, LAN Diagnostics, System Diagnostics, and System Performance. Data collector sets can be scheduled to run at certain times and certain days for a specified period of time. To specify how long a data collector set runs, you set a stop condition, explained later in the section "Scheduling Data Collector Sets."

Be aware that performance monitoring uses system resources. It takes memory to run Performance Monitor, CPU cycles to collect and display counter data, and disk resources to update log files. With Performance Monitor, however, you can select a remote computer as the target for monitoring. By monitoring remotely, you lessen the monitoring session's impact on the computer being monitored. You can also adjust the counter sampling interval to collect counter data less often than the default values. The more often counter data is collected, the greater the impact the monitoring session has on system resource use.

Scheduling Data Collector Sets

Running data collectors manually is fine when you're doing a quick real-time performance analysis, but to conduct longer-term studies, to measure performance during off hours, or to run them at times you're not available, you need to create a scheduled data collector set with these steps:

1. In the left pane of Performance Monitor, right-click the data collector set to schedule and click Properties. You can use a data collector set you created in the User Defined node or the predefined data collector set Server Manager Performance Monitor under the User Defined node. More predefined data collector sets are available under the System node.

2. Click the Schedule tab, and then click the Add button.

3. In the Folder Action dialog box, you can choose a beginning date, an expiration date, days of the week it should run, and the start time (see Figure 11-17). A new report is created each time the data collector set runs with the date and time appended to the report name.

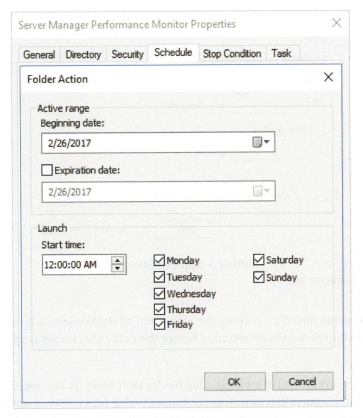

Figure 11-17   Scheduling a data collector set

4. If you want to run the data collector set for only a certain number of days, click the Expiration date check box, and enter the date on which the data collector set should stop running.

 Note

If a data collector set is still running when the expiration date is reached, it continues to run but doesn't start again.

5. Click OK, and then click the Stop Condition tab (see Figure 11-18). You can specify how long the data collector set should run each time it starts in units of seconds, minutes, hours, days, and weeks. In the Limits section, you have the following options:

- Restart the data collector set at limits: If this check box is selected, the data collector set saves a report when either limit has been reached and restarts to create a new report. This process continues until the overall duration is reached or the data collector set is manually stopped.

- Duration: If this check box is selected, the data collector set runs for the specified period within the overall duration. Enabling this limit makes sense only if you select the restart option.

- Maximum Size: If this check box is selected, the data collector set runs until it reaches a maximum size. However, if an overall duration is specified, that takes precedence.

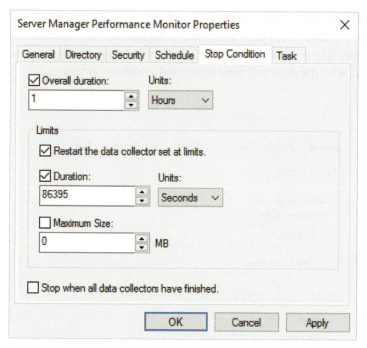

Figure 11-18   Setting a stop condition for a data collector set

If you have set an overall duration, clicking the *Stop when all data collectors have finished* check box allows the most recent counter data to be recorded before the data collector set stops.

Performance Alerts

Using a data collector set isn't limited to creating a log file for later analysis and reporting. You can configure one so that when a particular performance counter value falls below or above a certain threshold value, an alert is triggered. Alerts can write an entry to the Application event log and run a specific program or script. An alert can also trigger another data collector set to start collecting related data. An alert data collector set checks or "samples" the counter value at user-defined intervals. You want to sample often enough to make sure a problem doesn't go unnoticed for too long, but sampling too frequently can put an unnecessary load on the system. To create an alert, right-click User Defined under Data Collector Sets, point to New, and click Data Collector Set. Click Create manually (advanced), and then click Performance Counter Alert. From there, add the counters you wish to monitor and set the threshold value.

Performance Counters

The key to useful performance monitoring is determining not only when to monitor but also specifically what to monitor. There are literally hundreds of performance counters to choose from, and the value of your data collection sessions depends on carefully choosing the counters that will give you the best performance picture of the system you are monitoring. The following is a short list of performance counter categories, some of the performance counters in each category, and a description of what they measure:

- *Disk Counters*—Disk counters are broken into two general categories: physical disk and logical disk. A physical disk counter represents the physical hardware and all the partitions on the actual disk drive. Logical counters represent logical partitions such as drive letters, which might actually consist of a single partition on a single disk or a volume spread out over multiple physical disks as in the case of spanned or striped volumes, for example. Whether you choose the PhysicalDisk or LogicalDisk category, the following are some of the counters you can select:
  - Avg. Disk Queue Length: This counter refers to the number of disk read and write operations that are waiting to be serviced. A value higher than the number of disk spindles plus 2 on a sustained basis is an indication that the disk system is a performance bottleneck because the system is

having to wait for disk operations to complete. Faster disks or more disks to spread the load are possible remedies as is switching from mechanical disks to solid-state drives (SSD)s. However, high utilization of other systems such as the processor can also cause slow performance on input/output devices such as disk interfaces.

- **% Disk Time:** The percentage of time the disk is busy servicing read and write requests. A sustained value of 90% indicates a storage performance bottleneck. The Avg. Disk Queue Length is also likely to be high when this value is high.
- **% Idle Time:** This counter tells you the percentage of time the disk is not servicing requests. This counter can tell you that a disk is underused if the value is consistently high (the scale is 0 meaning always busy and 100 meaning never busy).
- **Disk Bytes/sec:** This is the total number of bytes transferred from and to the disk per second. This value by itself can't point to disk bottlenecks but can give you a general idea of how busy the disk system is.

- *Memory Counters*—An operating system and its running roles and applications need plenty of memory to operate efficiently. If a system lacks physical RAM, it begins using the paging file more, which will slow the system considerably. Because memory counters and paging file counters are tied together, they are both represented here. Here are a few key memory-related counters to monitor:
  - **Memory: Pages/sec:** This counter tells you how often the OS must read or write to disk to resolve hard page faults. A hard page fault is a condition in which running software attempts to access memory that is not currently mapped into physical RAM, and the OS must retrieve the data from disk. This counter is probably the primary indicator of whether memory usage is creating a bottleneck. A value higher than 20 often indicates there is insufficient memory to efficiently perform current workloads.
  - **Memory: Available Mbytes:** This counter simply tells you how much memory in megabytes is available for the operating system and running applications. Generally, if this value falls below about 10% of the total memory on the system, you should investigate other memory counters such as Pages/sec to see if adequate memory is available for the current workload.
  - **Paging File: % Usage:** This tells you how much of the paging file is in use. If this value reaches 100%, your paging file has reached capacity and your system could experience reliability problems. You should delete and recreate a larger page file if this occurs.

- *Processor Counters*—Processor counters tell you how much of your processor power is being used and the types of code being executed (privileged versus user) as well as how much delay is caused by code waiting to be executed. You can measure individual processors on multiprocessor or multicore systems or measure them as a total. You can find processor-related counters in both the Processor category and System category:
  - **Processor: % Processor Time:** This counter tells you what percentage of the time the processor is busy. Processor utilization frequently spikes, so it is not unusual to see this value hit 100% periodically; however, a sustained value of over 85 to 90% may indicate that the processing power of the system is inadequate for the workload. On the other hand, consistently low utilization may indicate that the system can handle more workloads. This counter, along with System: Processor Queue Length should be considered together.
  - **Processor: Interrupts/sec:** This counter tells you how many hardware interrupts the processor is processing per second. A sustained spike in this value could indicate hardware malfunctions.
  - **Processor: % Privileged Time:** This counter tells you the percentage of the time the processor is executing privileged code such as interrupt service routines, device drivers, and the Windows kernel. A high value could mean poorly written drivers. This value should generally be low in comparison to % User Time.
  - **Processor: % User Time:** This counter tells you the percentage of time the processor is executing user mode software, which includes applications and many Windows services. The majority of the processor time should be spent here compared to in privileged mode.

- System: Processor Queue Length: This counter tells you the number of threads that are waiting to be executed by the processor. Threads that are waiting mean system delays. Divide this value by the number of processor cores running and if the result is more than five, bottlenecks should be investigated (such as processes that are monopolizing CPU time). If there are no obvious bottlenecks, a CPU upgrade or an additional CPU (in multiprocessor systems) may be warranted.
- *Network Counters*—Network counters tell you the percentage of the bandwidth on your network interface that is being used as well as whether packets are having to wait to be transmitted. Network counters can also tell you raw usage statistics such as the number of bytes or packets sent and received and the number of errors or discarded packets.
  - Network Interface, Bytes Total/sec: This counter tells you the number of bytes sent and received on a network interface.
  - Network Interface, Current Bandwidth: This counter estimates the total number of bits per second that the interface can send and receive. To get the percent utilization of the interface, divide the Bytes Total/sec value by this value, and multiply by 8 (because this value is in bits per second versus bytes per second).
  - Network Interface, Output Queue Length: This counter tells you how many packets are waiting to be transmitted. A sustained value higher than 2 indicates a performance bottleneck, which may be resolved by upgrading the NIC or adding NIC teaming. However, high utilization of other systems such as the processor can also cause slow performance on input/output devices such as network interfaces.

Activity 11-1: Resetting Your Virtual Environment

Time Required: 5 minutes
Objective: Reset your virtual environment by applying the InitialConfig checkpoint or snapshot.
Required Tools and Equipment: ServerDC1, ServerDM1
Description: Apply the InitialConfig checkpoint or snapshot to ServerDC1 and ServerDM1.

1. Be sure the servers are shut down. In your virtualization program, apply the InitialConfig checkpoint or snapshot to ServerDC1 and ServerDM1.
2. When the snapshot or checkpoint has finished being applied, continue to the next activity.

Activity 11-2: Creating a Custom View in Event Viewer

Time Required: 10 minutes
Objective: Create a custom view to see data from multiple logs.
Required Tools and Equipment: ServerDC1
Description: Create a custom view by using available filtering options.

1. Start ServerDC1, and sign in as **Administrator**, if necessary. Open Server Manager, and click **Tools**, **Event Viewer** from the menu.
2. In the Actions pane, click **Create Custom View** to open the Create Custom View dialog box.
3. Leave the default **Any time** option in the Logged list box. Leave the Event level check boxes (Critical, Warning, Error, Information, and Verbose) unselected so that all event levels are recorded. (If you select a level here, only events meeting this level are recorded, but if they are all unselected, all event levels are recorded.)
4. If necessary, click the **By log** option button, click the **Event logs** list arrow, and click to expand **Applications and Services Logs**. Click the **Directory Service** and **DNS Server** check boxes (see Figure 11-19), and then click **OK**.
5. In the Save Filter to Custom View dialog box, type **DNS-DS** in the Name text box.
6. In the Select where to save the Custom view section, click **Custom Views**, and then click **OK**.
7. To view the results, in the left pane of Event Viewer, click to expand **Custom Views**, if necessary, and click **DNS-DS**. Events related to Directory Service (Active Directory) and DNS should be displayed in the center pane (see Figure 11-20).
8. Close Event Viewer and continue to the next activity.

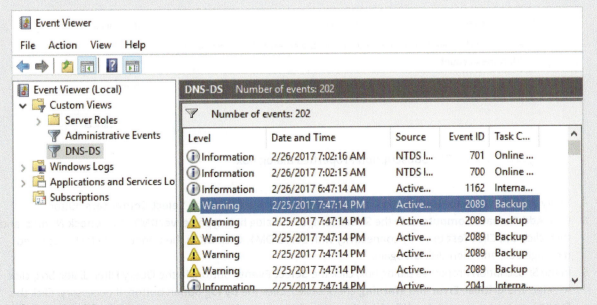

Create Custom View   ✕

Filter   XML

Logged: Any time   ⌄

Event level: ☐ Critical   ☐ Warning   ☐ Verbose

☐ Error   ☐ Information

◉ By log   Event logs: Directory Service,DNS Server   ⌄
                ⊞ ☐ Windows Logs
○ By source   Event sources: ⊟ ☑ Applications and Services Logs
                    ☐ Active Directory Web Services
                    ☐ DFS Replication
Includes/Excludes Event IDs: Enter   ☑ Directory Service   as. To
exclude criteria, type a minus sign   ☑ DNS Server
                    ☐ Hardware Events
                <All Event IDs>   ☐ Internet Explorer
                    ☐ Key Management Service
Task category: ⊞ ☐ Microsoft   ▾
                    ☐ Windows PowerShell
Keywords: ▾

User: <All Users>

Computer(s):   <All Computers

                                        ear

                                    Cancel

Figure 11-19   Selecting logs for a custom view

Event Viewer

File   Action   View   Help

◀ ▶ | 🔄 📷 | 🔲 | 📷

Event Viewer (Local) | DNS-DS   Number of events: 202
✔ Custom Views |
  > Server Roles | ▽ Number of events: 202
    Administrative Events | Level   Date and Time   Source   Event ID   Task C...
    DNS-DS | ⓘ Information   2/26/2017 7:02:16 AM   NTDS I...   701   Online ...
> Windows Logs | ⓘ Information   2/26/2017 7:02:15 AM   NTDS I...   700   Online ...
> Applications and Services Lo | ⓘ Information   2/26/2017 6:47:14 AM   Active...   1162   Interna...
  Subscriptions | ⚠ Warning   2/25/2017 7:47:14 PM   Active...   2089   Backup
                        | ⚠ Warning   2/25/2017 7:47:14 PM   Active...   2089   Backup
                        | ⚠ Warning   2/25/2017 7:47:14 PM   Active...   2089   Backup
                        | ⚠ Warning   2/25/2017 7:47:14 PM   Active...   2089   Backup
                        | ⚠ Warning   2/25/2017 7:47:14 PM   Active...   2089   Backup
                        | ⓘ Information   2/25/2017 7:47:14 PM   Active...   2041   Interna...

Figure 11-20   Using a custom view

Activity 11-3: Creating an Event Subscription

Time Required: 15 minutes
Objective: Create an event subscription.
Required Tools and Equipment: ServerDC1 and ServerDM1
Description: You have been asked to collect event data from two different systems in the Forwarded Events log so that they can be viewed in Event Viewer.

1. Sign in to ServerDC1 as **Administrator**, and start ServerDM1, if necessary.
2. On ServerDC1, open Event Viewer. In the left pane, right-click **Subscriptions** and click **Create Subscription**. In the message about starting the Windows Event Collector Service, click **Yes**.
3. In the Subscription Properties dialog box, type **ServerDM1 errors and warnings** in the Subscription name text box. The Destination log drop-down list is set to Forwarded Events by default (see Figure 11-21); leave this default setting.

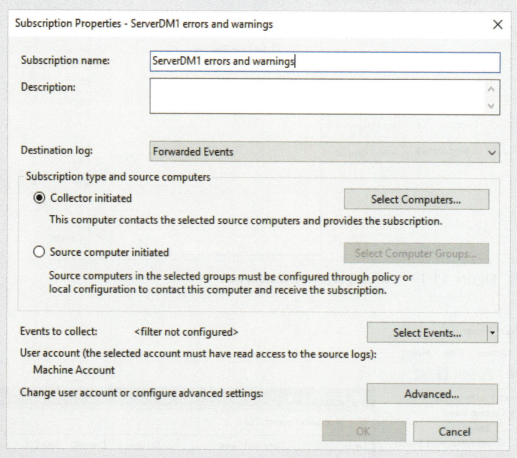

Figure 11-21 The Subscription Properties dialog box

4. Verify that the **Collector initiated** option button is selected, and click the **Select Computers** button.
5. Click **Add Domain Computers**. In the Select Computer dialog box, type **ServerDM1**, click **Check Names**, and then click **OK**. Click **Test** to verify connectivity with ServerDM1. Click **OK** in the Connectivity test succeeded message box, and then click **OK** again.
6. In the Subscription Properties dialog box, click the **Select Events** button. In the Query Filter dialog box, click to select the **Critical**, **Error** and **Warning** check boxes. Click the **By log** option button, if necessary. Click the **Event logs** list arrow, and click **Windows Logs** to collect events from the main log files. Notice that you can filter the subscription even more by event ID, keywords, user, and computer(s) (see Figure 11-22). Click **OK**.

Note

You might notice that the Query Filter dialog box looks the same as the Create Custom View dialog box. That's because the same parameters for determining what data is shown in a custom view are used to determine what data is included in a query filter.

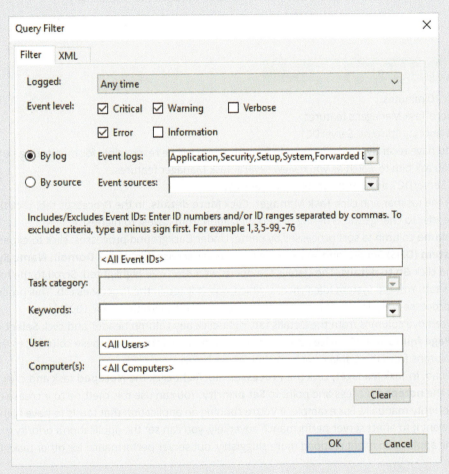

Figure 11-22 The Query Filter dialog box

7. In the Subscription Properties dialog box, click the **Advanced** button. In the Advanced Subscription Settings dialog box, click the **Specific User** option button. Click the **User and Password** button, type **Password01** in the Password text box, and click **OK**. Click **OK** to close the Advanced Subscription Settings dialog box and the Subscription Properties dialog box.

8. In the left pane of Event Viewer, click the **Subscriptions** node. The event subscription name is displayed in the middle pane. You can create event subscriptions for other servers and use different filter properties. Click to select the subscription name in the middle pane, and in the Actions pane, click **Runtime Status**. Verify that the current status is Active, and then click **Close**.

9. It might take a while before you see any events. However, to test your subscription, you can create an event manually. On ServerDM1, log on as the domain **Administrator** and open a command prompt window. Type **eventcreate /T Error /ID 1000 /L Application /D "Event to test Event Viewer subscriptions"** and press **Enter** to create an error-level event in the Applications log.

10. Sending the event to the Forwarded Events log on ServerDC1 might take a few minutes. In Event Viewer on ServerDC1, expand **Windows Logs** and click **Forwarded Events**. If the event isn't listed, wait a few minutes, and then right-click **Forwarded Events** and click **Refresh**. Eventually, the event should be listed.

11. You can also have an alert sent when a subscribed event arrives. In Event Viewer, right-click the **Forwarded Events** log and click **Attach a Task To this Log**.

12. The Create Basic Task Wizard starts. Accept the default task name, and then click **Next**. Click **Next** again. In the Action window, the Start a program option is the only one available; the other two have been deprecated. You could run a simple PowerShell or Visual Basic script that shows a message if you just want to be informed that a new event has arrived. For now, click **Cancel**. Close Event Viewer.

13. Shut down ServerDM1. Leave ServerDC1 running and continue to the next activity.

Activity 11-4: Exploring Task Manager

Time Required: 10 minutes
Objective: Explore Task Manager's features.
Required Tools and Equipment: ServerDC1
Description: You have recently hired a junior administrator who will be responsible for monitoring server performance. You ask him to watch as you review several Task Manager features.

1. Sign in to ServerDC1 as **Administrator**, if necessary.

2. Right-click the taskbar and click **Task Manager**. Click **More details**. In the Processes tab, click the **CPU** column header to change the ordering of CPU utilization from lowest to highest.

3. Click the **Name** column to sort processes by name. Under Background processes, click to expand **Domain Name System (DNS) Server**, and you see the DNS Server service. Right-click **Domain Name System (DNS) Server** and click **Go to details**. The Details tab opens with dns.exe highlighted. Scroll to the top of the list in the Details tab. You see System Idle Process, which wasn't listed in the Processes tab. This process runs when no other processes require CPU time, so it often shows CPU % utilization near 100%.

4. To add or remove columns from the Details tab, right-click any column header and click **Select columns**. Click the **Page faults** and **I/O writes** check boxes, and then click **OK** to add these columns to the display. To remove columns from the display, uncheck their check boxes.

5. Start Notepad. In Task Manager, click the **Processes** tab. Right-click the **Notepad** task and click **Go to details**.

6. Right-click the **notepad** process and point to **Set priority**. You can use this method to increase or decrease a process's priority manually. For example, if you're running an application that tends to have high CPU use but you don't want it to affect server performance adversely, you can set the application's priority to Below Normal or Low. The application might respond more sluggishly, but server performance for other tasks is better.

Caution ⚠

Use the Set Priority feature with care. Setting a higher priority can sometimes have unexpected and undesirable results. In particular, never set priority to Realtime unless an application's instructions specify it.

7. Click **End task**. When prompted to confirm, click **End process**. Notepad is removed from the running process list and its window closes. Ending a process is useful when a task is exhibiting problems and doesn't terminate on its own.

8. Click the **Performance** tab. Click **Open Resource Monitor** to see more detailed graphs of CPU, disk, network, and memory utilization. Explore each tab so that you're familiar with the information you can gather from this tool. Close Resource Monitor.

9. Click the **User**s tab, which lists users who are currently logged on interactively through a console connection, a remote desktop connection, or a Terminal Services connection. Click to expand **Administrator**. You see a list of processes started by the Administrator account. You can right-click any process to see the same menu available in the Processes tab.

10. Close Task Manager, and stay signed in for the next activity.

Activity 11-5: Using Performance Monitor

Time Required: 10 minutes
Objective: Use Performance Monitor to do a real-time check on CPU, memory, and disk use.
Required Tools and Equipment: ServerDC1
Description: You use Performance Monitor to create reports (line graph, histogram, and text report) showing real-time system utilization.

1. On ServerDC1, open Server Manager, and click **Tools**, **Performance Monitor** from the menu.
2. Click to expand **Monitoring Tools** in the left pane, if necessary, and click **Performance Monitor**. The view changes to a line graph of the % Processor Time counter showing the percentage of processor use.
3. Right-click the graph and click **Add Counters**. In the Add Counters dialog box, scroll up until you find LogicalDisk (the counters are in alphabetic order), and then click to expand **LogicalDisk**. Ctrl+click % **Disk Read Time** and % **Disk Write Time** to select both counters.
4. Click **_Total** in the Instances of selected object list box, and then click the **Add** button. Scroll through the counter list again, and click to expand **Memory**. Click % **Committed Bytes In Use**, click the **Add** button, and then click **OK**.
5. Performance Monitor displays a line graph with different colors representing the different metrics. Click the **Change graph type** icon (to the left of the green plus sign above the graph) to toggle from Line Chart to Histogram to Report and finally back to Line Chart.
6. Double-click any of the counters. In the Performance Monitor Properties dialog box (see Figure 11-23), you can change the line color, the scale, and style and width of line. Click **Cancel**.

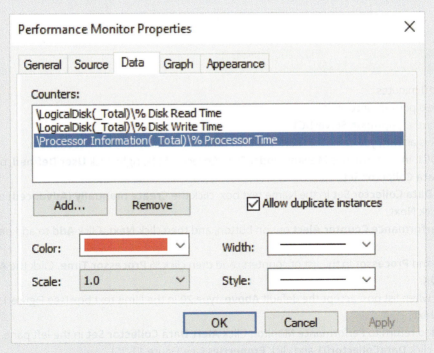

Figure 11-23   Performance Monitor Properties dialog box

7. Click the **highlight** icon in the tool bar (to the right of the red X). The line for the selected counter is highlighted.
8. Leave Performance Monitor open and continue to the next activity.

Activity 11-6: Creating a Performance Baseline Report with a Data Collector Set

Time Required: 10 minutes

Objective: Use data collector sets to create a performance baseline report.

Required Tools and Equipment: ServerDC1

Description: In this activity, you create a data collector set containing several performance metrics and then review the results as a report to see what utilization was like during the time data was collected.

1. On ServerDC1, in Performance Monitor, click to expand **Data Collector Sets** in the left pane.
2. Right-click the **User Defined** node, point to **New**, and click **Data Collector Set** to start the Create new Data Collector Set Wizard.
3. Type **Test Data Collector Set** in the Name text box. Accept the default setting **Create from a template (Recommended)**, and then click **Next**.
4. Click **System Performance** in the Template Data Collector Set list box, and then click **Next**.
5. In the *Where would you like the data to be saved?* window, accept the default setting %*systemdrive*%**PerfLogs**\ **Admin\Test Data Collector Set**, and then click **Next**.
6. In the Create the data collector set window, accept the default settings, and then click **Finish**.
7. In the left pane, under User Defined, right-click **Test Data Collector Set** and click **Start** to begin collecting data. The data collection should finish in about 60 seconds. In the right pane, you see the status change to Running. When the data collection is finished, the status changes to Stopped.
8. Click to expand **Reports**, **User Defined**, and **Test Data Collector Set**. Click the log file to see the report in the right pane.
9. Stay signed in for the next activity.

Activity 11-7: Creating a Performance Alert

Time Required: 10 minutes

Objective: Create a performance alert.

Required Tools and Equipment: ServerDC1

Description: In this activity, you create an alert that fires whenever CPU utilization exceeds 50%.

1. On ServerDC1, in Performance Monitor, under Data Collector Sets, right-click **User Defined**, point to **New**, and click **Data Collector Set**.
2. Type **Alert Data Collector Set** in the Name text box, click the **Create manually (Advanced)** option button, and then click **Next**.
3. Click the **Performance Counter Alert** option button, and then click **Next**. Click **Add** to add performance counters.
4. Click to expand **Processor** in the list of counters, and then click **% Processor Time**. Click the **Add** button, and then click **OK**.
5. In the Alert when list box, accept the default **Above**, type **20** in the Limit text box (see Figure 11-24), and then click **Next**.
6. Click **Finish** to return to Performance Monitor. Click **Alert Data Collector Set** in the left pane, and in the right pane, right-click **DataCollector01** and click **Properties** (see Figure 11-25).
7. In the Sample interval list box, set the value to 5 seconds. Click the **Alert Action** tab, and click **Log an entry in the application event log**. The event will actually get logged to Applications and Services Logs\Microsoft\ Windows\Diagnosis-PLA\Operational.
8. Click **OK** to return to Performance Monitor. Right-click **Alert Data Collector Set** in the left pane and click **Start**.

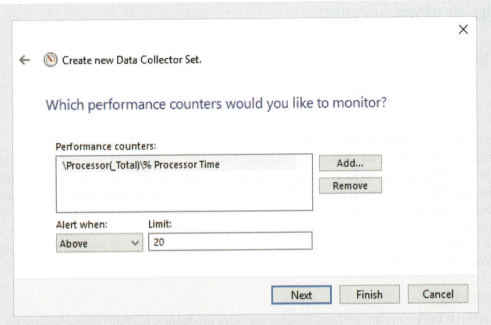

Figure 11-24   Selecting a performance counter to monitor

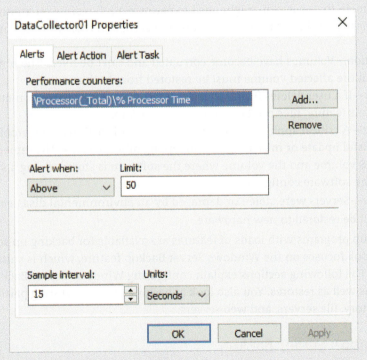

Figure 11-25   Configuring properties for a data collector set

9. Create some CPU activity by opening and closing Server Manager, Internet Explorer, and other applications. Check the event log occasionally in Event Viewer to see whether CPU utilization has exceeded 50%. In Event Viewer, navigate to Applications and Services Logs\Microsoft\Windows\Diagnosis-PLA\Operational. The event will have Event ID 2031.

10. After an event has been generated, right-click **Alert Data Collector Set** and click **Stop**.

11. Close Performance Monitor and continue to the next activity.

Backing Up Windows Servers

 **Certification**

- **70-740 – Maintain and monitor server environments:**
  Maintain server installations

Backing up servers and other devices is a mundane, often disliked, but critical task for a server administrator. It's one of those necessary evils that you hope you'll never need but you'll be thankful for when you do. Because data is stored in so many ways by so many different applications and services, it makes sense that there are different methods for creating backups and performing restores of that data. Windows Server Backup provides methods to back up and restore an entire system or just critical operating system components, and it recognizes special services like Active Directory and Hyper-V, making the backup and restore process easier in some circumstances than an all-or-nothing endeavor. This section discusses Windows Server Backup and the various methods available to create and restore backups.

Server Backup

A server backup is the cornerstone of any disaster recovery procedure. Backups are necessary for the following reasons, among others:

- *Server hardware failure*—The server can't start or no longer functions normally because of a hardware failure. In this case, you might need to perform a full restore on another server.
- *Disk failure*—Disk drives have failed and must be replaced, and their volumes must be restored from backup.
- *Volume corruption*—Volumes have become corrupted and can't be fixed. The physical disk might still be okay, but the affected volume must be restored from backup.
- *Deletion of files*—If a user deletes files that can't be recovered through other methods, such as the Previous Versions feature, files can be restored from backup.
- *Software failure*—A critical application or service no longer functions. This problem could be caused by an unsuccessful update or misconfiguration among other reasons. The remedy can include restoring the OS volume and the volume where the software is stored, doing a system restore, and restoring just the software configuration.
- *Theft or disaster*—Servers were stolen or damaged by an environmental disaster (such as fire or flood) and must be restored to new hardware.

Third-party backup programs with loads of features are available for backing up servers in an enterprise, but this book focuses on the Windows Server Backup feature, which is suitable for backing up an individual server. The following sections explain configuring Windows Server Backup to perform full and partial backups as well as restores. You also look at backing up and restoring particular roles such as Hyper-V, Active Directory, file servers, and web servers.

Configuring Windows Server Backup

The Tools menu in Server Manager includes a link for Windows Server Backup, but when you click it, you get a message stating that Windows Server Backup isn't installed. You need to install it with the Add Roles and Features Wizard or the PowerShell cmdlet `Install-WindowsFeature Windows-Server-Backup`. After installing it, you can configure backups with the Windows Server Backup console (see Figure 11-26), the `wbadmin` command-line program, or PowerShell cmdlets.

Configuring Backup Permissions

Backup is a critical function in any network, and it's important to assign the task of backing up servers to a reliable and responsible person. However, not just any user can perform backups on a server. By default, members of the local Administrators group, Backup Operators group, and Server Operators group

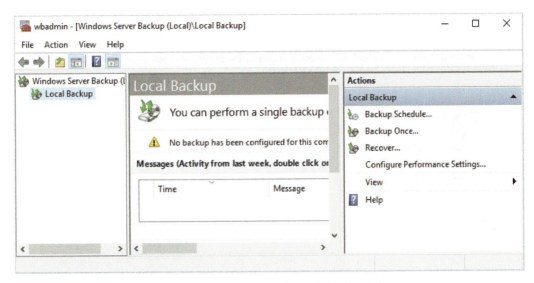

Figure 11-26   The Windows Server Backup console

can back up and restore files. Administrators have full rights to the server, and Backup Operators and Server Operators are given the following rights:

- Back up files and directories.
- Restore files and directories.
- Shut down the system.

If this list of rights doesn't suit your situation, you can assign each right separately. For example, you might want a user to be able to back up files but not restore them. You can assign the user only the *Back up files and directories* right without making the user a member of Backup Operators. You can assign rights to users or groups by editing the Local Security Policy or using group policies (in Computer Configuration, Policies, Windows Settings, Security Settings, Local Policies, User Rights Assignment). After installing the Windows Server Backup feature, you can perform the following tasks in the Windows Server Backup console:

- Create a scheduled backup job.
- Perform a one-time backup.
- Perform a recovery operation.
- Configure backup performance.

Configuring Backups

Whether you're scheduling a backup to occur regularly or are performing a one-time backup, you can configure the backup with the following options:

- *Full backup*—This backs up all data on all local volumes, including the system state. A **full backup** allows you to perform all types of server recoveries, which are discussed later in the section "Windows Server Recovery."
- *Custom backup*—This selects which data you want to back up from the following options (see Figure 11-27):
  - Bare metal recovery: A **bare metal recovery** backs up the critical volumes needed to recover a server's OS; data volumes aren't included. It includes the system state, the system reserved volume, and the volume where Windows is stored.
  - System state: A **system state backup** backs up boot files, Windows system files, and the Registry. On a domain controller (DC), the system state includes the Active Directory database and the SYSVOL folder. On a cluster server, a system state backup includes the cluster configuration, and on a certificate server, the certificate store is included.
  - EFI System Partition: Backs up files on the system partition, which includes the boot loader files, the boot manager, system volume information, and Windows Recovery Environment (RE).

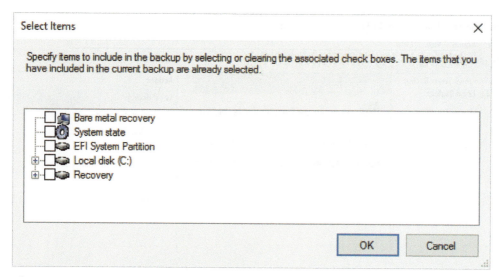

Figure 11-27 Selecting items to back up

- Individual volumes: Backs up only the volumes you select. If you choose this option, you can back up the entire volume or select specific files and folders. You can also exclude particular file types by file extension.
- Recovery: Backs up only the recovery partition.
- *Specify the destination*—Specify a dedicated hard disk (scheduled backup only), volume, or shared folder. The destination drive or share should have at least one and a half times the free space required to store the backup and can be one of the following:
  - DVD or other removable media: Only one-time backups can be stored on optical or removable media.
  - Internal hard drive: Both one-time backups and scheduled backups can be stored on an internal drive. For scheduled backups, you can dedicate the disk to backups, and it's no longer available for other purposes. (You see the disk in Disk Management but not File Explorer.) Dedicating a disk to backups is recommended but not required. You can use a volume on an internal disk to store backups along with other data. However, you can't store a bare metal recovery or full server backup on a critical volume (which is required to perform a bare metal recovery). If you use a volume to store the backup, it must be formatted as NTFS.
  - External hard drive: Similar to an internal hard drive, but this external drive has the advantage of being easily rotated with other drives, and backups can be stored off-site for disaster recovery.
  - Shared folder: Both one-time backups and scheduled backups can be stored on a shared folder. A single backup can be stored on a remote folder; any existing backups in the same location are overwritten. If you want to keep multiple backups, you must use an internal or external hard drive.

Note

There are other backup destination considerations: You can use a virtual hard disk as a backup destination, but it shouldn't be stored on a critical volume (the boot or system volume). You can't do a bare metal recovery from a backup stored on a dynamic disk. Tape drives aren't supported as a backup destination.

Performing a Scheduled Backup

To perform a **scheduled backup**, click Backup Schedule in the Actions pane of the Windows Server Backup console to start the Backup Schedule Wizard. You need to select a full or custom backup, as discussed previously, and then specify the times for the backup (see Figure 11-28). You can choose from once a day or multiple times throughout the day. In either case, you select the time the backup runs. By default, it runs at 9:00 p.m. once per day. Next, you specify the destination for the backup, as described previously. You can specify a hard disk that's dedicated for backups. External drives are preferable because you can remove them easily and store backups off-site. If you choose to dedicate a drive, it's formatted, and any existing volumes and data on the drive are deleted. If you don't have a drive to dedicate to backups, you can store the backup on another volume. However, you can't store a full server or system state backup on the Windows boot volume (usually C). If you choose a volume that includes other data, be aware that volume performance is severely affected when the backup is in progress. You can also store the backup on a network share, but only a single backup can be stored on a share, and any subsequent backups overwrite existing backups. Finally, you confirm the scheduled backup, and the backup begins at the scheduled time each day.

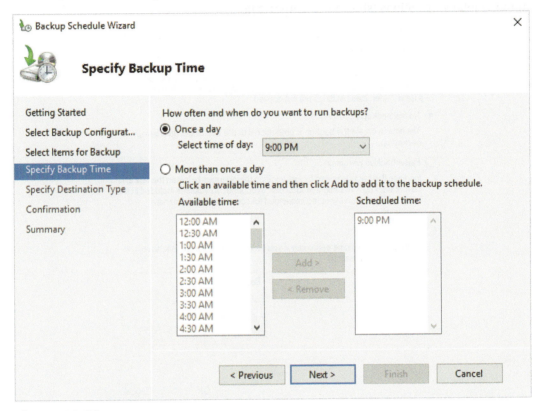

Figure 11-28   Scheduling a backup

You can have only one scheduled backup. If you click Backup Schedule after a scheduled backup has already been created, you're prompted to modify the existing scheduled backup or stop it. If you stop it and you're using a dedicated disk, the disk is released for normal use, and a drive letter is assigned to it.

Performing a One-Time Backup

A **one-time backup** creates a backup to a local volume or a share. The backup begins immediately, and the progress is shown in the Windows Server Backup console. You can close the console, and the backup continues to run. To configure a one-time backup, click Backup Once in the Actions pane to start the Backup Once Wizard. If you have any existing scheduled backups, you have the option to do the one-time backup using the options from one of the scheduled backups; otherwise, you select options as you do when creating a scheduled backup.

One-time backups shouldn't be used as the sole method of backing up your server. You should always have at least one regularly scheduled backup, and then use a one-time backup for particular situations, such as the following:

- Immediately before a software or hardware upgrade.
- Periodically, to store a full backup off-site, such as a once per month archival backup.
- To back up a volume not included in the scheduled backup.

- To back up a particular server role configuration after changes have been made to the configuration.
- To test the backup and restore process. You might want to verify that backups are working by backing up a volume and restoring it.

Configuring Backup Performance

Backup performance can be optimized for backups of entire volumes. Windows uses the Volume Shadow Copy Service (VSS) to perform full volume backups. VSS doesn't copy individual files; it copies the volume block by block, essentially making a mirror image of the volume. Windows Server Backup uses this image to create the backup. To optimize backup performance, click Configure Performance Settings in the Windows Server Backup console, which opens the Optimize Backup Performance dialog box. You can choose from the following options (shown in Figure 11-29):

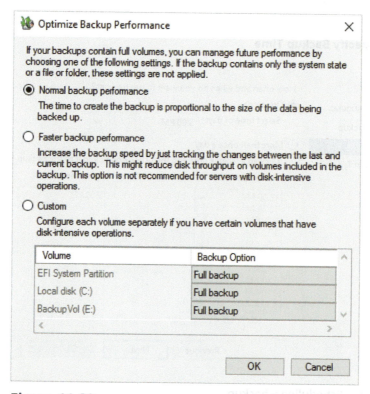

Figure 11-29 Optimizing backup performance

- *Normal backup performance*—This default setting is used with all backup types. The time needed to do the backup is proportional to the amount of data being backed up. The full contents of the source volume are transferred, but if a backup already exists on the destination, only the space required by the changed blocks is used.
- *Faster backup performance*—This option results in an **incremental backup** in which only the blocks that have changed since the last backup are transferred to the destination if there's an existing backup. Volumes used by disk-intensive applications shouldn't use this option because write performance on the source volume is decreased.
- *Custom*—You can choose a full backup or incremental backup for each volume.

Note

Even if you choose the incremental backup option, Windows Server Backup performs a full backup after 14 incremental backups have occurred or if more than 14 days have passed since the last full backup.

Configuring the Volume Shadow Copy Service

To configure the Volume Shadow Copy Service used for full volume backups, you can use the vssadmin command-line program. You can create and delete shadow copies and list existing shadow copies. In addition, you can revert a volume to an existing shadow, which overwrites the volume on a previously created shadow copy. The revert operation requires that no files be open on the volume to be reverted. To see the full list of vssadmin commands, enter vssadmin /? at a command prompt.

Backing Up Server Roles

Most server role data is stored in locations that are backed up when you perform a backup containing the system state, such as a system state or full server backup. If you restore the system state, data associated with the roles installed on the server is restored, too. A system state backup contains the following data, depending on which roles and features are installed:

- The Registry
- Boot files and Windows system files
- Component Services Class registration database
- Performance counter data
- Local users and groups
- Active Directory and SYSVOL
- Cluster configuration database
- Certificate Services database
- DFS namespace configuration
- Web Server role settings

In addition, some roles, features, applications, and services register themselves with Windows Server Backup so that you can recover application-specific data without having to do a more extensive recovery. When you perform a server recovery (discussed later in the section Windows Server Recovery), applications that have registered with Windows Server Backup are listed in the Select Application window and you have the option to restore only that application's data.

Performing Backups from the Command Line

Table 11-2 lists many PowerShell cmdlets you can use for Windows Server Backup operations. For detailed help and examples of using each cmdlet, type Get-Help *cmdletname* –detailed at a PowerShell prompt.

Table 11-2 PowerShell cmdlets for Windows Server Backup

Cmdlet	Description
Add-WBBackupTarget	Adds a backup storage location to the backup policy
Add-WBBareMetalRecovery	Adds to the backup policy items needed to perform a bare metal recovery
Add-WBSystemState	Adds to the backup policy items needed to perform a system state recovery
Add-WBVolume	Adds a volume to the list of items to be backed up
Get-WBBackupSet	Lists backups created for a server
Get-WBJob	Shows the backup job currently in operation
Get-WBPolicy	Gets the current backup policy
New-WBPolicy	Creates a new backup policy
Set-WBPolicy	Sets the backup policy used for scheduled backups
Set-WBSchedule	Sets the schedule for the backup policy
Start-WBBackup	Starts a one-time backup
Get-Command *-WB*	Lists all the Windows Backup Server PowerShell cmdlets

Table 11-3 lists many of the `wbadmin` commands you can use for Windows Server Backup operations. For a complete list of commands and examples of using them, see *http://technet.microsoft.com/en-us/library/cc742130.aspx*.

Table 11-3 `Wbadmin` commands for Windows Server Backup

Command	Description
`wbadmin enable backup`	Enables and configures a scheduled backup
`wbadmin disable backup`	Disables a scheduled backup
`wbadmin start backup`	Starts a one-time backup
`wbadmin get items`	Lists the items in a backup
`wbadmin start recovery`	Runs a recovery operation
`wbadmin start systemstaterecovery`	Runs a system state recovery operation
`wbadmin start systemstatebackup`	Runs a system state backup
`wbadmin start sysrecovery`	Starts a full server backup recovery
`wbadmin /?`	Lists all `wbadmin` commands

Note 📎

To perform most tasks with the `wbadmin` command, you must be a member of the Backup Operators or Administrators group. You must also open a command prompt window with elevated privileges (by right-clicking Start and clicking Command Prompt [Admin]) if you aren't signed in with the Administrator account.

Activity 11-8: Installing Windows Server Backup and Scheduling a Backup

Time Required: 10 minutes

Objective: Install Windows Server Backup and schedule a backup.

Required Tools and Equipment: ServerDC1, ServerDM1 (*Note:* ServerDC1 is not used in the activity, but it is the domain controller for the domain in which ServerDM1 is a member, so it should be running.)

Description: In this activity, you install Windows Server Backup with PowerShell on ServerDM1 and explore the Windows Server Backup console. You also explore the commands in PowerShell for performing Windows backup and restore procedures. Then, you schedule a backup.

1. Start ServerDM1 and sign in as the domain **Administrator**, if necessary. Be sure ServerDC1 is running.
2. On ServerDM1, open a PowerShell prompt. Type **Install-WindowsFeature Windows-Server-Backup** and press **Enter**. After the installation is finished, close the PowerShell window.
3. In Server Manager, click **Tools**, **Windows Server Backup**. In the left pane, click **Local Backup**. There's not much to see because you haven't performed a backup before. Look in the Actions pane to see what tasks you can perform.
4. Open a command prompt window. Type **wbadmin /?** and press **Enter** to see a list of options for performing backup and restore tasks with the `wbadmin` command. Close the command prompt window.
5. Open a PowerShell prompt. Type **Get-Command *-wb*** and press **Enter** to see the list of PowerShell cmdlets for performing backup and restore tasks. Close the PowerShell window.
6. Before you schedule a backup, you need to verify that you have a suitable disk online. Right-click Start and click Disk Management. If Disk 1 is offline, right-click it and click **Online**, then right-click it again and click **Initialize Disk** and click **OK**. Create a volume on Disk 1, name it **BackupVol** and accept the defaults for all other options. Close Disk Management.

7. In the Windows Server Backup console Actions pane, click **Backup Schedule**. In the Getting Started window, click **Next**.

8. In the Select Backup Configuration window, click **Custom** and click **Next**. Click **Add Items** and click the check box next to **System state** and click **OK**. Click **Next**.

9. In the Specify Backup Time window, review the options for scheduling the backup. You can perform the backup once per day or more than once per day, but you don't have any options for specific days of the week. Accept the default option **Once a day** and click **Next**.

10. In the Specify Destination Type window, click **Back up to a volume**, and click then **Next**.

11. In the Select Destination Disk window, only external disks are shown by default. Click **Add**. In the Add volumes dialog box, click **BackupVol**, and then click **OK**. Click **Next**.

12. In the Confirmation window, review the options you have selected, and click **Finish**. You see a message stating that when the first scheduled backup will occur. Click **Close**.

13. To see more backup options, click **Configure Performance Settings** in the Actions pane.

14. In the Optimize Backup Performance dialog box, review the options. If you want Windows Server Backup to perform incremental backups on subsequent backup runs, you would click the "Faster backup performance" option button. You can also click the Custom option button and choose the backup option (Full backup or Incremental backup) for each volume. For now, click **Cancel**.

15. If you want to begin the full backup, wait until the backup starts, and you see its status in the middle pane of the Windows Server Backup console. Otherwise, continue to the next activity where you stop the scheduled backup.

Activity 11-9: Performing a One-Time Backup of Selected Files

Time Required: 10 minutes

Objective: Perform a one-time backup of selected files.

Required Tools and Equipment: ServerDC1, ServerDM1 (*Note*: ServerDC1 is not used in the activity but it is the domain controller for the domain in which ServerDM1 is a member, so it should be running.)

Description: In this activity, you stop the scheduled backup, and then perform a one-time backup of selected files on ServerDM1.

1. Be sure ServerDC1 is running. First, you'll create a folder and some files to back up. On ServerDM1, create a folder named Docs on the C:\ drive and create two text files in the **Docs** folder named **File1** and **File2**.

2. In Windows Server Backup console, click **Backup Schedule** in the Actions pane. In the Modify Scheduled Backup Settings window, click the **Stop backup** option button, and then click **Next**.

3. In the Confirmation window click **Finish**. Click **Yes** to confirm. Click **Close**.

4. In the Actions pane, click **Backup Once**. In the Backup Options window, you see that you can base the one-time backup on the existing scheduled backup, if one exists. Accept the default option **Different options**, and then click **Next**.

5. In the Select Backup Configuration window, click the **Custom** option button, and then click **Next**.

6. In the Select Items for Backup window, click **Add Items**. Click to expand **Local disk (C:)**, and click to select **Docs**. You're backing up just a single folder so that the backup and restore run quickly. Click **OK** and then **Next**.

7. In the Specify Destination Type window, accept the default option **Local drives**, and then click **Next**.

8. In the Select Backup Destination window, click the **Backup destination** list arrow, if necessary, to select **BackupVol**. Click **Next**.

9. In the Confirmation window, click **Backup** to start the backup. You see its status in the Windows Server Backup Progress window. When the backup is finished, click **Close**.

10. Open File Explorer, and click the **BackupVol** drive. Double-click the **WindowsImageBackup** folder, and then double-click the **ServerDM1** folder. You see a number of folders including the folder Backup *date and time* (with *date and time* representing the date and time of the backup you created). Double-click the **Backup** folder to see a virtual disk and several XML documents. The virtual disk contains the files in the backup. Close File Explorer.

11. Stay signed in to ServerDM1 and continue to the next activity.

> **Tip**
>
> A virtual disk created with Windows Server Backup can be mounted and a drive letter assigned using Disk Management, allowing you to browse the contents of the backup without using the backup software.

Windows Server Recovery

 Certification

- **70-740 – Maintain and monitor server environments:**
  Maintain server installations

The reason you back up a server is so that you can recover lost data. Server recovery is a task you hope you never have to perform, but if you maintain a server for any length of time, a recovery of some sort is inevitable. Server recovery can mean different things, from recovery of a single file or folder to a full server restore. This section covers the following server recovery procedures:

- Recovering files, folders, and volumes
- System state recovery
- Bare metal recovery

Recovering Files, Folders, and Volumes

Windows Server Backup can recover single files, selected files and folders, or entire volumes. If you find you have to restore single files often because of accidental deletion or to recover a previous version of a file, you should enable the Shadow Copies feature on the volumes storing these documents. This feature enables users to restore files themselves in the Previous Versions tab of a shared or local folder's Properties dialog box.

Of course, Shadow Copies isn't always enabled on the volumes containing files that might need to be recovered; in that case, you have to turn to a backup of the volume. In addition, sometimes you need to restore an entire volume because of file system corruption or a failed drive. To recover a file or folder with Windows Server Backup, follow the procedure in Activity 11-10. To recover a file or folder at the command line, you can use the `wbadmin start recovery` command or the `Start-WBFileRecovery` PowerShell cmdlet. In both cases, you need to know the backup set's version identifier and the path of the file to recover. The following is an example of using `wbadmin` to recover the `D:\Docs\File1.txt` file from a backup with the version identifier 10/09/2017-21:00:

```
wbadmin start recovery —version:10/09/2017-2100 -itemType:File
  -items:D:\Docs\File1.txt
```

Using PowerShell, the same file recovery looks similar. In this example, the `$Backup` variable contains the backup set information:

```
Start-WBFileRecovery -Backupset $Backup
  -FilePathToRecover D:\Docs\File1.txt
```

If you need to restore an entire volume, you follow a procedure similar to restoring a single file or folder. You can't, however, do a volume recovery on a volume containing OS components. To perform a volume recovery involving OS components, you should perform a system state recovery or use the Windows Recovery Environment (Windows RE) to do a bare metal recovery.

Performing a System State Recovery

The procedure for a system state recovery varies depending on which server roles are installed. In particular, if you're restoring the system state of a DC, you need to decide whether to perform an authoritative restore or nonauthoritative restore of the Active Directory database and files as discussed later in "Active Directory Backup." You can do a system state recovery if you have any of the following backup types available:

- System state
- Bare metal recovery
- Full server

You can also restore the system state as a set of files to another location without affecting the current OS installation. If you restore the system state to the original location, the server restarts after the system state recovery is completed. Figure 11-30 shows the window in the Recovery Wizard where you can choose the location for the system state recovery.

Figure 11-30   Selecting the system state recovery location

Performing a Bare Metal Recovery

A bare metal recovery restores a server from a full server backup. You perform this task when your server has suffered catastrophic failure and can't boot to Windows. To do it, you need to be able to boot to the Windows installation medium. If you're restoring a physical server, you need an installation medium, such as a DVD, and if you're restoring a virtual machine, you can use an ISO file of the installation medium. To do a BMR, follow these steps:

1. Insert the installation medium into the system's DVD drive or configure a VM's DVD drive to point to an ISO file.

2. Boot the system you want to restore to from the installation medium. The Windows Setup process starts.

3. Confirm the language options. Select *Repair your computer* to start Windows Recovery Environment.

4. You see a menu with the following options: Continue (exits Windows RE and attempts to reboot the system), Troubleshoot (displays a menu where you can specify a system image recovery or open a command prompt window), and Turn off your PC (shuts down the computer). Select the Troubleshoot option, and then select System Image Recovery.

5. When prompted to select an OS to recover, choose Windows Server 2016.

6. Windows RE scans your system for a suitable backup. You're prompted to choose from the latest available system image or select a different system image, such as one on a share.

7. Next, you choose restore options. You can format and repartition disks, and you can exclude disks from the restore operation. For example, you might want to exclude data disks if you want only the Windows system disk to be restored. If necessary, you can load drivers for your disk controller if the disk isn't recognized. If you click the Advanced button, you see options to restart the computer and check for disk errors. (Both options are enabled by default.)

8. Finally, you have the option to review your choices and begin the restore procedure.

Activity 11-10: Recovering a File

Time Required: 10 minutes

Objective: Recover a file from backup.

Required Tools and Equipment: ServerDC1, ServerDM1 (*Note:* ServerDC1 is not used in the activity but it is the domain controller for the domain in which ServerDM1 is a member, so it should be running.)

Description: In this activity, you delete one of the files you backed up earlier and then recover it.

1. Be sure ServerDC1 is running. On ServerDM1, open File Explorer, and delete **C:\Docs\File1**. Leave File Explorer open.

2. In Windows Server Backup, click **Recover** in the Actions pane. In the Getting Started window, click **Next**.

3. In the Select Backup Date window, accept the default backup because you have only one backup, and then click **Next**.

4. In the Select Recovery Type window, accept the default option **Files and folders**. Review the other recovery types, most of which are grayed out because you don't have a suitable backup to perform them (see Figure 11-31). Click **Next**.

Figure 11-31 Selecting the recovery type

5. In the Select Items to Recover window, click to expand **ServerDM1** and **Local disk (C:)**, and click **Docs**. In the right pane, click **File1.txt**, and then click **Next**.

6. In the Specify Recovery Options window, you can recover the file to the original location or a new location. You also have the option to create a copy of the file if the original file exists, and you can choose to restore permissions to the file being recovered. Accept the default options, and then click **Next**.

7. In the Confirmation window, click **Recover**. In the Recovery Progress window, you see the progress of the recovery. After the recovery is finished, click **Close**.

8. In File Explorer, verify that the file has been recovered. Shut down all servers.

Backup and Recovery of Specific Roles

 **Certification**

- **70-740 – Maintain and monitor server environments:**
  Maintain server installations

The previous section primarily discussed using Windows Server Backup and the associated command-line tools to perform general backup and restore operations on a server. This section discusses particular considerations for backing up the following server roles:

- Hyper-V, including VMs
- Active Directory
- Internet Information Services (IIS)

Backing Up and Restoring Hyper-V

A Hyper-V backup includes two separate aspects:

- Backing up Hyper-V settings such as virtual switches, live migration settings, replication configuration, and so forth
- Backing up virtual machines and their guest operating systems and associated data

A full server backup or bare metal recovery backup on a Hyper-V host server includes the Hyper-V role, Hyper-V settings, and all the virtual machine settings and their guest OSs and data. A system state backup does not include Hyper-V settings or virtual machine data. So, if you have a full backup or bare metal recovery backup, you're covered in the event you need to restore Hyper-V, virtual machines, or both. However, suppose you want to back up only Hyper-V and its settings or one or more virtual machines? Windows Server Backup includes an option to do just that. If you choose a custom backup on a Hyper-V server, there is a Hyper-V node in the Select Items dialog box (highlighted in Figure 11-32). You can select to back up just the Hyper-V component, one or more virtual machines, or both the Hyper-V component and the virtual machines.

The virtual machines can be running or shut down when the backup occurs and the virtual machine settings, the virtual disks, and any checkpoints are backed up. Although you can install and run Windows Server Backup in each virtual machine's guest OS, performing a backup that way doesn't save the virtual machine settings in Hyper-V. The only advantages to backing up a VM from within the guest OS is that you can back up individual items of the guest OS such as files, volumes, or the system state. In addition, if the VM is using storage that is not supported by Windows Server Backup such as pass-through disks, shared VHDX, Fibre Channel, or iSCSI, the backup should be run from within the VM.

If you need to restore a VM or the Hyper-V host settings, you do so by selecting Hyper-V in the Select Recovery Type window in the Recovery Wizard. You can restore individual virtual machines, but you cannot restore part of a VM such as the system state; it's an all-or-nothing affair.

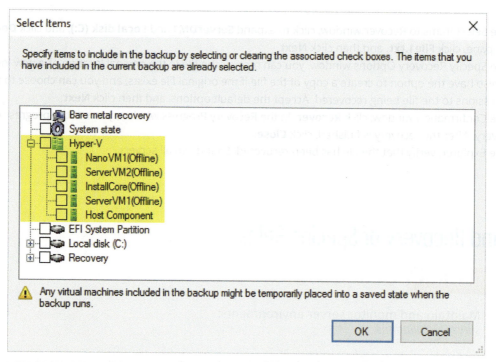

Figure 11-32   Backing up Hyper-V with Windows Server Backup

Backing Up and Restoring Active Directory

In this section, you learn how to recover Active Directory whether you need to recover from accidental object deletion or recover Active Directory from catastrophic failure.

Before getting into the details of how to maintain Active Directory, examine the two folders that hold most of the components of Active Directory:

- *NTDS*—By default, this folder is located in *%systemroot%* (usually C:\Windows). Here is a description of the some of the files it contains:
  - ntds.dit : The main Active Directory database.
  - edb.log : Place that holds a log of Active Directory transactions (changes). If Active Directory is shut down unexpectedly, changes that didn't get fully written to the database can be redone by using the data in this file to commit the changes. This file can grow to a maximum of 10 MB, and then new log files are created, named edb00001.log, edb00002.log, and so forth.
  - edb.chk : Stores information about the last committed transaction; used with edb.log to determine which transactions still need to be written to the database.
  - edbres00001.jrs : A placeholder file that simply takes up disk space. If the volume on which ntds.dit is stored fills up, this file and another named edbres00002.jrs are deleted to free disk space so that pending transactions can be committed to the database. After the changes are made, the DC is shut down, and the administrator must make disk space available before Active Directory can operate again.
- *SYSVOL*—By default, this folder is located in *%systemroot%*. It contains group policy templates, logon/logoff scripts, and DFS synchronization data.

During Active Directory installation, you can change the default location for these folders rather than accept the default *%systemroot%*. If you do, you don't have to do anything special to back them up because Windows recognizes the new location as part of the Windows system state. The Windows system state on a DC is composed of the same elements as on a non-DC plus the SYSVOL folder and the ntds.dit file.

Active Directory Backup

Active Directory is backed up when you perform any of the following types of backups on a DC: a full backup, backing up the volumes containing system recovery information, and a system state backup.

Although having a disaster recovery plan for all your servers that includes regular backups is a good idea, this chapter focuses on backing up Active Directory with system state backups.

Backing Up Active Directory with a System State Backup

A system state backup on a DC includes the Registry, boot files, the Active Directory database, the SYSVOL folder, some system files, and other files, depending on roles installed on the server. To perform a system state backup, you can run the Windows Server Backup tool or the wbadmin command:

```
wbadmin start systemstatebackup
```

Active Directory Restorations

An Active Directory restoration can be nonauthoritative or authoritative. A **nonauthoritative restore** restores the Active Directory database, or portions of it, and allows the data to be updated through replication by other domain controllers. An **authoritative restore** ensures that restored objects aren't overwritten by changes from other domain controllers through replication. The restored objects are replicated to other domain controllers.

Nonauthoritative Active Directory Restore

A nonauthoritative restore of Active Directory is usually done when the Active Directory database is corrupt or when you're doing a full server recovery. For this restore, you can stop Active Directory Domain Services or restart the DC in Directory Services Restore Mode (DSRM) before restoring from backup. The first option is preferable because it doesn't require a server restart. To stop Active Directory Domain Services, use one of the following methods:

- In the Services MMC, right-click the Active Directory Domain Services service and click Stop.
- At a command prompt, type net stop ntds and press Enter.
- At a PowerShell prompt, type Stop-Service ntds and press Enter.

To restart the DC in DSRM, press F8 when the server begins to boot to access the Advanced Boot Options menu and then select Directory Services Repair Mode. If pressing F8 doesn't work (for example, it can be very difficult to press F8 at the right time when booting a virtual machine), you can configure Windows to boot into DSRM using msconfig.exe. To do so, right-click Start, click Run, type msconfig, and press Enter. Click the Boot tab and click Safe boot and then click Active Directory repair (see Figure 11-33). Restart the system and Windows will boot into DSRM, bypassing the Advanced Boot Options menu.

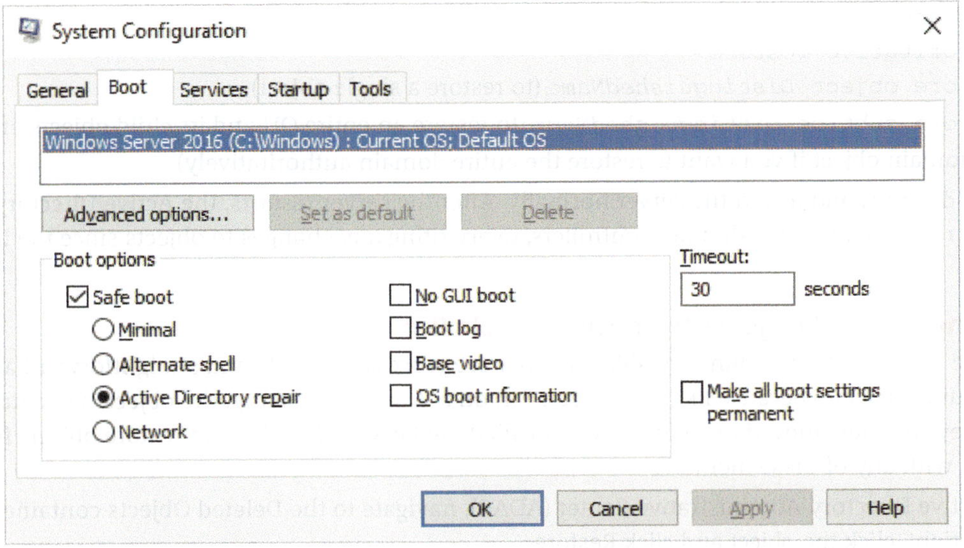

Figure 11-33   Using msconfig.exe to boot into DSRM

> **Note**
>
> When you boot into DSRM, you will need to log on with the local Administrator account instead of Domain\Administrator and use the DSRM password that was specified when Active Directory was installed.

After you have stopped Active Directory Domain Services or have booted into DSRM, run `wbadmin` to restore from a system state backup or from a backup that includes all critical volumes. After the restoration, restart the service or restart the server normally, and Active Directory replication updates the DC with any objects changed since the backup was created. If you have only one DC, any changes to Active Directory since the last backup are lost.

Authoritative Restore

With an authoritative restore, you can select specific Active Directory objects to be restored, or you can choose one or more containers and their contents, including the domain container. You can also choose to restore the SYSVOL folder authoritatively. A complete restore of an Active Directory domain should be a rare occurrence and a last-ditch effort to solve a major Active Directory problem because any changes made to objects on other DCs in the domain since the last backup will be lost. To perform an authoritative restore, follow these steps:

1. Boot the DC into DSRM.
2. Restore from the last system state backup by using the Recovery Wizard in Windows Server Backup or the `wbadmin` command.
3. Run `ntdsutil` to mark one or more objects as authoritative.
4. Restart the DC.

If you want the SYSVOL folder to be restored authoritatively, you have two options. If you're using the Recovery Wizard in Windows Server Backup, select the *Perform an authoritative restore of Active Directory files* option in the Select Location for System State Recovery window. If you're using `wbadmin`, include the `-authsysvol` parameter in the command.

After you have restored the system state from backup, you must use `ntdsutil` to mark one or more objects as authoritative before restarting the server. To mark an object or subtree as authoritative, enter these commands:

- `ntdsutil`
- `activate instance ntds`
- `authoritative restore`
- `restore object` *DistinguishedName* (to restore a single object)
- `restore subtree` *DistinguishedName* (to restore an entire OU and its child objects or specify the domain object if you want to restore the entire domain authoritatively)

Quit `ntdsutil`, and restart the server normally. After the server restarts, the Active Directory database is replicated to other domain controllers, overwriting any changes to objects since the last backup.

Recovering Deleted Objects from the Recycle Bin

If the Active Directory Recycle Bin is enabled, the restore process is simple and straightforward and doesn't require a backup because like the Recycle Bin on a Windows desktop, the objects were never really deleted. They were just moved to a special folder called the Recycle Bin. You can restore objects from the Recycle Bin with any of these methods:

- In Active Directory Administrative Center (ADAC), navigate to the Deleted Objects container, and then right-click the object and click Restore.

- Use the `Restore-ADObject` PowerShell cmdlet. For details on using this cmdlet, enter `Get-Help Restore-ADObject -detailed`.
- Use the `ntdsutil.exe` command.

The Active Directory Recycle Bin isn't enabled by default. After it's enabled, it can't be disabled without reinstalling the entire Active Directory forest. To enable it, all DCs must be running Windows Server 2008 R2 or later, and the forest functional level must be at Windows Server 2008 R2 or higher. The Recycle Bin is enabled with Active Directory Administrative Center or the following PowerShell cmdlet on the MCSA2016.local forest:

```
Enable-ADOptionalFeature -Identity "cn=Recycle Bin Feature,cn=Optional
    Features,cn=Windows NT,cn=Services,cn=Configuration,dc=MCSA2016,dc=local"
    -Scope ForestOrConfigurationSet -Target "MCSA2016.local"
```

Backing Up and Restoring IIS

Internet Information Services (IIS) is the web and application server role. A simple website with static HTML files is backed up when you perform a full backup or you can back up just the HTML files by backing up the C:\inetpub\wwwroot folder. If your website supports dynamic content, you need a backup program that supports the database software you are using to store the dynamic content. If you are using Microsoft SQL Server, backup and restore operations of the SQL database are supported by the Windows Server Backup program. If you want to back up only the IIS configuration files, you can back up the C:\Windows\System32\inetsrv folder, which contains most of the files that make up the IIS server role.

There is also a special command-line tool for managing and backing up IIS configuration files called `appcmd.exe`. You can use `appcmd` to maintain a separate backup for IIS, or you can use it to easily move your IIS configuration from one server to another. To create a backup with `appcmd` and name the backup IISbackup20171025, run the following from a command prompt:

```
appcmd add backup IISbackup20171025
```

The backup is stored as a folder in C:\Windows\System32\inetsrv\backup. To see a list of backups created by `appcmd`, run the following command:

```
appcmd list backup
```

To restore a backup made by `appcmd`, run the following command:

```
appcmd restore backup IISbackup20171025
```

If you want to copy the backup configuration to another IIS server, copy the backup folder from C:\Windows\System32\inetsrv\backup to the same folder on the destination server and run the `appcmd restore` command on the destination server.

Chapter Summary

- Monitoring performance is critical to maintaining server health. Windows Server 2016 includes tools such as Event Viewer, Task Manager, Resource Monitor, and Performance Monitor to help you check and analyze server performance.

- Event Viewer is useful for tracking down system or application problems and investigating security violations. Events are logged in two main categories: Windows logs, containing events that apply systemwide and events from applications, and Applications and Services logs, containing events from specific applications or system services.

- To help you isolate a problem or review log files more efficiently, Event Viewer offers several ways to search, filter, and sort event logs. Administrators can create event subscriptions to have logs from other systems written to a single log file, the Forwarded Events log.

- With Task Manager, you can see what's happening with processes running on the system in real time, so you can take action in a timely manner. When you start Task Manager, you see a list of applications running in the foreground on the system. These are applications that have a window currently open.

- Another tool for real-time monitoring is Resource Monitor, which shows CPU, memory, disk, and network use information for separate processes or the system as a whole in real time. You can also review processes that have stopped responding and close them if needed, check current file use by applications, and start, restart, pause, and end services.

- Performance Monitor can monitor real-time activity and review logs for historical information, and you can customize the data that's collected in logs. Alerts and tasks can be triggered based on user-defined thresholds, and a variety of reports can be generated.

- Data collector sets specify the performance counters you want to collect, how often to collect them, and how long to collect them. You can create multiple data collector sets that can be scheduled to capture different aspects of system performance and measure performance during different periods.

- Data collector sets can be configured so that when a particular performance counter value falls below or above a certain threshold value, an alert is triggered. Alerts can write an entry to the Application event log and run a specific program or script. An alert can also trigger another data collector set to start collecting related data.

- The key to useful performance monitoring is determining not only when to monitor but also specifically what to monitor. Some performance counter categories include Disk Counters, Memory Counters, Processor Counters, and Network Counters.

- A server backup is the cornerstone of any disaster recovery procedure. Backups are necessary for the following reasons: server hardware failure, disk failure, volume corruption, deletion of files, software failure, and theft or disaster.

- In Windows Server 2016 by default, members of the local Administrators group, Backup Operators group, and Server Operators group can back up and restore files. Administrators have full rights to the server, and Backup Operators and Server Operators are given the following rights: back up files and directories, restore files and directories, and shut down the system.

- When using Windows Server Backup, you can configure a backup to occur regularly or perform a one-time backup with the following options: full backup, custom backup, bare metal recovery, system state backup, EFI System Partition backup, recovery backup, and backup of separate volumes or files.

- A scheduled backup can dedicate a disk to the backup operation. You can have only one scheduled backup. A one-time backup creates a backup to a local volume or a share. The backup begins immediately.

- Most server role data are stored in locations that are backed up when you perform a backup containing the system state, such as a system state or full server backup. In addition, some roles, features, applications, and services register themselves with Windows Server Backup so that you can recover application-specific data without having to do a more extensive recovery.

- With the Windows Server Backup recovery options, you can recover files, folders, volumes, and the system state or perform a bare metal restore. The data to perform a system state recovery is included in the system state, bare metal recovery, and full server backup options.

- A full server backup or bare metal recovery backup on a Hyper-V host server includes the Hyper-V role, Hyper-V settings, and all the virtual machine settings and their guest OSs and data. A system state backup does not include Hyper-V settings or virtual machine data.

- Active Directory is backed up when you perform any of the following types of backups on a DC: a full backup, backing up volumes containing system recovery information, and a system state backup.

- An Active Directory restoration can be nonauthoritative or authoritative. A nonauthoritative restoration restores the Active Directory database, or portions of it, and allows it to be updated through replication by other domain controllers. An authoritative restore ensures that restored objects aren't overwritten by changes from other domain controllers through replication. The restored objects are replicated to other domain controllers.

- If you enable the Active Directory Recycle Bin, recovering deleted objects is simple and straightforward. It doesn't require a backup because like the Recycle Bin on a Windows desktop, the objects were never really deleted.

- The Internet Information Services (IIS) is the web and application server role. A simple website with static HTML files is backed up when you perform a full backup. However, if your website supports dynamic content, you need a backup program that supports the database software you are using to store the dynamic content.

Key Terms

<table>
<tr><td>authoritative restore</td><td>full backup</td><td>Performance Monitor</td></tr>
<tr><td>bare metal recovery</td><td>handle</td><td>Resource Monitor</td></tr>
<tr><td>baseline</td><td>incremental backup</td><td>scheduled backup</td></tr>
<tr><td>data collector set</td><td>nonauthoritative restore</td><td>system state backup</td></tr>
<tr><td>event subscription</td><td>one-time backup</td><td>Task Manager</td></tr>
<tr><td>Event Viewer</td><td>performance counter</td><td>thread</td></tr>
</table>

Review Questions

1. You can save event log information as a file in which format? (Choose all that apply.)
   a. Event log file format
   b. Log file format
   c. Tab delimited
   d. Comma delimited

2. Which subtypes of the Applications and Services logs in Event Viewer are hidden and disabled by default? (Choose all that apply.)
   a. Analytic   c. Debug
   b. Admin   d. Operational

3. Which of the following logs in Event Viewer do you use to create an event subscription?
   a. System   c. Security
   b. Forwarded Events d. Setup

4. In the Performance tab of Task Manager, which of the following components can you monitor? (Choose all that apply.)
   a. CPU use   c. Memory use
   b. Process use   d. Network adapters

5. In addition to monitoring system resources, you can do which of the following with Resource Monitor? (Choose all that apply.)
   a. Review and close processes that have stopped responding
   b. Delete files
   c. Control services
   d. See what files are in use by applications

6. Which of the following is (are) a source of data for Performance Monitor? (Choose all that apply.)
   a. Configuration information
   b. Event trace data

   c. Task Manager data
   d. Performance counters

7. Performance Monitor displays statistics in which of the following formats? (Choose all that apply.)
   a. Pie chart   c. Report
   b. Histogram   d. Line graph

8. What should you do to get a better idea of normal and abnormal system performance on your network?
   a. Talk to your users every day
   b. Create a baseline by recording monitor sessions at random times for later comparison
   c. Watch for certain thresholds to be exceeded
   d. Create a baseline by recording monitor sessions at peak and off-peak times for later comparison

9. An alert in Performance Monitor can write an event to which log?
   a. Security   c. Application
   b. System   d. Error

10. When can thresholds in a data collector set be configured to trigger an alert? (Choose all that apply.)
    a. The value in the counter falls below the threshold.
    b. The value in the counter is equal to the threshold.
    c. The value in the counter rises above the threshold.
    d. The value in the counter differs from the threshold by some percentage up or down.

11. The Users group has permission to do which of the following in Performance Monitor? (Choose all that apply.)
    a. View log files
    b. Access real-time data
    c. Create data collector sets
    d. Modify display properties

12. Which of the following counters refers to the quantity of disk read and write operations that are waiting to be serviced?
    a. Average Disk Queue Length
    b. Disk Bytes/sec
    c. % Disk Time
    d. % Idle Time

13. You have noticed that your system's performance has been degrading when running multiple applications on your server. You suspect that your system does not have enough memory to support the current workloads and is resolving too many hard page faults. Which memory counter would be the best counter to investigate to confirm your analysis?
    a. Paging File: % Usage
    b. Memory: Available MBytes
    c. Memory: Pages/sec
    d. Memory: Interrupts/sec

14. Which of the following situations typically require the availability of a backup created by Windows Server Backup? (Choose all that apply.)
    a. You need continuous availability of a network service.
    b. There's been accidental deletion of folders or files.
    c. You need to fail over to a replica VM.
    d. A server's registry appears to be corrupted.

15. You need to allow a junior administrator named jradmin to perform backup operations on a server named DataServ1. You don't want to give jradmin broader rights or permissions on the server, and this user shouldn't be able to restore files. What should you do?
    a. Add jradmin to the Backup Operators group.
    b. Add jradmin to the Server Operators group.
    c. Assign jradmin the Back up files and directories right.
    d. Add jradmin to the Allow list in the Software Restrictions policy.

16. Which of the following is true about a scheduled backup?
    a. You can create a separate schedule for each type of backup you want to perform.

b. You can specify a destination disk that's dedicated to backup jobs.
    c. Only one backup set is stored on the destination.
    d. You can't use a network share as the destination for a scheduled backup.

17. Which item is not included in a system state backup of a member server?
    a. Boot files
    b. The Registry
    c. SYSVOL
    d. Windows system files

18. What command-line program should you use to revert a volume to an existing shadow copy?
    a. `diskpart`   c. `wbadmin`
    b. `Start-Backup`   d. `vssadmin`

19. What feature can you enable in Windows Server 2016 to reduce the need to perform restore operations from a backup for files?
    a. Shadow copies   c. Disk quotas
    b. FSRM   d. Windows RE

20. Which of the following backup types should be performed on a Hyper-V host server to include the Hyper-V role, Hyper-V settings, and all the virtual machine settings and their guest OSs and data? (Choose all that apply.)
    a. System state
    b. Full server
    c. Bare metal recovery
    d. System checkpoint

21. Where would you find files related to logon and logoff scripts in an Active Directory environment?
    a. C:\Windows\NTDS
    b. %systemroot%\SYSVOL
    c. %Windir%\ntds.dit
    d. C:\Windows\edb.log

22. Within the NTDS file folder located in %systemroot%, which file is considered the main Active Directory database?
    a. `edb.dit`   c. `edb.log`
    b. `addb.dit`   d. `ntds.dit`

23. You have a domain controller that suffered a system crash, and you have to perform a full server recovery. You have two other DCs on the network, and they have been working fine during the two days the DC was offline. What type of Active Directory restore should you perform?
    a. Authoritative restore
    b. Shadow copy restore
    c. Nonauthoritative restore
    d. Bare metal recovery

24. Which of the following commands will allow you to back up the Registry, boot files, the Active Directory database, and the SYSVOL folder?

a. `robocopy C:\Windows`

b. `wbadmin start systemstatebackup`

c. `backup %systemroot%`
   `-selectsystemstate`

d. `ntdsutil create snapshot -source`
   `C:\Windows\ntds`

25. Which specific command-line tool will allow you to manage and back up IIS configuration files?

a. `appcmd.exe`

b. `resmon.exe`

c. `msconfig.exe`

d. `ntdsutil.exe`

Critical Thinking

The following activities give you critical thinking challenges. Case Projects offer a scenario with a problem to solve and for which you supply a written solution.

Case Project 11-1: Using System-Monitoring Tools

You recently became the server administrator for a company. As soon as you walked in the door, users were telling you the network is running slowly quite often, but they couldn't tell you when it happened or how much it slowed down. What tests and measurements could you use to try to determine what's going on?

Case Project 11-2: Recovering from Accidental Deletion

A junior administrator accidentally deleted the Sales OU, which contained 25 user accounts and 4 group accounts. You have five domain controllers in your network, two running Windows Server 2016, two running Windows Server 2008 R2, and one running Windows Server 2008. Explain what you need and the procedure for recovering the deleted objects.

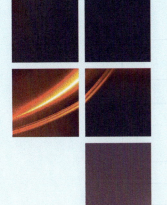

CHAPTER 12

NANO SERVER AND WINDOWS CONTAINERS

After reading this chapter and completing the exercises, you will be able to:

Describe Nano Server and its usage scenarios

Install and manage Nano Server

Create advanced Nano Server images

Describe Windows containers and appropriate usage scenarios

Deploy Windows containers

Manage Windows containers

Much of the buzz surrounding Windows Server 2016 as its release date approached centered on two separate but related new features: Nano Server and Windows containers. Nano Server takes Windows Server Core one step further in terms of Windows Server in a small footprint and low resource-usage package, and Windows containers takes the concept of "less is more" even further with respect to virtualization. Put the two together—Windows containers running on Nano Server—and you have a truly small-footprint, easy-to-deploy, and portable application environment with many of the isolation advantages of virtual machines (VMs).

In this chapter, you learn about Nano Server, a new headless deployment option for Windows Server 2016 that has a very small footprint, consumes few resources, and starts very quickly. It has limited usage scenarios because it supports only a few server roles and features, but it's likely to find a niche in virtual and cloud applications. Next, you'll learn about containers and the open source container management environment called *Docker*. Like Nano Server, containers are likely to be deployed in highly virtualized and cloud computing environments, but they might also find a spot in the bag of tricks of an administrator of a moderately sized datacenter.

Introducing Nano Server

 **Certification**

- **70-740 – Install Windows Servers in host and compute environments:**
  Install and configure Nano Server

Table 12-1 describes what you need for the hands-on activities in this chapter.

Table 12-1	Activity requirements	
Activity	**Requirements**	**Notes**
Activity 12-1: Resetting Your Virtual Environment	ServerHyperV	
Activity 12-2: Creating a Nano Server Base Image and Deploying It on a Virtual Machine	ServerHyperV	
Activity 12-3: Editing a Virtual Disk	ServerHyperV	
Activity 12-4: Working with External Virtual Switches	ServerHyperV	
Activity 12-5: Working with Internal Virtual Networks	ServerHyperV	
Activity 12-6: Working with Container Networks	ServerHyperV	

In Chapter 1, Nano Server was introduced as an even lighter-weight server than Server Core. Recall that Nano Server can be installed on a physical computer or as a virtual machine, but it's targeted application is as a specific-use virtual machine. As a refresher, here are the most common uses for Nano Server deployments:

- As a Hyper-V or container host
- As a cloud-based application server
- As a file server either part of a cluster (a scale-out file server) or standalone
- As a web server
- As a DNS server

Nano Server is not a general-purpose Windows server but is intended to be used as a tool to deploy a single, well-defined service. Nano Server is referred to as a **headless server** in which no traditional user interface is built in to manage Nano Server; rather, it is intended to be managed remotely using PowerShell, MMCs, or other remote management options. Applications running on Nano Server should be decoupled from any graphical user interface (GUI). For applications that require a GUI, the GUI should run remotely on another server with Desktop Experience installed or on a client version of Windows such as Windows 10.

Nano Server does have a user interface of sorts, the Nano Server Recovery Console (see Figure 12-1), that allows you to perform basic initial configuration tasks such as configuring a network interface and firewall rules so it can be managed remotely. As you can see in Figure 12-1, the tasks you can perform from the console are very limited.

Advantages of Nano Server

You might think that Nano Server provides limited functionality and presents some management challenges, and you would be right. So, why would you want to use Nano Server? Nano Server excels at three of the most important qualities you want in a server:

- *Availability*—Because the Nano Server image has only the roles, features, services, and drivers installed that are being used, Nano Server requires many fewer patches and security updates.

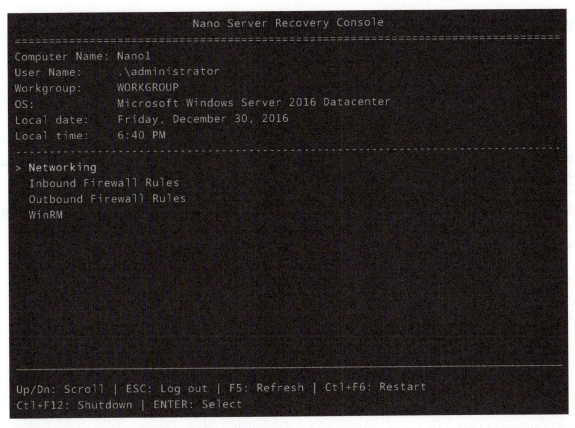

```
                    Nano Server Recovery Console
===============================================================================
Computer Name: Nano1
User Name:        .\administrator
Workgroup:        WORKGROUP
OS:               Microsoft Windows Server 2016 Datacenter
Local date:       Friday, December 30, 2016
Local time:       6:40 PM
- - - - - - - - - - - - - - - - - - - - - - - - - - - - - - - - - - - - - - - -
> Networking
  Inbound Firewall Rules
  Outbound Firewall Rules
  WinRM




Up/Dn: Scroll | ESC: Log out | F5: Refresh | Ctl+F6: Restart
Ctl+F12: Shutdown | ENTER: Select
```

Figure 12-1   The Nano Server Recovery Console

Fewer updates mean fewer reboots. Based on Microsoft research, Nano Server would have required only 2 critical updates over a period of 1 year compared with 8 for Server Core and 23 for the full server installation. Over the same period, Nano Server would have required only 3 reboots as a result of updates compared with 5 for Server Core and 11 for the full server. Fewer updates also means less time spent testing updates before deployment and generally a lower cost of maintenance.

- *Low resource utilization*—As mentioned, the Nano Server disk image contains only the binary files required for the installed features and devices, so the memory and disk footprint is very small. Kernel memory usage on Nano Server is only 61 MB compared with 139 MB for Server Core. The size of a dynamically expanding virtual disk is as small as 410 MB compared with over 6 GB for Server Core. In addition, the number of running processes on a base Nano Server installation is only 19 compared with around 30 for Server Core. Fewer running operating system processes means more CPU time for the applications and services you want your server to run.

- *Security*—Nano Server loads fewer than 75 services and drivers with fewer than 25 actually running. Server Core loads almost 100 services and drivers with almost 50 of them running. In addition, only 12 ports are open on a basic Nano Server installation whereas Server Core has more than 30 open ports. Fewer drivers, services, and ports means a smaller attack surface and a more secure server.

Although Nano Server does have its limitations, if your network needs DNS servers, Hyper-V servers, web servers, or file servers (and what network doesn't?), Nano Server is worth a look. Nano Server is still in its infancy; more use cases are on the horizon, particularly in cloud-based applications. Even if you don't see how it fits into your network now, it's likely that your datacenter will have a use for it in the near future.

Installing Nano Server

- **70-740 – Install Windows Servers in host and compute environments:**
  Install and configure Nano Server

Nano Server is not an installation option like Server Core and Desktop Experience. To install Nano Server, you create a virtual disk from files included on your Windows Server 2016 installation media using PowerShell. The virtual disk is used as the basis for a new virtual machine or to boot from a physical computer that supports booting from a virtual disk. Although you can install certain roles and features in Nano Server while it's running, it's best to include them when you create the Nano Server virtual disk. By doing so, you can create a library of Nano Server images with various roles already installed for easy deployment.

Nano Server Installation Requirements

Microsoft doesn't list installation requirements for Nano Server that are any different than those for the Server Core option of Windows Server 2016, but here's a quick summary:

- 1.4 GHz 64-bit processor
- 512 MB RAM
- 32 GB available disk space

As noted, the list of requirements are those officially specified by Microsoft for Windows Server 2016 including Nano Server; however, in practice, Nano Server can be run with much less RAM and disk space as discussed earlier. During some testing, a base installation of Nano Server in a Hyper-V VM with dynamic memory enabled required only 128 MB of start-up RAM and Hyper-V assigned just 156 MB of RAM to Nano Server after it was finished booting. The virtual hard disk required only about 550 MB of disk space on the Hyper-V host. A Nano Server VM running the DNS Server role required 192 MB of start-up RAM and 256 MB of RAM when Nano Server was fully booted. The virtual hard disk occupied less than 800 MB of disk space on the Hyper-V host. Granted, the servers tested were not under production workloads, but this example shows that the disk and memory footprint of Nano Server is far smaller than a Desktop Experience installation and even a Server Core installation.

Note 📎

Microsoft allows only customers with a Microsoft Software Assurance plan to deploy Nano Server. Microsoft Software Assurance plans come with volume license agreements. Nano Server is unlikely to be deployed in small business environments because small businesses rarely use enough servers to require a volume license agreement.

Installing Nano Server in a Virtual Machine

This section details how to install a base installation of Nano Server on a virtual machine. You'll need the Windows Server 2016 installation media because that's where the files needed to create the Nano Server virtual hard drive (VHD) are located. These steps assume that the installation media are available on a Hyper-V host server on the D: drive and that they will be copied to a folder named NanoServer on the server's C: drive. The general steps are as follows:

1. Copy the Nano Server image generator files from the installation media. Copy the D:\NanoServer\NanoServerImageGenerator folder from the installation media to the chosen location on your Hyper-V host. In this case, you would copy the folder to C:\NanoServer. In File Explorer, you will have a folder structure as shown in Figure 12-2.

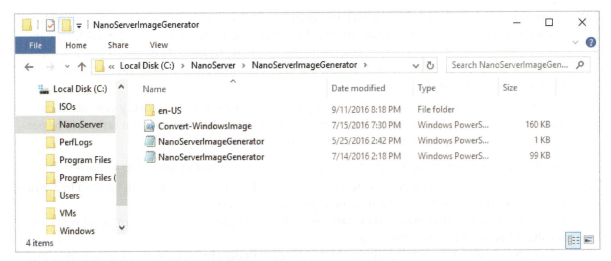

Figure 12-2   The NanoServerImageGenerator folder

2. Import the Nano Server image generator PowerShell module. Open a PowerShell window as Administrator and move to the NanoServerImageGenerator folder you copied to the host. Run the `Import-Module` PowerShell cmdlet (see Figure 12-3). This cmdlet imports the PowerShell cmdlets and scripts necessary to create and manage the Nano Server VHD images. There is no output generated if the cmdlet is successful, but if you want to see what the cmdlet does, add the `-Verbose` option. Note that this imports the NanoServerImageGenerator module for only this PowerShell session. If you quit PowerShell and later want to create more Nano Server images, you will need to run the `Import-Module` cmdlet again.

```
Windows PowerShell
Copyright (C) 2016 Microsoft Corporation. All rights reserved.

PS C:\Users\Administrator> cd \NanoServer\NanoServerImageGenerator\
PS C:\NanoServer\NanoServerImageGenerator> Import-Module .\NanoServerImageGenerator
PS C:\NanoServer\NanoServerImageGenerator> _
```

Figure 12-3   Running the `Import-Module` cmdlet

3. Create the Nano Server VHD using the `New-NanoServerImage` cmdlet, which is among the functions that were imported in the previous step. This cmdlet has many options, including the option to add certain roles such as Hyper-V, clustering, and file server. The basic options required to create a base Nano Server image and the remaining options are described later in the chapter. Use the `New-NanoServerImage` cmdlet to create a Nano Server VHD (or VHDX) image that can then be used as the basis for a new virtual machine (see Figure 12-4). You will be prompted for the Administrator password that will be used to sign in to the Nano Server recovery console. After some processing, the new VHD file will be created in the folder specified by the `-TargetPath` parameter.

```
PS C:\NanoServer\NanoServerImageGenerator> New-NanoServerImage -DeploymentType Guest -Edition Datacenter
-TargetPath C:\VMs\NanoVM1\NanoVM1.vhdx -MediaPath D:\ -BasePath .\Base -ComputerName NanoVM1

cmdlet New-NanoServerImage at command pipeline position 1
Supply values for the following parameters:
AdministratorPassword: **********
Done. The log is at: C:\NanoServer\NanoServerImageGenerator\Base\Logs\2017-01-01_15-27-40-14
```

Figure 12-4   Creating a Nano Server image

4. Create a new virtual machine and attach the virtual hard disk created in Step 3 to the new VM. When you create the new VM, simply specify the path of the Nano Server VHD (or VHDX) file in the Connect Virtual Hard Disk step if you create the VM using Hyper-V Manager. If you use the `New-VM` PowerShell cmdlet to create the VM, use the `-VHDPath` parameter to specify the path to the Nano Server virtual disk file.

5. Start the new VM and connect to it. You can sign in to the Nano Server Recovery Console and configure the network interface and firewall, if necessary. Most of the configuration tasks will be performed remotely using PowerShell Direct and other remote management tools.

Let's look at the parameters used in the `New-NanoServerImage` cmdlet from Step 3, above:

- `-DeploymentType`—Specify either Guest or Host. If the Nano Server image will be used in a virtual machine, specify Guest; if it will be used on a physical computer, specify Host.
- `-Edition`—Specify either Standard or Datacenter depending on which edition of Windows Server 2016 should be used to create the image.
- `-TargetPath`—Specify the full path and file name of the new virtual disk. You can specify a VHD or VHDX extension depending on which type of virtual disk you want. You can also create a WIM file instead of a VHD, which can be useful for some types of physical machine deployments. If the folder specified does not exist, it will be created.
- `-MediaPath`—This is the path to the root of the Windows Server 2016 installation media. After you have created the first Nano Server image, this parameter is no longer necessary.
- `-BasePath`—This is the path to a folder where the Nano Server WIM file and packages are copied from the Windows Server 2016 media that you specify with the `-MediaPath` parameter. If the folder doesn't already exist, it will be created. After the first Nano Server image is created, these files will be used to create subsequent Nano Server images.
- `-ComputerName`—This is the computer name assigned to the Nano Server image. Like any Windows computer name, it must be unique on the network.

The base Nano Server is not too useful because there are no roles and features installed. However, before we discuss how to add roles and features, let's take a look at creating a host Nano Server that runs on a physical computer.

> **Tip** ⓘ
>
> The PowerShell cmdlets to build a Nano Server image can become quite long, so Microsoft developed a graphical tool to build a Nano Server image you can download for free at *http://aka.ms/NanoServerImageBuilder*.

Installing Nano Server on a Physical Computer

Most Nano Server deployments are likely to be on virtual machines, but one of the important use cases for Nano Server is as a Hyper-V host. In production environments, that means deploying Nano Server to a physical computer. For testing purposes, you can use nested virtualization.

If you have already created a Nano Server image, you can skip Steps 1 and 2 outlined in the section "Installing Nano Server on a Virtual Machine"; otherwise, perform Steps 1 and 2 and then proceed with Step 3 using the `New-NanoServerImage` cmdlet but with some important differences as shown here:

```
New-NanoServerImage -DeploymentType Host -Edition Datacenter -TargetPath
  C:\VMs\NanoPhys1\NanoPhys1.vhdx -BasePath .\Base -ComputerName NanoPhys1
  -OEMDrivers -Compute
```

Here are the important differences in the `New-NanoServerImage` cmdlet to create an image for physical computer deployment instead of for virtual deployment:

- `-DeploymentType`—Use Host as the deployment type instead of Guest.
- `-OEMDrivers`—This parameter loads the standard Windows drivers that are needed to support devices such as network adapters and storage controllers on a variety of physical computers.
- `-Compute`—This parameter installs the Hyper-V role in the Nano Server image.

In addition to these parameters, the other difference is that you don't need the `-MediaPath` parameter because the necessary files are already copied to the folder specified with the `-BasePath` parameter. You can install drivers and roles after you create a base image, but if you know what role you are installing when you create the image, it's easier to specify it during creation. You'll learn about modifying a Nano Server image later in this chapter.

After the image is created, there are a few options for deploying it to a physical computer:

- *Dual boot on a computer that already has a Windows OS installed on it*—To use this option, you'll need a Windows computer such as Windows 10 or Windows Server 2016. Copy the Nano Server virtual disk file to the computer and mount the virtual disk. After mounting the virtual disk, open a command prompt as administrator and run `bcdboot D:\Windows`, replacing D: with the drive letter of the mounted virtual disk. Restart Windows, and you'll be presented with a boot menu. The Nano Server will be the first option in the menu.
- *Use PXE boot and WDS to install Nano Server on a bare-metal computer*—Using this option, you need to install and configure a Windows Deployment Services (WDS) server and add the Nano Server virtual disk or WIM file as an install image. Once WDS is configured, PXE boot the physical server on which you wish to install Nano Server. Select the Nano Server image from the Windows Setup screen, and Nano Server will install in just a few seconds.
- *Use WinPE to install Nano Server on a bare-metal machine*—You can download and install Windows Preinstallation Environment (WinPE) to a USB or DVD drive or PXE boot it from a WDS server. Once loaded, WinPE provides a command prompt with `diskpart.exe`, `dism.exe`, and `bcdboot.exe`, which allow you to prepare the hard disk and apply the Nano Server image. The details for doing so are beyond the scope of this book, but you can find an excellent article on the process by searching the Internet for "Deploying Nano Server to a Bare-Metal Machine."

Activity 12-1: Resetting Your Virtual Environment

Time Required: 5 minutes
Objective: Reset your virtual environment by applying the InitialConfig checkpoint or snapshot.
Required Tools and Equipment: ServerHyperV
Description: Apply the InitialConfig checkpoint or snapshot to ServerHyperV.

1. Be sure ServerHyperV is shut down. In your virtualization program, apply the InitialConfig checkpoint or snapshot to ServerHyperV.
2. Close your virtual machine environment.

Activity 12-2: Creating a Nano Server Base Image and Deploying It on a Virtual Machine

Time Required: 20 minutes
Objective: Create a Nano Server base image and deploy it on a virtual machine.
Required Tools and Equipment: ServerHyperV
Description: Copy the Nano Server image creation files to your server, import the necessary PowerShell module, and create a new Nano Server base image for deployment on a virtual machine. Then, create a virtual machine, connect the image to the VM, and start Nano Server.

1. Sign in to ServerHyperV as **Administrator** and open a PowerShell window.

2. Be sure the Windows Server 2016 installation media is available on drive D:. Type **dir d:** and press **Enter**, and you should see several folders including one named NanoServer. Type **xcopy d:\NanoServer\ NanoServerImageGenerator c:\NanoServer\NanoServerImageGenerator\ /e** and press **Enter**. The PowerShell script files are copied to C:\NanoServer.

3. Type **cd \NanoServer** and press **Enter**. Type **Import-Module .\NanoServerImageGenerator** and press **Enter**.

4. Now, create the Nano Server image. You'll create one with the VHDX disk type and place it in the folder C:\ VMs\NanoVM1. Type **New-NanoServerImage -DeploymentType Guest -Edition Datacenter -TargetPath C:\VMs\NanoVM1\NanoVM1.vhdx -MediaPath D:\ -BasePath .\Base -ComputerName NanoVM1** and press **Enter**.

5. When you are prompted for the Administrator password, type **Password01** and press **Enter**.

6. It will take some time for the image to be created. When the image is finished being created, type **dir c:\vms\ NanoVM1** and press **Enter** to verify that the virtual disk is there.

7. Next, you'll create a virtual machine and attach its hard drive to the Nano Server virtual disk. Type **New-VM -Name NanoVM1 -MemoryStartupBytes 256MB -VHDPath c:\VMs\NanoVM1\NanoVM1. vhdx -Generation 2 -Path C:\VMs\NanoVM1** and press **Enter**. (You could also create a new VM using Hyper-V Manager.)

8. Next, you'll connect the VM to a virtual switch so it can access the network. Type **Get-VMNetworkAdapter NanoVM1** and press **Enter**. Notice that the adapter is not connected to a switch.

9. Type **Connect-VMNetworkAdapter NanoVM1 -SwitchName PrivateNet** and press **Enter**. This connects all network adapters to the virtual switch PrivateNet, which should already be created on ServerHyperV.

10. Now, start the VM and connect to it. Type **Start-VM NanoVM1** and press **Enter**. To connect to the VM, type **vmconnect localhost NanoVM1** and press **Enter**. The vmconnect.exe command uses the syntax vmconnect *servername VMname*. You could also use Hyper-V Manager to connect to the VM.

11. You will see the Nano Server Recovery Console sign-in prompt (see Figure 12-5). Type **administrator**, press **Tab**, and then type **Password01** and press **Enter**.

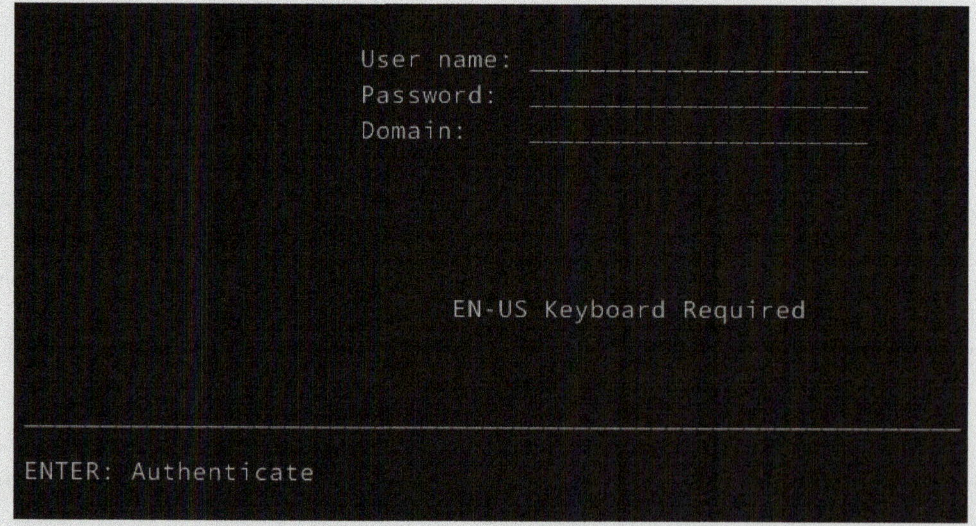

Figure 12-5 The Nano Server Recovery Console sign-in prompt

12. From the Nano Server Recovery Console, you can configure the network interface, firewall rules, and WinRM. You need to configure WinRM only if you are managing the server remotely. But you can also configure Nano Server using PowerShell Direct without any network configuration. Go to the PowerShell prompt

on ServerHyperV and type **Enter-PSSession -VMName NanoVM1** and press **Enter**. When prompted for credentials, type **administrator** and **Password01** and press **Enter** (see Figure 12-6). Your PowerShell session is now connected to NanoVM1.

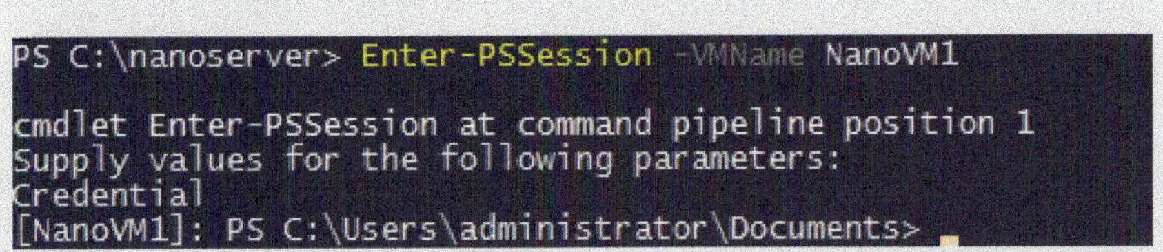

```
PS C:\nanoserver> Enter-PSSession -VMName NanoVM1

cmdlet Enter-PSSession at command pipeline position 1
Supply values for the following parameters:
Credential
[NanoVM1]: PS C:\Users\administrator\Documents>
```

Figure 12-6   Connecting to Nano Server with PowerShell Direct

13. Type **Get-ComputerInfo** and press **Enter** to see information similar to Figure 12-7 (you'll probably need to scroll up to see all the output). Notice the WindowsEditionId is called *ServerDataCenterNano* and the WindowsInstallationType is called *Nano Server*.

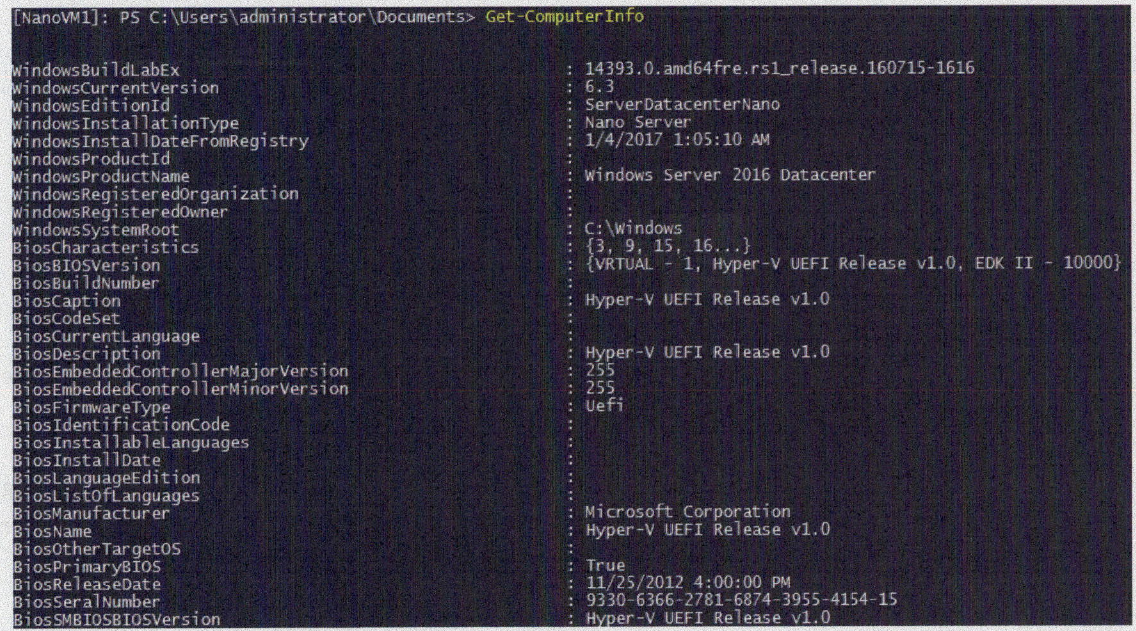

```
[NanoVM1]: PS C:\Users\administrator\Documents> Get-ComputerInfo

WindowsBuildLabEx                          : 14393.0.amd64fre.rs1_release.160715-1616
WindowsCurrentVersion                      : 6.3
WindowsEditionId                           : ServerDatacenterNano
WindowsInstallationType                    : Nano Server
WindowsInstallDateFromRegistry             : 1/4/2017 1:05:10 AM
WindowsProductId                           :
WindowsProductName                         : Windows Server 2016 Datacenter
WindowsRegisteredOrganization              :
WindowsRegisteredOwner                     :
WindowsSystemRoot                          : C:\Windows
BiosCharacteristics                        : {3, 9, 15, 16...}
BiosBIOSVersion                            : {VRTUAL - 1, Hyper-V UEFI Release v1.0, EDK II - 10000}
BiosBuildNumber                            :
BiosCaption                                : Hyper-V UEFI Release v1.0
BiosCodeSet                                :
BiosCurrentLanguage                        :
BiosDescription                            : Hyper-V UEFI Release v1.0
BiosEmbeddedControllerMajorVersion         : 255
BiosEmbeddedControllerMinorVersion         : 255
BiosFirmwareType                           : Uefi
BiosIdentificationCode                     :
BiosInstallableLanguages                   :
BiosInstallDate                            :
BiosLanguageEdition                        :
BiosListOfLanguages                        :
BiosManufacturer                           : Microsoft Corporation
BiosName                                   : Hyper-V UEFI Release v1.0
BiosOtherTargetOS                          :
BiosPrimaryBIOS                            : True
BiosReleaseDate                            : 11/25/2012 4:00:00 PM
BiosSerialNumber                           : 9330-6366-2781-6874-3955-4154-15
BiosSMBIOSBIOSVersion                      : Hyper-V UEFI Release v1.0
```

Figure 12-7   Result of the `Get-ComputerInfo` cmdlet

14. Set the IP address of NanoVM1 by typing **New-NetIPAddress -InterfaceAlias Ethernet -IPAddress 192.168.0.100 -PrefixLength 24** and press **Enter**.

15. Type **Get-NetIPAddress** and press **Enter**. All of the IP address settings are listed including the address you just set.

16. Many of the PowerShell commands you have used in full Windows installations work in Nano Server, but many are absent as well. Type **Get-Command** and press **Enter** to see the list of all functions and cmdlets. Now, type **Exit** and press **Enter** to return PowerShell to ServerHyperV and type **Get-Command** and press **Enter**. You see considerably more functions and cmdlets on ServerHyperV.

17. Open the Nano Server Recovery Console window and press **Ctrl+F12** and press **Enter** to shut down the server. Close the Virtual Machine Connection window and stay signed in to ServerHyperV for the next activity.

Creating Advanced Nano Server Images

 **Certification**

- 70-740 – Install Windows Servers in host and compute environments:
  Install and configure Nano Server

Now that you know how to create a basic Nano Server image, we'll look at some more installation scenarios in which you create a Nano Server image with one or more server roles pre-installed. We'll also take a look at deploying Nano Server packages, configuring packages already installed on Nano Server, and performing additional tasks such as joining Nano Server to a domain and modifying a Nano Server image with Windows updates among other Nano Server configuration tasks. As discussed, the `New-NanoServerImage` cmdlet has a number of parameters that allow you to perform several configuration tasks during image creation including role installation and network configuration. Many of these tasks are explored in the next section.

Deploying Nano Server Packages

The following list describes parameters that you can use with the `New-NanoServerImage` cmdlet for adding roles and features and for performing network configuration:

- `-Storage`—Installs the Storage package that includes the File Server role and other components needed to configure Nano Server as a file server.
- `-Compute`—Installs the Hyper-V package allowing Nano Server to be a virtualization host.
- `-Defender`—Installs the Windows Defender package.
- `-Clustering`—Installs the Clustering package. Clustering on Nano Server is currently supported for the Hyper-V and File Server roles.
- `-Containers`—Installs the Containers package, allowing Nano Server to host containerized packages. Containers are discussed later in this chapter.
- `-Packages`—Allows you to specify one or more packages to install. Several packages are available on the Windows Server 2016 installation media. These packages are copied to the Base\Packages folder specified by the `-BasePath` parameter in the `New-NanoServerImage` cmdlet. Other packages are available through online package repositories. Table 12-2 lists the name of the package and the role or feature it contains. Except where noted, you install these packages by including the `Packages` parameter followed by the package file name in the `New-NanoServerImage` cmdlet.

Table 12-2   Nano Server Packages

Package Name	Description
Microsoft-NanoServer-Compute-Package	Installs the Hyper-V role. To install this package, simply specify the `-Compute` parameter in the `New-NanoServerImage` cmdlet.
Microsoft-NanoServer-Containers-Package	Installs the Containers package. Use the `-Containers` parameter to install this package.
Microsoft-NanoServer-DCB-Package	Installs the Data Center Bridging package.
Microsoft-NanoServer-Defender-Package	Installs the Windows Defender package.
Microsoft-NanoServer-DNS-Package	Installs the DNS Server role.
Microsoft-NanoServer-DSC-Package	Installs the Desired State Configuration (DSC) package. Note that Nano Server does not support Group Policy, so configuration tasks that you might have used Group Policy for on a full server must be accomplished with DSC.

Table 12-2 Nano Server Packages (*continued*)

Package Name	Description
Microsoft-NanoServer-FailoverCluster-Package	Installs clustering services. Use the `-Clustering` parameter to install this package. Only Hyper-V and File Server roles can be clustered on Nano Server at this writing.
Microsoft-NanoServer-Guest-Package	Installs the drivers necessary for installing Nano Server as a guest OS in a Hyper-V VM. Use the `-DeploymentType Guest` parameter to install this package.
Microsoft-NanoServer-Host-Package	Installs the drivers necessary for installing Nano Server as a host OS on a physical machine. Use the `-DeploymentType Host` parameter to install this package.
Microsoft-NanoServer-IIS-Package	Installs the Internet Information Server (IIS) package allowing Nano Server to be configured as a web server.
Microsoft-NanoServer-OEM-Drivers-Package	Installs basic drivers needed for many physical machine deployments.
Microsoft-NanoServer-SCVMM-Compute-Package	Installs the System Center Virtual Machine Manager (SCVMM) package that installs the Hyper-V role and allows a Nano Server Hyper-V host to be managed by SCVMM. Use this package if you are monitoring Hyper-V. If you use this option, don't use the `-Compute` option.
Microsoft-NanoServer-SCVMM-Package	Installs the System Center Virtual Machine Manager (SCVMM) agent.
Microsoft-NanoServer-SecureStartup-Package	Installs the necessary files for configuring secure start-up that includes BitLocker, trusted platform module (TPM), volume encryption, and other functions necessary for secure start-up.
Microsoft-NanoServer-ShieldedVM-Package	Installs support for Hyper-V Shielded VMs when Nano Server is configured as a Hyper-V host. This option is available only when Nano Server is configured with the `-Version Datacenter` option.
Microsoft-NanoServer-SoftwareInventoryLogging-Package	Installs the Software Inventory Logging feature that allows administrators to log software inventory data.
Microsoft-NanoServer-Storage-Package	Installs the File Server role, Data Deduplication, Storage Replica, and iSCSI target features in addition to other features for creating a robust file server. Use the `-Storage` parameter to install this package.

Here are some examples of creating a Nano Server image with one or more roles and features pre-installed. In these examples, it is assumed you have already copied the NanoServer\NanoServerImageGenerator folder to a folder on your host computer and your PowerShell prompt is in that folder. In addition, you need to specify the -MediaPath parameter only if this is the first time creating a Nano Server image on this host.

- Nano Server host deployment with the Hyper-V role. In this cmdlet, you need to use the -DeploymentType Host, -Compute, and the -OEMDrivers parameters:

```
New-NanoServerImage -DeploymentType Host -Edition Datacenter -TargetPath
   C:\VMs\NanoHyperV1\NanoHyperV1.vhdx -MediaPath D:\ -BasePath
   .\Base -ComputerName NanoHyperV1 -Compute -OEMDrivers
```

- Nano Server guest deployment with the DNS Server role. In this cmdlet, you need to use the -DeploymentType Guest and -Packages parameters with the DNS package name.

```
New-NanoServerImage -DeploymentType Guest -Edition Datacenter -TargetPath
    C:\VMs\NanoDNS1\NanoDNS1.vhdx -MediaPath D:\ -BasePath .\Base -ComputerName
    NanoDNS1 -Packages Microsoft-NanoServer-DNS-Package
```

- Nano Server guest deployment with the file server and clustering functions. In this cmdlet, you need to use the `-DeploymentType Guest`, `-Storage`, and `-Clustering` parameters.

```
New-NanoServerImage -DeploymentType Guest -Edition Datacenter -TargetPath
    C:\VMs\NanoFileServer1\NanoFileServer1.vhdx -MediaPath D:\ -BasePath
    .\Base -ComputerName NanoFileServer1 -Storage -Clustering
```

Configuring Packages on Nano Server

Adding packages to a Nano Server image adds only the binary files for the package to the Nano Server image. You need to enable the features before you can begin using them. You can do this easily with PowerShell Direct on a virtual machine deployment or with PowerShell remoting on a physical deployment. You'll also need to import the PowerShell module if you want to use PowerShell to manage the feature. For example, if you have a Nano Server image with the DNS Server package installed and you have already created a Hyper-V VM for it named NanoDNS1, use the following process to enable and configure DNS:

1. Start the NanoDNS1 virtual machine.

2. Open a PowerShell prompt on the host computer and type `Enter-PSSession -VMName NanoDNS1`. Enter the administrator credentials for the Nano Server when prompted. Your PowerShell session is now connected to NanoDNS1.

3. Type `Get-WindowsOptionalFeature -Online`. You will see output similar to Figure 12-8.

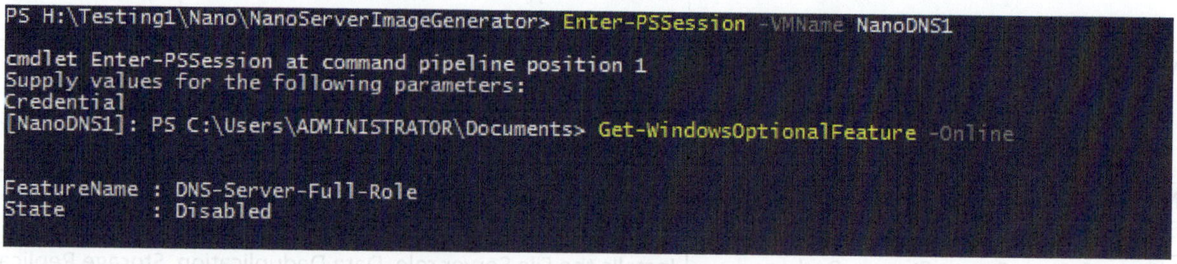

```
PS H:\Testing1\Nano\NanoServerImageGenerator> Enter-PSSession -VMName NanoDNS1

cmdlet Enter-PSSession at command pipeline position 1
Supply values for the following parameters:
Credential
[NanoDNS1]: PS C:\Users\ADMINISTRATOR\Documents> Get-WindowsOptionalFeature -Online


FeatureName : DNS-Server-Full-Role
State       : Disabled
```

Figure 12-8: Displaying installed features on Nano Server

4. Type `Enable-WindowsOptionalFeature -FeatureName DNS-Server-Full-Role -Online`.

5. To install the PowerShell module to manage DNS, type `Import-Module DnsServer`.

6. To verify the available PowerShell cmdlets for DNS, type `Get-Command *DNS*`. You will see a long list of cmdlets related to DNS Server. Figure 12-9 shows the results of Steps 4–6.

At this point, you can manage DNS Server on the Nano Server using PowerShell, you can manage it remotely with the DNS Server Manager MMC on a server with a GUI that has DNS Server installed, or you can manage it on a computer that has the remote server administration tools installed.

Some packages have a variety features that can be enabled or disabled. To see all the features available for a particular package, be sure to run the `Get-WindowsOptionalFeature -Online` cmdlet after you connect to Nano Server and then use `Enable-WindowsOptionalFeature` to enable specific features of the package.

Removing packages and disabling features require a similar process. To disable a feature, connect to the Nano Server with PowerShell and run the `Disable-WindowsOptionalFeature -FeatureName` *NameOfFeatureToDisable* `-Online` cmdlet. You can also remove a package entirely using `Remove-WindowsPackage -PackageName` *NameOfPackageToRemove* `-Online`. Be sure to use

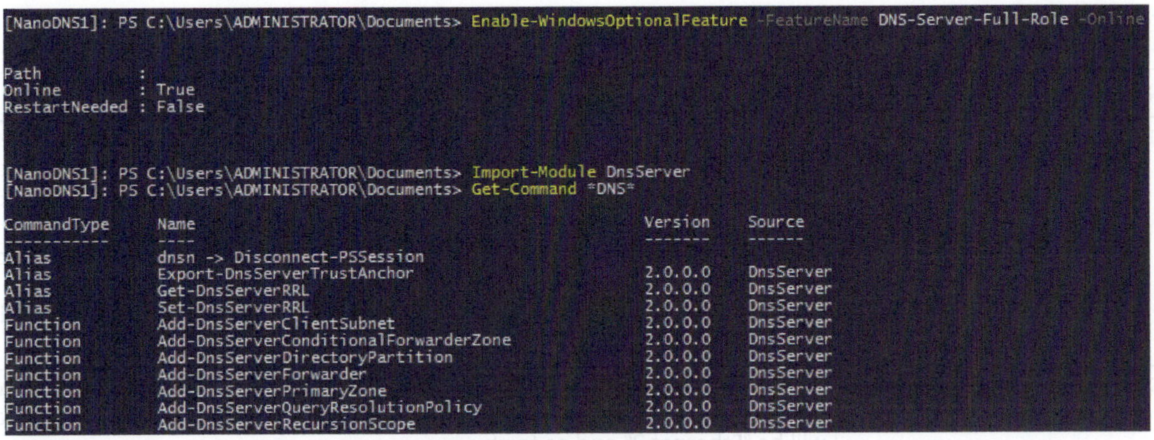

Figure 12-9:   Enabling the DNS Server role on Nano Server

`Get-WindowsPackage -Online` first so you have the exact name of the package you wish to remove. Note that enabling and disabling packages might require a reboot of Nano Server.

Configuring Nano Server Images

We've looked at deploying a base Nano Server image for both guest and physical deployment. We've also looked at installing various packages in the Nano Server image during image creation. In this section, we'll look at some additional configuration options that can be specified with the `New-NanoServerImage` cmdlet. Table 12-3 lists some of the more common configuration parameters. Examples using the parameters follow the table.

Table 12-3   `New-NanoServerImage` Configuration Parameters

Parameter	Function
`-DeploymentType`	Specifies the deployment type. Specifying `Guest` installs the Microsoft-NanoServer-Guest-Package, which includes the necessary drivers for deploying Nano Server in a virtual machine. Specifying `Host` installs the Microsoft-NanoServer-Host-Package, which includes some of the drivers needed for deploying Nano Server on a physical machine. This parameter is usually used along with `-OEMDrivers`.
`-Edition`	Specifies the Windows Server 2016 edition Nano Server should be based on. Options are `Standard` and `Datacenter`.
`-MaxSize`	Specifies the size in bytes (can also use MB and GB suffixes) for the maximum size of the dynamic virtual disk. The default is 4 GB so if that is suitable, this option is not required.
`-OEMDrivers`	Installs the OEMDrivers, which are the same drivers available when installing a regular Windows Server 2016 OS. This parameter is usually used with `-DeploymentType Host`.
`-AdministratorPassword`	Sets the administrator password used to sign in to the Nano Server Recovery Console. This parameter requires a secure string, which can be created using the `ConvertTo-SecureString` cmdlet. If omitted, you will be prompted for the administrator password.
`-DomainName`	Specifies a domain name to which the Nano Server should be joined. This parameter performs an offline domain join. The local computer on which the cmdlet is run must be a member of the specified domain.

(continues)

Table 12-3   `New-NanoServerImage` Configuration Parameters (*continued*)

Parameter	Function
`-DomainBlobPath`	Specifies the path to a domain blob and joins the image to that domain. Use this parameter when you want the Nano Server image to be joined to a different domain than the local computer. To create a domain blob, use the `djoin.exe` command. For example, to create a domain blob for a Nano Server named NanoDM1 that will belong to the MCSA2016.local domain, use this command: `djoin /provision /Domain MCSA2016.local /Machine NanoDM1 /SaveFile NanoDM1.blob`. Copy the NanoDM1.blob file to the server in which you will be creating the Nano Server image.
`-InterfaceNameOrIndex`	Specifies the name or index number of a network interface to configure. In a new image, the first interface name will be "Ethernet" and the second interface name will be "Ethernet 2" and so forth.
`-IPv6Address`	Specifies the IPv6 static address on the interface specified by the `-InterfaceNameOrIndex` parameter.
`-IPv6DNS`	Specifies one or more IPv6 DNS server addresses.
`-IPv4Address`	Specifies the IPv4 static address on the interface specified by the `-InterfaceNameOrIndex` parameter.
`-IPv4SubnetMask`	Specifies the IPv4 subnet mask on the interface specified by the `-InterfaceNameOrIndex` parameter.
`-IPv4Gateway`	Specifies the IPv4 default gateway address on the interface specified by the `-InterfaceNameOrIndex` parameter.
`-IPv4DNS`	Specifies one or more IPv4 DNS server addresses.

Here are some examples of using some of the parameters in Table 12-3. These commands assume that you have already created at least one Nano Server image and therefore don't need to specify the `-MediaPath` parameter and your PowerShell prompt is currently in the NanoServerImageGenerator folder.

- Base Nano Server guest deployment with IPv4 address, subnet mask, and default gateway configuration:

```
New-NanoServerImage -DeploymentType Guest -Edition Datacenter - TargetPath
    C:\VMs\Nano1\Nano1.vhdx -BasePath .\Base -ComputerName Nano1-InterfaceNameOrIndex
    "Ethernet" -Ipv4Address 192.168.0.100 -Ipv4SubnetMask 255.255.255.0
    -Ipv4Gateway 192.168.0.250
```

- Nano Server guest deployment with a maximum size virtual disk of 8 GB. IPv4 address, subnet mask, default gateway, and DNS server address are configured, and the image is joined to the domain MCSA2016.local. The host computer must already be a member of MCSA2016.local:

```
New-NanoServerImage -DeploymentType Guest -Edition Datacenter -TargetPath
    C:\VMs\NanoDM1\NanoDM1.vhdx -BasePath .\Base -ComputerName NanoDM1
    -InterfaceNameOrIndex "Ethernet" -Ipv4Address 192.168.0.100
    -Ipv4SubnetMask    255.255.255.0 -Ipv4Gateway 192.168.0.250 -Ipv4DNS
    192.168.0.1 -MaxSize 8GB -DomainName MCSA2016.local
```

- Nano Server guest deployment in which the image is joined to the domain *TestDom.local*. The host computer is currently a member of MCSA2016.local. You have created the domain blob NanoDM1. blob for TestDom.local and placed it in the C:\TestDomBlob folder:

```
New-NanoServerImage -DeploymentType Guest -Edition Datacenter - TargetPath
    C:\VMs\NanoDM1\NanoDM1.vhdx -BasePath .\Base -DomainBlobPath
    C:\TestDomBlob\NanoDM1.blob
```

Joining Nano Server to a Domain

There are two methods for joining Nano Server to a domain during image creation: join to the same domain as the host computer and join to a different domain. In both cases, you are performing an offline domain join in which the Nano Server will complete the joining process when it is first started. An **offline domain join** is a process that makes a computer a member of a domain without the computer having to contact a domain controller.

Join Nano Server to the Local Domain

With this option, you are joining Nano Server to the same domain as the host computer on which you create the Nano Server image. You need only to use the `-DomainName` *DomainToJoin* option where *DomainToJoin* is the name of the domain. Remember that the host computer must already be a member of this domain. The only other consideration is that the Nano Server must have a DNS server address configured that points to a DNS server responsible for that domain. Configuring the DNS server address can be done during image creation or afterward. The computer account in Active Directory is automatically created for you. Offline domain join requires that the account running the PowerShell cmdlet has administrator rights in the domain, so be sure you are signed in to the host computer with an account that has administrator rights in the domain you are joining.

Join Nano Server to a Different Domain

With this option, you are joining Nano Server to a domain different from the host computer's domain. The host computer could also be a standalone server. You use the `-DomainBlobPath` *PathToBlob* parameter where *PathToBlob* is the location of the domain blob. A **domain blob** is simply a file that contains the necessary information to perform an offline domain join. A domain blob is created with the `djoin.exe` command on a computer that is a member of the domain to which you want to join the Nano Server image. Let's say that our host computer is a standalone server and therefore not a member of any domain. We want to create a Nano Server image that is joined to the MCSA2016.local domain. To do so, perform the following steps:

1. Open an elevated command prompt on a server that is a member of the MCSA2016.local domain.

2. Type the following command. You should see output similar to Figure 12-10:

```
djoin /Provision /Domain MCSA2016.local /Machine NanoDM1 /SaveFile
   NanoDM1.blob
```

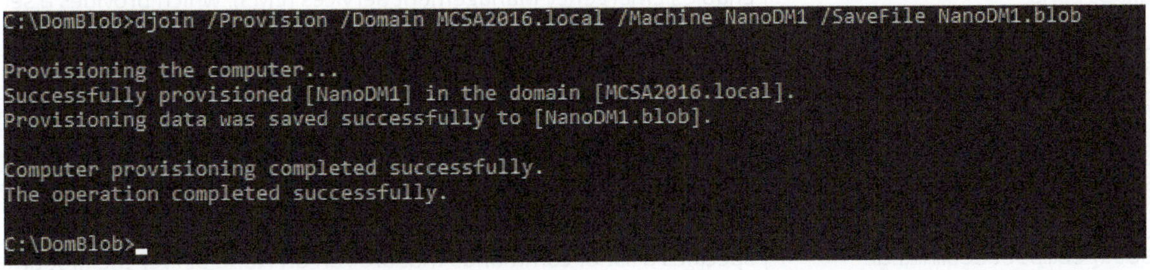

Figure 12-10 The results of the `djoin` command

3. Copy the NanoDM1.blob file created by the `djoin` command to a location on the server where you will create the Nano Server image. In this example, the NanoDM1.blob file is placed in the C:\NanoServer\Blobs folder.

4. On the host computer, create the Nano Server image with the `-DomainBlobPath` parameter and specify the path and file name of the domain blob. Because the computer name is part of the domain blob, do not specify the `-ComputerName` parameter. For example:

```
New-NanoServerImage -DeploymentType Guest -Edition Datacenter -TargetPath
   C:\VMs\NanoDM1\NanoDM1.vhdx -BasePath .\Base -DomainBlobPath
   C:\TestDomBlob\NanoDM1.blob
```

Advanced Nano Server Configuration Options

We've covered most of the Nano Server image creation parameters, but there are still some parameters that we haven't mentioned. Many of these parameters are for advanced deployment and debugging, so you might not ever need them. Nonetheless, some of them may be useful depending on your environment and the extent to which you deploy Nano Server. Table 12-4 lists the parameters we have not yet discussed.

Table 12-4 Advanced Nano Server parameters

Parameter	Function
-CopyFiles	Specifies a list of paths to files and directories that will be copied to the root of the image.
-DebugMethod	Enables kernel debugging via serial, network, USB, or FireWire interface.
-DebugComPort -DebugBaudRate -DebugRemoteIP -DebugPort -DebugKey -DebugChannel -DebugTargetName	Allows debugging parameters to be used if -DebugMethod is specified. For more information on these parameters, use the Get-Help NewNanoServerImage -Detail cmdlet. You might need to first run the Update-Help cmdlet to see detailed help information.
-Development	Puts Nano Server in a test mode in which unsigned drivers are allowed and debugger files are added.
-DriversPath	Specifies the path to driver files that will be added to the image. The drivers must be signed. Use this option when you need a driver that is not in the OEM drivers package such as for a disk controller or network interface.
-EMSBaudRate	Specifies the baud rate to connect via Emergency Management Services (EMS).
-EMSPort	Specifies a serial port number that will be used to connect via EMS. The default value is 1.
-EnableEMS	Enables Emergency Management Services (EMS), which provides a serial console connection to the boot loader menu.
-EnableRemoteManagementPort	Enables remote management using WinRM via TCP port 5985.
-ReuseDomainNode	Allows the server to join a domain when the computer account already exists in Active Directory.
-ServicingPackages	Specifies a list of servicing packages, which are .cab files you can download from the Microsoft Update site.
-SetupCompleteCommands	Specifies a list of commands that are run on Nano Server the first time it boots.
-UnattendPath	Specifies a path to an unattend file that Nano Server will use to perform configuration tasks such as setting the computer name, joining a domain, and setting IP addresses.

Editing Nano Server Images

You can configure Nano Server and install packages during Nano Server image creation, but you might need to make changes to an image after it has been created. You can do this with the Edit-NanoServerImage cmdlet. Almost all the parameters discussed that apply to New-NanoServerImage can be used with Edit-NanoServerImage with the exception of DeploymentType, Edition, MaxSize, and MediaPath. In addition, after the initial boot of a Nano Server image, you can't change the IP address settings and you can't use the `Development` or `SetupCompleteCommands` parameters. Also, you cannot edit a Nano Server image that is in use by a running VM. Here are some examples of using the `Edit-NanoServerImage` cmdlet.

- Configure the IP address of a Nano Server image:

```
Edit-NanoServerImage -TargetPath C:\VMs\Nano1\Nano1.vhdx -BasePath .\Base
  -InterfaceNameOrIndex "Ethernet" -Ipv4Address 192.168.0.100 -Ipv4SubnetMask
  255.255.255.0 -Ipv4Gateway 192.168.0.250 -Ipv4Dns 192.168.0.1
```

- Add the DNS Server role to a Nano Server image:

```
Edit-NanoServerImage -TargetPath C:\VMs\Nano1\Nano1.vhdx -BasePath .\Base
  -Package Microsoft-NanoServer-DNS-Package
```

- Add the Hyper-V role and clustering to a Nano Server image:

```
Edit-NanoServerImage -TargetPath C:\NanoPhys1\NanoPhys1.vhdx -BasePath .\Base
  -Compute -Clustering
```

- Join a Nano Server image to the same domain as the host computer:

```
Edit-NanoServerImage -TargetPath C:\NanoPhys1\NanoPhys1.vhdx -BasePath .\Base
  -DomainName MCSA2016.local
```

Note

You can run the `Edit-NanoServerImage` cmdlet multiple times on the same Nano Server image, if necessary.

Updating Nano Server Images

As you are aware, the Windows OS is updated periodically to resolve security vulnerabilities, fix bugs, and sometimes to add new features. Nano Server must also be updated from time to time, especially when the updates involve patching security vulnerabilities. You can apply Windows updates to Nano Server when you create a new Nano Server image using the `New-NanoServerImage` cmdlet or on an existing image using the `Edit-NanoServerImage` cmdlet. In either case, you use the `-ServicingPackagePath` parameter followed by the path to the update files that have a .cab extension. An example is:

```
Edit-NanoServerImage -TargetPath C:\VMs\Nano1\Nano1.vhdx -BasePath
  .\Base -ServicingPackagePath "C:\ServicingPackages\UpdateFile1.cab",
  "C:\ServicingPackages\UpdateFile2.cab"
```

You need first to download the updates from the Windows Catalog website at *www.catalog .update.microsoft.com*. The update files are distributed as .msu files, which you first must expand into .cab files using the `expand.exe` command. For example, if you need to update your image with update KB3192366, download the update from the Windows Catalog site to your host computer. The actual file name will be something like windows10.0-kb3192366-x64_af96b0015c04.msu, but you can rename the file to just kb3192366.msu. Then, run the following command: `expand kb3192366. msu -F:* C:\ServicingPackages`. The F:* parameter specifies that all .cab files should be extracted from the .msu file and placed in the C:\ServicingPackages folder that you should create ahead of time. You can use any folder or drive you want to store the update files. Then, run the `Edit-NanoServerImage` cmdlet specifying the path to the update files as in the previous example.

Introducing Windows Containers

- 70-740 – Implement Windows containers:
  Deploy Windows containers

In Chapter 1, we defined a **container** as a software environment in which an application can run but is isolated from much of the rest of the operating system and other applications. Containers are still types of virtualization, but whereas Hyper-V virtualizes the hardware environment, allowing multiple OSs to coexist on the same host, containers virtualize parts of the operating system, allowing containerized applications to have their own copy of critical OS structures, such as the registry, file system, and network configuration, while sharing the kernel, the host hardware, and possibly some runtime libraries. This is called *namespace isolation*. In this context, a **namespace** is all the parts of the OS that a specific application can see and interact with, such as the file system and the network. The host OS only lets the application running in a container see what it needs to run. The containerized application can't see other applications or the resources being used by other applications, so it can't interfere with them. That's how a container achieves **namespace isolation**. Further, the host OS can constrain the container to limit its host resource usage. For example, a container can be restricted to a certain percentage of the CPU, so even if the containerized application uses 100% of the CPU, it's only using 100% of the restricted amount. For example, if a container is constrained to 20% of the host CPU, that's the most it can use even if it is using 100% of it from the application's perspective.

If namespace isolation doesn't provide sufficient isolation, you can deploy a Hyper-V container in which each container has its own copy of the kernel and OS instance. To reiterate this concept, there are two types of containers supported by Windows Server 2016:

- *Windows Server containers*—A **Windows Server container** is an application environment that shares the host OS and kernel with the host OS and other Windows Server containers but has its own copy of user mode data structures such as the registry, file system, and network configuration.
- *Hyper-V containers*—A **Hyper-V container** is an application environment that provides OS and kernel isolation like a traditional VM but is not managed by Hyper-V Manager.

After an application is containerized, you have the option of deploying it as a Windows Server container or a Hyper-V container; in the case of a Hyper-V container, the VM is created and managed automatically. A Windows Server container has the benefit of very fast deployment compared with a Hyper-V container, but Hyper-V containers provide greater isolation.

A third deployment option is deploying containers in a Hyper-V virtual machine. In this scenario, the virtual machine is the container host and your physical host system must support nested virtualization because the Hyper-V role is installed in the virtual machine. All of these scenarios are explored in this chapter in "Deploying Windows Containers."

Note

Containers are supported by Windows 10 and Windows Server 2016; however, Windows 10 supports only Hyper-V containers.

The benefit of containers compared to full virtual machines is that containers use resources more efficiently while providing much of the application isolation provided by VMs. Because multiple containers running on the same host share some of the host computer's resources such as the kernel, deploying containerized applications uses less memory, disk space, and CPU compared with deploying each application in its own virtual machine. However, containers deployed on a host must all use the same base OS as the host computer, whereas each virtual machine has its own OS that can be different from the host OS and from other VM operating systems.

Certainly, containers are not a replacement for virtual machines, but there are some scenarios in which you might want to consider containers rather than virtual machines:

- When you want to deploy similar applications that use the same OS kernel
- When you want to package an application for fast deployment without worrying about dependencies and resource conflicts
- When an application consists of several lightweight components, or microservices, that can be easily scaled by adding additional containers

Containers are ideal for cloud providers for deploying Software as a Service (SaaS) applications when a single app can be deployed multiple times for multiple customers on a single host system. Each instance of the application runs independently of the others and each instance cannot affect the behavior of other instances. For example, if one instance of the application experiences a corrupted data structure, the other instances will continue to run, unaffected.

Deploying Windows Containers

- **70-740 – Implement Windows containers:**
  Deploy Windows containers

Windows containers can be deployed on Windows Server 2016 with Desktop Experience, Windows Server 2016 Server Core, and Windows Server 2016 Nano Server. These containers can be deployed on both physical computers and virtual machines as Windows Server containers or Hyper-V containers. Although the details of deploying and working with containers in each of these scenarios differ somewhat, all deployments require the same basic steps as follows:

- Configure the host OS as a container host.
- Install Docker on the container host.
- Install a base operating system.
- Create a Windows Server or Hyper-V container.
- Manage container networking, data volumes, and resources.

The following sections cover how to implement these steps in various scenarios, including deploying containers on Windows Server 2016 with Desktop Experience, Server Core, and Nano Server.

Implementing Containers on Windows Server 2016

The steps for implementing containers on Windows Server 2016 with Desktop Experience and Server Core are the same except that you can use Server Manager to install the Containers feature on Desktop Experience. We'll use command-line tools, which can be used on either installation of Windows Server 2016. The first thing you need to do is install the Containers feature using PowerShell. Because the server requires a restart after installing the Containers feature, add the `-Restart` option:

```
Install-WindowsFeature Containers -Restart
```

If you will be deploying Hyper-V containers or deploying containers inside VMs, you also need to install the Hyper-V role.

Installing Docker on a Windows Server 2016 Container Host

Docker is open source software that has been used in the Linux environment to implement containers for years. Rather than reinvent the wheel, Microsoft adapted Docker to the Windows environment. Docker is not part of Windows, so it can't be installed as a role or feature; you need to install it using PowerShell package management with the following cmdlets. The first cmdlet installs the Docker package management module and the second one installs Docker.

```
Install-Module DockerMsftProvider -Repository PSGallery -Force
Install-Package Docker -ProviderName DockerMsftProvider
```

You might be prompted to install the NuGet provider after you enter the first command and you will be asked if you want to trust the DockerDefault package after you enter the second command. Respond with Y in both cases. Next, you need to restart the computer. After the computer restarts, you can confirm that the Docker service is running with Task Manager (see Figure 12-11). The Docker service is represented by the `dockerd.exe` file, which was installed with the Docker package. The Docker service is also called the *Docker daemon* in the Linux world.

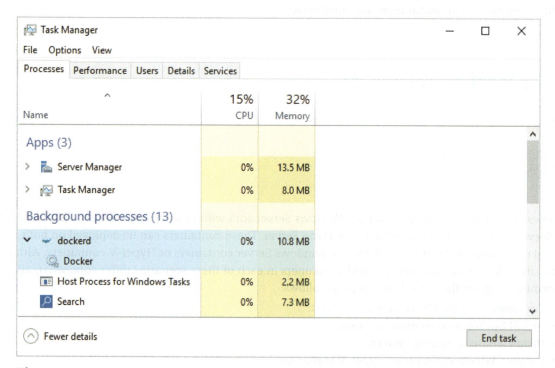

Figure 12-11   The Docker service running in Task Manager

> **Tip** ⓘ
>
> Learn more about Docker and Microsoft at *https://www.docker.com/microsoft*.

Installing a Base Operating System

The next step in deploying a container is to install a base operating system image using the Docker client. The Docker client is the executable file `docker.exe` that was installed with the Docker package. You install a base operating system image from the Docker Hub repository, which is a collection of Docker images maintained in the cloud. The base operating system you can deploy in a container depends somewhat on the OS running on the container host. Table 12-5 shows which base OS image can be deployed based on the OS running on the host machine.

Table 12-5	Container base operating system images supported on host OS	
Host OS	**Windows Server or Hyper-V container base OS image**
Windows Server 2016 Desktop Experience	Windows Server 2016 Server Core or Nano Server
Windows Server 2016 Server Core	Windows Server 2016 Server Core or Nano Server
Nano Server	Nano Server

Note 📎

Windows 10 also supports containers, but only Hyper-V containers, not Windows Server containers. On Windows 10 running Hyper-V, you can deploy a Hyper-V container with either the Server Core or Nano Server image.

There are various images available; some are preconfigured with applications. Microsoft provides a Windows Server 2016 Server Core image and Nano Server images. To download a Server Core image, run the following command from a PowerShell or command prompt:

```
docker pull microsoft/windowsservercore
```

In this command, the `pull` argument means to download the image, and `microsoft/windowsservercore` specifies that the image provider is Microsoft and the image name is windowsservercore. The download might take some time because it is about 5 GB. Figure 12-12 shows the results of the `docker pull` command while the file is downloading. In Figure 12-12, the first line of output says "Using default tag: latest." This indicates that Docker is downloading the image that has been tagged as "latest." There may be several versions of an image, and a **tag** is a way to differentiate them. By default, images are tagged as "latest," but when an image is created, you can specify a name such as ServerCore20171110 if you want to be more descriptive. If there is more than one image, you can include the `-a` option in the `docker pull` command to download all the images, or you can specify a particular tag name by adding `;Tag` after the image name where *Tag* is the tag assigned to the image.

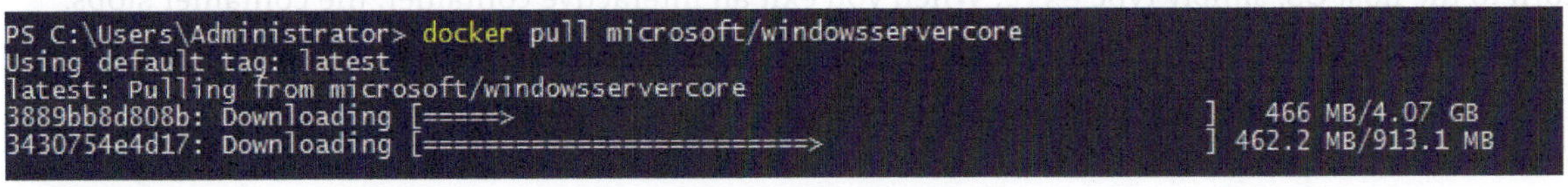

```
PS C:\Users\Administrator> docker pull microsoft/windowsservercore
Using default tag: latest
latest: Pulling from microsoft/windowsservercore
3889bb8d808b: Downloading [=====>                              ]  466 MB/4.07 GB
3430754e4d17: Downloading [==========================>         ]  462.2 MB/913.1 MB
```

Figure 12-12   Using Docker to pull an image from a repository

If you don't know the name of the image you want to download, you can use the `docker search` command as shown in Figure 12-13. The command in Figure 12-13 tells the Docker client to search for images that contain the keyword *microsoft*. As you can see, there are a number of images, many of them prebuilt for specific applications.

After images are downloaded, you can list them using the `docker images` command as shown in Figure 12-14. Two images have been downloaded, windowsservercore and nanoserver.

Creating a Windows Server 2016 Container

With an image downloaded, you create a container using the `docker run` command. The `docker run` command starts a container based on a specified image and runs a command or application. For example, you could start the container and have it execute a PowerShell script or a command prompt command. You can also run the container interactively, allowing you to, for example, type commands at a

```
PS C:\Users\Administrator> docker search microsoft
NAME                                DESCRIPTION                                 STARS
microsoft/aspnet                    ASP.NET is an open source server-side Web ...  561
microsoft/dotnet                    Official images for .NET Core for Linux an...  454
mono                                Mono is an open source implementation of M...  219
microsoft/mssql-server-linux        Official images for Microsoft SQL Server o...  182
microsoft/nanoserver                Windows Server 2016 Nano Server base OS im...  140
microsoft/windowsservercore         Windows Server 2016 Server Core base OS im...  133
microsoft/aspnetcore                Official images for running compiled ASP.N...  103
microsoft/iis                       Internet Information Services (IIS) instal...   95
microsoft/azure-cli                 Docker image for Microsoft Azure Command L...   79
microsoft/mssql-server-windows-express  Official Microsoft SQL Server Express Edit...   57
microsoft/mssql-server-windows      Official images for Microsoft SQL Server f...   31
microsoft/powershell                Official PowerShell Core releases from htt...   26
microsoft/aspnetcore-build          Official images for building ASP.NET Core ...   26
microsoft/oms                       Monitor your containers using the Operatio...   18
microsoft/vsts-agent                Official images for the Visual Studio Team...   16
microsoft/dotnet-samples            .NET Core Docker Samples                        13
microsoft/cntk                      CNTK images from github.com/Microsoft/CNTK...    6
microsoft/powershell-nightly        Nightly builds of PowerShell Core for CI         6
microsoft/applicationinsights       Application Insights for Docker helps you ...    4
microsoft/dotnet-nightly            Preview bits of the .NET Core CLI                3
```

Figure 12-13   Using Docker to search for images

```
PS C:\Users\Administrator> docker images
REPOSITORY                  TAG         IMAGE ID        CREATED         SIZE
microsoft/windowsservercore latest      4d83c32ad497    7 weeks ago     9.56 GB
microsoft/nanoserver        latest      d9bccb9d4cac    7 weeks ago     925 MB
PS C:\Users\Administrator>
```

Figure 12-14   Using Docker to list images

PowerShell or command prompt running in the container. The following command uses the `docker run` command to start an interactive PowerShell session.

```
docker run -it --name ContainerTest microsoft/windowsservercore powershell
```

In the previous command, the `-it` option specifies an interactive (-i) session with a terminal (-t) window. The `--name` option assigns a name to the container. If you omit this option, Docker assigns a random name to the container using two words separated by an underscore. The `microsoft/windowsservercore` parameter specifies the image to load and `powershell` is the command to run. The result of running this command is a PowerShell prompt running inside the container. To exit and return to the host OS, simply type `exit`. When you exit an interactive container, the container stops. To start and reconnect to the container, use the following commands. The first command restarts ContainerTest1 and the second command reconnects you to the container:

```
docker start ContainerTest1
docker attach ContainerTest1
```

When you are connected interactively to a container with a PowerShell prompt, you can type PowerShell and command prompt commands normally. For example, in Figure 12-15, the `Get-ComputerInfo | findstr "Windows"` and the `ipconfig` commands have been run in the container. The first command shows you that Server Core is running (the host is running Desktop Experience), and the second command shows the IP address configuration on the container, which is quite different from the IP configuration of the host computer. Network configuration of containers is discussed later in the chapter.

If you want to see all the containers on the host as well as their status, run the `docker ps -a` command on the host computer. In Figure 12-16, two containers exist: ContainerTest1, which is currently running, and ContainerTest2, which has been exited. The `-a` option in `docker ps -a` means to list all containers, including those that are not running.

You can also create a container without starting it using the `docker create` command. It uses the same options as the `docker run` command and has an initial status of Created.

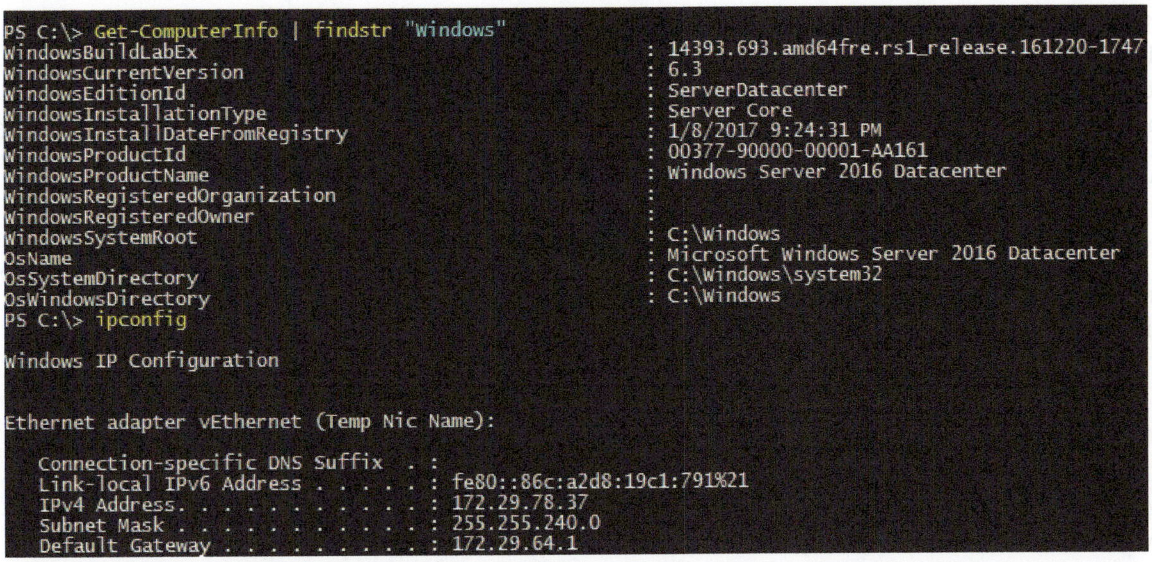

```
PS C:\> Get-ComputerInfo | findstr "Windows"
WindowsBuildLabEx                            : 14393.693.amd64fre.rs1_release.161220-1747
WindowsCurrentVersion                        : 6.3
WindowsEditionId                             : ServerDatacenter
WindowsInstallationType                      : Server Core
WindowsInstallDateFromRegistry               : 1/8/2017 9:24:31 PM
WindowsProductId                             : 00377-90000-00001-AA161
WindowsProductName                           : Windows Server 2016 Datacenter
WindowsRegisteredOrganization                :
WindowsRegisteredOwner                       :
WindowsSystemRoot                            : C:\Windows
OsName                                       : Microsoft Windows Server 2016 Datacenter
OsSystemDirectory                            : C:\Windows\system32
OsWindowsDirectory                           : C:\Windows
PS C:\> ipconfig

Windows IP Configuration


Ethernet adapter vEthernet (Temp Nic Name):

    Connection-specific DNS Suffix  . :
    Link-local IPv6 Address . . . . . : fe80::86c:a2d8:19c1:791%21
    IPv4 Address. . . . . . . . . . . : 172.29.78.37
    Subnet Mask . . . . . . . . . . . : 255.255.240.0
    Default Gateway . . . . . . . . . : 172.29.64.1
```

Figure 12-15   Running commands in a container

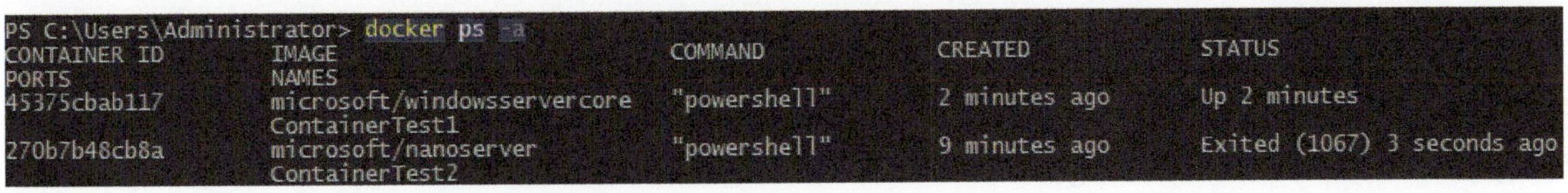

```
PS C:\Users\Administrator> docker ps -a
CONTAINER ID     IMAGE                          COMMAND        CREATED          STATUS
PORTS            NAMES
45375cbab117     microsoft/windowsservercore    "powershell"   2 minutes ago    Up 2 minutes
                 ContainerTest1
270b7b48cb8a     microsoft/nanoserver           "powershell"   9 minutes ago    Exited (1067) 3 seconds ago
                 ContainerTest2
```

Figure 12-16   Listing containers on the host

Creating a Hyper-V Container

The previous section showed how to create a Windows Server container. Creating a Hyper-V container is little different. Aside from the Containers feature, your host computer must also have the Hyper-V role installed. The only real difference is that you specify `--isolation=hyperv` option in the `docker run` command as follows:

```
docker run -it --isolation hyperv --name HyperVContainer
  microsoft/windowsservercore powershell
```

It takes a little longer to start a Hyper-V container than a Windows Server container, but other than that, you won't notice any difference between starting a Windows Server container and Hyper-V container. Of course, there is a difference in terms of resource usage and isolation because the Hyper-V container doesn't share the Windows kernel and other resources with the host.

Implementing Containers in a Virtual Machine

So far, we've discussed implementing containers on a physical host computer. You can implement containers in a Hyper-V virtual machine using the same procedures discussed earlier. The only difference is that if you want to create a Hyper-V container running in a virtual machine, the virtual machine must be configured for nested virtualization. Nested virtualization was discussed in detail in Chapter 7.

Implementing Containers on Nano Server

Implementing containers on Nano Server is much the same as it is in Windows Server 2016 Desktop Experience or Server Core. First, you need to install the Container feature in the Nano Server image. You can install the Container feature when you first create the Nano Server image using `New-NanoServerImage` with the `-Containers` parameter or on an existing Nano Server image using `Edit-NanoServerImage` with the `-Containers` parameter. These two cmdlets were discussed earlier in the chapter under "Installing Nano Server."

Installing Docker and Creating a Container on Nano Server

With the containers feature installed, you can install Docker on Nano Server. Start Nano Server and establish a remote PowerShell connection using the `Enter-PSSession` cmdlet. Once connected to the Nano Server with PowerShell, install Docker as you would on a regular installation of Windows Server 2016:

```
Install-Module DockerMsftProvider -Repository PSGallery -Force
Install-Package Docker -ProviderName DockerMsftProvider
```

With Docker installed, restart Nano Server and reconnect with `Enter-PSSession`. From there, follow the same procedure as for implementing containers on Windows Server 2016: Download a base image using `docker pull` and then create a container using `docker run`.

Note

If you are running Nano Server as a virtual machine, there are a couple things to be aware of: you cannot use PowerShell Direct to install Docker; you must use a WinRM PowerShell connection using `Enter-PSSession -ComputerName` instead of `Enter-PSSession -VMName`. If you want to run a Hyper-V container, the Hyper-V package must be installed on Nano Server and the Nano Server VM must be configured for nested virtualization.

Managing Daemon Start-up Options

When you first install Docker using the `Install-Package` cmdlet, the Docker daemon (service) starts automatically after you restart the computer. The default start-up options probably work for most scenarios, but there are a number of configurable options. The Docker daemon configuration is stored in the file daemon.json, and it is located in C:\ProgramData\docker\config. By default, this file doesn't exist so the daemon starts with default options. You can create the file with a simple text editor like Notepad using the format:

```
{
"optionName": optionParameters
"optionName": optionParameters
"optionName": optionParameters
}
```

You replace *optionName* and *optionParameters* with the option name and parameters you want to use. The option name must be enclosed in quotes, and option parameters that take a string value must also be enclosed in quotes. There are over two dozen options you can configure in the Windows Docker implementation. You need to add options only to the configuration file that you want to change. Any options not included in the file use the default value. An example daemon.json file might look like the following:

```
{
"bridge":"none"
"graph":"f:\\docker\images"
"group":"dockerAdmins"
"hosts":["tcp:0.0.0.0:2375"]
}
```

Here is a brief description of what each of the options does:

- `bridge`—When set to `"none"`, this option tells Docker not to configure a default network address translation (NAT) network. By default, a container is configured with an IP address in the range 172.16.0.0 through 172.31.0.0 with a default subnet mask of 255.255.240.0, and NAT is used to allow the container access to the external network. If the `"bridge": "none"` option is included, you must manually create a network using the `docker network create` command discussed later.

- `graph`—Sets the path where Docker will store images and containers. By default, the path is C:\ProgramData\docker. In the example, the path is set to F:\docker\images (note that this option requires a double backslash "\\" after the drive letter).
- `group`—By default, only members of the Administrators group can use Docker. Use this option to specify another group that can use Docker such as dockerAdmins in the example.
- `hosts`—Configures Docker to accept remote connections on a specific port. By convention, port 2375 is used for nonsecure connections, and port 2376 is used for secure connections.

Note 📎

For a list of all Docker daemon options available in Windows, see *https://docs.microsoft.com/en-us/virtualization/windowscontainers/manage-docker/configure-docker-daemon*.

Activity 12-3: Deploying a Windows Server Container

Time Required: 20 minutes
Objective: Deploy a Windows Server container.
Required Tools and Equipment: ServerHyperV, Internet access
Description: Install the Containers feature, install Docker, and download a Nano Server container image from a Docker repository. Then, deploy a container using the downloaded image.

1. On ServerHyperV, open a PowerShell window.
2. Type **Install-WindowsFeature Containers -Restart** and press **Enter**. The Containers feature is installed and the computer restarts. After the computer restarts, sign in and open a PowerShell window.
3. Type **Install-Module DockerMsftProvider -Repository PSGallery -Force** and press **Enter**. If you are prompted to install the NuGet provider, press **Enter** to confirm.
4. Type **Install-Package Docker -ProviderName DockerMsftProvider** and press **Enter**. When prompted to install software from DockerDefault, press **Y** and press **Enter**. Docker is now installed, but the service is not running.
5. Type **Restart-Computer** and press **Enter**. When the computer restarts, sign in and open a PowerShell prompt. To verify that Docker is running, type **Get-Service docker** and press **Enter**. You should see that the status is Running.
6. Now, you need to install a base operating system by downloading one from the Microsoft Docker repository. You'll use the `docker.exe` command for most of the next steps. Type **docker pull microsoft/nanoserver** and press **Enter**. It may take several minutes for the download to complete, depending on the speed of your Internet connection. The total download size for a Nano Server image is about 925 MB compared to about 5 GB for a Server Core image.
7. When the download is complete, you can verify the images on your local computer by typing **docker images** and pressing **Enter**. To search for Microsoft images on DockerHub, type **docker search microsoft** and press **Enter**. You see a list of images that contain the key word *microsoft*. (*Note:* During testing of this lab, the `docker search` command sometimes returned an error. If it does, just try it again, and it should work.)
8. Now it's time to run your first container. Type **docker run -it --name NanoPS1 microsoft/nanoserver powershell** and press **Enter**. After a short time, your prompt will change to PS C:\>, and you'll be connected to the container and running PowerShell.
9. To verify that you're in the container, type **Get-ComputerInfo | findstr "Windows"** and press **Enter**. The output shows the WindowsInstallationType of Nano Server.
10. Check your IP address configuration by typing **ipconfig /all** and pressing **Enter**. After running both commands, you'll see output similar to that in Figure 12-17. Notice that the IP address is in the range 172.16.00 to 172.31.0.0 (it's 172.28.116.31 in the figure). This tells you that the default NAT network is being used for this container.

```
PS C:\> Get-ComputerInfo | findstr "Windows"
WindowsBuildLabEx                                       : 14393.0.amd64fre.rs1_release.160715-1616
WindowsCurrentVersion                                   : 6.3
WindowsEditionId                                        : ServerDatacenterNano
WindowsInstallationType                                 : Nano Server
WindowsInstallDateFromRegistry                          : 3/8/2017 2:29:00 AM
WindowsProductId                                        :
WindowsProductName                                      : Windows Server 2016 Datacenter
WindowsRegisteredOrganization                           :
WindowsRegisteredOwner                                  :
WindowsSystemRoot                                       : C:\Windows
OsName                                                  : Microsoft Windows Server 2016 Datacenter
OsSystemDirectory                                       : C:\Windows\system32
OsWindowsDirectory                                      : C:\Windows
PS C:\> ipconfig /all

Windows IP Configuration

   Host Name . . . . . . . . . . . . : ec22e935e858
   Primary Dns Suffix  . . . . . . . :
   Node Type . . . . . . . . . . . . : Hybrid
   IP Routing Enabled. . . . . . . . : No
   WINS Proxy Enabled. . . . . . . . : No

Ethernet adapter vEthernet (Temp Nic Name):

   Connection-specific DNS Suffix  . :
   Description . . . . . . . . . . . : Hyper-V Virtual Ethernet Adapter #2
   Physical Address. . . . . . . . . : 00-15-5D-00-EA-C9
   DHCP Enabled. . . . . . . . . . . : No
   Autoconfiguration Enabled . . . . : Yes
   Link-local IPv6 Address . . . . . : fe80::2c2f:1861:b9ff:3883%19(Preferred)
   IPv4 Address. . . . . . . . . . . : 172.28.116.31(Preferred)
   Subnet Mask . . . . . . . . . . . : 255.255.240.0
   Default Gateway . . . . . . . . . : 172.28.112.1
   DNS Servers . . . . . . . . . . . : 172.28.112.1
                                       192.168.0.250
   NetBIOS over Tcpip. . . . . . . . : Disabled
```

Figure 12-17 `Get-ComputerInfo` and `ipconfig` in a container

11. Type **exit** and press **Enter** to return to the host PowerShell prompt. Type **ipconfig** and press **Enter**. Notice that new network adapter has been created on the host named *vEthernet* with IP address 172.28.112.1, which is the default gateway setting for the container. The host is used as the default gateway so the container can access the host's network.
12. Type **docker ps -a** and press **Enter** to see running containers. The status of the NanoPS1 container is Exited, which means that although the container is loaded, it's not running.
13. Type **docker start NanoPS1** and press **Enter** (being sure the capitalization in NanoPS1 matches the actual container name). Type **docker ps** and press **Enter** (you don't need the -a option because the -a option is needed only to list containers that aren't running as well as running containers). Notice that the status is Up.
14. Type **docker attach NanoPS1** and press **Enter** to connect to the container again. Press **Enter** again if you don't see the PowerShell prompt. Type **exit** and press **Enter** to return to the host.
15. Continue to the next activity.

Activity 12-4: Deploying a Hyper-V Container

Time Required: 20 minutes
Objective: Deploy a Hyper-V container.
Required Tools and Equipment: ServerHyperV
Description: Deploy a Hyper-V container using the Nano Server image.

1. On ServerHyperV, at the PowerShell prompt, type **docker create -it --isolation hyperv --name NanoH microsoft/nanoserver powershell** and press **Enter**. This creates the container and loads it but doesn't start it.
2. Because the container is not started, you are still at the host computer PowerShell prompt. Type **docker ps -a** and press **Enter**. You see two containers, one with status Created and the other with status Exited. Start the NanoPS1 container by typing **docker start NanoPS1** and pressing **Enter**.

3. Start the NanoH container by typing **docker start NanoH** and pressing **Enter**.

4. Type **docker ps** and press **Enter**. Both containers have the status Up.

5. The NanoPS1 container is running as a Windows Server container and the NanoH container is running as a Hyper-V container, but how can you tell? Type **docker inspect NanoPS1 | findstr Isolation** and press **Enter**. You see a single line of output that says "Isolation": "process",.

6. Now, type **docker inspect NanoH | findstr Isolation** and press **Enter**. You see a single line of output that says "Isolation": "hyperv",. Type **docker inspect NanoH** and press **Enter** you will see a bunch of detailed information about the container, including the network settings, volumes, memory settings, and so forth.

7. Type **docker stop NanoPS1 NanoH** and press **Enter** to stop both containers. Type **docker rm NanoPS1 NanoH** and press **Enter** to remove both containers. Type **docker ps -a** and press **Enter** to confirm there are not containers loaded.

8. Continue to the next activity.

Managing Windows Containers

Certification

- 70-740 – Implement Windows containers:
  Manage Windows containers

So far, you've learned about basic container implementation on Windows Server 2016 or Nano Server using Docker. This section looks at additional container configuration and management tasks using Docker as well as PowerShell. You'll also look at configuring Docker daemon start-up options, managing container networking, and managing volumes and resources. Finally, you'll see how to create and manage container images using a variety of tools.

Managing Containers with the Docker Daemon

The `docker.exe` program is the primary tool for working with containers. You have learned how to download a container image from the Microsoft repository using `docker pull` and how to deploy a container using `docker run`. We'll look at some more common tasks you might perform while working with containers and the associated Docker command.

Working with Containers

After you have deployed a container using `docker run` or `docker create`, there are several commands you can use to interact with and manage the container:

> **Tip** ⓘ
>
> To get help on using any Docker command, type `docker command --help` where *command* is run, create, start, and so forth.

- `docker ps`—This command lists running containers along with a variety of information about them including the container ID; the image that's running, such as nanoserver or windowsservercore; the command or app that is running in the container; when the container was created; and its current status. You'll use the `docker ps` command to see a list of running containers, and you can use the name of a container to perform additional Docker commands on it. Figure 12-18 shows the `docker ps -a` command (the output of the command has been modified for clarity). By default, `docker ps` shows only running containers. The -a option lists all containers, including stopped containers.

```
PS C:\Users\Administrator> docker ps -a
CONTAINER ID        IMAGE                         COMMAND         CREATED         STATUS                    NAMES
9613ec778db0        microsoft/nanoserver          "powershell"    12 seconds ago  Up 9 seconds              ContainerTest2
08e24cfee220        microsoft/windowsservercore   "cmd"           4 minutes ago   Created                   ContainerTest3
13f07df0f116        microsoft/nanoserver          "powershell"    8 hours ago     Up 8 minutes              HyperVContainer
45375cbab117        microsoft/windowsservercore   "powershell"    8 hours ago     Exited (0) 2 minutes ago  ContainerTest1
```

Figure 12-18   The `docker ps -a` command

- `docker rm`—This command deletes a container. You can use the name of the container or the container ID as in `docker rm ContainerTest2`. A container must first be stopped (indicated by the status Exited in the `docker ps -a` command) before it can be deleted. If the container cannot be stopped for some reason, you can use the `-force` option in the command.
- `docker stop`—This command stops a running container. Again, you can use the name or ID of the container.
- `docker start`—This command starts a container that is loaded but has a status of Exited or Created. After running this command, the container has a status of Up.
- `docker restart`—This command stops a running container and then starts it again. If the container is already stopped, this command will start it.
- `docker attach`—This command connects you to a container that was created to run in interactive mode. The container must be running. For example, if you exited a container or created a container using `docker create`, first run `docker start` and then run `docker attach` to begin or resume an interactive session.
- `docker exec`—This command executes a command in a running container. For example, if you wanted to see the IP configuration of the running container named ContainerTest2 without entering an interactive session, you could use this command: `docker exec ContainerTest2 ipconfig`. The output of the command is displayed, but you resume your prompt on the container host as in Figure 12-19.

```
PS C:\Users\Administrator> docker exec ContainerTest2 ipconfig

Windows IP Configuration

Ethernet adapter vEthernet (Temp Nic Name):

   Connection-specific DNS Suffix  . :
   Link-local IPv6 Address . . . . . : fe80::39e0:b7e9:621a:56d9%21
   IPv4 Address. . . . . . . . . . . : 172.29.75.74
   Subnet Mask . . . . . . . . . . . : 255.255.240.0
   Default Gateway . . . . . . . . . : 172.29.64.1
PS C:\Users\Administrator>
```

Figure 12-19   Results of the `docker exec` command

- `docker --help`—This command lists all the Docker commands along with a brief description.
- `docker command --help`—Use this command to get help on using any Docker command by replacing *command* with run, create, start, and so forth.

Tip ⓘ

Docker comes from the Linux world where, unlike Windows, everything is case sensitive. For example, ContainerTest2 is different than containertest2 when using Docker. Command options are also case sensitive, so `docker RM` won't work because the `rm` option must be lowercase.

Working with Container Images

This section looks at a few management tasks you can perform on container images using the Docker program:

- Listing container images
- Tagging container images
- Committing changes to images
- Removing images

Listing Container Images

After you have worked with container images for a while, you may have collected a few of them. To see a list of images that are available on the local computer, use the following command (see Figure 12-20):

```
docker images
```

```
C:\>docker images
REPOSITORY                   TAG        IMAGE ID        CREATED           SIZE
gtrepository                 CT2wPS     1d08481e0ede    21 minutes ago    967 MB
microsoft/nanoserver         GTTest1    2d15211bd861    32 minutes ago    931 MB
microsoft/windowsservercore  latest     4d83c32ad497    7 weeks ago       9.56 GB
microsoft/nanoserver         latest     d9bccb9d4cac    7 weeks ago       925 MB
```

Figure 12-20   Output of the `docker images` command

The `docker images` command lists the repository, tag, image ID, when it was created, and the size of the image. You can use the results of the command to select an image when creating an image using `docker run`. For example, notice in Figure 12-20 that there are two images with the repository label of microsoft/nanoserver. To differentiate the two images in the `docker run` command, you can specify the image ID, or you can specify the tag as in `docker run microsoft/nanoserver:GTTest1`. If you don't specify a tag, the "latest" tag is assumed as the default. If you have many images, you can include the repository name in the command to list only those images in a specific repository as in `docker images microsoft/nanoserver`.

Tagging Container Images

As mentioned earlier, a tag is a way to differentiate multiple versions of the same image. You can tag an image when it is created (for example, using the `docker build` command discussed later), and you can create a new tag for an existing image. For example, to create a new tag for the microsoft/nanoserver:latest image, you would use the following command:

```
docker tag microsoft/nanoserver microsoft/nanoserver:20170915
```

In that command, it is not necessary to specify the "latest" tag on the source image because "latest" is used as the default if no tag is specified. The `docker tag` command doesn't actually change the tag on the existing image; it creates a duplicate entry, almost like a file shortcut. As you can see in Figure 12-21, the image ID of the microsoft/nanoserver image is the same for both the "latest" and the "20170915" image. It's the same image just with two different tags.

```
C:\>docker tag microsoft/nanoserver microsoft/nanoserver:20170915

C:\>docker images
REPOSITORY                   TAG        IMAGE ID        CREATED           SIZE
gtrepository                 CT2wPS     1d08481e0ede    50 minutes ago    967 MB
microsoft/nanoserver         GTTest1    2d15211bd861    About an hour ago 931 MB
microsoft/windowsservercore  latest     4d83c32ad497    7 weeks ago       9.56 GB
microsoft/nanoserver         20170915   d9bccb9d4cac    7 weeks ago       925 MB
microsoft/nanoserver         latest     d9bccb9d4cac    7 weeks ago       925 MB
```

Figure 12-21   Tagging an image

When you use `docker tag`, you can also change the repository name, which also acts like a shortcut. So, for example, the following command changes the repository name to "nano" and gives the image the tag "20170915." In this way, you can refer to the image when performing other tasks such as `docker run` using the shorter name. If you don't specify a tag in the destination image name, it will use the default "latest."

```
docker tag microsoft/nanoserver nano:20170915
```

Committing Changes to Images

You can create a new image from changes you make in a container. For example, suppose you deploy a container image using `docker create microsoft/nanoserver powershell`. The image is loaded and is ready to run PowerShell. Suppose that you will frequently use this image. You can essentially save this container as a new image with the `powershell` command already integrated into the image using the following command:

```
docker commit nanoPowerShell nano/nanops
```

This command creates a new image in the nano/nanops repository with the tag "latest" because no tag was specified. Then, if you run the image using `docker run -it nano/nanops`, a container running PowerShell is started. Before you run `docker commit`, the container must not be running (in the Up state); it can be in the Exited or Created state. If you run `docker images` after running `docker commit`, you will see a new image listed with the repository name you specified. The size of the image will be shown as roughly the same size or much larger than the original image, but don't be fooled. When you commit an image, only the changes to the original image are actually saved, but the `docker images` command reports the total size, which includes the original image plus any saved changes.

Removing Images

If you have finished using an image or want to delete specific image tags, use the `docker rmi` command. If multiple images with the same ID (but different tags) exist, this command simply removes the instance of the image specified. If it is the last instance of the image, the image is deleted. For example, if you have two instances of the image of microsoft/nanoserver, one with the tag "latest" and the other with the tag "20170915," you can delete the latter with the following command:

```
docker rmi Microsoft/nanoserver:20170915
```

After running the command, Docker will respond with Untagged: microsoft/nanoserver:20170915. If you are deleting the last instance of the same image, Docker will print a second line of output similar to Untagged: microsoft/nanoserver@sha256:*32byteidentifier* where 32byteidentifier is the full 32 byte (256 bit) image identifier in hexadecimal.

Implementing Container Networks

As discussed previously, Docker configures the container network using **network address translation (NAT)**. NAT is the process in which the IP addresses in a packet are translated to different addresses when the packet leaves or enters a network. NAT is typically used to allow a network using private IP addresses to access the public Internet. By default, the container network uses an IP address in the range 172.16.0.0 to 172.31.0.0 and assigns a subnet mask of 255.255.255.240. This is the default setting, which can be changed using the daemon configuration file and when creating a container. To illustrate this, Figure 12-22 shows the `ipconfig` command being executed on a container. Next, the `ipconfig` command is executed on the host computer. In the figure, the container's network adapter is named vEthernet (Temp Nic Name), which is the default name given to a container's network adapter. The name vEthernet indicates that it is a virtual network adapter. Notice that the host computer has two network adapters: Ethernet 3 and vEthernet (HNS Internal NIC). The Ethernet 3 adapter is the adapter connected to the host network, and the vEthernet (HNS Internal NIC) is the virtual adapter used to communicate between the host and the container.

```
PS C:\Users\Administrator> docker exec NanoPS ipconfig

Windows IP Configuration


Ethernet adapter vEthernet (Temp Nic Name):

   Connection-specific DNS Suffix  . :
   Link-local IPv6 Address . . . . . : fe80::1537:5f18:4ee1:65dd%21
   IPv4 Address. . . . . . . . . . . : 172.29.69.254
   Subnet Mask . . . . . . . . . . . : 255.255.240.0
   Default Gateway . . . . . . . . . : 172.29.64.1
PS C:\Users\Administrator>
PS C:\Users\Administrator>
PS C:\Users\Administrator> ipconfig

Windows IP Configuration


Ethernet adapter Ethernet 3:

   Connection-specific DNS Suffix  . :
   Link-local IPv6 Address . . . . . : fe80::d005:66db:8123:52ec%6
   IPv4 Address. . . . . . . . . . . : 192.168.0.1
   Subnet Mask . . . . . . . . . . . : 255.255.255.0
   Default Gateway . . . . . . . . . : 192.168.0.250

Ethernet adapter vEthernet (HNS Internal NIC):

   Connection-specific DNS Suffix  . :
   Link-local IPv6 Address . . . . . : fe80::54c9:a4bc:3651:72df%15
   IPv4 Address. . . . . . . . . . . : 172.29.64.1
   Subnet Mask . . . . . . . . . . . : 255.255.240.0
   Default Gateway . . . . . . . . . :
```

Figure 12-22   IP address settings on a container and the host

The vEthernet adapter on the container has an address of 172.29.69.254 and a default gateway address of 172.29.64.1. The address of vEthernet (HNS Internal NIC) on the host is 172.29.64.1, making the host computer the default gateway for the container. When the container wants to communicate with the host network, it sends packets to the host's vEthernet adapter, which then performs a NAT operation on the packet's source address. The source address is translated to the host's Ethernet 3 adapter address, which in this case is 192.168.0.1. This allows the container to communicate with the host network and any networks the host is able to reach.

 Note

The host also acts as the container's DNS server. When the host receives DNS lookups from the container, it passes those requests along to a DNS server.

Configuring a NAT Network

You can change the default network settings by configuring the daemon.json file discussed earlier. If you want to use a different address for the NAT network, you can add an entry to the daemon.json file and then restart the Docker service. For example, to change the default network to 10.10.10.0/24:

```
{
"fixed-cidr":"10.10.10.0/24"
}
```

After you edit the daemon.json file, you must stop the Docker service, remove the default network, and restart the service from a PowerShell prompt as follows:

```
Stop-Service docker
Get-ContainerNetwork | Remove-ContainerNetwork
Start-Service docker
```

Any containers that were running when you stopped the service will need to be started again using `docker start`. The containers will now use the network specified in the daemon.json file.

As mentioned, you can also disable automatic network creation by adding the `"bridge":"none"` entry to the daemon.json file. If you do so, you need to create a network manually using the `docker network` command.

Port Mapping with NAT Networks

With a NAT network, devices on the host network cannot initiate communication with the container because its IP address is translated by the host computer. Port mapping allows the container host to forward packets for specific applications to containers hosting those applications. For example, if a container is hosting a web server, you would need the host to forward TCP ports 80 and 443 to the container using the following command:

```
docker run -p 80:80 -p 443:443 microsoft/nanoserver
```

Notice in the preceding command that the `-p` option is used twice. You can use it as many times as necessary—one for each port you wish to map. The parameter after the `-p` option is the *host port number:container port number*. The *host port number* is the port number with which external devices will attempt to contact the container, and the *container port number* is the port number on which the container service is listening. In the previous example, the port numbers are both the same but they need not be. For example, you could use 8008:80, which means the host will forward packets addressed to port 8008 to port 80 on the container. Container port mappings are shown in the PORTS column of the `docker ps` output, or you can use the `docker port` *ContainerName* command.

Deploying Other Network Types

Aside from NAT networks, Docker supports transparent and layer 2 bridge networks. A **transparent network** connects containers to the same network as the host so that a container's network adapter will have an IP address in the same IP subnet as the host's network adapter. This allows the container to communicate with devices on the host network without the address having to be translated. To create the transparent network Tran1 that uses a DHCP server that's already configured on the host network, use the following command:

```
docker network create -d transparent Tran1
```

Next, you need to connect containers to the network. You can connect a new container to the network using the `docker run` or `docker create` commands by adding the option `--network Tran1` as in this example:

```
docker run --network Tran1 microsoft/nanoserver
```

If you want to connect an existing container named *ContainerTest1* to the Tran1 network, make sure the container is stopped first and run this command:

```
docker network connect Tran1 ContainerTest1
```

The container will get its IP address configuration from a DHCP server running on the host network. If you don't have a DHCP server on the host network, you can create a static transparent network and assign a static IP address to a container. To create a static transparent network named *TranStatic* with a network ID of 192.168.0.0/24 and a default gateway address of 192.168.0.250, use the following command:

```
docker network create -d transparent --subnet 192.168.0.0/24 --gateway
  192.168.0.250 TranStatic
```

Next, create a container and assign it a static IP address and DNS server address; the default gateway will be automatically assigned:

```
docker run --network TranStatic --ip 192.168.0.101 --dns 192.168.0.200
   microsoft/nanoserver
```

> **Note** 🔗
>
> In the preceding `docker run` commands, you can add options such as `-it` and `--name` as well as any other options that `docker run` accepts.

A **layer 2 (L2) bridge network** is similar to a transparent network, but the container shares a MAC address with the container host. L2 bridge networks support only static addressing, and the container has a unique IP address in the same subnet as the host virtual adapter that is created when you created the L2 bridge network. These types of network are useful in advanced container deployment in private and public clouds when the container is running on a VM. When you create an L2 bridge network, you must specify the subnet and gateway in a manner similar to creating a static transparent network as follows:

```
docker network create -d l2bridge --subnet 192.168.0.0/24 --gateway
   192.168.0.250 BridgeNet1
```

Working with Container Data Volumes

Data that is created while the container is running and stored on its virtual volumes is not saved when a container is deleted (using `docker rm`). Each time a container is created, it starts fresh with no carryover from the previous time it was run. This is called **stateless operation**. You can save changes to the container with the `docker commit` command, but that saves the current state of the container as a new image. What if you want a container image to simply maintain data that is created or changed on its volumes between run times without having to commit changes and create a new image? You can do this by specifying a folder on the host computer and mapping it to a folder in the container. What's more, multiple containers can have access to the same data on the host volume, and you can assign containers read or read/write access to the data.

The following command maps the folder C:\HostData on the container host to the C:\ContainerData folder on a new container. The `-v` option specifies the volume mapping. By default, mapped volumes are read/write, but you can add `:ro` after the container folder name to make it read only.

```
docker run -v c:\HostData:c:\ContainerData Microsoft/nanoserver
```

After running this command, any data that is created in c:\HostData on the host computer will be seen in the c:\ContainerData folder in the container and vice versa. You can deploy additional containers with mappings to the same folder on the host, and all containers plus the host will have access to the same data.

Managing Container Resources

Resource control is one of the big advantages of using containers to run applications instead of running them directly on the host computer. Much as with a virtual machine, you can constrain, or limit, how much of a particular resource that a container can utilize including CPU, memory, and block I/O. To limit CPU resources, there are a number of options you can specify when the container is created using `docker run` or `docker create`:

- `--cpu-percent`—This Windows-only option specifies the percentage of the CPU a container may use. For example, if this value is set to 20, the container may use up to 20% of the host computer's CPU.
- `--cpu-count`—This Windows-only option limits the number of CPUs available to the container.

- `--cpu-shares`—This option specifies the proportion of the CPU that a container can use relative to other containers running on the same host. The default value is 1024. If you set this value to 0, the system will use the default value of 1024, so if you use this option, set it to a value higher or lower than 1024. For example, if you have three containers running and you want ContainerA to get half of the available CPU time and the other two to share the remaining half, you can set ContainerA's `cpu-shares` value to 2048 and leave the others to the default value of 1024. ContainerA will get 50% of the CPU time and the other two will share the remaining half at 25% each. This option can also be expressed as `-c`.
- `--cpuset-cpus`—This specifies which CPUs or CPU cores that a container can use in a multiprocessor or multicore system. Use numbers starting with 0. For example, if you want to limit the container to using only the third and fourth core on a 4-core CPU, you can use 2, 3 or 2-3.

  To see all the options for constraining CPU use, type `docker run --help | findstr cpu`. Some of the options for constraining memory include the following:

- `--memory`—Specifies the maximum amount of memory a container can use. Use the suffix b, k, m, or g to specify units (bytes, kilobytes, megabytes, or gigabytes). For example, to limit a container to using 2 MB, specify the option `--memory 2m`. This option can also be expressed as `-m`.
- `--kernel-memory`—Specifies the amount of kernel memory a container can use with a minimum allowed value of 4 MB. This option uses the same units as `--memory`.
- `--memory-reservation`—Specifies a memory soft limit, which must be less than the value specified by the `--memory` option. This option allows a certain amount of memory to be reclaimed by the host system if needed. For example, if you create a container with `--memory 400m` and `--memory-reservation 300m`, the host system can reclaim the difference between the 400m and 300m, ensuring the container has at least 300m to work with.
- `--memory-swap`—Specifies the amount of virtual memory (swap file) that the container can use. This value must be specified as the value of `--memory` plus the amount of virtual memory you wish the container to use. For example, if you create a container with `--memory 400m` and `--memory-swap 1000m`, the container can use up to 600m of virtual memory (the difference between `--memory-swap` and `--memory`). If this value is not specified, the system can use up to twice the amount of memory as virtual memory. For example, if you create a container with `--memory 400m` and don't specify `--memory-swap`, the container can use up to 800m as virtual memory. A `--memory-swap` value of -1 means the container can use unlimited virtual memory.

Managing Windows Containers with PowerShell

Docker is the primary tool for managing and working with containers and container images, but development is underway for a complete set of PowerShell tools to work with containers. Because the PowerShell module is under development, it is not included with Windows, but you can install the current Docker PowerShell module from a repository using the following PowerShell cmdlets:

```
Register-PSRepository -Name dockerps-dev -SourceLocation
    https://ci.appveyor.com/nuget/docker-powershell-dev
    Install-Module docker -Repository dockerps-dev -scope currentuser
```

After the module is installed, you can see all the cmdlets available by using the following cmdlet:

```
Get-Command -Module docker
```

As of this writing, there are about three dozen cmdlets, some of which are described in Table 12-6.

Note

For a complete list of Docker commands, see the Docker command reference at *https://docs.docker.com/engine/reference/commandline/cli/*.

Table 12-6   PowerShell cmdlets for managing containers

PowerShell Container cmdlet	Description (Docker equivalent, if any)
`Attach-Container`	Connects you to a container session (`docker attach`)
`Build-ContainerImage`	Builds a new container image from a Dockerfile (`docker build`)
`Commit-ContainerImage`	Creates a new image from an existing container (`docker commit`)
`Exec-Container`	Executes a command in a running container (`docker exec`)
`Load-ContainerImage`	Imports a container image from a compressed file (`docker import`)
`Pull-ContainerImage`	Downloads a container image from a repository (`docker pull`)
`Push-ContainerImage`	Uploads a container image to a Docker registry (`docker push`)
`Run-ContainerImage`	Loads and starts a container from a specified image (`docker run`)
`ConvertTo-ContainerImage`	Saves a loaded container to a container image (`docker commit`)
`Save-ContainerImage`	Exports a container image to a compressed file (`docker export`)
`Tag-ContainerImage`	Tags a container image (`docker tag`)
`Get-Container`	Displays currently loaded containers (`docker ps -a`)
`Get-ContainerImage`	Lists container images on the local computer (`docker images`)
`New-Container`	Creates a container from an image (`docker create`)
`Remove-Container`	Removes a container from memory (`docker rm`)
`Remove-ContainerImage`	Deletes a container image from the local computer (`docker rmi`)
`Start-Container`	Starts a container that is loaded but not running (`docker start`)
`Stop-Container`	Stops a container (`docker stop`)

Managing Container Images with Dockerfile, DockerHub, and Microsoft Azure

As you have seen, you can download container images from a repository and you can deploy containers using those images. You can create new container images from deployed containers using the `docker commit` command, and you can manage images using the `docker` command or PowerShell. In this section, you learn how to create new images using Dockerfile and how to manage images stored online using DockerHub and Microsoft Azure.

Creating Container Images with Dockerfile

Dockerfile is a feature of Docker in which you specify properties of a container image using a text file called a *dockerfile* and then use the `docker build` command to create the new image using the specifications in the dockerfile.

A dockerfile consists of a series of commands each of which is followed by one or more arguments. The commands are executed by the `docker build` command or `Build-ContainerImage` PowerShell cmdlet, and the result is a container image. Table 12-7 lists the most common Dockerfile commands, a description, and an example of its usage. The commands are customarily written in uppercase, but they need not be. The table lists the commands in alphabetical order, but the sample dockerfile shown later lists a typical order for the commands. Not all commands need be used in a dockerfile.

Table 12-7   Dockerfile commands

Command	Example	Description
ADD	ADD http://example.com/file.pdf c:/files/	Copies files and folders from the host or remote computer to the container image; local paths and URLs can be used as the source.
CMD	CMD powershell	Specifies a command to run when the container is started.
COPY	COPY C:/files/*.txt C:/Textfiles/	Copies files or folders from the host to the container; COPY and ADD are similar, but ADD has more options including copying files from URLs.
FROM	FROM microsoft/nanoserver	Specifies the base image to use for the container.
RUN	RUN md C:/SharedVol	Executes a command and creates a new layer to be added to the image.
USER	USER containeradmin	Sets the user name that is used when running the container image and any CMD or RUN commands.

The following is a basic dockerfile that creates a new image based on the Server Core image. It installs the DNS server role in the container, creates a new zone, adds a PowerShell script to the container, and runs the script. When the container is run, PowerShell is started. Lines that contain the hash or pound sign "#" are comments for documentation.

> **Note** ⬥
>
> In a dockerfile, file paths must use forward slashes "/" instead of backslashes "\".

```
# Dockerfile to create a container image with DNS installed with the
mcsa2016.local zone
# Base image
FROM microsoft/windowsservercore
# install DNS using PowerShell
RUN powershell -Command Install-WindowsFeature dns -IncludeManagementTools
RUN powershell -Command Add-DnsServerPrimaryZone mcsa2016.local -ZoneFile
mcsa2016.local.dns
# Copy the myscript.ps1 Powershell script file to the container and then run
the script
ADD myscript.ps1 C:/scripts/myscript.ps1
RUN powershell -executionpolicy bypass C:/scripts/myscript.ps1
CMD powershell
```

After you create the file, save it with the name *dockerfile* with no extension in a new folder. From the command prompt or PowerShell prompt, change to the folder where you saved the file and run the following command:

```
docker build -t dnscore .
```

In the previous command, the -t option specifies the image name to be saved, in this case dnscore, and the "." specifies that the dockerfile is in the current folder. Figure 12-23 shows the results of running the docker build command followed by docker images, which lists the new image.

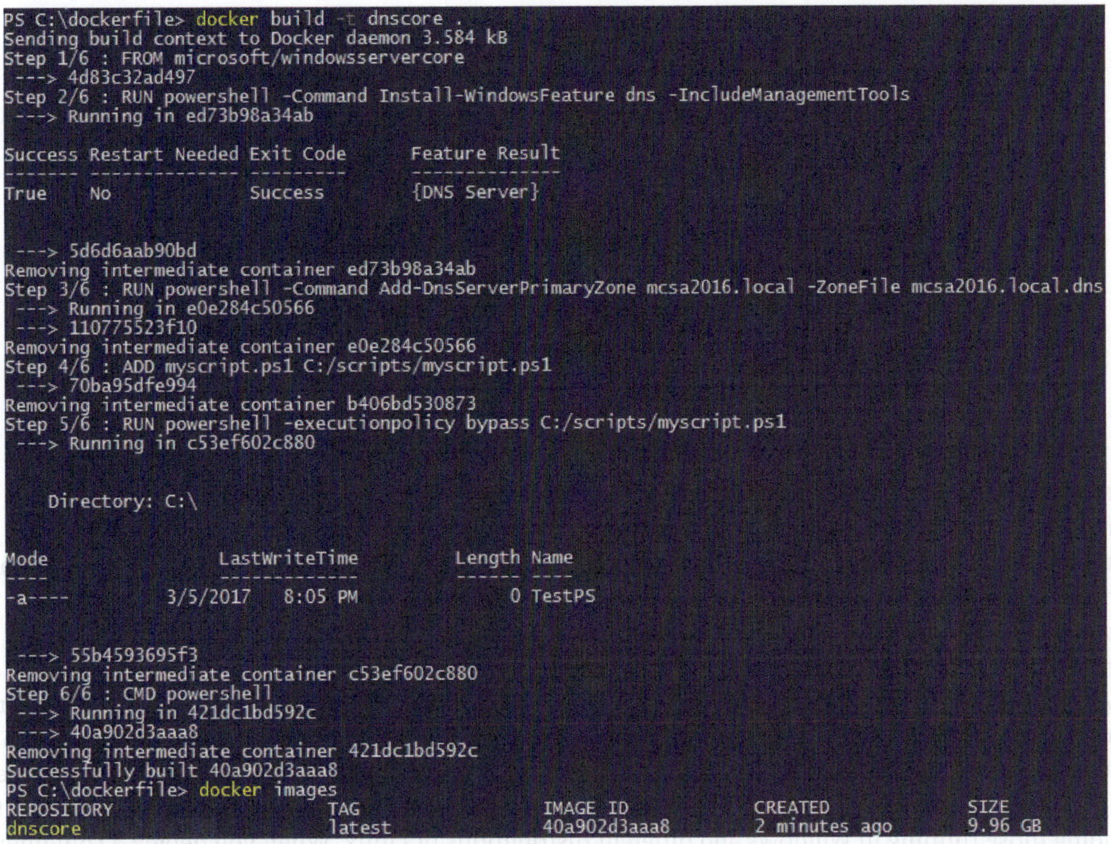

Figure 12-23   Results of the `docker build` command

When you run the container with the `-it` option, you are placed in a PowerShell prompt and can verify that the DNS Server service is running by running the `Get-Service DNS` cmdlet.

Managing Container Images with DockerHub

DockerHub is a public repository for Docker container images. You used it when you ran the `docker pull` command to download the Microsoft Nano Server image. Microsoft has additional images that have pre-installed features such as the dotnet development environment and the Microsoft Azure command-line interface. To see all the Microsoft images, open a browser to *https://hub.docker.com/u/microsoft/*.

Anybody can create an account with DockerHub and upload saved images, so you can share them with other people. To create an account, go to *http://hub.docker.com* and follow the instructions to create a new account. When you create an account, your image repository names will all begin with your username as in username/imagefile. After you log in to DockerHub, you can create a repository and set its visibility to public or private. You don't have to create a repository using the DockerHub website; however, any image you save to DockerHub will create a new repository if one doesn't already exist.

You can use `docker push` to save images to your DockerHub repository. For example, if you have an image named *gtomsho/dnscore* that you want to save to your DockerHub repository, first log in to the repository using `docker login` and then run `docker push`. When you run `docker login`, you'll be asked for your credentials. Figure 12-24 shows the process.

It's important to note that the image must be named with your login name. If you have an image that you wish to save to DockerHub that doesn't have your login name, use the `docker tag` command. For example, suppose that your image is simply dnscore and you want to save it to your repository and your username is jdoe. Add a tag to the image using the following command:

```
docker tag dnscore jdoe/dnscore
```

You can then free space on your local computer by removing Docker images using `docker rmi`.

```
PS C:\dockerfile> docker login
Login with your Docker ID to push and pull images from Docker Hub.
ub.docker.com to create one.
Username: gtomsho
Password:
Login Succeeded
PS C:\dockerfile> docker push gtomsho/dnscore
The push refers to a repository [docker.io/gtomsho/dnscore]
d55446814082: Pushed
6975ce53b523: Pushed
c5b258092f90: Pushed
67157983c8e8: Pushed
5971baf8ac82: Pushed
c28d44287ce5: Skipped foreign layer
f358be10862c: Skipped foreign layer
latest: digest: sha256:e4930fcc878482e70bf5581acedca95543a40f73563
```

Figure 12-24   Logging in to DockerHub and uploading an image

Manage Container Images Using Microsoft Azure

In an earlier chapter, we discussed using Microsoft Azure storage as a method for providing a failover cluster witness. You can also host containers in Azure with Azure Container Service. The Azure Container Service is primarily focused on deploying clusters of virtual machines that are configured to run containerized applications. Azure Container Service uses the familiar Docker container format so that your containers can run in the Azure cloud or on a traditional host computer.

As with Azure storage, you need an Azure subscription to use Azure Container Service. Once you are logged on to Azure, click the Marketplace and click Containers to search for existing containers you can deploy or create new containers using Azure Container Service (see Figure 12-25). Because Docker is open source, there are a variety of preconfigured containers running in different environments that you can try, including those running in Windows and different distributions of Linux. When you deploy a container in Azure, you are actually deploying a virtual machine that has the Containers feature and Docker already installed. Of course, with Azure, you can also deploy a traditional VM and manually install the Containers feature and Docker if you choose to do so. Either way, storage and management of the VM and container are through Microsoft Azure. Virtual machines and containers that you deploy in Microsoft Azure are fully compatible with your local computing environment as well.

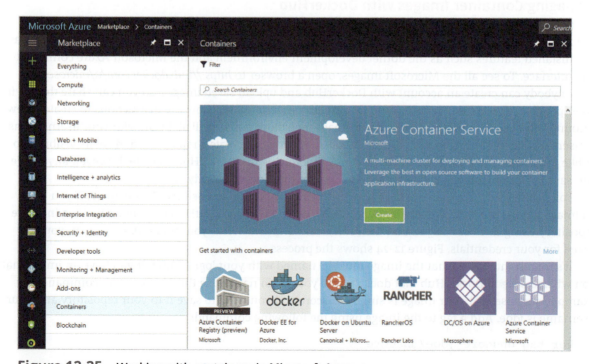

Figure 12-25   Working with containers in Microsoft Azure

Activity 12-5: Managing Container Images

Time Required: 20 minutes

Objective: Manage container images.

Required Tools and Equipment: ServerHyperV

Description: Work with container images using the `docker tag`, `docker commit`, and `docker rmi` commands.

1. On ServerHyperV at the PowerShell prompt, type **docker run -it --name NanoPS1 microsoft/nanoserver powershell** and press **Enter**.

2. You're connected to the container at a PowerShell prompt. Type **md docs** and press **Enter** to create a new folder in the container.

3. Type **cd docs** and press **Enter**. Now, you're going to create a couple of files. Nano Server isn't equipped with a text editor, but there other ways to create files. You'll use two of them. Type **echo Creating file 1 > file1.txt** and press **Enter**. Type **dir** and press **Enter** to see that file1.txt is created with length 40.

4. Type **New-Item file2.txt** and press **Enter**. Type **dir** and press **Enter** to see that there are now two files and file2.txt has length 0, which means that it's empty.

5. Type **exit** and press **Enter** to return to the host.

6. Type **docker commit NanoPS1 nano/nanops** and press **Enter**. This creates a new image based on the running container NanoPS1. The container saves it in a repository named nano/nanops (the repository name must be all lowercase).

7. Type **docker images** and press **Enter**. You see the new image with repository name nano/nanops.

8. Now, you'll create a new container from the saved image. Type **docker create -it --name NanoNew nano/nanops** and press **Enter**. You don't need to specify powershell at the end of the command because the container from which the image was saved was running PowerShell.

9. Type **docker start NanoNew; docker attach NanoNew** and press **Enter**. You can run multiple commands on one line separated by a semicolon. You are now attached to NanoNew.

10. Type **dir docs** and press **Enter**. You see the two files you created earlier. Remember that you can create new images based on existing containers and the state of the container such as start-up commands, files, and network settings are saved in the new image.

11. Type **exit** and press **Enter** to return to the host.

12. Type **docker rm NanoNew NanoPS1** and press **Enter** to remove both containers from memory. Type **docker tag nano/nanops nano/nanops:withDocs** and press **Enter**. This adds the tag withDocs to the image. Type **docker images** and press **Enter**. Notice that the two nano/nanops images have the same image ID, which means that they are the same image but with different tags.

13. Type **docker tag nano/nanops mynanoimage** and press **Enter**. Type **docker images** and press **Enter**. Now there are three images with the same image ID, just different repository names or tags. They are all the same image, just different shortcuts pointing to the same image. Also notice that the new image has the default tag of "latest" because you didn't specify a tag.

14. Type **docker rmi mynanoimage** and press **Enter**. The output of the command is Untagged: mynanoimage:latest. If you don't specify a tag, "latest" is assumed. Type **docker images** and press **Enter** to see that the image is gone. Type **docker rmi nano/nanops:withDocs** and press **Enter**.

15. To see details about an image, including its "parent" images (the image or images it was created from), type **docker image inspect nano/nanops** and press **Enter**. You see a lot of output but toward the top, you see a line named *Parent*, which tells you the image ID from which the image was created if it was created from an existing image. In the ContainerConfig section, you see the name of the image it was created from and the command that the image runs at start-up.

16. Continue to the next activity.

Activity 12-6: Working with Container Networks

Time Required: 20 minutes

Objective: Work with container networks.

Required Tools and Equipment: ServerHyperV

Description: In this activity, you work with container networks, create a static transparent network, and deploy a container with a static IP address.

1. On ServerHyperV, at the PowerShell prompt, type **docker network create -d transparent --subnet 192.168.100.0/24 --gateway 192.168.100.250 TranStatic** and press **Enter**. This creates the static transparent network TranStatic and assigns a default gateway.

2. Type **docker create -it --name NanoPS --network TranStatic --ip 192.168.100.1 nano/nanops** and press **Enter**.

3. Type **docker start NanoPS** and press **Enter**. Type **docker exec NanoPS ipconfig** and press **Enter**. This command tells the container to execute the command `ipconfig`. You see that the address of the container is 192.168.100.1 with a default gateway of 192.168.100.250.

4. Type **ipconfig** and press **Enter** to see the IP address configuration of the host computer. You see a virtual adapter with address 192.168.100.1, the same address of the container. The virtual adapter is how the container is able to communicate directly with the host network without having to go through network address translation.

5. Type **docker stop NanoPS** and press **Enter**.

6. Type **docker rm NanoPS** and press **Enter**.

7. Sign out or shut down the computer.

Chapter Summary

- Nano Server is not a general-purpose Windows server but is intended to be used as a tool to deploy a single, well-defined service. Nano Server is referred to as a *headless server*, and it is intended to be managed remotely using PowerShell, MMCs, or other remote management options.

- Nano Server excels at three of the most important qualities you want in a server: availability, low resource utilization, and security. If your network needs DNS servers, Hyper-V servers, web servers, or file servers, Nano Server is an excellent choice.

- Nano Server is not an installation option like Server Core and Desktop Experience. To install Nano Server, you create a virtual disk from files included on your Windows Server 2016 installation media using PowerShell.

- Most Nano Server deployments are likely to be on virtual machines, but one of the important use cases for Nano Server is as a Hyper-V host. In production environments, that means deploying Nano Server to a physical computer. For testing purposes, you can

- use nested virtualization. You can also install drivers and roles after you create a base image, but if you know what role you are installing when you create the image, it's easier to specify it during creation.

- Adding packages to a Nano Server image only adds the binary files for the package to the Nano Server image. You need to enable the features before you can begin using them. You can do this easily with PowerShell Direct on a virtual machine deployment or PowerShell remoting on a physical deployment.

- There are two methods for joining Nano Server to a domain during image creation: join to the same domain as the host computer and join to a different domain. In both cases, you are performing an offline domain join in which the Nano Server will complete the joining process when it is first started.

- You can configure Nano Server and install packages during Nano Server image creation, but you might need to make changes to an image after it has been created. You can do this with the `Edit-NanoServerImage` cmdlet.

- Nano Server must also be updated from time to time, especially when the updates involve patching security vulnerabilities. You can apply Windows updates to Nano Server when you create a new Nano Server image using the `New-NanoServerImage` cmdlet or on an existing image using the `Edit-NanoServerImage` cmdlet.

- Windows Server 2016 introduces Windows containers, a software environment in which an application can run but is isolated from much of the rest of the operating system and other applications.

- Containers are a type of virtualization, but containers virtualize parts of the operating system, allowing containerized applications to have their own copy of critical OS structures like the registry, file system, and network configuration while sharing the kernel, the host hardware, and possibly some runtime libraries. This is called *namespace isolation*.

- Windows Server 2016 supports two types of containers. A Windows Server container is an application environment that shares the host OS and kernel with the host OS and other Windows Server containers but has its own copy of user mode data structures such as the registry, file system, and network configuration. A Hyper-V container is an application environment that provides OS and kernel isolation like a traditional VM but is not managed by Hyper-V Manager.

- Windows containers can be deployed on Windows Server 2016 with Desktop Experience, Windows Server 2016 Server Core, and Windows Server 2016 Nano Server. They can be deployed on both physical computers and virtual machines as Windows Server containers or Hyper-V containers.

- Docker is open source software that has been used in the Linux environment to implement containers for years. Microsoft adapted Docker to the Windows environment. Docker is not part of Windows, so it can't be installed as a role or feature; you need to install it using PowerShell package management.

- To deploy a container, you install a base operating system image using the Docker client. The Docker client is the executable file `docker.exe` that was installed with the Docker package. You install a base operating system image from the DockerHub

repository that is a collection of Docker images maintained in the cloud.

- After you have downloaded an image, you can create a Windows Server 2016 Container by using the `docker run` command. The `docker run` command starts a container based on a specified image and runs a command or application.

- Implementing containers on Nano Server is much the same as it is in Windows Server 2016 Desktop Experience or Server Core. First, you need to install the Container feature in the Nano Server image. With the containers feature installed, you can install Docker on Nano Server.

- The `docker.exe` program is the primary tool for working with containers.

- Docker configures the container network using network address translation (NAT). NAT is typically used to allow a network using private IP addresses to access the public Internet. With a NAT network, devices on the host network cannot initiate communication with the container because its IP address is translated by the host computer. Port mapping allows the container host to forward packets for specific applications to containers hosting those applications.

- Data that is created while the container is running and stored on its virtual volumes is not saved when a container is deleted. You can save changes to the container with the `docker commit` command, but that saves the current state of the container as a new image.

- Resource control is one of the big advantages of using containers to run applications instead of running them directly on the host computer. Much as with a virtual machine, you can constrain, or limit, how much of a particular resource a container can utilize including CPU, memory, and block I/O.

- Dockerfile is a feature of Docker in which you specify properties of a container image using a text file called a *dockerfile* and then use the `docker build` command to create the new image using the specifications in the dockerfile.

- DockerHub is a public repository for Docker container images. You use it when you run the `docker pull` and `docker push` commands to download and upload Docker images from the online repository.

Key Terms

container
Docker
Dockerfile
DockerHub
domain blob
headless server

Hyper-V container
layer 2 (L2) bridge network
namespace
namespace isolation
network address
    translation (NAT)

offline domain join
stateless operation
tag
transparent network
Windows Server container

Review Questions

1. Windows 2016 Nano Server can provide you with some specific advantages when compared with Windows 2106 Server Core. Which of the following advantages are found in Nano Server? (Choose all that apply.)
   a. Fewer security updates
   b. Fewer running OS processes
   c. GUI
   d. Higher kernel memory usage

2. Which of the following type of servers would be ideal candidates to install and utilize Windows 2016 Nano Server? (Choose all that apply.)
   a. Active Directory server
   b. Hyper-V server
   c. DNS server
   d. Web server

3. You have decided to install and utilize Nano Server in your current network. What specific procedure should you perform when installing Windows 2016 Nano Server?
   a. Use PowerShell to create a new disk partition and use the files on the Windows Server 2016 installation media
   b. Convert an existing Server Core installation to a Nano installation
   c. Shrink an existing partition and install Windows Server 2016 Nano server
   d. Use PowerShell to create a virtual disk from files included on the Windows Server 2016 installation media

4. A system administrator needs to create and manage Nano Server VHD images. Which PowerShell cmdlet can an administrator use to import the cmdlets and scripts that facilitate the creation and management of Nano Server VHD images?
   a. `Import-Module`
   b. `Get-Module`
   c. `Import-ServerModule`
   d. `Get-NanoServerImage`

5. As a system administrator, you have been assigned the task of setting up a new Nano Server installation on a physical computer. The Nano Server image is already created and needs to be deployed to a physical computer. Which of the following options can be utilized to deploy Nano Server to a physical computer? (Choose all that apply.)
   a. Use PXE-boot and WDS to install Nano Server on a bare-metal machine
   b. Use WinPE to install Nano Server on a bare-metal machine
   c. Use PowerShell to convert a Server Core machine to Nano Server
   d. Dual boot to a computer that has a Windows OS installed

6. Which of the following PowerShell parameters will install the Hyper-V package that lets you utilize Nano Server as a virtualized host?
   a. `-Compute`
   b. `-Host`
   c. `-Clustering`
   d. `-Storage`

7. You have just completed the process of adding a specific package to a Nano Server image to add an additional feature. However, you have noticed the feature you needed on your Nano Server is not available for immediate use. What task must be performed before the newly added feature is available for use?
   a. Enable the package's binary files
   b. Enable the feature
   c. Remove the package's binary files
   d. Activate the feature using the cmdlet `Get-OptionalFeature`

8. You have decided to join Nano Server to a domain that is different from the host computer's domain. During this task, you will use a PowerShell cmdlet to point to a file that contains the information

to perform an offline domain join. What is the specific name of this type of file?

- **a.** Domain join file
- **b.** Domain path file
- **c.** Domain access file
- **d.** Domain blob file

9. Which of the following advanced Nano Server parameters will allow you to put Nano Server in a test mode that will allow you to use unsigned drivers?

- **a.** `-DebugDriver`
- **b.** `-Development`
- **c.** `-Driverpath`
- **d.** `-EnableEMS`

10. You have just finished creating a new Nano Server image. However, upon closer inspection, you realize that you did not configure your new image correctly. Which PowerShell cmdlet will allow you to edit your existing Server image?

- **a.** `Edit-NanoServer`
- **b.** `Setup-NanoServerImage`
- **c.** `Setup-NanoServer`
- **d.** `Edit-NanoServerImage`

11. When you create a virtual machine using Hyper-V, you generate a "virtualized" hardware environment that allows multiple operating systems to coexist on a single host. However, when you utilize a "containerized" application using Windows Server containers, you are creating an environment that shares very specific resources from the host machine. What specific resources are the containerized applications utilizing? (Choose all that apply.)

- **a.** Host operating system
- **b.** Second operating system in an isolated virtual machine
- **c.** Host kernel
- **d.** Virtual machine's kernel

12. Containers allow an application to see and interact only with certain parts of an operating system. Which of the following terms best describes the parts of the OS an application can see and interact with?

- **a.** Namespace
- **b.** Container
- **c.** Isolation
- **d.** Docker

13. Which of the following is an application environment that provides OS and kernel isolation like a traditional VM but is not managed by Hyper-V Manager?

- **a.** Windows Server container
- **b.** Hyper-V container
- **c.** Docker container
- **d.** Isolated container

14. When compared with virtual machines, containers are excellent alternatives for cloud providers who wish to provide which of the following services?

- **a.** Software as a Service
- **b.** Infrastructure as a Service
- **c.** Physical servers
- **d.** Platform as a Service

15. You are a system administrator and have been asked to design an environment that can deploy Windows containers. You are currently in the process of selecting an appropriate version of Windows Server. Which versions of Windows Server will support Windows containers? (Choose all that apply.)

- **a.** Windows Server 2016 without Desktop Experience
- **b.** Windows Server 2016 Nano Server
- **c.** 2016 Server Core
- **d.** Windows Server 2016 with Desktop Experience

16. Which of the following open source software projects has been adapted by Microsoft to implement containers within the Windows environment?

- **a.** KVM
- **b.** Hadoop
- **c.** Vagrant
- **d.** Docker

17. What specific command can be used to create a container after you have selected and downloaded an image from the Docker Hub repository?

- **a.** `docker exe`
- **b.** `docker run`
- **c.** `Get -docker`
- **d.** `docker start`

18. You have decided to create a Nano Server that will support the containers feature. However, you must first install the container feature in the Nano Server image. What parameter can you add to the PowerShell cmdlet *New-NanoServerImage* to install the container feature?

- **a.** `-DockerImage`
- **b.** `-Docker`
- **c.** `-Containers`
- **d.** `-DockerContainer`

19. You have recently decided that you would like to delete the Docker container AppTest. What command will delete the AppTest container after you have verified that the container has been stopped?

- **a.** `docker rm AppTest`
- **b.** `docker -remove AppTest`
- **c.** `container AppTest -delete`
- **d.** `container AppTest -remove`

20. You are currently editing and testing an existing container image and have decided you would like to be able to differentiate between multiple versions of the same image. What can be used to differentiate between multiple versions of the same image?
    a. Shortcut
    b. Pull
    c. Commit
    d. Tag

21. You have just been assigned the task of configuring your Docker containers to stop using NAT, the default container network configuration. The containers should be able to communicate with devices on the host network without the network addresses having to be translated or sharing the host's MAC address. What type of container network should you implement?
    a. Transparent
    b. Static
    c. Layer 2 (L2) bridge
    d. Dynamic

22. Which of the following options can be run with the `docker run` or `docker create` commands to specify the proportion of the CPU that a container can use relative to other containers running on the same host?
    a. `-cpu-percent`
    b. `-cpu-shares`
    c. `-cpuset-cpus`
    d. `-cpuset-count`

23. You have decided that you would like to limit the amount of memory a container may use to 3 megabytes. Which of the following options can be run with the `docker run` or `docker create` commands to specify that 3 megabytes are the maximum amount of memory the container can use?
    a. `-memory-limit 3m`
    b. `-memory 3m`
    c. `-memory-swap 3m`
    d. `-memory-reservation 3m`

24. What feature of Docker allows you the ability to specify properties of a container image using a text file?
    a. Containerfile
    b. Dockeredit
    c. Dockerfile
    d. Containeredit

25. When you are "pulling" a Microsoft Nano Server image for Docker, you are essentially pulling your image from what specific public repository?
    a. DockerImage
    b. Windows Server repository
    c. DockerRepo
    d. DockerHub

Critical Thinking

The following activities give you critical thinking challenges. Case Projects offer a scenario with a problem to solve and for which you supply a written solution.

Case Project 12-1: Choosing a Windows Server 2016 Installation Option

You have a Hyper-V server on which you want to create two virtual machines. The virtual machines should use the smallest footprint installation option available. One virtual machine will run the DNS Server role and the other will run the Active Directory Domain Services role. Which Windows Server 2016 installation option should you use for each of the VMs and why?

Case Project 12-2: Configuring a Container Network

You are beginning to implement containers. In your testing, you have used the default network configuration for the containers you have deployed. Now, it's time to begin using the containers in your production network. Your physical network is using a variety of IP networks including some in the range 172.16.0.0/12. You want to use NAT for your container network, but you want to be sure there are no address conflicts between your container networks and physical networks. What should you do?

MCSA Exam 70-740 Objectives

The table in this Appendix maps the exam objectives for Microsoft Certified Solutions Associate (MCSA) Exam 70-740, Installation, Storage, and Compute with Windows Server 2016, to the corresponding chapter and section title where the objectives are covered in this book. After each objective, the percentage of the exam that includes the objective is shown in parentheses.

MCSA Exam 70-740: Skill Measured	Chapter	Section
Install Windows Servers in host and compute environments (10–15%)		
Install, upgrade, and migrate servers and workloads	2, 3	
• Determine Windows Server 2016 installation requirements	2	Windows Server 2016 Editions and Requirements
• Determine appropriate Windows Server 2016 editions per workloads	2	Windows Server 2016 Editions and Requirements
• Install Windows Server 2016	2	Planning a Windows Server 2016 Installation
• Install Windows Server 2016 features and roles	2	Using Features on Demand
	3	Working with Server Roles and Features
• Install and configure Windows Server Core	2	Server Core: Windows That Doesn't Do Windows
• Manage Windows Server Core installations using Windows PowerShell, command line, and remote management capabilities	2	Server Core: Windows That Doesn't Do Windows
	3	Working with Server Roles and Features (Managing Server Roles with PowerShell)
	3	Managing Servers Remotely
	3	Configuring Services
• Implement Windows PowerShell Desired State Configuration (DSC) to install and maintain integrity of installed environments	3	Working with Server Roles and Features (Implementing Desired State Configuration)
• Perform upgrades and migrations of servers and core workloads from Windows Server 2008 and Windows Server 2012 to Windows Server 2016	2	Planning a Windows Server 2016 Installation
• Determine the appropriate activation model for server installation, such as Automatic Virtual Machine Activation (AVMA), Key Management Service (KMS), and Active Directory-based Activation	2	Planning a Windows Server 2016 Installation
Install and configure Nano Server	2, 12	
• Determine appropriate usage scenarios and requirements for Nano Server	2	Windows Server 2016 Editions and Requirements
	12	Introducing Nano Server

MCSA Exam 70-740: Skill Measured	Chapter	Section
• Install Nano Server	12	Installing Nano Server
• Implement Roles and Features on Nano Server	12	Creating Advanced Nano Server Images
• Manage and configure Nano Server	12	Installing Nano Server
	12	Creating Advanced Nano Server Images
• Manage Nano Server remotely using Windows PowerShell	12	Installing Nano Server
	12	Creating Advanced Nano Server Images
Create, manage, and maintain images for deployment	3, 6, 7	
• Plan for Windows Server virtualization	6	Installing Hyper-V
• Plan for Linux and FreeBSD deployments	7	Implementing Linux and FreeBSD Virtual Machines
• Determine considerations for deploying workloads into virtualized environments	6	Installing Hyper-V
• Update images with patches, hotfixes, and drivers	3	Working with Windows Install Images for Deployment
• Install roles and features in offline images	3	Working with Server Roles and Features (Managing Server Roles with PowerShell)
	3	Working with Windows Install Images for Deployment
• Manage and maintain Windows Server Core, Nano Server images, and VHDs using Windows PowerShell	3	Working with Windows Install Images for Deployment
Implement storage solutions (10–15%)		
Configure disks and volumes	4	
• Configure sector sizes appropriate for various workloads	4	Configuring Local Disks
• Configure GUID partition table (GPT) disks	4	Configuring Local Disks
• Create VHD and VHDX files using Server Manager or Windows PowerShell Storage module cmdlets	4	Working with Virtual Disks
• Mount virtual hard disks	4	Working with Virtual Disks
• Determine when to use NTFS and ReFS file systems	4	Configuring Local Disks
• Configure NFS and SMB shares using Server Manager	4	An Overview of File Sharing
	4	Creating Windows File Shares
• Configure SMB share and session settings using Windows PowerShell	4	Creating Windows File Shares
• Configure SMB server and SMB client configuration settings using Windows PowerShell	4	Creating Windows File Shares
• Configure file and folder permissions	4	Securing Access to Files with Permissions
Implement server storage	5	
• Configure storage pools	5	Using Storage Spaces
• Implement simple, mirror, and parity storage layout options for disks or enclosures	5	Using Storage Spaces

MCSA Exam 70-740: Skill Measured	Chapter	Section
• Expand storage pools	5	Using Storage Spaces
• Configure Tiered Storage	5	Using Storage Spaces
• Configure iSCSI target and initiator	5	Configuring iSCSI
• Configure iSNS	5	Configuring iSCSI
• Configure Datacenter Bridging (DCB)	5	Configuring iSCSI
• Configure Multi-Path IO (MPIO)	5	Configuring iSCSI
• Determine usage scenarios for Storage Replica	5	Storage Replica
• Implement Storage Replica for server-to-server, cluster-to-cluster, and stretch cluster scenarios	5	Storage Replica
Implement data deduplication	5	
• Implement and configure deduplication	5	Implementing Data Deduplication
• Determine appropriate usage scenarios for deduplication	5	Implementing Data Deduplication
• Monitor deduplication	5	Implementing Data Deduplication
• Implement a backup and restore solution with deduplication	5	Implementing Data Deduplication
Implement Hyper-V (20–25%)		
Install and configure Hyper-V	6, 7	
• Determine hardware and compatibility requirements for installing Hyper-V	6	Installing Hyper-V
• Install Hyper-V	6	Installing Hyper-V
• Install management tools	6	Installing Hyper-V
• Upgrade from existing versions of Hyper-V	6	Installing Hyper-V
• Delegate virtual machine management	6	Managing Virtual Machines (Delegation of VM Management)
• Perform remote management of Hyper-V hosts	6	Installing Hyper-V
• Configure virtual machines using Windows PowerShell Direct	6	Managing Virtual Machines (Non-Uniform Memory Access Support)
• Implement nested virtualization	7	Nested Virtualization
Configure virtual machine (VM) settings	6, 7	
• Add or remove memory in a running VM	6	Managing Virtual Machines
• Configure dynamic memory	6	Managing Virtual Machines
• Configure Non-Uniform Memory Access (NUMA) support	6	Managing Virtual Machines (Non-Uniform Memory Access Support)
• Configure smart paging	6	Managing Virtual Machines
• Configure Resource Metering	6	Managing Virtual Machines (Resource Metering)
• Manage Integration Services	6	Managing Virtual Machines
• Create and configure Generation 1 and 2 VMs and determine appropriate usage scenarios	6	Creating Virtual Machines in Hyper-V
• Implement enhanced session mode	6	Managing Virtual Machines (Enhanced Session Mode)

MCSA Exam 70-740: Skill Measured	Chapter	Section
• Create Linux and FreeBSD VMs	7	Implementing Linux and FreeBSD Virtual Machines
• Install and configure Linux Integration Services (LIS)	7	Implementing Linux and FreeBSD Virtual Machines
• Install and configure FreeBSD Integration Services (BIS)	7	Implementing Linux and FreeBSD Virtual Machines
• Implement Secure Boot for Windows and Linux environments	6	Creating Virtual Machines in Hyper-V
• Move and convert VMs from previous versions of Hyper-V to Windows Server 2016 Hyper-V	6	Installing Hyper-V
• Export and import VMs	6	Creating Virtual Machines in Hyper-V
• Implement Discrete Device Assignment (DDA)	6	Managing Virtual Machines (Discrete Device Assignment)
Configure Hyper-V storage	6, 7	
• Create VHDs and VHDX files using Hyper-V Manager	7	Working with Virtual Hard Disks
• Create shared VHDX files, configure differencing disks	7	Working with Virtual Hard Disks
• Modify virtual hard disks	7	Working with Virtual Hard Disks
• Configure pass-through disks	7	Working with Virtual Hard Disks
• Resize a virtual hard disk	7	Working with Virtual Hard Disks
• Manage checkpoints	6	Managing Virtual Machines (Checkpoints)
• Implement production checkpoints	6	Managing Virtual Machines (Checkpoints)
• Implement a virtual Fibre Channel adapter	7	Advanced Virtual Network Configuration (Configuring Fibre Channel Adapters)
• Configure storage Quality of Service (QoS)	7	Working with Virtual Hard Disks (Storage QoS)
Configure Hyper-V networking	7	
• Add and remove virtual network interface cards (vNICs)	7	Hyper-V Virtual Networks
• Configure Hyper-V virtual switches	7	Hyper-V Virtual Networks
• Optimize network performance	7	Advanced Virtual Network Configuration
• Configure MAC addresses	7	Advanced Virtual Network Configuration
• Configure network isolation	7	Hyper-V Virtual Networks
• Configure synthetic and legacy virtual network adapters	7	Advanced Virtual Network Configuration
• Configure NIC teaming in VMs	7	Advanced Virtual Network Configuration
• Configure virtual machine queue (VMQ)	7	Advanced Virtual Network Configuration
• Enable Remote Direct Memory Access (RDMA) on network adapters bound to a Hyper-V virtual switch using Switch Embedded Teaming (SET)	7	Advanced Virtual Network Configuration
• Configure Bandwidth Management	7	Hyper-V Virtual Networks
Implement Windows containers (5–10%)		
Deploy Windows containers	12	
• Determine installation requirements and appropriate scenarios for Windows containers	12	Introducing Windows Containers

MCSA Exam 70-740: Skill Measured	Chapter	Section
• Install and configure Windows Server container host in physical or virtualized environments	12	Deploying Windows Containers
• Install and configure Windows Server container host to Windows Server Core or Nano Server in a physical or virtualized environment	12	Deploying Windows Containers
• Install Docker on Windows Server and Nano Server	12	Deploying Windows Containers
• Configure Docker daemon start-up options	12	Deploying Windows Containers (Managing Daemon Start-up Options)
• Configure Windows PowerShell for use with containers	12	Managing Windows Containers (Managing Windows Containers with PowerShell)
• Install a base operating system	12	Deploying Windows Containers
• Tag an image	12	Managing Windows Containers (Working with Container Images)
• Uninstall an operating system image	12	Managing Windows Containers (Working with Container Images)
• Create Windows Server containers	12	Deploying Windows Containers
• Create Hyper-V containers	12	Deploying Windows Containers
Manage Windows containers	12	
• Manage Windows containers using the Docker daemon	12	Managing Windows Containers (Managing Containers with the Docker Daemon)
• Manage Windows containers using Windows PowerShell	12	Managing Windows Containers (Managing Windows Containers with PowerShell)
• Manage container networking	12	Managing Windows Containers (Implementing Container Networks)
• Manage container data volumes	12	Managing Windows Containers (Working with Container Data Volumes)
• Manage Resource Control	12	Managing Windows Containers (Managing Resource Control)
• Create new container images using Dockerfile	12	Managing Windows Containers (Managing Container Images with Dockerfile, DockerHub, and Microsoft Azure)
• Manage container images using DockerHub repository for public and private scenarios	12	Managing Windows Containers (Managing Container Images with Dockerfile, DockerHub, and Microsoft Azure)
• Manage container images using Microsoft Azure	12	Managing Windows Containers (Managing Container Images with Dockerfile, DockerHub, and Microsoft Azure)
Implement high availability (30–35%)		
Implement high availability and disaster recovery options in Hyper-V	9	
• Implement Hyper-V Replica	9	Configuring Virtual Machine Movement
• implement Live Migration	9	Configuring Virtual Machine Movement
• Implement Shared Nothing Live Migration	9	Configuring Virtual Machine Movement
• Configure CredSSP or Kerberos authentication protocol for Live Migration	9	Configuring Virtual Machine Movement
• Implement storage migration	9	Configuring Virtual Machine Movement

MCSA Exam 70-740: Skill Measured	Chapter	Section
Implement failover clustering	8, 9	
• Implement Workgroup, Single, and Multi-Domain clusters	8	Failover Cluster
	9	Advanced Failover Clusters (Creating Workgroup and Multi-Domain Clusters)
• Configure quorum	8	Failover Clusters
	9	Advanced Failover Clusters (Configuring Advanced Quorum Settings)
• Configure cluster networking	8	Failover Clusters (Configuring Failover Clustering)
• Restore single node or cluster configuration	9	Advanced Failover Clusters (Backing Up and Restoring Cluster Configuration)
• Configure cluster storage	8	Failover Clusters (Configuring Failover Clustering)
• Implement Cluster-Aware Updating	8	Failover Clusters (Cluster-Aware Updating)
• Implement Cluster Operating System Rolling Upgrade	9	Advanced Failover Clusters (Upgrading a Failover Cluster)
• Configure and optimize clustered shared volumes (CSVs)	8	Failover Clusters (Configuring Failover Clustering)
• Configure clusters without network names	9	Advanced Failover Clusters (Creating Active Directory–Detached Clusters)
• Implement Scale-Out File Server (SoFS)	9	Advanced Failover Clusters (Configuring Roles for High Availability)
• Determine different scenarios for the use of SoFS versus clustered File Server	9	Advanced Failover Clusters (Configuring Roles for High Availability)
• Determine usage scenarios for implementing guest clustering	9	Implementing High Availability in Hyper-V (Configure Guest Clustering)
• Implement a Clustered Storage Spaces solution using Shared SAS storage enclosures	9	Advanced Failover Clusters (Deploying Clustered Storage Spaces)
• Implement Storage Replica	9	Advanced Failover Clusters (Implementing Storage Replica with Failover Clusters)
• Implement Cloud Witness	9	Advanced Failover Clusters (Configuring Advanced Quorum Settings)
• Implement VM resiliency	9	Implementing High Availability in Hyper-V (Configure Guest Clustering)
• Implement shared VHDX as a storage solution for guest clusters	9	Implementing High Availability in Hyper-V (Configure Guest Clustering)
Implement Storage Spaces Direct	9	
• Determine scenario requirements for implementing Storage Spaces Direct	9	Implementing Storage Spaces Direct
• Enable Storage Spaces direct using Windows PowerShell	9	Implementing Storage Spaces Direct
• Implement a disaggregated Storage Spaces Direct scenario in a cluster	9	Implementing Storage Spaces Direct
• Implement a hyper-converged Storage Spaces Direct scenario in a cluster	9	Implementing Storage Spaces Direct
Manage failover clustering	8, 9	
• Configure role-specific settings including continuously available shares	9	Advanced Failover Clusters (Configuring Roles for High Availability)

MCSA Exam 70-740: Skill Measured	Chapter	Section
• Configure VM monitoring	9	Implementing High Availability in Hyper-V (Configuring Virtual Machine Monitoring)
• Configure failover and preference settings	8	Failover Clusters (Configuring a Cluster Role)
• Implement stretch and site-aware failover clusters	9	Implementing Stretch Clusters
• Enable and configure node fairness	9	Implementing High Availability in Hyper-V (Implement Node Fairness)
Manage VM movement in clustered nodes	9	
• Perform a live migration	9	Configuring Virtual Machine Movement (Live Migration)
• Perform a quick migration	9	Configuring Virtual Machine Movement (Quick Migration)
• Perform a storage migration	9	Configuring Virtual Machine Movement (Storage Migration)
• Import, export, and copy VMs	9	Configuring Virtual Machine Movement (VM Export and Import)
• Configure VM network health protection	9	Configuring Virtual Machine Movement (Configuring Virtual Machine Network Health Protection)
• Configure drain on shutdown	9	Implementing High Availability in Hyper-V (Configuring Highly Available Virtual Machines)
Implement Network Load Balancing (NLB)	8	
• Install NLB nodes	8	Configuring Network Load Balancing
• Configure NLB prerequisites	8	Configuring Network Load Balancing
• Configure affinity	8	Configuring Network Load Balancing (Configuring an NLB Cluster)
• Configure port rules	8	Configuring Network Load Balancing (Configuring an NLB Cluster)
• Configure cluster operation mode	8	Configuring Network Load Balancing
• Upgrade an NLB cluster	8	Configuring Network Load Balancing (Managing an NLB Cluster)
Maintain and monitor server environments (10–15%)		
Maintain server installations	10, 11	
• Implement Windows Server Update Services (WSUS) solutions	10	Installing the WSUS Role
	10	Configuring WSUS
• Configure WSUS groups	10	Configuring WSUS
• Manage patch management in mixed environments	10	Configuring WSUS
• Implement an antimalware solution with Windows Defender	10	Implementing Windows Defender
• Integrate Windows Defender with WSUS and Windows Update	10	Implementing Windows Defender
• Perform backup and restore operations using Windows Server Backup	11	Backing Up Windows Servers
	11	Windows Server Recovery

MCSA Exam 70-740: Skill Measured	Chapter	Section
• Determine backup strategies for different Windows Server roles and workloads, including Hyper-V Host, Hyper-V Guests, Active Directory, File Servers, and Web Servers using Windows Server 2016 native tools and solutions	11 11	Backing Up Windows Servers Backup and Recovery of Specific Roles
Monitor server installations	11	
• Monitor workloads using Performance Monitor	11	Monitoring a Windows Server
• Configure Data Collector Sets	11	Monitoring a Windows Server
• Determine appropriate CPU, memory, disk, and networking counters for storage and compute workloads	11	Monitoring a Windows Server
• Configure alerts	11	Monitoring a Windows Server
• Monitor workloads using Resource Monitor	11	Monitoring a Windows Server

GLOSSARY

A

access-based enumeration (ABE) A feature of a file share that shows only the files and folders to which a user has at least Read permission.

access control entry (ACE) An entry in a discretionary access control list (DACL); includes a security principal object and the object's assigned permissions. *See also* discretionary access control list (DACL).

activation A process in which a Windows operating system verifies the product key entered for an install product and registers the product with an activation server.

Active Directory The Windows directory service that enables administrators to create and manage users and groups, set networkwide user and computer policies, manage security, and organize network resources.

Active Directory-Based Activation (ADBA) An activation option that allows Windows computers that have a volume license key installed to activate when the computer joins the domain.

Active Directory–detached cluster A cluster configuration option that allows deploying a failover cluster without needing Active Directory for network name management.

active node A cluster member that's responding to client requests for a network application or service; also referred to as an *active server*.

administrative shares Hidden shares created by Windows that are available only to members of the Administrators group; they include the root of each volume, the \Windows folder, and IPC$. Hidden shares' names end with a dollar sign.

Aggregated policy A storage QoS policy that applies the minimum and maximum I/O operations per second (IOPS) values to a set of virtual disks working as a whole.

authoritative restore A method of restoring Active Directory data from a backup to ensure that restored objects aren't overwritten by changes from other domain controllers through replication.

automatic disk An option for a physical disk in Storage Spaces that will be used as Storage Spaces sees fit when a virtual disk is created.

Automatic Virtual Machine Activation (AVMA) An activation option that lets you install Windows Server 2016 in Hyper-V virtual machines without having to manage the product key for each virtual machine.

autonomous mode A WSUS server mode that decentralizes administration of update approvals and client groups; the default option when you install WSUS.

B

backplane A connection system that uses a printed circuit board instead of traditional cables to carry signals.

bare metal recovery A backup option that includes the system state, the system reserved volume, and the volume where Windows is stored.

baseline A record of performance data gathered when a system is performing well under normal operating conditions that can be used as a point of reference.

basic disk A traditional Windows or DOS disk arrangement in which the disk is partitioned into primary and extended partitions. A basic disk can't hold volumes spanning multiple disks or be part of a RAID.

block-level replication A Windows Server feature that provides block-level file replication between storage devices, primarily for the purpose of fault tolerance and disaster recovery.

block-level storage A storage replication strategy in which individual data blocks on the disk are copied as they change, as opposed to file-level replication, which replicates entire files as they change.

boot image   An image file containing the Windows Preinstallation Environment (PE) that allows a client computer to access a WDS server so that it can access an install image. *See also* Windows Preinstallation Environment (PE).

boot volume   The volume where the \Windows folder is located; usually the C drive but doesn't have to be. Also referred to as the *boot partition*.

build   A specific compilation of the operating system that determines which updates have been incorporated into the OS installation.

C

capture image   A special boot image that creates an install image from a reference computer. *See also* install image *and* reference computer.

checkpoint   A partial copy of a virtual machine made at a specific moment that is used to restore the VM to its state when the checkpoint was taken. Also called a *snapshot*.

clean installation   A Windows OS installation in which the OS is installed on a new disk partition; it's not an upgrade from any previous version of Windows.

client access point   A name and IP address by which clients can access a clustered service in a failover cluster. *See also* failover cluster.

client affinity value   An option specified in multiple host filtering modes that determines whether the same or a different host handles successive requests from the same client.

client-side targeting   A method for adding computers to WSUS groups in which a registry setting on the client machine instructs the client to add itself to the specified WSUS group.

cloud computing   A collection of technologies for abstracting the details of how applications, storage, network, and other computing resources are delivered to users.

cloud witness   A new quorum witness option introduced in Windows Server 2016 that allows you to specify a resource in Microsoft Azure to act as the cluster witness.

Cluster-Aware Updating (CAU)   A failover cluster feature in Windows Server that automates software updates on cluster servers while maintaining cluster service availability. *See also* failover cluster.

cluster heartbeat   Communication between cluster nodes that provides the status of each cluster member to the cluster quorum. The cluster heartbeat, or lack of it, informs the cluster when a server is no longer communicating.

Cluster Operating System Rolling Upgrade   A Windows Server 2016 OS upgrade option that can upgrade a Windows Server 2012 R2 cluster to a Windows Server 2016 cluster without taking the workloads offline.

cluster operation mode   A cluster parameter that specifies the type of network addressing used to access the cluster: Unicast, Multicast, or IGMP multicast.

cluster server   A Windows server that participates in a failover cluster; also referred to as a *cluster node* or *cluster member*. *See also* failover cluster.

cluster shared volume   A storage option in a failover cluster in which all cluster nodes have access to the shared storage for read and write access. *See also* failover cluster.

clustered application   An application or service installed on two or more servers participating in a failover cluster; Also called a *clustered service*. *See also* failover cluster.

column   A property of a virtual disk that indicates the number of physical disks it is using.

compute host   A server that provides processing, storage, networking, and memory resources needed to run an application, usually as a virtual machine and often as a cluster member.

container   A software environment in which an application can run but is isolated from much of the rest of the operating system and other applications.

core cluster resources   Resources in a failover cluster that include the quorum resource, which is usually the witness disk or witness share; the IP address resource that provides the cluster IP address; and the network name resource that provides the cluster name.

Current Branch   A feature update option that causes WSUS clients to download and install feature updates as soon as they are available.

Current Branch for Business   A feature update option that causes WSUS clients to download and install feature updates after Microsoft has verified that the feature is suitable for enterprise installations.

D

data center bridging (DCB)   An enhancement to Ethernet that provides additional features for use in enterprise data centers, especially where server clustering and storage area networks (SANs) are in use.

data collector set   Settings that specify the performance counters you want to collect, how often to collect them, and how long to collect them.

data deduplication   A technology that reduces the amount of storage necessary to store an organization's data.

Datacenter Edition   A Windows Server 2016 edition intended primarily for organizations using virtualization on a large scale.

Dedicated policy   A storage QoS policy that applies the minimum and maximum values to each virtual disk to which the policy is applied.

Deployment Image Servicing and Management (dism.exe)   A command-line tool for updating an image file with patches, drivers, hotfixes, and service packs without having to re-create the entire image.

Desired State Configuration (DSC)   A feature that allows you to manage and maintain servers with simple declarative statements.

differencing disk   A dynamically expanding virtual disk that uses a parent/child relationship in which the parent disk is a dynamically expanding or fixed size disk with an OS installed and possibly some applications and data. The differencing disk is a child of the parent. Changes are made only to the differencing disk; the parent disk remains unaltered.

direct-attached storage (DAS)   A storage medium directly connected to the server using it but differs from local storage in that it includes externally connected HDDs in an enclosure with a power supply.

disaggregated Storage Spaces Direct deployment   A server cluster configuration with two separate clusters: an S2D cluster and a Hyper-V cluster.

discover image   An image file that can be used to boot a client computer that can't use PXE, usually from a CD/DVD or flash device.

Discrete Device Assignment (DDA)   A new feature in Windows Server 2016 Hyper-V that gives a VM exclusive access to hardware devices on the host computer.

discretionary access control list (DACL)   A list of security principals; each has permissions that define access to an object. *See also* security principal.

disk drive   A physical component with a disk interface connector (such as SATA or SCSI) and a power connector.

Docker   Open source software that is used in the Linux and Windows environment to implement containers.

Dockerfile   A feature of Docker in which you specify properties of a container image using a text file called a *dockerfile*.

DockerHub   A public repository for Docker container images.

domain blob   A file that contains the necessary information to perform an offline domain join.

domain controller (DC)   A Windows server that has Active Directory installed and is responsible for allowing client computers to access domain resources.

downstream server   A server in a multiple-server WSUS deployment that accesses other (upstream) WSUS servers for synchronizing updates.

drain on shutdown   A feature in Windows Server 2016 that drains roles automatically and live-migrates VMs to another cluster node before the Hyper-V server shuts down.

dual parity space   A parity space that can recover from simultaneous failure of two disks.

dynamic disk   A disk arrangement that can hold up to 128 volumes, including spanned volumes, striped volumes, and RAID volumes.

Dynamic Memory   A Hyper-V feature that allows an administrator to set startup, minimum, and maximum memory allocation values for each VM.

dynamic quorum   A feature that assigns a cluster node vote dynamically depending on whether the node is an active member of the cluster. If a node is no longer active in the cluster, its vote is removed.

dynamic witness   A quorum feature in Windows Server 2012 R2 in which the cluster determines whether to give the witness a quorum vote based on whether there's an odd or even number of cluster nodes.

dynamically expanding disk   A virtual hard disk in which the .vhd file is very small when created but can expand as additional space is needed.

 E

effective access   The access that a security principal has to a file system object when taking sharing permissions, NTFS permissions, and group memberships into account. *See also* security principal.

effective permissions   The combination of permissions assigned to an account from explicit and inherited permissions; determines an account's effective access to an object. *See also* effective access.

emulated drivers   Legacy drivers installed on a VM that are used when Integration Services isn't installed; also called *legacy drivers*.

enclosure awareness   A resiliency feature in Storage Spaces in which Storage Spaces associates each copy of file data with a particular JBOD enclosure so that if an enclosure goes offline, the data is retained in another enclosure.

Enhanced Session mode   A Hyper-V feature that provides improved interaction and device redirection between the host computer and the guest OS.

Essentials Edition   A Windows Server 2016 edition suitable for small businesses with 25 or fewer users. Some services, such as Active Directory and DNS, are installed automatically during OS installation.

event subscription   A feature in Event Viewer that allows an administrator to collect event logs from other systems.

Event Viewer   An MMC snap-in that allows you to review the events recorded in logs on your local computer as well as other computers on the network.

explicit permission   A permission assigned by adding a user's account to an object's DACL.

extended partition   A division of disk space on a basic disk that can be divided into logical drives; can't be marked active and can't hold the Windows system volume.

external virtual switch   A virtual switch in which one of the host's physical network adapters is bound to the virtual network switch, allowing virtual machines to access a LAN connected to the host.

F

failback options   Settings that specify that a cluster should revert to the most preferred owner when that server is available again. The failback can occur immediately or between certain hours of the day.

failover   The ability of a server to recover from network hardware failure by having redundant hardware that can immediately take over for a device failure.

failover affinity   A method that allows failover to occur to a node in the same site before failing over to a node in a different site.

failover cluster   Two or more servers appearing as a single server to clients. One server is considered the active server, and other servers are passive. The active server handles all client requests for the clustered application, and the passive servers wait in standby mode until the active server fails.

failover options   Settings that specify how many times a service attempts to restart or fail over to another server in the specified period.

fault domain   A property of a cluster that has name, type, description, and location values.

feature file store   A network share containing the files required to install roles, role services, and features on Windows Server 2016 servers. *See also* Features on Demand.

feature update   An update that adds new features or enhances existing features within the OS.

Features on Demand   A feature in Windows Server 2016 that enables you to remove the files used to install roles and features and free up the disk space these files normally consume.

file and folder permissions   The permissions that give both network users and interactive users fine-grained access control over folders and files.

file-level storage   A type of storage that the client has access to only as files and folders.

file system   The method and format an OS uses to store, locate, and retrieve files from electronic storage media.

filtering mode   An option in a port rule that specifies whether multiple hosts or a single host responds to traffic identified by the port rule. Multiple host is the default mode and allows scalability. Single host mode specifies that the server with the highest priority value handles traffic.

fixed provisioning   A method of creating virtual disks that allocates all space for the virtual disk from the storage pool immediately.

fixed size disk   A virtual hard disk in which the disk's full size is allocated on the host system when it's created.

formatting   The process of preparing a disk with a file system used to organize and store files.

full backup   A backup option that backs up all data on all local volumes, including the system state.

G

guest clustering   A clustering feature that requires two or more VMs with a guest OS installed and configured for failover clustering; the failover clustering occurs in the VM's guest OS.

guest OS   The operating system running in a virtual machine installed on a host computer. *See* virtual machine (VM).

GUID Partitioning Table (GPT)   A disk-partitioning method that supports volume sizes up to 18 exabytes.

H

handle   A reference to a resource on the computer; often associated with open files but can also be associated with a block of memory or other data structures an application is using.

handling priority   An NLB parameter used in single host mode that determines which host handles all traffic meeting the port rules' criteria. *See also* filtering mode and network load balancing (NLB).

headless server   A server in which no traditional user interface is built in to manage the server. Rather, it is intended to be managed remotely using PowerShell, MMCs, or other remote management options.

heartbeat   A signal sent between cluster nodes informing them that a node is up and running.

high availability   A network or computer configuration in which data and applications are almost always available, even after a system failure.

highly available virtual machine   A virtual machine (VM) that allows you to make applications and services highly available by installing them on a VM residing on a Hyper-V server configured for high availability.

host computer   The physical computer on which virtualization software is installed and virtual machines run.

hot-add   A high-end feature that allows adding hardware (usually memory, processors, or disk drives) to a system while it's running.

hot backup site   A location that duplicates much of the main site's IT infrastructure and can be switched to if a disaster occurs at the main site.

hot-replace   A high-end feature that allows replacing faulty hardware (usually memory, processors, or disk drives) in a system while it's running.

hot spare disk   An option for a physical disk in storage spaces that will allow the disk to sit idle until it is needed to repair a volume due to disk failure.

hotfix   An update to Windows that fixes a bug within a limited scope.

hyper-converged Storage Spaces Direct deployment   A server cluster configuration that incorporates both the storage and the Hyper-V role within the same cluster.

Hyper-V container   An application environment that provides OS and kernel isolation like a traditional VM but is not managed by Hyper-V Manager.

Hyper-V Replica   A feature in Windows Server 2016 that periodically replicates changes in a VM to a mirror VM hosted on another Hyper-V server.

hypervisor   The virtualization software component that creates and monitors the virtual hardware environment, which allows multiple virtual machines to share physical hardware resources.

I

image file   A file containing other files, much like a zip file containing multiple files; WDS image files can be one of three formats: .wim, .vhd, and .vhdx.

image group   A container for organizing images with common properties.

incremental backup   A backup in which only the blocks that have changed since the last backup are transferred to the destination if there is an existing backup.

inherited permission   A permission that comes from an object's parent instead of being assigned explicitly. *See also* explicit permission.

in-place upgrade   An upgrade that replaces the existing OS with the new OS but maintains all the roles and features installed on the existing OS.

install image   An image file containing the OS being deployed to client computers.

Integrated Scripting Environment (ISE)   A PowerShell development environment that helps in creating PowerShell scripts.

Integration Services   A software package installed on a VM's guest OS that includes enhanced drivers for the guest OS and improves performance and functionality for IDE and SCSI storage devices, network interfaces, and mouse and video devices. It also integrates the VM with the host OS better to provide services such as data exchange, time synchronization, OS shutdown, and others.

internal virtual switch   A virtual switch that isn't bound to any of the host's physical NICs. However, a host virtual NIC is bound to the internal virtual switch, which allows virtual machines and the host computer to communicate with one another, but VMs can't access the physical network.

Internet Storage Name Service (iSNS)   An IP-based protocol used to communicate between iSNS clients and servers for allowing iSCSI devices to discover and monitor one another.

iSCSI initiator   An iSCSI client that sends iSCSI commands to an iSCSI target. *See also* iSCSI target.

iSCSI logical unit number (LUN)   A reference ID to a logical drive the iSCSI initiator uses when accessing storage on the iSCSI target server.

iSCSI qualified name (IQN)   An identifier for iSCSI targets and initiators used to identify the iSCSI device in an iSCSI connection.

iSCSI target   A logical storage space made available to iSCSI clients by a server running the iSCSI Target Server role service.

J

just a bunch of disks (JBOD)   A disk arrangement in which two or more disks are abstracted to appear as a single disk to the OS but aren't arranged in a specific RAID configuration.

K

Key Management Service (KMS)   A service that activates Windows using a computer configured as a KMS host instead of having to connect with Microsoft servers via the Internet.

L

layer 2 (L2) bridge network   A network that is similar to a transparent network but the container shares a MAC address with the container host.

live migration   An application or service installed on two or more servers participating in a failover cluster; also called a *clustered service*.

load balancing   A feature of NIC teaming that distributes traffic between two or more interfaces, providing an increase in overall network throughput that server is able to maintain.

load balancing and failover (LBFO)   A network interface configuration that allows multiple network interfaces to work in tandem to provide increased bandwidth, load balancing, and fault tolerance. Also called *NIC teaming*.

load weight   An NLB parameter that allows configuring how much network traffic, as a percentage, each node should handle. *See also* network load balancing (NLB).

local configuration manager (LCM)   A configuration manager responsible for sending (pushing) and receiving (pulling) configurations, applying configurations, monitoring, and reporting discrepancies

between the desired state and the current state of a server.

local storage   Storage media with a direct and exclusive connection to the computer's system board through a disk controller.

logical unit number (LUN)   A logical reference point to a unit of storage that could refer to an entire array of disks, a single disk, or just part of a disk.

M

manual disk   An option for a physical disk in storage spaces that will allow an administrator to choose which disks will be used when creating a virtual disk.

Master Boot Record (MBR)   A disk-partitioning method that supports volume sizes up to 2 TB.

member server   A Windows server that's in the management scope of a Windows domain but doesn't have Active Directory installed.

Microsoft Hyper-V Server 2016   A Windows Server 2016 edition that is a free download with no licensing costs that allows you to make a server a Hyper-V virtualization server.

mirror space   A resilient storage layout in Storage Spaces that is similar to a RAID 1 volume. Can be configured as a two-way or three-way mirrored volume. *See also* three-way mirror.

mirrored volume   A volume that uses space from two dynamic disks and provides fault tolerance. Data written to one disk is duplicated, or mirrored, to the second disk. If one disk fails, the other disk has a good copy of the data, and the system can continue to operate until the failed disk is replaced; also called a *RAID 1 volume*.

multicasting   A network communication method for delivering data to multiple computers on a network simultaneously.

Multipath IO (MPIO)   This provides fault tolerance for Windows storage networks, including iSCSI SANs.

Multipoint Premium Server   A Windows Server 2016 edition intended for volume licensing customers in academic markets. Multipoint Premium Server allows multiple users to share one Windows computer, each with its own Windows environment settings.

N

namespace   The parts of the operating system that a specific application can see and interact with, such as the file system and the network.

namespace isolation   An isolated environment that allows containerized applications to have their own copy of critical OS structures such as the registry, file system, and network configuration while sharing the kernel, the host hardware, and possibly some runtime libraries.

nested virtualization   The ability to run a virtual machine on a virtual machine.

network address translation (NAT)   The process by which the IP addresses in a packet are translated to different addresses when the packet leaves or enters a network. NAT is typically used to allow a network using private IP addresses to access the public Internet.

network-attached storage (NAS)   A storage device that has an enclosure, a power supply, slots for multiple HDDs, a network interface, and a built-in OS tailored for managing shared files and folders.

network boot   The process by which a computer loads and runs an OS that it retrieves from a network server.

network client   The part of the OS that sends requests to a server to access network resources.

network connection   The network interface, network protocol, and network client and server software working together on a Windows computer.

Network File System (NFS)   The native file-sharing protocol in UNIX and Linux OSs; also supported by Windows Server 2016.

network interface   The network interface card and the device driver software working together.

network load balancing (NLB)   A Windows Server feature that uses server clusters to provide scalability and fault tolerance. *See also* server cluster.

network protocol   Software that specifies the rules and format of communication between devices on a network.

network server software   The part of the OS that receives requests for shared network resources and makes these resources available to a network client.

NFS data store   An NFS share on a Windows failover cluster that provides a highly available storage solution for applications using NFS. *See also* Network File System (NFS).

NIC teaming   A network interface configuration that allows multiple network interfaces to work in tandem to provide increased bandwidth, load balancing, and fault tolerance. Also called *load balancing and failover (LBFO)*.

node fairness   A new failover cluster feature in Windows Server 2016 that helps optimize usage of failover cluster node members.

nonauthoritative restore   A method of restoring Active Directory data from a backup that restores the database, or portions of it, and allows the data to be updated through replication by other domain controllers.

Non-Uniform Memory Access (NUMA)   A system memory architecture used in multiprocessor systems that allows processors to efficiently share memory.

NT File System (NTFS)   A file system used on Windows OSs that supports compression, encryption, and file and folder permissions.

NUMA spanning   The allocation of additional memory from a different NUMA node.

O

object owner   Usually the user account that created the object or a group or user who has been assigned ownership of the object. An object owner has special authority over that object.

offline domain join   A process that makes a computer a member of a domain without the computer having to contact a domain controller.

offline files   A feature of shared folders that allows users to access the contents of shared folders when not connected to the network; also called *client-side caching*.

one-time backup   A backup type that creates a backup to a local volume or a share; the backup begins immediately.

operating system environment (OSE)   All or part of an operating system instance or all or part of a virtual operating system instance, which includes Windows Server 2016 installed as a virtual machine or a Hyper-V container.

P

page file   A system file in Windows used as virtual memory and to store dump data after a system crash.

parameter   An input to a command or PowerShell cmdlet.

parity space   A resilient storage layout in Storage Spaces that is similar to a RAID 5 volume and requires at least three disks.

partition   A logical unit of storage that can be formatted with a file system; similar to a volume but used with basic disks.

partitioned A cluster status that can occur if communication fails between cluster servers, resulting in two or more subclusters, each with the objective of handling the clustered service. *See also* cluster server.

passive node A cluster member that's not currently responding to client requests for a clustered application but is in standby in case the active node fails; also called a *passive server*.

pass-through disk A physical disk attached to the host system that's placed offline so that it can be used by a VM instead of or in addition to a virtual disk.

patches Software updates normally intended to fix security vulnerabilities and software bugs.

patch management A procedure that enables administrators to control which product updates to allow as well as the source and timing of these updates.

performance counter A performance metric from OS components and applications.

Performance Monitor A performance monitoring tool that uses a variety of data sources to examine how roles, services, and applications affect the performance of a computer.

permission inheritance A method for defining how permissions are transmitted from a parent object to a child object.

permissions A property of the file system that specifies which users can access a file system object (a file or folder) and what users can do with the object if they're granted access.

port rule A setting that specifies which type of TCP or UDP traffic that an NLB cluster should respond to and how the traffic is distributed among cluster members. *See also* network load balancing (NLB).

PowerShell A command-line interactive scripting environment that provides the commands needed for most management tasks in a Windows Server 2016 environment.

Preboot eXecution Environment (PXE) A network environment built into many NICs that allows a computer to boot from an image stored on a network server.

preferred owner The server selected as the active server for a service or an application.

prestaging A feature that enables you to perform a basic unattended installation by specifying the computer name, selecting the boot and install images a client should receive, and joining the client to the domain.

primary partition A division of disk space on a basic disk used to create a volume. It can be assigned a drive letter, be marked active, and contain the Windows system volume.

primordial pool A collection of physical disks available to be added to a storage pool.

private cloud A cloud computing service provided by a company's internal IT department. *See* cloud computing.

private virtual switch A virtual switch with no host connection to the virtual network, thereby allowing VMs to communicate with one another. However, there's no communication between the private virtual network and the host.

production checkpoint A checkpoint that is supported for production virtual machines and uses backup technology in the guest OS to create the checkpoint.

public cloud A cloud computing service provided by a third party. *See* cloud computing.

Q

quality update An update that fixes software defects and enhances security.

quick migration A migration option available only between Hyper-V servers in a failover cluster; usually results in a minute or more of downtime, depending on how much memory the VM uses.

quorum A database containing cluster configuration information about the status of each node (active or passive) for clustered applications. In a server or communication failure, it's also used to determine whether the cluster is to remain online and which servers should continue to participate in the cluster.

R

RAID 5 volume A volume that uses space from three or more dynamic disks and uses disk striping with parity to provide fault tolerance. When data is written, it's striped across all but one of the disks in the volume. Parity information derived from the data is written to the remaining disk, which is used to re-create lost data after a disk failure.

recovery point A checkpoint that can be generated automatically so that you can revert to an earlier server state if there's an unplanned failover and the VM is in an unworkable state.

redundant array of independent disks (RAID)
A disk configuration that uses space on multiple disks to form a single logical volume. Most RAID configurations provide fault tolerance, and some enhance performance.

reference computer   A computer used as a prototype or template from which a capture image is created in WDS.

reparse point   Metadata associated with a file that is used by a particular application or service that accesses the file.

replica mode   A WSUS server mode that centralizes administration of update approvals and client groups.

replica server   In the Hyper-V Replica feature, the Hyper-V server where replication is enabled.

resilience   Another term for fault tolerance; indicates a disk arrangement's capability to maintain data if a disk fails.

resource metering   A Hyper-V feature that allows vendors of large-scale virtualization to measure customer use of VM resources for billing purposes.

Resource Monitor   A monitoring tool that shows CPU, memory, disk, and network use information for separate processes or the system as a whole in real time.

role services   Services that can be installed in Server Manager to add functions to the main role. *See also* server role.

rolling upgrade   An NLB cluster upgrade method that involves taking each cluster node offline, upgrading the host, and then bringing it back online. *See also* network load balancing (NLB).

root domain controller   The first domain controller installed in an Active Directory forest. *See also* domain controller (DC).

S

scale-out file server (SoFS)   A highly available share option that provides the reliability of failover clusters and the load distribution of an NLB because client connections are distributed among all nodes in the cluster.

scheduled backup   A backup type that allows specifying how often a backup occurs and dedicating a disk to backups.

security descriptor   A file system object's security settings composed of the DACL, owner, and SACL. *See also* discretionary access control list (DACL) and system access control list (SACL).

security principal   An object that can be assigned permission to access the file system; includes user, group, and computer accounts.

Serial ATA (SATA)   A common disk interface technology that's inexpensive, fast, and reliable with transfer speeds up to 6 Gb/s; used in both client computers and low-end servers and replaces the older parallel ATA (PATA) technology.

serial attached SCSI (SAS)   A serial form of SCSI with transfer rates up to 6 Gb/s and higher; the disk technology of choice for servers and high-end workstations. *See also* small computer system interface (SCSI).

server cluster   A group of two or more servers configured to respond to a single virtual IP address.

server features   Components you can install that provide functions to enhance or support an installed role or add a standalone feature.

Server Message Block (SMB)   A client/server Application-layer protocol that provides network file sharing, network printing, and authentication.

server operating system   OS designed to emphasize network access performance and run background processes rather than desktop applications.

server role   A major function or service that a server performs.

server role migration   An upgrade in which you perform a clean install of Windows Server 2016 and migrate existing server roles to the new OS.

server-side targeting   A method for adding computers to WSUS groups in which the server takes action to add the computer to the WSUS group.

service   A task or process that runs in the background.

service dependencies   The services that a specific service depends on to operate.

service pack   A collection of bug fixes, security updates, and new features that can be installed on an OS to bring it up to date.

share permissions   The permissions applied to shared folders that protect files accessed across the network; the only method for protecting files on FAT volumes.

shared-nothing live migration   A live migration done between Hyper-V servers that have no common storage.

shared virtual hard disk (shared VHDX)   A virtual hard disk configured on a VM in a guest cluster that's used for shared storage among VMs in the guest cluster instead of traditional SAN storage.

simple space   A simple volume created in Storage Spaces that has no fault tolerance or resilience.

simple volume   A volume that resides on a single disk, basic or dynamic.

single-root I/O virtualization (SR-IOV)   An advanced feature in Hyper-V that enhances the virtual network adapter's performance by bypassing the virtual switch software on the parent partition.

site-aware cluster   A new feature in Windows Server 2016 that allows an administrator to assign a name to a physical location (site) and assign cluster nodes to each location.

small computer system interface (SCSI)   An older parallel bus disk technology still used on some servers but has reached its performance limits at 640 MB/s transfer rates.

smart paging   A Hyper-V feature that uses a file on the host computer for temporary memory storage when a sudden surge in memory requirements exceeds the physical amount of memory available.

solid state drive (SSD)   A type of storage medium that uses flash memory, has no moving parts, and requires less power than a traditional HDD. It is also faster and more shock resistant than a traditional HDD but costs more per gigabyte and doesn't have as much capacity as an HDD.

spanned volume   A volume that extends across two or more physical disks, for example, a simple volume that has been extended to a second disk is a spanned volume.

split vote   A quorum situation in which no quorum can be reached.

standalone server   A Windows server that isn't a domain controller or a member of a domain.

standard checkpoint   A checkpoint that captures the state of a virtual machine, including the running state, if desired. A standard checkpoint should not be used in production VMs.

Standard Edition   A Windows Server 2016 edition suitable for most businesses that need a full-featured server and might need to use virtualization on a moderate scale.

standby mode   A cluster node that isn't active.

stateless operation   An operation state that allows a container to start fresh and not carry over any information from the previous time it was run.

storage appliance   A storage device that has an enclosure, a power supply, slots for multiple HDDs, a network interface, and a built-in OS tailored for managing shared storage.

storage area network   A storage technology that uses high-speed networking technologies to give servers fast access to large amounts of shared disk storage.

storage layouts   The method used to create a virtual disk with Storage Spaces; includes simple, mirror, and parity. *See also* Storage Spaces.

storage migration   A VM migration process used to move a VM's storage from one volume to another without moving the VM to another Hyper-V server.

storage pool   A collection of physical disks from which virtual disks and volumes are created and assigned dynamically.

storage Quality of Service (QoS)   A feature on virtual machines that enables administrators to specify minimum and maximum performance values for virtual hard disks.

Storage Replica   A Windows Server feature that provides block-level file replication between storage devices, primarily for the purpose of fault tolerance and disaster recovery.

Storage Spaces   A feature in Windows Server 2016 that provides flexible provisioning of virtualized storage.

Storage Spaces Direct (S2D)   A new feature in Windows Server 2016 that extends the storage pool concept on a single server to multiple servers in a failover cluster.

stretch cluster   A cluster in which the servers are located in different geographical locations. A stretch cluster is primarily used in disaster recovery scenarios.

striped volume   A volume that extends across two or more dynamic disks, but data is written to all disks in the volume equally.

synthetic driver   A driver installed on a VM with Integration Services that's optimized for use in the Hyper-V environment.

synthetic network adapter   A network adapter that uses synthetic drivers in Hyper-V and offers much better performance than legacy network adapters. *See also* synthetic driver.

system access control list (SACL) Defines the settings for auditing access to an object.

system state backup A backup option that backs up boot files, Windows system files, and the registry. On a domain controller (DC), the system state includes the Active Directory database and the SYSVOL folder.

system volume The volume that contains the files the computer needs to find and load the Windows OS. Also referred to as the *system partition*.

T

tag A way to differentiate multiple versions of the same image by specifically tagging the image.

Task Manager A monitoring tool that lets you view running processes and the resources they are consuming.

thin provisioning A method for creating virtual disks whereby the virtual disk expands dynamically and uses space from the storage pool as needed until it reaches the specified maximum size.

thread The smallest piece of program code that Windows can schedule for execution.

three-way mirror A resilient storage layout, requiring at least five disks, that maintains data if one disk (two-way mirror) fails or two disks (three-way mirror) fail.

tie breaker for 50% node split A feature in Windows Server 2012 R2 in which a cluster is partitioned into an equal numbers of nodes, and the dynamic quorum feature is used to change node votes to break the tie. *See also* dynamic quorum.

tiered storage A feature of Storage Spaces that combines the speed of solid state drives with the low cost and high capacity of hard disk drives.

transparent network A network that connects containers to the same network as the host so that a container's network adapter will have an IP address in the same IP subnet as the host's network adapter.

U

UNC path The format used to specify a shared folder on a remote Windows computer. It uses the syntax *server**share*[*subfolder*][*file*]. The parameters in brackets are optional.

upstream server A server in a multiple-server WSUS deployment that other (downstream) WSUS servers use for synchronizing updates.

V

variable A temporary storage location that holds values, whether numeric, strings, or objects.

VHD Set A new VHD option in Windows Server 2016 designed specifically for shared virtual hard disks that enables backup of virtual machine groups and online disk resizing, and supports Hyper-V Replica.

virtual desktop infrastructure (VDI) A sector of private cloud computing whereby users access their desktops through a private cloud; the OS and applications run on servers in a corporate data center rather than on the local computer.

virtual disk Files stored on the host computer that represent a virtual machine's hard disk.

virtual hard disk Files stored on a physical disk drive that emulate a physical disk but have additional capabilities for virtual machines and general Windows storage applications.

virtual instance An installation of Windows Server 2016 in a Hyper-V virtual machine.

virtual IP address The IP address by which networking services provided by an NLB cluster are accessed by network clients. A DNS host record should exist for the cluster name mapped to this address. *See also* network load balancing (NLB).

virtual machine (VM) The virtual environment that emulates a physical computer's hardware and BIOS.

virtual machine monitoring A feature introduced in Windows Server 2012 that allows monitoring resources, applications, and services running on highly available VMs. *See also* highly available virtual machine.

virtual machine network health protection A failover cluster feature that automatically live-migrates a virtual machine to another node if its network connection fails.

virtual machine queue (VMQ) A feature of virtual network interfaces (vNICs) that accelerates vNIC performance by delivering packets from the external network directly to the vNIC.

virtual network A network configuration created by virtualization software and used by virtual machines for network communication.

virtual processor The virtual representation of a physical processor or processor core residing on the host that can be assigned to a virtual machine.

virtualization   A technology that uses software to emulate multiple hardware environments, allowing multiple operating systems to run on the same physical server simultaneously.

virtualization software   The software for creating and managing virtual machines and creating the virtual environment in which a guest OS is installed.

volume   A logical unit of storage that can be formatted with a file system.

W

wdsnbp.com   A bootstrap program; a WDS component that a WDS client downloads when performing a network boot.

Windows Deployment Services (WDS)   A server role that facilitates installing Windows OSs across a network.

Windows domain   A group of Windows computers that share common management and are subject to rules and policies that an administrator defines.

Windows Imaging Format (WIM)   The most common image file type used by WDS and the method used to store installation files on a Windows installation DVD.

Windows Preinstallation Environment (PE)   A minimal OS that has only the services needed to access the network, work with files, copy disk images, and jump-start a Windows installation.

Windows Remote Management (WinRM)   A Windows feature that provides a command-line interface for performing a variety of remote management tasks.

Windows Server container   An application environment that shares the host OS and kernel with the host OS and other Windows Server containers but has its own copy of user mode data structures such as the registry, file system, and network configuration.

Windows Server Update Services (WSUS)   A server role that makes it possible for administrators to take control of Microsoft product updates on computers running Windows.

Windows Storage Server   A Windows Server 2016 edition focused on making a computer a storage appliance. Storage Server can be configured as a network-attached storage device for file sharing applications or as a block-level iSCSI storage device for shared storage applications.

Windows workgroup   A small collection of Windows computers whose users typically have something in common, such as the need to share files or printers with each other. No computer has authority or control over another. Logons, security, and resource sharing are decentralized. Also called a *peer-to-peer network*.

witness disk   Shared storage used to store cluster configuration data and help determine the cluster quorum.

INDEX